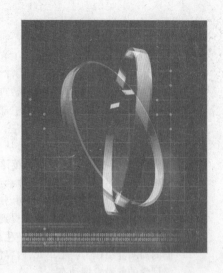

统计学专业英语

（第三版）

王忠玉　主编

English in Statistics
(Third Edition)

内容提要

本书内容分为三部分:第一部分是英译汉常用的翻译方法和技巧;第二部分是专业英文选读,内容涉及描述统计学、数理统计学(也就是推断统计学)、指数理论、数据科学与大数据、高等专题等五个方面;第三部分是指数和缺失数据与估算参考译文。

与同类书籍相比,本书具有三大特点:(1)将英译汉翻译常用方法和技巧与统计学专业翻译技巧融合在一起,特别注重从目前统计学英文期刊、教材与专著中提炼出专业术语、常用句型、翻译技巧等;(2)统计英语原文选编,提供一些选自于最新统计学英文文献中的部分内容,让学生真正在学习中体会到原汁原味的专业特色,并且在每一章节之后都提供一个词汇表,解释一些比较难的词语或词组,还有特定专业术语或词组等。例如,这部分专业英语涉及目前中文课本中没有提到的"两个分布等价定义"、"位置参数"、"尺度参数(或标度参数)"、"稳定分布"、"熵"、"生成函数"等;(3)关注统计学前沿领域,将数据科学和大数据的简明介绍作为一个单元,内容包括历史演变、概念及方法,目的在于拓宽知识视野,了解统计学的前沿发展动态。

本书适合于统计学、数学、应用数学、经济数学等专业高年级本科生以及研究生专业英语教学用书或者双语教学用书,也可作相关专业研究生教学参考书。

图书在版编目(CIP)数据

统计学专业英语/王忠玉主编. —3 版. —哈尔滨:哈尔滨工业大学出版社,2015.4(2020.8 重印)
ISBN 978 - 7 - 5603 - 5333 - 3

Ⅰ.①统… Ⅱ.①王… Ⅲ.①统计学-英语-高等学校-教材 Ⅳ.①H31

中国版本图书馆 CIP 数据核字(2015)第 079673 号

策划编辑	刘培杰
责任编辑	张永芹 邵长玲
封面设计	孙茵艾
出版发行	哈尔滨工业大学出版社
社　　址	哈尔滨市南岗区复华四道街 10 号 邮编 150006
传　　真	0451 - 86414749
网　　址	http://hitpress.hit.edu.cn
印　　刷	哈尔滨市工大节能印刷厂
开　　本	787mm×1092mm　1/16　印张 33　字数 603 千字
版　　次	2015 年 4 月第 3 版　2020 年 8 月第 4 次印刷
书　　号	ISBN 978 - 7 - 5603 - 5333 - 3
定　　价	68.00 元

(如因印装质量问题影响阅读,我社负责调换)

第3版序言

最近几年,有关大数据内容的探讨、专题会议和研究越来越多,并已经引起许多高校如计算机专业与统计学专业等领域研究者及教师的高度关注。另一方面,商业公司纷纷参与或创建有关大数据研究院或研究所,这种发展充分显示出"大数据"时代已经来临。大数据潮流来势凶猛,正在引发诸多领域的新发展、新动态、新趋势。

在 Forrester 分析师布赖恩·霍普金斯(Brian Hopkins)和鲍里斯·埃韦尔松(Boris Evelson)撰写的"首席信息官,请用大数据扩展数字视野"报告中,他们提出了大数据的四个典型特征:海量(Volume)、多样性(Variety)、高速(Velocity)和易变性(Variability)。

和以往数据相比,大数据具有诸多新颖的特点。如果从结构特征来看,有结构化数据和非结构化/半结构化数据。如果从获取和处理方式来看,有动态(流式/增量式/线上数据)/实时数据和静态(线下数据)/非实时数据。如果从关联特征来看,则有无关联/简单关联数据(键值记录型数据)和复杂关联数据(图数据)。另外,大数据来自于应用行业,具有极强的行业应用需求特性。数据规模极大,达到 PB 甚至 EB 量级,超过任何传统数据库系统的处理能力。如何处理大数据给传统计算技术带来极大挑战,大多数传统算法在面向大数据处理时都面临问题,需要重写。

探究大数据的理论及方法已经呈现新的视角、新的范式。图灵奖获得者吉姆·格雷(Jim Gray,1944年1月12日—2007年1月28日,大数据浪潮的先驱者,1998年获得计算机科学界的诺贝尔奖——图灵奖)认为,数据密集型科学发现(data-intensive scientific discovery)将成为科学技术发展的第四种范式,这四种范式分别是:

- 实验科学:几千年前,描述自然现象。
- 理论科学:过去几百年,牛顿定律、麦克斯方程之类的理论。
- 计算科学:过去几十年,模拟复杂现象。
- 数据科学:当今,数据密集型科学(理论、实验和模拟的统一)。

将人类科学研究的历史划分为四个阶段,这有助于我们理解为什么数据科学正在成为一种全新的科学研究方式。

比如,在计算科学中,数据计算具有两个特征:(1)模型驱动(model-driven);(2)经验决策(rule-based decision)。在新兴的数据科学中,数据计算则呈现新的特征:①数据驱动(data-driven);②数据驱动决策(data-driven decision)。当然,大数据的发展和研究也面临着许多挑战,例如大数据的异构性、非结构型,表现出多源、异构、多模,还有结构化困难和建模困难,如何将媒体数据(比如图像)转化成结构化数据统计描述等等。

最近,出现了数据科学的称谓。这是一个新兴的交叉学科领域,推进学科发展的因素无非两个:一个是外界需求,另一个是专业人才。美国加州大学伯克利分校统计系的郁彬(Yu Bin)教授提出,一个合格的数据科学家应具备的基本素质和技能,可概括为 SDC^3:

Statistics (S) 统计学;
Domain (science) knowledge (D) 深厚的(科学)知识;
Computing (C) 计算技术;
Collaboration ("team work") (C) 团队的合作能力;
Communication (to outsiders) (C) 与外界沟通能力。并认为

$$Data\ Science = SDC^3$$

美国统计学家吴建民(C. F. Jeff Wu)教授早在1998年的一个学术会议上就曾建议:

Statistics → Data Science
Statisticians → Data Scientists

Several good names have been taken up: computer, information science, material science, cognitive science. "Data Science" is likely the remaining good name reserved for us.

由此可见,统计学是数据科学中最重要的组成部分之一。

为了适应这一技术变革趋势与新兴的社会需求,伊利诺伊大学香槟分校(University of Illinois Urbana Champaign)从2011年起举办"数据科学暑期研究班";哥伦比亚大学从2013年起开设"应用数据科学"课程,并从2013年起开设相关培训项目,还计划从2014年起设立硕士学位,2015年设立博士学位;纽约大学从2013年秋季起设立"数据科学"硕士学位。在英国,邓迪大学从2013年起设立"数据科学"科学硕士学位。

特别提及的是,美国的德克萨斯大学奥斯汀分校(The University of Texas Austin)的自然科学学院(College of Natural Sciences)索性将统计系改名为统计及数据科学系(Department of Statistics and Data Sciences),而其他大学例如美国的西弗吉尼亚大学(West Virginia University)统计系硕士研究生设有数据科学方向(Master of Data Science)。还有斯坦福大学统计学系研究生层面教育也有数据科学方向。

对于中国的情况来说,香港中文大学从2008年起设立"数据科学商业统计"科学硕士学位;复旦大学从2007年起开设数据科学讨论班,2010年开始招

收数据科学博士研究生,并从 2013 年起开设"数据科学"课程;北京航空航天大学于 2012 年设立大数据工程硕士学位。

除了理工学院的有关专业关注数据科学教育外,在国际范围内多所大学的管理学院或商学院陆续创建新专业"商务数据分析"(Business Analytics),关于 Business Analytics(BA)的解释如下:Business analytics is the practice of iterative, methodical exploration of an organization's data with emphasis on statistical analysis。美国南加州大学的马歇尔商学院,就专门开设商业数据分析(Business Analytics)的硕士项目。在项目介绍中,第一句话就是,商业数据分析是现在全美增长最迅速的领域。而旧金山州立大学也成立了类似项目,学制只需一年半,其中一年学习知识,半年学校帮助寻找实习机会。此外,新西兰奥塔哥大学的商学院(Otago Business School)研究生也设有商业数据科学方向(Master of Business Data Science),欧洲的伦敦城市大学也开设了数据科学硕士研究生的教育。如果考察这些数据科学研究生课程内容,可以发现大多数课程都是关于统计学理论及方法的,当然更少不了"数据科学"课程。

Gartner 咨询公司预测,大数据将为全球带来 440 万个 IT 新岗位和上千万个非 IT 岗位。麦肯锡公司预计,美国到 2018 年深度数据分析人才缺口将达 14 万~19 万人,能够分析数据帮助公司获得经济效益的技术及管理人才有 150 万人的缺口。

在中国,真正能够理解与应用大数据的创新人才,或者更准确地说,是研究数据科学的复合型人才,也同样是拥有未来广阔前景的稀缺性资源。2014 年 7 月,深圳国泰安教育技术股份有限公司就曾发布了一个《大数据建设白皮书》,旨在推动大数据学科和教育的发展,促进产学研的良好结合。

本书第 3 版的修订工作正是在这样的背景下修订完成的。和第 2 版内容相比,第 3 版变动主要包括以下几个方面:

(1)增加了数据科学及大数据的单元内容,这个单元仅仅是一个粗略的概述,并不能代替"大数据"或"数据科学"的课程,目的只是希望增加这部分选学内容来初步了解和认识什么是数据科学、大数据,开阔视野。在这个单元中,我们安排了有关的 Analytics 和 Big Data Analytics。*Analytics* 杂志给出的 analytics 定义是"用数学、运筹学、统计学影响商业决策",这里将 analytics 译成分析学或者分析方法。

计算机技术和网络的发展,使得计算资源变得更加丰富,从而使得数据搜集的能力、数据存储的能力以及数据处理的能力极大地丰富,为 analytics 的普及提供技术基础。数学、统计学、计算机科学的发展使得人们能运用更复杂的数学模型与算法分析数据,这些都进一步地丰富 analytics 分析数据的手段。另一方面,哲学、经济学、管理学、社会学、心理学的发展使得理性在决策中占据越来越重要的地位,这些学科的发展为 analytics 提供了思想与理论的准备。

从 2008 年开始,IBM 等跨国公司开始在 analytics 的名义下重新组织或完善自己的产品线。以 Analytics 为名的杂志于 2008 年开始发行,美国的一些大学也开始授予 analytics 的理学硕士学位。

（2）增加了描述统计学的多节内容。

（3）对原来第 2 版的 Unit 2 习题做了彻底更新，增大了习题数量，同时提供多项选择试题，并将部分习题答案放在刘培杰数学工作室网站上（http://lpj.hit.edu.cn），方便教师和学生的参考使用。另外，附录中增加了关于数据大小阶的常用英文表示法。

（4）将 Unit Five Econometric Models 内容删减下来作为教学补充资料，放在刘培杰数学工作室网站上，也就是提供给那些希望选用此部分内容的教师及学生。

另外，本书提供了有关数学所用的 PPT 及基本章节的 MP3 有声读物.

最后，选用关于大数据的漫画，来查看一下自己对这英文意思的理解如何？当然，关于更多的大数据专业性含义，只有了解和学习大数据知识之后，才能更深刻地知晓。（Fig. 1）

Fig. 1　What are "Big Data"?

本书第 3 版的修订写作筹划工作，花费一年多的时间准备，感谢曾经参与第 3 版资料整理的有关人员，包括深圳国泰安教育技术股份有限公司的常艳，英国帝国理工大学的朱煊繁同学，黑龙江大学的王天元，哈工大的周丽媛、杨菲同学，以及哈工大王延青老师还有一些同学也参与了本书的编写，包括黄炜、黄庆佳、刘禹辰、王妍妍、刘伟、王荣峰、张颖、刘云峰、徐雪、申江华、陈静、许瑶、江妍妍，对于他们的帮助及支持表示感谢。

书中难免存在纰漏与错误，希望广大教师及学生指正。联系方式：h20061111@126.com。

王忠玉

2015 年 3 月

前 言

作为一名统计学或应用数学专业的大学生,还有数量经济学专业研究生,要想跟踪当代统计学或应用数学、数量经济学理论及应用研究前沿,除了具备坚实的数学基础与相应的专业知识之外,还要具有相当的专业英语知识,就如何培育和训练坚实的基本技能而言,大致有下述几种途径:(1)在教师的指导下,一道道地做练习题,培养扎实的对统计问题或者经济现象进行抽象的能力;(2)仔细研读名著,与名师大家交流,聆听精彩的演讲和讲座;(3)潜心研究当代顶尖级统计学及相关应用领域的期刊论文,弄懂其研究方法与结构,学习写作学术论文的基本知识。而要实现上述目标,就必须掌握坚实的统计学专业英语。

作者在哈尔滨工业大学攻读博士学位以及后来在吉林大学数量经济研究中心做博士后研究期间,研究并翻译普利斯卡的《数理金融学引论》(Stanley R. Pliska. Introduction to Mathematical Finance. 2000,王忠玉译,经济科学出版社,2003年),后来又研读伍德里奇的《横截面与面板数据的经济计量分析》(Jeffrey M. Wooldridge. Econometric Analysis of Cross Section and Panel Data. 2002. MIT Press,王忠玉译,中国人民大学出版社,2007年)和科埃里等人的《效率与生产率分析引论》(Tim Coelli, etc. An Introduction to Efficiency and Productivity Analysis, 2nd, 2005. Springer,王忠玉译,中国人民大学出版社,2007年),还有《微观经济计量学:方法与应用》(A. Colin Cameron and Pravin K. Trivedi. Microeconometrics: Methods and Applications. Cambridge University Press, 2005)等著作,深感数理统计学作为数理金融学(或更宽泛地讲金融经济学)、经济计量学等领域中一个极为重要的研究工具的重要性,从而激发了编写一本既适合于统计学和应用数学等专业的高年级本科生,又适合于数量经济学专业研究生教学的专业英语教材的想法。

为了避免让学生重复学习以往曾学过的专业内容,本教材编写时既注重比较新颖的知识,又注重与以往学过的专业课程内容较少重复或者不重复,这样做的目的就是使学习专业英语和提升数理统计学知识有机地结合起来。比如,在第Ⅱ部分中,特别选取了目前国内经济计量经济学教材中不曾涉及的涵盖广义线性回归模型的经济计量的内容,还有指数性质的检验方法等,而在高等专题里特别地给出中文统计学课本没有提及的两个分布等价的定义、尺度参数、稳定分布等。作者的这种想法与构思曾得到南开大学张晓峒教授的赞许。当然，这种新颖的编写方法和尝试的教学效果究竟如何，还有待于教学实践及广大读者的检验。

统计专业英文内容包括五单元：

Unit One 首先介绍统计学的含义和重要性、描述统计、推断统计、有序变量、定类变量一些基本的概念，阐述均值、中位数、众数、标准差、方差以及分组数据的均值、方差等，此外还有各种各样的图示法，包括直方图、相对频数多边图、分位数等。

Unit Two 介绍事件及概率、随机变量及其分布、数学期望的概念，把离散变量与连续变量的两种情况以一种统一形式加以阐述，重点阐述矩生成函数的定义及其性质、大数定律、中心极限定律、统计推断的点估计和区间估计，特别地对假设检验中的两类错误类型、功效函数、沃尔德检验、似然比检验等加以详细阐明，最后给出最小二乘法估计量的推导过程、性质以及高斯-马尔可夫定理等。在附录中，提供换元积分法、分部积分法、泰勒序列展开式、Cramer-Rao 不等式、矩阵代数的某些公式的推导。

Unit Three 介绍引入统计指数的背景，系统地阐明综合指数、拉氏指数、派式指数、费希尔指数、Törnqvist 指数、数量指数、质量指数、环比指数、定基指数，特别地介绍统计指数公理化的一些性质。

Unit Four 阐述经济计量学中联立方程组的一些基本概念，而这些内容从本质上讲，正是线性统计模型在经济计量领域的应用。介绍参数方法、半参数方法、非参数方法、结构式、简化式、随机过程、遍历性、同期不相关等概念。

Unit Five 以一种更严谨的方式介绍进一步学习和研究高等数理统计学所必需的一些有关随机变量及其分布方面的知识，而且这部分里的一些概念在现代数理统计学的应用中广泛出现，比如"两个分布等价的定义、位置、尺度参数、稳定分布、熵、生成函数"等。

依据不同专业不同学时，本书的教学内容安排可以设计如下：

(1)统计专业和应用数学专业的本科教学：Unit One→Unit Two→Unit Three(或者 Unit Four)(34 学时)；或者 Unit One→Unit Two→Unit Three(或者 Unit Four)→Unit Five(51 学时)。

(2)数量经济专业研究生：Unit One→Unit Two→Unit Four→(34 学时)；或者 Unit One→Unit Two→Unit Four→Unit Five(51 学时)。

当然，不同高校的任课教师可依据个人偏好而进行不尽相同的内容取舍组合及编排。

在本书编写过程中，作者曾得到南开大学张晓峒教授的支持，吉林大学商学院数量经济学专业硕士研究生高敬一、郑佳，以及哈尔滨工业大学硕士研究生赵黎同学的帮助,还有李洪轩、刘晓阳、宋蕾、华夏同学为英译汉翻译技巧的个别章节进行文字录入工作,在此对张晓峒教授以及上述同学的帮助表示感谢。

本书能够顺利地出版,得益于哈尔滨工业大学出版社刘培杰先生的大力支持,在此对他的帮助表示感谢。同时,感谢高敬一在搜集资料方面的帮助。

最后,也要感谢吉林大学数量经济研究中心以及我的博士后导师赵振全教授为我提供的舒适而宽松的学术研究条件,为编写本书创造了良好的科研氛围。

此外,对编辑王勇钢、翟新烨的辛勤劳动表示感谢。

在本书编写中难免存在不足之处,请广大读者指正。

王忠玉

2006.12

电子邮箱:h20061111@126.com

CONTENTS

第Ⅰ部分　英译汉常用方法与技巧

第1章　翻译概述
- 1.1　翻译与翻译标准 …… 1
- 1.2　翻译过程 …… 3
- 1.3　怎样做好翻译 …… 5

第2章　句子与句型
- 2.1　句子 …… 7
- 2.2　句型 …… 10
- 2.3　第一种句型<S+V> …… 11
- 2.4　第二种句型<S+V+C> …… 12
- 2.5　第三种句型<S+V+O> …… 14
- 2.6　第四种句型<S+V+O1+O2> …… 16
- 2.7　第五种句型<S+V+O+C> …… 19
- 2.8　特殊句型 …… 22
- 2.9　强调句型 …… 24

第3章　相关词的翻译技巧
- 3.1　词义的选择 …… 30
- 3.2　词义的引申 …… 36
- 3.3　词类的转换 …… 37
- 3.4　词的增译 …… 42
- 3.5　词的省译 …… 45
- 3.6　重复法 …… 48
- 3.7　代词的翻译 …… 50
- 3.8　形容词的翻译 …… 53
- 3.9　副词及比较级的翻译 …… 56
- 3.10　介词的翻译 …… 60

第4章　被动语态的翻译
- 4.1　译成汉语被动句 …… 65
- 4.2　译成汉语主动句 …… 66
- 4.3　译成汉语无主句 …… 67
- 4.4　习惯译法 …… 67

第 5 章　定语从句的翻译
　　5.1　主句与从句合起来译 …………………………………………………… 69
　　5.2　主句与从句分开译 ……………………………………………………… 70
　　5.3　特殊定语从句的译法 …………………………………………………… 72
　　5.4　译成简单句 ……………………………………………………………… 72
　　5.5　几点说明 ………………………………………………………………… 73

第 6 章　其他从句的翻译
　　6.1　主语从句的翻译 ………………………………………………………… 75
　　6.2　表语从句的翻译 ………………………………………………………… 76
　　6.3　宾语从句的翻译 ………………………………………………………… 78
　　6.4　同位语从句的翻译 ……………………………………………………… 79
　　6.5　状语从句的翻译 ………………………………………………………… 80

第 7 章　否定形式的翻译
　　7.1　全部否定 ………………………………………………………………… 83
　　7.2　部分否定 ………………………………………………………………… 85
　　7.3　双重否定 ………………………………………………………………… 85
　　7.4　意义否定 ………………………………………………………………… 86
　　7.5　问答中的否定 …………………………………………………………… 87
　　7.6　前缀与后缀的否定 ……………………………………………………… 88
　　7.7　带有否定词的短语译法 ………………………………………………… 90

第 8 章　专业名词与数词翻译
　　8.1　专业术语的译法 ………………………………………………………… 95
　　8.2　数量的增加和倍数的译法 ……………………………………………… 99
　　8.3　数量减少的译法 ………………………………………………………… 101
　　8.4　不定数量的译法 ………………………………………………………… 103
　　8.5　近似数的译法 …………………………………………………………… 104
　　8.6　带有数词的短语译法 …………………………………………………… 105
　　8.7　大数英语表示法 ………………………………………………………… 106
　　8.8　一些数学算式写法与读法 ……………………………………………… 108

第 9 章　长句的翻译
　　9.1　长句的分析 ……………………………………………………………… 111
　　9.2　长句的译法 ……………………………………………………………… 112

第 II 部分　专业英文选读

Unit One　Descriptive Statistics
　　1.1　Introduction to Statistics ………………………………………………… 117
　　1.2　Population and Sample ………………………………………………… 120
　　1.3　Measurement Scales …………………………………………………… 123

1.4	The Process of a Statistical Study	125
1.5	Several Variables	127
1.6	Measures of Location	130
1.7	Measures of Dispersion	136
1.8	Grouped Data	139
1.9	Graphics	143
1.10	An Example	147
1.11	Proofs of the Results in this Chapter	150
Exercises		151

Unit Two Mathematical Statistics

2.1	Event and Probability	153
2.2	Random Variable and Distribution	156
2.3	Mathematical Expectation	165
2.4	Transformation of Variables	177
2.5	Moment-Generating Function	179
2.6	Law of Large Numbers and Central Limit Theorem	184
2.7	Statistical Inference	190
2.8	Testing Hypothesis	206
2.9	Regression Analysis	215
Appendix 2A	Integration by Substitution	227
Appendix 2B	Integration by Parts	227
Appendix 2C	Taylor Series Expansion	228
Appendix 2D	Cramer-Rao Inequality	228
Appendix 2E	Some Formulas of Matrix Algebra	232
Appendix 2F	Bayes' Theorem	233
Exercises		236

Unit Three Index Numbers

3.1	Introduction	268
3.2	Conception and Notation	270
3.3	Formula for Price Index Numbers	272
3.4	Quantity Index Numbers	275
3.5	Properties of Index Numbers: The Test Approach	280

Unit Four Missing Data and Imputation

4.1	Introduction	284
4.2	Missing Data Assumptions	287
4.3	Handing Missing Data without Models	290
4.4	Observed-Data Likelihood	292
4.5	Regression-Based Imputation	293

Unit Five Advanced Topics

  5.1 Measures and Measure Spaces ……………………………………… 297
  5.2 Random Variables and Distributions …………………………………… 299
  5.3 Type of Distribution ……………………………………………………… 302
  5.4 Moment Characteristics ………………………………………………… 303
  5.5 Shape Characteristies …………………………………………………… 305
  5.6 Entropy …………………………………………………………………… 307
  5.7 Generating Function and Characteristic Function …………………… 308
  5.8 Decomposition of Distributions ………………………………………… 311
  5.9 Stable Distributions ……………………………………………………… 312
  5.10 Random Vectors and Multivariate Distributions ……………………… 312
  5.11 Conditional Distributions ………………………………………………… 315
  5.12 Moment Characteristics of Random Vectors ………………………… 316
  5.13 Conditional Expectations ……………………………………………… 318
  5.14 Regressions ……………………………………………………………… 319
  5.15 Cenerating Function of Random Vectors ……………………………… 319
  Appendix 5A Properties of Conditional Expectations …………………… 321
  Appendix 5B Properties of Conditional Variances ……………………… 323

Unit Six Data Science and Dig Data

  6.1 From Data to Wisdom …………………………………………………… 324
  6.2 Data Science …………………………………………………………… 327
  6.3 Big Data ………………………………………………………………… 344
  6.4 Analytics ………………………………………………………………… 353
  6.5 Big Data Analytics ……………………………………………………… 367

第Ⅲ部分 参考译文

第3单元 指数译文

  3.1 引言 ……………………………………………………………………… 386
  3.2 概念与符号 ……………………………………………………………… 387
  3.3 价格指数公式 …………………………………………………………… 388
  3.4 数量指数 ………………………………………………………………… 390
  3.5 指数性质:检验方法 …………………………………………………… 394

第4单元 缺失数据与估算

  4.1 引言 ……………………………………………………………………… 397
  4.2 缺失数据假设 …………………………………………………………… 399
  4.3 非模型处理缺失数据 …………………………………………………… 401
  4.4 观测数据似然函数 ……………………………………………………… 403
  4.5 基于回归的估算 ………………………………………………………… 404

附 录

附录Ⅰ	常用数学运算和统计学常用的符号及读法	406
附录Ⅱ	概率论数理统计惯用符号及其含义	409
附录Ⅲ	统计学常用英文词汇汉译表	410
附录Ⅳ	网上概率和统计学期刊	454
附录Ⅴ	统计学专业软件	461
附录Ⅵ	希腊字母读音表	477
附录Ⅶ	基数与序数的英文表示汇总表	478
附录Ⅷ	概率论及统计学历史大事	479
附录Ⅸ	数据阶常用英文表示法	481
附录Ⅹ	计算机系统存储单位数据表示	482
附录Ⅺ	大数据常用术语(含定义)表	483
附录Ⅻ	数据科学与统计学的比较	486
附录ⅩⅢ	数据科学各构成部分关系框架	488
附录ⅩⅣ	哈佛大学统计系本科生及研究生课程纵览	489
附录ⅩⅤ	生日与星座	491

参考文献 ······ 492

第Ⅰ部分　英译汉常用方法与技巧

第1章　翻译概述

1.1　翻译与翻译标准

1.1.1　翻译

翻译是指用一种语言把另外一种语言所表达的内容准确、完整地重新表达出来的活动,也是一项艰苦的、艺术性的再创作。使用不同语言的民族要想达到相互交流、相互了解的目的,就需要通过翻译。

翻译活动的范围非常广泛,依据不同的内容与形式,通常可分为如下几个种类:

(1)按照语言来分,有外语译成本族语,本族语译成外语两种。如英译汉、汉译英等。

(2)按照工作来分,有口译与笔译。口译是口头翻译,笔译是文字翻译。

(3)按照译文表达原文的确切和完整程度来分,有等值翻译与非等值翻译。表达确切和完整的为等值翻译,而表达不完整、不确切的为非等值翻译。如节译、选译等。

(4)按照译文体裁来分,翻译有文学翻译、政论翻译和科技翻译。

1.1.2　翻译标准

翻译有一定的标准,这是衡量译文好坏的尺度与标准。清末时期,文学家和翻译家严复曾提出"信(faithfulness)——就是忠实原文;

达(expressiveness)——就是表达清楚;雅(elegance)——就是文字古雅"的翻译标准。这是一种过去的说法,虽然仍有许多学者认为,这三项要求还是衡量翻译水平的基本准则,但是,当代学者则有适应新时代、新要求的翻译标准和内容。当代,国内翻译界的学者主张,把翻译标准概括为"忠实、通顺"四个字。

所谓"忠实",一方面要忠于原作的内容,要把原作的内容准确、完整地表达出来,不得随意篡改、增删;另一方面,还要保持原作的风格,即原作的民族风格、时代风格、语言风格等。如果原作是通俗的口语体,那么就不能译成文绉绉的书面语体;如果原作是古代风格的,那么就不能译成现代风格的。总之,翻译必须"保存着原作的风姿"。

"忠实"这个标准对科技翻译更为重要。因为科学技术文献的任务在于准确而系统地论述某一类科技问题,它要求高度的准确性。因此,对于科技翻译来说,要特别强调其准确性,尤其是专业术语、定义、定理和结论的翻译更应该给予特别的重视。

所谓"通顺",是指译文语言必须通顺易懂,符合本民族语言的说法与规范。译文力求做到:结构合理,逻辑清晰,不能出现逐词死译、硬译或乱译的现象。

对于科技英语的特点和用途而言,其翻译除了原则上要满足上述的两个标准之外,还应该要求:准确规范、通俗易懂、简洁明晰。

科技文献的主要功能是论述科学事实、探讨科学问题、传播科学知识、记录科学实验、总结科学经验等。这就要求科技文献翻译首先必须是准确规范。所谓准确,就是忠实地、不折不扣地传达原文的全部信息内容。所谓规范,就是译文要符合所涉及的科学技术或者某个专业领域的专业语言表达规范。要想做到这一点,译者必须充分地理解原文所表达的内容,其中包括对原文词汇、语法、逻辑关系以及科学内容的理解。

所谓通俗易懂,指译文的语言符合译语语法结构及表达习惯,易于为读者所理解和接受。换句话说,译文语言须明白易懂、文理通顺、结构合理、逻辑关系清楚,没有死译、硬译、语言晦涩难懂的现象。

所谓简洁明晰,就是指译文简洁精炼、一目了然,要尽量避免繁琐、冗赘和不必要的重复。在科技英语翻译中,准确的译文必须是通顺的,而译文的通顺必须以准确为基础和前提。倘若准确但不通顺,则准确的意义尽失;倘若通顺而又不准确,则背离了翻译的基本原则及标准。在做到准确和通顺的要求上,如果能做到简洁,则应是科技英语翻译的理想境界。

本书所论述的翻译问题属于科技翻译的范畴,重点介绍统计学方面的一些内容。

1.2 翻译过程

翻译是一种创造性的语言活动,它并不比创作容易,需要付出艰巨的劳动。创作可以选择熟悉的内容写作,而翻译就不能完全由自己做主了。有时,为了准确地译出一个句子或者词组,要反复推敲很长时间。翻译家严复曾说:"一名之立,旬月踌躇",就是这个道理。作家鲁迅曾讲过:"我向来总是以为翻译比创作容易,因为至少是无须构思,但到真的一译,就会遇到难关,比如一个名词或动词,写不出,创作时候可以回避,翻译上却不成,也还得想,一直弄到头昏眼花,好像在脑子里面摸一个急于要开箱子的钥匙,却没有。"(《'题未定'草》)这段话生动地表述了翻译工作的艰巨性。

要想准确地将英语翻译成汉语,通常必须经过如下三个阶段:理解、表达、校核。

1.2.1 理解阶段

阅读理解与翻译是密不可分的。要做到"忠实、通顺",进行翻译时要做到如下几点。

(1)首先必须仔细阅读英语原文;对原文有透彻的理解,然后把所理解的东西用汉语确切地表达。在处理一个句子、一个段落、一篇文章时,要从英语到汉语,从汉语到英语,反复推敲,仔细研究。

(2)其次,要理解上下文的逻辑关系。有时候,原文里的一个词、词组或一个句子,可能有几种不同的意思,只有经过逻辑推理才能决定哪一种是确切的译法。如:Please let me know if you need my help,本句有两个意思:(a)如果你需要帮助,就请告诉我。(b)请告诉我,你是否要我帮助。

(3)还要理解原文所涉及的事物。有些的文章具有其特定的历史背景、典故或专业术语,如果不能深刻地理解,就很难译成恰当的汉语。比如,Sir Richmond died that night in *the small hours*。"the small hours"这一词组不能按其字面翻译。美国人提到"the small hours"时,指的是凌晨 1~3 点钟这段时间,可译作"半夜三更"。因此,本句可译为:雷茨门爵士在那天半夜里去世了。

比如,He did it *step by slow step*。在这里,原句中的 step by slow step 是由 step by step 变化而来的。step by step 的意思是"一步一步地",即"逐渐""渐渐"。中间加了个 slow 问题就复杂了,那么应该怎样翻译呢?从语法结构上分析,这里的 slow 只形容后一个 step,似乎与前面一个 step 无关,所以才会产生误解,认为是"越来越慢"的意思。其实,这里的 slow 是修饰整个成语 step by step 的,从语义分析可将其看成是副词状语,其意思应该是"慢慢地、一步一步

(地)",所以全句可以译成:他一步一步地做,进行得很慢。或者:他从容不迫,一步一步地进行。

英语中由一个名词重复,中间加一个 by 构成的类似习语很多,如 little by little / bit by bit (一点一点地), drop by drop (一滴一滴地), page by page (逐页地), door by door (挨门挨户地)等。在这些习语的 by 后面加上一个形容词,可以表示各种各样的意思。

例如,He scrutinized the book page by extremely meticulous page, trying to find any clue others might missed. 他极端仔细地一页一页地阅读这本书,想从中发现别人可能错过的线索。

还是以 step by step 为例,就应该理解和猜得出下面说法的确切含义:step by quick step, step by careful step, step by happy step, step by smiling step.

1.2.2 表达阶段

表达是理解的结果,是把已经理解了的原文选择适当的译文语言材料重新表达出来。表达的好坏通常与理解的深度及对译文语言掌握的程度有关。对原文理解正确了,翻译才能表达正确。在翻译表达上有许多具体方法和技巧。

最基本的方法有:直译法和意译法。直译就是基本保持原文的表达形式及内容,不做大的改动,同时要求语言通顺易懂,表达清楚明白。直译所强调的是"形似",主张把原文内容按照原文的形式,比如词序、语序、语气、结构、修辞方法等,用译语表达出来。

有时候不宜采用直译的方法,就应该采用意译法。意译是指将原文所表达的内容以一种释义性的方式用译语把其意义表达出来。意译所强调的是"神似",也就是不拘泥于原文在词序、语序、语法结构等方面的形式,用译语的习惯表达方式把原文的本意翻译出来。

例如:Arguably, there are no new results in the book, but, *like Monday morning quarterbacking*, we can look backwards and see better ways to say and do things. 这一句可翻译成:或许本书中没有崭新的结果,但是可以像事后诸葛亮那样,我们能够看到以最佳方式来阐述结果以及推演。这句中斜体部分若按原文逐词直译为"好像星期一上午的担任重要前卫"使人听了不知所云,所以只能意译。因为这里 "Monday morning quarterbacking" is an American term for the fact that it is easy to be critical of decisions that have already been made, but it is a lot more difficult to make good decisions in real-time.

由于英汉语言各有其特点和形式,在词汇、语法、惯用法、表达方式等有相同之处,所以,翻译时就必须采用不同的手段,或采用直译或采用意译,而有时候必须采用意译和直译相结合的手法,要以完整、准确、通顺地表达出原文的意义为翻译的最终目的。

1.2.3 核校阶段

核校是理解与表达的进一步深化,是对原作内容进一步核实,对译文语言进一步推敲,是使译文符合标准必不可少的一个阶段。核校通常有初校、复校、定稿三个步骤:初校是在初稿出来之后,对照原文进行核校,看有没有漏译或错误的地方;复校是脱离原文,看译文是否合本族语的规范,是否通顺;定稿是在初校和复校的基础上,再次对照原文,进行一次仔细地、认真地核校,如果所有问题均已解决,译文才能定稿。核校阶段对于科技文献的翻译尤为重要,因为这类文章中公式数字较多,要有高度的精确性,绝不能疏忽大意有任何差错。

1.3 怎样做好翻译

要想做好翻译工作,必须做到下述一些基本要求。

1.3.1 不断提高外语水平

要做到这一点,通常可以从下述几个方面着手:①加强基本功的训练。多读多听,多背多记;多写多说,多译多改。②不断地扩大自己的词汇量。词汇掌握得越多,翻译起来就越容易,速度就越快。③熟练地掌握语法,做到概念清楚、条理分明、能分析、会辨认。

1.3.2 不断提高汉语水平

汉语水平不高,词语贫乏,翻译起来往往就会笔不从心,词不达意;译文既不通顺,又不符合汉语语法和习惯规范。汉语水平高,翻译起来就会得心应手,文笔流畅。

1.3.3 具有严肃认真的工作态度和精益求精的工作精神

对于自己不懂的问题,理解不深的词句,必须设法解决,不能马虎了事;在科技文献中,特别是数学和统计学里,定义、定律、公式、数字、图表、结论等,更不能有半点差错。

1.3.4 具有广博的知识

通常,科技文献往往涉及很多方面。要想做好翻译工作,除了要求译者既要具有一定的专业知识,还要掌握各种学科的基本常识和广泛的现实生活知识。不了解所译的专业内容,就会影响自己的理解和译文的质量。缺乏较广泛的一般性知识就会给翻译工作带来一定的困难。因此,各种知识知道得越多、越广泛,翻译起来就越容易、越方便。

1.3.5　掌握基本的翻译方法和技巧

熟悉相关的翻译理论,掌握常用的翻译方法和技巧,是从事科技翻译工作必不可少的条件之一。

第 2 章 句子与句型

2.1 句 子

　　句子是表达思想和进行交际的基本语言单位,要想正确地理解和研究文章内容,就应该从句子开始。只有切实弄懂写作句子的基本方法和技巧,才能为真实理解篇章奠定坚实的语言基础。
　　把单词聚集起来表达一个意思的句子。通常,句子是由作为主题的主语部分和叙述主题的谓语部分两个要素组成。

2.1.1 句子

　　运用一个单词或几个单词表达一种思想、感情、欲望等的称为句子。写句子时,通常以大写字母开始,以句号(.)或者感叹号(!)、问号(?)结束。句子是根据某种意图说出或写出的,除句子形式和意思之外,根据语境和文章内容去理解也是很重要的。
　　(1)运用 <主语部分 + 谓语部分> 形式的句子
　　一般句子由作为主题的部分和叙述它的部分组成,前者叫主语部分(Subject),后者叫谓语部分(Predicate)。换句话说,主语是句子描述的核心,大多数情况下,在主动句中,主语是动作的发出者,而在被动句中,主语是动作的承受者。
　　除 there be 句型和倒装句句型之外,主语一般位于谓语之前。比如,下面两个句子:

	主语部分	谓语部分	功能
(a)	I (我)	agree. (同意)	同意
(b)	What sort of information (什么类型的信息)	can be found on the Internet ? (能在因特网上找到?)	提问

像(a)句一样,主语和谓语各只有1个单词;也有像(b)句一样,主、谓语各是由几个单词组成的。但是,无论是(a)句或者(b)句,只有主语或只有谓语,所表达的意思都不完整,这种情况不叫句子。

(2)不用 <主语部分+谓语部分> 形式的句子

在句子中,还有不同时具备主语、谓语两个要素的情况。出现这样情形,大致有如下几种句子。

① 祈使句

在祈使句中,主语 you 往往都省略。这时,动词形式应该运用原形。

Lend me this book, please.（请把这本书借给我。）

* 即使形式是祈使句,但作用是请求。

② 省略主语（口语）

Thank you for your kindness.（谢谢你的好意。）

"How's things?" "(They) Couldn't be better."

（"怎么样?""很好。"）

③ 省略 <主语+be 动词>（口语）

(I am) Sorry I won't be there.（抱歉,我不能去那里。）

"Could you mail this letter?" "(That'd be) No problem."

（"你能帮我邮这封信吗?""没问题。"）

"(I will) See you later!" "Yes, goodbye!"

（"待会儿见!""再见!"）

"How kind (it is) of you (to help me)!" "Not at all!"

（"谢谢你帮忙!""没有什么!"）

* 根据情况可以加进或省略 to help 等。

④ 感情表达,或者是呼吁的语句。

My God!（天哪!）

Mom!（妈妈!）

⑤ 对前面发言的应答,或根据场面而使用的表达。

"Thanks." "Not at all."

（"谢谢。""不客气。"）

"Meaning what?" "Meaning that I wish you would change your mind."

（"什么意思?""就是要你改变你的想法。"）

* 一般来说,即使省略了什么,也能根据对话语境或前后关系,知道其意思。

⑥ 谚语

Out of sight, out of mind.（不见易忘。）

First come, first served. (先到先得。)

2.1.2 主语部分和谓语部分的构成

主语部分和谓语部分各由几个单词构成的,作为主语部分中心的名词或相当于名词的单词叫主语。

在科技英语中,主语的形式主要有以下几种:
(1) 名词、名词性代词以及其他可以起到名词作用的词;
(2) 动名词(这时,句子的谓语必定为单数第三人称形式);
(3) 动词不定式(这时,句子的谓语必定为单数第三人称形式,并且往往可以用形式主语 it 的句型);
(4) 主语从句(这时,句子的谓语必定为单数第三人称形式,并且往往可以用形式主语 it 的句型)。

作为谓语部分中心的单词叫谓语动词或动词。谓语是表示动作的,在主动句中表示主语发出的动作,而在被动句中则表示主语所承受的动作,有时谓语还表示特征、状态等。谓语一般位于主语之后(there be 句型和倒装句除外)。

科技英语中的谓语形式通常有以下几种:
(1) 单个实义动词(属于单一式);
(2) 系动词+表语(属于复合式);
(3) 助动词+主要动词(或半助动词+动词不定式)(属于复合式);
(4) 情态动词+主要动词(属于复合式);
(5) there+ { be / 某些不及物动词(exist, appear, seem, result)。 / 不及物动词

一般说来,谓语有明显的时态和语态形式,所以在分析和认识一个复杂又冗长的句子时,应首先找出谓语,然后确定主语,接着再找出其他成分。

例如,下面三个句子:

	主语部分	谓词部分
(a)	The **telephone** on my desk (我桌上的电话	**rang** persistently and loudly. 大声地响了很久。)
(b)	**George and Karl** (乔治和卡尔	**are** good friends. 是好朋友。)
(c)	The **picture** of the accident (这张事故的照片	**makes** me sick. 使我恶心。)

(a)句和(c)句中的主语部分有 on my desk 和 of the accident 作限定主语的修饰语(冠词也是修饰语)。(b)句中 George 和 Karl 两个都是主语。

谓语部分,rang/are/makes 各是谓语动词。根据谓语动词种类的不同,跟在它们后面的单词,分别起副词修饰语、补语、宾语的作用。在(a)句中,persistently 和 loudly 起副词修饰语的作用;(b)句中的 friends 作(主语)补语;(c)句中的 me 起宾语,sick 起(宾格)补语的作用。

主语部分的主语(S),谓语部分的谓语动词(V),以及宾语(O)和补语(C),这4个是句子的主要因素。

2.1.3 主谓一致的几点说明

(1) not only A but also B 作主语时,句子的谓语与 B 一致。

(2) A as well as B 作主语时,句子的谓语与 A 一致。

(3) either A or B 或 neither A nor B 作主语时,句子的谓语与 B 一致。

(4) A rather than (together with, but, except, plus 等) B 作主语时,句子的谓语与 A 一致。

(5) 表示时间、距离、温度等的复数名词作主语时,句子的谓语常用单数形式(但表示时间的复数名词有时也可用复数的谓语形式)。

(6) "more than one + 单数名词" 作主语时,句子的谓语用单数形式。

(7) "one and half + 复数名词" 作主语时,句子的谓语用单数形式; "one or two + 复数名词" 作主语时,句子的谓语用复数形式。

(8) "a set / kind / piece / type / sort / form / pair of + 复数名词" 作主语时,句子的谓语一般要用单数形式。

(9) there be 的单复数形式一般与靠近的第一个名词一致。

(10) 如果在由 and 连接作主语的两个单数名词前面有 every, each, no 等修饰词,谓语用单数形式。

(11) 有些集合名词作主语时,如果作为一个整体看待,则谓语用单数形式;若强调其一个一个成员时,则谓语用复数形式。科技会议通知书中偶尔会出现这种情况。

2.2 句 型

2.2.1 句子要素和五种基本句型

句子成分与词类一样,是句子的部件。分析清楚句子成分对正确理解句子的含义极为重要。通常,英语句子的一般语序如下:

①主动句:主语→谓语(→ 宾语 → 宾语补足语);

②被动句:主语→谓语(→ 状语/ 主语补足语 / 保留宾语)。

一般情况下,在一个句子中,定语在名词前后,状语位置则更灵活。

除主语之外,动词用什么样的句子要素(宾语、补语),以这个为基准对句子加以分类,基本上有以下五种句型。这里把它们称为五种基本句型。

Ⅰ. 主语 + 动词 (S+V)

Everybody **laughed**. (每个人都笑了。)

Ⅱ. 主语 + 动词 + 补语 (S+V+C)

His eyes **are** blue. (他的眼睛是蓝色的。)

Ⅲ. 主语 + 动词 + 宾语 (S+V+O)

Foreigners **admire** the Great Wall. (外国人赞美长城。)

Ⅳ. 主语 + 动词 +(直接)宾语+(间接)宾语 (S+V+O1+O2)

I **gave** him my address. (我把我的地址给了他。)

Ⅴ. 主语 + 动词 + 宾语 + 补语 (S+V+O+C)

I **found** the box empty. (我发现箱子是空的。)

* 在Ⅰ,Ⅱ,Ⅲ句中,有时会各加上不能删除的附加语。加上后就分别成了第一句型<S+V+A>、第二句型< S+V+C+A>、第三句型< S+V+O+A>句型。

2.2.2 动词种类和五种基本句型

不及物动词、及物动词以及完全动词、不完全动词和句型的关系如下所示。其中"○"表示需要用宾语或补语,"×"表示不需要。

	不及物动词		及物动词	
	完全不及物动词	不完全不及物动词	完全及物动词	不完全及物动词
宾语	×	×	○	○
补语	×	○	×	○
句型	Ⅰ	Ⅱ	Ⅲ,Ⅳ	Ⅴ

2.3 第一种句型 <S+V>

这种句型的动词不用宾语和补语,叫完全不及物动词。

2.3.1 第一种句型用的动词

不及物动词多是完全不及物动词,但单独使用并不很多。

"Here is how you should do it , **See**?" "**I see**. I'll try it."

("这里写着应该怎么做,明白了吗?"

"知道了。我试试。")

【确认】

"How's this?" "That **will do**."
("怎么样?""可以。") 【承诺】
Years **passed**. (岁月可逝。)
有时也会没有修饰动词的语句,但一般说来,修饰语都伴随着副词语句。
The sun **is shining** brightly.
(太阳闪闪发光。)
The meeting **ended** at three in the afternoon.
(会议是下午3点结束的。)
He **has been waiting** for an hour.
(他等了一个钟头。)
The bedroom curtains **have faded** at the edges.
(卧室窗帘的边缘褪色了。)

2.3.2 \<S+V+A\>

有时,用在完全不及物动词的句子里的副词性语句,去掉它句子就不成立。这就是所谓的附加语(A)。

Mother is in the kitchen. (母亲在厨房。)

像这样,需要附加语的完全不及物动词,还有 **be**, **live**, **stand**, **stay** 等。与普通的修饰语(M)区别,特别需要附加语(A)的第一种句型,变成(S+V+A)后成为第一种句型的特别句型。

2.4 第二种句型 \<S+V+C\>

这个句型的动词需要补语,所以称为不完全不及物动词。主语和补语之间,可以看到<主语=补语>的关系,这种补语叫主语补语。能成为补语的是名词、代词、形容词、非谓语动词、短语以及从句。

2.4.1 用于第二种句型的动词

不完全不及物动词,分为以下4种。
(1)表示状态的动词"是……"
① be 组:be , lie, sit, stand 等。
"May I use this phone?" "**Be my guest**." 【承诺】
("可以借用一下电话吗?""您请便。")
Do we have to **lie** *flat* on the ground?
(我们必须躺在地上吗?)

The students **sat** *still*, listening to the lecture.
(学生们安静地坐着听讲。)
② keep 组：continue，hold，keep，remain，stay 等。
He kept quite calm.（他极为冷静。）
He remained silent.（他保持沉默。）
We stayed roommates for four years.
(我们是4年室友。)
(2) 表示状态变化的动词"成为……"
become，come，get，grow，make，turn，fall，go，run 等。
① become：比 get 更严谨的说法。多用于过去时和现在完成时。
English **has become** my favorite subject.
(英语开始成为我喜欢的科目。)
Suddenly her face was pale.
(突然她的脸变青了。)
＊be 有时也相当口语的"变成……"。比 become 更口语化。
② get：重视变化发生的初始阶段。多用于进行时。
补语 angry，dark，excited，sleepy，tires，wet 等。
We **are getting** *older* day by day.
(我们一天一天老起来。)
③come：平常的，或者是向好的状态变化。多用于习惯句。
补语 alive，cheap，clean，easy，true，untied 等。
Everything **will come** *right* in the end.
(什么事最终都将顺利。)
④ go：向不希望的状态变化。比 turn 或 grow 更普通的说法。
补语 bald，bankrupt，dizzy，mad，stale，wrong 等。
The milk **has gone** *bad*.（牛奶变坏了。）
⑤ grow：逐渐起的变化。较严谨的说法。也受旧式的影响。
补语 cold，cool，dark，old，sick，uneasy 等。
The children **are growing** *tired*.
(孩子们疲倦起来。)
⑥ fall：突然变成某种状态，多用于习惯句。
补语 flat，ill，quite，short，sick，silent 等。
While he was studying, he **fell** *asleep*.
(他学习的时候睡着了。)
⑦ turn：向与目前不同的方向或状态显著地变化。

补语 **cold**, **green**, **pale**, **rainy**, **sour**, **stormy** 等。
The leaves **turned** *red* as the days passed.
(树叶随着时间而变成红色。)
(3) 表示外表的动词:"看起来……" 如 **appear**, **look**, **seem** 等。
He **seemed** *surprised* by my ignorance.
(他对我的无知看上去很吃惊。)
She **looked** *troubled* by the news.
(她对这条新闻看上去很烦恼。)
He **appears** *happy* in his new job.
(他对新工作表现出很高兴。)
(4) 感觉动词:**feel**, **smell**, **sound**, **taste** 等。
Peaches **taste** *sweet*. (桃子尝起来是甜的。)
These lilies **smell** *lovely*. (这些百合花闻起来很香。)
"How about going to Hawaii?" "<u>**Sounds** *great*</u>!"   【同意】
("去夏威夷怎么样?""听起来不错!")

2.4.2 \<S+V+C+A\>

成为\<S+V+C\>句型中补语的形容词,有时会跟\<of +名词\>等带有介词的短语,构成相当于一个动词的\<be+形容词+介词\>结构。

这种场合,从句型上看,\<S+V+C\>中的 C(形容词)作为不可删除的附加语(A)使成为带有\<of+名词\>等的形式,这也可看成是\<S+V+C+A\>这种第二种句型的特例。

另外,这种带有介词的短语,也可以用 that 从句改写,这时就要去掉介词。
比如:
He is very **fond** *of playing the guitar.*
(他非常喜欢弹吉他。)
→ He **likes** *playing the guitar* very much.
＊playing 以后是 likes 的宾语。
I am **sure** *of his honesty.*
(我相信他的诚实。)
→ I am **sure** *that he is honest.*
＊考虑前面的 of the fact 被省略的话,that 从句应该是名词从句。

2.5 第三种句型 \<S+V+O\>

这种句型的动词,有宾语但不需要补语,称为完全及物动词。

2.5.1 第三种句型的一般形式

成为宾语的是名词、代词以及名词性从句。例如:
Most of us probably **eat** too much meat.
(我们大都可能肉吃太多了。)
Heaven **helps** those who help themselves.
(天助自助之人。)
﹡修饰宾语 those 的 who 以后的修饰从句,成为<S+V+O>句子结构。
I **want** to have some apple pie.
(我想吃些苹果馅饼。)
At last he **stopped** looking for the pearl.
(最后他停止了寻找珍珠。)
We must **decide** when to start.
(我们必须决定何时出发。)
The settlers **learned** that the land in the valley was fertile.
(开拓者知道山谷的土地是很肥沃的。)

2.5.2 <S+V+O+A>

第三句型的句子,根据动词的不同,在普通宾语后面伴有介词短语,形成意思完整的句子。如果把这些语句删除掉,作为句子就不完整,我们把它看成附加语(A)。<S+V+O+A>是第三种句型的特殊句型。下面是一些例子。

(1)需要表示动作方向或目标的动词
He **put** his hands in his pockets.
(他把他的手放在兜里。)
﹡若没有 in his pockets 的话,句子就会显得不自然。
She **introduced** me to her brother.
(她把我介绍给她哥哥。)
﹡从内容背景来看,当介绍对象很清楚的时候,可以用这样的句子:Allow me to introduce my brother. (请允许我来介绍我哥哥。)

(2)成语中用<及物动词+宾语+介词>的句子结构
通常,不同的及物动词使用的介词也不同。比如:
The man **robbed** him of all his money.
(那个男人偷了他所有的钱。)
Bees **provide** us with honey.
(蜜蜂给我们提供了蜂蜜。)

* 在美语中，也说 Bees provide us honey.

2.6 第四种句型 <S+V+O1+O2>

这种句型的动词，是用间接宾语和直接宾语的及物动词，叫施动词。用于"为……"的是间接宾语(O1)，用于"把……"是直接宾语(O2)。间接宾语主要是人，直接宾语是物。

2.6.1 用第四种句型的动词

施动词根据意思分为"给予……"意思的 give 组和"为……买"的意思的 buy 组。

(1) give 组

allot	（分配）	award	（授予）
give	（给予）	grant	（给予）
hand	（交给）	lend	（借给）
offer	（提供）	pass	（传递）
pay	（付款）	promise	（允诺）
read	（阅读）	sell	（卖）
send	（发送）	show	（出示）
teach	（教）	tell	（告诉）
throw	（掷、投）	write	（写）

例如：
I **gave** him some advice.（我给了他一些忠告。）
He **handed** the salesclerk the money.（他把钱递给店员。）
The girl **lent** her friend her new bicycle.
（女孩把她的新自行车借给了朋友。）
He **told** his brother the story.（他把这件事告诉了弟弟。）
We **showed** him some pictures of London.
（我们给他看了一些伦敦的照片。）
属于这组的动词，间接宾语和直接宾语语序相反时，成为间接宾语的语句前要加 to 。这样形成的句子又变成了第三种句型。比如：

I	gave	some advice		him.
He	handed	the money		the salesclerk.
The girl	lent	her new bicycle	to	her friend.
He	told	the story		his brother.
We	showed	some pictures of London		him.

* give 是"给予"的意思,它后面的直接宾语和间接宾语都不能省略,但 tell 等两个宾语都可省略。

I know, so I'll **tell** you.(我知道,我告诉你。)

I know, but I won't **tell**.(我知道,但我不说。)

(2) **buy** 组

buy	(买)	call	(叫喊)
cook	(烹调)	find	(找到)
get	(得到)	make	(制作)
order	(订餐)	prepare	(准备)
save	(储存)	spare	(抽出(时间))

He **bought** his daughter a dress.(他给女儿买了件套裙。)

I will **find** you a vacant seat.(我给你找空位。)

I've **ordered** you some dessert.(我给你要了些甜点。)

Get me a nice video camera.(给我一个好的录像机。)

属于这一组的动词,间接宾语和直接宾语顺序相反时,间接宾语前加 for。

He	bought	a dress		his daughter.
I	will find	a vacant seat	for	you.
I	've ordered	some dessert		you.
	Get	a nice video camera		me.

* 这种句型的直接宾语,像上例所示不定式很多。

* choose(选择)不常在这种句型中使用。

(3) **bring** 等

根据 bring 和 leave 等意思,有时会用 to 或 for。这时,to 和 for 都表示它本来的意思。"To"表示"方向","for"表示"为了"。

Bring the money *to* me here.

(把钱拿到我这里来。)

I have **brought** your heavy suitcase *for* you.

（我把你最重的箱子给你带过来了。）

He **left** a pretty fortune *to* his wife.

（他给妻子留下了一笔可观的遗产。）

I **left** some cookies *for* him.

（我给他留了些小甜饼。）

＊注意：leave A to B 的意思是"把 A 遗留给 B"。

(4) 其他组

① (a) ask 当间接宾语和直接宾语相反时，不是加 to 而加 of，ask a question of A 这是一个比较严谨的说法，实际上不太用。另外，在 question 以外，没有这种形式。

The teacher **asked** me a very difficult question.

（教师问了我一个很难的问题。）

→ The teacher **asked** a very difficult question *of* me.

Can I **ask** you a favor?

（能请你帮忙吗？）

→Can I **ask** a favor *of* you？

＊"请求"时用 of 的形式比较多。

(b) play 在<play O2 on O1>句中，表示从<（人）O1 给 O2（玩耍）>的意思时，把这句可以换成〈play O1 O2〉句型。

He **has played** a mean trick *on me*.

→ He **has played** *me* a mean trick.

（他给我玩鬼把戏。）

② 顺序不变的词

用 **cost**, **envy**, **save**, **spare** 等词时顺序不改变。

This computer has **saved** us a lot of work.

（这台电脑省了我们很多工作。）

I **envy** you your trip to Europe.

（羡慕你去欧洲旅游。）

＊I envy you. 和 I envy your trip. 作为句子都可以成立，上句中的 you 和 your trip 两个都可以认为是(直接)宾语。

2.6.2 不定式或从句作直接宾语

(1) 不定式

① to 不定式

She **promised** (me) *to keep* the secret.（她答应我保守秘密。）

→She **promised**(me) *that she would keep the secret.*

* promised O1 to do 时,间接宾语 O1(特别是 1、2 人称代词)通常被省略。

* 一般<S+V+O+to do>句型,不属于五种基本句型,就直接用这样的形式即可。

②疑问词+to 不定词

Would you please **advise** me *which to buy*?(能否告诉我买哪个?)

My sister **taught** me *how to fold* paper into a crane.
(我姐姐教我如何叠纸鹤。)

(2)名词从句

①that 从句

I **convinced** him that he was wrong.(我发现他错了。)

注:在<S+V+O+that 从句>中不能省略 O 的动词:通常不能省略 that 从句前名词的宾语的动词有:assure(保证)、convince(说服)、inform(告知)、notify(通知)、persuade(说服)、tell(告诉)等。

★ <S+V+O+that 从句>句型里,看上去能但实际不能去掉的动词。

下面的动词,从意思上讲可以从这个句子结构中去掉,但实际是不能去掉的,必须注意。例如,不可以说 suggest me that...,只能说 suggest *to me* that...

expect	(期望、认为)	explain	(阐明、解释)
order	(命令)	propose	(提议)
recommend	(推荐)	require	(强迫)
request	(请求)	suggest	(建议)
urge	(极力主张)	want	(要求)

②疑问词从句

This book **shows** you how a car works.
(这本书告诉你车是怎样工作的。)

★ 用于< S+ V + O + 疑问词从句> 句型的动词

advise	(劝告)	ask	(问)
instruct	(教导)	remind	(使想起)
show	(出示)	teach	(教)
tell	(讲述)	warn	(警告)

2.7　第五种句型 <S+V+O+C>

这种句型的及物动词需要宾格补语,称为不完全及物动词。在宾语和宾格补语之间,有<主语+谓语>的关系。

They **called** him *Jim*. (他们叫他吉姆。)

I **want** him to be honest. (我要他诚实。)

2.7.1 把名词、形容词、短语作为宾格补语的动词

(1) make 组　表达"把……做成"意思时,如果没有相当于"……"的语句(宾格补语)句子就不成立。比如:

No wise bird **makes** its own nest *dirty*.
(聪明的鸟是不会弄脏自己的巢穴的。)

We **chose** Mr. Gray *chairperson* of the meeting.
(我们选格雷先生为这次会议主席。)

She **named** her cat *Sally*.
(她把她的猫叫莎丽。)

The news of his injury **turned** her *pale*.
(听到他受伤了,她脸色变得苍白。)

Anger **drove** him *blind*.
(愤怒使他盲目。)

He always **leaves** everything *in order*.
(他总是把事情做得井井有条。)

表达"把……形成(某种状态)"这样意思的动词,除上例以外,还有 **get**, **lay**, **let**, **render**, **set** 等。另外,除宾格补语用名词的动词外,还有 **appoint**(任命),**declare**(宣布),**elect**(选举),**vote**(表决)等。

(2) paint 组　主要表示动作的结果所产生的状态。即使没有表示状态的宾格补语句子也成立。例如:

Mr. Johnson **painted** the fence *white*.
(约翰逊先生把栅栏漆成白色。)

* 刷涂料的结果是栅栏变成了白色,所以因为有了 white,其结果状态很清楚。

She **boiled** the egg *hard*. (她把鸡蛋煮硬。)

He **pushed** the door *open*. (他把门打开。)

* open 虽是形容词,但感觉像构成动名词的副词一样。所以 *push open the door* 的语序也可以。这种形式和结果相比,"打开"这一动作感觉更强烈。特别适合宾语长的情况。

★ 表示动作结果产生状态的动词

bake	（烘）	beat	（打）
burn	（燃烧）	color	（着色）
cut	（切）	dye	（染）
lick	(舔)	wash	（洗）
wipe	（擦）		

(3) **think** 组　表达"认为"意思的动词，省略了 to be。在宾语和补语之间，有时也会加上 to be。例如：

Alice **thinks** her husband (to be) a great musician.
（艾丽丝认为她的丈夫是一个伟大的音乐家。）

＊用 Alice thinks (that) her husband is a great musician. 更口语化。

I **consider** his words (to be) very important.
（我认为他的话很重要。）

2.7.2　用不定式、分词作宾格补语的动词

主要以使役动词、感觉动词为主。

(1) 使役动词

The black suit **made** Susan *look* thin.
（黑色的套装使苏珊看上去更苗条。）

No one can **get** the car *to start*.
（没有人能发动这辆车。）

I cannot **have** you *doing* that.
（我不能让你干那种事。）

I could not **make** myself *understood* in German.
（我说德语时还不能让别人听懂。）

(2) 感觉动词

I *heard* something *crash* against the wall.
（我听到什么东西碰撞到墙上的声音。）

I *saw* some little fish *swimming* about in the water.
（我看见一些小鱼在水里游。）

Did you *hear* your name *called*?
（你听到有人喊你的名字了吗？）

(3) 其他

The management **wants** all the employees *to be punctual*.
（管理部门要求所有的职工都准时。）

＊这句从意思上讲，可以认为 all the employees to be punctual 全部都是

want 的宾语,但考虑到 all the employees to be punctual 这一关系,可以把 all the employees 看成 want 的宾语,把 to be punctual 可看成是宾格补语。只是一般不把<S + V + O + to do>句型归入五种基本句型里。这样,只要理解这个句型就可以了。

2.8 特殊句型

2.8.1 <There + be 动词 + 主语>

当人们表示某种不特定的东西存在时,用 There is (are , was 等)句子结构。英语中要表达"桌上有花瓶"这句时,一般不说:A vase is on the table. 而说:There is a vase on the table.

这种句子结构的 be 动词,原则上是和后面的名词的数、人称相一致,一般主语可考虑是 be 动词后面的名词。句首 there 本身并没有明确的意思,发音也是弱读。这种句子结构是<动词+主语>的形式,属于第 1 类句型。

There **are** five in my family.
(我家 5 口人。)

"Would you show me how to do it ?" "**Sure**, *there's* **nothing to it**."
("能教我怎么做吗?" "可以,其实没什么。") 【承诺】

There **used to be** a small park just around the corner.
(过去在拐角处有一个小小的公园。)

there is... 句子结构中的 there ,意思上并不是主语,但在变疑问句时,在语法上起主语的作用。

Is **there** a vase on the desk?
(桌上有花瓶吗?)

﹡加上附加疑问的场合也同样。

There is no one in the room, *is there*?
(房间里没有人,是吗?)

I don't want **there** *to be* any misunderstanding.
(我不希望有任何误解。)

﹡成为不定式意思上的主语。

There *being* nothing to do, I went to bed.
(没什么事可做,我睡觉了。)

﹡成为分词结构意思上的主语,文语型。

She insisted on **there** *being* a third party.

(她坚持第三方的存在。)

* 成为动名词意思上的主语。

跟在 there 后面的单词,除 be 动词外还有 come, live, remain, stand 等。

There once **lived** a great king.(曾有一位伟大的国王。)

There **followed** a long silence.(接着是长时间的沉默。)

2.8.2 常见的 It 句型与译法

在科技文献中,it 作形式主语的句型非常多,现将常见句型及其译法介绍如下。

(1)it is +形容词+ that... 例如:

it is possible that...	有可能,是可能的
it is impossible that...	不可能,是不可能的
it is obvious that...	显然,很明显
it is clear that...	显然,很明显,自然
it is necessary that...	必须,有必要,是必要的
it is important that...	重要的是,是重要的
it is essential that...	必需,是必不可少的
it is appropriable that...	是适当的
it is notable that...	值得注意的是

(2)it is + 名词 + that... 例如:

it is a fact that...	事实上
it is a wonder that...	令人奇怪的是
it is no wonder that...	难怪,无怪乎
it is no use that...	是无用的
it is the case that...	事实是这样的
it is a good thing that...	好在
it is common practice that...	通常是
it is a common knowledge that...	众所周知
it is no matter that...	是无关紧要的
it is worth notice that...	值得注意的是
it is no harm that...	是无害的

(3)it + 不及物动词 + that... 例如:

it seems that...	似乎,看来
it appears that...	似乎,看来
it follows that...	从而,于是,由此可见

it turns out that… 结果是,结果表明
it stands to reason that… 显然,有理
it goes without saying that… 显然,不言而喻

(4) it + 被动语态 + that… 例如:

it is said that… 据说,有人说
it is known that… 众所周知,大家知道
it is believed that… 大家相信,人们相信,据信
it is learned that… 据说,据闻
it is found that… 人们发现,据发现
it is considered that… 据估计,人们认为
it is assumed that… 假定,假设
it is estimated that… 据估计,有人估计
it is claimed that… 有人宣称,据称
it is stressed that… 应强调,有人强调说
it is expected that… 预期,人们希望
it is supposed that… 假定,据推测

(5) it + 动宾结构、系表结构或其他 + that… 例如:

it makes no matter that… 无关紧要
it seems impossible that… 似乎是不可能的
it seems possible that… 似乎是可能的
it used to be said that… 常说,常言
it has been made clear that… 已经很清楚

2.9 强调句型

把句中特定部分的意思特别加强的叫强调。在英语中,强调句子成分的手段多种多样。在口语中一般借助语调的变化来表示,也就是重读句中要强调的某个词或某个部分;在书面语中可以通过词汇手段、语法手段或修辞手段来进行强调,以加强语势。

下面介绍科技英语中最常见的几种强调形式。

2.9.1 用语法手段表示强调

语法手段表强调指的是英语中某些固定的强调句型,表示强调的句型主要有"it"强调句。

(1) it 强调句型

It is (was) + 被强调的部分 { 主语 / 宾语 / 状语 / 介词宾语 } + that (who/ whom)...

换句话说, it 强调句结构为:"It is (was) + 被强调的部分 + that (who/whom) + 句子的其他成分", 这种强调句除不能强调谓语动词之外, 其他句子成分, 如主语、宾语、宾语补足语、状语等都可以强调。

it 强调句型一般情况下, 翻译成"正是……""就是……"或"是……"。而当引出疑问句的疑问词、引出名词从句的连接代词和连接副词时, 通常译为"究竟""到底"。

it 强调句有肯定、否定和疑问三种形式。把句中 it is/was/...that/which/who 这三个词去掉后, 留下来的部分仍是一个语法完整的句子。在 it 强调句中, it 既不是代词, 又不是形式主语, 它没有实际意义。

无论强调上述哪种成分, 均可使用 that; 当强调表示事物的主语或宾语时, 也可以使用 which; 当强调作主语的人时, 多用 who。

不论强调什么成分, it 强调句型中的 be 均用单数第三人称形式。假如被强调的句子谓语为现在的某一时态或将来时态时, 一般用 is; 如果是过去的任何时态, 一般用 was。不过, 在某些科技文献中, 也可用 has been, will be, may be, can be, must be, must have been 等来表达。

①强调主语

It will be space ***that*** will represent the new cutting edge of humanity.
(代表人类探索新前沿的将是太空。)

It is what this chapter describes ***that*** is very important.
(正是这一章的内容极为重要。)【本句强调的是一个主语从句】

No one knows what ***it is that*** composes the field itself.
(没有人知道, 到底是什么东西构成了场本身。)
【强调句型出现在宾语从句中, 由于 what 引导宾语从句, 所以它位于从句句首, 而不是位于 is 与 that 之间】

It must be the wind ***that*** makes it so cold.
(一定是因为风, 所以天气这么冷。)

②强调宾语

It is the flow of electrons, not the electrons themselves ***that*** we call an electric current.
(我们正是把电子的流动, 而不是电子本身, 称为电流。)

It is the losses caused by fiction ***that*** we must try to overcome by various means.

(我们必须想尽各种办法来克服的,是由摩擦引起的各种损耗。)

【本句强调的是动词不定式 to overcome 的宾语】

③强调状语

It is to observe the earth ***that*** satellites carry TV cameras far into space.

(正是为了观测地球,卫星把电视摄像机带入遥远的太空。)

It is appropriate to ask why ***it is that*** alpha particles are given off by heavy nuclei.

(完全有理由发问:阿尔法粒子到底为什么是由重原子核发射出来的呢?)

【本句强调的是动词不定式 to ask 的宾语从句引导词——连接副词 why,由于它引导从句,所以位于从句句首】

It must have been much later ***that*** Man learned to cook food by heating it with boiling water or with steam.

(想必是很久以后,人类才学会用开水或蒸汽加热的方法来烧煮食物。)

④强调介词宾语

As matter of fact, the word "function" is used in both cases, but ***it is*** the former sense in ***which*** it most frequently appears in what follows.

(事实上,"function"这个词可用于上述两种情况,不过在下文中,最经常出现的是它的第一种意思。)

What is it that this sequence "tends to"?

(这个数列到底趋于什么值?)

【本句强调的是 to 的介词宾语——引出疑问句的疑问代词 what,所以它位于句首,而且由于是疑问句的关系,is 被放在 it 之前】

注:(i) 过去时的强调:

按照下列两点区分强调的句子结构和形式主语句子结构:关于过去的句子,有时用<it is...that...>,但通常用<it was...that...>。强调 yesterday 或 last year 等表示过去时的副词语句时,原则上用<it is...that...>。

(ii) 强调句句子结构和形式主语句子结构:

(a)去掉 It is 和 that 把剩下的语序复原,如果是一个完整的句子就是强调句子结构。被强调的单词是代词的时候,主语和宾语有时可以替换。例如:

(It was) Tom (that) lost hit watch. (是汤姆丢失了表。)

【强调句子结构】

It is a fact that the world is round. (地球是圆的,这是事实。)

【形式主语句子结构。因为本句去掉 It is 和 that 时,不能成为完整句子】

(b) It is 和 that 之间的单词,如果是形容词或与它类似的语句是形式主语句子结构,如果是名词、代词、副词(短语、从句)多是强调句子结构。比如:

It is true that he broke the record. (他破记录是真的。)
【形式主语句子结构】

It was a police officer that signalled him to stop. (是警察示意他停下。)
【形式主语句子结构】

(2) it 强调句型几点注意:

① 如果被强调的主语或宾语是人时,可用 that 也可用 who。例如:

It is a policeman who (that) my son wants to be. (我儿子想当的就是警察。)

② 如果被强调的是人称代词,该人称代词可以用主格,也可以用宾格。非正式文体中多用宾格。例如:

It is he (him) that is to blame. (该受责备的是他。)

③ 如果原句中含有 not...until,转变成强调句时,其结构为:It is (was) not until...that... 比如,I didn't get your letter until yesterday.

→ It wasn't until yesterday that I got your letter.

(直到昨天我才收到你的来信。)

④ 如果原句是一般疑问句,其强调结构为:Is(Was) it...that... 如果原句是特殊疑问句,其强调结构为:特殊疑问词+is (was) it that... 例如:

Was it at eight o'clock that you began to work? (你是在八点钟开始工作的吗?)

Where was it that you met him? (你是在什么地方遇到他的?)

Why was it that he couldn't answer the question?
(他为什么不能回答这个问题?)

2.9.2 用词汇手段表示强调

英语中有些词在句中起强调作用,强调句中的动词、名词、数词、形容词、副词等。常见的形式如下:

(1) 用助动词 do 强调谓语动词

① 在一般句型中,do (does, did) 常用来强调谓语动词的语气,在句中要重读,且需符合下列两个条件:(i)句子是肯定句;(ii) 句子中的谓语动词是一般现在时或一般过去时。

助动词 do 强调形式为:

$$\left.\begin{array}{l}\text{do}\\\text{does}\\\text{did}\end{array}\right\}+动词原形$$

这种强调形式在科技英语中(do)一般翻译为"的确""确实",有时译为"真的""一定""务必""实际""却"等。例如:

This function ***does satisfy*** the given differential equation.

(这个函数的确满足给定的微分方程。)

Liquids can support neither tensions nor shears, but they ***do tend*** to resist compression. (液体既不能支撑张力,也不能支撑切力,不过它们却趋于阻止压力。)

② 在祈使句中,do 表示强意的请求,而不是命令,有时它可以使邀请对方的心意更加客气、热情、友好,而且亲切,此时的 do 可译为"务""务必"等。例如:

Please ***do sit*** down. (务请坐下。)

Do be careful! (请务必小心谨慎!)

Do tell me all about it. I'll keep it a dead secret. (请告诉我吧,我一定严守秘密。)

(2)用 good 强调名词或形容词

① 形容词 good 置于名词或形容词之前,可以起到强调作用,在不同的句子中可译为:"足足""整整""狠狠地""相当""很"等。例如:

It'll take you a ***good four hours*** to get there.

(到达那里足足需要你四个小时。)

His father gave him a ***good beating***.

(他父亲狠狠地揍了他一顿。)

I covered a ***good hundred miles*** that day.

(那天我整整走了一百英里。)

除 good 之外,cool, solid, clear 等词也可以用来表强调。比如:

His father earns a ***cool thousand dollars*** a month.

(他父亲每月能挣足足一千美元。)

The snake measures ten ***clear feet*** long. (蛇足有十英尺长。)

② 形容词 good 和 and 结合起来,构成 good and …表强调,程度副词作状语,相当于 very, thoroughly, completely 等,强调 and 之后的形容词或副词。例如:

These apples are ***good and ripe***. (这些苹果完全熟透了。)

He drove ***good and fast***. (他开车相当快。)

When it was **good and dark**, he left his home。
(当天完全黑了时,他离开了家。)

除 good 之外,形容词 nice, fine, sweet, rare, lovely 等词也可以与 and 连用表强调。例如:

The building stands **nice and high**. (这座建筑挺高。)

It was **lovely and cool** there. (那儿非常凉爽。)

(3) 用 very 强调名词

very 常用在 the, this, that 或物主代词 my, his, our, your 之后,加强名词的语意,意为"正是""就是""仅仅""甚至"等。其 very 强调形式为:

$$\left.\begin{array}{l}the\\this\\no\\\text{物主代词}\end{array}\right\} + very + 名词$$

例如:

The very gravity prevents us from flying beyond the atmosphere.
(正是重力,使我们不至于飞离大气层。)

The alternating current is **the very** current that makes radio possible.
(交流电就是使无线电成为可能的那种电流。)

At **this very** moment the telephone rang.
(就在这个时候电话铃响了。)

The fault is **your very** own. (这完全是你自己的错。)

(4) 用 only 强调名词

only 常置于单数名词之前,以加强名词的语意,意为"唯一的""仅有的""最合适的""无与伦比的"等。比如:

This is the **only book** of its kind in the world.
(这本书是世界上仅有的一本。)

Mr Brown is the **only person** able to do it.
(布朗先生是唯一能胜任的人。)

She is the **only woman** for the position.
(她是那个职位的最佳人选。)

3

第 3 章　有关词的翻译技巧

3.1　词义的选择

在现代英语中,一词多用和多义的现象比较普遍,经常是同一个词可以属于几种词类,具有不同的词义。所谓一词多类就是指一个词往往属于几个不同的词类,具有几个不同的意义。一词多义是指一个词在同一个词类中,具有几个不同的词义。因此,在众多的词义中,选择出一个最确切的词义是正确理解原文所表达的思想的基本环节,是翻译成功的基础。一般来说,词义的选择与确定可从以下几个方面来考虑。

3.1.1　根据词类选择词义

根据词类选择词义的方法主要是针对一些兼类词,因为这些词在句中所承担的成分不同,其词性不同,词义也不同。因此,要选择正确的词义,首先要确定该词在句中属于哪一种词类,然后再进一步确定其词义。

在下面的各句中,measure 一词分属几个不同的词类,请比较。

(1) The thickness of a tooth *measured* along the pitch circle is one half the circular pitch.

沿节圆所测得的齿厚是周长的一半。(*measure* 是及物动词,意为"测量")

(2) The earthquake *measured* 6.5 on the Richter scale.

这次地震震级为 6.5 里氏震级。(*measure* 是不及动词,意为"有",译成"为")

(3) We must reflect what *measured* to take in case of any accidental collapse of a bed.

我们必须考虑一下如果床层意外崩塌应采取什么措施。(*measure* 是名词,复数时意为"措施")

3.1.2　根据上下文选择词义

英语中的同一个词,同一词类,在不同场合经常有不同的含义,这就要求译者根据上下文的联系,以及句型来确定某个词在特定场合下的词义。这里以 *power* 一词为例,请比较。

(1) The fourth *power* of three is eighty-one.

3 的 4 次方是 81。(*power* 系名词,意为"方")

(2) Energy is the *power* to do work.

能是做功的能力。(*power* 系名词,意为"能力")

(3) *Power* can be transmitted over a long distance.

电力可以输送到遥远的地方。(*power* 系名词,意为"电力")

(4) This is a 20 *power* binoculars microscope.

这是一架 20 倍的双目显微镜。(*power* 系名词,意为"放大率",译成"倍")

(5) Friction causes a loss of *power* in every machine.

摩擦引起每台机器的功率损耗。(*power* 系名词,意为"功率")

3.1.3　根据词的搭配来选择词义

英语的一词多义往往也体现在词与词的搭配上。不同搭配方式,可以生产不同的词义。

以 idle 为例,请比较。

idle capacity	备用容量
idle coil	闲圈
idle current	无功电流
idle frequency	中心频率
idle motion	空转
idle roll	传动轧辊
idle wheel(gear)	惰轮
idle contact	间隔接点
idle space	有害空间
idle stroke	慢行程

再以 large 为例,请比较。

large current	强电流
large pressure	高电压
large amount of electric power	大量的电力

large loads　　　　　　　　重载
large-screen receiver　　　宽屏电视接收机
large capacity　　　　　　高容量
large growing　　　　　　生长快的

3.1.4　根据科学和专业选择词义

在英语中,同一个词在不同的科学领域或专业中往往具有不同的词义。因此,在选择词义时,应考虑到阐述内容所涉及的概念属于哪种学科、何种专业。以英语名词 carrier 为例,请比较。

邮政业:"邮递员"　　　　　军事:"航空母舰"
运输业:"搬运工"　　　　　化学:"载体"
医药学:"带菌者,媒介物"　　车辆制造:"底盘"
无线电:"载波"　　　　　　机械行业:"托架,传导管"

附:英语中一词同类多义或一词多类多义的现象非常普遍,下面把与统计学相关的一些常见词选列出来:

account　计算;说明;叙述;理由;缘故;重要性,价值,用处,好处;以为,认为;考虑;解释

work　工作,操作;功;事业;手工;作品,著作;工厂,工件;起作用,引起,产生

solution　解答,解决;解式,解法;溶解;溶液;溶体

class　种类;等级;班级,年级;阶级;将……归类;把……分等级

condition　状况,状态,情况;形势;条件;地位;以……为条件;检查;调解

draw　拉,拖,拔,抽;提取;吸,吸收;引起,引出;草拟;划,画;制图;吸引物

mean　意思是,意味着;表示,打算;中间的,平均的;中央,中间;平均数;方法,手段,工具

measure　量度,尺寸;计量方法;计量单位;量具;程度,限度;测量,测定;有……长;有……高;有……宽

section　部分;分割,分段;地段,区;组;派;科;切面

set　放,摆;固定;规定;装置;调整;出,移动,推动;配合;镶;落,固定的;套;组

range　排列;分类,编入,列入;调整;对准;测距;平行,并列;范围;限程;射程,距离

time　时间;时候;机会;时代,时期;次,回;倍数;定时……,定期……;记录……时间;使……调和

subject　题目,主题;科目,学科;主体;材料;从属的,支配的;以……为条

件的;使……服从于,从……属于;使……受
    object   物体;对象;目的;宾语;反对;提出……作为反对的理由
    course   进行,过程;航线,航向;方针,方法;教程;课程
    level   水平;水平线,水平面,水平仪;级;层;高度;程度;水平的;相等的,水准测量
    point   点;尖端;地点;时刻;问题;要点;目的;指向;瞄准
    round   圆形的,球形的;整数的,完全的;圆形物;周;次;回;环绕,环行;周围;到处
    unit   单位,单元;部分;组合;机组;部件;成分

3.1.5 依据名词的数来选择词义

名词的数是一个语法范畴,是数量概念的语法表现。一般说来,英语名词的数指名词的单、复数形式。

名词的最基本分类是可数名词和不可数名词。可数名词通常有单复数形式;不可数名词一般没有单复数之分。在语言实际运用中,可以发现,有些可数名词的复数形式与其相对应的单数名词在词义表达上意义迥然不同,大大超越"数量变化"带来的差别,而有些不可数名词有时也以复数形式出现,但它们的词义却完全不同。

因此,在科技英语中,翻译名词时,可以依据名词的数确定合适的词义。科技英语中,下列一些名词就是这类词。比如,下面一些名词的单复数形式就具有不同的含义。

名 词	单数词义	复数词义
advice	意见,劝告,建议	报告,消息
authority	凭据,根据,权威	上级,当局
charge	电荷,负荷	费用
compass	罗盘,指南针	圆规
content	容量,含量	目录,内容
custom	习惯,风俗	海关,关税
development	加工,发展,研制,设计	情况,现象,设备,装置
dimension	尺寸,尺度	面积,大小,容积
divider	除法器,分压器,除数	两脚规
eye	观察力,注意力,眼睛表情	眼睛
element	元素,元件	原理

名 词	单数词义	复数词义
facility	方便,条件	设备,装置;机构
function	作用,功能,功用,函数	职责,任务
fundamental	主要成分,基波,基音	原理,基础,根本法则,原则
good	利益,好处	商品,货物
import	输入	进口商品
main	主线,干线	电源
manner	方式,态度	礼貌,风俗
mean	项,平均值	手段,方法,工具
minute	瞬间,一会儿	会议记录
particular	特点,特色	细节
paper	纸,报纸	论文,考卷,文件,记录
proportion	比例,比	面积,大小
remark	注意,陈述,评论	附注,摘要,要点,备考
scale	标度,尺度	天平,秤
score	计算,成绩	许多,二十
spirit	精神,灵感	酒精
time	时间,时刻,时节	倍数;时代,日子,时势
water	水	矿泉,水面;河,湖,海
work	功,工作	著作,工厂,机件

下面就这一类词进行词义辨析,比如:

1. age(年龄,成年),ages(很长一段时期,时代)

Children usually begin school at the age of six.

儿童一般6岁上学。

He is under age.

他未成年。

We haven't seen each other for ages.

我们彼此长时期未见。

Our ancestors lived on hunting in the primitive ages.

祖先们在原始时代靠打猎为生。

2. eye(观察力,注意力,眼睛的某种表情、样子),eyes(眼睛)

Nothing escaped his eye.
他观察到一切。
He has a quick eye for mistakes.
他敏于发现错误。
How his eye is lit up with a proud joy!
他发亮的目光显得多么得意洋洋!
The girl's eyes filled with tears.
女孩的眼睛充满了泪水。

3. time(时间,时刻,时节),times(时代,日子,时势)
Time and tide wait for no man.
岁月不等人。
What time do you get up?
你几点起床?
The times are different.
时代不同了。
What wonderful times we live in!
我们生活在多么了不起的时代啊!

4. afterward, afterwards(以后,编后记):英国人只用 afterwards,美国人 afterwards 和 afterward 通用。
They lived happily ever afterwards.
以后他们一直幸福地生活着。
She will come afterward.
她随后会来的。(美式用法)

5. manner(方式,态度),manners(礼貌,风俗)
Please decorate the wedding room in a European manner.
请用欧洲风格装饰新房。
My father's manner showed his frankness.
我父亲的态度说明了他的坦率。
Our guests have manner as well as good manners.
我们的客人不但很有礼貌而且举止大方。
My friend wants to read a novel of manners.
我的朋友想看一本社会风俗小说。

6. custom(习惯,风俗),customs(海关,关税)
It is the custom of certain foreigners to do so.
这种做法是某些外国人的习惯。

How long will it take us to pass the customs？办完海关手续要多长时间？

7. paper(纸),papers(论文,考卷,文件)

I need a blank sheet of paper to write a letter.

我需要一张白纸写封信。

The teacher hopes to read our term papers soon.

老师希望早日读到我们的学年论文。

I'm very busy with correcting the papers.

我正忙于阅卷。

8. look(看,脸色,神态),looks(外貌,面容)

I'd like to go and have a look at them.

我要去看一看他们。

A serious look passed over his face.

他脸上显出一副严肃的神色。

Don't judge a man by his looks.

不要凭容貌来判断一个人。

3.2　词义的引申

在翻译过程中,译者经常会遇到英语句子中的一些单词和词组,无法从字典等工具书找到其直接、恰当、准确的释义。如果硬要牵强附会,照搬字典里的某个释义,那么译文定会晦涩难懂,不符合汉语语言规范和翻译所要求的标准。遇到这种情况,译者可以结合上下文,根据语气、逻辑关系、搭配习惯及全句的技术含义等方面的情况,在准确理解原文含义的基础上,按照汉语的表达习惯,对词义加以引申。

3.2.1　技术性引申

技术性引申的目的主要是使译文中涉及科学技术概念的词语符合技术语言规范。例如:

(1) After the spring has been closer to its *sold height*, the compressive force is removed.

弹簧被压缩到接近并紧高度之后,就没有压力了。

(2) The adjustment screw has *stops* at both sides.

调整螺钉的两端设有定位块。

(3) The *probe* was on the course for Saturn.

探测器在去土星的轨道上。

3.2.2 修辞性引申

修辞性引申的目的是为了使译文语言流畅,文句通顺,符合汉语的表达习惯。例如:

Computers come in a *wide variety of* sizes and capabilities.
计算机大小不一,能力各异。

3.2.3 具体化引申

把原有的语句中含义较概括、抽象、笼统的词引申为意思较为具体的词,尤其是将不定代词进行具体化引申,避免造成译文概念不清或不符合汉语表达习惯的情况出现。例如:

(1) While this restriction on the size of the circuit holds, *the law is valid.*
只要电路尺寸符合上述的限制,这条定律就能适用于该电路。

(2) This suggests that matter can be converted into energy, and *vice versa*.
这就是说物质可以转化为能量,能量也可以转化为物质。

(3) The data types arrays and records are *native* to many programming languages.
数组和记录在大多数高级语言中都是固有数据类型。

3.2.4 抽象化引申

有些词在英语中比较具体、形象,如果在译文中不需要强调它的具体名称或具体说明,汉译时,则可以把它抽象化或概括化,用比较抽象的或概括的语言来表达。例如:

(1) Quantum chemistry is still *in its infancy*.
量子化学仍处于发展初期。

(2) Chemical control will do most of *things* in pest control.
化学防治能在病虫害防治中起主要作用。

3.3 词类的转换

由于汉英两种语言结构与表达方式的不同,有些句子在英译汉时不能逐词对译。为了更好地传达原文的思想内容,使译文更符合汉语的表达习惯、更加通顺自然,在翻译时,常常需要进行词类的转换,即英语中的某一词类,并不一定为汉语中的相应词类,而要作适当的转换。词类转换主要有以下四种情况。

3.3.1 转译为动词

英语与汉语相比,英语句子中往往只有一个谓语动词,而汉语句子中动词用得比较多,很可能有几个动词或动词性结构一起连用。例如:

The shadow cast by an object is long or short *according* as the sun is *high up* in the heaven or *near* the horizon.

物体投影的长短取决于太阳是高挂天空还是靠近地平线。

该句中副词 according 转译为动词"取决于",形容词短语 high up 转译为动词"高挂",介词 near 也转译为动词"靠近"。

因此,可以看出根据需要,英语中的名词、形容词、副词、动词和介词在翻译时均可以转换为汉语的动词。

1. 名词转译为动词

(1) These depressing pumps ensure contamination-free *transfer* of abrasive and aggressive fluids such as acids, dyes and alcohol among others.

在输送酸、染料、醇以及其他摩擦力大、腐蚀性强的流体时,这类压缩泵能够保证输送无污染。(名词 transfer 转译为动词)

(2) Despite all the *improvements*, rubber still has a number of limitations.

尽管改进了很多,但合成橡胶仍有一些缺陷。

(3) High precision implies a high degree of exactness but with no *implication* as to accuracy.

高精度意味着高度的精确度,但并不表明具有准确性。(名词 implication 转译为动词)

2. 形容词转译为动词

一些表示心理活动、心理状态的形容词作表语时,通常可以转译为动词。有些具有动词意义的形容词也可以转译为汉语的动词。例如:

(1) The circuits are connected in parallel in the interest of a *small* resistance.

将电路并联是为了减小电阻。(形容词 small 转译为动词)

(2) Once inside the body, vaccine separates from the gild particles and becomes "*active*".

一旦进入体内,疫苗立即与微金粒分离并"激活"。(形容词 active 转译为动词)

3. 副词转译为动词

英语中很多副词在古英语中曾是动词。在翻译时常常可以将副词转译为汉语的动词,尤其当它们在英语句子中作表语时。例如:

(1) If one generator is out of order, the other will produce electricity *instead*.

如果一台发电机发生故障,另一台便代替它发电。(副词 *instead* 转译为动词)

(2) The fatigue life test is *over*.

疲劳寿命试验结束了。(副词 *over* 转译为动词)

4. 介词转译为动词

英语中很多介词在古英语中曾是动词,在翻译时也可以常常将介词转译为汉语的动词。例如:

(1) This type of film develops *in* twenty minutes.

冲洗此类胶片需要20分钟。(介词 *in* 转译为动词)

(2) An analog computer manipulates data *by* analog means.

模拟计算机采用模拟方式处理数据。(介词 *by* 转译为动词)

3.3.2 转译为名词

英语中的动词、代词和形容词等也可以转译为汉语的名词。

1. 动词转译为名词

(1) Boiling point *is defined* as the temperature at which the vapor pressure is equal to that of the atmosphere.

沸点的定义就是气压等于大气压时的温度。(is defined as 译为"定义")

(2) Black holes *act* like huge drains in the universe.

黑洞的作用像宇宙中巨大的吸管。(动词 *act* 转译为名词)

2. 代词转译为名词

所谓代词转译为名词,实际上就是将代词所代替的名词翻译出来,我们也可以称之为"还原"。例如:

The radioactivity of the new element is several million times stronger than *that* of uranium.

新元素的放射性是铀的几百万倍。

3. 形容词转译为名词

(1) Television is *different* from radio in that it sends and receivers a picture.

电视和收音机的区别在于电视发送和接受的是图像。(形容词 *different* 转译为名词)

(2) About 20 kilometers *thick*, this giant umbrella is made up of a layer of ozone gas.

地球的这一巨型保护伞由一层臭氧组成,其厚度约为20千米。(形容词

thick 转译为名词)

4. 副词转译为名词

除了动词、代词和形容词可以转译为名词外,有时副词、介词甚至连词也可以转译为名词。

(1) The device is shown *schematically* in Fig. 2.

图 2 是这种装置的简图。(副词 *schematically* 转译为名词)

(2) Administrative personnel should be *mathematically* informed if they are to make wise decision.

管理人员要作出明智的决策,就应该懂得数学。(副词 *mathematically* 转译为名词)

3.3.3 转译为形容词

1. 名词转译为形容词

Gene mutation is of great *importance* in breeding new varieties.

在新品种培育方面,基因突变是非常重要的。(名词 *importance* 转译为形容词)

2. 副词转译为形容词

当英语动词转译为汉语的名词时,修饰该英语动词的副词往往随之转译为汉语的形容词。例如:

(1) This communication system is *chiefly characterized* by its simplicity of operation.

这种通讯系统的主要特点是操作简单。(动词 *characterized* 转译为名词"特点";副词 *chiefly* 转译为形容词"主要")

(2) Earthquakes are *closely related* to faulting.

地震与断层的产生有密切的关系。(动词 *related* 转译为名词"关系";副词 *closely* 转译为形容词"密切的")

3. 动词转译为形容词

(1) Light waves *differ* in frequency just as sound waves do.

同声波一样,光波也有不同的频率。(动词 *differ* 转译为形容词)

(2) The range of the spectrum in which heat is *radiated* mostly lies within the infrared portion.

辐射热的光谱段大部分位于红外区。(动词 *radiated* 转译为形容词)

3.3.4 转译为副词

1. 形容词转译为副词

英语中能转译成汉语副词的主要是形容词。形容词转译为副词有以下三种情况。

(1) 当英语的名词转译成汉语的动词时,原来修饰名词的英语形容词就相应地转译为汉语的副词。例如:

①In case of use without conditioning the electrode, *frequent calibrations* are required.

如果在使用前没有调解电极,则需要经常校定。(名词 calibrations 转译为动词"校定",形容词 frequent 则转译为副词"经常")

②A *further word of caution* regarding the selection of standard sized of materials is necessary.

必须进一步提醒关于选择材料的标准规格之事宜。(名词词组 word of caution 转译为动词"提醒",形容词 further 则转译为副词"进一步")

(2) 在"系动词+表语的句型"结构中,作表语的名词转译为汉语的形容词时,原来修饰名词的英语形容词就相应地转译为汉语的副词。例如:

①This experiment is an *absolute necessity* in determining the solubility.

对确定溶解度来说,这次试验是绝对必要的。(名词 necessity 转译为形容词"必要的",形容词 absolute 转译为副词"绝对")

②These characteristics of nonmetal are of *great importance*.

非金属的这些特性是非常重要的。(名词 importance 转译为形容词"重要的",形容词 great 转译为副词"非常")

(3) 除了以上两种形式外,其他形式的形容词也可以转译为副词。

①In actual tests this point is *difficult* to obtain.

在实际的测试中,很难测到这个点。(形容词 difficult 转译为副词)

②There is *superficial* similarity between the two devices.

这两个装置在表面上有相似之处。(形容词 superficial 转译为副词)

2. 动词转译为副词

当英语句子中的谓语动词后面的补定式短语或分词转译为汉语句子中的谓语动词时,原来的谓语动词就相应地转译为汉语的副词。例如:

Rapid evaporation *tends* to make the steam wet.

快速蒸发往往使蒸汽的湿度加大。(动词 tends 转译为副词)

3. 名词转译为副词

英语中一些具有副词含义的名词有时也可以转译为副词,例如:

(1) Quasi-stars were discovered in 1963 as a result of an *effort* to overcome the shortcomings of radio telescopes.

类星体是 1963 年发现的,是人们努力克服射电望远镜的缺点所取得的一项成果。(名词 *effort* 转译为副词)

(2) Each sample must be submitted with full *particular* of its source.

每个样品均应详细标明其来源。(名词 particular 转译为副词)

从以上的例句中可以看出,不同词类之间的相互转译现象还是很普遍的,并且是多种多样的,绝对不仅仅局限于以上介绍的几种。词类能否转译或转译为何种词类,由于处理方法不同,也可能有不同的转译方法,译者可以根据对专业技术的理解,以及汉语语言的表达习惯灵活使用。

3.4 词的增译

所谓词的增译就是在译文中增加英语原文省略或原文中无其词而有其义的词语。增译的目的在于使译文既能准确地表达原文的含义,又能更符合汉语的表达习惯和语法修辞。比如下面的句子:

Combine digital technology with advanced software, smaller and more powerful microprocessors, and exponential growth in fiber and wireless bandwidth, and you get something far more powerful-seamless, universal connectivity.

把数字技术与先进的软件,体积更小、功能更强大的微型处理器以及快速增长的光纤和无线频带宽度发展相结合,你会获得功能更强大的无缝隙全方位的连接。

这句的翻译是根据原文所要表达的意思,虽无其词但有其义地在形容词前增译了名词"体积","功能";二是根据汉语的表达习惯和修辞要求在"无线频带宽度"这个具体名词后增译了抽象名词"发展";三是分析专业技术的含义,在 fiber "纤维"前增译了"光"字,便译成"光纤"。

从以上例句可以看出,无论是根据什么原则进行增译,译者首先要理解原句的内容与结构,并结合一些专业技术术语的表达规范,用符合汉语表达习惯的语言,完整、准确、流畅地将原文的意思翻译出来。

3.4.1 增译名词

增译名词最常见的就是在名词后增译名词。另外还可以在动词后或形容词前增译名词。例如:

A new kind of computer—*small*, *cheap*, *fine* is attracting increasing attention.

一种新型的计算机越来越引起人们的注意——这种计算机体积小,价格低,性能优。(在三个形容词 small,cheap,fine 前分别增译名词"体积""价格""性能")

3.4.2　增译动词、形容词

根据语义和表达的需要可以在名词前后增译动词。例如:

The next stage of space travel is a space station.

宇宙飞行的下一步是建立航天站。

根据原文所要表达的含义,结合上下文,在部分名词后适当地增译形容词,使译文能更加准确地表达原意。例如:

(1) *Speed* and *reliability* are the chief advantage of the electronic computer.

速度快、可靠性高是电子计算机的主要优点。(名词 *Speed* 和 *reliability* 后分别增译了形容词"快"和"高")

(2) Perhaps the most important difference between these helicopters is their *power sources*.

也许这些直升机之间的最重要区别在于它们的动力源不同。(名词短语 *power sources* 后增译了形容词"不同")

3.4.3　增译副词

根据原文的上下文,有些动词前可以增译副词,在不改变原意的基础上,可使译文更加符合汉语的修辞需要和表达习惯。例如:

Scientists *believe* that a way to improve the power of the brain may soon be possible.

科学家们深信,不久便有可能找到一种方法来改善大脑的功能。

3.4.4　增译代词

所谓的增译代词是指通过在句首增译"人们""有人""我们"等泛指代词,将英语的被动句翻译为汉语的主动句。有时,翻译英语的主动句也增译代词,这完全是为了遵循汉语的表达习惯。例如:

With the popularity of USB peripherals, *it* is believed USB interfaces would become a standard feature for monitors.

随着 USB 外部设备的普及,人们相信 USB 接口会成为显示器的标准部件。(增译了"人们")

3.4.5 增译量词

英语中的量词是很有限的,表示数量概念时往往是数词或不定冠词(a/an)与可数名词直接连用;而汉语却习惯于根据事物的形状、特征或材料,用不同的量词来表示不同事物数量的概念。因此,翻译时应根据汉语的表达习惯增加适当的量词。增译量词主要有三种情况:一是在数词或不定冠词后增译量词;二是在指示代词或定冠词之后增译量词;三是在少数表示数量的形容词与名词之间增译量词,例如:

This machine has *two settings*, fast and slow.

这台机器的速度有快有慢两个挡。(增译量词"台"和"个")

3.4.6 增译表示名词复数的词

如果英语原句中的名词为复数,汉译时,可根据具体情况增译适当的表示复数概念的词:"们""各种""种种""许多""大量""几个""一些"等。例如:

For *reasons* the alternating current is more widely used than the direct current.

由于种种原因,交流电比直流电用的更为广泛。(reasons 译为种种原因)

3.4.7 增译概括性的词

所谓概括词,就是指类似"两种""三类""双方""等等""种种"等词语。增译概括性的词就是将所罗列的事物用概括性的词语进行总结概括,使译文更加清晰明了。例如:

The vapor pressure changes with the temperature, the pressure, and the kind of liquid.

蒸汽压力随温度、压力和液体类型这三种因素的变化而变化。(增译"这三种因素")

3.4.8 增译连接词

为了使译文更富有逻辑、更符合汉语的表达习惯、更加通顺流畅,可以适当地在译文中增加一些表示原因、条件、目的、结果、让步、假设等连接词。例如:

As the nature of the soil often varies considerably on the same construction site, the capacity of the soil to support loads also varies.

即便在同一施工场地,由于地基的性质有很大差异,土体的承载力也不相同。(增译"由于")

3.4.9 增译转折词

当英语原句子中没有转折词,但是在翻译时,为了使译文的语句通顺、符合汉语的表达方式,可在译文中适当地增译转折词。这种增译不是依据句法结构,而是根据语义要求来进行的。例如:

Ice and water consist of the same substance in different forms.

冰和水由相同的物质构成,但形态不同。(增译"但")

3.5 词的省译

在科技英语的翻译过程中,严格地说,对原文内容的翻译是不允许有任何删略的。但是,由于英汉两种语言表达方式的不同,英语句子中有些词如果硬是要译成汉语,反而会使得译文晦涩难懂;如果不译出来,则会使译文更能通顺、准确地表达出原文的思想内容。因此,学习和掌握省译的方法及技巧也是必要的。一般来讲,词的省译主要体现在下述几个方面。

3.5.1 连词的省略

英语中的连词用得很多,词与词、短语与短语、句子与句子之间的关系通常都是通过一定的连词连接起来的,所以一般不能省略。而汉语则不然,连词用得较少,句子的结构通常是按时间顺序和逻辑关系排列的,语序固定、关系明确,一般不需使用那么多的连词。所以有些并列连词和主从连词往往可以省略不译。例如:

(1) The body possesses a definite store of potential energy *while* it is in the elevated position.

把物体举高,它就具有一定势能的储存。(省略 *while*)

(2) The average speed of all molecules remains the same *as long as* the temperature is constant.

温度不变,所有分子的平均速度也就不变。(省略 *as long as*)

3.5.2 代词的省略

1. 用来代替句中曾出现过的某一名词的人称代词或指示代词 that (those),有时可省略不译。例如:

Today's engines are of much greater difference from *those* used in the past.

现在的发动机与过去所使用的有很大的不同。(省略 *those*)

2. 英语中的人称代词 we, you 及不定代词 one 在句中作主语时,往往含有泛指的意思,可省略不译。例如:

(1) By analysis, *we* mean analyzing the contradictions in things.
所谓分析,就是分析事物的矛盾。(省略 *we*)

(2) Since the airplane's mass is not given, *we* can find it by using this formula.
既然飞机的质量未给出来,可用这条公式把它求出。(省略 *we*)

(3) If *you* know the frequency, *you* can find the wave length.
如果知道频率,就可求出波长。(省略两个 *you*)

(4) *You* also need the acceleration before *you* can substitute in the force formula.
需要先求出加速度,才能代入力的公式。(省略两个 *you*)

3. 根据汉语习惯,某些用作宾语或同位语的反身代词,可省略不译。例如:

(1) A gas distributed *itself* uniformly throughout a container.
气体均匀地分布在整个容器中。(省略 *itself*)

(2) Why do we feel cooler when we fan *ourselves*?
我们为什么感到凉快些?(省略 *ourselves*)

4. 英语中某些作定语的物主代词,因其关系明确可省略不译。例如:

The mass of one unit of volume of a material is called *its* density.
物质单位体积的质量叫做密度。(省略 *its*)

3.5.3 动词的省略

1. 谓语动词的省略

谓语动词是英语句子中必不可少的一个成分。但汉语则不然,句中可以没有动词,而直接用形容词、名词或词组作谓语。所以有些谓语动词省略不译,句子则更为通顺流利。例如:

The charged capacitor *behaves* as a secondary battery.
充了电的电容器就像一个蓄电池一样。(省略 *behaves*)

2. 重复动词的省略

在复合句中,如果从句中的谓语动词与主句中的谓语动词相同,往往可省略不译。例如:

(1) When heated, gases act in exactly the same way as liquid *acts*.
气体受热时所发生的变化与液体完全一样。(省略 *acts*)

(2) It is clear that solids expand and contract as liquids and gases *do*.
显然,固体像液体和气体一样,也膨胀和收缩。(省略 *do*)

3.5.4　介词的省略

英语句子词与词之间的关系通常都是用介词来表示的。而汉语则不然,词与词之间的关系在许多情况下通过语序和逻辑关系表示。所以英译时,许多介词往往可以省略。例如:

The first electronic computer was produced *in* our country *in* 1958.
1958 年我国生产了第一台电子计算机。(省略两个介词 *in*)

3.5.5　冠词的省略

英语中的冠词用得很多,而汉语中却无冠词,所以翻译时往往可以省略。例如:

The gear box contained in *the* headstock makes it possible to run *the* lathe at various speeds.
装在车床头的齿轮箱能使车床以各种速度运转。(省略三个定冠词 *the*)

3.5.6　引导词的省略

1. 在"there + be(或其他不及物动词)+主语……"句型中,there 本身没有任何词汇意义,所以汉译时一律省略。例如:

(1) *There* are many substances through which currents will not flow at all.
有许多物质是电流根本不能通过的。

(2) *There* exist neither perfect insulators nor perfect conductors.
既没有理想的绝缘体,也没有理想的导体。

2. 在英语中,常用引导词 it 作为先行主语或宾语(即形式主语或宾语),而把作为实际主语或宾语的动词不定式、动名词以及从句放在后面。这种结构中的 it 没有实际意义,可以省略不译。例如:

(1) *It* is a common knowledge *that weight is a pull exerted on an object by the earth.*
众所周知,重量是地球作用在物体上的引力。

(2) At one time *it* was though *that all atoms of the same element were exactly alike.*
曾经一度为人公认,同一种元素的所有原子都是完全相同的。

3. 强调句中的先行形式主语 it,本身没有意义,也可以省略不译。例如:

(1) *It* is only when an object is heated *that* the average speed of molecules is increased.

只是当物体受热时,分子的平均速度才增大。

(2) *It* is the gravitation *which* makes the satellites move round the earth.

是地球引力使卫星绕地球运行。

3.5.7 同义词或近义词的省略

英语中有一些同义词或近义词经常连用,表示强调,使其意义更加明确;或者表示一个名词的不同说法。在英译汉时,根据实际情况只译出一个即可。例如:

(1) To be sure, the change of the earth is slow *but*, *nevertheless*, it is continuous.

确实,地球变化很缓慢,但是这一变化确是连续不断的。(*but* 和 *nevertheless* 都含有"但是""然而"的意思,所以只译出一个,省略一个)

(2) The mechanical energy can be changed back into electrical energy by means of *generator* or *dynamo*.

利用发电机能把机械能再转变成电能。(*generator* 和 *dynamo* 都是"发电机"的意思,所以只译出一个,省略一个)

3.6 重 复 法

避免重复是英语修辞的一大特点。英语中经常出现一个动词后面接几个宾语或表语,或大量使用代词可以避免重复使用名词的现象。但汉语的表达方式则有所不同,有时为了使译文更加生动、富有表现力,在翻译时常常对重要或关键性的词语加以重复。

重复法在翻译科技英语时是经常用到的,其目的就是为了使译文的表达更准确。重复法不同于增译法:增译法主要是在译文中根据需要增补新的词语,而重复法则是重复在译文中已出现过的词语。

3.6.1 重复名词

1. 在英语句子中,当并列连词 and, as well as, not only...but also, not...but, either...or, both...and, neither...nor 等连接两个并列成分时,其相应的核心名词在汉译时为了译文的修辞需要,可以重复翻译该名词。例如:

The *weight* of a neutron is about the same as a proton.

中子的重量和质子的重量差不多相等。

2. 在有些较长的定语从句中,翻译时译文可以重复关系代词所代替的名词。例如:

(1) The controller translates these into detail through its feedback system *which* relies on sensors in the hand that measure the force applied.

控制器通过它的反馈系统把这些命令转换成细节,而反馈系统依靠的是(假)手中能测定用力大小的传感器。

(2) Big corporations also have *their* own troubles.

大公司也有大公司的难处。

3. 当英语句子中几个形容词共同修饰名词时,被修饰的名词在译成汉语时常常可以重复。例如:

(1) The three most important effects of an electric current are heating, magnetic and chemical *effects*.

电流三种最重要的效应是热效应、磁效应和化学效应。

(2) Computers can operate on either analogue or digital *information*.

计算机能够根据模拟信息或数字信息进行运算。

3.6.2 重复动词

在英语句子中,如果并列连词 as well as, not only…but also, but, not…but, either…or, both…and, neither…nor 等连词连接两个并列成分,且只有一个谓语动词时,汉译时为了译文的修辞需要,可以重复翻译该动词。例如:

(1) The internal combustion engines can *operate* on kerosene as well as on benzene.

内燃机不仅能用汽油开动,而且能用航空煤油开动。

(2) Alternating stress not only *varies* in magnitude but also in direction.

角变应力不仅大小变化,而且方向也变化。

(3) Money is not only a means of exchange but also a means of measuring the value of men's labour.

货币不仅是交换的手段,而且是衡量人们劳动价值的手段。

3.7 代词的翻译

3.7.1 人称代词的译法

1. 第一人称代词与第二人称代词的译法

在英语中,第一人称代词 we 与第二人称代词 you,基本上相当于汉语中的"我们""你、你们"。在含有普遍规律及一般真理的句子中,当它们在句中作主语时,通常含有泛指的意义,用来指一般的人。这个时候,经常可以省略不用翻译;然而,也可以照译,只要符合汉语的习惯就行。例如:

(1) *You* can find the density of a body providing *you* know its mass and volume.

只要知道物体的质量和体积,就可以求出其密度。(省略 *you*)

(2) By acceleration *we* mean the rate of change of velocity with time.

所谓加速度,是指速度随时间的变化率。(省略 *we*)

2. 第三人称代词的译法

(1) 译成代词:如果第三人称代词所指代的意思在译文中明确清晰,那么常常就译成代词。然而,要注意英文中的第三人称代词有性和数的区别,单数基本上相当于汉语中的"他""她""它",复数通常译成汉语中的"他们""她们""它们"。但是,实际上落实到具体的翻译中并不是如此简单。汉语中的"他""她""他们"通常用来代替人,代物时一般用"它""它们"。而英语中的 he,she,有时却是用来代替物,特别是代替国家、党派、船只、自然界,甚至动物等。因此,在具体英文翻译时,英语代词如果代物,一般不能译成"他""她""她们",而应译成"它""它们"等。有时,人称代词的复数形式 they 也可译成"它",而单数形式"it"却译成"他们",这主要与所代替的名词是集体名词还是物质名词有关。

① When water freezes and becomes solid, we call *it* ice.

当水冻结成固体时,我们称它为冰。

② Small as a drop of water is, *it* is a big world of atom.

一滴水虽小,但它却是一个巨大的原子世界。

(2) 译成所代替的名词:为了明确代词所代替的事物,使译文更确切明了,不产生歧义,有时可以把代词译成所代替的名词,而不管代词出现在所代名词之前或之后。有时,在把代词译成名词的同时,还可以把这一代词所指名词译

成代词,以免重复,使文字更流畅。例如:

①To be sure, the change of the earth is slow, but nevertheless, *it* is continuous.

确实,地球变化很缓慢,但是这一变化却是连续不断的。

②Since the electrons are very light, we think of *them* as adding no weight at all to the atom.

由于电子的重量非常轻,我们通常认为电子没有给原子增加任何重量。

(3)略去不译:如果译文确切明了,而且前面已有主语,而后文中的主语是用来代替该主语的代词时,这个代词往往略去不译。此外,即使代词用作其他成分,省略后并不影响对意思的理解时,也可以省略。

①The law of reflection holds good for all surfaces, whether *they* are rough or smooth, plane or curved.

反射定律对一切表面都适用,不管是粗糙的还是光滑的,平面的还是弯曲的。(省略 *they*)

②When you throw a ball into the air, *it* will go up high if you are strong.

当你把一个球抛向空中时,如果你力气大,就抛得高。(省略 *it*)

(4)颠倒译法:由于英汉两种语言的次序不同,有时需要先译成代词,然后再译所代名词,这时就必须把代词与所指代名词颠倒翻译。有时,英语的时间、条件、让步状语从句在后,主句在前,而汉语习惯从句在前,主句在后。因此,翻译时要先把从句中的代词译成所代名词,然后再把主句中所代名词译成代词"它们"或"其"。例如:

①*The body* possesses a definite store of potential energy while it is in the elevated position.

把物体举高时,它具有一定的势能。

②*Many laws of nature* actually exist in nature though they have not yet been discovered.

虽然许多自然规律还没有被发现,但是它们确实在自然界中存在。

③*The structure of an atom* can be accurately described though we cannot see *it*.

即使我们看不见原子结构,但是能准确地描述它。

3.7.2 不定代词的译法

one 是英语中常见的一个不定代词。它可以用来指人,也可以指物。在句子中,通常作为主语、表语、宾语和定语等。由于作用不同,译法各不相同。

1. one 代替名词时的译法

(1) 代替前面名词的译法:在同一个句中,为了避免词的重复,往往可用 one 代替前面曾出现过的某一个可数名词。这时它有复数形式 ones。其前面可有形容词或指示代词等所表示的定语说明,其后可有介词短语、分词短语或定语从句。在翻译时,通常把 one 译成它所代替的名词。

①For nearly two thousand years it was believed that all heavy objects fell faster than light *ones*. This is a mistaken idea.

将近两千年来,人们都认为一切重物比轻物落得快些。这是一个错误的概念。(*ones* 代替 objects,其前面有形容词"light"作为定语,译成"物体")

②The normal state for a body to be in is *one* of rest or of uniform motion in a straight line.

物体所处的正常状态,就是静止状态或做匀速直线运动的状态。(*one* 代替 state,其后面介词短语"of rest or of..."作为定语,译成"状态")

(2) 代替后面名词的译法:在"one of + 复数名词"的结构中,one 代替着后面复数名词中的一个。翻译时,通常先从后面译起,把 one of... 译成"……的一个""……的一种……""……之一"等。例如:

①It is well known that laser is *one of* the most sensational developments in recent years.

众所周知,激光是近年来轰动一时的科学成就之一。

②Inertia is known to be *one of* the fundamental characteristics of object.

大家知道,惯性是物体的基本特性之一。

2. one 作为泛指代词的译法

(1) one 单独使用时,往往含有泛指的意思,用来指任何人。可译成"人""人们""一个人""每个人""我们""谁"等,也可以依据文意略去不译。例如:

①*One* should add here that inertia of a given object is measured by its mass.

这里,我们想补充一点:给定物理的惯性都是以它的质量来测量的。(*One* 译成"我们")

②Modesty helps *one* to go forward, whereas conceit makes one lag behind. This is a truth we must always bear in mind.

虚心使人进步,骄傲使人落后,我们应该永远记住这个真理。(*one* 译成"人")

(2) one 与 who 连用时,通常表示"一种人"或"一类人"。Who 引导的是一个定语从句。一般译成"人"或者根据汉语习惯灵活处理。例如:

①*One who* does not study and work hard can not hope to accomplish much.

不努力学习和工作的人,不能指望有多大的成就。

②Nothing in the world is difficult for *one who* sets his mind to it.

世上无难事,只怕有心人。

(3)one 指人时,有反身代词"oneself"和所有格形式"ones",可译成复合不定代词 someone(有人,某人),anyone(任何人,无论谁),everyone(每人,人人),no one(无人,没有人)等。翻译时,要依据文意来灵活处理。例如:

①*No one* has ever found a way to create energy out of nothing.

从来就没有一个人曾经想出凭空创造能量的方法来。(*No one* 译成"没有一个人")

②This *anyone* can see who has tried to run on a highly polished floor or on ice.

这个道理对曾试图在极光滑的地板上或者冰面上跑步的人来说,是很清楚的。(who 所引导的是一个定语从句,说明"*anyone*"译成"……的人")

3. one 的其他用法

(1)当句子中出现过两个人或者事物,下面要分别叙述时,通常用"one...the other"或"one...one..."等形式来表示。汉译时,一般译成"一种……另一种的……"、"一个……另一个……"等。例如:

There are two kinds of electric currents: *one* is the direct current and *the other* is the alternating current.

电流有两种:一种是直流电,另一种是交流电。

(2)one 与 another 可构成相互代词,一般有"one another"与"one another's"两种形式。在句子中可作宾语或定语。英译汉时,前者译成"互相",后者译成"互相的"等。例如:

Although the molecules of a gas move very fast, they do get very far before they collide with *one another*.

气体分子虽然运动很快,但是它们走不远就要互相碰撞。(作介词 with 的宾语)

3.8　形容词的翻译

在英语中的形容词不仅数量多,而且使用率也非常高。英语中的形容词既可以单独使用,又可以用来修饰名词及某些代词,在句子中主要作为定语、表语、宾语补足语,也可以作状语。

3.8.1 直译

大多数作为前置定语与少数作为后置定语的形容词以及表语的形容词,在翻译时通常可直接译出,也就是译为汉语的定语"的"字结构,也可省略"的"字。例如:

(1) This machine has two settings, *fast and slow*.

这台机器的速度有快慢两个挡。

(2) The econometric *all-purpose* regression tool is the normal linear regression model.

经济计量中的用于各种用途的回归工具是正态线性回归模型。

3.8.2 转译

许多形容词在翻译时,可视具体情况而转译成名词、动词与副词。

1. 译成名词

在形容词前加上定冠词用来表示一类人或物时,可将该形容词转译为名词,这是最常见的形容词转译为名词的现象。此外,还有下述的两种情况,英语形容词可转译为名词。

(1) 在英语句子中,起表语作用的形容词,汉译时有时可转译为名词。例如:

The metal may be *fluid*, *plastic*, *elastic*, *ductile* or *malleable*.

金属具有流动性、塑性、弹性、延展性或韧性。

(2) 在"as + 形容词 + as"或"形容词比较级 + than"句型中,其中的形容词经常可译为名词。例如:

Gases are much less *viscous* than liquids.

气体的粘滞性大大小于液体。

2. 译成动词

(1) 一些与系动词连用的表示心理活动和心理状态的形容词作表语时,通常可转译为动词。这些形容词常见的有:sure, certain, careful, anxious, able, familiar, available 等。

These systems are *able* to execute multiple threads concurrently rather than serially.

这些系统能够并行地而不是串行地执行任务。

(2) 有些具有动词意义的形容词,也可转译成为汉语的动词。例如:

The impulse is *dependent* upon the duration of shock wave as well as its pressure.

脉冲的大小取决于冲击波的延续时间及其压力。

3. 译成副词

形容词转译为副词有两种情况：

（1）当英语的名词转译为汉语的动词时，原来修饰名词的英语形容词就相应地转译为汉语的副词。例如：

The imitation of living systems, be it direct or indirect, is very useful for devising machines, hence the *rapid* development of bionics.

对生物的模仿，不管是直接的还是间接的，对于机械设计都是很有用处的，因此仿生学才得以迅速发展。

（2）当英语的名词转译为汉语的形容词时，原来修饰名词的英语形容词就相应地转译为汉语的副词。例如：

With *slight* modification each type can be used for all three systems.

每一种型号只要稍加改动就能应用于这三种系统。

3.8.3　形容词作为前置定语的译法

所谓的形容词作前置定语是指形容词作定语放在被修饰的名词之前。这种情况下，一般译为汉语的"的"字结构，在译文中仍然起定语作用。不过，也有两种比较特殊的译法。

（1）译为短语

在许多情况下，形容词作为前置定语不能直接译出"的"字，而经常与被修饰的名词一起译成约定俗成的短语，在科技英语中，经常译为特定的专业术语。

In *semiparametric modeling*, the distribution of the endogenous variable is left unspecified.

在半参数建模中，内生变量的分布不用设定。

（2）译为主谓结构

形容词作为前置定语，可以翻译成"的"字结构，作所修饰名词的定语，但是有时根据汉语的表达习惯译成汉语的主谓结构更为通顺、合理。例如：

Advantages include *lower operating temperatures*, *reduced power usage*, *clean compact design* and an exclusive shaft seal design.

其优点包括运行温度低、耗能小、设计紧凑以及独特的轴密封。（译成主谓结构）

其优点包括低的运行温度、小的耗能、紧凑的设计以及独特的轴密封。

(译成"的"结构,但是不如翻译成主谓结构表达得流畅)

3.9 副词及比较级的翻译

副词修饰动词、形容词和其他副词以及全句,用来表示时间、地点、程度、方式、条件等概念,按照其功能可分为普通副词、疑问副词、关系副词和连接副词。副词修饰动词时,其位置比较灵活,可放在句首、句尾、助动词或情感动词之后;修饰形容词和其他副词时,须放在被修饰的词之前;副词作定语时,一般放在修饰的名词之后。副词在句子中可以作为状语、表语和定语。

3.9.1 副词的一般译法

这里所要讨论的副词的一般译法是指英语中的普通副词的范畴,其汉译时都可采用直译法。

1. 加"地"字译法

所谓加"地"字译法,是指在翻译副词时在其后面加上"地"字,特别是翻译形容词或名词派生的表示方式的副词。例如:

To understand *better* matter and energy in the natural world is the purpose of chemistry.

更好地理解自然界的物质与能量是化学研究的目的。

2. 加"上"或"下"字译法

所谓加"上"或"下"字译法,是指在翻译副词时在其后面加"上"字或"下"字,特别是在翻译表示程度、状况的副词时。例如:

Morphologically and anatomically the leaf is the most variable plant organ.

从形态学和解剖学上看,叶子是最富有变化的植物器官。

3. 转译法

有些副词,在汉译时依据汉语的表达习惯,可以转译为动词、形容词和名词。

(1)副词转译为动词

副词在英文句子中可以作表语和状语时,翻译时经常可转译成汉语的动词。例如:

Our experiment was finished two weeks *ahead* of schedule.

我们的试验比计划提前两周。

(2)副词转译为形容词

当英语的动词转译为汉语的名词时,修饰该英语动词的副词往往转译成汉语的形容词。例如:

Today all the *naturally* occurring elements that exist on earth have been isolated.

今天地球上所有存在的天然元素都已被离析出来。

(3)副词转译为名词

The device is shown *schematically* in Fig. 2.

图 2 是这种装置的简图。

3.9.2　形容词与副词的比较级译法

1. 原级比较的译法

(1)肯定式原级的译法:当两个事物的某一属性在比较之下,其程度一样时,用"as+原级+ as"的结构来表示,第一个 as 为副词,在主句中作状语;第二个 as 为连词,引导的是比较状语从句,从句经常有省略现象。汉译时,通常把这种结构译成"和……一样""像……那样""与……同样"等。例如:

①The velocity of light is *as great as* that of radio waves in vacuum.

光的速度和无线电波在真空中的速度一样快。

②The heat of the sun is *as necessary* to life *as* the light.

对于生命而言,太阳的热与光同样是必需的。

(2)否定式原级的译法:当两个事物进行比较,其程度一方不如另一方时,用"not so + 原级 + as"来表示;如果强调两者之间的不同时,用"not as+原级+ as"来表示。汉译时,一般把前者译成"……不如……""……不及……""……不像……""……没有……那样……"等;而后者译成"……和……不一样……""……和……不同"。例如:

①Sound travels *not so* fast in gases *as* in liquids.

声音在气体中不如在液体中传播得那么快。

②The line *AB* is *not as long as* the line *CD*, but a little longer.

AB 线和 CD 线不一样长,AB 线稍长一些。

(3)如果在"as...as..."的结构中有具体的数字及倍数,其词序为"数字或倍数 + as+ 原级 + as..."。其中的数字或倍数可以看成是后面形容词或副词的状语。翻译时,数字照译不减,把倍数译成"……是……的几倍""……为……的几倍""……是……的几倍"通常把这种结构译成"和……一样",或者"……比……n-1 倍"。例如:

①The oxygen atom is *nearly* 16 *times as heavy as* the hydrogen atom.

氧原子的重量差不多是氢原子的16倍。

②The speed of sound in water is *about four times as great as* in air.

声音在水中的速度比在空气中的大3倍左右。

(4)英语中有许多形容词本身就带有比较级的含义,后面被比较的部分要求用介词to引出。这类词有:

superior...	优于……,……比……优越
preferable to...	优于……,胜过……,……比……还好
inferior to...	次于……,不及……,……比……差
junior to...	少于……,低于……,……比……小
senior...	……比……年长

Conductivity of semiconductor material is *inferior to* that of conductor.

半导体材料的导电性比导体差。

2. 比较级比较的译法

(1)当两个事物或人进行比较,一方的程度高于另一方时,英语中常用:"比较级 + than"的结构来表示。than是一个连词,引导的是比较状语从句。该从句常常有省略现象。汉译时,通常把这种结构译成"比……""较……""比……更……""较之……""较……更……"等。比如:

①The robot is a *lighter*, *more portable* piece of equipment *than* an NC machine tool.

与数控机床相比,机器人是一种重量更轻、更便于携带的设备。

②These atoms are separated by distances *larger than* their diameters.

这些原子相隔距离的长度超过了它们的直径。

(2)两者比较时,如果一方的程度或数量不及另一方,则用"less ... than"的结构来表示。汉译时,一般译成"比……小""不如……""不像……""没有那么……"等。例如:

①In liquids, the force of attraction between molecules is *less than* it is in solids.

液体分子之间的吸引力比固体分子之间的吸引力小。

②Electrical and magnetic quantities are *less simple than* length, mass or time.

电量和磁量不像长度、质量或时间那么简单。

(3)如果比较级之前有much(……得多),far(……得多),still(更,还),even(还要,更),a lot(……得多),a little(稍微),a bit(……一点),a great deal(……得多),considerably(……相当地……,得多)等词作状语,通常表示程度上的差别,含有强调的作用。汉译时,一般要译出上述词的意思。例如:

Much greater magnification can be obtained with the electron microscope.

使用电子显微镜,可以获得大得多的放大倍数。

(4)如果英语句子以"the + 比较级……,the + 比较级……"的形式出现,则一方的程度和性质随另一方而变化。通常第一个是关系副词,引导比较状语从句;第二个是指示副词,在主句中作状语。这种句型中,往往是倒置语序,省略了某些成分。汉译时,先译从句,后译主句,译成"越……,(就)越……""愈……,(就)愈……"。例如:

①*The greater* the force and the longer the distance moved, *the greater* the work performed.

力愈大,通过的距离愈远,所做的功就愈多。

②*The faster* an object moves, *the greater* is the air resistance.

物体运动越快,其空气阻力越大。

(5)带有比较级的词组、习语及常见译法。

英语中有许多这种比较级的词组、习语及固定结构,例如:

more than...	大于……,不止……,多过……
more and less...	或多或少,多少,左右
not less than...	至少……,不小于……,不下于……
no less than...	有……之多,至少有……多
not more ... than ...	不如……,不及……,不比……
not more than ...	不超过……,至多……
no more ... than...	并不比……更……,跟……同样不……
no more than ...	仅仅……,只不过……
no later than...	决不迟于
no longer...	不再,已不
any longer...	再,更
more than all	尤其
two or more	两个或两个以上

①These elements are so combined that the elements can *no longer* be identified.

这些元素经过这样的化合之后,就不能再辨认出来了。

②A compound is substance made up of *two or more* elements.

化合物是由两种或两种以上的元素构成的。

3. 最高级比较的译法

(1)形容词和副词的最高级是指在三个或三个以上的人或事物的比较中

表示最高、最低、最大、最小等概念。形容词最高级前面通常要加定冠词 the,句中经常有介词短语 of...,in...,among...等词以及限制定语或定语从句等所表示的比较范围。汉译时把最高级译为"最"等。例如:

①It is well known that water is *the most common* and *the most important* liquid *in* the world.

众所周知,水是世界上最普遍的也是最重要的液体。

②It may be safely said that light moves *fastest* in the world.

可以有把握地说,在世界上光传播得最快。

(2) most 有时虽然在形式上与形容词或副词连用,但是已不表示比较,而是含有 very 的意思,所以译成"很"、"非常"等。这时之前一般没有定冠词,有时可有不定冠词 a。例如:

①Wave motion is one of *most common* motions.

波运动是一种非常普遍的运动。

②The design of an aircraft is *a most complicated* matter, so is its manufacture.

飞机的设计是一件极其复杂的事,其制造也是如此。

3.10 介词的翻译

介词是一种虚词,表示词与词之间的关系。在英语中应用得相当广泛而灵活。同一个词与不同的介词搭配后常常具有不同的意义。翻译时,不仅要依据具体情况,采用适当的词汇手段或句法手段把其意义表达出来,而且还必须根据汉语的表达习惯,要正确处理介词及介词短语在句中的作用。

3.10.1 直译

译成介词

英语中的介词,按其具体使用情况通常可以翻译成汉语中相应的介词,比如"往、向、从、在、关于、对于、为了、除了、由于"等。例如:

(1) *In* the everyday life, we see things moving about *on* the ground or *in* the air.

在日常生活中,我们看见许多东西在地面上或在空中运动着。(介词 *in* 译成"在……中",而 *on* 译成"在……上")

(2) The third law of motion states that *to* every action there is an equal and opposite reaction.

运动第三定律指出:对每一个作用力都有一个大小相等方向相反的反作用

力。(介词 to 译成"对")

(3) For many reasons the alternating current is more widely used than the direct current.

由于种种原因,交流电比直流电用得广泛。(介词 for 译成"由于")

3.10.2 转译

许多介词在翻译时可以转译成为连词或动词等。

1. 译成连词

英语中的介词,按其搭配关系及使用的具体场合,有时可以译成汉语中的连词,比如"和、同、与、由于、因为、如果、虽然、当……时"等。例如:

(1) Since the advent of jet aircraft, travel has been speeded up.

自从喷气式飞机出现以后,旅行的速度加快了。(介词 since 译成"自从……以后")

(2) Colour is to light what pitch is to sound.

颜色与光的关系就好比音调与声音的关系。(介词 to 译成"与")

2. 译成动词

英语中的介词译成汉语中动词的方式很多,特别是用作表语的介词与作状语的介词短语中的介词。按其具体使用情况通常可以翻译成汉语中相应的介词,比如"往、向、从、在、关于、对于、为了、除了、由于"等。例如:

(1) It is clear that numerical control is the operation of machine tools by numbers.

显然,数控就是机床采用数字操纵。(介词 by 译成"采用")

(2) Without air, the earth would undergo extreme changes in temperature.

没有空气,地球温度就会发生剧变。(介词 without 译成"没有")

(3) When there is no force acting on a body, the body is in equilibrium.

如果没有外力作用于物体,物体便处于平衡状态。(系词 is+介词 in 译成"处于")

3.10.3 省译

根据汉语的表达习惯及需要,英语中的一些介词在汉译时可以省略不译。

(1) 当英语中的被动句译成汉语中的主动句,其中被动语态的行为主体译成句子的主语时,介词 by 省略不译。例如:

① We were deeply impressed by the exhibition on artistic handcrafts.

手工艺品展览给我们留下了深刻的印象。(介词 by 省略不译)

(2)被动句中带有介词的地点状语,以及表示与主语有关的某一方面及某一位置的带有介词的补足语译成主语时,这些介词省略不译。例如:

①When water freezes, it becomes larger *in* volume instead of smaller.

水结成冰时,其体积变得更大而不是更小。(介词 *in* 省略不译)

②More electron microscopes will be produced *in* the plant next year.

明年该厂将生产更多的电子显微镜。(介词 *in* 省略不译)

(3)动词不定式短语前由"介词 for+名词或宾格代词"所表示的逻辑主语,通常介词省略不译。例如:

It is demonstrated that it takes a year *for* the earth to go around the sun.

业已证实,地球绕太阳转一周需用一年时间。(介词 *for* 省略不译)

(4)英语中某些表示时间或其他关系的介词,往往省略不译。例如:

①It is well known that China had possessed the accurate value *for* π over 1,300 years before Europe.

众所周知,中国求出 π 的精确值比欧洲早 1,300 多年。(介词 *for* 省略不译)

②The earth makes one complete rotation on its axis *in* every 24 hours.

地球每 24 小时正好自转一周。(介词 *in* 省略不译)

(5)在句型中,当带有介词的地点状语或介词"of+名词"表示的定语译成句中主语时,这些介词可省略不译。例如:

①If there were no frictional losses *in* a machine, the machine would be 100 per cent efficient.

如果机械没有摩擦损失,那其效率就是百分之百。(介词 *in* 省略不译)

②According to the way of taking-off and landing, there are two kinds *of* airplanes, i. e. seaplanes and landplanes.

按照起飞和着陆方式,飞机可分为两种:水上飞机和陆上飞机。(介词 *of* 省略不译)

3.10.4　介词短语的译法

介词所支配的名词、代词或作用相当于名词的其他词类或者短语,就叫介词的宾语。介词及其宾语一起构成的短语叫做介词短语。介词短语通常在句中作状语及定语,有时也可作表语、宾语补语或主语补语。下面,介绍作状语与定语的译法。

1. 作状语的译法

(1) 译成相应的成分：介词短语作状语时，通常译成汉语的相应成分。例如：

①*In steady flight* the four forces balance that act on an airplane.

在稳定飞行中，作用于飞机上的四种力是平衡的。（介词 *In steady flight* 译成"在稳定飞行中"，作状语）

②Not *until* 1788 was a method of producing an electric current discovered.

直到1788年，人们才发现了产生电流的方法。（介词 *until* 译成"直到……才"）

(2) 译成其他成分、分句或从句：介词短语作状语时，根据句子的结构、特征、意思以及汉语的表达习惯，也可以译成其他成分。例如：

①Some features of the nucleon structure emerge *from these relations*.

这些关系式展示了核子结构的某些特征。（介词短语 *from these relations* 译成"这些关系式"，作主语）

②*In freezing water to ice*, only the physical aspects of matter are changed.

水凝结成冰时，只是物质物理方面的变化。（介词短语 *In freezing water to ice* 译成条件从句"水凝结成冰时"）

2. 常见介词+动名词的译法

英语中的介词若与动名词连用，构成介词短语作状语，其译法比较固定。几种常见的多义介词与动名词连用的译法如下：

(1) 介词 in + 动名词：在……时；在……中；在……过程中
(2) 介词 on + 动名词：在……时；在……之后；一……就……
(3) 介词 for + 动名词：为了……；要……；用来……；以……
(4) 介词 by + 动名词：用……方法；通过……；借助于……

①*In producing missiles and rockets*, reinforced plastics are also used.

在生产导弹和火箭时，也使用强化塑料。（介词 in+ 动名词短语译成"在……时"）

②*For reaching the speed to take off*, the airplane is running along the runway.

为了达到起飞速度，飞机正沿着跑道滑跑。（介词 for+ 动名词短语译成"为了……"）

3.10.5 作定语的译法

1. 译成加"的"字结构

当介词短语作定语说明句中另一个名词或代词等时，通常把介词省略，在

短语之后加"的"字,放在它所修饰的词之前。例如:

(1) Documents *for the World Wide Web* are written in HTML.

万维网的文件是用 HTML(超文本标记语言)编写而成的。

(2) In the absence of the action *of external* force, a body *at rest* remains at rest and a body *in motion* remains in motion at a constant speed in a straight line.

在不受外力的作用时,静止的物体一直保持静止,运动的物体一直做匀速直线运动。

2. 不加任何词译出

依据汉语表达习惯,英语中用介词短语所表示的定语,有时可以不加任何词(如"的")而译在所修饰的词之前。特别是,当介词短语说明事物的性质、用途、来源、领导关系等,或者它所修饰的词已构成专门术语时,更是这样。例如:

(1) It is well known that steel, essentially, is an alloy *of iron and carbon*.

众所周知,钢本质上就是一种铁碳合金。

(2) The formula *for kinetic* energy is applicable to any object that is moving.

动能公式适用于任何运动的物体。

第 4 章 被动语态的翻译

科技英语文献中,使用被动语态非常普遍,这是因为:第一,被动结构比主动结构更少主观色彩,描述客观事物,进行逻辑推理,正需要这种特性;第二,被动结构更能突出要论证、说明的对象,把它放在句子主语的地位上,更能引人注目;第三,在很多情况下,被动结构比主动结构更简短。

当然,英语科技论文中主动语态也有增多的趋势,比如常见到"This paper reports..." "The author concluded..." "We made the analysis..." "The researchers have carried out..."等等。因此,在学习和研究文献时,有意识地观察和掌握被动语态运用的同时,也要记住主动和被动句式交替使用的特点,以便今后自己写作英文论文时做到句型多样化,达到客观准确地揭示事物现象和变化规律。

4.1 译成汉语被动句

英文中被动语态的句子,经常可以译成汉语的被动句,这时可加"被""由""为""靠""所""叫""受""把""得到""受到""加以""予以""为……所……""是……的"等词译出。但视具体情况也可以不加任何词直接译出。例如:

(1) This new idea *is* now *being accepted* by more and more people.
这种新观念正在为越来越多的人所接受。

(2) The laws of motion *will be discussed* in the text article.
运动定律将在下文中予以讨论。

(3) Electricity itself *has been known* to man for thousands of years.
电为人类所知已有好几千年了。

(4) The words "work" and "power" *are* often *confused* or *interchanged* in colloquial use.

在日常生活中,"功"和"功率"是常被混淆或相互代用的两个词。

4.2　译成汉语主动句

(1)当英语被动句中的主语为无生命的名词,且句中一般没有由介词 by 引导的行为主体时,这种句子常常可译成汉语的主动句,而不需加什么词。例如:

①The prices *were raised* sharply in a few days.

几天内,物价就大幅度提高了。

②It is clear that a body can *be changed* under certain condition.

显然,在一定条件下物体能够带电。

③The speed of the molecules *is increased* when they are heated.

当分子受热时,其速度就增加。

④Every moment of every day, energy *is being transformed* from one form into another.

每时每刻,都有能量由一种形式变为另一种形式。

(2)当被动句中有地点状语,由介词"by"引导的方式状语及"from"等表示的其他状语时,有时可以把这种状语译成主语,将介词省略,而把原主语译成宾语,这样,更符合汉语的习惯。例如:

①The sunlight and water *are needed* by plants.

植物需要阳光和水分。

②Recently, some new kinds of steel *have been developed* in our country.

最近,我国研制出了一些新品种的钢。

③Questions *are invited*.

欢迎提问题。

④It is well known that the compass *was invented* in *China* four thousands years ago.

众所周知,中国在四千年前发明了指南针。

(3)如果英语中某些要求宾语及宾语补语的动词为被动语态,翻译时往往可在其前加"人们""大家""有人""众人""我们"等含有泛指意义的词做主语,而把原句中的主语译成宾语。例如:

①Rubber *is found* a good insulating material.

人们发现橡胶是一种很好的绝缘材料。

②Sliver *is known* to be the best conductor.

大家都知道,银是最好的导体。

③Gases are frequently *regarded as* compressible, liquids as incompressible.

人们通常认为气体是可压缩的,而液体是不可压缩的。

4.3　译成汉语无主句

英语中许多被动语态的句子,往往可以译成汉语中的无主句,这时被动句中的主语就译成了无主句中的宾语。这种译法在科技文章中颇为常见,因为一般不需要指出动作的发出者是谁。有时,还可以在句中原主语之前加"把""将""使""给""对"等词译出。例如:

(1) Air resistance must *be given* careful consideration when the aircraft is to be manufactured.

要制造飞行器,必须仔细考虑空气阻力问题。

(2) Whenever work is being done, energy is *being converted* from one form into another.

凡做功,都是把能从一种形式转换成另一种形式。

(3) Much greater magnification can *be obtained* with the electron microscope.

使用电子显微镜,能获得大的多的放大倍数。

4.4　习惯译法

(1)英语中,为使用上下文紧密衔接,句子前后平衡,有时可把被动语态中的过去分词放在句首,而把主句放在助动词"be"之后,形成倒装结构。这种句子在翻译时,词序一般不需变动,而常在主语之前加"……的是……""……有……"等词译出。这是一种习惯译法,科技文章中甚多。例如:

In an ordinary atom the number of protons are the same as that of electrons. *Clustered* together with these protons *are* neutrons.

在普通原子里,质子数和电子数相等。与这些质子集结在一起的是中子。

(2)英语中以"it"作形式主语,以被动语态作谓语,其后跟一个由 that 引导的主语从句的结构很多。这种结构在译成汉语时,除把 it 一律省略外,通常有两种处理方法:一是在被动语态之前加"人们""有人""我们""大家""据……"等词译出;于是,不加任何词直接译出。例如:

①*It was estimated* that the power of an average horse is equal to 550 foot-pounds per second.

我们估计,一匹普通马的功率等于 550 英尺·磅/秒。

②Not very many years ago, *it was supposed* that life was altogether absent in the deeper parts of the sea.

没有多少年以前,人们还认为,海洋深处完全没有生命。

实际上,上述句型可以概括成为"It+被动语态+that..."的形式。下面列出有关以 it 作为形式主语的英语被动语态的一些常用形式。

(i) 不加主语的常用形式

It is reported that ...	据报道……
It is said that ...	据说/有人说……
It has been announced that ...	已经宣布……
It should be noted that ...	应当指出……
It must be pointed out that ...	必须指出……
It will be seen from this that ...	由此可见……
It is preferred that ...	最好……
It has been proved that ...	已证明……
It can be seen that ...	可以看出/可见……
It is understood that ...	不用说/很清楚……

(ii) 加主语的常用形式

It is believed that ...	有人相信……
It is well known that ...	大家知道(众所周知)……
It was told that ...	有人曾经说……
It will be said that ...	有人会说……
It is noticed that ...	有人指出/注意到……
It is asserted that ...	有人主张/有人认为……
It is generally agreed that ...	人们通常认为……

# 第 5 章 定语从句的翻译

修饰名词或代词的从句称为定语从句。定语从句是由关系代词 that, which, who, (whom, whose) 和关系副词 when, where, why 引导的。定语从句所修饰的词叫做先行词。定语从句一般放在先行词的后面。

5.1 主句与从句合起来译

在英语中的限制性定语从句,均位于它所修饰的词之后,一般为全句必不可少的成分,如果省去,主句就会发生意义上的变化,甚至由于意义不完全而不知所云,因此翻译时,常常把从句融合在主句中,省去关联词,在从句之后加"的"来修饰主句中有关的词。例如:

(1) The bodies *which may either repel or attract each other* are called electrified body.

人们把互相排斥的或互相吸引的物体叫带电体。

(2) Matter is the name *that is given to all substances of each kind*.

物质是赋予所有各类物体的共同名称。

(3) Air moves from places *where he pressure is high* to places *where the pressure is low*.

空气从压力高的地方流向压力低的地方。

(4) AIDS is only contracted from an exchange of blood or semen *that contained the HIV virus*.

只有通过含有 HIV 病毒的血液或精液的交流才会感染上艾滋病。

5.2 主句与从句分开译

当从句与其所修饰的词之间的关系不很密切,只是起一种补充说明的作用,如果省去,并不影响主句的意思时,常常可以按其顺序,把主句与从句分开翻译,译成并列句或状语从句。这种译法常见与非限制性定语从句,但限制性定语从句有时也可采用。

5.2.1 译成并列句

如果从句较长,结构较复杂,或者意思上的独立性较强,通常可把主句与从句分开译,已成并列句。

1. 重复关联所代替的词,有时还可在这些词之前加指示代词"这""这个""这些"等,是译文更加明确。例如:

(1) Ultrasonic sounds produce pulsed signals, *by means of which various defects in metals can be detected.*

超声波产生脉冲信号,用这些信号能查处金属中各种缺陷。

(2) Inertia is that property of matter *because of which force is needed to accelerate a baby.*

惯性是物质的一种属性,由于这一属性,如果使物体产生加速度,就必须施加一个作用力。

(3) Archimedes' principle applies to liquids, *by which we mean all liquids and gases.*

阿基米德原理适用于一切流体,这里所谓的流体指的是一切液体和气体。

2. 当从句在意思上与主句相矛盾或语气突然转折时,除重复关联词所代替的词之外,还可加连词"但""而""却""但是""可是"等,使译文语气连贯。例如:

(1) Matter is composed of molecules *that ate composed of atoms.*

物质是由分子组成的,而分子是由原子组成的。

(2) Mechanical energy can be changed to electrical energy, *which in turn can be changed to mechanical energy.*

机械能能转变为电能,而电能又能转变为机械能。

3. 翻译时也可不必重复关联词所代替的词,而将其译成人称代词"它""它们""他""他们"等,使句子简明扼要。例如:

(1) The simplest atom is the hydrogen atom *that contains one proton and one electron.*

最简单的原子是氢原子,它只包含一个质子和一个电子。

(2) The control unit is an important part of the computer, *which can cause the machine to operate according to man's wishes.*

控制单元是计算机的重要组成部分,它能使机器按人们的意愿进行操作。

4. 以 whose 引导的定语从句分译时,通常将 whose 译成"它的""他的""她的""他们的""它们的"等词。例如:

(1) A vector can be resolved into two or more other vectors *whose sum is equal to the original vector.*

一个向量可以分解为两个或两个以上不同的向量,其综合等于原来的向量。

(2) The sun is an enormous mass of gases *whose temperature and pressure increase towards the center.*

太阳是一个巨大的气团,它的温度和压力越接近中心越高。

5. 以"where"引导的定语从句分译的情况。例如:

See Fig. 1 ~ 9, *where the plate lies on three rest buttons.*

见图 1 ~ 9,图中平板放在三个定位钮上。

5.2.2 译成状语从句

当定语从句在内容上含有时间、原因、条件、让步、目的、结果等状语意思时,往往可在其前加相应的连词,已成状语从句。例如:

(1) A body *that contains only atoms which same general properties* is called an element.

一个物体,如果它包含的原子性质都相同,则称之为元素。(译成条件状语从句)

(2) Anyone *who thinks that rational knowledge need not be derived from perceptual knowledge* is an idealist.

如果以为理性认识可以不从感性认识得来,他就是一个唯心论者。(译成条件状语成句)

(3) Engels, *whose native language was German*, could read and write in several foreign languages.

虽然恩格斯的母语是德语,他却能用好几门外语来阅读和写作。(译成让步状语成句)

5.3 特殊定语从句的译法

5.3.1 which 引导的特殊定语从句的译法

以 which 引导的特殊定语从句,通常是说明整个主句的,是用来对主句所述的事物或现象加以总结概括,补充说明或承上启下的,其前都有逗号分开。所以翻译时,主句与从句分译,通常把"which"译成"这……",但有时也可译成"从而……""因而……"。例如:

(1) The sun heats the earth, *which makes it possible for plants to grow*.

太阳晒热大地,这就使植物有可能生长。

(2) Energy can neither be created nor destroyed, *which is the universally accepted law*.

能量既不能被创造也不能被消灭,这是一条公认的规律。

(3) All forces occur in pair, *which may conveniently be spoken of as action and reaction*.

所有的力都是成对出现的,这很方便的称为作用和反作用。

5.3.2 as 引导的特殊定语从句的译法

以"as"引导的特殊定语从句,有点像插入成分,通常对主句所作的陈述进行附加说明。这种从句可在主句之前、之中或之后。翻译时主句与从句分译,通常把"as"译成"这""如""像"等词。例如:

(1) Levers and pulleys, *as show in the experiment*, change motion from one direction to another.

如实验所示,杠杆和滑轮改变了运动的方向。

(2) Power is equal to work divided by the time, *as has been said before*.

功率等于功除以时间,这在前面已经讲到。

(3) Electrons, *as one knows*, are minute negative charges of electricity.

如大家所知,电子是微小的负电荷。

5.4 译成简单句

当英语中定语从句的结构比较简单,且主句又多为"there+be+主语+……"句型时,或者主句虽不是这种句型,但从句与其所修饰的词关系比较密切,意思上的联系不可分割时,往往可以把从句作为主句,把主句并进去,而把复合句译

成简单句。例如:

(1) There is nothing *that does not contain contradiction*; without contradiction nothing would exist.

没有什么事物是不包含矛盾的。没有矛盾就没有世界。

(2) In a conductor there are a lager number of electrons *which move freely from atom to atom*.

导体中有大量的电子在原子与原子之间自由活动。

(3) With the introduction of the electronic computer, there is no complicated problem *but can be solved quickly*.

由于采用了电子计算机,任何复杂的问题都能迅速计算出来。

5.5 几点说明

1. 英语中定语从句的翻译比较复杂,虽然限制性定语从句常常与主句合起来译,但非限制性的定语从句有时也可这样翻译。有些句子合起来译或分开译均可以,所以上面所介绍的几种翻译方法,决不能生搬硬套,而应考虑具体情况既要考虑英语句子的结构和意义,又要考虑汉语的表达习惯,才能使译文通顺易懂,确切明了。例如:

A semiconductor means a material *whose conductivity range between that of conductors and insulators*.

半导体指的是这样的材料,它的导电性介于导体和绝缘体之间。(或译成:半导体指的是导电性介于导体和绝缘体之间的材料。)

2. 分隔定语从句:英语中的定语从句通常紧跟在它所修饰的词之后,但有时也可被其他成分所分隔,这种情况在科技文章中颇为常见。翻译时应特别注意。有的与主句合起来译,有的分开译,有的译成简单句。视具体情况,灵活处理。

(1) 当从句所修饰的词之后有介词短语、分词短语、形容词短语所表示的定语或状语时,从句往往放在这些成分之后,形成与它所修饰的词的分隔情况。例如:

①Yet there exist complex computations in science and engineering *which people are unable to make*.

到目前为止在科学和工程方面还存在许多人们无能为力的复杂计算。

②We have made a number of creative advances in theoretical research and applied sciences *which are up to advanced world levels*.

我们在理论研究和应用科学方面,获得了不少具有世界先进水平的创造性成就。

（2）当主句的结构比较简单而从句又是修饰主句中的主语时或者从句本身较长而又带有另一从句时，为了使句子匀称，往往可把从句放在主句谓语或其他成分之后，形成从句与主句所修饰的词分隔开。例如：

①In industry certain mixtures of metals or ally are known to have been greatly developed *that will resist the action of acids.*

我们知道，在工业上已经研制出了能耐酸的某些金属混合物，即合金。

②Here serious problems are encountered *which have only been partly solved.*

这里遇到一些尚未完全解决的重大问题。

③No machine exists *which can not be made reasonably safe.*

没有什么机器不可以制造得安全可靠。

第 6 章 其他从句的翻译

6.1 主语从句的翻译

在复合句中起主语作用的从句称为主语从句。引导主语从句的词有关系代词 what 和连接代词以及连接副词 who, what, which, when, where, how, why, 还有连词 that, whether 等。

英语中的主语从句有两种句型：①从属连词或者关联词位于句首的从句+主语谓语+其他成分；②形式主语 it+谓语+that(whether)引导的从句。在翻译时，语序一般不变，依次译出。但是，有时也可以变换，在第一种句型中先译从句，再译主句。在第二种句型中，先译从句，再译主句。这主要与汉语的表达习惯有关。如果先译从句，那么有时可以在主句之前加"这"译出。例如：

(1) *What you are doing* seems very difficult.

你正在做的事似乎很难。

(2) *Whatever he saw and heard on his trip* gave him a very deep impression.

此行所见所闻都给他留下了深刻的印象。

(3) *Who else may object*, I shall approve.

不管什么人反对，我都要赞成。

(4) It is very important *whether we should maintain our present standard of living*.

我们是否该维持目前的生活水平，这一点很重要。

(5) It is a matter of common experience that *bodies are lighter in water than they are in air*.

物体在水中比在空气中轻，这是大家共有的经验。

(6) *Whether you come or not* is up to you.

来不来由你自己决定。

【注】 ①由 what 引导的从句相当于一个名词加一个定语从句,表示"所……的"这类东西。

②由连词 that 引导的从句在大多数情况下都是用作形式上的主语,把从句移到句子后面去。例如:

That the majority are for the plan is obvious.

大多数人都赞成这个计划,这是很明显的。

或者表述成:It is obvious *that the majority are for the plan*.

另外,虽然下面的句型不是主语句型,但却是两个经常出现的实用句型:

(i) it follow + that 从句(当然……,由此可得……)

From this evidence, it follow that he is not the murder.

由证据判断,他当然不可能是凶手。

it doesn't follow + that 从句(未必……)

Although she is poor, it doesn't follow that she is dishonest.

虽然她很穷,却未必不诚实。

(ii) It occurs to + 人 + that 从句(某人突然想起……)

等于 It strikes + 人 + that 从句

It occurs to me that I should ask him for help.

等于 It strikes me that I should ask him for help.

我突然想起,我应该向他求助。

6.2 表语从句的翻译

在系动词(主要是 to be)后面作表语用的从句叫表语从句。表语从句一般由关系代词 that 和连接代词或连接副词 what, who, when, where, how 或连词 that, as if, whether 等引导。

6.2.1 英语中的表语从句

通常总是位于主句和系动词(主要是 be)之后,翻译时顺序一般不变。例如:

(1) The fact is *that I cannot afford to buy the car at all*.

事实是我根本买不起那辆小车。

(2) The question is *what a diesel engine is, how it works and how it differs from a gasoline engine*.

问题在于什么是柴油机,它是怎样工作的,它和汽油机有何区别。

(3) That was *what he wanted*.

那正是他想要的。

(4) It is very important *whether we should maintain our present standard of living*.

我们是否该维持目前的生活水平,这一点很重要。

(5) One reason for this is *that you don't have enough sleep*.

引起这的一个原因是你睡眠不足。

(6) This is *where Salt Lake City now lies*.

这就是盐湖城现在所在的位置。

6.2.2 表语从句的几种常见句型及其译法

下列句型在翻译成汉语时,既可以先译主句,后译从句,也可以先译从句,后译主语,依据汉语的表达习惯而灵活处理。

1. 在"that (this) is why ..."句型中,如果先译主句,后译从句,通常译成"这就是为什么……""这就是为什么……的原因""这就是……的缘故"等。如果先译从句,后译主句,一般译成"……原因就在这里""……理由就在这里"等。例如:

(1) *This is why* the jet engine can work at all altitudes.

这就是喷气发动机能在任何高度上工作的原因。

(2) Iron combines easily with oxygen. *That is why* it is never found pure in nature.

铁很容易与氧化合,这就是在自然界中从未发现纯铁的缘故。

2. 在"that (this) is because ..."句型中,通常先译主句,后译从句,译成"这是因为……""这是因为……的缘故""这是由于……的缘故"等。例如:

(1) It often happens, however, that thinking lags behind reality; *this is because* mans cognition is limited by numerous social conditions.

然而,思想落后于实际的事是常有的,这是因为人的认识受到了许多社会条件的限制的缘故。

(2) *This is because* people engaged in changing reality are usually subject to numerous limitations; ...

这是因为从事现实变革的人们,常常受着许多的限制;……

3. 在"this is what ..."句型中,如果先译主句,后译从句,译成"这就是……的……内容""这就是……的含义"等。如果先译从句,再译主句,通常译成"……就是这个道理""……就这个意思"等。例如:

(1) *This is what* the equation means.

这就是此方程式的含意。

(2) *This is what* we have discussed in this article.

这就是我们在本文中所讨论的内容。

(3) *This is what* is meant by "failure is the mother of success" and "a fall into the pit, a gain in your wit."

所谓"失败乃成功之母""吃一堑,长一智"就是这个道理。

4. 在"It is just as ..."句型中,通常先译主句,后译从句,译成"这正像……的那样""这正如……的那样"等。例如:

It is just as Lenin stated, "Without revolutionary theory there can be no revolutionary movement".

这正像列宁所说的那样,"没有革命的理论就不会有革命的运动"。

6.3 宾语从句的翻译

修饰名词或代词的从句称为定语从句。定语从句是由关系代词 that, which, who (whom, whose)和关系副词 where, when, why 引导的。定语从句一般放在先行词的后面。

1. 英语中的宾语从句,通常用作主句中及物动词的宾语,该动词可能是变化了的谓语形式或者动词原形所表示的命令形式,也可能是用作主语、表语、定语、状语的动词不定式或分词及物动词的形式;有时,也可作某些形容词或介词的宾语,且位于这些词之后。翻译时,顺序一般不变。例如:

(1) Have you heard *what happened to her yesterday*?

你听说她昨天出了什么事吗?

(2) He refuses to do *what he thinks to be wrong*.

他拒绝做他认为是错误的事情。

(3) He never accepts *what the professors say as authoritative*.

他从不把教授的话看成是绝对的真理。

(4) Please tell me *where I can get the book*.

请告诉我在哪儿能搞到那本书。

(5) Let's see *how we can finish the work in time*.

我们想想有什么办法能及时完成这项工作。

(6) In learning a language, it is important to find out *how speakers of that language show politeness*.

学习一种语言,要领悟应用这种语言的人怎样表示礼貌,这很重要。

(7) Most scientists agree *that computers cannot completely take the place of*

human beings.

大多数科学家认为,计算机不能完全代替人脑。

此外,在由 that 引导的宾语从句中,常常可以省略。例如:

I hear (that) *physics isn't easy*.

我听说物理不那么容易学。

2. 英语中的介词等之后,如果跟有宾语从句,常常可译成并列句的分句,用"除……之外""除了……""此外……""只是……""但……"等词译出;在 in 之后,如果跟有宾语从句,经常可以译成原因状语从句,用"因为……""在于……""是因为……"等词译出。例如:

(1) She talked about *what it meant to grow up*.

他谈论一个人的成长意味着什么。

(2) This reminds me of *how she helped me when I was in difficulties*.

这使我想起在我有困难时她是怎么帮助我的。

(3) Thank you for *what you've done for me*.

感谢你为我做了这些事。

(4) She walked to *where the pianist was sitting*.

她走到钢琴家坐着的地方。

(5) Ideas of *what are good manners* are not always the same in different countries.

什么叫做很有礼貌,不同的国家看法往往不同。

【注】 介词后面的宾语从句一般不用 that 引导。

6.4 同位语从句的翻译

用作同位语的从句称为同位语从句。它通常跟在 idea, fact, news, suggestion 等名词的后面,用以说明名词所表示的具体内容。引导同位语从句的词有连词 that 与连接副词 how, where, when 等。

英语中的同位语从句与其所修饰的名词在地位上是同等的,只起进一步揭示其内容的作用。从句常用 that 与 whether 引导,它们在从句中不担任任何成分。这种从句译成汉语时,一般有两种处理方法:一是把从句译成一个独立的句子,并在其前加"即""这"等词,或在从句所修饰的名词之后加冒号或破折号;二是用"的"字把从句译在它所修饰的词之前。究竟采用哪种译法方式,要视具体情况而定。例如:

(1) We are familiar with the idea *that all matter consists of atoms*.

我们都熟悉这样一个概念,即一切物质都由原子组成。

(2) You have no idea *how worried I was*.

你不知道我当时多么担心。

(3) He put forward a proposal *that they should set a deadline for handing in the plan*.

他提出建议,他们应该订出一个交计划的期限。

(4) The fact *that he had not said anything* surprised everybody.

他一言不发使大家十分吃惊。

(5) I don't agree to the view *that all people are selfish*.

我不同意人都是自私的这一观点。

(6) The foreign journalists got the impression *that the majority of the Chinese supported the economic reform*.

外国记者的印象是中国大多数人民都支持经济改革。

(7) He made a promise *that he would never smoke again*.

他保证再不吸烟了。

6.5 状语从句的翻译

修饰动词、形容词或者副词等的从句称为状语从句。状语从句可以用来表示时间、地点、原因、目的、结果、条件、让步、比较、方式等几个方面。状语从句在句子中的位置是相当灵活的,既可放在句首,又可放在句末。

1. 时间状语从句:这种从句一般由 when, whenever, while, as, before, after, since, until, as soon as, once 等词连词引导。例:

(1) *When he got to the airport*, the flight had already left.

他到达机场时,班机已经起飞了。

(2) *While we were discussing the text*, he brought up an interesting question.

在我们讨论课文的时候,他提出了一个有趣的问题。

(3) I'll give you an answer after I have thought everything over.

我考虑好以后,会给你个答复。

(4) I'll tell him to phone you *as soon as he comes back to the office*.

他一回到办公室,我就告诉他给你去电话。

(5) *Once he makes up his mind*, he'll never change.

一旦他下了决心,决不改变。

【注】 在时间状语从句中,不用将来时,例如:

When practice is over, Jane will go home.

2. 地点状语从句:这类从句一般由 where, wherever 等词引导。例如:

(1) The delegation was warmly received *wherever it went*.

代表团所到之处总是受到热情的接待。

(2) These things must be taken to the room *where they are usually kept*.

这些东西必须送到经常存放它们的那间屋里去。

3. 原因状语从句:这类从句一般由 because, as, since 等词引导。例如:

(1) We had to put off the match *because it was raining hard*.

因为雨下得很大,我们不得不推迟比赛。

(2) *Since everybody has come*, we can set off.

既然大家都到了,我们可以出发了。

(3) *As the train was two hours late*, we strolled round the neighbourhood.

因为火车晚点两个小时,我们在附近转了转。

4. 目的状语从句:这类从句一般用 so that, in order that, for fear that 等词引导。例如:

(1) He spends his spare time studying English *in order that he might read foreign material on the latest technology*.

为了能够阅读最新技术方面的外文资料,他利用业余时间学习英文。

(2) She spoke slowly *so that we could follow her easily*.

她讲得很慢,以便我们可以跟上她。

(3) She took a raincoat with her *for fear that it should rain*.

她怕天会下雨,带了一件雨衣。

5. 条件状语从句:这类从句最常用的引导词有 if, unless, as (so) long as, provided that, on condition that 等。例如:

(1) I won't wait for him *unless he phones me*.

他若不给我打电话,我就不等他。

(2) You can camp here *provided that you leave no mess*.

只要不把这儿弄脏,你们可以在这儿宿营。

(3) He said he would attend the meeting *on condition that he was not asked to speak*.

他说只要人们不请他发言他会参加会议的。

6. 让步状语从句:这类从句一般由 although, though, even if, whatever, whoever, however, whether, no matter what (who, how...) 等词引导。例如:

(1) *Different as the forms of matter are*, they are nothing but matter in motion.

虽然物质的形式各不相同,但它们都不过是运动中的物质。

(2) He couldn't solve the problem *however hard he tried*.

不管他怎么想方设法也解决不了这个难题。

(3) *Even if you are not fond of modern music*, you shouldn't miss this concert.

即使你不喜欢现代音乐,你也该去听一听这次音乐会。

7. 比较状语从句:比较从句是提出另一个事实或情况和主句中的事实或情况相比较。这类从句一般以 as 或 than 引导。通常用的句型有 as...as..., not as (so)...as..., more...than..., the more...the more...等。例如:

(1) The price was a lot *more than they planned to append*.

这价格远远超出了他们计划花的钱。

(2) A telephone call would be *nicer than a letter*.

打电话比写信要好。

(3) *The more she worried*, *the more* nervous she got.

她越担心就越紧张。

第 7 章 否定形式的翻译

英语和汉语一样,在表达的形式上有肯定形式和否定形式之分。一般来说,翻译时应把肯定形式译成肯定形式,否定形式译成否定形式。但是,由于两种语言的表达手段和表达习惯不同,如果生搬硬套,把英语中的肯定形式千篇一律地都译成汉语中的肯定形式,或者把英语中的否定形式都译成汉语中的否定形式,不仅译文不通,不符合汉语习惯,甚至会成为误译,所以翻译时,往往需作反面处理。这是说英语中的否定形式,有时可以译成汉语中的肯定形式,而英语中的肯定形式反而可译成汉语中的否定形式。

英语中否定形式的表达法很多,归纳起来大致可分为六类:全部否定、部分否定、双重否定、意义否定、问答中的否定、前缀与后缀的否定。现分述如下。

7.1 全部否定

英语中的全部否定通常是用下列一些否定词来表达的。这类否定句一般仍译为否定句,但否定词的词序有时有所变动,究竟怎样变动,视句子的意思而定。这类否定词常见的有:

no	不,没有
not	不,不是
none	没人,谁都不;一点不,都不
nobody	没人,谁也不
nothing	没有任何东西,什么也不
nohow	决不,毫不;无论如何不
never	从不,决不,千万不
nor	也不
neither	两个都不,……也不

neither ... nor　　既不……也不……，两者都不

(1) We usually regard energy as not occupying space.

通常认为能不占有空间。

(2) A gas has neither definite size nor definite shape.

气体既没有一定的体积，也没有一定的形状。

(3) Neither problem has been solved.

两个问题哪个也没解决。

(4) Nothing is hard in this world, if you dare to scale the heights.

世上无难事，只要肯登攀。

1. 英语中表示信念或推测等意义的动词 expect, think, believe, suppose, imagine 等否定式时，如果其后带有 that 引导的宾语从句(that 可省略)或动词不定式表示的宾语补语，这种否定并非真正的否定，而是从句中谓语及宾语补语否定的转移。所以翻译时，应把这类动词的否定式译成肯定，而把其后从句中的谓语或宾语补语译成否定。

(1) I don't think that he can operate the new type of computer.

我认为他不会操作这种新型计算机。

(2) Seeing a ball flying, we don't expect the ball to fly forever.

我们看到球飞滚时，认为它不会永远飞下去。

(3) Ordinarily one does not believe air to have weight.

人们通常认为空气没有重量。

(4) I don't suppose he will come tomorrow.

我认为他明天不会来。

2. 在"not ... because ..."的结构中，有时 not 否定的并不是语句中的谓语，而是 because 引导的状语从句，主要根据句子的逻辑来确定。例如：

(1) Plastics for industrial purposes are not valuable because they are colourful.

工业用的塑料不因为五颜六色而才有价值。

(2) The motor did not stop running because the fuel was finished.

这台电动机不是因为燃料用完了才停止运转。

(3) He did not come because he wanted to see comrade Li.

他不是因为要看李同志才来的。

【注】① not 为否定副词，通常用来构成谓语动词的否定形式。谓语动词若为行为动词(be 除外)，其否定式还需加 do(does, did)。

② no 为否定形容词，通常是用来否定名词、动名词及形容词的，且常位于这类词之前。no 的否定语气比 not 更强。

③ nor 为否定连词,通常位于句首,句子用倒装语序。

7.2 部分否定

英语中的部分否定是由 all, every, each, both, always, much, many, often, everybody, everything, total, totally, whole, wholly complete, completely 等词与 not 结合而构成的。Not 可在上述词之前,也可在谓语中。不论 not 在什么地方,通常都译成"不全是""不都是""不总是""不是都""未必都""并非""全非""不多""不常"等。例如:

(1) Thus, friction is not always an evil.
这样说来,摩擦并非总是不好的。
(2) An engine may not always do work at its rated horsepower.
发动机并非始终以额定马力做功。
(3) Not all substances exist in all three states.
并非所有的物质都有三态。
(4) Both of the answers are not right.
两种答案并非都对。
(5) All that glitters is not gold.
闪光者未必都是金子。

7.3 双重否定

双重否定通常是由 no(not)等与某些表示否定意义的词连用而构成,表示否定的否定。译成汉语时,可以是肯定形式,也可以保持双重否定的形式,视汉语的习惯而定。这种否定形式最常见的有:

no (not)... no(not)...	没有……没有……;没有……不……
no (not)...but...	没有……不
no (not)...without...	没有……不……;除……不……
no (none)...the less...	不因……就不……
no (not)...unless...	没有……就不……;除非……才
not...until(till)...	不到……不……;直到……才……
no (none)...other than...	不是别的,正是……;就是……
not but that...	并非……不……;虽然……
not...a little...	不少,很多……

(1) No flow of water occurs unless there is a difference in pressure.

没有压差,水就不会流动。

(2) Bearings should not be unboxed or unwrapped until the moment for fitting has arrived.

不到安装的时候,不应启动包装箱或包装纸。

(3) No machine can be made completely frictionless.

没有摩擦作用的机器是造不出来的。

(4) There is no law that has not exceptions.

凡是规律都有例外。

7.4 意义否定

英语中有些动词、名词、副词、介词、连词、形容词及词组在形式上是肯定的,但在含义上往往是否定的。所以翻译时,应作反面的处理。这类词组常见的有:

too ... to ...	太……不……
too ... for ...	太……不……
far from ...	一点也不……;远非……;没有……反而
free form ...	没有,免于
safe form ...	免于
keep from ...	使……不受;避开;阻止;免于
save form ...	使……不受;避开;阻止
protect from ...	使……不受;避开;阻止
but for ...	若非;如果没有
anything but ...	绝不是
instead of ...	而不(是)……;代替……
prevent from ...	不……;阻止……
in place of ...	代替……
out of ...	缺乏……;脱离……;在……外
in lieu of ...	代替
in vain ...	无效;徒然
short of ...	缺少;没……
rather than ...	而不是;与其……不如……
miss	失败;没有
refuse	拒绝
ignore	忽略;不顾

overlook	忽略；忽视
exclude	排除；除去
fail	失败；缺乏
few	几乎没有；很少
neglect	忽略；忽视
absence	缺少；缺乏
exclusion	排除；除去
but that	若非；要不是
without	没有；不必
except	除……之外

(1) It is gravity that keeps us from falling off.

正是重力使我们不会从地球上掉出去。

(2) So instead of using weight as a standard we use mass, because that doesn't change.

因此，我们用质量作为标准而不用重量，因为质量不会变化。

(3) Note that we talk about mass, rather than weight.

注意，我们讲到的是质量而不是重量。

(4) On freezing water becomes larger in volume instead of smaller.

水在结冰时体积变得较大，而不是较小。

(5) Very few of the everyday things around us are really pure states of matter.

我们周围的日常用品几乎没有是纯态的。

7.5 问答中的否定

英语问答中的否定形式是多种多样的，其回答中的否定词"no"，和肯定词"yes"是针对事实的，而汉语中的则往往是针对问题的。因此，在翻译时，有时可把英语中的否定词译成肯定。例如：

(1) Air is not a solid, is it? No, it isn't.

空气不是固体，对吧？对的，它不是固体。

(2) Have you not yet finished your experiment? No, we have't.

你们还没有做完实验吗？是的，还没有。

(3) Won't you come? Yes, I will. (No, I won't.)

你不来吗？不，我来。（是的，我不来。）

7.6 前缀与后缀的否定

英语中否定的表示,还可通过具有否定意义的前缀或后缀来表达。

1. 具有否定意义的前缀

(1) anti- 表示"反,防,抗,非,逆,解"等意义。例如:
proton(质子)—— antiproton(反质子)
missile(导弹)—— antimissile(反导弹的)
freeze(冻结)—— antifreeze(防冻)
jamming(干扰)—— antijamming(抗干扰)
clocking(顺时针方向)—— anticlockwise(逆时针方向)

(2) im-, in-, il-, ir- 表示"不,无,非"等意义。例如:
possible(可能的)—— impossible(不可能的)
accurate(精确的)—— inaccurate(不精确的)
regular(规则的)—— irregular(不规则的)
finite(有限的)—— infinite(无限的)
elastic(弹性的)—— inelastic(非弹性的)
logical(逻辑的)—— illogical(不合逻辑的)

(3) un- 表示"去,非,无,未,失"等意义。例如:
equal(相等的)—— unequal(不相等的)
stable(稳定的)—— unstable(不稳定的)
known(已知的)—— unknown(未知的)
common(普通的)—— uncommon(非凡的)
limited(有限的)—— unlimited(无限的)

(4) de- 表示"去,解,反,失,除,减,脱"等意义。例如:
composition(合成)—— decomposition(分解)
oxidation(氧化)—— deoxidation(脱氧)
modulation(调制)—— demodulation(反调制)
ionization(电离)—— deionization(去电离)
formation(形成)—— deformation(失真,变形)

(5) dis- 表示"不,无,放,非,解除"等意义。例如:
order(秩序)—— disorder(无秩序)
charge(充电)—— discharge(放电)
approve(赞成)—— disapprove(不赞成)
junction(连接)—— disjunction(分离,分开)

proportion(比例)——disproportion(不成比例)
(6) non- 表示"不,非,无"等意义。例如：
metal(金属)——non-metal(非金属)
conductor(导体)——non-conductor(非导体)
stop(停止)——non-stop(不停的)
uniform(均匀的)——nonuniform(不均匀的)
ductile(有延性的)——nonductile(无延性的)
(7) counter- 表示"反,抗,抵,逆"等意义。例如：
action(作用)——counteraction(反作用)
force(力,力量)——counterforce(对抗能力)
current(电流)——countercurrent(逆流)
balance(平衡)——counterbalance(抗衡)
motion(运动)——counter-motion(反向运动)
(8) under- 表示"不足,欠,不"等意义。例如：
production(生产)——underproduction(生产不足)
speed(速度)——underspeed(速度不足)
proof(合格的)——underproof(不合格的)
damp(阻尼)——underdamp(欠阻尼)
firing(点火)——underfiring(欠火)

2. 具有否定意义的后缀

(1) -free 表示"无……的""免于……的"等意义。例如：
oil（油）——oil-free(无油的)
dust（灰尘）——dust-free(无尘的)
error（误差）——error-free(无误差的)
ice(冰)——ice-free(无冰的)
rent(租金)——rent-free(租金免付的)
(2) -less 表示"没有……的""无……的""不……的"等意义。例如：
weight（重量）——weightless（失重的）
point（要点）——pointless（不得要领的）
colour(颜色)——colourless（无色的)
sound（声音）——soundless（无声的）
stain（污斑）——stainless（无垢的;有锈的）

7.7 带有否定词的短语译法

英语中带有否定词的短语或习语很多不能逐字死译,有的甚至并不表示否定意义。应该按照句子的具体意义处理。现在,把科技文献中常见的这类短语、习语以及习惯介绍如下:

and what not	等等,诸如此类
as likely as not	或许,多半,很可能
as often as not	时常,屡次
at no time	决不,从来没有
by no means	决不,绝不是
by no manner of means	决不,绝不是
by no rate	绝没有
cannot be otherwise than	……只能
cannot but (+inf.)	不得不;不禁
cannot fail (+inf.)	不定要
cannot ... too ...	应尽量
care nothing about(for)...	对……漠不关心
come to no good	结果不佳
come to nothing	失败,毫无结果
cut no ice	无效,无益
do no good	无用,无关系
for no other reason than ...	只因为……这个理由
for nothing	徒然;无缘无故
had it not been for ...	若非,倘若没有
have no occasion (+inf.)	没有……理由
have no part in ...	和……一点关系也没有
have neither part not lot in...	和……一点关系也没有
have nothing in common with...	与……毫无共同之处
have nothing to do with	与……完全无关
if for nor other reason than	即使……也好;若只是由于……理由
if it had not been for ...	要不是……的话
if not	不然的话
in neither case	在两种情况下都不

in no case	决不
in no degree	毫不
in no respect	绝不是
in no sense	绝不是
in no time	立刻
in no way (wise)	决不
it does not matter	没关系;无影响
it is no matter	无关紧要
it is not the case	情况并非如此
it is nothing but	不外是,不过是
it makes no matter	无关紧要
it was not long before	不久
leave no stones unturned	用尽方法
leave no means untried	用尽方法
leave nothing to be desired	完备无缺
less than no time	立刻
little or no	几乎没有
little or nothing	几乎没有;简直没有
lose no time	乘机,不失时机,立即
make no doubt	不用怀疑
make nothing of	不懂,不认为困难
more often than not	多半,时常
neither here nor there	不必要的;没关系的
never mind	没关系
never more	决不再
never fail of	务必,非要
never fail to	必定
next to nothing	几乎没有,极少
no... at all	一点也没有
no better than...	与……差不多;简直是
no end of...	无限的,无数的
no less	仍旧,依然
no less than	至少,不少于
no less... than	……和……同样;正好,不亚于
no longer	不再,已不

no matter	不要紧,无关紧要
no matter how ...	不管怎样
no matter how much	不管多少
no matter what	无论什么
no matter when	无论何时
no matter where	无论何处
no matter whether	不论……是否
no matter which	无论哪个
no matter who	无论谁
no more	不再
no more than	不过,仅仅
no more ... than ...	与……同样不
no sooner ... than	刚一……就……,立即
no sort of ...	毫不
no ... whatever	什么也不
none but	谁都不,除……外谁也不
none the less	虽然……但是,仍然,还是
none the more	虽……仍旧,还是
not a bit	一点也不,毫不
not a few	许多,不少
not a little	很多,不少
not ... any longer	不再,已不
not ... any more	不再
not ... any more than	仅仅,不过
not at all	毫不,完全不
not by any means	绝不是
not for to seek	很明白,不难找到
not for the world	决不
not in any way	无论如何
not in the least	毫不,并不,一点也不
not less than	不少于
not long since	就在不久以前
not more than	仅仅,不超过
not ... on any consideration	决不
not the case of	并非如此

not the least	很少，很，全无
not to mention(to say)	更谈不上，更不必说
not to speak of	更不必讲
not yet	尚未，还不
nothing but	仅是，正是；不过是
nothing else than	无非是
nothing in the world	一点也不
nothing of kind	绝不是那样
nothing short of	完全是，简直是
nothing to speak of	不值一谈，微不足道
nothing wrong with …	没问题，没毛病
on no account	决不
on no consideration	决不
only not	简直是，几乎跟……一样
pay no regard to …	不顾
seldom or never	简直不；极难得
spare no efforts(+inf.)	尽力；不遗余力
spare no pains	极力；不怕费力
there could be no question	是不可能的
there is no lack of	不缺，有很多的
take no account of	不计，不考虑
think nothing of …	轻视
to no avail	无用
to no effect	无效，徒劳
to no purpose	无结果，白白地
to say nothing of	更不用说
under no account	决不
under (in) no circumstances	在任何情况下……都不，决不
upon no time	决不
were it not for …	若不是，要不是
whether or no (not)	是否，无论如何
will not do for …	当作……用不行
with no difficulty	轻而易举地

例如：

(1) Since probability distributions for counts are *not yet* standard in the

econometric literature, their properties are explored in some detail in this chapter.

对计数情况来说,由于其概率分布尚未成为计量经济学文献的标准内容,所以本章以某种详细方式来探讨它们的性质。

(2) Energy is *nothing but* the capacity to do work.

能量正是做功的能力。

第8章 专业名词与数词翻译

8.1 专业术语的译法

8.1.1 专业术语译法

专业术语是指特定的专业知识或学科中的专业名词或者词组。专业术语是各种专业翻译中的核心内容,虽然这些专业术语在各专业使用中显而易见,但是对于翻译者来说,要特别关注专业术语英语的中文翻译与译法,尤其是对一些新的专业术语如何翻译成中文则要仔细斟酌。通常,专业术语的英文译法大致有下述几种。

1. 意译

意译就是按原词的意义翻译。意译法使用最普通,统计专业术语在可能的情况下应该尽可能采用这种译法。例如:

pie chart	饼分图
pot chart	散点图
national account	国民核算、国民账户
index numbers	指数
degrees of freedom	自由度
panel data	面板数据
cross-section	横截面,截面
national income aggregates	国民总收入
base period	基期
central tendency	中心趋势,集中趋势
weighted harmonic mean	加权调和平均(值)

weighted geometric average　　加权几何平均(值)

2. 音译

音译就是译成读音与原词相同的汉字。例如：

logic	逻辑
copy	拷贝
trust	托拉斯
motor	马达,摩托

(1)计量单位和各种新材料的名称,一般采用音译,必要时可加注释。例如：

ton	吨
pound	磅
bit	比特
gallon	加仑
vaseline	凡士林(石油冻)
watt	瓦特(瓦)
volt	伏特(伏)
bushel	蒲式耳

(2)有一些科技术语,随着历史的发展已经被人们所熟悉或者掌握,往往又由音译转为意译,或者音译与意译兼用。例如：

modern	摩登的,现代的
combine	康拜因,联合收割机
laser	莱塞,激光
seminar	习明纳尔,课堂讨论
microphone	麦克风,扩音器

3. 音意兼译

音意兼译就是把原词的一部分音译,而另一部分意译。

(1)由人名构成的专业术语,一般采用音意兼译。例如：

Hausman test	豪斯曼(Hausman)检验
Heckman regression	赫克曼(Heckman)回归
Wald statistic	沃尔德(Wald)统计量
Weibull distribution	威布尔(Weibull)分布
Einstein equation	爱因斯坦方程
Archimedes' principle	阿基米德原理

(2)由人名构成的科技术语被人们熟悉之后,通常只取人名第一音节,然

后加"氏"字译出。例如：

Laspeyres index	拉氏指数
Paasche index	派氏指数
Fisher index	费氏指数/费希尔指数
Törnqvist index	特氏指数/特恩奎斯特指数

(3) 有一些词以音译为主，但可在词头或者词尾加上表意的词。例如：

Marxism	马克思主义
logic	逻辑性
Jacobian	雅可比行列式，函数行列式

4. 形象译法

原文用字母等表示事物，译文也可按照事物的内容或者外形用各种办法来表示。例如：

t-test	t 检验
F statistic	F 统计量
p-value	p 值
F distribution	F 分布

8.1.2 准专业术语译法

1. 准专业术语的翻译

除了上述介绍的专业术语翻译之外，还有就是作者认为的"准专业术语"的翻译应该引起人们的关注和研究。

准专业术语

名词群(noun cluster)，即利用一个以上的名词作为定语修饰名词的现象。在科技文献中，名词群的出现和增多的趋势是与科技人员追求简短快捷的表达有关。比如：

(1) random walk chain（随机游走链）；

(2) random utility model（随机效用模型）；

(3) simple panel data model（简单面板数据模型）；

(4) random effects model（随机效应模型）；

(5) finite-sample correction term（有限样本修正项）；

(6) measurement error model（测量误差模型）；

(7) extreme value theory（极值理论）。

在现代数理统计学和高等经济计量学中，经常出现的一些专业行话术语也越来越多，对于这些行话及术语的翻译也应该纳入到专业术语之中。例如：

(1) A can be shown to be B.
可以证明,A 是 B。
(2) It shows that A be B.
可以证明,A 是 B。
(3) Somebody shows that A be B.
某人已经证明,A 是 B。

可见,同样是表述"可以证明"这件事就有多种不同的表达方式。

再比如,在刻画"收敛"概念时,有下述几种既有联系,又有区别的收敛概念:

convergence in probability	依概率收敛
convergence in distribution	依分布收敛
mean-square convergence	均方收敛
almost sure convergence	几乎必然收敛

2. 通用数学术语的翻译

由于现代科技发展的日新月异,各种学科越来越重视数学方法的广泛应用,使得数学术语及符号经常出现在统计学、经济学等许多学科之中,因此,对于熟悉和掌握通用数学术语的英文翻译显得尤为重要。

非语言符号(non-verbal sign)

统计学专业英语中经常运用各种各样的公式、符号、图形、表格等,已经形成一套非语言符号系统,承担着语言符号的信息职能。由于这类非语言符号具有叙述简明、形象、直观的特点,尤其是在当今统计学界具有统一性和通用性,因此越来越受到人们的重视。例如:

if and only if	当且仅当
a plus or minus b	$a \pm b$
a is greater than b	$a > b$
a is greater than or equal to b	$a \geqslant b$
a is less than b	$a < b$
x approaches infinity	$x \to \infty$
the second power of 5 is 25	$5^2 = 25$
y is a function of x	$y = f(x)$
the absolute value of a	$|a|$
the value of function f at a	$f(a)$
common logarithm of x	$\lg x$
log x to the base 10	$\lg x$
n factorial	$n!$

【注】 可参看8.7节和8.8节的有关内容。

8.2　数量的增加和倍数的译法

1. 在"increase(be, go up...) + by +数字或倍数+..."的结构中,by后表示的是净增加数或倍数,所以照译不减。如果是倍数,应译成"增加……"。例如:

(1) This year the output of our factory *has increased by three times* as compared with that of 1990.

今年我厂的产量比1990年增加了三倍。

(2) The fuselage of this aircraft *is by 5 feet longer* than the fuselage of that one.

这种飞机的机身比那种飞机的机身长5英尺。

(3) New boosters can *increase* the payload by 120%.

新型助推器能使有效负载增加到120%。

2. 在"increase(rise, grow, go up, multiply, be...)+数词+times 或 fold+..."结构中,英语均表示增加后的结果,所以应译成"增加了 $n-1$ 倍""增加到 n 倍""为……的 n 倍""n 倍于……"。例如:

(1) In 2000, the output value of Beijing's heavy industry *increased* 3.8 *times* as against 2002.

2000年与2002年相比,北京重工业产量增长了2.8倍。

(2) The volume of gas in tube A *is three times* that in tube B.

试管A内的气体体积是试管B内气体体积的3倍。

(3) The sales of industrial electronic products *have multiplied* 6 *times* since 2000.

自2000年以来工业电子产品销售值增加了5倍。

(4) Total output value of Shanghai's light industry between 1990 and 2002 grew 13 fold, that the textile industry went up 4.3 fold.

1990年到2002年,上海轻工业总产值增长了12倍,纺织工业总产值增长了3.3倍。

3. 在"数字或倍数+比较级(more, higher, better, longer, faster, greater, broader...)+than+..."的结构中,比较级之前表示净增加的数或倍数,英汉两种语言习惯相同,所以照译不减,通常译成"比……""较……"等。例如:

(1) Water conducts heat *about* 20 *times better than* air does.

水的导热能力较空气约强20倍。

(2) The volume of the earth *is* 49 *times larger than* that of the moon.

地球的体积比月球的体积大 49 倍。

(3) Wheel A turns *twenty percent faster than* wheel B.

A 轮转动比 B 轮快 20%。

4. 在"倍数或数字+ as +形容词或副词+ as +..."的结构中,如果第一个 as 之前为数字,照译不减;如果是倍数,通常译成"是……的 n 倍""为……的 r 倍""比……$n-1$ 倍"等。例如:

(1) The speed of sound in water is *about four times as great as* in air.

水中的声速约为空气中的 4 倍。

(2) The resistance is 3 *times as great as* the effort.

阻力是作用力的 3 倍。

(3) The oxygen atom is nearly 16 *times as heavy as* the hydrogen atom.

氧原子的重量几乎是氢原子的 16 倍。

(4) The machine, after modified, can produce 4 *times as many products as* before in a given period of time.

这台机器改装之后在所给的时间内能够生产的产品为以前的 4 倍。

5. 在"as many as..."结构中,常见的形式及其译法如下。

(1) "... as many(much, large, fast, high, long...) again as+..."或"again as many(much, large, fast, high, long...) as +..."通常译成"是……的两倍""两倍于……""比……多(大,快,高,长……)一倍"。

(2) "... half as many(much, large, fast, high, long...) again+..."或"half as many(much, large, fast, high, long...) as+..."通常译成"是……的一倍半""有……一倍半那么多""比……多(大,快,高,长……)半倍"等。例如:

①The year we have produced *as many tractors again as* they.

今年我们生产的拖拉机是他们的 2 倍。

②This machine turns *half as fast again as* that one.

这台机器转动的比那台快半倍。

③The leads of the new condenser are *as long again as* those of the old.

新型电容器的引线有老式的两倍长。

④The antenna is *half again as high as* that one.

这根天线比那根高一半。

6. 在带有 double, treble 等的句子中, double, twice, two fold 通常译成"为……的两倍""增加一倍""翻一番"; treble 译成"为……的三倍""增至三倍""增加两倍"; quadruple 译成"为……的四倍""增至四倍""增加三倍"。例如:

(1) As the high voltage *was* abruptly *trebled* all the valves burnt.

由于高压突然增加了两倍,所有的电子管都烧坏了。

(2) By the end of 2005, the total mileage if railways open to traffic nearly *quadrupled that just before liberation in* 1949.

到 2005 年底,我国铁路通车的里程差不多为 1949 年解放的 12 倍。

(3) If the resistance is *doubled* without changing the voltage, the current becomes only half as strong.

如果电压不变,电阻增加一倍,电流就减小一半。

7. 在"表示增加意义的谓语+by+ a factor of + 数词"的结构中,尽管有介词 by,翻译时仍应减一,译成"$n-1$ 倍"。例如:

(1) The speed exceeds the average speed *by a factor of* 3.5.

该速度超过平均速度 2.5 倍。

(2) In case of electronic scanning the beam width *is broader by a factor of two*.

电子扫描时,波束宽度展宽一倍。

(3) The error probability of binary AM is greater than for binary FM *by a factor of at least* 6.

二进制调幅的误差概率比二进制调频至少大 5 倍。

【注】 在 2,4,7 几种结构中,如果倍数是一个相当大的近似值,差一倍没有多大的意义时,往往可以照译不必减一。例如:

The sun is 330,000 times as large as the earth.

太阳比地球大 33 万倍(太阳的大小是地球的 33 万倍)。

8.3 数量减少的译法

1. 在"reduce (fall, drop, lower, decrease…)+ by + 数字"的结构中,by 表示纯减少的数量,所以照译不减。例如:

(1) The cost of radio receivers *decreased by* 60%.

收音机的成本降低了 60%。

(2) An increase in the oxygen content of a coal by 1 per cent reduces the calorific value *by about* 1.7 *per cent*.

煤的含氧量增加 1%,其热值下降约 1.7%。

(3) Prices for chemical fertilizer, insecticides and diesel oil *have dropped by one-third to two thirds* compared with 1990.

化肥、农药、柴油的价格比 1990 年降低了三分之一到三分之二。

2. 在"reduce(drop, decrease…)+介词 to + 数字"的结构中,to 表示"到"的意思,所以通常译成"降到……""减少到……"。例如:

(1) By using this new process, the loss of metal *was reduced to* 20%.

采用这种新工艺,金属耗损降到20%。

(2) Hot gas is fed to the cooler, where its temperature *drops to* 20℃.

热气体加到冷却器,其温度降低到20℃。

3. 如果英语中减少的是倍数,通常应换算成分数或百分数来表示,因为汉语中一般很少讲"减少……倍",而说"减少了几分之几"或"减少了百分之几"。把倍数换算成分数的方法是:把倍数作分母,用1作分子,表示减少后的结果,译成"减少到几分之一""减为几分之一"。例如:

  shorten...3 times   缩短了三分之二;缩短到三分之一
  reduce...by a factor of 7 降低七分之六;降到七分之一
  a four-fold reduction   减少四分之三;减少为四分之一

(1) Switching time of the new type transistor *is shortened three times*.

新型晶体管的开关时间缩短了三分之二(或缩短到三分之一)。

(2) The new equipment will *reduce* the error, probability by a factor of 7.

新设备将使误差概率降低七分之六(或降到七分之一)。

(3) The principle advantage over the old-fashioned machine *is a four-fold reduction* in weight.

与旧式机器相比的主要优点是重量减少了四分之三。

【注】 如果减少的倍数里面有小数点,则应进一步换算成分数。如 reduce 3.5 times,汉语里不说"减少到三点五分之一"。所以应换算成整数分母。即"减少了七分之五"或"减少到七分之二"。如果换算成分数仍不符合汉语习惯,则应进一步换算成百分数。如 shorten 8.2 times 换算成整数分母,即"缩短到四十一分之五"或"缩短了四十一分之三十六",仍不符合汉语习惯,应进一步换算成"缩短了87.8%"或"缩短到12.2%"。

4. 英语中" half as many (much, long, fast...) as..."" twice thinner than...""reduce by one half...""halve..." 等结构,均表示"减少一半"的意思。翻译时,根据具体句子的意思恰当译出。例如:

(1) They have produced *half as much steel as* us.

他们生产的钢比我们生产的少一半。

(2) *Reducing* the date *by one-half* will double the duration of each symbol interval.

数据率减小一半,将使每一符号间隔的持续时间延长一倍。

(3) The leads of new condenser are *half as long as* those of the old, yet the functions are the same.

新型电容器的导线比老式的短一半,但作用相同。

8.4 不定数量的译法

不定数量表示"若干,多少,大量,不少,成千上万"等概念。英语中的不定数量的表示形式很多,常见的如下。

1. 在 lot, number, score, ten, hundred, thousand, million 等词之后加 s,或组成词组表示:

lots of...	许多,大量
numbers of...	许多,若干
scores of...	许多,好几十
hundreds of...	许多,几百
thousands of...	成千上万,几千
tens of thousands of...	成千上万,几万
hundreds of thousands of...	无数,千万个,几十万
many thousands of...	成千上万
thousands upon thousands of...	成千上万,无数
millions	千百万,几百万

2. 由某些代词或其他词组表示

many (of)...	许多
much (of)...	许多
some (of)...	一些,几个,若干
a bit of...	少量,一点
a crowd of...	许多
a few...	一些,几个,少数
a good few...	不少,相当多
a great quantity of...	大量,许多
a little...	一些,不多
a lot of...	许多,大量
a multitude of...	许多,大量
a number of...	若干,许多
a particle of...	若干,许多
a portion of...	若干,一部分
a quantity of...	一些
a small amount of...	少量
a small quantity of...	少量

a small number of...	少量
a store of...	大量,许多
a wealth of...	大量
a world of...	许多,许许多多,大量
anything of...	很少,一点
how many(much)	多少
plenty of...	许多,若干
some few (little)	少量,少许

3. 修饰数量的形容词一览表

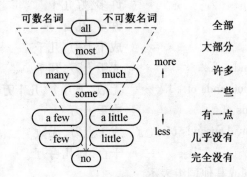

8.5 近似数的译法

近似数是由含有"上下,左右,多于,少于,以上,以下"等概念的副词、介词、形容词等与数字连用而构成的,常见的表示法及其译法如下。

1. "over, above, more, than + 数字"或者是"数字 + odd",通常译成"……多""……以上""……有余"等。例如:

over two years	两年以上
above 20 pounds	二十多磅
more than 90 degrees	九十多度
more than 50 elements	五十多种元素
thirty odd years	三十余年
twenty and odd days	二十多天

2. under, below, less than+数字,通常译成"……以下""不到……""不足……""少于……"等。例如:

below six temperatures	六度以下
under two years	不到两年
less than 60 miles	不足 60 英里

below eighty dollars	八十元以下
less than ten grams	不到十克

3. "some, about, toward(s), nearly, more or less+数字",或者"数字+or so"通常译成"……左右""……上下""大约……""将近……""几乎……"等。例如：

about 90 yards	约 90 码
toward(s)4 o'clock	将近 4 点钟
some 10 answers	大约 10 个答案
nearly one tenth	近乎十分之一
more or less 20 metres	20 米左右
nine kilometers or so	9 公里左右
toward(s)30 feet	约 30 英尺
about 50 per cent	大约百分之五十

4. 在"from...to...""...to...""between...and...""..."的空隙中用数字,通常译成"从……到……""……到……""在……之间"等。例如：

five to ten horse-power	5 到 10 马力
from twenty to thirty yards	从 20 码到 30 码
six-twelve volts	6 到 12 伏
between nine and thirty ohms	在 9 到 30 欧姆之间

8.6　带有数词的短语译法

英语中有许多词组,短语或者习语包含数词,往往并不表示具体数量,甚至与数量无关,通常有习惯译法。现将科技书中常见的一些介绍如下：

a few tenths of	十分之几,有几成
a long hundred	一百二十
a hundred and one	许多
a hundred and one ways	千方百计
a thousand and one	许多的,无数的,各种各样的
last but one(two)	倒数第二(三)
on second thought	重新考虑,改变主意
ten to one	十之八九,十有八九
twenty to one	十之八九,十有八九
by hundred percent	百分之百地,全部地
two over three	三分之二

by ones or twos	三三两两地,零零落落地
by (in) twos and threes	三三两两
in two twos	立即,转眼
two by two	两个两个地
five to five	五比五,五对五
at sixes and sevens	乱七八糟
second to none	首屈一指
within a factor of ten	在一个数量级(内)
fifty-fifty	平均地,各半
twenty more grams	再二十克
five more tons	再五吨
four metres too long	长过四米
the second half	后一半
two figures	二位数
three figures	三位数
four figures	四位数

8.7 大数英语表示法

这一节阐述大数英语数词的构词方式与算术值的关系。

在英语中,自 million 开始的大数数词除个别数词外,在构词上有一定规律。只要了解和认识这种规律,就容易而正确地掌握大数数词。

英语大数数词是由代表幂数的前缀与词根-illion 构成的派生词。由于美国英语和英国英语的大数名称的构成方式不同,因此词根-illion 在两种英语中含意不同。这也是同一大数数词(如 billion)在两种英语中算术值不同的原因。

1. 英国英语大数词

英国英语中数词从 milliard(十亿)开始,除 billion 是 milliard 的 1,000 倍外、后面大数均为前面数值的 1 百万倍。前缀表示词根的幂数,因而词根-illion 表示"百万"。例如:

billion = million^2, trillion = million^3

2. 美国英语大数数词

美国大数数词是从中世纪法语的大数系统演变而来的。不过,现在法语的大数系统已采用英国英语的命名方式。美国大数数词的前缀表示 1 千的幂数,词根-illion 表示"1 千",其算术值等于 1 千的前缀数加 1 次方。例如:

billion = $1,000^{2+1}$, trillion = $1,000^{3+1}$

由此可见，只要记住各大数数词前缀的含义，就可知道该数词的准确算术值。一些常见前缀的幂数含义如下：

表 8.1　常见前缀的幂数含义

centi-,	100	undeci-,	11
bi-,	2	duodeci-,	12
tri-,	3	tredeci-,	13
quadric-,	4	quattuordeci-,	14
quinti-,	5	quindeci-,	15
sexti-,	6	sexdeci-,	16
septi-,	7	septendeci-,	17
octi-,	8	octodeci-,	18
non-,	9	novemdeci-,	19
deci-,	10	centi-,	20

鉴于英美两种英语中常见大数数词及其算术值的差异很大，有必要深入细致地加以总结和梳理，为此我们整理出下面内容：

表 8.2　英美两种英语中常见大数数词及其算术值

	［英］	［美］
billion	$1,000,000^{2}$	$1,000^{2+1}$
trillion	$1,000,000^{3}$	$1,000^{3+1}$
quadrillion	$1,000,000^{4}$	$1,000^{4+1}$
quintillion	$1,000,000^{5}$	$1,000^{5+1}$
sextillion	$1,000,000^{6}$	$1,000^{6+1}$
septillion	$1,000,000^{7}$	$1,000^{7+1}$
octillion	$1,000,000^{8}$	$1,000^{8+1}$
nonillion	$1,000,000^{9}$	$1,000^{9+1}$
decillion	$1,000,000^{10}$	$1,000^{10+1}$
undecillion	$1,000,000^{11}$	$1,000^{11+1}$
duodecillion	$1,000,000^{12}$	$1,000^{12+1}$
tredecillion	$1,000,000^{13}$	$1,000^{13+1}$

续表

	[英]	[美]
quattuordecillion	$1,000,000^{14}$	$1,000^{14+1}$
quindecillion	$1,000,000^{15}$	$1,000^{15+1}$
sexdecillion	$1,000,000^{16}$	$1,000^{16+1}$
septendecillion	$1,000,000^{17}$	$1,000^{17+1}$
octodecillion	$1,000,000^{18}$	$1,000^{18+1}$
novemdecillion	$1,000,000^{19}$	$1,000^{19+1}$
vigintillion	$1,000,000^{20}$	$1,000^{20+1}$
centillion	$1,000,000^{100}$	$1,000^{100+1}$

总之，当人们知道所阅读英文内容美国英语还是英国英语时，就可根据上述规律准确迅速知道大数数词的算术值。

8.8 一些数学算式的写法与读法

1. 分数

$\frac{1}{2}$	a half or one half
$\frac{1}{3}$	a third or one third
$\frac{1}{4}$	a quarter or one quarter; or one fourth
$\frac{1}{5}$	a fifth
$\frac{3}{5}$	three fifths
$1\frac{1}{2}$	one and a half
$6\frac{7}{9}$	six and seven-ninths
$\frac{20}{9}$	twenty over nine
$\frac{217}{356}$	two hundred and seventeen over three hundred and fifty-six

2. 小数

5.4	five point four
0.9	zero point nine or point nine; or nought point nine
0.06	zero point zero six or point zero six; or nought point nought six
10.25	ten point two five

3. 百分数

10%	ten percent
56%	fifty-six percent
102%	a hundred and two percent

4. 数学算式

$1+1=2$	One plus one equals two.
$9-8=1$	Nine minus eight equals one.
$2 \times 2=4$	Two times two is four.
$9 \div 3=3$	Nine divided by three makes three.
x^2	x square
2^4	two to the power of four (or the fourth power of two)
$\sqrt{9}$	the square root of nine
$\sqrt[3]{27}$	the cube root of twenty seven
$\sqrt[5]{64}$	the fifth root of sixty-four
y^{-10}	y to the minus tenth (power)
$3x=5$	three times x equals 5
$x^2+y^2=10$	x squared with y squared equals 10
$(a+b-c \times d) \div e = f$	a plus b minus c multiplied by d, all divided by e equals f
$4\,567 \div 23 = 198$ 余 13	twenty-three into four thousand five hundred and sixty-seven goes on one hundred and ninety-eight times, and thirteen remainder
Σ	the sum of the terms indicated; summation of; sigma
Π	the product of the terms indicated
$\bar{a}$	bar; the mean value of a

$\hat{x}$	caret
$\tilde{x}$	tilde
$n!$	factorial n
$\in$	is an element of ; is member of set
$\notin$	is not an element of
$\subset$	is included in; is a subset of
$\supset$	contains as a subset
e^x, $\exp x$	exponential function (to the base) of x
$\ln x$, $\log e^x$	log x to the base e; natural logarithm of x
$\log a^x$	log x to the base a; logarithm to the base a of x
$a = b$	a equals b; a is b; or a is equal to b
$a \neq b$	a is not equal to b; a is not b
$a \approx b$	a is approximately equal to b
$a \equiv b$	a is identically equal to b; a is of identity to b
$\lim_{x \to a} f(x)$	the limit of $f(x)$ as x approaches a is b
df	total differential of the function f
$\frac{df}{dx}$, df/dx, f', Df	derivative of the function f with respect to x
$\frac{\partial f}{\partial x}$, $\partial f / \partial x$, $\partial x \, f$, $D_x f$	partial derivative of the function f with respect to x, where f is a function of x and another variable (or variables)
$\int f(x) \, dx$	an indefinite integral of the function f or the set of indefinite integral of the function f
$\int_a^b f(x) \, dx$	definite integral of the function f from a to b

第 9 章 长句的翻译

9.1 长句的分析

英语中的长句既有简单句,又有并列句和复合句,其中以并列句与复合句居多。有时,一个长句就是一个较长的段落。形成长句的原因很多,但归纳起来有如下几点。

1. 句中的并列成分多:并列主语、并列谓语、并列宾语、并列定语或并列状语等。

2. 句中的短语多:介词短语、分词短语、不定式短语、动名词短语或形容词短语等。有时,短语中的某些词又有另外的短语或从句说明。

3. 并列句和从句多:有时,并列句和复合句交错在一起,甚至从句又可被另外的从句所说明。

4. 句中的附加成分多:插入语、同位语或独立成分等。

翻译长句时,首先抓住全句的中心内容,弄清各部分之间的语法关系及逻辑关系,分清上下层次以及前后联系,然后根据汉语的特点、习惯和表达方式,正确地译出原文的意思,不必过分拘泥原文的形式。例如:

(1) To illustrate, the solution of the mathematical equations for the trajectory of a space rocket would require nearly two years of work by one computer operating an ordinary adding machine, while an electronic computing machine can do the same job in several seconds without any error.

举例来说,一个计算机工作者用一架普通加法机来解决一种宇宙火箭轨道的数学方程式,差不多需要两年的工作时间,而一台电子计算机却可以毫无误差地在几秒钟之内就能完成同样的工作。

语法分析:该句是一个以 while 连接的并列句。在第一个句子中,to

illustrate 为插入语,介词短语 for the trajectory 为修饰 equations 的定语,分词短语 operating ... machine 为修饰 one computer 的定语。在第二句子中,介词短语 in several seconds 以及 without any error 分别为时间状语和方式状语。

(2) It is well known that radioactive atoms are very valuable in all sorts of ways, because we can use them to do things which are not possible with ordinary atoms that are not radioactive.

众所周知,放射性原子在各个方面都是很有价值的,因为可以用它来做出普通非放射性原子所不能做的事情。

语法分析:在该复合句中,共有四个从句,各自修饰其前的一个句子。that 引导的为主语从句,because 引导的为原因状语从句,which 和 that 引导的均为定语从句,分别修饰名词 things 和 atoms。

9.2 长句的译法

一般来说,对长句的翻译可采用:顺序法、逆序法、分译法、综合法等翻译方式。

1. 顺序法

如果长句的叙述层次依次连接,与汉语的习惯大体相同,可按原文顺序翻译。有时,为了使前后语气衔接,可以增加一些必要的词语。

(1) We must define a market as any area (A) over which buyers and sellers are in such close touch with another (B), that the prices in one part of the market affect the prices paid in other parts (C).

分析:这个句子是一个主从复合句,它是由一个主句和一个带有状语从句的定语从句组成的。"We must define a market as any area(我们应该把市场解释为这样一个领域)"是主句,也是全句的中心。over which 开始一直到句末是先行词 area 的定语从句,其中有一个以 that 引导的状语从句。

全句共有三层意思:(A)我们应该把市场解释为这样的一个领域;(B)通过这个领域买方和卖方彼此密切接触;(C)从而市场上一部分价格影响着其他价格。原文的这三层意思的逻辑关系、表达顺序完全符合汉语的表达习惯,因此可以按原句顺序译出。

(2) Modern means of communication are so rapid (A) that a buyer can find out what a seller is asking (B), and can accept it (C) if he wishes (D), although he may thousands of miles away (E).

分析:本句也是一个主从复合句,它是由 Modern means of communication are so rapid 加 that 引导的结果状语从句构成的,其中结果状语从句又是一个主从复合句,它是由带有一个宾语从句 what price a seller is asking 和一个条件状语从句 if he wishes 的主句加上 although 引导的让步状语从句构成的。

全句共有五层意思:(A)现代的通信手段如此迅速;(B)以至于买方能知道卖方的要价是多少;(C)而且他可以接受这一要价;(D)如果他们愿意的话;(E)尽管他可能在数千英里之外。原句五层意思的逻辑关系、表达次序与汉语表达习惯基本一致。因此,本句可译为:现代的通信手段如此迅速,以至于买主虽然在数千里之外,买主也能知道他的要价是多少,而且如果愿意的话他可以接受这一要价。

2. 逆序法

有些英语长句的表达顺序与汉语的表达习惯不同,甚至完全相反,这样就必须从原文的后面译起,逆着原文的顺序翻译。

<u>Differences of this type result</u> (A) <u>because in accounting there are alternative ways</u> (B), <u>all of which are quite legal</u> (C), <u>to treat many kinds of business transactions</u> (D).

分析:这个句子也是一个主从复合句,它是由主句 Different of this type result 加由 because 引导的、由带有一个非限制性定语从句的原因状语从句构成的。to 引导的动词不定式短语在 because 引导的状语从句中做从句 alternatives ways 的定语。

全句共有四层意思:(A)这种差别产生了;(B)由于会计核算时有可能有供选择的方法;(C)这些方法都是合法的;(D)来处理各种业务往来。

按照汉语习惯,通常原因在前,结果在后,这样,本句可以逆着原文的顺序译出。即:"由于在处理各种业务往来时具有可供互相替换的会计核算的方法,而这些方法都是合法的,因此,这种差别就产生了。"

3. 分译法

下面这个句子并不长,但是英语中的两个疑问词 how 和 why 一定要分开翻译。how 讲的是区别的内容,why 询问的是区别的原因。

How and why do monopolies behave differently from firms in more competitive industries?

参考译文:垄断企业的行为与竞争激烈行业中的厂商有什么区别,他们行为区别的原因是什么?

有时,英语长句中主句或从句与修饰语之间的关系并不十分密切,翻译时可以按照汉语的习惯把长句中的从句或短语化为短句,分开来叙述。看下面的例子:

Since its establishment, the SEC (the Securities and Exchange Commission) has worked with organizations of professional accounts to establish groups that are given the primary responsibilities to work out the detailed rules that become generally accepted accounting principles.

句中有两个限制性定语从句,如果拘泥于定语从句的前置翻译法,就会形成以下译文:自成立以来,证券交易委员会与职业会计团体成立承担制定形成公认会计原则的详细规则的主要责任的小组。

这样的译文读起来非常费劲。如果我们把从句化成短句,并且将其与被修饰的名词分开,就会形成以下比较好的译文:

参考译文:自成立以来,证券交易委员会与职业会计合作团体合作成立了专门小组,这些专门小组的主要任务就是制定出详细规则,进而形成公认的会计原理。([注]"小组"前面增加"专门"二字,把定语从句的限制性灵活地体现了出来,这是采用的"增词法")

再举一个例子:

The 29th Annual Meeting of the World Economic Forum closes tonight after six days of discussions among world business, government and media leaders on "responsible globality — managing the impact of globalization".

本句从开始到 among 基本可以顺译,即:第二十九届世界经济论坛年会经过六天的讨论之后于今晚闭幕。Among 后讲的是参加讨论的人员和讨论的内容,句法上是一个短语,我们必须将其译成一个句子,与前面的分开,即:来自世界各地的大公司主管、政界领袖以及传媒巨头,讨论了世界经济全球化的责任问题,即如何应付经济全球化的冲击。

4. 综合法

在翻译中,有些英语长句需要按照时间先后或逻辑顺序,采取有顺有逆、有主有次,各种翻译方法和技巧灵活、综合使用的方法。

考虑下面例子:

Claims are even made that more detailed U.S. accounting requirements make it more difficult for U.S. companies to compete with international competitors that operate in countries with less revealing accounting rules.

我们经过阅读研究,分析如下:

(1) claims are even made 是一个被动语态的句子,应该翻译成主动态。即:"有人甚至提出这样的看法"。

(2) 从 that 开始是一个同位语从句,具体讲了看法的具体内容。

(3) 同位语从句中的主语 more detailed U.S. accounting requirements 可以译成一个简单句:美国对会计报表要求得越详细。

(4) Make it more difficult 中的 it 是形式宾语,真正宾语是带逻辑主语的不定式:for U. S. companies to compete with international competitors 我们应直接翻译成:就会使美国公司与国际竞争对手竞争时更为不利。

根据 that 定语从句的内容,应该意识到它表达了美国公司之所以在竞争中处于不利地位的原因,因此可以大胆译成原因状语:因为这些竞争对手所在国不存在如此清晰的会计规则。

(5)最后做适当的润色,译文可以是:甚至有人提出这样的看法,美国对会计报表要求的越是详细,就会使美国公司与某些国际竞争对手的竞争遭遇更多的困难,因为这些竞争对手所在的国家不存在如此清晰的会计规则。

再比如,对下面的句子,我们分析如下:

We tend to forget that labor is the most important resource of all, as has been demonstrated by the speed with which nations devastated by war recover if they have skilled labor forces.

(1)主句可以采用顺译法,即:我们常有这样的倾向,忘记劳动力是所有资源中最为重要的。

(2)As 引出的是一个非限制性定语从句,as 代表的是 labor is the most important resource of all,从句里是被动语态,应把它译成主动态,即:速度体现了劳动力资源的重要性。

(3)The speed 后面是一个定语从句,具体说明"速度"。这个定语从句尽管很长,而且又有 if 引出的条件从句,我们可以将其译成一个长长的短语,并且将 speed 转换成副词,即:战后那些拥有熟练技术劳动力的国家能迅速地从战争废墟中得以恢复充分地体现了这一点。

(4)进行调整以后的参考译文可以是:我们常有这种倾向,忘记劳动力是所有资源中最重要的。战后那些拥有熟练技术工人的国家能迅速从战争废墟中得以恢复充分体现了劳动力资源的重要性。

下面看一看对下述三个较长句子的分析与翻译:

Another source of interest in the nature of GAAP is the fact that managers and other employees often receive part of their pay based on reaching stated targets for net income and are thus directly concerned with how net income is computed.

(1)主句是一个主系表结构的句子,可以顺译。即:另一个对公认的会计原理发生兴趣的原因是因为这个事实。

(2)That 引出的是一个同位语从句,具体描述 fact 的内容。同位语从句由两个并列句构成,thus 表示这两个并列句是因果关系。全局可译成:经理和另外一些雇员部分工资与实现净收益的目标挂钩,因此他们会直接关心净收益的计算方法。

(3)进行校核和润色可形成以下译文:另一个对公认会计原则性质发生兴

趣的原因是由于这一事实:经理和雇员部分薪水经常与是否实现净收益的目标挂钩,因此他们会直接关心净收益的计算方法。

What we mean is that the financial manager best serves the owners of the business by identifying goods and services that add value to the firm because they are desired and valued in the free marketplace.

(1) 一开始的系表结构采用顺译,即:我们的意思是。

(2) 表语从句相当复杂,其中的主句也可以顺译,即:财务管理人员最好地为公司的业主服务。

(3) by 加动名词说明通过什么方法来为业主服务。通过确定生产能够给公司增添价值的产品和提供劳务来为业主们服务。

(4) because 从句讲了决定生产的这些产品或劳务之所以能够给公司增值的原因是它们符合市场的需求,能够卖到好价钱。

第Ⅱ部分　专业英文选读

All knowledge is, in the final analysis, history.
All sciences are, in the abstract, mathematics.
Alljudgments are, in their rationale, are statistics.
—— The famous statistician, C. R. Rao in 《Statistics and Truth》, 1989

Unit One　Descriptive Statistics

1.1　Introduction to Statistics

1.1.1　Why statistics matter

Are you aware of the extent to which statistics enter your life? You will probably have read in the newspaper or heard on news programmes, of such statistics as "average earning" and the "Index of Retail Prices". These kinds of statistics are used in negotiations that lead to decisions that can have major effects on live standards.

Have you ever seen people standing around, usually in busy shopping centres, clutching clip-boards and stopping the occasional passer-by to ask questions? Perhaps you may have had someone calling at your home asking for your help with a survey of some kind, or have been asked to complete a questionnaire. The results of such surveys may be used to influence the types and qualities of goods and services that you are offered in the future.

Every ten years in Great Britain all households must complete a census return which is used to compile statistics on population patters and developments. These statistics have an effect on government planning for the provision of housing, services such as schools and hospitals, and development of industry.

In an environment where statistics play such an important role it is in the interests of us all to know more about them: how they are collected, analyzed and used.

In other words, statistics is the science of collecting, organizing, analyzing, and interpreting data in order to make decisions. In general data consist of information coming from observations, counts, measurements, or responses. The singular for data is datum.

1.1.2 The meaning of statistics

The word statistics has two meanings:

(1) In the plural sense it means collections of numerical facts and is widely used when reference is made to facts and figures on such things as population, crime and education. Statisticians call the figures which have been collected *data*.

(2) In the singular sense it means the science (or art) of dealing with statistical data. The collection, analysis and interpretation of data is called *statistical method*, and it is with this sense of the word that we are mainly concerned in this book.

There are two subdivisions of statistical method:

(1) **Descriptive statistics** This deals with the compilation and presentation of data in various forms such as tables, graphs and diagrams. The purpose of descriptive statistics to display and pass on information from which conclusions can be drawn and decisions made. Businesses, for example, use descriptive statistics when presenting their annual accounts and reports, and the Government is a particularly prolific provider of descriptive statistics.

In sum descriptive statistics is the branch of statistics that involves the organization, summarization, and display of data.

(2) **Mathematical or inductive statistics** This deals with the tolls of statistics, the techniques that are used to analyze the data and to make estimates or draw conclusions from the data.

In fact, inductive statistics is inferential statistics, is the branch of statistics that involves using a sample to draw conclusions about a population. A basic tool in the study of inferential statistics is probability.

1.1.3 The growth and importance of statistics

Statistics have been collected since the earliest times. Rulers needed to have information about the population and their possessions so that taxes could be levied to maintain the state and the court, and it was also essential for them to be aware of military strength of the nation. In the sixteenth century the word "statist" was used to describe a politician — a dealer in facts about the state, its Government and its people.

With the growth of the population and the advent, in the eighteenth and nineteenth centuries, of the industrial revolution and accompanying agricultural revolution there was a need for a greater volume of statistics on an increasing variety of subjects. In this country the Government also began to intervene more and more in the affairs of the people and of business and to attempt to control the workings of the economy. It therefore required information on:

(1) production;
(2) earnings;
(3) expenditure;
(4) imports and exports.

As time went on, the Government took over many of the activities that had been part of the private sector of the economy, such as education and health services. It was vital therefore for information to be available on:

(5) population growth or decline;
(6) disease and its incidence;
(7) housing conditions.

All this led to an enormous expansion in the volume of statistics that have been and are being collected Government over the last few decades. For Government to make sensible decisions, however, these data need to be correctly collected, processed and analyzed.

Words and Expressions

Index of Retail Prices 零售价格指数
negotiation *n.* 商议,流通
clutch *v.* 紧握,抱紧,抓紧
clip-boards 写字夹板,带弹簧夹的写字板
passer-by *n.* 路人,过路人
questionnaire *n.* 调查表,问卷
survey *v.* 调查,视察
census *n.* 人口普查
numerical *adj.* 数字的,用数表示的; *n.* 数字,数词
population *n.* 总体,对象总体,全域;人口

annual accounts 年度账目

prolific *adj.* 多育的,结果实的;有生产力的;富于创造力的;多产……的（of）;肥沃的;丰富的;富于……的（in）

descriptive statistics 描述统计学

mathematical statistics 数理统计学

inductive statistics 归纳统计学

inferential statistics 推断统计学

possession *n.* 拥有,占有,领地,财产（常用复数）

statist *n.* 统计学员,统计学家

working *n.* 工作方式,运作

private *adj.* 私有的,私营的,私人的

health services 公共医疗卫生服务,健康服务

vital *adj.* 至关重要的,重大的,所必需的

disease *n.* 疾病

incidence *n.* 流行范围,影响范围

process *v.* 加工,处理 *n.* 过程;进程;方法

decline *v.* 倾斜;衰退,减退;（物价的）下落;衰弱

1.2 Population and Sample

To further continue our study, we need to "talk the talk." Statistics has its own jargon, terms beyond descriptive statistics and inferential statistics, that need to be defined and illustrated. The concept of a population is the most fundamental idea in statistics.

The **population** is the complete collection of individual or objects are of interest to the sample collector. The population of concern must be carefully defined and is considered fully defined only when its membership list of elements is specified. The set of "all students who have ever attended a U. S. college" is an example of a well-defined population.

Typically, we think of a population as a collection of people. However, in statistics the population could be a collection of animals, manufactured objects, whatever. For example, the set of all redwood trees in California could be a population.

There are two kinds of populations: finite and infinite. When the membership of population can be (or could be) physically listed, the population is said to be **finite**. When the membership is unlimited, the population is **infinite**. The books in your college library form a finite population; the OPAC (Online Public Access Catalog, the computerized card catalog) lists the exact membership. All the registered voters in the United States form a very large finite population; if necessary, a composite of all voter lists from all voting precincts across the United States could be compiled. On the other hand, the population of all people who might use aspirin and the population of all 40-watt light bulbs to be produced by Sylvania are infinite. Large populations are difficult to study; therefore, it is customary to select a sample, or a subset of a population, and study data in sample. A **sample** consists of the individuals, objects, or measurements selected form the population by the sample collector.

Statisticians are interested in particular **variables** of a sample or a population. That is, they examine one or more characteristics of interest about each individual element of a population or sample. Things like age, hair color, height, and weight are variables. Each variable associated with one element of a population or sample has a value. That value, called the **data value**, may be a number, word, or symbol. For example, when Bill Jones entered college at age "23," his hair was "brown," he was "71 inches" tall, and he weighed "183 pounds." These four data values are the values for the variables as applied to Bill Jones.

The set of values collected from the variable from each of the elements that belong to the sample is called data. The set of 25 heights (or weight, ages, and hair colors) collected from students is an example of set of data. To collect a set of data, a statistician would do an **experiment**, which is a planned activity whose results yield a set of data. An experiment includes the activities for both selecting the elements and obtaining the data values.

The "average" age at time of admission for all students who have ever attended our college and the "proportion" of students who were older than 21 years of age when they entered college are examples of two population parameters. A **parameter** is a value that describes the entire population. Often a Greek letter is used to symbolize the name of a parameter. These symbols will be assigned as we study specific parameters.

For every parameter there is a corresponding sample statistic. The statistic is numerical value summarizing the sample data and describing the sample the same way the parameter describes the population.

The "average" height, found by using the set of 25 height, is an example of sample statistic. A statistic is a value that describes a sample. Most sample statistics are found with the aid of formulas and are typically assigned symbolic names that are letters of the English alphabet (for example, $\bar{x}, s$, and r).

In fact, there is difference between population and sample. The main difference between a population and sample has to do with how observations are assigned to the data set. Look at Fig. 1.1.

Apopulation includes each element from the set of observations that can be made.

A sample consists only of observations drawn from the population.

Definition:

The population in a statistical study is the complete set of people or things being studied.

The sample is the subset of the population from which the raw data are actually obtained.

(Population) parameters are specific characteristics of the population that a statistical study is designed to estimate.

(Sample) statistics are numbers or observations that summarize the raw data.

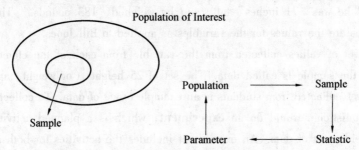

We measure the sample using statistics in order to draw
inferences about the parameters of the population

Fig. 1.1 Population vs Sample.

Words and Expressions

membership *n.* 会员身份(或资格、地位),会籍;党籍;团籍。【生】从属关系
    a ~ card 会员证,a ~ fee 会费。

sample *n.* 样品,标本,榜样;(化验的)取样。【统】样本
    vt. 取……的样品,尤指用样品来检验;【统】抽样调查,抽样

parameter *n.* 限制因素;决定因素【数】参数;参量

statistic *n.* 【统】统计量

statistics *n.* [复]统计;统计资料。【统】单数,统计学

finite *adj.* 有限的;【数】有穷的,有限的
infinite *adj.* 无限的,无穷的;无数的,许许多多的;极大的
   n. 无限,无穷;无限的事物。【数】无穷大
measure *vt.* 量,测量;估量,衡量;斟酌,权衡
   ~ *the distance* 测量距离; ~ *one's words* 斟酌词句
measurement *n.* 测量法;度量,测量,(量得的)尺寸,大小;长(或宽度、深)度
draw *vt.* 拉,拉动;引领;使行动;提取;领取;推断出;形成
   ~ a tooth 拔牙; ~ a knife 拔刀; ~ money from one's account 提取存款;
draw conclusion 得出结论
complete *adj.* (用以强调)完全的;完成的;达到结尾的;完整的
   vt. 完成,使完满;完成或结束;填写(表格)。

1.3 Measurement Scales

A very important dimension of any observed data is the measurement scale of the individual data series. In this subsection we discuss this important dimension and raise some of the issues related to the modeling of data measured on different scales.

The number of classifications introduced above increases substantially by realizing that the discrete-continuous dichotomy can be classified further according to the measurement scale bestowed on the set in question.

The measurement scales are traditionally classified into four broad categories.

1.3.1 Ratio Scale

Variables in this category enjoy the richest mathematical structure in their range of values, where for any two values along the scale, say x_1 and x_2:

(a) The ratio (x_1/x_2) is a meaningful quantity (there exists a natural origin for the measurement system),

(b) The distance (x_1-x_2) is a meaningful quantity, and

(c) There exists a natural ordering (ascending or descending order) of the values along the scale; the comparison $x_2 \leqslant$ or $\geqslant x_1$ makes sense.

Economic variables such as consumption and inflation be long to this category. For any two values x_1 and x_2 of a variable in this category, it is meaningful to ask the question:

How many times is x_1 bigger than x_2?

1.3.2 Interval scale

A variable is said to be an interval variable if its measurement system is bestowed with (b) ~ (c) but not (a), e. g. , temperature, systolic blood pressure. For any two values x_1 and x_2 of a variable in this category it is meaningful to ask the question:

How much do x_1 and x_2 differ?

1.3.3 Ordinal scale

A variable belongs to this category if it is bestowed with (c) only, e. g. grading (excellent, very good, good, failed), income class (upper, middle, lower). For such variables the ordering exists but the distance between categories is not meaningfully quantifiable. For any two values x_1 and x_2 of a variable in this category it is meaningful to ask the question:

Is x_1 bigger or smaller than x_2?

1.3.4 Nominal scale

A variable is said to be nominal if its measurement system is blessed with none of the above. The variable denotes categories which do not even have a natural ordering, e. g. marital status (married, unmarried, divorced, separated), gender (male, female, other), employment status (employed, unemployed, other). Due to the nature of such variables the modeler should be careful in attributing numerical values to avoid misleading inferences. For any two values x_1 and x_2 of a variable in this category the only meaningful question to ask:

Is x_1 different from x_2?

The above measurement scales have been considered in a descending hierarchy from the highest (ratio, the richest in mathematical structure) to the lowest (nominal). It is important to note that statistical concepts and methods designed for one category of variables do not necessarily apply to variables of other categories. For instance, the mean, variance, and covariance (the building blocks of regression analysis) make no sense in the case of ordinal and nominal variables, he median makes sense in the case of ordinal but not in the case of nominal variables. In the latter case the only measure of location that has a meaning is the mode. The only general rule for the methods of analysis of different measurement-scale variables one can state at this stage is that a method appropriate for a certain measurement-scale in the hierarchy is also appropriate for the scales above but not below.

It is important to note that in the statistical literature there is widespread confusion between the measurement scales and three different categorizations: discrete/continuous, qualitative/ quantitative and categorical/non-categorical variables. Discrete variables can be measured on all four scales and continuous variables can sometimes be grouped into a small number of categories. Categorical variables are only variables that can be measured on either the ordinal or the nominal scales but the qualitative variables category is fuzzy. In some books qualitative variables are only those measured on the nominal scale but in some others it also includes ordinal variables.

Words and Expressions

observed data 观察数据,观测数据,观察资料
dimension *n.* 尺寸;方面;规模;范围.【数】维,维数
inflation *n.* 膨胀;充气;【经】通货膨胀;自负
dichotomy *n.* 两分,二分法,分离
bestow *vi.* ~ sth (on/upon sb)(将……)给予,授予,献给 to give sth to sb
fuzzy *adj.* 覆有绒毛的;毛茸茸的;紧鬈的;拳曲的
　　【数】模糊的, fuzzy number 模糊数; fuzzy mathematics 模糊数学

1.4　The Process of a Statistical Study

Statistical studies are conducted in many different ways and for many different purposes, but they all share a few characteristics. To get the basic ideas, consider the Nielsen ratings, which are used to estimate the numbers of people watching various television shows. These ratings are used, for example, to determine the most popular television show of the week.

Nielsen's goal is to draw conclusions about the viewing habits of all Americans. In the language of statistics, we say that Nielsen is interested in the population of all Americans. The characteristics of this population that Nielsen seeks to learn—such as the number of people watching each television show—are called population parameters.

Nielsen seeks to learn about the population of all Americans by studying a much smaller sample of Americans in depth. More specifically, Nielsen has devices (called "people meters") attached to televisions in 5,000 homes, so the people who live in these homes make up the sample of Americans that Nielsen studies. The individual measurements that Nielsen collects from the sample, such as who is watching each show at each time, constitute the raw data. Nielsen then consolidates these raw data into a set of numbers that characterize the sample, such as the percentage of young male viewers watching Lost. These numbers are called sample statistics.

Suppose the Nielsen ratings tell you that Lost was last week's most popular show, with 22 million viewers. You probably know that no one actually counted all 22 million people. But you may be surprised to learn that the Nielsen ratings are based on the television-viewing habits of people in only 5,000 homes. To understand how Nielsen can draw a conclusion about millions of Americans from 5,000 homes, we need to investigate the principles behind statistical research.

Because Nielsen does not study the entire population of all Americans, it cannot actually measure any population parameters. Instead, the company tries to infer reasonable values for population parameters from the sample statistics (which it did measure).

The process of inference is simple in principle, though it must be carried out with great care. For example, suppose Nielsen finds that 7% of the people in its sample watched Lost. If this sample accurately represents the entire population of all Americans, then Nielsen can infer that approximately 7% of all Americans watched the show. In other words, the sample statistic of 7% is used as an estimate for the population parameter.

Once Nielsen has estimates of the population parameters, it can draw general conclusions about what Americans were watching. The process used by Nielsen Media Research is similar to that used in many statistical studies.

Fig. 1.2 summarizes the general relationships among a population, a sample, the sample statistics, and the population parameters.

1.4.1 Basic Steps in a Statistical Study

1. State the goal of your study precisely. That is, determine the population you want to study and exactly what you'd like to learn about it.

2. Choose a representative sample from the population.

3. Collect raw data from the sample and summarize these data by finding sample statistics of interest.

4. Use the sample statistics to infer the population parameters.

5. Draw conclusions: Determine what you learned and whether you achieved

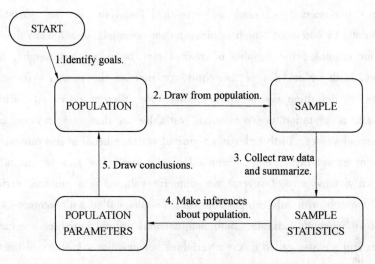

Fig. 1.2 Elements of a statistical study

your goal.

Words and Expressions

Nielsen ratings 尼尔森收视率,又称尼尔森收视率统计
television show 电视节目;电视剧
viewing habit 指看电视的习惯,甚至是电视瘾
raw data 【统】原始数据
viewer *n.* 观察者;观看者;电视观众;(幻灯片)观看器
a person watching television 电视观众
in depth 深入地;全面深入地
people meters 收视纪录器
television-viewing habit 看电视的习惯
Nielsen Media Research 尼尔森媒体研究公司
representative sample 【统】代表样本

1.5 Several Variables

Statistics is a process for converting information into knowledge and making knowledge useful for the advancement of science. Many scientists use statistical methods to analyze their data in order to better understand a given research problem at hand and to help discover the unknown, and they regard statistical analysis to be integral part of their research. Statistics as presented in this chapter is a collection of analytic methods for scientific research and for practical applications.

The fundamental element of statistical analysis is the variable, the characteristic or outcome, which is measured or counted. In a human development study, for example, the variable of interest may be infant birthweight, length of gestation, birth order, sex of the child, or race of the mother. These, as all variables, by definition assume different values for different individuals. Birthweight and length of gestation are continuous variables in that they assume any of a continuum of values. Birth order is an ordinal variable because the values, the first birth, the second birth, etc., form a logical order. The race of an individual, which can assume any of several non-numeric values, is a nominal variable. A nominal variable with only two possible values is also called a dichotomous variable; sex is a dichotomous variable. Both nominal and ordinal variables are categorical variables and are also called discrete variables because the values are distinct and do not fall on a continuum.

Variables associated with time, weight, or dimension are continuous variables. As rule of thumb, a variable that can be *measured* as opposed to counted is a continuous variable. Due to the limitation of measuring scales, continuous variables are expressed in discrete units; weight is expressed in grams or pounds, length of gestation in months or weeks. The accuracy of the measurement of a continuous variable depends on the refinement of the scale: weight expressed in grams is more accurate than in kilograms. The following are additional examples of continuous variables:

(1) the time a clock stops;
(2) the distance of visibility on a specific day;
(3) the height of a college student;
(4) the level of cholesterol in a sample of blood.

Observed values of variables are expressed numerically so that the study data can be statistically analyzed. When a variable cannot be expressed numerically, such as a categorical variable, we record the number of observations falling into each category of the variable thus providing numbers for analysis, such as the number of students in a class, the number of dots on the faces of a pair of dice, the number of whales caught each year,. etc. .

Statistical data are a group of measurements, or observations, of some variable common to many people (or things) in a study, but they are different from personal data. They are non-personal. For example, are, sex, weight and height of a particular child are the child's personal data. However, these same measurements are detached from the child if the child is one of a group of children in a statistical study. These measurements become the data of one of many children and are treated in exactly the same way as those of any other child in the group. The fact that they relate to a particular child is disregarded.

Statistical data are different from personal data in yet other respects. First, they possess some properties not found in personal data. A group of observations, which forms a distribution, can be organized and summarized by what is know as descriptive statistics. Descriptive statistics describe the location, the dispersion and the pattern of the distribution by using numerals, tabulations, or graphics.

Further, the information derived from statistical analysis can be used to make inferences about some unknowns, such as the mean intelligence level of college students in California, the life expectancy of a newborn child, etc. It is property that makes statistics an important analytical tool in scientific research. This chapter is devoted to the discussion of descriptive statistics. In subsequent chapters, we shall present various methods of analysis for making statistical inference about unknowns.

In the study of statistical methods, we deal mostly with symbols and formulas, and little with numerical values. Numerical computations and numerical results are mainly for illustration, clarification, and introduction of concepts. While any symbol may be chosen to represent a variable, the process of representing variables in symbols and expressing procedures in formulas is fundamental to the study of statistical methods. When the symbols in a formula are understood, the formula can be applied to a large number of problems.

Words and Expressions

convert *v.* 变换,转换,转化;改造,改装;兑换,更换
infant *n.* 婴儿,幼儿(未满七岁)
gestation *n.* 妊娠(期),怀孕(期);酝酿,孕育
race *n.* 人种;种族,民族;氏族,家族,家系,系统;门第
continuous variable 连续变量
ordinal variable 定序变量;有序变量
nominal variable 名义变量
dichotomous *adj.* 两分的;对生的;二歧的;二叉的
discrete variable 离散变量
categorical variables 分类变量;定类变量

continuum $n.$ (pl) 连续统,闭联集
space-time continuum 时空连续
accuracy $adj.$ 正确,准确(度);精确 firing accuracy 命中率 with accuracy 正确地
accurate $adj.$ 准确的,精密的
refinement $adj.$ 精炼,提炼,提纯,纯化,精制;高尚,优雅
visibility $n.$ 能见性(度);可见物;可见度;可见距离;视界
cholesterol $n.$ (生物化学)胆固醇,胆甾醇
observed values 可观测值
dot $n.$ 点;圆点;句点;(数学)小数点;相乘的符号。
detach $v.$ 分开,分离,拆开 be detached from... 脱离
disregard $v.$ 不理,不顾,不管;蔑视,轻视
location $n.$ 定位;位置,场所,地点
dispersion $n.$ 分散,散开;散布,传播;离散(统计学)离中趋势
tabulation $n.$ 制表,造册,表格
graphics $n. pl.$ 用作单数,(建筑或工程的)绘图学,制图学
expectancy $n.$ 预期,期望,期待;期望的东西
life expectance 估计寿命
newborn $adj.$ 新生的,初生的,再生的,复活的
analytical tool 分析工具

1.6 Measures of Location

Table 1.1 contains ages of 400 HIV positive men which will be used for illustration of descriptive statistics. These men constitute a sample; $n=400$ is the sample size. The variable in this example is age, denoted by a symbol, Y. Thus y_1 denotes the age of the first man in the sample, y_2 the age of the second man, etc. As the identities of the 400 men are not of concern, the symbol y_1 may represent any one of the 400 ages, y_2 may represent any other age, etc. Here we let $y_1 = 49$ years, $y_2 = 42$ years, ..., $y_{400} = 27$ years.

Table 1.1 Ages (last birthday in years) of 400 HIV positive men, San Francisco

49	40	28	31	27	27	32	34	27	32
42	36	28	32	33	40	28	25	47	40
28	38	35	32	23	39	31	26	31	31
40	51	32	29	30	28	34	29	34	36
42	38	37	28	27	28	38	38	40	33

Table 1.1 (Continued)

52	37	45	35	39	28	33	30	40	37
37	32	33	32	28	49	31	30	33	29
37	33	41	44	37	29	31	54	36	34
40	38	47	42	42	36	37	28	35	32
30	36	28	28	30	28	34	28	34	37
41	33	30	38	42	41	49	43	38	38
40	30	33	35	26	47	42	49	40	36
37	30	50	44	33	28	37	29	34	38
34	50	38	47	29	35	38	34	38	32
38	27	37	34	29	32	34	41	40	39
36	28	33	33	44	31	36	25	42	38
31	37	32	28	43	35	26	29	34	38
26	30	39	30	30	36	36	32	29	35
35	40	50	28	50	32	29	37	32	26
32	34	25	40	44	49	31	26	26	34
40	34	43	33	34	37	28	29	25	24
42	42	44	35	34	34	31	41	40	25
41	28	34	38	26	29	35	37	32	39
38	30	35	36	49	34	29	27	41	35
30	41	40	39	28	39	29	29	32	27
27	27	34	38	36	37	30	47	30	33
29	31	32	39	31	34	31	39	29	29
27	44	33	30	43	26	34	33	40	44
34	39	39	33	42	37	52	34	26	29
52	40	40	32	31	30	28	30	35	33
37	33	30	33	32	45	32	35	27	48
34	39	27	30	31	30	33	30	43	31
46	41	37	44	26	36	39	29	33	32
30	34	32	49	30	39	46	37	31	39
33	29	34	44	33	39	32	42	48	34
28	36	25	30	30	27	27	37	26	31
27	34	49	36	35	35	33	29	32	31
29	30	25	30	43	30	43	28	37	47
31	29	33	42	37	33	34	28	42	34
33	27	36	35	35	41	31	52	32	27

Statistical analysis can derive some meaning from a data set. The first question one might ask about the ages in Table 1.1 is: How old were these men on the average? Or, what value might represent the 400 ages? Here we are seeking a measure of the "central" value or "central tendency," or the "location" of a group of observations. The following are the three most commonly used measures of location: The mean, the median, and the mode.

1.6.1 Mean

The mean, or the arithmetic mean (represented by $\bar{y}$), of a group of observations is the sum of the observations divided by the number of the observations. In formula, the mean of n observations, $y_1, \cdots, y_n$, is given by

$$\bar{y} = \frac{y_1 + y_2 + \cdots + y_n}{n} = \frac{1}{n}(\sum_{i=1}^{n} y_i) \tag{1.1}$$

For the example data in Table 1.1:

$$\bar{y} = \frac{49+42+\cdots+27}{400} = \frac{13,923}{400} = 34.81 \text{ years}$$

Thus the mean age of the 400 men was 34.81 years.

Some properties of mean

(1) The mean also represents the balancing point of a group of observations, where the value of each observation is represented by a point on a horizontal scale. This balancing point is the center of gravity. Take the following set of four numbers

$$(1, 4, 7, 8)$$

so that the mean is $\bar{y} = 5$. These numbers and the mean can be demonstrated graphically in Fig. 1.3.

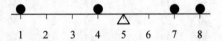

Fig. 1.3 Observed values and their mean

If a unit weight is attached to each one of the four points (assuming the line is weightless), the line segment will be balanced at the point of the mean, $\bar{y}=5$. This example illustrates an important property of the mean: the sum of the differences, called deviations, between each observation and the mean equals zero. In the present example

$$(4-5)+(8-5)+(7-5)+(8-5) = 0$$

An algebraic proof of this property is given in Section 1.7.

(2) If a constant a is added to each observation y_i, the mean is increased by the constant a. That is, the mean of $(a+y_1, a+y_2, \cdots, a+y_n)$ is $a+\bar{y}$.

(3) If each observation y_i is multiplied by a constant b, the mean is multiplied

by the constant b. That is, the mean of $(by_1, by_2, \ldots, by_n)$ is $b\bar{y}$.

The last two properties can be combined to give a basic rule of the mean: The mean of a linear function of observations is equal to the linear function of the mean. That is, the mean of $(a+by_1, \ldots, a+by_n)$ is $a+b\bar{y}$.

1.6.2 Median

In the computation of the mean, the observations $y_1, y_2, \ldots, y_n$ need not be ordered. Formula (1.1) will yield the same value for the mean regardless of the value in the group each y_i represents. In the computation of the median, however, we require that the observations be ordered so that $y_1 < y_2 < \ldots < y_n$. The median (M_d) of an ordered group of observations is the value that divides the observations into two equal subgroups. The same number of observations is above and below the median. If the number of observations n is odd

$$M_d = \left(\frac{n+1}{2}\right) \text{th observation} \qquad (1.2)$$

To find the median of the five numbers (9, 4, 14, 10, 8), we first order them: (4, 8, 9, 10, 14) and then use formula (1.2) to locate the $(\frac{5+1}{2})$th, or the third ordered value. That is $M_d = 9$.

When the number of observations n is even, the median is the average of two middle values. For example, the median of the $n = 4$ numbers (4, 8, 9, 14) is $\frac{(4+1)}{2} = 2.5$th ordered value which is $\frac{(8+9)}{2} = 8.5$. Similarly, the median age of the 400 men in Table 1.1 is the average of the 200th and 201st ordered values, which is $M_d = 34.5$ years.

Remark 1.1

When n is even, any number between the two middle values has the property of the median. In the example (4, 8, 9, 10), 8.25 can be the median, as there are two numbers (9 and 14) greater than 8.25 and two numbers (4 and 8) less than 8.25. By convention, however, we use the average of the two middle values as the median.

Remark 1.2

The mean of a distribution is a more sensitive measure of location than the median is, in the sense that the mean is affected by every one of the observations, while the median may not be. In the example (4, 8, 9, 10, 14), both the mean and the median are equal to 9. If one of the observations is changed, the value of the mean changes as well. The mean of (4, 8, 9, 10, 14) is $\bar{y}=9$ and the mean (4, 8, 9, 10, 149) is $\bar{y}=36$; but in both these cases the median remains $M_d=9$. Which of the two measures is a better representation observations? The mean or the median? The choice is dependent on the nature of the data and the purpose of the study. If one needs a measure that takes into account every observed value in a sample, the mean is preferred. If a data set is likely to have a few extremely high values or a few extremely low values that will inappropriately influence the distribution, then the median is a better choice. Most data dealing with personal income, for example, are described by the median because it is not unduly affected by the extremely wealthy or by the very poor and, therefore, it is more representative of the income of an entire group.

1.6.3 Mode

The mode (M_o) of a group of observations is the value of that observation which occurs most frequently. For example, the mode of the distribution (4, 8, 9, 9, 10, 14) is $M_o=9$. The distribution in this example is also symmetric with respect to the value $y=9$, as shown in the Fig. 1.4.

Fig. 1.4 The mean, the median, and the mode coincide in a symmetric distribution

The mean, the median, and the mode all equal 9. Generally, in a symmetric (unimodal) distribution of observations, the mean, the median, and the mode coincide. However, the converse is not necessarily true. The three measures of location in a distribution may also coincide in an asymmetric distribution. In the group (4, 8, 9, 9, 11, 13), for example, the three measures of location all equal 9, but the distribution is asymmetric. Thus symmetry of a (unimodal) distribution implies that the three measures of location are equal, but equality of the three measures does not necessarily imply that the distribution is symmetric. See Fig. 1.5.

When a distribution in non-symmetric and three measures of location are distinct, the distribution is skewed. A distribution may be skewed to the right (positively skewed) or skewed to the left (negatively skewed). A distribution skewed to the right usually has more extreme values to the right of the median and

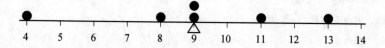

Fig. 1.5 The mean, the median, and the mode coincide in a asymmetric distribution

the mean is greater than the median. A distribution skewed to the left has the mean smaller than the median. The mode usually is on the other side of the median from the mean. For example, the distribution of the numbers (8, 9, 9, 11, 13, 16) is skewed to the right, where the mean ($\bar{y}=11$) is greater than the median ($M_d=10$), and the median is greater than the model ($M_o=9$); the mean and the mode are on the two sides of the median, or $9<10<11$. See Fig. 1.6., Fig. 1.7 shows a symmetric distribution and a skewed distribution (to the right) of continuous variables.

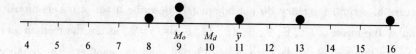

Fig. 1.6 The mean, the median, and the mode in a positively skewed distribution

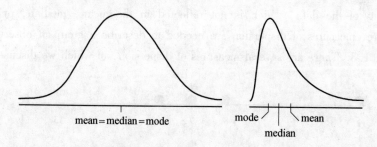

Fig. 1.7 A symmetric distribution and a positively skewed distribution

A distribution may have more than one mode. A distribution with one mode is called a unimodal distribution, while a distribution which has two or more modes is called a bimodal or multimodal distribution.

Words and Expressions

HIV (human immunodeficiency virus) 人类免役缺陷病毒,艾滋病病毒
virus *n.* 病毒
positive men 化验呈阳性的人

central tendency 中心趋势
balancing point 对称点,平衡点
mean *n.* 均值
arithmetic mean 算术均值
median *n.* 中位数
odd *adj.* 奇数的,单数的,单只的
even *adj.* 偶数的,平的,平滑的,一致的
unduly *adv.* 不适当地,过度地,不正当地
unimodal *adj.* 单峰的
multimodal *adj.* 多峰的

1.7 Measures of Dispersion

In the example $(4, 8, 9, 9, 10, 14)$ in Fig. 1.4, the mean, the median, and the model all equal 9, showing that the data are centered at the point $y = 9$. But measures of central tendency do not adequately describe a set of observations. For example, the mean of $(7, 8, 9, 9, 10, 11)$ is also $\bar{y} = 9$, as are the median and the mode. But the two sets of data are quite different from one another. The numbers in $(7, 8, 9, 9, 10, 11)$ are closer to one another, and to the mean, than are the numbers in $(4, 8, 9, 9, 10, 14)$. The difference is in the dispersion or the variability of the data, which is not reflected in the mean, median, or mode. Therefore, measures of dispersion are needed to describe a group of observations. See Fig. 1.8. There are several measures of dispersion, of which we discuss three.

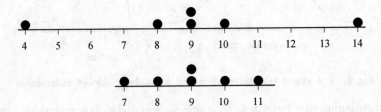

Fig. 1.8 Two distributions with the same central values but different dispersions

1.7.1 Range

The range of a group of observations is the largest value minus the smallest value in the group, or

$$\text{Range} = \text{largest } y - \text{smallest } y \tag{1.3}$$

A large value of the range indicates a large dispersion of the observations. In Fig. 1.6, the range of (4, 8, 9, 9, 10, 14) is 14−4 = 10, while the range of (7, 8, 9, 9, 10, 11) is 11 − 7 = 4. Therefore, the first set of observations has a large dispersion than the second. The range is a very simple concept and is easy to determine, sometimes by inspection alone. But since it depends only on two extreme values and is not affected by any other values in a set of observations, the range is not affected by any other values in a set of observations, the range is not a sensitive measure of dispersion. For example, the range of (4, 6, 9, 9, 12, 14) is also 14−4 = 10. But the numbers in (4, 6, 9, 9, 12, 14) are more different from one another, and from the mean, than are the numbers in (4, 8, 9, 9, 10, 14). A more precise measure of dispersion of a set of data is the variance.

1.7.2 Variance and standard deviation

The variance of a sample of n observations is defined as the sum of squared deviations of observations from the mean divided by $n-1$, or

$$S_Y^2 = \frac{1}{n-1} \sum_{i=1}^{n} (y_i - \bar{y})^2 \tag{1.4}$$

The variance of a sample of observations takes into account the deviation of every y_i from the mean. The value of the variance is zero when all the n observations are identical; in this case there is no variability. The variance increases as the variability, or the deviations $y_i - \bar{y}$, increase. The variance of a sample of observations reflects quantitatively the degree of dispersion in the sample.

In formula (1.4), each derivation $(y_i - \bar{y})$ is squared to assure that the variance is a positive measure. If each deviation is not squared, the sum of the deviations $(y_i - \bar{y})$ is zero, as shown in Sec. 1.8 as a property of the mean. Also the fact that the sum of n squared deviations is divided by $n-1$, not by n, may appear strange at first glance, but it is intuitively justifiable. There are only $n-1$ *independent* deviations because any one of the deviations can be expressed in terms of the other $n-1$ deviations. For example $(y_1 - \bar{y}) = -[(y_2 - \bar{y}) + \cdots + (y_n - \bar{y})]$. In three observations (1, 2, 6) with $y = 3$ we have $(1-3) = -[(2-3) + (6-3)]$.

The standard deviation is defined as the (positive) square root of the variance, or

$$S_Y = \sqrt{\frac{1}{(n-1)} \left[\sum_{i=1}^{n} (y_i - \bar{y})^2 \right]} \tag{1.5}$$

Some properties of variance and standard deviation

(1) If a constant a is added to each observation in the data set, the variance is

not changed. In other words, a change of the location of a distribution has no effect on the dispersion of the distribution. In formula

$$S^2_{a+Y} = S^2_Y \tag{1.6}$$

(2) If each observation is multiplied by a constant b, then the variance is multiplied by a factor b^2 or

$$S^2_{bY} = b^2 S^2_Y \tag{1.7}$$

Both properties can be summarized as: the variance of a linear function of Y, $a+bY$, is equal to b^2 time the variance of Y, or

$$S^2_{a+bY} = b^2 S^2_Y \tag{1.8}$$

If follows that the standard deviation of a linear function of Y, $a+bY$, is equal to b times the standard deviation of Y.

Table 1.2 shows the range, the variance, and the standard deviation of each of the three examples. The sample variance for the ages in Table 1.1 is

Table 1.2

Sample	R	S^2_Y	S_Y
(7,8,9,10,11)	4	2.0	1.41
(4,8,9,9,10,14)	10	10.4	3.22
(4,6,9,9,12,14)	10	13.6	3.69

$$S^2_Y = \frac{1}{399}\left[\sum_{i=1}^{400}(y_i - 34.81)^2\right] = \frac{1}{399}[(49 - 34.81)^2 + (42 - 34.81)^2 + \cdots + (27 - 34.81)^2] = 39.95$$

where y_i denotes the age and the standard deviation is $S_Y = \sqrt{39.95} = 6.24$ years

Two alternative formulas for the variance

For easier computation, for combining two or more variances, or for the partition of sums of squares, two alternative formulas of the variance are available

$$S^2_Y = \frac{1}{n-1}\left[\sum_{i=1}^{n} y_i^2 - n(\bar{y}^2)\right] \tag{1.9}$$

and

$$S^2_Y = \frac{1}{n-1}\left[\sum_{i=1}^{n} y_i^2 - \frac{\left(\sum_{i=1}^{n} y_i\right)^2}{n}\right] \tag{1.10}$$

1.7.3 Covariance Cov (X, Y), or $S_{x,y}$

The covariance between two variables, X and Y, is a measure of the variation of X and Y jointly. In a sample of n pairs of observations, (x_1, y_1), $(x_2, y_2), \ldots, (x_n, y_n)$, the formula for the covariance is

$$\text{Cov}(X,Y) = \frac{1}{n-1} \sum_{i=1}^{n} (x_i - \bar{x})(y_i - \bar{y}) \tag{1.11}$$

The covariance may be positive, negative, or equal to zero. If Y increases as X increases, $\text{Cov}(X,Y) > 0$; if Y decreases as X increases, $\text{Cov}(X,Y) < 0$; if one of the variables is constant, or if the distribution of one variable remains the same for different values of the other variable, the covariance is zero.

The computational formulas for the covariance are

$$\text{Cov}(X,Y) = \frac{1}{n-1} \left[\sum_i x_i y_i - \frac{1}{n} \sum_i x_i \sum_i y_i \right] = \frac{1}{n-1} \left(\sum_i x_i y_i - n \overline{xy} \right) \tag{1.12}$$

Words and Expressions

variability *n.* 可变性,变异性
inspection *n.* 检查,检验;审查
range *n.* 极差
variance *n.* 方差
standard deviation 标准差
independent *adj.* 独立的
covariance *n.* 协方差
positive *adj.* 正的,实际的,积极的
negative *adj.* 负的,阴性的,消极的

1.8 Grouped Data

A data set generated from a research project usually is voluminous unordered, confusing and even chaotic. Before attempting any statistical analysis, we need to rearrange and reduce the mass of data to a simple and compact form so that some meaningful information can be derived. The most effective form is the frequency distribution, which consists of a number of ordered intervals (or classes) and the number of observations falling into each interval, or the frequency. A data set in this form is called grouped data. A typical frequency distribution is shown in Table 1.3.

The following terms are associated with a frequency distribution.

Relative frequency ($\frac{f_i}{n}$) is the proportion of observations in a specific interval.

Cumulative frequency (F_i) is the total number of observations up to the upper limit of a specific interval. That is, $F_i = f_1 + \cdots + f_i$, for $i = 1, \cdots, k$; and $F_k = n$.

Table 1.3 A frequency table

Class or Interval L_i to L_i+1	Midpoint y_i	Frequency f_i	Relative Frequency $\dfrac{f_i}{n}$	Cumulative Frequency F_i	Relative-cumulative Frequency $\dfrac{f_i}{n}$
(1)	(2)	(3)	(4)	(5)	(6)
L_1 to L_2	y_1	f_1	$\dfrac{f_1}{n}$	F_1	$\dfrac{F_1}{n}$
L_2 to L_3	y_2	f_2	$\dfrac{f_2}{n}$	F_2	$\dfrac{F_2}{n}$
L_3 to L_4	y_3	f_3	$\dfrac{f_3}{n}$	F_3	$\dfrac{F_3}{n}$
$\vdots$	$\vdots$	$\vdots$	$\vdots$	$\vdots$	$\vdots$
L_k to L_k+1	y_k	f_k	$\dfrac{f_k}{n}$	F_k	$\dfrac{F_k}{n} = 1$
Total	$-^*$	n	1.0	$-^*$	$-^*$

* The sum of this column has no meaning.

Relative-cumulative frequency ($\dfrac{f_i}{n}$) is the proportion of observations up to the upper limit of a specific interval.

Construction of a frequency distribution from a given set of data involves the determination of the number of intervals (k), the width of the interval (w), the limits of the intervals (L_i, L_{i+1}), and the corresponding frequencies (f_i). The number of intervals is usually set between 8 and 20 that there will be enough intervals to show the general pattern of the distribution, but not too many so that the pattern is lost. The range of a data set divided by the number of intervals gives the approximate width of the interval. Generally, the width of the interval is an integer and is constant for all the k intervals. The first interval must include the smallest number in a data set and the last interval includes the largest. The midpoint of the interval should be a convenient number for computation. From the upper limit of the first interval, marking a length of w consecutively $k-1$ times gives all the k intervals. Finally, tallying all the n numbers in a data set yields a frequency distribution. The entire grouping process can be done on a computer.

Computational formulas for grouped data

In computing the mean, the median, and the variance from a frequency distribution, we make the assumption that the observations in each interval are uniformly distributed in the interval and that the midpoint of the interval, denoted by y_i, represents all the observations in the interval. It follows that the formula of the mean is

$$\bar{y} = \frac{f_1 y_1 + f_2 y_2 + \cdots + f_k y_k}{\sum_{i=1}^{k} f_i} = \frac{1}{n} [\sum_{i=1}^{k} f_i y_i] \qquad (1.13)$$

The formula for the variance is

$$S_Y^2 = \frac{f_1(y_1 - \bar{y})^2 + f_2(y_2 - \bar{y})^2 + \cdots + f_k(y_k - \bar{y})^2}{(n-1)} =$$

$$\frac{1}{n-1} [\sum_{i=1}^{k} f_i (y_i - \bar{y})^2] = \qquad (1.14)$$

$$\frac{1}{n-1} \left[\sum_{i=1}^{k} f_i (y_i)^2 - \frac{(\sum_{i=1}^{k} f_i y_i)^2}{n} \right] = \qquad (1.15)$$

$$\frac{1}{n-1} [\sum_{i=1}^{k} f_i (y_i)^2 - n(\bar{y})^2] \qquad (1.16)$$

The formula for the standard deviation for grouped data, as in the case for ungrouped data, is the (positive) square root of the variance, or

$$S_Y = \sqrt{S_Y^2} \qquad (1.17)$$

The formula for the median for a set of grouped data is

$$M_d = L + \left[\frac{\frac{n}{2} + F}{f} \right] w \qquad (1.18)$$

where

L = the lower limit of the interval containing the median value

F = the cumulative frequency up to L

f = the frequency in the interval containing the median value

w = the width of the interval containing the median value

The key to calculating the median from grouped data is the assumption of a uniform distribution of the f observations in the interval containing the median. By definition, the median is the value of the $(\frac{n}{2})$th observation in a sample, or the value of the $(\frac{n}{2} - F)$ the observation in the interval containing the median. Under the uniform distribution assumption, the ratio of the difference (M_d-L) to the width of the interval (w) is equal to the ratio of the two corresponding frequencies $(\frac{n}{2}-F)$ to f, that is

$$\frac{M-L}{w} = \frac{\frac{n}{2}-F}{f} \tag{1.19}$$

Solving Eq. (1.19) for M_d yields the formula in (1.18). Fig. 1.9 shows a graphic illustration of formula (1.19).

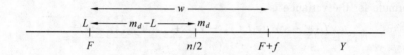

Fig. 1.9 Determination of the median for grouped data

In deriving the formulas for the grouped data, we made an assumption of uniform distribution of f_i observations in each interval. This assumption generally is acceptable when the sample size is moderately large. For the special case of the 400 ages in Table 1.4, we have computed the mean, median, variance, and standard deviation from both grouped and ungrouped data, and presented them in Table 1.5. The two sets of numerical values differ only slightly from one another, indicating that the uniform distribution assumption is acceptable in this case.

Table 1.4 Frequency distribution of age $n=400$ men

Interval (in years) L_i to L_i+1	Midpoint y_i	Frequency f_i	Relative Frequency $\frac{f_i}{n}$	Cumulative Frequency F_i	Relative-cumulative Frequency $\frac{f_i}{n}$
(1)	(2)	(3)	(4)	(5)	(6)
22–26	24	10	0.025 0	10	0.025 0
26–30	28	78	0.195 0	88	0.220 0
30–34	32	103	0.257 5	191	0.477 5
34–38	36	88	0.220 0	279	0.697 5
38–42	40	62	0.155 0	341	0.852 5
42–46	44	31	0.077 5	372	0.930 0
46–50	48	18	0.045 0	390	0.975 0
50–54	52	9	0.022 5	399	0.997 5
54–58	56	1	0.002 5	400	1.000 0
Total	–*	400	1.000 0	–*	–*

* This sum has no meaning.

Table 1.5 Descriptive statistics of the ages of 400 men

		Ungrouped (Table 1.1)	Grouped (Table 1.4)
Sample size	n	400	400
Mean	$\bar{y}$	35.31	35.3
Median	M_d	34.0	34.4
Variance	S_Y^2	39.95	40.39
Standard deviation	S_Y	6.24	6.4

Words and Expressions

voluminous *adj.* 庞大的,著书多的,容积大的,丰满的,长篇的
chaotic *adj.* 混乱的,无秩序的
grouped data 分组数据
frequency *n.* 次数,频数,出现率;频度,频率
frequency distribution 频率分布,频数分布
cumulative frequency 累加频数,累加频率
relative cumulative frequency 相对累加频数,相对累加频率
tallying *v.* 计算,总结(up);记录;使符合
uniformly distributed 均匀分布的
moderately *adv.* 适度地,适中地

1.9 Graphics

Graphics is another way of summarizing a mass of data in a simple form. A visual impression is direct and immediate and can convey much information quite effectively. Graphical representation has been extensively used to present summary information in many areas, including survey data, census figures, the national budget, and commercial advertising. The graphics most relevant to statistical analysis are the histogram, the frequency polygon and the cumulative frequency polygon.

1.9.1 Histogram

A histogram is a graphic representation of a (relative) frequency distribution. It consists of k rectangles, one for each interval, placed side by side on b horizontal axis. The base of each rectangle is the width of the interval, and the height is equal to the relative frequency ($\frac{f_i}{n}$). When the base of each rectangle is taken as a unit length, the area of each rectangle is $1 \times (\frac{f_i}{n})$, or equal to $\frac{f_i}{n}$, the relative frequency. It follows that the area of a histogram is the sum of the relative frequencies, or unity. If the height of each rectangle is equal to the frequency, f_i, then the area of a histogram is equal to the sample size, n. The two histograms are identical, except that the scales are different; the height of each rectangle is the relative frequency in one histogram, while it is the frequency f_i in the other. One may have two scales for a histogram — one on each side of the histogram. When relative frequencies are used, the name "relative frequency" histogram is more descriptive; the simple name "histogram" is used when there is no ambiguity. A relative frequency histogram has the advantage that it is consistent with the concept of probability, or proportion (cf. Fig. 1.10).

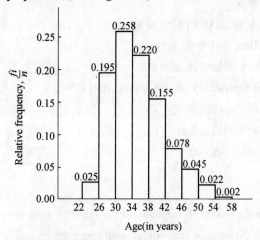

Fig. 1.10 Histogram: Age distribution of 400 HIV position men

1.9.2 Relative frequency polygon

A relative frequency polygon also is a graphic representation of the distribution. It is constructed by line segments connecting midpoints at the top of neighboring rectangles in the relative frequency histogram. The polygon is completed by creating two additional intervals, each with a zero frequency, one below the first interval and the other above the last interval. The two midpoints on the horizontal axis are then connected by lines with the points in the first and the last intervals, respectively.

These $k+1$ lines plus the base line constitute a polygon as shown in Fig. 1.11. The area of a relative frequency polygon, as in the case of a histogram, is equal to unity.

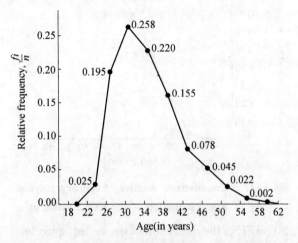

Fig. 1.11 Relative frequency polygon: Age distribution of 400 HIV position men

1.9.3 Cumulative frequency polygon

A cumulative frequency polygon is yet another graphic representation of a frequency distribution or, more accurately, of a cumulative relative frequency distribution. It is constructed using lines connecting points over the upper limit of each interval with a height equal to the cumulative (relative) frequency of that interval ($\frac{f_i}{n}$). While for a histogram or a relative frequency polygon, the proportion of observations falling in a region is represented by an area, for a cumulative frequency polygon the proportion is represented by the height of a point on the polygon. The height of the point on the polygon over the upper limit of the last (the kth) interval is equal to unity, because it represents the proportion of all the observations in the sample. The numbers in Fig. 1.12 are the cumulative relative frequencies ($\frac{f_i}{n}$).

1.9.4 Percentiles and quartiles and interquartile range

The pth percentile in a sample is the point that divides the ordered observations into two pieces with p percent below and $(100-p)$ percent above that point. When p

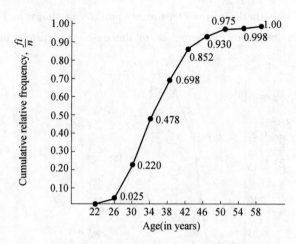

**Fig. 1.12 Cumulative (relative) frequency polygon:
Age distribution of 400 HIV Position men**

is equal to 25, 50 or 75, the percentiles are called quartiles. Thus the 25th percentile is the first quartile, the 50th percentile is the second quartile, and the 75th percentile is the third quartile. The 50th percentile, or the second quartile, is the median of a distribution. The distance between the first quartile and the third quartile is called the interquartile range, which is yet another measure of variability of observations in a sample. By definition, the interquartile range in a sample contains 50 percent of the observations. A large interquartile range indicates a high variability of the observations; a small interquartile range indicates a low variability.

Percentiles and quartiles usually are used in large samples and are determined from a frequency distribution. Their formulas are similar to the formula for the median. The first quartile, for example, is given by

$$Q_1 = L_1 + \left(\frac{\frac{n}{4} - F_1}{f_1} \right) \times w_1 \qquad (1.20)$$

where L_1 denotes the lower limit of the interval where the first quartile is located, F_1 is the cumulative frequency up to L_1, f_1 is the frequency in the interval, and w_1 is the width of the interval. The formula for the third quartile is

$$Q_3 = L_3 + \left(\frac{\frac{3n}{4} - F_3}{f_3} \right) \times w_3 \qquad (1.21)$$

where L_3, F_3, f_3 and w_3 are similarly defined as L_1, F_1, f_1, and w_1 for the first quartile.

Words and Expressions

commercial advertising 商业广告
histogram n. 直方图
frequency polygon 频率多边图,频数多边图
rectangle n. 矩形,长方形
ambiguity n. 可作两种或多种解释;含糊;意义不明确
at the top of 处于顶峰,高居首位
percentile n. 百分位数
quartile n. 四分位数
interquartile range 四分位数间距

1.10 An Example

In Table 1.1 are ages (on last birthday) of a random sample of $n = 400$ men taken from census information of the Castro district in San Francisco. Each of these men was found to be antibody positive to the human immunodeficiency virus (HIV), the AIDS virus. We use this data set to illustrate descriptive statistics.

Frequency distribution The smallest and largest values in the group are 24 years and 54 years, respectively, giving the range $54 - 24 = 30$ years. Using $k = 9$ intervals and $w = 4$ years as the width of each interval, we let the first interval be (22-26) and mark from the point 26 a width of $w = 4$ years consecutively 8 times to determine all the 9 intervals as shown in Table 1.4, column (1). Tallying the $n = 400$ ages consecutively yields the frequencies in the 9 intervals and the frequency distribution in column (3). Note that the intervals are of exact age; two neighboring intervals overlap by one point. The first two intervals, for example, have a common point at (exactly) 26 years. Since age is a continuous variable, there are no persons whose ages are *exactly* 26 years at any given moment. Also, as the reported ages are those at last birthday, an age of 26 years should be entered in interval (26-30), an age of 30 years in interval (30-34), etc.

Relative frequencies, cumulative frequencies, and relative-cumulative frequencies are shown in columns (4) ~ (6) respectively.

Mean, mode, and standard deviation As the intervals in column (1) are exact ages, the midpoint in column (2) for each interval is equally distant from the lower and the upper limit of the interval. For example, the midpoint of the first interval is $24 = \frac{(22+26)}{2}$. Using formulas (1.13) and (1.15), we find the mean age $\bar{Y} = 35.3$ years, the variance $S_Y^2 = 40.39$, and hence the standard deviation $S_Y = 6.4$ years. The mode is $M_o = 32$ years.

Median To use formula (1.18) to compute the median, first look for the interval which contains the $(\frac{n}{2})$th, or the 200th, ordered observation. The interval is (34–88). Next, identify the lower limit $L = 34$, the cumulative frequency $F = 191$, the frequency $f = 88$, and the width of the interval $w = 4$ years. Finally, substitute these values in formula (1.18) to obtain the median

$$M_d = 34 + \left(\frac{200-191}{88}\right) \times 4 = 34.3 \text{ (years)}$$

As the mode $M_o = 32$ years, the median $M_d = 34.4$ years and the mean $\bar{Y} = 35.3$ years, and $M_o < M_d < \bar{Y}$, the distribution is skewed to the right, or positively skewed.

Quartiles and interquartile range From the cumulative frequencies in column (5), we find that the first quartile Q_1 is located in the interval (30–34), and the third quartile Q_3 is in the interval (38–42). Using formula (1.20), we compute the first quartile

$$Q_1 = 30 + \left(\frac{100-88}{103}\right) \times 4 = 30.5 \text{ (years)}$$

Using formula (1.21), we have the third quartile

$$Q_3 = 38 + \left(\frac{300-279}{62}\right) \times 4 = 39.4 \text{ (years)}$$

Therefore, the interquartile range is from 30.5 years to 39.4 years, which contains 50 percent of the ages in the sample.

Histogram, frequency polygon, and cumulative frequency polygon
Following the instructions in Sec. 1.5, a histogram, a relative frequency polygon and a cumulative polygon have been prepared (Figs. 1.8 ~ 1.10, respectively).

The histogram in Fig. 1.8 and the relative frequency polygon in Fig. 1.9 are subject to similar interpretation. First of all, the height of each rectangle in the histogram and the height of each point in the polygon are equal, and equal to the relative frequency in the interval, denoted by a number, The area of the histogram and the area under the polygon are both equal to unity. Further, the area to the left (or right) of a point is the proportion of men (observations) who were younger (or older) than the age represented by the point. And finally, the area between any two points is the proportion of men (observations) whose ages were between the ages represented by the two points. For example, the area to the left of 30 is 0.22 (=0.025+0.195), which means that 22 percent of the men in the sample were younger than 30 years of (exact) age. Similarly, 2.4 percent (=0.022+0.002) of the men were older than 50 years of age. Finally, 63.3 percent (=0.258+0.220+ 0.155) of them were between 30 and 42 years of age.

In the cumulative (relative) frequency polygon in Fig. 1.10, the height of each point, denoted by a number, is cumulative relative frequency up to the corresponding interval. Generally, the height of any point on a line segment on the polygon represents the proportions of men (observations) who were younger than the age represented by the point on the horizontal axis.

As the sample size n and the number of intervals k increase indefinitely, the proportions become probabilities, each rectangle in the histogram reduces to a (vertical) straight line (which is known as the density function), the relative frequency polygon approaches a smooth curve, and the cumulative frequency polygon tends to an S-shaped curve (known as the distribution function). The probability density, the smooth curve, and the S-shaped curve, each describes the probability distribution of a continuous variable. Thus the graphics, as presented in this chapter, are an important first step to the understanding of the probability distribution.

A final remark This chapter contains only a few of the many possible techniques included in descriptive statistics. The use of descriptive statistics is more of an art than a science. The choice of the specific descriptive method often depends on the subject matter under study, the focus of the investigator, or the impression one wishes to convey. The choice is semantic; the availability of a large variety of descriptive statistics allows a wide range of ways to express the same information. British statesman Benjamin Disraeli once remarked — "there are lies, damned lies and statistics." Quite possibly, the Victorian Prime Minister was puzzled by the number of ways one can present information with statistics. Today, it may be equally appropriate to say "there are lies, damned lies and politics."

Words and Expressions

overlap *v.* 交叠,(物体)部分重叠
AIDS virus 艾滋病病毒,获得性免疫缺陷综合征(Acquired Immune Deficiency Syndrome)病毒
antibody *n.* (医学)抗体
first of all 首先,第一
smooth curve 光滑曲线

straight line 直线
only a few 仅仅少数,一点点
under study 正在研究之中
probability distribution 概率分布
semantic *adj.* 语义(学)的
damned *adj.* 该死的;被罚的;讨厌的,糟透的

1.11 Proofs of the Results in this Chapter

In the following proofs $\sum$ is written for $\sum_{i=1}^{n}$ for simplicity.

1. The sum of the deviations of each observation from the mean equals zero.

$$\sum(y_i - \bar{y}) = \sum y_i - \sum \bar{y} = \sum y_i - n\bar{y} = \sum y_i - \sum y_i = 0 \quad (1.22)$$

2. The mean of a linear function of a variable is equal to the linear function of the variable. Or, the mean of $a+by$ is $a+b\bar{y}$

$$\frac{1}{n}\sum(a + by_i) = \frac{1}{n}(\sum a + b\sum y_i) = \frac{1}{n}(na + nb\bar{y}) = a + b\bar{y} \quad (1.23)$$

Note $\quad \sum a = a + a + \cdots + a = na$

3. The variance of a linear function of a variable, $a+bY$, is equal to b^2 times the variance of the variable Y

$$S_{a+bY}^2 = \frac{1}{n-1}\sum[(a + by_i) - (a + b\bar{y})]^2 =$$

$$\frac{1}{n-1}\sum[by_i - b\bar{y}]^2 =$$

$$\frac{b^2}{n-1}\sum[(y_i - \bar{y})^2] = b^2 S_Y^2 \quad (1.24)$$

4. $\sum(y_i - \bar{y})^2 = \sum y_i^2 - \frac{(\sum y_i)^2}{n}$ Since

$$(y_i - \bar{y})^2 = y_i^2 - 2\bar{y}y_i + \bar{y}^2 \quad (1.25)$$

$$\sum(y_i - \bar{y})^2 = \sum y_i^2 - 2\bar{y}\sum y_i + n\bar{y}^2 = \sum y_i^2 - 2n\bar{y}^2 + n\bar{y}^2 =$$

$$\sum y_i^2 - n\bar{y}^2 = \sum y_i^2 - n\left(\frac{\sum y_i}{n}\right)^2 =$$

$$\sum y_i^2 - \frac{(\sum y_i)^2}{n} \quad (1.26)$$

Exercises

1. Please translate statistics quotes of the beginning of the each unit.

(1) All knowledge is, in the final analysis, history.

All sciences are, in the abstract, mathematics.

All judgments are, in their rationale, are statistics.

—— The famous statistician, C. R. Rao in 《Statistics and Truth》, 1989

(2) There are three kinds of lies: lies, damned lies, and statistics.

—— Benjamin Disraeli

(3) Statistics are like a bikini. What they reveal is suggestive, but what they conceal is vital.

—— Professor in Baruch College, Aaron Levenstein

(4) Genius is one percent inspiration and ninety nine percent perspiration.

—— T. A. Edison

(5) There are two kinds of statistics, the kind you look up and the kind you make up.

—— Rex Stout

(6) To understand God's thoughts we must study statistics, for these are the measure of his purpose.

—— Florence Nightingale

2. The weights of club members

The members of a sports club, 60 male adults, had their weights recorded, in pounds. The weights are given in the table below.

171	160	144	132	154	160	160	158	148	160	131	153
131	165	139	163	149	149	140	149	150	161	136	144
165	174	153	149	157	169	147	156	149	171	149	154
153	149	147	154	145	158	160	152	156	138	167	142
165	155	140	155	158	147	149	169	148	174	150	144

Construct a cumulative frequency table for these weights, using classes of width 5lb, starting at 129.5lb. Hence draw a cumulative frequency graph, and use this to find the median and semi-interquartile range.

Use the grouped frequency table to calculate the mean and standard deviation, and compare them with the values obtained using the original, ungrouped, data.

3. Histogram for catches of fish

A keen angler kept a record of the weight of each of his last 51 catches of fish.

The weights, recorded to the nearest 0.1 kg, are as given in the following table.

Weight/kg	0.0–0.4	0.5–0.9	1.0–1.2	1.3–1.7	1.8–2.1	2.2–3.7	3.8–5.2
Frequency	9	12	8	8	8	4	2

Draw a histogram for the data, and use it to calculate the modal class.

4. Distribution of examination marks

The following table shows the number of candidates who scored $0, 1, \ldots, 10$ marks for a particular question in an examination.

Mark	0	1	2	3	4	5	6	7	8	9	10
No. of Candidates	8	10	49	112	98	86	54	37	28	12	6

Calculate the mean, median and mode of the distribution of marks. What feature of the distribution is suggested by the fact that the mean is greater than the median?

There are three kinds of lies: lies, damned lies, and statistics.
—— Benjamin Disraeli

Unit Two Mathematical Statistics

In this unit, the statistical methods used in the proceeding chapters are summarized. Mood, Graybill and Bose (1974), Hogg and Craig (1995) and Stuart and Ord (1991, 1994) are good references in Sections 2.1 ~ 2.8, while Judge, Hill, Griffiths and Lee (1980) and Greene (1993, 1997, 2000) are representative textbooks in Section 2.9.

2.1 Event and Probability

2.1.1 Event

We consider an *experiment* whose outcome is not known in advance but an event occurs with probability, which is sometimes called a *random experiment*. The *sample space* of an experiment is the set of all possible outcomes. Each element of a sample space is called an *element* of the sample space or a *sample point*, with represents each outcome obtained by the experiment. An *event* is any collection of outcomes contained in the sample space, or equivalently a subset of the sample space. A *simple event* consists of exactly one element and a *compound event* consists of more than one element. Sample space is denoted by Ω and sample point is given by ω.

Suppose that event A is a subset of sample Ω. Let ω be a sample point in event A. Then, we say that a sample point ω is contained in a sample space A, which is denoted by $\omega \in A$.

A set of the sample points which does not belong to event A is called the *complementary event* of A, which is denoted by A^c. An event that does not have any sample point is called the *empty event*, denoted by $\emptyset$. Conversely, an event which includes all possible sample points is called the *whole event*, represented by Ω.

Next, consider two events A and B. A set consisting of the whole sample points which belong to either event A or event B is called the *sum event*, which is denoted by $A \cap B$. A set consisting of the whole sample points which belong to both event A and event B is called the *product event*, denoted by $A \cap B$. When $A \cap B = \emptyset$, we say that events A and B are *mutually exclusive*.

Example 2.1

Consider an experiment of casting a die. We have six sample points, which are denoted by $\omega_1 = \{1\}$, $\omega_2 = \{2\}$, $\omega_3 = \{3\}$, $\omega_4 = \{4\}$, $\omega_5 = \{5\}$ and $\omega_6 = \{6\}$, where ω_i represents the sample point that we have i. In this experiment, the sample space is given by $\Omega = \{\omega_1, \omega_2, \omega_3, \omega_4, \omega_5, \omega_6\}$. Let A be the event that we have even numbers and B be the event that we have multiples of three. Then, we can write as $A = \{\omega_2, \omega_4, \omega_6\}$ and $B = \{\omega_3, \omega_6\}$. The complementary event of A is given by $A^c = \{\omega_1, \omega_3, \omega_5\}$, which is the event that we have odd numbers. The sum event of A and B is written as $A \cup B = \{\omega_2, \omega_3, \omega_4, \omega_6\}$, while the product event is $A \cap B = \{\omega_6\}$. Since $A \cap A^c = \emptyset$, we have the fact A and A^c are mutually exclusive.

Example 2.2

Cast a coin three times. In this case, we have the following eight sample points

$$\omega_1 = (H,H,H), \ \omega_3 = (H,H,T), \ \omega_3 = (H,T,H), \ \omega_4 = (H,T,T)$$
$$\omega_5 = (T,H,H), \ \omega_6 = (T,H,T), \ \omega_7 = (T,T,H), \ \omega_8 = (T,T,T)$$

where H represents head while T indicates tail. For example, (H, T, H) means that the first flip lands head, the second flip is tail and the third one is head. Therefore, the sample space of this experiment can be written as

$$\Omega = \{\omega_1, \omega_2, \omega_3, \omega_4, \omega_5, \omega_6, \omega_7, \omega_8\}$$

Let A be an event that we have two heads, B be an event that we obtain at least one tail, C be an event that we have head in the second flip, and D be an event that we obtain tail in the third flip. Then, the events A, B, C and D are give by

$$A = \{\omega_2, \omega_3, \omega_5\}$$
$$B = \{\omega_2, \omega_3, \omega_4, \omega_5, \omega_6, \omega_7, \omega_8\}$$
$$C = \{\omega_1, \omega_2, \omega_5, \omega_6\}$$
$$D = \{\omega_2, \omega_4, \omega_6, \omega_8\}$$

Since A is a subset of B, denoted by $A \subset B$, a sum event is $A \cup B = B$, while a product event is $A \cap B = A$. Moreover, we obtain $C \cap D = \{\omega_2, \omega_6\}$ and $C \cup D = \{\omega_1, \omega_2, \omega_4, \omega_5, \omega_6, \omega_8\}$.

2.1.2 Probability

Let $n(A)$ be the number of sample points in A. We have $n(A) \leq n(B)$ when $A \subseteq B$. Each sample point is equally likely to occur. In the case of Example 2.1 (Section 2.1.1), each of the six possible outcomes has probability 1/6 and in Example 2.2 (Section 2.1.1), each of the eight possible outcomes has probability 1/8. Thus, the probability which the event A occurs is defined as

$$P(A) = \frac{n(A)}{n(\Omega)}$$

In Example 2.1, $P(A) = 3/6$ and $P(A \cap B) = 1/6$ are obtained, because $n(\Omega) = 6$, $n(A) = 3$ and $n(A \cap B) = 1$. Similarly, in Example 2.1, we have $P(C) = 4/8$, $P(A \cap B) = P(A) = 3/8$ and so on. Note that we obtain $P(A) \leq P(B)$ because of $A \subseteq B$.

It is known that we have the following three properties on probability

$$0 \leq P(A) \leq 1 \tag{2.1}$$
$$P(\Omega) = 1 \tag{2.2}$$
$$P(\emptyset) = 0 \tag{2.3}$$

$\emptyset \subseteq A \subseteq \Omega$ implies $n(\emptyset) \leq n(A) \leq n(\Omega)$. Therefore, we have

$$\frac{n(\emptyset)}{n(\Omega)} \leq \frac{n(A)}{n(\Omega)} \leq \frac{n(\Omega)}{n(\Omega)} = 1$$

Dividing by $n(\Omega)$, we obtain

$$P(\emptyset) \leq P(A) \leq P(\Omega) = 1$$

Because $\emptyset$ has no sample point, the number of the sample point is given by $n(\emptyset) = 0$ and accordingly we have $P(\emptyset) = 0$. Therefore, $0 \leq P(A) \leq 1$ is obtained is (2.1). Thus, (2.1) ~ (2.3) are obtained.

When events A and B are mutually exclusive, i.e., when $A \cap B = \emptyset$, then $P(A \cup B) = P(A) + P(B)$ holds. Moreover, since A and A^c are mutually exclusive, $P(A^c) = 1 - P(A)$ is obtained. Note that $P(A \cup A^c) = P(\Omega) = 1$ holds. Generally, unless A and B are not exclusive, we have the following formula

$$P(A \cup B) = P(A) + P(B) - P(A \cap B)$$

which is known as the *addition rule*. In Example 2.1, each probability is given by $P(A \cup B) = 2/3$, $P(A) = 1/2$, $P(B) = 1/3$ and $P(A \cap B) = 1/6$. Thus, in the example we can verify that the above addition rule holds.

The probability which event A occurs, given that event B has occurred, is called the *conditional probability*, i. e.

$$P(A|B) = \frac{n(A \cap B)}{n(B)} = \frac{P(A \cap B)}{P(B)}$$

or equivalently

$$P(A \cap B) = P(A|B)P(B)$$

which is called the *multiplication rule*. When event A is *independent* of event B, we have $P(A \cap B) = P(A)P(B)$, which implies that $P(A|B) = P(A)$. Conversely, $P(A \cap B) = P(A)P(B)$ implies that A is independent of B. In Example 2.2, because of $P(A \cap C) = 1/4$ and $P(C) = 1/2$, the conditional probability $P(A|C) = 1/2$ is obtained. From $P(A) = 3/8$, we have $P(A \cap C) \neq P(A)P(C)$. Therefore, A is not independent of C. As for C and D, since we have $P(C) = 1/2$, $P(D) = 1/2$ and $P(C \cap D) = 1/4$, we can show that C is independent of D.

Words and Expressions

in advance 预先,事前
simple event 简单事件
compound event 复合事件
complementary event 对立事件,互补事件
empty event 空事件
whole event 全事件
sum event 和事件
product event 积事件
mutually exclusive 互补相交的,互不相容的,互斥的
cast *v.* 投,掷,抛
die *n.* 骰子
flip *v.* 掷,弹,轻击;*n.* 抛,弹
addition rule 加法规则
conditional probability 条件概率
multiplication rule 乘法规则
independent *adj.* 独立的

2.2 Random Variable and Distribution

2.2.1 Univariate Random Variable and Distribution

The *random variable* X is defined as the real value function on sample space Ω.

Since X is a function of a sample point ω, it is written as $X=X(\omega)$. Suppose that $X(\omega)$ takes a real value on the interval I. That is, X depends on a set of the sample point ω, i.e., $\{\omega; X(\omega) \in I\}$, which is simply written as $X \in I$.

In Example 2.1 (Section 2.1.1), suppose that X is a random variable which takes the number of spots up on the die. Then, X is a function of ω and takes the following values

$$X(\omega_1)=1,\ X(\omega_2)=2,\ X(\omega_3)=3$$
$$X(\omega_4)=4,\ X(\omega_5)=5,\ X(\omega_6)=6$$

In Example 2.2 (Section 2.1.1), suppose that X is a random variable which takes the number of heads. Depending on the sample point ω_i, X takes the following values

$$X(\omega_1)=3,\ X(\omega_2)=2,\ X(\omega_3)=2,\ X(\omega_4)=1$$
$$X(\omega_5)=2,\ X(\omega_6)=1,\ X(\omega_7)=1,\ X(\omega_8)=0$$

Thus, the random variable depends on a sample point.

There are two kinds of random variables. One is a *discrete random variable*, while another is a *continuous random variable*.

Discrete Random Variable and Probability Function Suppose that the discrete random variable X takes $x_1, x_2, \ldots$, where $x_1 < x_2 < \ldots$ is assumed. Consider the probability that X takes x_i, i.e., $P(X=x_i)=p_i$, which is a function of x_i. That is, a function of x_i, say $f(x_i)$, is associated with $P(X=x_i)=p_i$. The function $f(x_i)$ represents the probability in the case where X takes x_i. Therefore, we have the following relation

$$P(X=X_i)=p_i=f(x_i),\ i=1,\ 2,\ldots$$

where $f(x_i)$ is called the probability function of X.

More formally, the function $f(x_i)$ which has the following properties is defined as the probability function

$$f(x_i) \geq 0,\ i=1,\ 2,\ldots$$
$$\sum_i f(x_i) = 1$$

Furthermore, for an even A, we can write a probability as the following equation

$$P(X \in A) = \sum_{x_i \in A} f(x_i)$$

In Example 2.2 (Section 2.1.1), all the possible values of X are 0, 1, 2 and 3. (note that X denotes the number of heads when a die is cast three times) That is, $x_1=0$, $x_2=1$, $x_3=2$ and $x_4=3$ are assigned in this case. The probability that X takes x_1, x_2, x_3 or x_4 is given by

$$P(X=0)=f(0)=P(\{\omega_8\})=\frac{1}{8}$$

$$P(X=1)=f(1)=P(\{\omega_4,\omega_6,\omega_7\})=P(\{\omega_4\})+$$

$$P(\{\omega_6\})+P(\{\omega_7\})=\frac{3}{8}$$

$$P(X=2)=f(2)=P(\{\omega_2,\omega_3,\omega_5\})=P(\{\omega_2\})+$$

$$P(\{\omega_3\})+P(\{\omega_5\})=\frac{3}{8}$$

$$P(X=3)=f(3)=P(\{\omega_1\})=\frac{1}{8}$$

which can be written as

$$P(X=x)=f(x)=\frac{3!}{x!\,(3-x)}\left(\frac{1}{2}\right)^3,\ x=0,\ 1,\ 2,\ 3$$

For $P(X=1)$ and $P(X=2)$, note that each sample point is mutually exclusive. The above probability function is called the *binomial distribution* Thus, it is easy to check $f(x)\geqslant 0$ and $\sum_x f(x)=1$ in Example 2.2.

Continuous Random Variable and Probability Density Function Whereas a discrete random variable assumes at most a countable set of possible values, a continuous random variable X takes any real number within an interval I. For the interval I, the probability which X is contained in A is defined as

$$P(X\in I)=\int_I f(x)\,dx$$

For example, let I be the interval between a and b for $a<b$. Then, we can rewrite $P(X\in I)$ as follows

$$P(a<X<b)=\int_a^b f(x)\,dx$$

Where is $f(x)$ called the *probability density function* of X, or simply the *density function* of X.

In order for $f(x)$ to be a probability density function, $f(x)$ has to satisfy the following properties

$$f(x)\geqslant 0$$

$$\int_{-\infty}^{+\infty} f(x)\,dx=1$$

For a continuous random variable, note as follows

$$P(X=x)=\int_x^x f(t)\,dt=0$$

In the case of discrete random variables, $P(X=x_i)$ represents the probability which

X takes x_i, i. e., $p_i = f(x_i)$. Thus, the probability function $f(x_i)$ itself implies probability. However, in the case of continuous random variables, $P(a<X<b)$ indicates the probability which X lies on the interval (a,b).

Example 2.3

As an example, consider the following function
$$f(x) = \begin{cases} 1, & \text{for } 0<x<1 \\ 0, & \text{otherwise} \end{cases}$$

Clearly, since $f(x) \geq 0$ for $-\infty < x < +\infty$ and $\int_{-\infty}^{+\infty} f(x) dx = [x]_0^1 = 1$, the above function can be a probability density function. In fact, it is called a *uniform distribution*.

Example 2.4

As another example, consider the following function
$$f(x) = \frac{1}{\sqrt{2\pi}} e^{-\frac{1}{2}x^2}$$

for $-\infty < x < +\infty$, Clearly, we have $f(x) \geq 0$ for all x. We check whether $\int_{-\infty}^{+\infty} f(x) dx = 1$. First of all, we define I as $I = \int_{-\infty}^{+\infty} f(x) dx$ To show $I=1$, we may prove $I^2 = 1$ because of $f(x) > 0$ for all x, which is shown as follows

$$I^2 = \left(\int_{-\infty}^{+\infty} f(x) dx \right)^2 = \left(\int_{-\infty}^{+\infty} f(x) dx \right) \left(\int_{-\infty}^{+\infty} f(y) dy \right) =$$

$$\left(\int_{-\infty}^{+\infty} \frac{1}{\sqrt{2\pi}} \exp\left(-\frac{1}{2}x^2\right) dx \right) \left(\int_{-\infty}^{+\infty} \frac{1}{\sqrt{2\pi}} \exp\left(-\frac{1}{2}y^2\right) dy \right) =$$

$$\frac{1}{2\pi} \int_{-\infty}^{+\infty} \int_{-\infty}^{+\infty} \exp\left(-\frac{1}{2}(x^2+y^2)\right) dxdy =$$

$$\frac{1}{2\pi} \int_0^{2\pi} \int_0^{+\infty} \exp\left(-\frac{1}{2}r^2\right) r dr d\theta =$$

$$\frac{1}{2\pi} \int_0^{2\pi} \int_0^{+\infty} \exp(-s) ds d\theta = \frac{1}{2\pi} 2\pi [-\exp(-s)]_0^{+\infty} = 1$$

In the fifth equality, integration by substitution is used. See Appendix 2.1 for the integration by substitution. $x = r\cos\theta$ and $y = r\sin\theta$ are taken for transformation, which is a one-to-one transformation from (x,y) to (r,θ). Note that $0<r<+\infty$ and $0<\theta<2\pi$. The Jacobian is given by

$$J = \begin{vmatrix} \frac{\partial x}{\partial r} & \frac{\partial x}{\partial \theta} \\ \frac{\partial y}{\partial r} & \frac{\partial y}{\partial \theta} \end{vmatrix} = \begin{vmatrix} \cos\theta & -r\sin\theta \\ \sin\theta & r\cos\theta \end{vmatrix} = r$$

In the inner integration of the sixth equality, again, integration by substitution is utilized, where transformation is $s = \frac{1}{2}r^2$.

Thus, we obtain the result $I^2 = 1$ and accordingly we have $I = 1$ because of $f(x) \geq 0$. Therefore, $f(x) = e^{-\frac{1}{2}x^2}/\sqrt{2\pi}$ is also taken as a probability density function. Actually, this density function is called the standard normal probability density function.

Distribution Function   The *distribution function* (or the *cumulative distribution function*), denoted by $F(x)$, is defined as
$$P(X \leq x) = F(x)$$
which represents the probability less than x. The properties of the distribution function $F(x)$ are given by
$$F(x_i) \leq F(x_i) \text{ for } x_1 < x_2$$
$$P(a < X \leq b) = F(b) - F(a) \text{ for } a < b$$
$$F(-\infty) = 0, F(+\infty) = 1$$
The difference between the discrete and continuous random variables is given by

(1) Discrete random variable (see Fig. 2.1)
$$F(x) = \sum_{i=1}^{r} f(x_i) = \sum_{i=1}^{r} p_i$$
where r denotes the integer which satisfies $x_r \leq x < x_{r+1}$
$$F(x_i) - F(x_i - \varepsilon) = f(x_i) = p_i$$
where ε is a small positive number less than $x_i - x_{i-1}$.

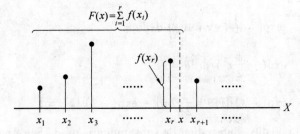

Note that r is the integer which satisfies $x_r \leq x \leq x_{r+1}$

Fig. 2.1   Probability Function $f(x)$ and Distribution Function $F(x)$ (Discrete Random Variable)

(2) Continuous random variable (see Fig. 2.2)
$$F(x) = \int_{-\infty}^{x} f(t) \, dt$$
$$F'(x) = f(x)$$

$f(x)$ and $F(x)$ are displayed in Fig. 2.1 for a discrete random variable and Fig. 2.2 for a continuous random variable.

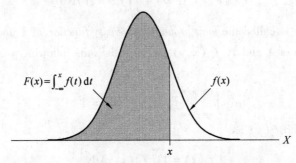

Fig. 2.2　Density Function $f(x)$ and Distribution Function $F(x)$ (Continuous Random Variable)

2.2.2　Multivariate Random Variable and Distribution

We consider two random variables X and Y in this section. It is easy to extend to more than two random variables.

Discrete Random Variables　Suppose that discrete random variables X and Y take $x_1, x_2, \ldots$, and $y_1, y_2, \ldots$, respectively. The probability which event $\{\omega | X(\omega) = x_i, \text{ and } Y(\omega) = y_i\}$ occurs is given by
$$P(X = x_i, Y = y_j) = f_{xy}(x_i, y_j)$$
where $f_{xy}(x_i, y_j)$ represents the *joint probability function* of X and Y. In order for $f_{xy}(x_i, y_j)$ to be a joint probability function, $f_{xy}(x_i, y_j)$ has to satisfies the following properties
$$f_{xy}(x_i, y_j) \geq 0, i, j = 1, 2, \ldots$$
$$\sum_i \sum_j f_{xy}(x_i, y_j) = 1$$
Define $f_x(x_i)$ and $f_y(y_j)$ as
$$f_x(x_i) = \sum_j f_{xy}(x_i, y_j), \ i = 1, 2, \ldots$$
$$f_y(y_j) = \sum_i f_{xy}(x_i, y_j), \ j = 1, 2, \ldots$$
Then, $f_x(x_i)$ and $f_y(y_j)$ are called the *marginal probability functions* of X and Y. $f_x(x_i)$ and $f_y(y_j)$ also have the properties of the probability functions, i.e., $f_x(x_i) \geq 0$ and $\sum_i f_x(x_i) = 1$, and $f_y(y_j) \geq 0$ and $\sum_j f_y(y_j) = 1$.

Continuous Random Variables　Consider two continuous random variables X and Y. For a domain D, the probability which event $\{\omega | (X(\omega), Y(\omega)) \in D\}$

occurs is given by
$$P((X,Y) \in D) = \iint_D f_{xy}(x,y)\,dxdy$$
where $f_{xy}(x,y)$ is called the *joint probability density function* of X and Y or the *joint density function* of X and Y. $f_{xy}(x,y)$ has to satisfy the following properties
$$f_{xy}(x,y) \geq 0$$
$$\int_{-\infty}^{+\infty}\int_{-\infty}^{+\infty} f_{xy}(x,y)\,dxdy = 1$$
Define $f_x(x)$ and $f_y(y)$ as
$$f_x(x) = \int_{-\infty}^{+\infty} f_{xy}(x,y)\,dy$$
for all x and y
$$f_y(y) = \int_{-\infty}^{+\infty} f_{xy}(x,y)\,dx$$
where $f_x(x)$ and $f_y(y)$ are called the *marginal probability density functions* of X and Y or the *marginal density functions* of X and Y.

For example, consider the event $\{\omega \mid a<X(\omega)<b,\ c<Y(\omega)<d\}$, which is a specific case of the domain D. Then, the probability that we have the event $\{\omega \mid a<X(\omega)<b,\ c<Y(\omega)<d\}$ is written as
$$P(a < X < b, c < Y < d) = \int_a^b\int_c^d f_{xy}(x,y)\,dxdy$$

The mixture of discrete and continuous random variables is also possible. For example, let X be a discrete random variable and Y be a continuous random variable. X takes $x_1, x_2,\ldots$ The probability which both X takes x_i and Y takes real numbers within the interval I is given by
$$P(X = x_i, Y \in I) = \int_I f_{xy}(x_i,y)\,dy$$
Then, we have the following properties
$$f_{xy}(x_i,y) \geq 0$$
for all y and $i = 1, 2, \ldots$
$$\sum_i \int_{-\infty}^{+\infty} f_{xy}(x_i,y)\,dy = 1$$
The marginal probability function of X is given by
$$f_x(x_i) = \int_{-\infty}^{+\infty} f_{xy}(x_i,y)\,dy$$
for $i = 1, 2, \ldots$ The marginal probability density function of Y is
$$f_y(y) = \sum_i f_{xy}(x_i,y)$$

2.2.3 Conditional Distribution

Discrete Random Variable The *conditional probability function* of X given $Y=y_j$ is represented as

$$P(X=x_i \mid Y=y_j) = f_{x\mid y}(x_i \mid y_j) = \frac{f_{xy}(x_i,y_j)}{f_y(y_j)} = \frac{f_{xy}(x_i,y_j)}{\sum_i f_{xy}(x_i,y_j)}$$

The second equality indicates the definition of the conditional probability, which is shown in Section 2.1.2. The features of the conditional probability function $f_{x\mid y}(x_i\mid y_j)$ are

$$f_{x\mid y}(x_i \mid y_j) \geq 0, i=1,2,\ldots$$

$$\sum_i f_{x\mid y}(x_i \mid y_j) = 1 \text{ (for any } j)$$

Continuous Random Variable The *conditional probability density function* of X given $Y=y$ (or the *conditional density function* of X given $Y=y$) is

$$f_{x\mid y}(x \mid y) = \frac{f_{xy}(x,y)}{f_y(y)} = \frac{f_{xy}(x,y)}{\int_{-\infty}^{+\infty} f_{xy}(x,y)\,\mathrm{d}x}$$

The properties of the conditional probability density function $f_{x\mid y}(x\mid y)$ are given by

$$f_{x\mid y}(x \mid y) \geq 0$$

$$\int_{-\infty}^{+\infty} f_{x\mid y}(x \mid y)\,\mathrm{d}x = 1 \text{ (for any } Y=y)$$

Independence of Random Variables For discrete random variables X and Y, we say that X is *independent* (or *stochastically independent*) of Y if and only if $f_{xy}(x_i,y_j) = f_x(x_i)f_y(y_j)$. Similarly, for continuous random variables X and Y, we say that X is independent of Y if and only if

$$f_{xy}(x,y) = f_x(x)f_y(y)$$

When X and Y are stochastically independent, $g(X)$ and $h(Y)$ are also stochastically independent, where $g(X)$ and $h(Y)$ are functions of X and Y.

2.2.4 Several Distribution

We now list some the most commonly used discrete random variables and their probability distributions, see following Table 2.1. Similarly, there are some the most commonly used continuous random variables and their probability distributions, see following Table 2.2.

Table 2.1 discrete random variables and their probability distributions

Distribution	$P(X=t)$	Parameters
Uniform	$\dfrac{1}{b-a+1}$, $(t=a, a+1,\ldots,b)$	a,b
Binomial	$\binom{n}{t}p^t(1-p)^t$, $(t=0,1,\ldots,n)$	n,p
Poisson	$\dfrac{\exp(-\lambda)\lambda^t}{t!}$, $(t=0, 1, 2,\ldots)$	λ
Hypergeometric	$\dfrac{\binom{M}{t}\binom{N-M}{n-t}}{\binom{N}{n}}$ $t_1 \leq t \leq t_2$ where $t_1 = \max(0, n-N-M)$ $t_2 = \min(M, n)$	M,N,n
Geometirc	$p(1-p)^t$, $(t=0, 1, 2,\ldots)$	p

Table 2.2 continuous random variables and their probability distributions

Distribution	pdf $f_X(t)$	Parameters
Uniform	$\begin{cases}\dfrac{1}{b-a}, & (a \leq t \leq b) \\ 0, & (\text{elsewhere})\end{cases}$	a,b
Normal	$\dfrac{1}{\sigma\sqrt{2\pi}}\exp\left(-\dfrac{(t-\mu)^2}{2\sigma^2}\right)$, $(t \in \mathbf{R})$	μ,σ
Cauchy	$\dfrac{1}{\pi(1+t^2)}$, $t \in \mathbf{R}$	
Gamma	$\begin{cases}\dfrac{1}{\Gamma(\alpha)\beta^\alpha}\exp\left(\dfrac{-t}{\beta}\right)t^{\alpha-1}, & (t>0) \\ 0, & (t \leq 0)\end{cases}$	α,β

Words and Expressions

random variable 随机变量
spot *n*. 点数
discrete random variable 离散随机变量
continuous random variable 连续随机变量
probability function 概率函数
binominal distribution 二项式分布

probability density function 概率密度函数
density function 密度函数
uniform distribution 一致分布,均匀分布
integration by substitution 积分换元法
one-to-one 一对一的
Jacobian n. 雅可比行列式,函数行列式
joint probability function 联合概率函数
marginal probability function 边际概率函数
joint probability density function 联合概率密度函数
marginal probability density function 边际概率密度函数
independence n. 独立性,无关性
stochastically independent 随机独立的
if and only if 当且仅当
Poisson distribution 泊松分布
Hypergeometric distribution 超几何分布
Geometirc distribution 几何分布
Cauchy distribution 柯西分布
Gamma distribution 伽玛分布,Γ 分布

2.3 Mathematical Expectation

2.3.1 Univariate Random Variable

Definition of Mathematical Expectation: let $g(X)$ be a function of random variable X. The mathematical expectation of $g(X)$, denoted by $E(g(X))$, is defined as follows

$$E(g(X)) = \begin{cases} \sum_i g(x_i)p_i = \sum_i g(x_i)f(x_i), \text{Discrete Random Variable} \\ \int_{-\infty}^{+\infty} g(x)f(x)\,dx, \text{Continuous Random Variable} \end{cases}$$

The following three functional forms of $g(X)$ are important.

1. $g(X) = X$

The expectation of X, $E(X)$, is know as *mean* of random variable X

$$E(X) = \begin{cases} \sum_i x_i f(x_i), \text{Discrete Random Variable} \\ \int_{-\infty}^{+\infty} x f(x)\,dx, \text{Continuous Random Variable} \end{cases}$$

$$\mu \text{ (or } \mu_x)$$

When a distribution of X is symmetric, mean indicates the center of the distribution.

2. $g(X) = (X-\mu)^2$

The expectation of $(X-\mu)^2$ is known as *variance* of random variable X, which is denoted by $V(X)$.

$$V(X) = E((X-\mu)^2) = \begin{cases} \sum_i (x_i - \mu)^2 f(x_i), \text{Discrete Random Variable} \\ \int_{-\infty}^{+\infty} (x-\mu)^2 f(x) dx, \text{Continuous Random Variable} \end{cases} =$$

$$\sigma^2 \text{ (or } \sigma_x^2)$$

If X is broadly distributed, $\sigma^2 = V(X)$ becomes large. Conversely, if the distribution is concentrated on the center, σ^2 becomes small. Note that $\sigma = \sqrt{V(X)}$ is called the *standard deviation*.

3. $g(X) = e^{\theta X}$

The expectation of $e^{\theta X}$ is called the *moment-generating function*, which is denoted by $\varnothing(\theta)$

$$\varnothing(\theta) = E(e^{\theta X}) = \begin{cases} \sum_i e^{\theta x_i} f(x_i), \text{Discrete Random Variable} \\ \int_{-\infty}^{+\infty} e^{\theta x} f(x) dx, \text{Continuous Random Variable} \end{cases}$$

Note that the definition of e is given by

$$e = \lim_{x \to 0}(1+x)^{\frac{1}{x}} = \lim_{h \to 0}(1+\frac{1}{h})^h = 2.718\ 281\ 828\ 459\ 05$$

The moment-generating function plays an important role in statistics, which is discussed in Section 2.5.

In Examples 2.5 ~ 2.8, mean, variance and the moment-generating function are computed.

Example 2.5

In Example 2.2 of flipping a coin three times (Section 2.1.1), we see in Section 2.2.1 that the probability function is written as the following binomial distribution

$$P(X=x) = f(x) = \frac{n!}{x!\ (n-x)!} p^x (1-p)^{n-x}$$

$$\text{for } x = 0, 1, 2, \cdots, n$$

where $n = 3$ and $p = 1/2$. When X has the binomial distribution above, we obtain $E(X), V(X)$ and $\varnothing(\theta)$ as follows.

First, $\mu = E(X)$ is computed as

$$\mu = E(X) = \sum_x x f(x) = \sum_x x \frac{n!}{x!(n-x)!} p^x (1-p)^{n-x} =$$

$$\sum_x \frac{n!}{(x-1)!(n-x)!} p^x (1-p)^{n-x} =$$

$$np \sum_x \frac{(n-1)!}{(x-1)!(n-x)!} p^{x-1}(1-p)^{n-x} =$$

$$np \sum_{x'} \frac{n'!}{x'!(n'-x')!} p^{x'}(1-p)^{n'-x'} = np$$

where $n' = n-1$ and $x' = x-1$ are set.

Second, in order to obtain $\sigma^2 = V(X)$, we rewrite $V(X)$ as

$$\sigma^2 = V(X) = E(X^2) - \mu^2 = E(X(X-1)) + \mu - \mu^2$$

$E(X(X-1))$ is given by

$$E(X(X-1)) = \sum_x x(x-1)f(x) =$$

$$\sum_x x(x-1)\frac{n!}{x!(n-x)!} p^x (1-p)^{n-x} =$$

$$\sum_x \frac{n!}{(x-2)!(n-x)!} p^x (1-p)^{n-x} =$$

$$n(n-1)p^2 \sum_x \frac{(n-2)!}{(x-2)!(n-x)!} p^{x-2}(1-p)^{n-x} =$$

$$n(n-1)p^2 \sum_{x'} \frac{n'!}{x'!(n'-x')!} p^{x'}(1-p)^{n'-x'} =$$

$$n(n-1)p^2$$

where $n' = n-2$ and $x' = x-2$ are re-defined. Therefore, $\sigma^2 = V(X)$ is obtained as

$$\sigma^2 = V(X) = E(X(X-1)) + \mu - \mu^2 =$$

$$n(n-1)p^2 + np - n^2 p^2 =$$

$$-np^2 + np = np(1-p)$$

Finally, the moment-generating function $\emptyset(\theta)$ is represented as

$$\emptyset(\theta) = E(e^{\theta x}) = \sum_x e^{\theta x} \frac{n!}{x!(n-x)!} p^x (1-p)^{n-p} =$$

$$\sum_x \frac{n!}{x!(n-x)!} (pe^\theta)^x (1-p)^{n-p} = (pe^\theta + 1 - p)^n$$

In the last equality, we utilize the following formula

$$(a+b)^n = \sum_{k=0}^n \frac{n!}{x!(n-x)!} a^x b^{n-x}$$

which is called the *binomial theorem*.

Example 2.6

As an example of continuous random variables, in Section 2.2.1 the uniform distribution is introduced, which is given by

$$f(x) = \begin{cases} 1, & \text{for } 0<x<1 \\ 0, & \text{otherwise} \end{cases}$$

When X has the uniform distribution above, $E(X)$, $V(X)$ and $\phi(\theta)$ are computed as follows

$$\mu = E(X) = \int_{-\infty}^{+\infty} xf(x)\,dx = \int_0^1 x\,dx = \left[\frac{1}{2}x^2\right]_0^1 = \frac{1}{2}$$

$$\sigma^2 = V(X) = E(X^2) - \mu^2 = \int_{-\infty}^{+\infty} x^2 f(x)\,dx - \mu^2 =$$

$$\int_0^1 x^2\,dx - \mu^2 = \left[\frac{1}{3}x^3\right]_0^1 - \left(\frac{1}{2}\right)^2 = \frac{1}{12}$$

$$\phi(\theta) = E(e^{\theta x}) = \int_{-\infty}^{+\infty} e^{\theta x} f(x)\,dx = \int_0^1 e^{\theta x}\,dx =$$

$$\left[\frac{1}{\theta}e^{\theta x}\right]_0^1 = \frac{1}{\theta}(e^\theta - 1)$$

Example 2.7

As another example of continuous random variables, we take the standard normal distribution

$$f(x) = \frac{1}{\sqrt{2\pi}} e^{-\frac{1}{2}x^2}, \quad \text{for } -\infty < x < +\infty$$

When X has a standard normal distribution, i.e., when $X \sim N(0, 1)$, $E(X)$, $V(X)$ and $\phi(\theta)$ are as follows.

$E(X)$ is obtained as

$$E(X) = \int_{-\infty}^{+\infty} xf(x)\,dx = \frac{1}{\sqrt{2\pi}} \int_{-\infty}^{+\infty} x e^{-\frac{1}{2}x^2}\,dx =$$

$$\frac{1}{\sqrt{2\pi}} [-e^{-\frac{1}{2}x^2}]_{-\infty}^{+\infty} = 0$$

because $\lim_{x \to \pm\infty} -e^{-\frac{1}{2}x^2} = 0$.

$V(X)$ is computed as follows

$$V(X) = E(X^2) = \int_{-\infty}^{+\infty} x^2 f(x)\,dx = \int_{-\infty}^{+\infty} x^2 \frac{1}{\sqrt{2\pi}} e^{-\frac{1}{2}x^2}\,dx =$$

$$\frac{1}{\sqrt{2\pi}} \int_{-\infty}^{+\infty} x \frac{d(-e^{-\frac{1}{2}x^2})}{dx}\,dx =$$

$$\frac{1}{\sqrt{2\pi}}[x(-e^{-\frac{1}{2}x^2})]\Big|_{-\infty}^{+\infty} + \frac{1}{\sqrt{2\pi}}\int_{-\infty}^{+\infty} e^{-\frac{1}{2}x^2}dx =$$

$$\int_{-\infty}^{+\infty} \frac{1}{\sqrt{2\pi}} e^{-\frac{1}{2}x^2}dx = 1$$

The first equality holds because of $E(X) = 0$. In the fifth equality, use the following integration formula, called the *integration by parts*

$$\int_a^b h(x)g'(x)dx = [h(x)g(x)]\Big|_a^b - \int_a^b h'(x)g(x)dx$$

where we take $h(x) = x$ and $g(x) = -e^{-\frac{1}{2}x^2}$ in this case. See Appendix 2.2 for the integration by parts. In the sixth equality, $\lim_{x\to\pm\infty} -xe^{-\frac{1}{2}x^2} = 0$ is utilized. The last equality is because the integration of the standard normal probability density function is equal to one (see Section 2.2.1 for the integration of the standard normal probability density function).

$\phi(\theta)$ is derived as follows

$$\phi(\theta) = \int_{-\infty}^{+\infty} e^{\theta x} f(x)dx = \int_{-\infty}^{+\infty} e^{\theta x} \frac{1}{\sqrt{2\pi}} e^{-\frac{1}{2}x^2}dx =$$

$$\int_{-\infty}^{+\infty} \frac{1}{\sqrt{2\pi}} e^{-\frac{1}{2}x^2+\theta x}dx = \int_{-\infty}^{+\infty} \frac{1}{\sqrt{2\pi}} e^{-\frac{1}{2}((x-\theta)^2-\theta^2)}dx =$$

$$e^{\frac{1}{2}\theta^2}\int_{-\infty}^{+\infty} \frac{1}{\sqrt{2\pi}} e^{-\frac{1}{2}(x-\theta)^2}dx = e^{\frac{1}{2}\theta^2}$$

The last equality holds because the integration indicates the normal density with mean θ and variance one.

Example 2.8

When the moment-generating function of X is given by $\phi_x(\theta) = e^{\frac{1}{2}\theta^2}$ (i.e., X has a standard normal distribution), we want to obtain the moment-generating function of $Y = \mu + \sigma X$.

Let $\phi_x(\theta)$ and $\phi_y(\theta)$ be the moment-generating functions of X and Y, respectively. Then, the moment-generating function of Y is obtained as follows

$$\phi_y(\theta) = E(e^{\theta y}) = E(e^{\theta(\mu+\sigma x)}) = e^{\theta\mu}E(e^{\theta\sigma X}) = e^{\theta\mu}\phi_x(\theta\sigma) =$$

$$e^{\theta\mu}e^{\frac{1}{2}\sigma^2\theta^2} = \exp(\mu\theta + \frac{1}{2}\sigma^2\theta^2)$$

Some Formulas of Mean and Variance

1. Theorem

$$E(aX+b) = aE(X) + b$$

where a and b are constant.

Proof When X is a discrete random variable

$$E(aX + b) = \sum_i (ax_i + b)f(x_i) = a\sum_i x_i f(x_i) + b\sum_i f(x_i) = aE(X) + b$$

Note that we have $\sum_i x_i f(x_i) = E(X)$ from the definition of mean and $\sum_i f(x_i) = 1$ because $f(x_i)$ is a probability function.

If X is a continuous random variable

$$E(aX + b) = \int_{-\infty}^{+\infty} (ax + b)f(x)\,dx =$$

$$a\int_{-\infty}^{+\infty} xf(x)\,dx + b\int_{-\infty}^{+\infty} f(x)\,dx$$

Similarly, note that we have $\int_{-\infty}^{+\infty} xf(x)\,dx = E(X)$ from the definition of mean and $\int_{-\infty}^{+\infty} f(x)\,dx = 1$ because $f(x)$ is a probability density function.

2. Theorem

$$V(X) = E(X^2) - \mu^2$$

where
$$\mu = E(X)$$

Proof

$$V(X) = E((X - \mu)^2) = E(X^2 - 2\mu X - \mu^2) = E(X^2) - 2\mu E(X) + \mu^2 = E(X^2) - \mu^2$$

The first equality is due to the definition of variance.

3. Theorem

$$V(aX+b) = a^2 V(X)$$

where a and b are constant.

Proof From the definition of the mathematical expectation, $V(aX+b)$ is represented as

$$V(aX+b) = E(((aX+b) - E(aX+b))^2) = E((aX - a\mu)^2) = E(a^2(X-\mu)^2) = a^2 E((X-\mu)^2) = a^2 V(X)$$

The first and the fifth equalities are from the definition of variance. We use $E(aX+b) = a\mu + b$ in the second equality.

4. Theorem

The random variable X is assumed to be distributed with mean $E(X) = \mu$ and variance $V(X) = \sigma^2$. Define $Z = (X-\mu)/\sigma$. Then, we have $E(Z) = 0$ and $V(Z) = 1$.

Proof $E(X)$ and $V(X)$ are obtained as

$$E(Z) = E\left(\frac{X-\mu}{\sigma}\right) = \frac{E(X)-\mu}{\sigma} = 0$$

$$V(Z) = V\left(\frac{1}{\sigma}X - \frac{\mu}{\sigma}\right) = \frac{1}{\sigma^2}V(X) = 1$$

The transformation from X to Z is known as normalization or standardization.

2.3.2 Bivariate Random Variable

Definition

Let $g(X, Y)$ be a function of random variables X and Y. The mathematical expectation of $g(X,Y)$, denoted by $E(g(X, Y))$, is defined as

$$E(g(X,Y)) = \begin{cases} \sum_i \sum_j g(x_i, y_j) f(x_i, y_j), \\ \text{Discrete Random Variable} \\ \int_{-\infty}^{+\infty} \int_{-\infty}^{+\infty} g(x,y) f(x,y) \,\mathrm{d}x \mathrm{d}y, \\ \text{Continuous Random Variable} \end{cases}$$

The following four functional forms are important, i.e., mean, variance, covariance and the moment-generating function.

1. $g(X,Y) = X$

The expectation of random variable X, i.e., $E(X)$, is given by

$$E(X) = \begin{cases} \sum_i \sum_j x_i f(x_i, y_j), \text{Discrete Random Variable} \\ \int_{-\infty}^{+\infty} \int_{-\infty}^{+\infty} x f(x,y) \,\mathrm{d}x \mathrm{d}y, \text{Continuous Random Variable} \end{cases}$$

The case of $g(X,Y) = Y$ is exactly the same formulation as above, i.e., $E(Y) = \mu_y$.

2. $g(X,Y) = (X-\mu_x)^2$

The expectation of $(X-\mu_x)^2$ is known as variance of random variable X, which is denoted by $V(X)$ and represented as follows

$$V(X) = E((X-\mu_x)^2) = \begin{cases} \sum_i \sum_j (x_i - \mu_x)^2 f(x_i, y_j), \\ \text{Discrete Random Variable} \\ \int_{-\infty}^{+\infty} \int_{-\infty}^{+\infty} (x-\mu_x)^2 f(x,y) \,\mathrm{d}x \mathrm{d}y, \\ \text{Continuous Random Variable} \end{cases} = \sigma_x^2$$

The variance of Y is also obtained in the fashion, i.e., $V(Y) = \sigma_y^2$.

3. $g(X,Y) = (X-\mu_x)(Y-\mu_y)$

The expectation of $(X-\mu_x)(Y-\mu_y)$ is known as *covariance* of X and Y, which

is denoted by Cov(X, Y) and written as
$$\text{Cov}(X,Y) = E((X - \mu_x)(Y - \mu_y)) =$$
$$\begin{cases} \sum_i \sum_j (x_i - \mu_x)(y_j - \mu_y) f(x_i, y_j) & \text{(Discrete Case)} \\ \int_{-\infty}^{+\infty} \int_{-\infty}^{+\infty} (x - \mu_x)(y - \mu_y) f(x,y) \, dxdy & \text{(Continuous Case)} \end{cases}$$

Thus, covariance is defined in the case of bivariate random variables.

4. $g(X,Y) = e^{\theta_1 X + \theta_2 Y}$

The mathematical expectation of $e^{\theta_1 X + \theta_2 Y}$ is called the moment-generating function, which is denoted by $\phi(\theta_1, \theta_2)$ and written as
$$\phi(\theta_1, \theta_2) = E(e^{\theta_1 X + \theta_2 Y}) =$$
$$\begin{cases} \sum_i \sum_j e^{\theta_1 x_i + \theta_2 y_j} f(x_i, y_j) & \text{(Discrete Case)} \\ \int_{-\infty}^{+\infty} \int_{-\infty}^{+\infty} e^{\theta_1 x + \theta_2 y} f(x,y) \, dxdy & \text{(Continuous Case)} \end{cases}$$

In Section 2.5, the moment-generating function in the multivariate cases is discussed in more detail.

Some Formulas of Mean and Variance

We consider two random variables X and Y. Some formulas are shown as follows.

1. Theorem
$$E(X+Y) = E(X) + E(Y)$$

Proof For discrete random variables X and Y, it is given by
$$E(X + Y) = \sum_i \sum_j (x_i + y_j) f_{xy}(x_i, y_j) =$$
$$\sum_i \sum_j x_i f_{xy}(x_i, y_j) + \sum_i \sum_j y_j f_{xy}(x_i, y_j) =$$
$$E(X) + E(Y)$$

For continuous random variables X and Y, we can show
$$E(X + Y) = \int_{-\infty}^{+\infty} \int_{-\infty}^{+\infty} (x + y) f_{xy}(x,y) \, dxdy =$$
$$\int_{-\infty}^{+\infty} \int_{-\infty}^{+\infty} x f_{xy}(x,y) \, dxdy + \int_{-\infty}^{+\infty} \int_{-\infty}^{+\infty} y f_{xy}(x,y) \, dxdy =$$
$$E(X) + E(Y)$$

2. Theorem
$$E(XY) = E(X) E(Y)$$

when X is independent of Y.

Proof For discrete random variables X and Y

$$E(XY) = \sum_i \sum_j x_i y_j f_{xy}(x_i, y_j) = \sum_i \sum_j x_i y_j f_x(x_i) f_y(y_j) =$$
$$\left(\sum_i x_i f_x(x_i)\right)\left(\sum_j y_j f_y(y_j)\right) = E(X)E(Y)$$

If X is independent of Y, the second equality holds, i.e., $f_{xy}(x_i, y_j) = f_x(x_i) f_y(y_j)$. For continuous random variables X and Y

$$E(XY) = \int_{-\infty}^{+\infty} \int_{-\infty}^{+\infty} xy f_{xy}(x, y) \, dx dy =$$
$$\int_{-\infty}^{+\infty} \int_{-\infty}^{+\infty} xy f_x(x) f_y(y) \, dx dy =$$
$$\left(\int_{-\infty}^{+\infty} x f_x(x) \, dx\right) \left(\int_{-\infty}^{+\infty} y f_y(y) \, dy\right) =$$
$$E(X)E(Y)$$

When X is independent of Y, we have $f_{xy}(x, y) = f_x(x) f_y(y)$ in the second equality.

3. Theorem
$$\text{Cov}(X, Y) = E(XY) - E(X)E(Y)$$

Proof For both discrete and continuous random variables, we can rewrite as follows
$$\text{Cov}(X, Y) = E((X - \mu_x)(Y - \mu_y)) =$$
$$E(XY - \mu_x Y - \mu_y X + \mu_x \mu_y) =$$
$$E(XY) - E(\mu_x Y) - E(\mu_y X) + \mu_x \mu_y =$$
$$E(XY) - \mu_x E(Y) - \mu_y E(X) + \mu_x \mu_y =$$
$$E(XY) - \mu_x \mu_y - \mu_y \mu_x + \mu_x \mu_y = E(XY) - \mu_x \mu_y =$$
$$E(XY) - E(X)E(Y)$$

In the fourth equality, the theorem in Section 2.3.1 is used, i.e., $E(\mu_x Y) = \mu_x E(Y)$ and $E(\mu_y X) = \mu_y E(X)$.

4. Theorem
$$\text{Cov}(X, Y) = 0$$
when X is independent of Y.

Proof From the above two theorems, we have $E(XY) = E(X)E(Y)$ when X is independent of Y and $\text{Cov}(X, Y) = E(XY) - E(X)E(Y)$. Therefore, $\text{Cov}(X, Y) = 0$ is obtained when X is independent of Y.

5. Definition

The *correlation coefficient* between X and Y, denoted by ρ_{xy}, is defined as

$$\rho_{xy} = \frac{\text{Cov}(X, Y)}{\sqrt{V(X)} \sqrt{V(Y)}} = \frac{\text{Cov}(X, Y)}{\sigma_x \sigma_y}$$

When $\rho_{xy}>0$, we say that there is a *positive correlation* between X and Y. As ρ_{xy} approaches 1, we say that there is a *strong positive correlation* between X and Y. When $\rho_{xy}<0$, we say that there is a *negative correlation* between X and Y. As ρ_{xy} approaches -1, we say that there is a *strong negative correlation* between X and Y.

6. Theorem

$$\rho_{xy}=0$$

when X is independent of Y.

Proof When X is independent of Y, we have $\text{Cov}(X,Y)=0$. Therefore, we can obtain the result $\rho_{xy} = \dfrac{\text{Cov}(X,Y)}{\sqrt{V(X)}\sqrt{V(Y)}} = 0$. However, note that $\rho_{xy}=0$ does not mean the independence between X and Y.

7. Theorem

$$V(X \pm Y) = V(X) \pm 2\text{Cov}(X,Y) + V(Y)$$

Proof For both discrete and continuous random variables, $V(X \pm Y)$ is rewritten as follows

$$V(X+Y) = E(((X \pm Y) - E(X \pm Y))^2) =$$
$$E(((X-\mu_x) \pm (Y-\mu_y))^2) =$$
$$E((X-\mu_x)^2 \pm 2(X-\mu_x)(Y-\mu_y) + (Y-\mu_y)^2) =$$
$$E((X-\mu_x)^2 \pm 2E((X-\mu_x)(Y-\mu_y)) + E(Y-\mu_y)^2) =$$
$$V(X) \pm 2\text{Cov}(X,Y) + V(Y)$$

8. Theorem

$$-1 \leq \rho_{xy} \leq 1$$

Proof Consider the following function of t: $f(t) = V(Xt-Y)$, which is always greater than or equal to zero because of the definition of variance. Therefore, for all t, we have $f(t) \geq 0$. $f(t)$ is rewritten as follows

$$f(t) = V(Xt-Y) = V(Xt) - 2\text{Cov}(Xt,Y) + V(Y) =$$
$$t^2 V(X) - 2t\text{Cov}(X,Y) + V(Y) =$$
$$V(X)\left(t - \frac{\text{Cov}(X,Y)}{V(X)}\right)^2 + V(Y) - \frac{(\text{Cov}(X,Y))^2}{V(X)}$$

In order to have $f(t) \geq 0$ for all t, we need the following condition

$$V(Y) - \frac{(\text{Cov}(X,Y))^2}{V(X)} \geq 0$$

because the first term in the last equality is nonnegative, which implies

$$\frac{(\text{Cov}(X,Y))^2}{V(X)V(Y)} \leq 1$$

Therefore, we have
$$-1 \leq \frac{\text{Cov}(X,Y)}{\sqrt{V(X)}\sqrt{V(Y)}} \leq 1$$

From the definition of correlation coefficient, i. e., $\rho_{xy} = \frac{\text{Cov}(X,Y)}{\sqrt{V(X)}\sqrt{V(Y)}}$, we obtain the result: $-1 \leq \rho_{xy} \leq 1$.

9. Theorem
$$V(X \pm Y) = V(X) + V(Y)$$
when X is independent of Y.

Proof From the theorem above, $V(X \pm Y) = V(X) \pm 2\text{Cov}(X,y) + V(Y)$ generally holds. When random variables X and Y are independent, we have $\text{Cov}(X, Y) = 0$. Therefore, $V(X+Y) = V(X) + V(Y)$ holds, when X is independent of Y.

10. Theorem
For n random variables $X_1, X_2, \ldots, X_n$
$$E(\sum_i a_i X_i) = \sum_i a_i \mu_i$$
$$V(\sum_i a_i X_i) = \sum_i \sum_j a_i a_j \text{Cov}(X_i, X_j)$$

where $E(X_i) = \mu_i$ and a_i is a constant value. Especially, when $X_1, X_2, \ldots, X_n$ are mutually independent, we have the following
$$V(\sum_i a_i X_i) = \sum_i a_i^2 V(X_i)$$

Proof For mean of $\sum_i a_i X_i$, the following representation is obtained
$$E(\sum_i a_i X_i) = \sum_i E(a_i X_i) = \sum_i a_i E(X_i) = \sum_i a_i \mu_i$$

The first and second equalities come from the previous theorems on mean.

For variance of $\sum_i a_i X_i$, we can rewrite as follows
$$V(\sum_i a_i X_i) = E(\sum_i a_i (X_i - \mu_i))^2 =$$
$$E(\sum_i a_i (X_i - \mu_i))(\sum_j a_j (X_j - \mu_j)) =$$
$$E(\sum_i \sum_j a_i a_j (X_i - \mu_i)(X_j - \mu_j)) =$$
$$\sum_i \sum_j a_i a_j E((X_i - \mu_i)(X_j - \mu_j)) =$$
$$\sum_i \sum_j a_i a_j \text{Cov}(X_i, X_j)$$

When $X_1, X_2, \ldots, X_n$ are mutually independent, we obtain $\text{Cov}(X_i, X_j) = 0$ for all

$i \neq j$ from the previous theorem. Therefore, we obtain
$$V(\sum_i a_i X_i) = \sum_i a_i^2 V(X_i)$$
Note that $\text{Cov}(X_i, X_i) = E((X_i - \mu)^2) = V(X_i)$.

11. Theorem

n random variables $X_1, X_2, \ldots, X_n$ are mutually independently and identically distributed with μ mean and variance σ^2. That is, for all $i = 1, 2, \ldots, n$, $E(X_i) = \mu$ and $V(X_i) = \sigma^2$ are assumed. Consider arithmetic average $\bar{X} = (1/n) \sum_i^n X_i$. Then, mean and variance of $\bar{X}$ are given by
$$E(\bar{X}) = \mu, \quad V(\bar{X}) = \frac{\sigma^2}{n}$$

Proof The mathematical expectation of $\bar{X}$ is given by
$$E(\bar{X}) = E\left(\frac{1}{n} \sum_{i=1}^n X_i\right) = \frac{1}{n} E\left(\sum_{i=1}^n X_i\right) =$$
$$\frac{1}{n} \sum_{i=1}^n E(X_i) = \frac{1}{n} \sum_{i=1}^n \mu = \frac{1}{n} n\mu = \mu$$

$E(aX) = aE(X)$ in the second equality and $E(X+Y) = E(X) + E(Y)$ in the third equality are utilized, where X and Y are random variables and a is a constant value. For these formulas, see Section 2.3.1 and this section.

The variance of $\bar{X}$ is computed as follows
$$V(\bar{X}) = V\left(\frac{1}{n} \sum_{i=1}^n X_i\right) = \frac{1}{n^2} V\left(\sum_{i=1}^n X_i\right) = \frac{1}{n^2} \sum_{i=1}^n V(X_i) =$$
$$\frac{1}{n^2} \sum_{i=1}^n \sigma^2 = \frac{1}{n^2} n\sigma^2 = \frac{\sigma^2}{n}$$

We use $V(aX) = a^2 V(X)$ in the second equality and $V(X+Y) = V(X) + V(Y)$ for X independent of Y in the third equality, where X and Y denote random variables and a is a constant value. For these formulas, see Section 2.3.1 and this section.

Words and Expressions

univariate *n.* 单变量,一元变量,一维变量
standard deviation *n.* 标准差
moment-generating function 矩母函数,矩生成函数
binominal theorem 二项式定理
integration by parts 分部积分法
bivariate *n.* 两变量,二元变量,二维变量

normalization *n*. 正规化
standardization *n*. 标准化
correlation coefficient 相关系数
positive correlation 正相关
negative correlation 负相关
arithmetic average 算术平均值

2.4 Transformation of Variables

Transformation of variables is used in the case of continuous random variables. Based on a distribution of a random variable, a distribution of the transformed random variable is derived. In other words, when a distribution of X is known, we can find a distribution of Y using the transformation of variables, where Y is a function of X.

2.4.1 Univariate Case

Distribution of $Y = \psi^{-1}(X)$: Let $f_x(x)$ be the probability density function of continuous random variable X and $X = \psi(Y)$ be a one-to-one transformation. Then, the probability density function of Y, i.e. $f_y(y)$, is given by
$$f_y(y) = |\psi'(y)| f_x(\psi(y))$$
We can derive the above transformation of variables from X to Y as follows. Let $f_x(x)$ and $F_x(x)$ be the probability density function and the distribution function of X, respectively. Note that $F_x(x) = P(X \leq x)$ and $f_x(x) = F'_x(x)$.

When $X = \psi(Y)$, we want to obtain the probability density function of Y. Let $f_y(y)$ and $F_y(y)$ be the probability density function and the distribution function of Y, respectively.

In the case of $\psi'(X) > 0$, the distribution function of Y, $F_y(y)$, is rewritten as follows
$$F_y(y) = P(Y \leq y) = P(\psi(Y) \leq \psi(y)) =$$
$$P(X \leq \psi(y)) = F_x(\psi(y))$$
The first equality is the definition of the cumulative distribution function. The second equality holds because $\psi'(Y) > 0$. Therefore, differentiating $F_y(y)$ with respect to y, we can obtain the following expression
$$f_y(y) = F'_y(y) = \psi'(y) F'_x(\psi(y)) = \psi'(y) f_x(\psi(y)) \qquad (2.4)$$
Next, in the case of $\psi'(X) < 0$, the distribution function of Y, $F_y(y)$, is rewritten as follows

$$F_y(y) = P(Y \leq y) = P(\psi(Y) \geq \psi(y)) = P(X \geq \psi(y)) =$$
$$1 - P(X < \psi(y)) = 1 - F_x(\psi(y))$$

Thus, in the case of $\psi'(X) < 0$, pay attention to the second equality, where the inequality sign is reversed. Differentiating $F_y(y)$ with respect to y, we obtain the following result

$$f_y(y) = F'_y(y) = -\psi'(y)F'_x(\psi(y)) = -\psi'(y)f_x(\psi(y)) \qquad (2.5)$$

Note that $-\psi'(Y) > 0$.

Thus, summarizing the above two cases, i.e., $\psi'(X) > 0$ and $\psi'(X) < 0$, equations (2.4) and (2.5) indicate the following result

$$f_y(y) = |\psi'(y)| f_x(\psi(y))$$

which is called the *transformation of variables*.

Example 2.9

When X has a standard normal density function. i.e., when $X \sim N(0, 1)$, we derive the probability density function of Y, where $Y = \mu + \sigma X$.

Since we have

$$X = \psi(Y) = \frac{Y - \mu}{\sigma}$$

$\psi'(y) = 1/\sigma$ is obtained. Therefore, the density function of Y, $f_y(y)$, is given by

$$f_y(y) = |\psi'(y)| f_x(\psi(y)) = \frac{1}{\sigma\sqrt{2\pi}} \exp\left(-\frac{1}{2\sigma^2}(y-\mu)^2\right)$$

which indicates the normal distribution with mean μ and variance σ^2, denoted by $N(\mu, \sigma^2)$.

On Distribution of $Y = X^2$ As an example, when we know the distribution function of X as $F_x(x)$, we want to obtain the distribution function of Y, $F_y(y)$, where $Y = X^2$. Using $F_x(x)$, $F_y(y)$ is rewritten as follows

$$F_y(y) = P(Y \leq y) = P(X^2 \leq y) = P(-\sqrt{y} \leq X \leq \sqrt{y}) =$$
$$F_x(\sqrt{y}) - F_x(-\sqrt{y})$$

Therefore, when we have $f_x(x)$ and $Y = X^2$, the probability density function of Y is obtained as follows

$$f_y(y) = F'_y(y) = \frac{1}{2\sqrt{y}}(f_x(\sqrt{y}) + f_x(-\sqrt{y}))$$

2.4.2 Multivariate Cases

Bivariate Case   Let $f_{xy}(x, y)$ be a joint probability density function of X and Y. Let $X = \psi_1(U, V)$ and $Y = \psi_2(U, V)$ be a one-to-one transformation from $(X, Y,)$

to (U, V). Then, we obtain a joint probability density function of U and V, denoted by $f_{uv}(u,v)$, as follows

$$f_{uv}(u,v) = |J| f_{xy}(\psi_1(u,v), \psi_2(u,v))$$

where J is called the *Jacobian* of the transformation, which is defined as

$$J = \begin{vmatrix} \dfrac{\partial x}{\partial u} & \dfrac{\partial x}{\partial v} \\ \dfrac{\partial y}{\partial u} & \dfrac{\partial y}{\partial v} \end{vmatrix}$$

Multivariate Case let $f_x(x_1, x_2, \ldots, x_n)$ be a joint probability density function of $X_1, X_2, \ldots, X_n$. Suppose that a one-to-one transformation from $(X_1, X_2, \ldots, X_n)$ to $(Y_1, Y_2, \ldots, Y_n)$ is given by

$$X_1 = \psi_1(Y_1, Y_2, \ldots, Y_n)$$
$$X_2 = \psi_2(Y_1, Y_2, \ldots, Y_n)$$
$$\vdots$$
$$X_n = \psi_n(Y_1, Y_2, \ldots, Y_n)$$

Then, we obtain a joint probability density function of $Y_1, Y_2, \ldots, Y_n$, denoted by $f_y = (y_1, y_2, \ldots, y_n)$, as follows

$$f_y(y_1, y_2, \ldots, y_n) =$$
$$|J| f_x(\psi_1(y_1, \ldots, y_n), \psi_2(y_1, \ldots, y_n), \ldots, \psi_n(y_1, \ldots, y_n))$$

Where J is called the Jacobian of the transformation, which is defined as

$$J = \begin{vmatrix} \dfrac{\partial x_1}{\partial y_1} & \dfrac{\partial x_1}{\partial y_2} & \cdots & \dfrac{\partial x_1}{\partial y_n} \\ \dfrac{\partial x_2}{\partial y_1} & \dfrac{\partial x_2}{\partial y_2} & \cdots & \dfrac{\partial x_2}{\partial y_n} \\ \vdots & \vdots & & \vdots \\ \dfrac{\partial x_n}{\partial y_1} & \dfrac{\partial x_n}{\partial y_2} & \cdots & \dfrac{\partial x_n}{\partial y_n} \end{vmatrix}$$

Words and Expressions

transformation of variables 变量变换,变数变换
one-to-one transformation ——变换
Jacobian of transformation 变换的雅可比行列式

2.5 Moment-Generating Function

2.5.1 Univariate Case

As discussed in Section 2.3.1, the moment-generating function is defined as

$\phi(\theta)=E(e^{\theta X})$. In this section, several important theorems and remarks of the moment-generating function are summarized.

For a random variable X, $\mu'_n \equiv E(X^n)$ is called the nth moment of X. Then, we have the following first theorem.

1. Theorem
$$\phi^{(n)}(0) = \mu'_n \equiv E(X^n)$$

Proof First, from the definition of the moment-generating function, $\phi(\theta)$ is written as
$$\phi(\theta) = E(e^{\theta X}) = \int_{-\infty}^{+\infty} e^{\theta x} f(x) \, dx$$

The nth derivative of $\phi(\theta)$, denoted by $\phi^{(n)}(\theta)$, is
$$\phi^{(n)}(\theta) = \int_{-\infty}^{+\infty} x^n e^{\theta x} f(x) \, dx$$

Evaluating $\phi^{(n)}(\theta)$ at $\theta=0$, we obtain
$$\phi^{(n)}(0) = \int_{-\infty}^{+\infty} x^n f(x) \, dx = E(X^n) \equiv \mu'_n$$

where the second equality comes from the definition of the mathematical expectation.

2. Remark
Let X and Y be two random variables. When the moment-generating function of X is equivalent to that of Y, we have the fact that X has the same distribution as Y.

3. Theorem
Let $\phi(\theta)$ be the moment-generating function of X. Then, the moment-generating function of Y, where $Y=aX+b$, is given by $e^{b\theta}\phi(a\theta)$.

Proof Let $\phi_y(\theta)$ be the moment-generating function of Y. Then, $\phi_y(\theta)$ is rewritten as follows
$$\phi_y(\theta) = E(e^{\theta Y}) = E(e^{\theta(aX+b)}) = e^{b\theta} E(e^{a\theta X}) = e^{b\theta} \phi(a\theta)$$

Note that $\phi(\theta)$ represents the moment-generating function of X.

4. Theorem
Let $\phi_1(\theta), \phi_2(\theta), \ldots, \phi_n(\theta)$ be the moment-generating functions of X_1, $X_2, \ldots, X_n$, which are mutually independently distributed random variables. Define $Y = X_1 + X_2 + \ldots + X_n$. Then, the moment-generating function of Y is given by $\phi_1(\theta)\phi_2(\theta)\ldots\phi_n(\theta)$, i.e.
$$\phi_y(\theta) = E(e^{\theta Y}) = \phi_1(\theta)\phi_2(\theta)\ldots\phi_n(\theta)$$

where $\phi_y(\theta)$ represents the moment-generating function of Y.

Proof The moment-generating function of Y, i.e., $\phi_y(\theta)$, is rewritten as

$$\phi_y(\theta) = E(e^{\theta Y}) = E(e^{\theta(X_1+X_x+\ldots+X_n)}) =$$
$$E(e^{\theta X_1})E(e^{\theta X_2})\ldots E(e^{\theta X_n}) =$$
$$\phi_1(\theta)\phi_2(\theta)\ldots\phi_n(\theta)$$

The third equality holds because $X_1, X_2, \ldots, X_n$ are mutually independently distributed random variables.

5. Theorem

When $X_1, X_2, \ldots, X_n$ are mutually independently and identically distributed and the moment-generating function of X_i is given by $\phi(\theta)$ for all i, the moment-generating function of Y is represented by $(\phi(\theta))^n$, where $Y = X_1 + X_2 + \ldots + X_n$.

Proof Using the above theorem, we have the following
$$\phi_y(\theta) = \phi_1(\theta)\phi_2(\theta)\ldots\phi_n(\theta) = \phi(\theta)\phi(\theta)\ldots\phi(\theta) = (\phi(\theta))^n$$
Note that $\phi_i(\theta) = \phi(\theta)$ for all i.

6. Theorem

When $X_1, X_2, \ldots, X_n$ are mutually independently and identically distributed and the moment-generating function of X_i is given by $\phi(\theta)$ for all i, the moment-generating function of $\overline{X}$ is represented by $\left(\phi\left(\dfrac{\theta}{n}\right)\right)^n$, where
$$\overline{X} = (1/n)\sum_{i=1}^{n} X_i$$

Proof Let $\phi_{\overline{X}}(\theta)$ be the moment-generating function of $\overline{X}$
$$\phi_{\overline{X}}(\theta) = E(e^{\theta \overline{X}}) = E(e^{\frac{\theta}{n}\sum_{i=1}^{n} X_i}) = \prod_{i=1}^{n} E(e^{\frac{\theta}{n} X_i}) = \prod_{i=1}^{n}\left(\phi\left(\frac{\theta}{n}\right)\right)^n$$

Example 2.10

For the binomial random variable, the moment-generating function $\phi(\theta)$ is known as
$$\phi(\theta) = (pe^\theta + 1 - p)^n$$
which is discussed in Example 2.5 (Section 2.3.1). Using the moment-generating function, we check whether $E(X) = np$ and $V(X) = np(1-p)$ are obtained when X is a binomial random variable.

The first and the second-derivatives with respect to θ are given by
$$\phi'(\theta) = npe^\theta(pe^\theta + 1 - p)^{n-1}$$
$$\phi''(\theta) = npe^\theta(pe^\theta + 1 - p)^{n-1} + n(n-1)p^2 e^{2\theta}(pe^\theta + 1 - p)^{n-2}$$
Evaluating at $\theta = 0$, we have
$$E(X) = \phi'(0) = np, \quad E(X^2) = \phi''(0) = np + n(n-1)p^2$$
Therefore, $V(X) = E(X^2) - (E(X))^2 = np(1-p)$ can be derived. Thus, we can

make sure that $E(X)$ and $V(X)$ are obtained from $\phi(\theta)$.

2.5.2 Multivariate Cases

Bivariate Case As discussed in Section 2.3.2, for two random variables X and Y, the moment-generating function is defined as $\phi(\theta_1,\theta_2) = E(e^{\theta_1 X+\theta_2 Y})$. Some useful and important theorems and remarks are shown as follows.

1. Theorem

Consider two random variables X and Y. let $\phi(\theta_1,\theta_2)$ be the moment-generating function of X and Y. Then, we have the following result

$$\frac{\partial^{j+k}\phi(0,0)}{\partial\theta_1^j \partial\theta_2^k} = E(X^j Y^k)$$

Proof Let $f_{xy}(x,y)$ be the probability density function of X and Y. From the definition, $\phi(\theta_1,\theta_2)$ is written as

$$\phi(\theta_1,\theta_2) = E(e^{\theta_1 X+\theta_2 Y}) = \int_{-\infty}^{+\infty}\int_{-\infty}^{+\infty} e^{\theta_1 x+\theta_2 y} f_{xy}(x,y)\,dxdy$$

Taking the jth derivative of $\phi(\theta_1,\theta_2)$ with respect to θ_1 and at the same time the kth derivative with respect to θ_2, we have the following expression

$$\frac{\partial^{j+k}\phi(\theta_1,\theta_2)}{\partial\theta_1^j \partial\theta_2^k} = \int_{-\infty}^{+\infty}\int_{-\infty}^{+\infty} x^j y^k e^{\theta_1 X+\theta_2 Y} f_{xy}(x,y)\,dxdy$$

Evaluating the above equation at $(\theta_1,\theta_2) = (0,0)$, we can easily obtain

$$\frac{\partial^{j+k}\phi(0,0)}{\partial\theta_1^j \partial\theta_2^k} = \int_{-\infty}^{+\infty}\int_{-\infty}^{+\infty} x^j y^k f_{xy}(x,y)\,dxdy \equiv E(X^j Y^k)$$

2. Remark

Let (X_i, Y_i) be a pair of random variables. Suppose that the moment-generating function of (X_1, Y_1) is equivalent to that of (X_2, Y_2). Then, (X_1, Y_1) has the same distribution function as (X_2, Y_2).

3. Theorem

Let $\phi(\theta_1,\theta_2)$ be the moment-generating function of (X,Y). The moment-generating function of X is given by $\phi_1(\theta_1)$ and that of Y is $\phi_2(\theta_2)$. Then, we have the following facts

$$\phi_1(\theta_1) = \phi(\theta_1,0), \phi_2(\theta_2) = \phi(0,\theta_2)$$

Proof Again, the definition of the moment-generating function of X and Y is represented as

$$\phi(\theta_1,\theta_2) = E(e^{\theta_1 X+\theta_2 Y}) = \int_{-\infty}^{+\infty}\int_{-\infty}^{+\infty} (e^{\theta_1 x+\theta_2 y}) f_{xy}(x,y)\,dxdy$$

When $\phi(\theta_1,\theta_2)$ is evaluated at $\theta_2 = 0, \phi(\theta_1,0)$, is rewritten as follows

$$\phi(\theta_1, 0) = E(e^{\theta_1 X}) = \int_{-\infty}^{+\infty} \int_{-\infty}^{+\infty} e^{\theta_1 x} f_{xy}(x,y) \,dx\,dy =$$

$$\int_{-\infty}^{+\infty} e^{\theta_1 x} \left(\int_{-\infty}^{+\infty} f_{xy}(x,y) \,dy \right) dx =$$

$$\int_{-\infty}^{+\infty} e^{\theta_1 x} f_x(x) \,dx = E(e^{\theta_1 X}) = \phi_1(\theta_1)$$

Thus, we obtain the result: $\phi(\theta_1, 0) = \phi_1(\theta_1)$. Similarly, $\phi(0, \theta_2) = \phi_2(\theta_2)$ can be derived.

4. Theorem

The moment-generating function of (X, Y) is given by $\phi(\theta_1, \theta_2)$. Let $\phi_1(\theta_1)$ and $\phi_2(\theta_2)$ be the moment-generating functions of X and Y, respectively. If X is independent of Y, we have

$$\phi(\theta_1, \theta_2) = \phi_1(\theta_1) \phi_2(\theta_2)$$

Proof From the definition of $\phi(\theta_1, \theta_2)$, the moment-generating function of X and Y is rewritten as follows

$$\phi(\theta_1, \theta_2) = E(e^{\theta_1 X + \theta_2 Y}) = E(e^{\theta_1 X}) E(e^{\theta_2 Y}) = \phi_1(\theta_1) \phi_2(\theta_2)$$

The second equality holds because X is independent of Y.

Multivariate Case For multivariate random variables $X_1, X_2, \ldots, X_n$, the moment-generating function is defined as

$$\phi(\theta_1, \theta_2, \ldots, \theta_n) = E(e^{\theta_1 X_1 + \theta_2 X_2 + \cdots + \theta_n X_n})$$

1. Theorem

If the multivariate random variables $X_1, X_2, \ldots, X_n$ are mutually independent, the moment-generating function of $X_1, X_2, \ldots, X_n$, denoted by $\phi(\theta_1, \theta_2, \ldots, \theta_n)$, is given by

$$\phi(\theta_1, \theta_2, \ldots, \theta_n) = \phi_1(\theta_1) \phi_2(\theta_2) \cdots \phi_n(\theta_n)$$

where $\phi_i(\theta) = E(e^{\theta X_i})$.

Proof From the definition of the moment-generating function in the multivariate cases, we obtain the following

$$\phi(\theta_1, \theta_2, \ldots, \theta_n) = E(e^{\theta_1 X_1 + \theta_2 X_2 + \cdots + \theta_n X_n}) =$$
$$E(e^{\theta_1 X_1}) E(e^{\theta_2 X_2}) \cdots E(e^{\theta_n X_n}) =$$
$$\phi_1(\theta_1) \phi_2(\theta_2) \cdots \phi_n(\theta_n)$$

2. Theorem

Suppose that the multivariate random variables $X_1, X_2, \ldots, X_n$ are mutually independently and identically distributed X_i has a normal distribution with mean μ and variance σ^2, i.e., $X_i \sim N(\mu, \sigma^2)$. Let us define $\hat{\mu} = \sum_{i=1}^{n} a_i X_i$, where a_i, $i =$

$1, 2, \ldots, n$, are assumed to be known. Then, $\hat{\mu}$ has a normal distribution with mean $\mu \sum_{i=1}^{n} a_i$ and variance $\sigma^2 \sum_{i=1}^{n} a_i^2$, i.e., $\hat{\mu} \sim N(\mu \sum_{i=1}^{n} a_i, \sigma^2 \sum_{i=1}^{n} a_i^2)$

Proof From Example 2.8 and Example 2.9, it is shown that the moment-generating function of X is given by $\phi_x(\theta) = \exp(\mu\theta + \frac{1}{2}\sigma^2\theta^2)$, when X is normally distributed as $X \sim N(\mu, \sigma^2)$.

Let $\phi_{\hat{\mu}}$ be the moment-generating function of $\hat{\mu}$

$$\phi_{\hat{\mu}} = E(e^{\theta\hat{\mu}}) = E(e^{\theta \sum_{i=1}^{n} a_i X_i}) = \prod_{i=1}^{n} E(e^{\theta a_i X_i}) =$$

$$\prod_{i=1}^{n} \phi_x(a_i\theta) = \prod_{i=1}^{n} \exp(\mu a_i \theta + \frac{1}{2}\sigma^2 a_i^2 \theta^2) =$$

$$\exp(\mu \sum_{i=1}^{n} a_i \theta + \frac{1}{2}\sigma^2 \sum_{i=1}^{n} a_i^2 \theta^2)$$

which is equivalent to the moment-generating function of the normal distribution with mean $\mu \sum_{i=1}^{n} a_i$ and variance $\sigma^2 \sum_{i=1}^{n} a_i^2$, where μ and σ^2 in $\phi_x(\theta)$ is simply replaced by $\mu \sum_{i=1}^{n} a_i$ and $\sigma^2 \sum_{i=1}^{n} a_i^2$ in $\phi_{\hat{\mu}}(\theta)$, respectively.

Moreover, note as follows. When $a_i = 1/n$ is taken for all $i = 1, 2, \ldots, n$, i.e., when $\bar{\mu} = \bar{X}$ is taken, $\bar{\mu} = \bar{X}$ is normally distributed as: $\bar{X} \sim N(\mu, \sigma^2/n)$. The readers should check difference between Theorem 11 of subsection 2.3.2 and this theorem.

Words and Expressions

moment n. 矩;动差;动量;adj. 片刻的,瞬间的,力矩的;
mutually independently distributed 相互独立的分布
independently and identically distributed 独立同分布的

2.6 Law of Large Numbers and Central Limit Theorem

2.6.1 Chebyshev's Inequality

In this section, we introduce Chebyshev's inequality, which enables us to find upper and lower bounds given a certain probability.

Theorem
Let $g(X)$ be a nonnegative function of the random variable X, i.e., $g(X) \geq$

0. If $E(g(X))$ exists, then we have
$$P(g(X) \geq k) \leq \frac{E(g(X))}{k}$$
for a positive constant value k.

Proof We define the discrete random variable U as follows
$$U = \begin{cases} 1, & \text{if } g(X) \geq k \\ 0, & \text{if } g(X) < k \end{cases} \tag{2.6}$$
Thus, the discrete random variable U takes 0 or 1. Suppose that the probability function of U is given by
$$f(u) = P(U = u)$$
where $P(U=u)$ is represented as
$$P(U = 1) = P(g(X) \geq k)$$
$$P(U = 0) = P(g(X) < k)$$
Then, in spite of the value which U takes, the following equation always holds
$$g(X) \geq kU \tag{2.7}$$
which implies that we have $g(X) \geq k$ when $U=1$ and $g(X) \geq 0$ when $U=0$, where k is a positive constant value. Therefore, taking the expectation on both sides, we obtain
$$E(g(X)) \geq kE(U)$$
where $E(U)$ is given by
$$E(U) = \sum_{u=0}^{1} uP(U = u) = 1 \times P(U = 1) + 0 \times P(U = 0) =$$
$$P(U = 1) = P(g(X) \geq k) \tag{2.8}$$
Accordingly, substituting equation (2.8) into equation (2.7), we have the following inequality
$$P(g(X) \geq k) \leq \frac{E(g(X))}{k}$$

Chebyshev's Inequality Assume that $E(X) = \mu$, $V(X) = \sigma^2$, and λ is a positive constant value. Then, we have the following inequality
$$P(|X - \mu| \geq \lambda\sigma) \leq \frac{1}{\lambda^2}$$
or equivalently
$$P(|X - \mu| < \lambda\sigma) \geq 1 - \frac{1}{\lambda^2}$$
which is called *Chebyshev's inequality*.

Proof Take $g(X) = (X-\mu)^2$ and $k = \lambda^2\sigma^2$. Then, we have

$$P((X-\mu)^2 \geq \lambda^2\sigma^2) \leq \frac{E(X-\mu)^2}{\lambda^2\sigma^2}$$

which implies

$$P(|X-\mu| \geq \lambda\sigma) \leq \frac{1}{\lambda^2}$$

Note that $E(X-\mu)^2 = V(X) = \sigma^2$.

Since we have $P(|X-\mu| \geq \lambda\sigma) + P(|X-\mu| < \lambda\sigma) = 1$, we can derive the following inequality

$$P(|X-\mu| < \lambda\sigma) \geq 1 - \frac{1}{\lambda^2} \tag{2.9}$$

An Interpretation of Chebyshev's inequality $1/\lambda^2$ is an upper bound for the probability $P(|X-\mu| \geq \lambda\sigma)$. Equation (2.9) is rewritten as

$$P(\mu-\lambda\sigma < X < \mu+\lambda\sigma) \geq 1 - \frac{1}{\lambda^2}$$

That is, the probability that X falls within $\lambda\sigma$ units of μ is greater than or equal to $1-1/\lambda^2$. Taking an example of $\lambda = 2$, the probability that X falls within two standard deviations of its mean is at lest 0.75.

Furthermore, note as follows. Taking $\varepsilon = \lambda\sigma$, we obtain as follows

$$P(|X-\mu| \leq \varepsilon) \leq \frac{\sigma^2}{\varepsilon^2}$$

i.e.

$$P(|X-E(X)| \geq \varepsilon) \leq \frac{V(X)}{\varepsilon^2} \tag{2.10}$$

which inequality is used in the next section.

Remark Equation (2.10) can be derived when we take $g(X) = (X-\mu)^2$, $\mu = E(X)$ and $k = \varepsilon^2$ in equation (2.6). Even when we have $\mu \neq E(X)$, the following inequality still hold

$$P(|X-\mu| \geq \varepsilon) \leq \frac{E((X-\mu)^2)}{\varepsilon^2}$$

Note that $E((X-\mu)^2)$ represents the mean square error (MSE). When $\mu = E(X)$, the mean square error reduces to the variance.

2.6.2 Law of Large Numbers (Convergence in probability)

Law of Large Numbers Assume that $X_1, X_2, \ldots, X_n$ are mutually independently and identically distributed with mean $E(X_i) = \mu$ and variance $V(X_i) = \sigma^2 < \infty$ for all i. Then, for any positive value ε, as $n \to \infty$, we have the

following result
$$P(|\bar{X}_n - \mu| > \varepsilon) \to 0$$
where $\bar{X}_n = (1/n)\sum_{i=1}^{n} X_i$. We say that $\bar{X}_n$ converges to μ in probability.

Proof Using (2.10), Chebyshev's inequality is represented as follows
$$P(|\bar{X}_n - E(\bar{X}_n)| > \varepsilon) \leq \frac{V(\bar{X}_n)}{\varepsilon^2}$$
where X in (2.10) is replaced by $\bar{X}_n$. As in Section 2.3.2, we have $E(\bar{X}_n) = \mu$ and $V(\bar{X}_n) = \sigma^2/n$, which are substituted into the above inequality. Then, we obtain
$$P(|\bar{X}_n - \mu)| > \varepsilon) \leq \frac{\sigma^2}{n\varepsilon^2}$$
Accordingly, when $n \to \infty$, the following equation holds
$$P(|\bar{X}_n - \mu| > \varepsilon) \leq \frac{\sigma^2}{n\varepsilon^2} \to 0$$
That is, $\bar{X}_n \to \mu$ is obtained as $n \to \infty$, which is written as: $p \lim \bar{X}_n = \mu$. This theorem is called the *law of large numbers*.

The condition $P(|\bar{X}_n - \mu| > \varepsilon) \to 0$ or equivalently $P(|\bar{X}_n - \mu| < \varepsilon) \to 1$ is used as the definition of *convergence in probability*. In this case, we say that $\bar{X}_n$ converges to μ in probability.

Theorem

In the case where $X_1, X_2, \ldots, X_n$ are not identically distributed and they are not mutually independently distributed, we assume that
$$m_n = E\left(\sum_{i=1}^{n} X_i\right) < \infty$$
$$V_n = V\left(\sum_{i=1}^{n} X_i\right) < \infty$$
$$\frac{V_n}{n^2} \to 0 \quad \text{as} \quad n \to \infty$$
Then, we obtain the following result
$$\frac{\sum_{i=1}^{n} X_i - M_n}{n} \to 0$$
That is, $\bar{X}_n$ converges to $\lim_{n \to \infty} \frac{m_n}{n}$ in probability. This theorem is also called the law of large numbers.

2.6.3 Central Limit Theorem

$X_1, X_2, \ldots, X_n$ are mutually independently and identically distributed with $E(X_i) = \mu$ and $V(X_i) = \sigma^2$ for all i. Both μ and σ^2 are finite. Under the above assumptions, when $n \to \infty$, we have

$$P\left(\frac{\overline{X}_n - \mu}{\sigma/\sqrt{n}} < x\right) \to \int_{-\infty}^{x} \frac{1}{\sqrt{2\pi}} e^{-\frac{1}{2}u^2} du$$

which is called the *central limit theorem*.

Proof Define $Y_i = \frac{X_i - \mu}{\sigma}$ We can rewritten as follows

$$\frac{\overline{X}_n - \mu}{\sigma/\sqrt{n}} = \frac{1}{\sqrt{n}} \sum_{i=1}^{n} \frac{X_i - \mu}{\sigma} = \frac{1}{\sqrt{n}} \sum_{i=1}^{n} Y_i$$

Since $Y_1, Y_2, \ldots, Y_n$ are mutually independently and identically distributed, the moment-generating function of Y_i is identical for all i, which is denoted by $\phi(\theta)$. Using $E(Y_i) = 0$ and $V(Y_i) = 1$, the moment-generating function of Y_i, $\phi(\theta)$, is rewritten as

$$\phi(\theta) = E(e^{Y_i\theta}) = E(1 + Y_i\theta + \frac{1}{2}Y_i^2\theta^2 + \frac{1}{3!}Y_i^3\theta^3 + \ldots) =$$

$$1 + \frac{1}{2}\theta^2 + O(\theta^3)$$

In the second equality, $e^{Y_i\theta}$ us approximated by the Taylor series expansion around *theta* $= 0$. See Appendix 2.3 for the Taylor series expansion. $O(x)$ implies that it is a polynomial function of x and the higher-order terms but it is dominated by x. In this case, $O(\theta^3)$ is a function of $\theta^3, \theta^4, \ldots$ Since the moment-generating function is conventionally evaluated at $\theta = 0$, θ^3 is the largest value of $\theta^3, \theta^4, \ldots$ and accordingly $O(\theta^3)$ is dominated by θ^3 (in other words, $\theta^4, \theta^5, \ldots$ are small enough, compared with θ^3).

Define Z as

$$Z = \frac{1}{\sqrt{n}} \sum_{i=1}^{n} Y_i$$

Then, the moment-generating function of Z, i.e., $\phi_z(\theta)$, is given by

$$\phi_z(\theta) = E(e^{Z\theta}) = E(e^{\frac{\theta}{\sqrt{n}}\sum_{i=1}^{n} Y_i}) = \prod_{i=1}^{n} E(e^{\frac{\theta}{\sqrt{n}} Y_i}) =$$

$$\left(\phi\left(\frac{\theta}{\sqrt{n}}\right)\right)^n = \left(1 + \frac{1}{2}\frac{\theta^2}{n} + O\left(\frac{\theta^3}{n^{\frac{3}{2}}}\right)\right)^n =$$

$$\left(1 + \frac{1}{2}\frac{\theta^2}{n} + O(n^{-\frac{3}{2}})\right)^n$$

We consider that n goes to infinity. Therefore, $O\left(\dfrac{\theta^3}{n^{\frac{3}{2}}}\right)$ indicates a function of $n^{-\frac{3}{2}}$.

Moreover, consider $x = \dfrac{1}{2}\dfrac{\theta^2}{n} + O(n^{-\frac{3}{2}})$. Multiply n/x on both sides of $x = \dfrac{1}{2}\dfrac{\theta^2}{n} + O(n^{-\frac{3}{2}})$. Then, we obtain $n = \dfrac{1}{x}\left(\dfrac{1}{2}\theta^2 + O(n^{-\frac{1}{2}})\right)$. Substitute $n = \dfrac{1}{x}\left(\dfrac{1}{2}\theta^2 + O(n^{-\frac{1}{2}})\right)$ into the moment-generating function of Z, i.e., $\phi_Z(\theta)$. Then, we obtain

$$\phi_Z(\theta) = \left(1 + \frac{1}{2}\frac{\theta^2}{n} + O(n^{-\frac{3}{2}})\right)^n = (1+x)^{\frac{1}{x}(\frac{\theta^2}{2}+O(n^{-\frac{1}{2}}))} =$$

$$((1+x)^{\frac{1}{x}})^{\frac{\theta^2}{2}+O(n^{-\frac{1}{2}})} \to e^{\frac{\theta^2}{2}}$$

Note that $x \to 0$ when $n \to \infty$ and that $\lim\limits_{x \to 0}(1+x)^{1/x} = e$ as in Section 2.2.3. Furthermore, we have $O(n^{-\frac{1}{2}}) \to 0$ as $n \to \infty$.

Since $\phi_Z(\theta) = e^{\frac{\theta^2}{2}}$ is the moment-generating function of the standard normal distribution (see Section 2.3.1 for the moment-generating function of the standard normal probability density), we have

$$P\left(\frac{\overline{X}_n - \mu}{\sigma/\sqrt{n}} < x\right) \to \int_{-\infty}^{x} \frac{1}{\sqrt{2\pi}} e^{-\frac{1}{2}u^2} du$$

or equivalently

$$\frac{\overline{X}_n - \mu}{\sigma/\sqrt{n}} \to N(0,1)$$

The following expression is also possible

$$\sqrt{n}(\overline{X}_n - \mu) \to N(0, \sigma^2) \qquad (2.11)$$

Corollary 1

When $E(X_i) = \mu$, $V(X_i) = \sigma^2$ and $\overline{X}_n = (1/n)\sum_{i=1}^{n} X_i$, note that

$$\frac{\overline{X}_n - E(\overline{X}_n)}{\sqrt{V(\overline{X}_n)}} = \frac{\overline{X}_n - \mu}{\sigma/\sqrt{n}}$$

Therefore, we can rewrite the above theorem as

$$P\left(\frac{\overline{X}_n - E(\overline{X}_n)}{\sqrt{V(\overline{X}_n)}} < x\right) \to \int_{-\infty}^{x} \frac{1}{\sqrt{2\pi}} e^{-\frac{1}{2}u^2} du$$

Corollary 2

Consider the case where $X_1, X_2, \ldots, X_n$ are not identically distributed any they are

not mutually independently distributed. Assume that
$$\lim_{n\to\infty} nV(\bar{X}_n) = \sigma^2 < \infty$$
where $\bar{X}_n = (1/n) \sum_{i=1}^{n} X_i$. Then, when $n \to \infty$, we have

$$P\left(\frac{\bar{X}_n - E(\bar{X}_n)}{\sqrt{V(\bar{X}_n)}} < x\right) = P\left(\frac{\sum_{i=1}^{n} X_i - E(\sum_{i=1}^{n} X_i)}{\sqrt{V(\sum_{i=1}^{n} X_i)}} < x\right) \to \int_{-\infty}^{x} \frac{1}{\sqrt{2\pi}} e^{-\frac{1}{2}u^2} du$$

Words and Expressions

Chebyshev's inequality 切比雪夫不等式
in spite of 不管,不顾,尽管
mean square error (**MSE**) 均方误差
law of large numbers 大数定律
convergence in probability 依概率收敛
reduce *v.* 简化,约简;化为;折合
infinity *n.* 无穷大
central limit theorem 中心极限定理
corollary *n.* 推论

2.7 Statistical Inference

2.7.1 Point Estimation

Suppose that the functional form of the underlying distribution on population is known but the parameter θ included in the distribution is not known. The distribution function of population is given by $f(x;\theta)$. Let $x_1, x_2, \ldots, x_n$ be the n observed data drawn from the population distribution. Consider estimating the parameter θ using the n observed data. Let $\hat{\theta}_n(x_1, x_2, \ldots, x_n)$ be a function of the observed data $x_1, x_2, \ldots, x_n$. Suppose that $\hat{\theta}_n(x_1, x_2, \ldots, x_n)$ is constructed from the purpose of estimating the parameter θ. $\hat{\theta}_n(x_1, x_2, \ldots, x_n)$ takes a certain value given the n observed data. Then, $\hat{\theta}_n(x_1, x_2, \ldots, x_n)$ is called the *point estimate* of θ, or simply the *estimate* of θ.

Example 2.11

Consider the case of $\theta = (\mu, \sigma^2)$, where the unknown parameters contained in population is given by mean and variance. A point estimate of population mean μ is given by

$$\hat{\mu}_n(x_1, x_2, \ldots, x_n) \equiv \bar{x} = \frac{1}{n} \sum_{i=1}^{n} x_i$$

A point estimate of population variance σ^2 is

$$\hat{\sigma}_n^2(x_1, x_2, \ldots, x_n) \equiv s^2 = \frac{1}{n-1} \sum_{i=1}^{n} (x_i - \bar{x})^2$$

An alternative point estimate of population variance σ^2 is

$$\tilde{\sigma}_n^2(x_1, x_2, \ldots, x_n) \equiv s^{**2} = \frac{1}{n} \sum_{i=1}^{n} (x_i - \bar{x})^2$$

2.7.2 Statistic, Estimate and Estimator

The underlying distribution of population is assumed to be known, but the parameter θ, which characterizes the underlying distribution, is unknown. The probability density function of population is given by $f(x;\theta)$. Let $X_1, X_2, \ldots, X_n$ be a subset of population, which are regarded as the random variables and are assumed to be mutually independent. $x_1, x_2, \ldots, x_n$ are taken as the experimental values of the random variables $X_1, X_2, \ldots, X_n$. In statistics, we consider that n-variate random variables $X_1, X_2, \ldots, X_n$ takes the experimental values $x_1, x_2, \ldots, x_n$ by chance. There, the experimental values and the actually observed data series are used in the same meaning.

As discussed in Section 2.7.1, $\hat{\theta}_n(x_1, x_2, \ldots, x_n)$ denotes the point estimate of θ. In the case where the observed data $x_1, x_2, \ldots, x_n$ are replaced by the corresponding random variables $X_1, X_2, \ldots, X_n$, a function of $X_1, X_2, \ldots, X_n$, i.e., $\hat{\theta}(x_1, x_2, \ldots, x_n)$, is called the estimator of θ, which should be distinguished form the estimate of θ, i.e., $\hat{\theta}(x_1, x_2, \ldots, x_n)$.

Example 2.12

Let $X_1, X_2, \ldots, X_n$ denote a random sample of n from a given distribution $f(x;\theta)$. Consider the case of $\theta = (\mu, \sigma^2)$.

The estimator of μ is given by $\bar{X} = (1/n) \sum_{i=1}^{n} X_i$, while the estimate of μ is $\bar{x} = (1/n) \sum_{i=1}^{n} x_i$. The estimator of σ^2 is $S^2 = \sum_{i=1}^{n} (X_i - \bar{X})^2 / (n-1)$ and the estimate of σ^2 is $S^2 = \sum_{i=1}^{n} (x_i - \bar{x})^2 / (n-1)$.

There are numerous estimators and estimates of θ. All of $(1/n)\sum_{i=1}^{n} X_i$, $(X_1 + X_n)/2$, median of $(X_1, X_2, \ldots, X_n)$ and so on are taken as the estimators of μ. Of course, they are called the estimates of θ when X_i is replaced by x_i for all i. Similarly, both $S^2 = \sum_{i=1}^{n}(X_i - \bar{X})^2/(n-1)$ and $S^{*2} = \sum_{i=1}^{2}(X_i - \bar{X})^2/n$ are the estimators of σ^2. We need to choose one out of the numerous estimators of θ. The problem of choosing an optimal estimator out of the numerous estimators is discussed in Sections 2.7.4 and 2.7.5.

In addition, note as follows. A function of random variables is called a *statistic*. The statistic for estimation of the parameter is called an estimator. Therefore, an estimator is a family of a statistic.

2.7.3 Estimation of Mean and Variance

Suppose that the population distribution is given by $f(x; \theta)$. The random sample $X_1, X_2, \ldots, X_n$ are assumed to be drawn from be population distribution $f(x; \theta)$, where $\theta = (\mu, \sigma^2)$. Therefore, we can assume that $X_1, X_2, \ldots, X_n$ are mutually independently and identically distributed, where "identically" implies $E(X_i) = \mu$ and $V(X_i) = \sigma^2$ for all i.

Consider the estimators of $\theta = (\mu, \sigma^2)$ as follows.

1. The estimator of population mean μ is

$$\bar{X} = \frac{1}{n}\sum_{i=1}^{n} X_i$$

2. The estimators of population variance σ^2 are

$$S^{*2} = \frac{1}{n}\sum_{i=1}^{n}(X_i - \mu)^2$$

when μ is known

$$S^2 = \frac{1}{n-1}\sum_{i=1}^{n}(X_i - \bar{X})^2$$

$$S^{**2} = \frac{1}{n}\sum_{i=1}^{n}(X_i - \bar{X})^2$$

Properties of $\bar{X}$ From Theorem 11 of Subsection 2.3.2, mean and variance of $\bar{X}$ are obtained as follows

$$E(\bar{X}) = \mu, \qquad V(\bar{X}) = \frac{\sigma^2}{n}$$

Properties of S^{*2}, S^2 and S^{**2} The expectation of S^{*2} is

$$E(S^{*2}) = E\left(\frac{1}{n}\sum_{i=1}^{n}(X_i - \mu)^2\right) = \frac{1}{n}E\left(\sum_{i=1}^{n}(X_i - \mu)^2\right) =$$

$$\frac{1}{n}\sum_{i=1}^{n}E((X_i - \mu)^2) = \frac{1}{n}\sum_{i=1}^{n}V(X_i) =$$

$$\frac{1}{n}\sum_{i=1}^{n}\sigma^2 = \frac{1}{n}n\sigma^2 = \sigma^2$$

where $E((X_i-\mu)^2) = V(X_i) = \sigma^2$ is used in the fourth and fifth equalities.

Next, the expectation of S^2 is given by

$$E(S^2) = E\left(\frac{1}{n-1}\sum_{i=1}^{n}(X_i - \bar{X})^2\right) = \frac{1}{n-1}E\left(\sum_{i=1}^{n}(X_i - \bar{X})^2\right) =$$

$$\frac{1}{n-1}E\left(\sum_{i=1}^{n}((X_i - \mu) - (\bar{X} - \mu))^2\right) =$$

$$\frac{1}{n-1}E\left(\sum_{i=1}^{n}((X_i - \mu)^2 - 2(X_i - \mu)(\bar{X} - \mu) + (\bar{X} - \mu)^2)\right) =$$

$$\frac{1}{n-1}E\left(\sum_{i=1}^{n}(X_i - \mu)^2 - 2(\bar{X} - \mu)\sum_{i=1}^{n}(X_i - \mu) + n(\bar{X} - \mu)^2\right) =$$

$$\frac{1}{n-1}E\left(\sum_{i=1}^{n}(X_i - \mu)^2 - n(\bar{X} - \mu)^2\right) =$$

$$\frac{n}{n-1}E\left(\frac{1}{n}\sum_{i=1}^{n}(X_i - \mu)\right) - \frac{1}{n-1}E((\bar{X} - \mu)^2) =$$

$$\frac{1}{n-1}\sigma^2 - \frac{n}{n-1}\frac{\sigma^2}{n} = \sigma^2$$

$\sum_{i=1}^{n}(X_i - \mu) = n(\bar{X} - \mu)$ is used in the sixth equality. $E((1/n)\sum_{i=1}^{n}(X_i - \mu)^2) = E(S^{*2}) = \sigma^2$ and $E((\bar{X}-\mu)^2) = V(\bar{X}) = \sigma^2/n$ are required in the eighth equality.

Finally, the mathematical expectation of S^{**2} is represented by

$$E(S^{**2}) = E\left(\frac{1}{n}\sum_{i=1}^{n}(X_i - \bar{X})^2\right) =$$

$$E\left(\frac{n-1}{n}\frac{1}{n-1}\sum_{i=1}^{n}(X_i - \bar{X})^2\right) =$$

$$E\left(\frac{n-1}{n}S^2\right) = \frac{n-1}{n}E(S^2) = \frac{n-1}{n}\sigma^2 \neq \sigma^2$$

Summarizing the above results, we obtain as follows

$$E(S^{*2}) = \sigma^2, E(S^2) = \sigma^2, E(S^{**2}) = \frac{n-1}{n}\sigma^2 \neq \sigma^2$$

2.7.4 Point Estimation: Optimality

As mentioned in the previous sections, θ denotes the parameter to be estimated. $\hat{\theta}_n(X_1, X_2, \ldots, X_n)$ represents the estimator of θ, while $\hat{\theta}_n(x_1, x_2, \ldots, x_n)$ indicates the estimate of θ. Hereafter, in the case of no confusion, $\hat{\theta}_n(x_1, x_2, \ldots, x_n)$ is simply written as $\hat{\theta}_n$.

As discussed above, there are numerous candidates of the estimator $\hat{\theta}_n$. The desired properties which $\hat{\theta}_n$ have to satisfy include unbiasedness, efficiency and consistency.

Unbiasedness One of the desirable features that the estimator of the parameter should have is given by

$$E(\hat{\theta}_n) = \theta \tag{2.12}$$

which implies that $\hat{\theta}_n$ is distributed around θ. When the condition (2.12) holds, $\hat{\theta}_n$ is called the unbiased estimator of θ. $E(\hat{\theta}_n) - \theta$ is defined as bias.

As an example of unbiasedness, consider the case of $\theta = (\mu, \sigma^2)$. Suppose that $X_1, X_2, \ldots, X_n$ are mutually independently distributed with mean μ and variance σ^2. Consider the following estimators of μ and σ^2.

1. The estimator of μ is

$$\bar{X} = \frac{1}{n}\sum_{i=1}^{n} X_i$$

2. The estimators of σ^2 are

$$S^2 = \frac{1}{n-1}\sum_{i=1}^{n}(X_i - \bar{X})^2$$

$$S^{**2} = \frac{1}{n}\sum_{i=1}^{n}(X_i - \bar{X})^2$$

Since we have obtained $E(\bar{X}) = \mu$ and $E(S^2) = \sigma^2$ in Section 2.7.3, $\bar{X}$ and S^2 are unbiased estimators of μ and σ^2. However, we have obtained the result $E(S^{**2}) \neq \sigma^2$ in Section 2.7.3 and therefore S^{**2} in not an unbiased estimator of σ^2. Thus, according to the criterion of unbiasedness, S^2 is preferred to S^{**2} for estimation of σ^2.

Efficiency Consider two estimators, i.e., $\hat{\theta}_n$ and $\tilde{\theta}_n$. Both are assumed to be unbiased. That is, we have the following condition: $E(\hat{\theta}_n) = \theta$ and $E(\tilde{\theta}_n) = \theta$. When $V(\hat{\theta}_n) < V(\tilde{\theta}_n)$, we say that $\hat{\theta}_n$ is more efficient than $\tilde{\theta}_n$. The estimator which is widely distributed is not preferred.

Consider as many unbiased estimators as possible. The unbiased estimator with the least variance is known as the efficient estimator. We have the case where an efficient estimator does not exist.

In order to obtain the efficient estimator, we utilize Cramer-Rao inequality. Suppose that X_i has the probability density function $f(x_i;\theta)$ for all i, i.e., X_1, $X_2,\ldots,X_n$ are mutually independently and identically distributed. For any unbiased estimator of θ, denoted by $\hat{\theta}_n$, it is known that we have the following inequality

$$V(\hat{\theta}_n) \geq \frac{\sigma^2(\theta)}{n} \tag{2.13}$$

where

$$\sigma^2(\theta) = \frac{1}{E\left(\left(\frac{\partial \log f(X;\theta)}{\partial \theta}\right)^2\right)} = \frac{1}{V\left(\frac{\partial \log f(X;\theta)}{\partial \theta}\right)} = \frac{1}{E\left(\frac{\partial^2 \log f(X;\theta)}{\partial \theta^2}\right)} \tag{2.14}$$

which is known as the Cramer-Rao inequality. See Appendix 2.4 for proof of the Cramer-Rao inequality.

When there exists the unbiased estimator $\hat{\theta}_n$ such that the equality in (2.13) holds, $\hat{\theta}_n$ becomes the unbiased estimator with minimum variance, which is the efficient estimator. $\sigma^2(\theta)/n$ is called the Cramer-Rao lower bound.

Example 2.13 (Efficient Estimator)

Suppose that $X_1, X_2, \ldots, X_n$ are mutually independently, identically and normally distributed with mean μ and variance σ^2. Then, we show that $\bar{X}$ is an efficient estimator of μ.

When $\sigma^2 < \infty$, form Theorem 11 of Subsection 2.3.2, $V(\bar{X})$ is given by σ^2/n in spite of the distribution of X_i, $i=1,2,\ldots,n$

On the other hand, because we assume that X_i is normally distributed with mean μ and variance σ^2, the probability density function of X_i is given by

$$f(x;\mu) = \frac{1}{\sqrt{2\pi\sigma^2}} \exp\left(-\frac{1}{2\sigma^2}(x-\mu)^2\right)$$

The Cramer-Rao inequality is represented as

$$V(\bar{X}) \geq \frac{1}{nE\left(\left(\frac{\partial \log f(X;\mu)}{\partial \mu}\right)^2\right)} \tag{A}$$

where the logarithm of $f(X;\mu)$ is written as

$$\log f(X;\mu) = -\frac{1}{2}\log(2\pi\sigma^2) - \frac{1}{2\sigma^2}(X-\mu)^2$$

Therefore, the partial derivative of $f(X;\mu)$ with respect to μ is

$$\frac{\partial \log f(X;\mu)}{\partial \mu} = \frac{1}{\sigma^2}(X-\mu)$$

Accordingly, the Cramer-Rao inequality in this case is written as

$$V(\bar{X}) \geq \frac{1}{nE\left(\left(\frac{1}{\sigma^2}(X-\mu)\right)^2\right)} = \frac{1}{n\frac{1}{\sigma^4}E((X-\mu)^2)} = \frac{\sigma^2}{n} \qquad (B)$$

From (A) and (B), variance of $\bar{X}$ is equal to the lower bound of Cramer-Rao inequality, i.e., $V(\bar{X}) = \frac{\sigma^2}{n}$, which implies that the equality included in the Cramer-Rao inequality holds. Therefore, we can conclude that the sample mean $\bar{X}$ is an efficient estimator of μ.

Example 2.14 (Linear Unbiased Minimum Variance Estimator)

Suppose that $X_1, X_2, \ldots, X_n$ are mutually and identically distributed with mean μ and variance σ^2 (note that the normality assumption is excluded from Example 2.13). Consider the following linear estimator: $\hat{\mu} = \sum_{i=1}^{n} a_i X_i$. Then, we want to show $\hat{\mu}$ (i.e., $\bar{X}$) is a *linear unbiased minimum variance estimator* if $a_i = 1/n$ for all I, i.e., if $\hat{\mu} = \bar{X}$.

Utilizing Theorem of Subsection 2.3.2, when $E(X_i) = \mu_i$ and $V(X_i) = \sigma^2$ for all i, we have: $E(\hat{\mu}) = \mu \sum_{i=1}^{n} a_i$ and $V(\hat{\mu}) = \sigma^2 \sum_{i=1}^{n} a_i^2$.

Since $\hat{\mu}$ is linear in X_i, $\hat{\mu}$ is called a linear estimator of μ. In order for $\hat{\mu}$ to be unbiased, we need to have the condition: $E(\hat{\mu}) = \mu \sum_{i=1}^{n} a_i = \mu$. That is, if $\sum_{i=1}^{n} a_i = 1$ is satisfied, $\hat{\mu}$ gives us a *linear unbiased estimator*. Thus, as mentioned in Example 2.12 of Section 2.7.2, there are numerous unbiased estimators.

The variance of $\hat{\mu}$ is given by $\sigma^2 \sum_{i=1}^{n} a_i^2$. We obtain the value of a_i which minimizes $\sum_{i=1}^{n} a_i^2$ with the constraint $\sum_{i=1}^{n} a_i = 1$. Construct the Lagrange function as follows

$$L = \frac{1}{2}\sum_{i=1}^{n} a_i^2 + \lambda\left(1 - \sum_{i=1}^{n} a_i\right)$$

where λ denotes the Lagrange multiplier. The $\frac{1}{2}$ in front of the first term appears to make life easier later on and does not affect the outcome. To determine the optimum values, we set the partial derivatives of L with respect to a_i and λ equal to zero, i. e.

$$\frac{\partial L}{\partial a_i} = a_i - \lambda = 0, i = 1, 2, \ldots, n$$

$$\frac{\partial L}{\partial \lambda} = 1 - \sum_{i=1}^{n} a_i = 0$$

Solving the above equations, $a_i = \lambda = 1/n$ is obtained. Therefore, when $a_i = 1/n$ for all i, $\hat{\mu}$ has minimum variance in a class of linear unbiased estimators. That is, $\bar{X}$ is a *linear unbiased minimum variance estimator*.

The linear unbiased minimum variance estimator should be distinguished from the efficient estimator discussed in Example 2.13. The former does not requires the assumption on the underlying distribution. The latter gives us the unbiased estimator which variance is equal to the Cramer-Rao lower bound, which is not restricted to a class of the linear unbiased estimators. Under the assumption of normal population, the linear unbiased minimum variance estimator leads to the efficient estimator. However, both are different in general. In addition, note that the efficient estimator does not necessarily exist.

Consistency Let $\hat{\theta}_n$ be an estimator of θ. Suppose that for any $\varepsilon > 0$ we have the following

$$P(|\hat{\theta}_n - \theta|) > \varepsilon \to 0 \text{ (as } n \to \infty\text{)}$$

which implies that $\hat{\theta} \to \theta$ as $n \to \infty$. Then, we say that $\hat{\theta}_n$ is a *consistent estimator* of θ. That is, the estimator which approaches the true parameter value as the sample size is large is called the consistent estimator of the parameter.

Example 2.15

Suppose that $X_1, X_2, \ldots, X_n$ are mutually independently and identically distributed with mean μ and variance σ^2. Assume that σ^2 is known. Then, it is shown that $\bar{X}$ is a consistent estimator of μ.

From (2.10), Chebyshev's inequality is given by

$$P(|X - E(X)| > \varepsilon) \leq \frac{V(X)}{\varepsilon^2}$$

for a random variable X. Here, replacing X by $\bar{X}$, we obtain $E(\bar{X})$ and $V\bar{X}$ as follows

$$E(\bar{X}) = \mu, V(\bar{X}) = \frac{\sigma^2}{n}$$

because $E(X_i) = \mu$ and $V(X_i) = \sigma^2 < \infty$ are assumed for all i.

Then, when $n \to \infty$, we obtain the following result

$$P(|\bar{X} - \mu| > \varepsilon) \leq \frac{\sigma^2}{n\varepsilon^2} \to 0$$

which implies that $\bar{X} \to \mu$ as $n \to \infty$. Therefore, we can conclude that $\bar{X}$ is a consistent estimator of μ.

Summarizing the results up to now, $\bar{X}$ is an unbiased, minimum variance and consistent estimator of population mean μ. When the distribution of X_i is assumed to be normal for all i, $\bar{X}$ leads to an unbiased, efficient and consistent estimator of μ.

Example 2.16

Suppose that $X_1, X_2, \ldots, X_n$ are mutually independently, identically and normally distributed with mean μ and variance σ^2. Consider $S^{**2} = \frac{1}{n}\sum_{i=1}^{n}(X_i - \bar{X})^2$, which is an estimate of σ^2.

In Remark of Section 2.6.1, X and μ are replaced by S^{**2} and σ^2. Then, we obtain the following inequality

$$P(|S^{**2} - \sigma^2| < \varepsilon) \geq 1 - \frac{E((S^{**2} - \sigma^2)^2)}{\varepsilon^2}$$

We compute $E((S^{**2} - \sigma^2)^2)$. Since $(n-1)S^2/\sigma^2 \sim \chi^2(n-1)$, we obtain $E((n-1)S^2/\sigma^2) = n-1$ and $V((n-1)S^2/\sigma^2) = 2(n-1)$, where $S^2 = \frac{1}{n-1}\sum_{i=1}^{n}(X_i - \bar{X})^2$.

Therefore, $E(S^2) = \sigma^2$ and $V(S^2) = 2\sigma^4/(n-1)$ can be derived. Using $S^{**2} = S^2(n-1)/n$, we have the following

$$E((S^{**2} - \sigma^2)^2) = E\left(\left(\frac{n-1}{n}S^2 - \sigma^2\right)^2\right) =$$

$$E\left(\left(\frac{n-1}{n}(S^2 - \sigma^2) - \frac{\sigma^2}{n}\right)^2\right) =$$

$$\frac{(n-1)^2}{n^2}E((S^2 - \sigma^2)^2) + \frac{\sigma^4}{n^2} =$$

$$\frac{(n-1)^2}{n^2}V(S^2) + \frac{\sigma^4}{n^2} = \frac{(2n-1)^2}{n^2}\sigma^4$$

Therefore, as $n \to \infty$, we obtain

$$P(|S^{**2} - \sigma^2| < \varepsilon) \geq 1 - \frac{1}{\varepsilon^2}\frac{(2n-1)}{n^2}\sigma^4 \to 1$$

Because $S^{**2} \to \sigma^2$, S^{**2} is a consistent estimator of σ^2. Thus, S^{**2} is not unbiased (see Section 2.7.3), but is consistent.

Words and Expressions

construct *v.* 构成,建造,建筑,铺设,架设;构想,创立
point estimate 点估计
by chance 意外,偶然地
estimate *n.* 估计值,估计
estimator *n.* 估计量
statistic *n.* 统计量
optimality *n.* 最优性
unbiased estimator 无偏估计量
efficient estimator 有效估计量
unbiasedness *n.* 无偏性
efficiency *n.* 有效性
consistent estimator 一致估计量
bias *n.* 偏差,偏倚
Lagrange multiplier 拉格朗日乘子

2.7.5 Maximum Likelihood Estimator

In Section 2.7.4, the properties of the estimators $\bar{X}$ and S^2 are discussed. It is shown that $\bar{X}$ is an unbiased, efficient and consistent estimator of μ under normality assumption and that S^2 is an unbiased estimator of σ^2. Note that S^2 is not efficient but consistent (we do not check these features of S^2 in this chapter).

The population parameter θ depends on a functional form of the population distribution $f(x;\theta)$. It corresponds to (μ, σ^2) in the case of the normal distribution and β in the case of the exponential distribution. Now, in more general cases, we want to consider how to estimate θ. The maximum likelihood estimator gives us one of the solutions.

Let $X_1, X_2, \ldots, X_n$ be mutually independently and identically distributed random samples. X_i has the probability density function $f(x;\theta)$. Under these assumptions, the joint density function of $X_1, X_2, \ldots, X_n$ is given by

$$f(x_1, x_2, \ldots, x_n; \theta) = \prod_{i=1}^{n} f(x_i; \theta)$$

where θ denotes the unknown parameter.

Given the actually observed data $x_1, x_2, \ldots, x_n$, the joint density $f(x_1,$

$x_2,\ldots,x_n;\theta)$ is regarded as a function θ, i. e.

$$l(\theta) = l(\theta;x) = l(\theta;x_1,x_2,\ldots,x_n) = \prod_{i=1}^{n} f(x_i;\theta)$$

$l(\theta)$ is called the *likelihood function*.

Let $\hat{\theta}_n$ be the θ which maximizes the likelihood function. Replacing $x_1,x_2,\ldots,x_n$ by $X_1,X_2,\ldots,X_n$, $\hat{\theta}_n = \hat{\theta}_n(X_1,X_2,\ldots,X_n)$, is called the *maximum likelihood estimator*, which $\hat{\theta}_n(x_1,x_2,\ldots,x_n)$ is called the *maximum likelihood estimate*.

That is, solving the following equation

$$\frac{\partial l(\theta)}{\partial \theta} = 0$$

the maximum likelihood estimator $\hat{\theta}_n \equiv \hat{\theta}_n(X_1,X_2,\ldots,X_n)$ is obtained.

Example 2.17

Suppose that $X_1, X_2, \ldots, X_n$ are mutually independently, identically and normally distributed with mean μ and variance σ^2. We derive the maximum likelihood estimators of μ and σ^2. The joint density (or the likelihood function) of $X_1,X_2,\ldots,X_n$ is written as

$$f(x_1,x_2,\ldots,x_n;\mu,\sigma^2) = \prod_{i=1}^{n} f(x_i;\mu,\sigma^2) =$$

$$\prod_{i=1}^{n} \frac{1}{\sqrt{2\pi\sigma^2}} \exp\left(-\frac{1}{2\sigma^2}(x_i-\mu)^2\right) =$$

$$(2\pi\sigma^2)^{-n/2} \exp\left(-\frac{1}{2\sigma^2}\sum_{i=1}^{n}(x_i-\mu)^2\right) =$$

$$l(\mu,\sigma^2)$$

The logarithm of the likelihood function is given by

$$\log l(\mu,\sigma^2) = -\frac{n}{2}\log(2\pi) - \frac{n}{2}\log(\sigma^2) - \frac{1}{2\sigma^2}\sum_{i=1}^{n}(x_i-\mu)^2$$

which is called the *log-likelihood function*. For maximization of the likelihood function, differentiating the log-likelihood function $\log l(\mu,\sigma^2)$ with respect to μ and σ^2, the first derivatives should be equal to zero, i. e.

$$\frac{\partial \log l(\mu,\sigma^2)}{\partial \mu} = \frac{1}{\sigma^2}\sum_{i=1}^{n}(x_i-\mu) = 0$$

$$\frac{\partial \log l(\mu,\sigma^2)}{\partial \sigma^2} = -\frac{n}{2}\frac{1}{\sigma^2} + \frac{1}{2\sigma^4}\sum_{i=1}^{n}(x_i-\mu)^2 = 0$$

Let $\hat{\mu}$ and $\hat{\sigma}^2$ be the solution which satisfies the above two equations. Solving the two equations, we obtain the maximum likelihood estimates as follows

$$\hat{\mu} = \frac{1}{n}\sum_{i=1}^{n} x_i = \bar{x}$$

$$\hat{\sigma}^2 = \frac{1}{n}\sum_{i=1}^{n}(x_i - \mu)^2 = \frac{1}{n}\sum_{i=1}^{n}(x_i - \bar{x})^2 = s^{**2}$$

Replacing x_i by X_i for $i = 1, 2, \ldots, n$, the maximum likelihood estimators of μ and σ^2 are given by $\bar{X}$ and S^{**2}, respectively. Since $E(\bar{X}) = \mu$, the maximum likelihood estimator of μ, $\bar{X}$, is an unbiased estimator. However, because of $E(S^{**2}) = \frac{n-1}{n}\sigma^2 \neq \sigma^2$ as shown in Section 2.7.3, the maximum likelihood estimator of σ^2, S^{**2}, is not an unbiased estimator.

Properties of Maximum Likelihood Estimator   For small sample, the maximum likelihood estimator has the following properties.

(1) The maximum likelihood estimator is not necessarily unbiased in general, but we often have the case where we can construct the unbiased estimator by an appropriate transformation.

For instance, in Example 2.17, we find that the maximum likelihood estimator of σ^2, S^{**2}, is not unbiased. However, $\frac{n}{n-1}S^{**2}$ is an unbiased estimator of σ^2.

(2) If the efficient estimator exists, i.e., if there exists the estimator which satisfies the equality in the Cramer-Rao inequality, the maximum likelihood estimator is efficient.

For large sample, as $n \to \infty$, the maximum likelihood estimator of θ, $\hat{\theta}_n$, has the following property

$$\sqrt{n}(\hat{\theta}_n - \theta) \to N(0, \sigma^2(\theta)) \tag{2.15}$$

where

$$\sigma^2(\theta) = \frac{1}{E\left(\left(\frac{\partial \log f(X;\theta)}{\partial \theta}\right)^2\right)}$$

(2.15) indicates that the maximum likelihood estimator has consistency, asymptotic unbiasedness, asymptotic efficiency and asymptotic normality. Asymptotic normality of the maximum likelihood estimator comes from the central limit theorem discussed in Section 2.6.3. Even though the underlying distribution is not normal, i.e., even though $f(x; \theta)$ is not normal, the maximum likelihood estimator is asymptotically normally distributed. Note that the properties of $n \to \infty$ are called the asymptotic properties, which include consistency, asymptotic normality and so on.

By normalizing, as $n \to \infty$, we obtain as follows

$$\frac{\sqrt{n}(\hat{\theta}_n - \theta)}{\sigma(\theta)} = \frac{\hat{\theta}_n - \theta}{\sigma(\theta)/\sqrt{n}} \to N(0,1)$$

As another representation, when n is large, we can approximate the distribution of $\hat{\theta}_n$ as follows

$$\hat{\theta}_n \sim N\left(\theta, \frac{\sigma^2(\theta)}{n}\right)$$

This implies that when $n \to \infty$, $\hat{\theta}_n$ approaches the lower bound of Cramer-Rao inequality: $\sigma^2(\theta)/n$, which property is called an asymptotic efficiency.

Moreover, replacing θ in variance $\sigma^2(\theta)$ by $\hat{\theta}_n$, when $n \to \infty$, we have the following property

$$\frac{\hat{\theta}_n - \theta}{\sigma(\hat{\theta}_n)/\sqrt{n}} \to N(0,1) \qquad (2.16)$$

which also comes from the central limit theorem.

Practically, when n is large, we approximately use as follows

$$\hat{\theta}_n \sim N\left(\theta, \frac{\sigma^2(\hat{\theta}_n)}{n}\right) \qquad (2.17)$$

Proof (2.15) By the central limit theorem (2.11) of Section 2.6.3

$$\frac{1}{\sqrt{n}} \sum_{i=1}^{n} \frac{\partial \log f(X_i; \theta)}{\partial \theta} \to N\left(0, \frac{1}{\sigma^2(\theta)}\right) \qquad (2.18)$$

where $\sigma^2(\theta)$ is defined in (2.14), i.e., $V(\partial \log f(X_i;\theta)/\partial \theta) = 1/\sigma^2(\theta)$. As shown in (2.46) of Appendix 2.4, note that $E(\partial \log f(X_i;\theta)/\partial \theta) = 0$. We can apply the central limit theorem, taking $\partial \log f(X_i;\theta)/\partial \theta$ as the ith random variable.

By performing the first order Taylor series expansion around $\hat{\theta}_n = \theta$, we have the following approximation

$$0 = \frac{1}{\sqrt{n}} \sum_{i=1}^{n} \frac{\partial \log f(X_i; \hat{\theta}_n)}{\partial \theta} = \frac{1}{\sqrt{n}} \sum_{i=1}^{n} \frac{\partial \log f(X_i; \theta)}{\partial \theta} + \frac{1}{\sqrt{n}} \sum_{i=1}^{n} \frac{\partial^2 \log f(X_i; \theta)}{\partial \theta^2} (\hat{\theta}_n - n) + \cdots$$

Therefore, the following approximation also holds

$$\frac{1}{\sqrt{n}} \sum_{i=1}^{n} \frac{\partial \log f(X_i; \theta)}{\partial \theta} \approx -\frac{1}{\sqrt{n}} \sum_{i=1}^{n} \frac{\partial^2 \log f(X_i; \theta)}{\partial \theta^2} (\hat{\theta}_n - \theta)$$

From (2.18) and the above equation, we obtain

$$-\frac{1}{n} \sum_{i=1}^{n} \frac{\partial^2 \log f(X_i; \theta)}{\partial \theta^2} \sqrt{n}(\hat{\theta}_n - \theta) \to N\left(0, \frac{1}{\sigma^2(\theta)}\right)$$

The law of large numbers indicates as follows

$$-\frac{1}{n}\sum_{i=1}^{n}\frac{\partial^2 \log f(X_i;\theta)}{\partial \theta^2} \to -E\left(\frac{\partial^2 \log f(X_i;\theta)}{\partial \theta^2}\right) = \frac{1}{\sigma^2(\theta)}$$

where the last equality is from (2.14). Thus, we have the following relation

$$-\frac{1}{n}\sum_{i=1}^{n}\frac{\partial^2 \log f(X_i;\theta)}{\partial \theta^2}\sqrt{n}(\hat{\theta}_n - \theta) \to$$

$$\frac{1}{\sigma^2(\theta)}\sqrt{n}(\hat{\theta}_n - \theta) \to N(0, \frac{1}{\sigma^2(\theta)})$$

Therefore, the asymptotic normality of the maximum likelihood estimator is obtained as follows

$$\sqrt{n}(\hat{\theta}_n - \theta) \to N(0, \sigma^2(\theta))$$

Thus, (2.15) is obtained.

2.7.6 Interval Estimation

In Sections 2.7.1 ~ 2.7.5, the point estimation is discussed. It is important to known where the true parameter value of θ is likely to lie.

Suppose that the population distribution is given by $f(x;\theta)$. Using the random sample $X_1, X_2, \ldots, X_n$ drawn from the population distribution, we construct the two statistics, say, $\hat{\theta}_U(X_1, X_2, \ldots, X_n; \theta^*)$ and $\hat{\theta}_L(X_1, X_2, \ldots, X_n; \theta^{**})$, where θ^* and θ^{**} denote the constant values which satisfy

$$P(\theta^* < \hat{\theta}_n < \theta^{**}) = 1 - \alpha \qquad (2.19)$$

for $\theta^{**} > \theta^*$. Note that $\hat{\theta}_n$ depends on $X_1, X_2, \ldots, X_n$ as well as θ, i.e., $\hat{\theta}_n \equiv \hat{\theta}_n(X_1, X_2, \ldots, X_n; \theta)$. Now we assume that we can solve (2.19) with respect to θ, which is rewritten as follows

$$P(\hat{\theta}_L(X_1, X_2, \ldots, X_n; \theta^*) < \theta < \hat{\theta}_U(X_1, X_2, \ldots, X_n; \theta^{**})) = 1 - \alpha$$
(2.20)

(2.20) implies that θ lies on the interval $(\hat{\theta}_L(X_1, X_2, \ldots, X_n; \theta^*), \hat{\theta}_U(X_1, X_2, \ldots, X_n; \theta^{**}))$ with probability $1 - \alpha$. Depending on a function of $\hat{\theta}_n(X_1, X_2, \ldots, X_n; \theta)$, we possibly have the situation that θ^* and θ^{**} are switched with each other.

Now, we replace the random variables $X_1, X_2, \ldots, X_n$ by the experimental values $x_1, x_2, \ldots, x_n$. Then, we say that the interval

$$(\hat{\theta}_L(X_1, X_2, \ldots, X_n; \theta^*), \hat{\theta}_U(X_1, X_2, \ldots, X_n; \theta^{**}))$$

is called the $100 \times (1-\alpha)\%$ *confidence interval* of θ. Thus, estimating the interval is known as the *interval estimation*, which is distinguished from the point estimation. In the interval, $\hat{\theta}_L(X_1, X_2, \ldots, X_n; \theta^*)$ is known as the *lower bound* of the confidence interval, while $\hat{\theta}_U(X_1, X_2, \ldots, X_n; \theta^{**})$ is the *upper bound* of the confidence interval.

Given probability α, the $\hat{\theta}_L(X_1, X_2, \ldots, X_n; \theta^*)$ and $\hat{\theta}_U(X_1, X_2, \ldots, X_n; \theta^{**})$ which satisfies equation (2.20) are not unique. For estimation of the unknown parameter θ, it is more optimal to minimize the width of the confidence interval. Therefore, we should choose θ^* and θ^{**} which minimizes the width

$$\hat{\theta}_U(X_1, X_2, \ldots, X_n; \theta^{**}) - \hat{\theta}_L(X_1, X_2, \ldots, X_n; \theta^*)$$

Interval Estimation of $\bar{X}$: let $X_1, X_2, \ldots, X_n$ be mutually independently and identically distributed random variables. X_i has a distribution with mean μ and variance σ^2. From the central limit theorem

$$\frac{\bar{X} - \mu}{\sigma/\sqrt{n}} \to N(0,1)$$

Replacing σ^2 by its estimator S^2 (or S^{**2})

$$\frac{\bar{X} - \mu}{S/\sqrt{n}} \to N(0,1)$$

Therefore, when n is large enough

$$P(z^* < \frac{\bar{X} - \mu}{S/\sqrt{n}} < z^{**}) = 1 - \alpha$$

where z^* and z^{**} ($z^* < z^{**}$) are percent points from the standard normal density function. Solving the inequality above with respect to μ, the following expression is obtained

$$P\left(\bar{X} - z^{**}\frac{S}{\sqrt{n}} < \mu < \bar{X} - z^*\frac{S}{\sqrt{n}}\right) = 1 - \alpha$$

where $\hat{\theta}_L$ and $\hat{\theta}_U$ correspond to $\bar{X} - z^{**}S/\sqrt{n}$ and $\bar{X} - z^*S/\sqrt{n}$, respectively.

The length of the confidence interval is given by

$$\hat{\theta}_U - \hat{\theta}_L = \frac{S}{\sqrt{n}}(z^{**} - z^*)$$

which should be minimized subject to

$$\int_{z^*}^{z^{**}} f(x)\,dx = 1 - \alpha$$

i. e.

$$F(z^{**}) - F(z^*) = 1 - \alpha$$

where $F(\cdot)$ denotes the standard normal cumulative distribution function.

Solving the minimization above, we can obtain the conditions that $f(z^*) = f(z^{**})$ for $z^* < z^{**}$ and that $f(x)$ is symmetric. Therefore, we have

$$-z^* = z^{**} = z_{\alpha/2}$$

where $z_{\alpha/2}$ denotes the $100 \times \alpha/2$ percent point from the standard normal density function.

Accordingly, replacing the estimators $\bar{X}$ and S^2 by their estimates $\bar{x}$ and s^2, the $100 \times (1-\alpha)\%$ confidence interval of μ is approximately represented as

$$\left(\bar{x} - z_{\alpha/2}\frac{s}{\sqrt{n}}, \bar{x} + z_{\alpha/2}\frac{s}{\sqrt{n}}\right)$$

for large n.

For now, we do not impose any assumptions on the distribution of X_i. If we assume that X_i is normal, $\sqrt{n}(\bar{X}-\mu)/S$ has a t distribution with $n-1$ degrees of freedom for any n. Therefore, $100 \times (1-\alpha)\%$ confidence interval of μ is given by

$$\left(\bar{x} - t_{\alpha/2}(n-1)\frac{s}{\sqrt{n}}, \bar{x} + t_{\alpha/2}(n-1)\frac{s}{\sqrt{n}}\right)$$

where $t_{\alpha/2}(n-1)$ denotes the $100 \times \alpha/2$ percent point of the t distribution with $n-1$ degrees of freedom.

Interval Estimation of $\hat{\theta}_n$ Let $X_1, X_2, \ldots, X_n$ be mutually independently and identically distributed random variables. X_i has the probability density function $f(x_i; \theta)$. Suppose that $\hat{\theta}_n$ represents the maximum likelihood estimator of θ.

From (2.17), we can approximate the $100 \times (1-\alpha)\%$ confidence interval of θ as follows

$$\left(\hat{\theta}_n - z_{\alpha/2}\frac{\sigma(\hat{\theta}_n)}{\sqrt{n}}, \hat{\theta}_n + z_{\alpha/2}\frac{\sigma(\hat{\theta}_n)}{\sqrt{n}}\right)$$

Words and Expressions

likelihood function 似然函数
maximum likelihood estimator 最大似然估计量
maximum likelihood estimate 最大似然估计值
log-likelihood function 对数似然函数
asymptotic properties 渐近性质
switch *v.* 转换,转变
confidence interval 置信区间
interval estimation 区间估计
lower bound 下界
upper bound 上界
impose *v.* 利用（on upon）,施加影响（on upon）

2.8 Testing Hypothesis

2.8.1 Basic Concepts in Testing Hypothesis

Given the population distribution $f(x;\theta)$, we want to judge from the observed values $x_1, x_2, \ldots, x_n$ whether the hypothesis on the parameter θ, e. g. $\theta = \theta_0$, is correct or not. The hypothesis that we want to test is called the *null hypothesis*, which is denoted by $H_0 : \theta = \theta_0$. The hypothesis against the null hypothesis, e. g. $\theta \neq \theta_0$, is called the *alternative hypothesis* which is denoted by $H_1 : \theta \neq \theta_0$.

Type I and Type II Errors When we test null hypothesis H_0, as shown in Table 2.1 we have four cases, i. e., ①we accept H_0 when H_0 is true, ②we reject H_0 when H_0 is true, ③we accept H_0 when H_0 is false, and ④ we reject H_0 when H_0 is false. ① and ④ are correct judgments, while ② and ③ are not correct. ② is called a *type I error* and ③ is called a *type II error*. The probability which a type I error occurs is called the *significance level*, which is denoted by α, and the probability of committing a type II error is denoted by β. Probability of ④ is called the *power* or the *power function*, because it is a function of the parameter θ, see Table 2.3.

Table 2.3 Type I and Type II Errors

	H_0 is true	H_0 is false
Acceptance of H_0	Correct judgment	Type II Error (Probability β)
Rejection of H_0	Type I Error (Probability α = Significance Level)	Correct judgment ($1-\beta$ = Power)

Testing Procedures

The testing procedure is summarized as follows.

1. Construct the null hypothesis (H_0) on the parameter.

2. Consider an appropriate statistic, which is called a *test statistic*. Derive a distribution function of the test statistic when H_0 is true.

3. From the observed data, compute the observed value of the test statistic.

4. Compare the distribution and the observed value of the test statistic. When the observed value of the test statistic is in the tails of the distribution, we consider that H_0 is not likely to occur and we reject H_0.

The region that H_0 is unlikely to occur and accordingly H_0 is rejected is called *the rejection region* or the *critical region*, denoted by R. Conversely, the region that H_0 is likely to occur and accordingly H_0 is accepted is called the *acceptance region*, denoted by A.

Using the rejection region R and the acceptance region A, the type I and II errors and the power are formulated as follows. Suppose that the test statistic is give by $T=T(X_1,X_2,\ldots,X_n)$. The probability of committing a type I error, i.e., the significance lever α, is given by

$$P(T(X_1,X_2,\ldots,X_n) \in R | H_0 \text{ is true}) = \alpha$$

which is the probability that rejects H_0 when H_0 is true. Conventionally, the significance level $\alpha = 0.1, 0.05, 0.01$ is chosen in practice. The probability of committing a type II error, i.e., β, is represented as

$$P(T(X_1,X_2,\ldots,X_n) \in A | H_0 \text{ is not true}) = \beta$$

which corresponds to the probability that accepts H_0 when H_0 is not true. The power is defined as $1-\beta$, i.e.

$$P(T(X_1,X_2,\ldots,X_n) \in R | H_0 \text{ is not true}) = 1-\beta$$

which is the probability that rejects H_0 when H_0 is not true.

2.8.2 Power Function

Let $X_1, X_2, \ldots, X_n$ be mutually independently, identically and normally distributed with mean μ and variance σ^2. Assume that σ^2 is known.

In Fig. 2.3, we consider the hypothesis on the population mean μ, i.e., the null hypothesis $H_0:\mu=\mu_0$ against the alternative hypothesis $H_1:\mu=\mu_1$, where $\mu_1 > \mu_0$ is taken. The dark shadow area corresponds to the probability of committing a type I error, i.e., the significance level, while the light shadow area indicates the probability of committing a type II error. The probability of the right-hand side of f^* in the distribution under H_1 represents the power of the test, i.e., $1-\beta$.

In the case of normal population, the distribution of sample mean $\bar{X}$ is given by

$$\bar{X} \sim N\left(\mu, \frac{\sigma^2}{n}\right)$$

For the distribution of $\bar{X}$, see the moment-generating function of $\bar{X}$ in Theorem of Subsection 2.5.2. By normalization, we have

$$\frac{\bar{X}-\mu}{\sigma/\sqrt{n}} \sim N(0,1)$$

Therefore, under the null hypothesis $H_0:\mu=\mu_0$, we obtain

$$\frac{\bar{X}-\mu_0}{\sigma/\sqrt{n}} \sim N(0,1)$$

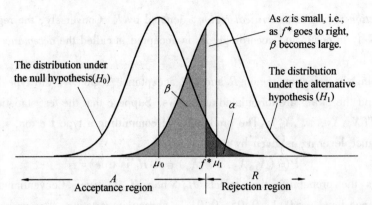

Fig. 2.3 Type I Error (α) and Type II Error (β)

where μ is replaced by μ_0. Since the significance level α is the probability which rejects H_0 when H_0 is true, it is given by

$$\alpha = P\left(\bar{X} > \mu_0 + z_\alpha \frac{\sigma}{\sqrt{n}}\right)$$

where z_α denotes $100 \times \alpha$ percent point of the standard normal density function. Therefore, the rejection region is given by

$$\bar{X} > \mu_0 + z_\alpha \sigma/\sqrt{n}$$

Since the power $1-\beta$ is the probability which rejects H_0 when H_1 is true, it is given by

$$1 - \beta = P\left(\bar{X} > \mu_0 + z_\alpha \frac{\sigma}{\sqrt{n}}\right) = P\left(\frac{\bar{X} - \mu}{\sigma/\sqrt{n}} > \frac{\mu_0 - \mu_1}{\sigma/\sqrt{n}} + z_\alpha\right) =$$

$$1 - P\left(\frac{\bar{X} - \mu_1}{\sigma/\sqrt{n}} < \frac{\mu_0 - \mu_1}{\sigma/\sqrt{n}} + z_\alpha\right) =$$

$$1 - F\left(\frac{\mu_0 - \mu_1}{\sigma/\sqrt{n}} + z_\alpha\right)$$

where $F(\cdot)$ represents the standard normal cumulative distribution function, which is given by

$$F(x) = \int_{-\infty}^{x} 2(\pi)^{-1/2} \exp\left(-\frac{1}{2}t^2\right) dt$$

The power function is a function of μ_1, given μ_0 and α.

2.8.3 Testing Hypothesis on Population Mean

Let $X_1, X_2, \ldots, X_n$ be mutually independently, identically and normally distributed with mean μ and variance σ^2. Assume that σ^2 is known.

Consider testing the null hypothesis $H_0: \mu = \mu_0$. When the null hypothesis H_0 is true, the distribution of $\bar{X}$ is given by

$$\frac{\bar{X} - \mu_0}{\sigma/\sqrt{n}} \sim N(0,1)$$

Therefore, the test statistic is given by: $\sqrt{n}(\bar{X}-\mu_0)/\sigma$, while the test statistic value is: $\sqrt{n}(\bar{x}-\mu_0)/\sigma$, where the sample mean $\bar{X}$ is replaced by the observed value $\bar{x}$.

Depending on the alternative hypothesis, we have the following three cases.

1. **The alternative hypothesis** $H_1: \mu < \mu_0$ (one-sided test)

We have $P\left(\dfrac{\bar{X}-\mu_0}{\sigma/\sqrt{n}} < -z_\alpha\right) = \alpha$. Therefore, when $\dfrac{\bar{X}-\mu_0}{\sigma/\sqrt{n}} < -z_\alpha$, we reject the null hypothesis $H_0: \mu = \mu_0$ at the significance level α.

2. **The alternative hypothesis** $H_1: \mu > \mu_0$ (one-sided test)

We have $P\left(\dfrac{\bar{X}-\mu_0}{\sigma/\sqrt{n}} > z_\alpha\right) = \alpha$. Therefore, when $\dfrac{\bar{X}-\mu_0}{\sigma/\sqrt{n}} > z_\alpha$, we reject the null hypothesis $H_0: \mu = \mu_0$ at the significance level α.

3. **The alternative hypothesis** $H_1: \mu \neq \mu_0$ (two-sided test)

We have $P\left(\left|\dfrac{\bar{X}-\mu_0}{\sigma/\sqrt{n}}\right| > z_{\alpha/2}\right) = \alpha$. Therefore, when $\left|\dfrac{\bar{X}-\mu_0}{\sigma/\sqrt{n}}\right| > z_{\alpha/2}$, we reject the null hypothesis $H_0: \mu = \mu_0$ at the significance level α.

When the sample size n is large enough, the testing procedure above can be applied to the cases: ①the distribution of X_i is not known and ② σ^2 is replaced by its estimator S^2 (in the case where σ^2 is not known).

2.8.4 Wald Test

From (2.16), under the null hypothesis $H_0: \theta = \theta_0$, as $n \to \infty$, the maximum likelihood estimator $\hat{\theta}_n$ is distributed as follows

$$\frac{\hat{\theta}_n - \theta_0}{\sigma(\hat{\theta}_n)/\sqrt{n}} \sim N(0,1)$$

For $H_0: \theta = \theta_0$ and $H_1: \theta \neq \theta_0$, replacing $X_1, X_2, \ldots, X_n$ in $\hat{\theta}_n$ by the observed values $x_1, x_2, \ldots, x_n$, we obtain the following testing procedure

1. If we have

$$\left|\frac{\hat{\theta}_n - \theta_0}{\sigma(\hat{\theta}_n)/\sqrt{n}}\right| > z_{\alpha/2}$$

we reject the null hypothesis H_0 at the significance level α, because the probability which H_0 occurs is small enough.

2. As for $H_0: \theta=\theta_0$ and $H_1: \theta>\theta_0$, if we have
$$\frac{\hat{\theta}_n - \theta_0}{\sigma(\hat{\theta}_n)/\sqrt{n}} > z_\alpha$$
we reject H_0 at the significance level α.

3. For $H_0: \theta=\theta_0$ and $H_1: \theta<\theta_0$, when we have the following
$$\frac{\hat{\theta}_n - \theta_0}{\sigma(\hat{\theta}_n)/\sqrt{n}} < -z_\alpha$$
we reject H_0 at the significance level α.

The testing procedure introduced here is called the *Wald test*.

Example 2.18

$X_1, X_2, \ldots, X_n$ are mutually independently, identically and exponentially distributed. Consider the following exponential probability density function
$$f(x;\gamma) = \gamma e^{-\gamma x}$$
for $0<x<\infty$.

Using the Wald test, we want to test the null hypothesis $H_0: \gamma=\gamma_0$ against the alternative hypothesis $H_1: \gamma \neq \gamma_0$.

Generally, as $n\to\infty$, the distribution of the maximum likelihood estimator of the parameter γ, $\hat{\gamma}_n$, is asymptotically represented as
$$\frac{\hat{\gamma}_n - \gamma}{\sigma(\hat{\gamma}_n)/\sqrt{n}} \sim N(0,1)$$
where
$$\sigma^2(\gamma) = \left(E\left(\left(\frac{d\log f(X;\gamma)}{d\gamma}\right)^2\right)\right)^{-1} = -\left(E\left(\frac{d^2\log f(X;\gamma)}{d\gamma^2}\right)\right)^{-1}$$
See (2.14) and (2.16) for the above properties on the maximum likelihood estimator.

Therefore, under the null hypothesis $H_0: \gamma=\gamma_0$, when n is large enough, we have the following distribution
$$\frac{\hat{\gamma}_n - \gamma_0}{\sigma(\hat{\gamma}_n)/\sqrt{n}} \sim N(0,1)$$
As for the null hypothesis $H_1: \gamma \neq \gamma_0$ against the alternative hypothesis $H_1: \gamma \neq \gamma_0$, if we have
$$\left|\frac{\hat{\gamma}_n - \gamma_0}{\sigma(\hat{\gamma}_n)/\sqrt{n}}\right| > z_{\alpha/2}$$
we can reject H_0 at the significance level α.

We need to derive $\sigma^2(\gamma)$ and $\hat{\gamma}_n$ to perform the testing procedure. First, $\sigma^2(\gamma)$ is given by

$$\sigma^2(\gamma) = -\left(E\left(\frac{d^2 \log f(X;\gamma)}{d\gamma^2}\right)\right)^{-1} = \gamma^2$$

Note that the first- and the second-derivatives of $\log f(X;\gamma)$ with respect to γ are given by

$$\frac{d\log f(X;\gamma)}{d\gamma} = \frac{1}{\gamma} - X, \frac{d^2 \log f(X;\gamma)}{d\gamma^2} = -\frac{1}{\gamma^2}$$

Next, the maximum likelihood estimator of γ, i.e., $\hat{\gamma}_n$, is obtained as follows. Since $X_1, X_2, \ldots, X_n$ are mutually independently and identically distributed, the likelihood function $l(\gamma)$ is given by

$$l(\gamma) = \prod_{i=1}^{n} f(x_i;\gamma) = \prod_{i=1}^{n} \gamma e^{-\gamma x_i} = \gamma^n e^{-\gamma \sum x_i}$$

Therefore, the log-likelihood function is written as

$$\log l(\gamma) = n\log \gamma - \gamma \sum_{i=1}^{n} x_i$$

we obtain the value of γ which maximizes $\log l(y)$. Solving the following equation

$$\frac{d\log l(\gamma)}{d\gamma} = \frac{n}{\gamma} - \sum_{i=1}^{n} x_i = 0$$

the maximum likelihood estimator of γ, i.e., $\hat{\gamma}_n$ is represented as

$$\hat{\gamma}_n = \frac{n}{\sum_{i=1}^{n} X_i} = \frac{1}{\overline{X}}$$

Then, we have the following

$$\frac{\hat{\gamma}_n - \gamma}{\sigma(\hat{\gamma}_n)/\sqrt{n}} = \frac{\hat{\gamma}_n - \gamma}{\hat{\gamma}_n/\sqrt{n}} \to N(0,1)$$

where $\hat{\gamma}_n$ is given by $1/\overline{X}$.

For $H_0: \gamma = \gamma_0$ and $H_1: \gamma \neq \gamma_0$, if we have

$$\left|\frac{\hat{\gamma}_n - \gamma_0}{\hat{\gamma}_n/\sqrt{n}}\right| > z_{\alpha/2}$$

We reject H_0 at the significance level α.

2.8.5 Likelihood Ratio Test

Suppose that the population distribution is given by $f(x;\theta)$, where $\theta = (\theta_1, \theta_2)$. Consider testing the null hypothesis $\theta_1 = \theta_1^*$ against the alternative hypothesis $H_1: \theta_1 \neq \theta_1^*$, using the observed values $(x_1, x_2, \ldots, x_n)$ corresponding to the random sample $(X_1, X_2, \ldots, X_n)$.

Let θ_1 and θ_2 be $1 \times k_1$ and $1 \times k_2$ vectors, respectively. Therefore, $\theta = (\theta_1, \theta_2)$ denotes a $1 \times (k_1 + k_2)$ vector. Since we take the null hypothesis as $H_0 : \theta_1 = \theta_1^*$, the number of restrictions is given by k_1, which is equal to the dimension of θ_1.

The likelihood function is written as

$$l(\theta_1, \theta_2) = \prod_{i=1}^{n} f(x_i; \theta_1, \theta_2)$$

Let $(\tilde{\theta}_1, \tilde{\theta}_2)$ be the maximum likelihood estimator of (θ_1, θ_2). That is, $(\tilde{\theta}_1, \tilde{\theta}_2)$ indicates the solution of (θ_1, θ_2), obtained from the following equations

$$\frac{\partial l(\theta_1, \theta_2)}{\partial \theta_1} = 0, \frac{\partial l(\theta_1, \theta_2)}{\partial \theta_2} = 0$$

The solution $(\tilde{\theta}_1, \tilde{\theta}_2)$ is called the *unconstrained maximum likelihood estimator*, because the null hypothesis $H_0 : \theta_1 = \theta_1^*$ is not taken into account.

Let $\hat{\theta}_2$ be the maximum likelihood estimator of θ_2 under the null hypothesis $H_0 : \theta_1 = \theta_1^*$. That is, $\hat{\theta}_2$ is a solution of the following equation

$$\frac{\partial l(\theta_1^*, \theta_2)}{\partial \theta_2} = 0$$

The solution $\hat{\theta}_2$ is called the *constrained maximum likelihood estimator* of θ_2, because the likelihood function is maximized with respect to θ_2 subject to the constraint $\theta_1 = \theta_1^*$.

Define λ as follows

$$\lambda = \frac{l(\theta_1^*, \hat{\theta}_2)}{l(\tilde{\theta}_1, \tilde{\theta}_2)}$$

which is called the *likelihood ratio*.

As n goes to infinity, it is known that we have

$$-2\log \lambda \sim \chi^2(k_1)$$

where k_1 denotes the number of the constraints.

Let $\chi_\alpha^2(k_1)$ be the $100 \times \alpha$ percent point from the chi-square distribution with k_1 degrees of freedom. When $-2\log \lambda > \chi_\alpha^2(k_1)$, we reject the null hypothesis $H_0 : \theta_1 = \theta_1^*$ at the significance level α. If $-2\log \lambda$ is close to zero, we accept the null hypothesis. When $(\theta_1^*, \hat{\theta}_2)$ is close to $(\tilde{\theta}_1, \tilde{\theta}_2)$, $-2\log(\lambda)$ approaches zero.

The likelihood ratio test is useful in the case where it is not easy to derive the distribution of $(\tilde{\theta}_1, \tilde{\theta}_2)$.

Example 2.19

$X_1, X_2, \ldots, X_n$ are mutually independently, identically and exponentially

distributed. Consider the following exponential probability density function
$$f(x;\gamma) = \gamma e^{-\gamma x}$$
for $0 < x < \infty$.

Using the likelihood ratio test, we want to test the null hypothesis $H_0: \gamma = \gamma_0$ against the alternative hypothesis $H_1: \gamma \neq \gamma_0$. Remember that in Example 2.18 we test the hypothesis with the Wald test.

In this case, the likelihood ratio is given by
$$\lambda = \frac{l(\gamma_0)}{l(\hat{\gamma}_n)}$$
where $\hat{\gamma}_n$ is derived in Example 2.18, i. e.
$$\hat{\gamma}_n = \frac{n}{\sum_{i=1}^{n} X_i} = \frac{1}{\overline{X}}$$

Since the number of the constraint is equal to one, as the sample size n goes to infinity we have the following asymptotic distribution
$$-2\log \lambda \to \chi^2(1)$$
The likelihood ratio is computed as follows
$$\lambda = \frac{l(\gamma_0)}{l(\hat{\gamma}_n)} = \frac{\gamma_0^n e^{-\gamma_0 \sum X_i}}{\hat{\gamma}_n^n e^{-n}}$$

If $-2\log \lambda > \chi_\alpha^2(1)$, we reject the null hypothesis $H_0: \mu = \mu_0$ at the significance level α. Note that $\chi_\alpha^2(1)$ denotes the $100 \times \alpha$ percent point from the chi-square distribution with one degree of freedom.

Example 2.20

Suppose that $X_1, X_2, \ldots, X_n$ are mutually independently, identically and normally distributed with mean zero and variance σ^2.

The normal probability density function with mean μ and variance σ^2 is given by
$$f(x;\mu,\sigma^2) = \frac{1}{\sqrt{2\pi\sigma^2}} e^{-\frac{1}{2\sigma^2}(x-\mu)^2}$$

By the likelihood ratio test, we want to test the null hypothesis $H_0: \mu = \mu_0$ against the alternative hypothesis $H_1: \mu \neq \mu_0$.

The likelihood ratio is given by
$$\lambda = \frac{l(\mu_0, \tilde{\sigma}^2)}{l(\hat{\mu}, \hat{\sigma}^2)}$$
where $\tilde{\sigma}^2$ is the constrained maximum likelihood estimator with the constrain $\mu = \mu_0$,

while (μ, σ^2) denotes the unconstrained maximum likelihood estimator. In this case, since the number of the constraint is one, the asymptotic distribution is as follows

$$-2\log \lambda \to \chi^2(1)$$

Now, we derive $l(\mu_0, \tilde{\sigma}^2)$ and $l(\hat{\mu}, \hat{\sigma}^2)$. $l(\mu, \sigma^2)$ is written as

$$l(\mu, \sigma^2) = f(x_1, x_2, \ldots, x_n; \mu, \sigma^2) = \prod_{i=1}^{n} f(x_i; \mu, \sigma^2) =$$

$$\prod_{i=1}^{n} \frac{1}{\sqrt{2\pi\sigma^2}} \exp\left(-\frac{1}{2\sigma^2}(x_i - \mu)^2\right) =$$

$$(2\pi\sigma^2)^{-n/2} \exp\left(-\frac{1}{2\sigma^2} \sum_{i=1}^{n} (x_i - \mu)^2\right)$$

The log-likelihood function $\log(\mu, \sigma^2)$ is represented as

$$\log(\mu, \sigma^2) = -\frac{n}{2}\log(2\pi) - \frac{n}{2}\log(\sigma^2) - \frac{1}{2\sigma^2} \sum_{i=1}^{n} (x_i - \mu)^2$$

For the numerator of the likelihood ratio, under the constraint $\mu = \mu_0$, maximize $\log l(\mu_0, \sigma^2)$ with respect to σ^2. Since we obtain the first-derivative

$$\frac{\partial \log l(\mu_0, \sigma^2)}{\partial \sigma^2} = -\frac{n}{2} \frac{1}{\sigma^2} + \frac{1}{2\sigma^4} \sum_{i=1}^{n} (x_i - \mu_0)^2 = 0$$

the constrained maximum likelihood estimator $\tilde{\sigma}^2$ is given by

$$\tilde{\sigma}^2 = \frac{1}{n} \sum_{i=1}^{n} (x_i - \mu_0)^2$$

Therefore, replacing σ^2 by $\tilde{\sigma}^2$, $l(\mu_0, \tilde{\sigma}^2)$ is written as

$$l(\mu_0, \tilde{\sigma}^2) = 2(\pi\tilde{\sigma}^2)^{-n/2} \exp\left(-\frac{1}{2\tilde{\sigma}^2} \sum_{i=1}^{n} (x_i - \mu_0)^2\right) = (2\pi\tilde{\sigma}^2)^{-n/2} \exp\left(-\frac{n}{2}\right)$$

For the denominator of the likelihood ratio, because the unconstrained maximum likelihood estimators are obtained as

$$\hat{\mu} = \frac{1}{n} \sum_{i=1}^{n} x_i, \quad \hat{\sigma}^2 = \frac{1}{n} \sum_{i=1}^{n} (x_i - \hat{\mu})^2$$

$l(\hat{\mu}, \hat{\sigma}^2)$ is written as

$$l(\hat{\mu}, \hat{\sigma}^2) = (2\pi\hat{\sigma}^2)^{-n/2} \exp\left(-\frac{1}{2\hat{\sigma}^2} \sum_{i=1}^{n} (x_i - \hat{\mu})^2\right) = (2\pi\hat{\sigma}^2)^{-n/2} \exp\left(-\frac{n}{2}\right)$$

Thus, the likelihood ratio is given by

$$\lambda = \frac{l(\mu_0, \tilde{\sigma}^2)}{l(\hat{\mu}, \hat{\sigma}^2)} = \frac{(2\pi\tilde{\sigma}^2)^{-n/2} \exp\left(-\frac{n}{2}\right)}{(2\pi\hat{\sigma}^2)^{-n/2} \exp\left(-\frac{n}{2}\right)} = \left(\frac{\tilde{\sigma}^2}{\hat{\sigma}^2}\right)^{-n/2}$$

Asymptotically, we have
$$-2\log \lambda = n(\log \tilde{\sigma}^2 - \log \hat{\sigma}^2) \sim \chi^2(1)$$
When $-2\log\lambda > \chi^2_\alpha(1)$, we reject the null hypothesis $H_0: \mu = \mu_0$ at the significance level α.

Words and Expressions

null hypothesis 零假设,原假设
alternative hypothesis 备择假设,对立假设
significance level 显著性水平
power function 势函数,幂函数
testing procedures 检验方法,检验程序
test statistic 检验统计量
rejection region 拒绝区域
critical region 临界区域,判别区域
acceptance region 接受区域
Wald test 沃尔德检验
first-derivatives 一阶导数
second-derivatives 二阶导数
unconstrained maximum likelihood estimator 无约束极大似然估计量
constrained maximum likelihood estimator 约束极大似然估计量
likelihood ratio 似然比
numerator *n*. 分子
denominator *n*. 分母;(爱好、见解等的)标准

2.9 Regression Analysis

2.9.1 Setup of the Model

When $(X_1, Y_1), (X_2, Y_2), \ldots, (X_n, X_n)$ are available, suppose that there is a linear relationship between Y and X, i.e.
$$Y_i = \beta_1 + \beta_2 X_i + u_i \tag{2.21}$$
for $i = 1, 2, \ldots, n$.

X_i and Y_i denote the ith observations. Y_i is called the *dependent variable* or the *unexplanatory variable*, while X_i is known as the *independent variable* or the *explanatory variable*. β_1 and β_2 are unknown *parameters* to be estimated. u_i is the unobserved *error term* assumed to be a random variable with mean zero and variance

σ^2. β_1 and β_2 are called the *regression coefficients*.

X_i is assumed to be nonstochastic, but Y_i is stochastic because depends on the error u_i. The error terms $u_1, u_2, \ldots, u_n$ are assumed to be mutually independently and identically distributed. It is assumed that u_i has a distribution with mean zero, i.e., $E(u_i) = 0$ is assumed. Taking the expectation on both sides of equation (2.21), the expectation of Y_i is represented as

$$E(Y_i) = E(\beta_1 + \beta_2 X_i + u_i) = \beta_1 + \beta_2 X_i + E(u_i) =$$
$$\beta_1 + \beta_2 X_i \qquad (2.22)$$

for $i = 1, 2, \ldots, n$. Using $E(Y_i)$ we can rewrite (2.21) as $Y_i = E(Y_i) + u_i$. Equation (2.22) represents the true regression line.

Let $\hat{\beta}_1$ and $\hat{\beta}_2$ be estimators of $\hat{\beta}_1$ and $\hat{\beta}_2$. Replacing (β_1, β_2) by $(\hat{\beta}_1, \hat{\beta}_2)$, equation (2.21) turns out to be

$$Y_i = \hat{\beta}_1 + \hat{\beta}_2 X_i + e_i \qquad (2.23)$$

for $i = 1, 2, \ldots, n$, where e_i is called the *residual*. The residual e_i is taken as the experimental value of u_i.

We define $\hat{Y}_i$ as follows

$$\hat{Y}_i = \hat{\beta}_1 + \hat{\beta}_2 X_i \qquad (2.24)$$

for $i = 1, 2, \ldots, n$, which is interpreted as the predicted value of Y_i. Equation (2.24) indicates the estimated repression line, which is different from equation (2.22). Moreover, using $\hat{Y}_i$ we can rewrite (2.23) as $Y_i = \hat{Y}_i + e_i$.

Equations (2.22) and (2.24) are displayed in Fig. 2.4. Consider the case of $n = 6$ for simplicity. × indicates the observed data series. The true regression line (2.22) is represented by the solid line, while the estimated repression ling (2.24) is drawn with the dotted line. Based on the observed data, β_1 and β_2 are estimated as: $\hat{\beta}_1$ and $\hat{\beta}_2$.

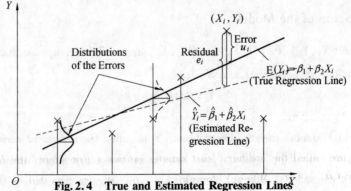

Fig. 2.4 **True and Estimated Regression Lines**

In the next section, we consider how to obtain the estimates of β_1 and β_2, i.e., $\hat{\beta}_1$ and $\hat{\beta}_2$.

2.9.2 Ordinary Least Squares Estimation

Suppose that $(X_1, Y_1), (X_2, Y_2), \ldots, (X_n, Y_n)$ are available. For the regression model (2.21), we consider estimating β_1 and β_2. Replacing β_1 and β_2 by their estimates $\hat{\beta}_1$ and $\hat{\beta}_2$, remember that the residual e_i is given by

$$e_i = Y_i - \hat{Y}_i = Y_i - \hat{\beta}_1 - \hat{\beta}_2 X_i$$

The sum of squared residuals is defined as follows

$$S(\hat{\beta}_1, \hat{\beta}_2) = \sum_{i=1}^{n} e_i^2 = \sum_{i=1}^{n} (Y_i - \hat{\beta}_1 - \hat{\beta}_2 X_i)^2$$

It might be plausible to chose the $\hat{\beta}_1$ and $\hat{\beta}_2$ which minimize the sum of squared residuals, i.e., $S(\hat{\beta}_1, \hat{\beta}_2)$. This method is called the *ordinary least squares* (OLS) *estimation*. To minimize $S(\hat{\beta}_1, \hat{\beta}_2)$ with respect to and , we set the partial derivatives equal to zero

$$\frac{\partial S(\hat{\beta}_1, \hat{\beta}_2)}{\partial \hat{\beta}_1} = -2 \sum_{i=1}^{n} (Y_i - \hat{\beta}_1 - \hat{\beta}_2 X_i) = 0$$

$$\frac{\partial S(\hat{\beta}_1, \hat{\beta}_2)}{\partial \hat{\beta}_2} = -2 \sum_{i=1}^{n} X_i(Y_i - \hat{\beta}_1 - \hat{\beta}_2 X_i) = 0$$

which yields the following two equations

$$\bar{Y} = \hat{\beta}_1 + \hat{\beta}_2 \bar{X} \tag{2.25}$$

$$\sum_{i=1}^{n} X_i Y_i = n\bar{X}\hat{\beta}_1 + \hat{\beta}_2 \sum_{i=1}^{n} X_i^2 \tag{2.26}$$

where $\bar{Y} = (1/n) \sum_{i=1}^{n} Y_i$ and $\bar{X} = (1/n) \sum_{i=1}^{n} X_i$. Multiplying (2.25) by $n\bar{X}$ and subtracting (2.26), we can derive $\hat{\beta}_2$ as follows

$$\hat{\beta}_2 = \frac{\sum_{i=1}^{n} X_i Y_i - n\overline{XY}}{\sum_{i=1}^{n} X_i^2 - n\bar{X}^2} = \frac{\sum_{i=1}^{n} (X_i - \bar{X})(Y_i - \bar{Y})}{\sum_{i=1}^{n} (X_i - \bar{X})^2} \tag{2.27}$$

From equation (2.25), $\hat{\beta}_1$ is directly obtained as follows

$$\hat{\beta}_1 = \bar{Y} - \hat{\beta}_2 \bar{X} \tag{2.28}$$

When the observed values are taken for Y_i and X_i for $i = 1, 2, \ldots, n$, we say that $\hat{\beta}_1$ and $\hat{\beta}_2$ are called the *ordinary least squares estimates* (or simply the *lest squares estimates*) of $\hat{\beta}_1$ and $\hat{\beta}_2$. When Y_i for $i = 1, 2, \ldots, n$, are regarded as the random sample, we say that $\hat{\beta}_1$ and $\hat{\beta}_2$ are called the *ordinary least squares estimators* (or the *least squares estimators*) of $\hat{\beta}_1$ and $\hat{\beta}_2$.

2.9.3 Properties of Least Square Estimator

Equation (2.27) is rewritten as

$$\hat{\beta}_2 = \frac{\sum_{i=1}^{n}(X_i - \bar{X})(Y_i - \bar{Y})}{\sum_{i=1}^{n}(X_i - \bar{X})^2} = \frac{\sum_{i=1}^{n}(X_i - \bar{X})Y_i}{\sum_{i=1}^{n}(X_i - \bar{X})^2} - \frac{\bar{Y}\sum_{i=1}^{n}(X_i - \bar{X})}{\sum_{i=1}^{n}(X_i - \bar{X})^2} =$$

$$\sum_{i=1}^{n} \frac{X_i - \bar{X}}{\sum_{i=1}^{n}(X_i - \bar{X})^2} Y_i = \sum_{i=1}^{n} \omega_i Y_i \qquad (2.29)$$

In the third equality, $\sum_{i=1}^{n}(X_i - \bar{X}) = 0$ is utilized because of $\bar{X} = (1/n)\sum_{i=1}^{n} X_i$. In the fourth equality, ω_i is defined as

$$\omega_i = \frac{X_i - \bar{X}}{\sum_{i=1}^{n}(X_i - \bar{X})^2}$$

ω_i is nonstochastic because X_i is assumed to be nonstochastic. ω_i has the following peoperites

$$\sum_{i=1}^{n} \omega_i = \sum_{i=1}^{n} \frac{X_i - \bar{X}}{\sum_{i=1}^{n}(X_i - \bar{X})^2} = \frac{\sum_{i=1}^{n}(X_i - \bar{X})}{\sum_{i=1}^{n}(X_i - \bar{X})^2} = 0 \qquad (2.30)$$

$$\sum_{i=1}^{n} \omega_i X_i = \sum_{i=1}^{n} \omega_i (X_i - \bar{X}) = \frac{\sum_{i=1}^{n}(X_i - \bar{X})^2}{\sum_{i=1}^{n}(X_i - \bar{X})^2} = 1 \qquad (2.31)$$

$$\sum_{i=1}^{n} \omega_i^2 = \sum_{i=1}^{n} \left(\frac{X_i - \bar{X}}{\sum_{i=1}^{n}(X_i - \bar{X})^2} \right)^2 = \frac{\sum_{i=1}^{n}(X_i - \bar{X})^2}{\left(\sum_{i=1}^{n}(X_i - \bar{X})^2\right)^2} = \frac{1}{\sum_{i=1}^{n}(X_i - \bar{X})^2} \qquad (2.32)$$

The first equality of equation (2.31) comes from equation (2.30).

From now on, we focus only on $\hat{\beta}_2$, because usually β_2 is more important than β_1 in the regression model (2.21). In order to obtain the properties of the least squares estimator $\hat{\beta}_2$, we rewrite equation (2.29) as

$$\hat{\beta}_2 = \sum_{i=1}^{n} \omega_i Y_i = \sum_{i=1}^{n} \omega_i (\beta_1 + \beta_2 X_i + u_i) =$$

$$\beta_1 \sum_{i=1}^{n} \omega_i + \beta_2 \sum_{i=1}^{n} \omega_i X_i + \sum_{i=1}^{n} \omega_i u_i =$$

$$\beta_2 + \sum_{i=1}^{n} \omega_i u_i \qquad (2.33)$$

In the fourth equality of (2.33), equations (2.30) and (2.31) are utilized.

Mean and Variance of $\hat{\beta}_1$: $u_1, u_2, \ldots, u_n$ are assumed to be mutually independently and identically distributed with mean zero and variance σ^2, but they are not necessarily normal. Remember that we do not need normality assumption to obtain mean and variance but the normality assumption is required to test a hypothesis.

From equation (2.33), the expectation of $\hat{\beta}_2$ is derived as follows

$$E(\hat{\beta}_2) = E(\beta_2 + \sum_{i=1}^{n} \omega_i u_i) = \beta_2 + E(\sum_{i=1}^{n} \omega_i u_i) =$$

$$\beta_2 + \sum_{i=1}^{n} \omega_i E(u_i) = \beta_2 \qquad (2.34)$$

It is shown from (2.34) that the ordinary least squares estimator $\hat{\beta}_2$ is an unbiased estimator of $\hat{\beta}_2$.

From (2.33), the variance of $\hat{\beta}_2$ is computed as

$$V(\hat{\beta}_2) = V(\beta_2 + \sum_{i=1}^{n} \omega_i u_i) = V(\sum_{i=1}^{n} \omega_i u_i) = \sum_{i=1}^{n} V(\omega_i u_i) =$$

$$\sum_{i=1}^{n} \omega_i^2 V(u_i) = \sigma^2 \sum_{i=1}^{n} \omega_i^2 = \frac{\sigma^2}{\sum_{i=1}^{n} (X_i - \bar{X})^2} \qquad (2.35)$$

From Theorem of Subsection 2.3.1, the second and the fourth equalities hold. The third equality holds because $u_1, u_2, \ldots, u_n$ are mutually independent (see the theorem Subsection 2.3.2). The last equality comes from equation (2.32).

Thus, $E(\hat{\beta}_2)$ and $V(\hat{\beta}_2)$ are given by (2.34) and (2.35).

Gauss-Markov Theorem

It has been discussed above that $\hat{\beta}_2$ is represented as (2.29), which implies that $\hat{\beta}_2$ is a linear estimator, i.e., linear in Y_i. In addition, (2.34) indicates that $\hat{\beta}_2$ is an unbiased estimator. Therefore, summarizing these two facts, it is shown that $\hat{\beta}_2$ is a *linear unbiased estimator*. Furthermore, here we show that $\hat{\beta}_2$ has minimum variance within a class of the linear unbiased estimators.

Consider the alternative linear unbiased estimator $\tilde{\beta}_2$ as follows

$$\tilde{\beta}_2 = \sum_{i=1}^{n} c_i Y_i = \sum_{i=1}^{n} (\omega_i + d_i) Y_i$$

where $c_i = \omega_i + d_i$ is defined and d_i is nonstochastic. Then, $\tilde{\beta}_2$ is transformed into

$$\tilde{\beta}_2 = \sum_{i=1}^{n} c_i Y_i = \sum_{i=1}^{n} (\omega_i + d_i)(\beta_1 + \beta_2 X_i + u_i) =$$

$$\beta_1 \sum_{i=1}^{n} \omega_i + \beta_2 \sum_{i=1}^{n} \omega_i X_i + \sum_{i=1}^{n} \omega_i u_i +$$

$$\beta_1 \sum_{i=1}^{n} d_i + \beta_2 \sum_{i=1}^{n} d_i X_i + \sum_{i=1}^{n} d_i u_i =$$

$$\beta_2 + \beta_1 \sum_{i=1}^{n} d_i + \beta_2 \sum_{i=1}^{n} d_i X_i + \sum_{i=1}^{n} \omega_i u_i + \sum_{i=1}^{n} d_i u_i$$

Equations (2.30) and (2.31) are used in the forth equality. Taking the expectation on both sides of the above equation, we obtain

$$E(\tilde{\beta}_2) = \beta_2 + \beta_1 \sum_{i=1}^{n} d_i + \beta_2 \sum_{i=1}^{n} d_i X_i + \sum_{i=1}^{n} \omega_i E(u_i) + \sum_{i=1}^{n} d_i E(u_i) =$$

$$\beta_2 + \beta_1 \sum_{i=1}^{n} d_i + \beta_2 \sum_{i=1}^{n} d_i X_i$$

Note that d_i is not a random variable and that $E(u_i) = 0$. Since $\tilde{\beta}_2$ is assumed to be unbiased, we need the following conditions

$$\sum_{i=1}^{n} d_i = 0, \quad \sum_{i=1}^{n} d_i X_i = 0$$

When these conditions hold, we can rewrite $\tilde{\beta}_2$ as

$$\tilde{\beta}_2 = \beta_2 + \sum_{i=1}^{n} (\omega_i + d_i) u_i$$

The variance of $\tilde{\beta}_2$ is derived as

$$V(\tilde{\beta}_2) = V(\beta_2 + \sum_{i=1}^{n} (\omega_i + d_i) u_i) = V(\sum_{i=1}^{n} (\omega_i + d_i) u_i) =$$

$$\sum_{i=1}^{n} V((\omega_i + d_i) u_i) = \sum_{i=1}^{n} (\omega_i + d_i)^2 V(u_i) =$$

$$\sigma^2 (\sum_{i=1}^{n} \omega_i^2 + 2 \sum_{i=1}^{n} \omega_i d_i + \sum_{i=1}^{n} d_i^2) =$$

$$\sigma^2 (\sum_{i=1}^{n} \omega_i^2 + \sum_{i=1}^{n} d_i^2)$$

From unbiasedness of $\tilde{\beta}_2$, using $\sum_{i=1}^{n} d_i = 0$ and $\sum_{i=1}^{n} d_i X_i = 0$, we obtain

$$\sum_{i=1}^{n} \omega_i d_i = \frac{\sum_{i=1}^{n}(X_i - \bar{X})d_i}{\sum_{i=1}^{n}(X_i - \bar{X})^2} = \frac{\sum_{i=1}^{n} X_i d_i - \bar{X}\sum_{i=1}^{n} d_i}{\sum_{i=1}^{n}(X_i - \bar{X})^2} = 0$$

which is utilized to obtain the variance of $\tilde{\beta}_2$ in the third line of the above equation.

From (2.35), the variance of $\tilde{\beta}_2$ is given by: $V(\tilde{\beta}_2) = \sigma^2 \sum_{i=1}^{n} \omega_i^2$. Therefore, we have

$$V(\tilde{\beta}_2) \geq V(\tilde{\beta}_2)$$

because of $\sum_{i=1}^{n} d_i^2 \geq 0$. When $\sum_{i=1}^{n} d_i^2 = 0$, i.e., when $d_1 = d_2 = \ldots = d_n = 0$, we have the equality: $V(\tilde{\beta}_2) = V(\tilde{\beta}_2)$. Thus, in the case of $d_1 = d_2 = \ldots = d_n = 0$, $\tilde{\beta}_2$ is equivalent to $\tilde{\beta}_2$.

As shown above, the least squares estimator $\tilde{\beta}_2$ given us the *linear unbiased minimum variance estimator*, or equivalently the *best linear unbiased estimator* (BLUE), which is called the *Gauss-Markov theorem*.

Asymptotic Properties of $\tilde{\beta}_2$ we assume that as n goes to infinity we have the following

$$\frac{1}{n}\sum_{i=1}^{n}(X_i - \bar{X})^2 \to M < \infty$$

where M is a constant value. Form (2.32), we obtain

$$n\sum_{i=1}^{n} \omega_i^2 = \frac{1}{(1/n)\sum_{i=1}^{n}(X_i - \bar{X})} \to \frac{1}{M}$$

Note that $f(x_n) \to f(m)$ when $x_n \to m$, where m is a constant value and $f(\cdot)$ is a function.

Here, we show both consistency of $\hat{\beta}_2$ and asymptotic normality of $\sqrt{n}(\hat{\beta}_2 - \beta_2)$. First, we prove that $\hat{\beta}_2$ is a consistent estimator of β_2. As in (2.10), Chebyshev's inequality is given by

$$P(|X - \mu| > \varepsilon) \leq \frac{\sigma^2}{\varepsilon^2}$$

where $\mu = E(X)$ and $\sigma^2 = V(X)$. Here, we replace X, $E(X)$ and $V(X)$ by $\hat{\beta}_2$

$$E(\hat{\beta}_2) = \beta_2, V(\hat{\beta}_2) = \sigma^2 \sum_{i=1}^{n} \omega_i^2 = \frac{\sigma^2}{\sum_{i=1}^{n}(X_i - \bar{X})}$$

respectively. Then, when $n \to \infty$, we obtain the following result

$$P(|\hat{\beta}_2 - \beta_2| > \varepsilon) \leq \frac{\sigma \sum_{i=1}^{n} \omega_i^2}{\varepsilon^2} = \frac{\sigma^2}{\varepsilon^2 \sum_{i=1}^{n} (X_i - \bar{X})} \to 0$$

where $\sum_{i=1}^{n} \omega_i^2 \to 0$ because $n \sum_{i=1}^{n} \omega_i^2 \to 1/M$ from the assumption. Thus, we obtain the result that $\hat{\beta}_2 \to \beta_2$ as $n \to \infty$. Therefore, we can conclude that $\hat{\beta}_2$ is a consistent estimator of β_2.

Next, we want to show that $\sqrt{n}(\hat{\beta}_2 - \beta_2)$ is asymptotically normal. Noting that $\hat{\beta}_2 = \beta_2 + \sum_{i=1}^{n} \omega_i u_i$ as in (2.33) from Corollary 2 of Section 2.6 (central limit theorem), asymptotic normality is shown as follows

$$\frac{\sum_{i=1}^{n} \omega_i u_i - E(\sum_{i=1}^{n} \omega_i u_i)}{\sqrt{V(\sum_{i=1}^{n} \sqrt{n} \omega_i u_i)}} = \frac{\sum_{i=1}^{n} \omega_i u_i}{\sigma \sqrt{\sum_{i=1}^{n} \omega_i^2}} =$$

$$\frac{\hat{\beta}_2 - \beta_2}{\sigma / \sqrt{\sum_{i=1}^{n}(X_i - \bar{X})^2}} \to N(0,1)$$

where $E(\sum_{i=1}^{n} \omega_i u_i) = 0$, $V(\sum_{i=1}^{n} \omega_i u_i) = \sigma^2 \sum_{i=1}^{n} \omega_i^2$, and $\sum_{i=1}^{n} \omega_i u_i = \hat{\beta}_2 - \beta_2$ are substituted in the second equality. Moreover, we can rewrite as follows

$$\frac{\hat{\beta}_2 - \beta_2}{\sigma / \sqrt{\sum_{i=1}^{n}(X_i - \bar{X})^2}} = \frac{\sqrt{n}(\hat{\beta}_2 - \beta_2)}{\sigma / \sqrt{(1/n) \sum_{i=1}^{n}(X_i - \bar{X})^2}} \to$$

$$\frac{\sqrt{n}(\hat{\beta}_2 - \beta_2)}{\sigma / \sqrt{M}} \to N(0,1)$$

or equivalently

$$\sqrt{n}(\hat{\beta}_2 - \beta_2) \to N(0, \frac{\sigma^2}{M})$$

Thus, asymptotic normality of $\sqrt{n}(\hat{\beta}_2 - \beta_2)$ is shown.

Finally, replacing σ^2 by its consistent estimator s^2, it is known as follows

$$\frac{\hat{\beta}_2 - \beta_2}{s \sqrt{\sum_{i=1}^{n}(X_i - \bar{X})^2}} \to N(0,1) \tag{2.36}$$

where s^2 is defined as

$$s^2 = \frac{1}{n-2} \sum_{i=1}^{n} e_i^2 = \frac{1}{n-2} \sum_{i=1}^{n} (Y_i - \hat{\beta}_1 - \hat{\beta}_2 X_i)^2 \qquad (2.37)$$

which is a consistent and unbiased estimator of σ^2.

Thus, using (2.36), in large sample we can construct the confidence interval discussed in Section 2.7.6 and test the hypothesis discussed in Section 2.8.

Exact Distribution of $\hat{\beta}_2$ We have shown asymptotic normality of $\sqrt{n}\,(\hat{\beta}_2 - \beta_2)$, which is one of large sample properties. Now, we discuss the small sample properties of $\hat{\beta}_2$. In order to obtain the distribution of $\hat{\beta}_2$ in small sample, the distribution of the error term has to be assumed. Therefore, the extra assumption is that $u_i \sim N(0, \sigma^2)$. Writing equation (2.33), again, $\hat{\beta}_2$ is represented as

$$\hat{\beta}_2 = \beta_2 + \sum_{i=1}^{n} \omega_i u_i$$

First, we obtain the distribution of the second term in the above equation. From Theorem of multivariate case of Section 2.5.2, $\sum_{i=1}^{n} \omega_i u_i$ is distributed as

$$\sum_{i=1}^{n} \omega_i u_i \sim N(0, \sigma^2 \sum_{i=1}^{n} \omega_i^2)$$

which is easily shown using the moment-generating function. Therefore, from Example 2.9 of Section 2.4, $\hat{\beta}_2$ is distributed as

$$\hat{\beta}_2 = \beta_2 + \sum_{i=1}^{n} \omega_i u_i \sim N(\beta_2, \sigma^2 \sum_{i=1}^{n} \omega_i^2)$$

or equivalently

$$\frac{\hat{\beta}_2 - \beta_2}{\sigma / \sqrt{\sum_{i=1}^{n} \omega_i^2}} = \frac{\hat{\beta}_2 - \beta_2}{\sigma / \sqrt{\sum_{i=1}^{n} (X_i - \bar{X})^2}} \sim N(0,1)$$

for any n.

Moreover, replacing σ^2 by its estimator s^2 defined in (2.37), it is known that we have

$$\frac{\hat{\beta}_2 - \beta_2}{s / \sqrt{\sum_{i=1}^{n} (X_i - \bar{X})^2}} \sim t(n-2)$$

where $t(n-2)$ denotes t distribution with $n-2$ degrees of freedom. Thus, under normality assumption on the error term u_i, the $t(n-2)$ distribution is used for the confidence interval and the testing hypothesis in small sample.

2.9.4 Multiple Regression Model

In Sections 2.9.1 ~ 2.9.3, only one independent variable, i.e., X_i, is taken into the repression model. In this section, we extend it to more independent variables, which is called the *multiple regression*. We consider the following regression model

$$Y_i = \beta_1 X_{i,1} + \beta_2 X_{i,2} + \ldots + \beta_k X_{i,k} + u_i = X_i \beta + u_i$$

for $i = 1, 2, \ldots, n$, where X_i and $\boldsymbol{\beta}$ denote a $1 \times k$ vector of the independent variables and a $k \times 1$ vector of the unknown parameters to be estimated, which are represented as

$$X_i = (X_{i,1}, X_{i,2}, \ldots, X_{i,k}), \boldsymbol{\beta} = \begin{pmatrix} \beta_1 \\ \beta_2 \\ \vdots \\ \beta_k \end{pmatrix}$$

$X_{i,j}$ denotes the ith observation of the jth independent variable. The case of $k = 2$ and $X_{i,1} = 1$ for all i is exactly equivalent to (2.21). Therefore, the matrix form above is a generalization of (2.21). Writing all the equations for $i = 1, 2, \ldots, n$, we have

$$Y_1 = \beta_1 X_{1,1} + \beta_2 X_{1,2} + \ldots + \beta_k X_{1,k} + u_1$$
$$Y_2 = \beta_1 X_{2,1} + \beta_2 X_{2,2} + \ldots + \beta_k X_{2,k} + u_2$$
$$\vdots$$
$$Y_n = \beta_1 X_{n,1} + \beta_2 X_{n,2} + \ldots + \beta_k X_{n,k} + u_n$$

which is rewritten as

$$\begin{pmatrix} Y_1 \\ Y_2 \\ \vdots \\ Y_n \end{pmatrix} = \begin{pmatrix} X_{1,1} & X_{1,2} & \ldots & X_{1,k} \\ X_{2,1} & X_{2,2} & \ldots & X_{2,k} \\ \vdots & \vdots & & \vdots \\ X_{n,1} & X_{n,2} & \ldots & X_{n,k} \end{pmatrix} \begin{pmatrix} \beta_1 \\ \beta_2 \\ \vdots \\ \beta_n \end{pmatrix} + \begin{pmatrix} u_1 \\ u_2 \\ \vdots \\ u_n \end{pmatrix}$$

Again, the above equation is compactly rewritten as

$$Y = X\beta + u \tag{2.38}$$

where Y, X and u are denoted by

$$Y = \begin{pmatrix} Y_1 \\ Y_2 \\ \vdots \\ Y_n \end{pmatrix}, X = \begin{pmatrix} X_{1,1} & X_{1,2} & \ldots & X_{1,k} \\ X_{2,1} & X_{2,2} & \ldots & X_{2,k} \\ \vdots & \vdots & & \vdots \\ X_{n,1} & X_{n,2} & \ldots & X_{n,k} \end{pmatrix}, u = \begin{pmatrix} u_1 \\ u_2 \\ \vdots \\ u_n \end{pmatrix}$$

Utilizing the matrix form (2.38), we derive the ordinary least squares estimator of β, denoted by $\hat{\beta}$. In equation (2.38), replacing β by $\hat{\beta}$, we have the following equation

$$Y = X\hat{\beta} + e$$

where e denotes a $1 \times n$ vector of the residuals. The ith element of e is given by e_i. The sum of squared residuals is written as follows

$$S(\hat{\boldsymbol{\beta}}) = \sum_{i=1}^{n} e_i^2 = e'e = (Y - X\hat{\boldsymbol{\beta}})'(Y - X\hat{\boldsymbol{\beta}}) =$$
$$(Y' - \hat{\boldsymbol{\beta}}'X')(Y - X\hat{\boldsymbol{\beta}}) =$$
$$Y'Y - Y'X\hat{\boldsymbol{\beta}} - \hat{\boldsymbol{\beta}}'X'Y + \hat{\boldsymbol{\beta}}X'X\hat{\boldsymbol{\beta}} =$$
$$Y'Y - 2Y'X\hat{\boldsymbol{\beta}} + \hat{\boldsymbol{\beta}}'X'X\hat{\boldsymbol{\beta}}$$

See Appendix 2.5 for the transpose in the fourth equality. In the last equality, note that $\hat{\boldsymbol{\beta}}'X'Y = Y'X'\hat{\boldsymbol{\beta}}$ because both are scalars. To minimize with $S(\hat{\boldsymbol{\beta}})$ respect to $\hat{\boldsymbol{\beta}}$, we set the first derivative of $S(\hat{\boldsymbol{\beta}})$ equal to zero, i.e.

$$\frac{\partial S(\hat{\boldsymbol{\beta}})}{\partial \boldsymbol{\beta}} = -2X'Y + 2X'X\hat{\boldsymbol{\beta}} = 0$$

See Appendix 2.5 for the derivatives of matrices. Solving the equation above with respect to $\hat{\boldsymbol{\beta}}$, the ordinary least squares estimator of $\boldsymbol{\beta}$ is given by

$$\hat{\boldsymbol{\beta}} = (X'X)^{-1}X'Y \tag{2.39}$$

See Appendix 2.5 for the inverse of the matrix. Thus, the ordinary least squares estimator is derived in the matrix form.

Now, in order to obtain the properties of $\hat{\boldsymbol{\beta}}$ such as mean, variance, distribution and so on, (2.39) is rewritten as follows

$$\hat{\boldsymbol{\beta}} = (X'X)^{-1}X'Y = (X'X)^{-1}X'(X\boldsymbol{\beta} + u) =$$
$$(X'X)^{-1}X'X\boldsymbol{\beta} + (X'X)^{-1}X'u =$$
$$\boldsymbol{\beta} + (X'X)^{-1}X'u \tag{2.40}$$

Taking the expectation on both sides of equation (2.40), we have the following

$$E(\hat{\boldsymbol{\beta}}) = E(\boldsymbol{\beta} + (X'X)^{-1}X'u) = \boldsymbol{\beta} + (X'X)^{-1}X'E(u) = \boldsymbol{\beta}$$

because of $E(u) = 0$ by the assumption of the error term u_i. Thus, unbiasedness of $\hat{\boldsymbol{\beta}}$ is shown.

The variance of $\hat{\boldsymbol{\beta}}$ is obtained as

$$V(\hat{\boldsymbol{\beta}}) = E((\hat{\boldsymbol{\beta}} - \boldsymbol{\beta})(\hat{\boldsymbol{\beta}} - \boldsymbol{\beta})') = E((X'X)^{-1}X'u((X'X)^{-1}X'u')) =$$
$$E((X'X)^{-1}X'uu'X(X'X)^{-1}) =$$
$$(X'X)^{-1}X'E(uu')X(X'X)^{-1} =$$
$$\sigma^2(X'X)^{-1}X'X(X'X)^{-1} = \sigma^2(X'X)^{-1}$$

The first equality is the definition of variance in the case of vector. In the fifth equality, $E(uu') = \sigma^2 I_n$ is used, which implies that $E(u_i^2) = \sigma^2$ for all i and $E(u_i u_j) = 0$ for $i \neq j$. Remember that $u_1, u_2, \ldots, u_n$ are assumed to be mutually independently and identically distributed with mean zero and variance σ^2.

Under normality assumption on the error term u, it is known that the distribution of $\hat{\boldsymbol{\beta}}$ is given by
$$\hat{\boldsymbol{\beta}} \sim N(\boldsymbol{\beta}, \sigma^2(\boldsymbol{X'X})^{-1})$$
Taking the jth element of $\hat{\boldsymbol{\beta}}$, its distribution is give by
$$\hat{\beta}_j \sim N(\beta_j, \sigma^2 a_{jj})$$
i. e.
$$\frac{\hat{\beta}_j - \beta_j}{\sigma \sqrt{a_{jj}}} \sim N(0,1)$$
where a_{jj} denotes the jth diagonal element of $(\boldsymbol{X'X})^{-1}$.

Replacing σ^2 by its estimator s^2, we have the following t distribution
$$\frac{\hat{\beta}_j - \beta_j}{s \sqrt{a_{jj}}} \sim t(n-k)$$
where $t(n-k)$ denotes the t distribution with $n-k$ degrees of freedom. s^2 is taken as follows
$$s^2 = \frac{1}{n-k} \sum_{i=1}^{n} e_i^2 = \frac{1}{n-k} e'e = \frac{1}{n-k}(\boldsymbol{Y} - \boldsymbol{X}\hat{\boldsymbol{\beta}})'(\boldsymbol{Y} - \boldsymbol{X}\hat{\boldsymbol{\beta}})$$
which leads to an unbiased estimator of σ^2.

Using the central limit theorem, without normality assumption we can show that as $n \to \infty$, under the condition of $(1/n)\boldsymbol{X'X} \to \boldsymbol{M}$ we have be following result
$$\frac{\hat{\beta}_j - \beta_j}{s \sqrt{a_{jj}}} \to N(0,1)$$
where $\boldsymbol{M}$ denotes a $k \times k$ constant matrix.

Thus, we can construct the confidence interval and the testing procedure, using the t distribution under the normality assumption or the normal distribution without the normality assumption.

Words and Expressions

dependent variable 因变量
unexplanatory variable 未解释变量
independent variable 自变量
error term 误差项
regression coefficients 回归系数
residual *n*. 残差
solid line 实线
dotted line 点线

plausible *adj.* 似乎合理的;似乎可能的
ordinary least squares (OLS) estimation 普通最小二乘估计
ordinary least squares estimate 普通最小二乘估计值
ordinary least squares estimator 普通最小二乘估计量
linear unbiased estimator 线性无偏估计量
class of the linear unbiased estimator 线性无偏估计量类
linear unbiased minimum variance estimator 线性无偏最小方差估计量
best linear unbiased estimator 最佳(最优)线性无偏估计量
sum of squared residuals 残差平方和

Appendix 2A Integration by Substitution

Univariate Case For a function of x, $f(x)$, we perform integration by substitution, using $x = \psi(y)$. Then, it is easy to obtain the following formula

$$\int f(x)\,\mathrm{d}x = \int \psi'(y) f(\psi(y))\,\mathrm{d}y$$

which formula is called the *integration by substitution*.

Proof Let $F(x)$ be the integration $f(x)$, i.e.

$$F(x) = \int_{-\infty}^{x} f(t)\,\mathrm{d}t$$

which implies that $F'(x) = f(x)$.

Differentiation $F(x) = F(\psi(y))$ with respect to y, we have

$$f(x) \equiv \frac{\mathrm{d}F(\psi(y))}{\mathrm{d}y} = \frac{\mathrm{d}F(x)}{\mathrm{d}x}\frac{\mathrm{d}x}{\mathrm{d}y} = f(x)\psi'(y) = f(\psi(y))\psi'(y)$$

Bivariate Case For $f(x,y)$, define $x = \psi_1(u,v)$ and $y = \psi_2(u,v)$

$$\iint f(x,y)\,\mathrm{d}x\mathrm{d}y = \iint J f(\psi_1(u,v), \psi_2(u,v))\,\mathrm{d}u\mathrm{d}v$$

where J is called the *Jacobian*, which represents the following determinant

$$J = \begin{vmatrix} \dfrac{\partial x}{\partial u} & \dfrac{\partial x}{\partial v} \\ \dfrac{\partial y}{\partial u} & \dfrac{\partial y}{\partial v} \end{vmatrix} = \frac{\partial x}{\partial u}\frac{\partial y}{\partial v} - \frac{\partial x}{\partial v}\frac{\partial y}{\partial u}$$

Appendix 2B Integration by Parts

Let $h(x)$ and $g(x)$ be functions of x. Then, we have the following formula

$$\int h(x) g'(x)\,\mathrm{d}x = h(x) g(x) - \int h'(x) g(x)\,\mathrm{d}x$$

which is called the *integration by parts*.

228 English in Statistics

Proof Consider the derivative of $f(x)g(x)$ with respect to x, i.e.

$$(f(x)g(x))' = f'(x)g(x) + f(x)g'(x)$$

Integrating the above equation on both sides, we have

$$\int (f(x)g(x))' dx = \int f'(x)g(x) dx + \int f(x)g'(x) dx$$

Therefore, we obtain

$$f(x)g(x) = \int f'(x)g(x) dx + \int f(x)g'(x) dx$$

Thus, the following result is derived

$$\int f(x)g'(x) dx = f(x)g(x) - \int f'(x)g(x) dx$$

When we want to integrate $f(x)g'(x)$ within the range between a and b for $a<b$, the above formula is modified as

$$\int_a^b f(x)g'(x) dx = [f(x)g(x)]_a^b - \int_a^b f'(x)g(x) dx$$

Appendix 2C Taylor Series Expansion

Consider approximating $f(x)$ around $x = x_0$ by the Taylor series expansion. Then, $f(x)$ is approximated as follows

$$f(x) = f(x_0) + f'(x_0)(x - x_0) + \frac{1}{2!}f''(x_0)(x - x_0)^2 +$$

$$\frac{1}{3!}f'''(x_0)(x - x_0)^3 + \ldots = \sum_{n=0}^{\infty} \frac{1}{n!} f^{(n)}(x_0)(x - x_0)^n$$

where $f^{(n)}(x_0)$ denotes the nth derivative of $f(x)$ evaluated at $x = x_0$. Note that $f^{(0)}(x_0) = f(x_0)$ and $0! = 1$.

In addition, the following approximation is called the kth order Taylor series expansion

$$f(x) \approx \sum_{n=0}^{k} \frac{1}{n!} f^{(n)}(x_0)(x - x_0)^n$$

Appendix 2D Cramer-Rao Inequality

As seen in (2.13) and (2.14), the Cramer-Rao inequality is given by

$$V(\hat{\theta}_n) \geq \frac{\sigma^2(\theta)}{n}$$

where

$$\sigma^2(\theta) = \frac{1}{E\left(\left(\frac{\partial \log f(X;\theta)}{\partial \theta}\right)^2\right)} = \frac{1}{V\left(\frac{\partial \log f(X;\theta)}{\partial \theta}\right)} =$$

$$-\frac{1}{E\left(\dfrac{\partial^2 \log f(X;\theta)}{\partial \theta^2}\right)}$$

Proof We prove the above inequality and the equalities in $\sigma^2(\theta)$. The likelihood function $l(\theta;x) = l(\theta;x_1,x_2,\ldots,x_n)$ is a joint density of $X_1, X_2, \ldots, X_n$. Therefore, the integration of $l(\theta;x_1,x_2,\ldots,x_n)$ with respect to $x_1,x_2,\ldots,x_n$ is equal to one. See Section 2.7.5 for the likelihood function. That is, we have the following equation

$$1 = \int l(\theta;x)\,\mathrm{d}x \qquad (2.41)$$

where the likelihood function $l(\theta;x)$ is given by $l(\theta;x) = \prod_{i=1}^{n} f(x_i;\theta)$ and $\int \ldots \mathrm{d}x$ implies n-tuple integral.

Differentiating both sides of equation (2.41) with respect to θ, we obtain the following equation

$$0 = \int \frac{\partial l(\theta;x)}{\partial \theta}\,\mathrm{d}x = \int \frac{1}{l(\theta;x)} \frac{\partial l(\theta;x)}{\partial \theta} l(\theta;x)\,\mathrm{d}x =$$

$$\int \frac{\partial \log l(\theta;x)}{\partial \theta} l(\theta;x)\,\mathrm{d}x = E\left(\frac{\partial \log l(\theta;X)}{\partial \theta}\right) \qquad (2.42)$$

which implies that the expectation of $\partial \log l(\theta;x)/\partial \theta$ is equal to zero. In the third equality, note that $\mathrm{d}\log x/\mathrm{d}x = 1/x$ Now, let $\hat{\theta}_n$ be an estimator of θ. The definition of the mathematical expectation of the estimator $\hat{\theta}_n$ is represented as

$$E(\hat{\theta}_n) = \int \hat{\theta}_n l(\theta;x)\,\mathrm{d}x \qquad (2.43)$$

Differentiating equation (2.43) with respect to θ on both sides, we can rewrite as follows

$$\frac{\partial E(\hat{\theta}_n)}{\partial \theta} = \int \hat{\theta}_n \frac{\partial l(\theta;x)}{\partial \theta}\,\mathrm{d}x = \int \hat{\theta}_n \frac{\partial \log l(\theta;x)}{\partial \theta} l(\theta;x)\,\mathrm{d}x =$$

$$\int (\hat{\theta}_n - E(\hat{\theta}_n)) \left(\frac{\partial \log l(\theta;x)}{\partial \theta} - E\left(\frac{\partial \log l(\theta;x)}{\partial \theta}\right)\right) \cdot$$

$$l(\theta;x)\,\mathrm{d}x = \mathrm{Cov}\left(\hat{\theta}_n, \frac{\partial \log l(\theta;X)}{\partial \theta}\right) \qquad (2.44)$$

In the second equality, $\mathrm{d}\log x/\mathrm{d}x = 1/x$ is utilized. The third equality holds because of $E(\partial \log l(\theta;X)/\partial \theta) = 0$ from equation (2.42).

For simplicity of discussion, suppose that θ is a scalar. Taking the square on both sides of equation (2.44), we obtain the following expression

$$\left(\frac{\partial E(\hat{\theta}_n)}{\partial \theta}\right)^2 = \left(\mathrm{Cov}\left(\hat{\theta}_n, \frac{\partial \log l(\theta;X)}{\partial \theta}\right)\right)^2 =$$

$$\rho^2 V(\hat\theta_n) V\left(\frac{\partial \log l(\theta;X)}{\partial \theta}\right) \leq$$

$$V(\hat\theta_n) V\left(\frac{\partial \log l(\theta;X)}{\partial \theta}\right) \tag{2.45}$$

where ρ denotes the correlation coefficient between $\hat\theta_n$ and $\partial \log l(\theta;X)/\partial\theta$. Note that we have the definition of ρ is given by

$$\rho = \frac{\mathrm{Cov}\left(\hat\theta_n, \frac{\partial \log l(\theta;X)}{\partial \theta}\right)}{\sqrt{V(\hat\theta_n)} \sqrt{V\left(\frac{\partial \log l(\theta;X)}{\partial \theta}\right)}}$$

Moreover, we have $-1 \leq \rho \leq 1$ (i.e., $\rho^2 \leq 1$). Then, the inequality (2.45) is obtained, which is rewritten as

$$V(\hat\theta_n) \geq \frac{\left(\frac{\partial E(\hat\theta_n)}{\partial \theta}\right)^2}{V\left(\frac{\partial \log l(\theta;X)}{\partial \theta}\right)} \tag{2.46}$$

When $E(\hat\theta_n) = \theta$, i.e., when $\hat\theta_n$ is an unbiased estimator of θ, the numerator in the right-hand side of equation (2.46) is equal to one. Therefore, we have the following result

$$V(\hat\theta_n) \geq \frac{1}{V\left(\frac{\partial \log l(\theta;V)}{\partial \theta}\right)} = \frac{1}{E\left(\left(\frac{\partial \log l(\theta;X)}{\partial \theta}\right)^2\right)}$$

Note that we have $V(\partial \log l(\theta;X)/\partial\theta) = E((\partial \log l(\theta;X)/\partial\theta)^2)$ in the equality above, because of $E(\partial \log l(\theta;X)/\partial\theta) = 0$.

Moreover, the denominator in the right-hand side of the above inequality is rewritten as follows

$$E\left(\left(\frac{\partial \log l(\theta;X)}{\partial \theta}\right)^2\right) = E\left(\left(\sum_{i=1}^{n} \frac{\partial \log f(X_i;\theta)}{\partial \theta}\right)^2\right) =$$

$$\sum_{i=1}^{n} E\left(\left(\frac{\partial \log f(X_i;\theta)}{\partial \theta}\right)^2\right) =$$

$$nE\left(\left(\frac{\partial \log f(X;\theta)}{\partial \theta}\right)^2\right) =$$

$$n\int_{-\infty}^{+\infty} \left(\frac{\partial \log f(x;\theta)}{\partial \theta}\right)^2 f(x;\theta)\,dx$$

In the first equality, $\log l(\theta;X) = \sum_{i=1}^{n} \log f(X_i;\theta)$ is utilized. Since X_i, $i=1, 2, \ldots, n$, are mutually independent, the second equality holds. The third equality holds because $X_1, X_2, \ldots, X_n$ are identically distributed.

Therefore, we obtain the following inequality

$$V(\hat{\theta}_n) \geq \frac{1}{E\left(\left(\frac{\partial \log f(\theta;X)}{\partial \theta}\right)^2\right)} = \frac{1}{nE\left(\left(\frac{\partial \log f(X;\theta)}{\partial \theta}\right)^2\right)} = \frac{\sigma^2(\theta)}{n}$$

which is equivalent to (2.13).

Next, we prove the equalities in (2.14), i.e.

$$-E\left(\frac{\partial^2 \log f(X;\theta)}{\partial \theta^2}\right) = E\left(\left(\frac{\partial \log f(X;\theta)}{\partial \theta}\right)^2\right) = V\left(\frac{\partial \log f(X;\theta)}{\partial \theta}\right)$$

Differentiating $\int f(x;\theta) dx = 1$ with respect to θ, we obtain as follows

$$\int \frac{\partial f(x;\theta)}{\partial \theta} dx = 0$$

We assume that the range of x does not depend on the parameter θ and that $\partial f(x;\theta)/\partial \theta$ exists. The above equation is rewritten as

$$\int \frac{\partial \log f(x;\theta)}{\partial \theta} f(x;\theta) dx = 0 \qquad (2.47)$$

or equivalently

$$E\left(\frac{\partial \log f(X;\theta)}{\partial \theta}\right) = 0 \qquad (2.48)$$

Again, differentiating equation (2.47) with respect to θ

$$\int \frac{\partial^2 \log f(x;\theta)}{\partial \theta^2} f(x;\theta) dx + \int \frac{\partial \log f(x;\theta)}{\partial \theta} \frac{\partial f(x;\theta)}{\partial \theta} dx = 0$$

i.e.

$$\int \frac{\partial^2 \log f(x;\theta)}{\partial \theta^2} f(x;\theta) dx + \int \left(\frac{\partial \log f(x;\theta)}{\partial \theta}\right)^2 f(x;\theta) dx = 0$$

i.e.

$$E\left(\frac{\partial^2 \log f(x;\theta)}{\partial \theta^2}\right) + E\left(\left(\frac{\partial \log f(x;\theta)}{\partial \theta}\right)^2\right) = 0$$

Thus, we obtain

$$-E\left(\frac{\partial^2 \log f(x;\theta)}{\partial \theta^2}\right) = E\left(\left(\frac{\partial \log f(x;\theta)}{\partial \theta}\right)^2\right)$$

Moreover, from equation (2.48), the following equation is derived

$$E\left(\left(\frac{\partial \log f(x;\theta)}{\partial \theta}\right)^2\right) = V\left(\frac{\partial \log f(x;\theta)}{\partial \theta}\right)$$

Therefore, we have

$$-E\left(\frac{\partial^2 \log f(X;\theta)}{\partial \theta^2}\right) = E\left(\left(\frac{\partial \log f(X;\theta)}{\partial \theta}\right)^2\right) = V\left(\frac{\partial \log f(X;\theta)}{\partial \theta}\right)$$

Thus, the Cramer-Rao inequality is derived as

$$V(\hat{\theta}_n) \geq \frac{\sigma^2(\theta)}{n}$$

where

$$\sigma^2(\theta) = \frac{1}{E\left(\left(\frac{\partial \log f(X;\theta)}{\partial \theta}\right)^2\right)} = \frac{1}{V\left(\frac{\partial \log f(X;\theta)}{\partial \theta}\right)} = -\frac{1}{E\left(\frac{\partial^2 \log f(X;\theta)}{\partial \theta^2}\right)}$$

Appendix 2E Some Formulas of Matrix Algebra

1. Let $A = \begin{pmatrix} a_{11} & a_{12} & \cdots & a_{1k} \\ a_{21} & a_{22} & \cdots & a_{2k} \\ \vdots & \vdots & & \vdots \\ a_{l1} & a_{l2} & \cdots & a_{lk} \end{pmatrix} = [a_{ij}]$, which is a $l \times k$ matrix, where a_{ij}

denotes ith row and jth column of A. The transpose of A, denoted by A', is defined as

$$A' = \begin{pmatrix} a_{11} & a_{21} & \cdots & a_{l1} \\ a_{12} & a_{22} & \cdots & a_{l2} \\ \vdots & \vdots & & \vdots \\ a_{1k} & a_{2k} & \cdots & a_{lk} \end{pmatrix} = [a_{ij}]$$

where the ith row of is the ith column of A.

2. $(Ax)' = x'A'$

where A and x are a $l \times k$ matrix and a $k \times 1$ vector, respectively.

3. $a' = a$

where a denotes a scalar.

4. $\dfrac{\partial a'x}{\partial x} = a$

where a and x are $k \times 1$ vectors.

5. $\dfrac{\partial x'Ax}{\partial x} = (A+A')x$

where A and x are a $k \times k$ matrix a $k \times 1$ vector, respectively.
Especially, when A is symmetric.

$$\frac{\partial x'Ax}{\partial x} = 2Ax$$

6. Let A and B be $k\times k$ matrices, and I_k be a $k\times k$ identity matrix (one in the diagonal elements and zero in the other elements).

When $AB=I_k$, B is called the inverse of A, denoted by $B=A^{-1}$.

That is, $AA^{-1}=A^{-1}A=I_k$.

7. Let A be a $k\times k$ matrix and x be a $k\times 1$ vector.

If A is a positive definite matrix, for any x we have
$$x'Ax>0$$
If A is a positive semidefinite matrix, for any x we have
$$x'Ax\geqslant 0$$
If A is a negative definite matrix, for any x we have
$$x'Ax<0$$
If A is a negative semidefinite matrix, for any x we have
$$x'Ax\leqslant 0$$

Appendix 2F Bayes' Theorem

Bayes' Theorem provides the technique for calculating a posterior distribution from the prior and the likelihood function.

Definition

A partition is a collection of events $A_1,\ldots,A_n\subset\Omega$ such that $A_i\cap A_j=\varnothing$ whenever $i\neq j$, and $A_1\cup\ldots\cup A_n\subset\Omega$.

The idea of the theorem is the following. Suppose a point is chosen at random, and we want to know in which of the A_i it lies. Even if we cannot observe this, we may be able to observe whether or not it lies in another event B, and by taking account of the degree to which B overlaps each of the A_i we may make a new inference about the probability of x lying in A_i. See Fig. 2.5.

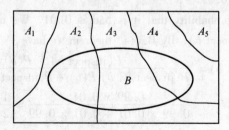

Fig. 2.5

Theorem 1

Suppose that B is an event and $A_1,\ldots,A_n$ a partition. Then

$$P(A_i \mid B) = \frac{P(B \mid A_i)P(A_i)}{\sum_{j=1}^{n} P(B \mid A_j)P(A_j)}$$

Proof Using the definition of conditional probability we can write

$$P(A_i \mid B) = \frac{P(B \mid A_i)P(A_i)}{P(B)}$$

It remains to expand the $P(B)$ term. We have

$$P(B) = \sum_{j=1}^{n} P(B_i \cap A_j) = \sum_{j=1}^{n} P(B \mid A_j)P(A_j)$$

where the first equality holds because the A_j from a partition, and the second follows from the definition of conditional probability.

We remark that the expression

$$P(B) = \sum_{j=1}^{n} P(B \mid A_j)P(A_j)$$

is called the *law (or theorem) of total probability*.

The initial probability $P(A_i)$ is called the *prior probability*, and the updated probability $P(A_i \mid B)$ is the *posterior probability*. The term $P(B \mid A_i)$ is called the likelihood. Bayes' theorem is often written in the form $P(A_i \mid B) \propto (P(B \mid A_i)P(A_i))$, and then $1/\sum_{j=1}^{n} P(B \mid A_j)P(A_j)$ is the constant of proportionality required to ensure that the total probability equals 1.

Example

Components produced on a production line are either good, g or bad, b, with probabilities $P(g) = 0.99$. $P(b) = 0.01$. Visual inspection can be used to identify good and bad components, and is rather effective in the sense that good components are identified as good with probability 0.99, and bad components are identified as bad with probability 0.99.

Suppose prior probability that it is bad is 0.01. We need to determine the probability $P(b \mid \text{inspect } b)$. By Bayes' theorem we have

$$P(b \mid \text{inspect } b) = \frac{P(\text{inspect } b \mid b)P(b)}{P(\text{inspect } b \mid b) P(b) + P(\text{inspect } b \mid g)P(g)} = \frac{0.99 \times 0.01}{0.99 \times 0.01 + 0.01 \times 0.99} = \frac{1}{2}$$

The version of Bayes' theorem for continuous variables, or vectors of continuous variables, is the following.

Theorem 2

let $\underline{X}$ and $\underline{\Phi}$ be continuous random vectors with joint probability density function

$f(\underline{x}, \underline{\theta})$. Let $f(\underline{x}|\underline{\theta})$ and $f(\underline{\theta}|\underline{x})$ be corresponding conditional densities, and $f(\underline{\theta}) = \int f(\underline{x}, \underline{\theta}) \mathrm{d}\underline{x}$ the marginal density of $\underline{\Phi}$. Then

$$f(\underline{\theta}|\underline{x}) = \frac{f(\underline{x}|\underline{\theta})f(\underline{\theta})}{\int f(\underline{x}|\underline{\theta})f(\underline{\theta})\mathrm{d}\underline{\theta}}$$

Proof By definition of the conditional probability density
$$f(\underline{x}|\underline{\theta})f(\underline{\theta}) = f(\underline{x}, \underline{\theta}) = f(\underline{\theta}|\underline{x})f(\underline{x})$$
Hence if $f(\underline{\theta}) > 0$ and $f(\underline{x}) > 0$
$$f(\underline{\theta}|\underline{x}) = \frac{f(\underline{x}|\underline{\theta})f(\underline{\theta})}{f(\underline{x})} = \frac{f(\underline{x}|\underline{\theta})f(\underline{\theta})}{\int f(\underline{x}|\underline{\theta})f(\underline{\theta})\mathrm{d}\underline{\theta}}$$

The application of this theorem is as follows. The prior distribution on the parameter $\underline{\Phi}$ is $f_0(\underline{\theta})$. If we have a sample of n lifetimes $x_1, \ldots, x_n$ with joint density $f(x_1, \ldots, x_n|\underline{\theta})$, then the posterior density of $\underline{\Phi}$ given the observations is

$$f_1(\underline{\theta}|x_1, \ldots, x_n) = \frac{f(x_1, \ldots, x_n|\underline{\theta})f_0(\underline{\theta})}{\int f(x_1, \ldots, x_n|\underline{\theta})f_0(\underline{\theta})\mathrm{d}\underline{\theta}}$$

The function $f_1(x_1, \ldots, x_n|\underline{\theta})$ considered as a function of θ is also called the *likelihood* of given the observation $x_1, \ldots, x_n$, and is written
$$L(\underline{\theta}|x_1, \ldots, x_n)$$
One can write the above expression as
$$f_1(\underline{\theta}|x_1, \ldots, x_n) \propto L(\underline{\theta}|x_1, \ldots, x_n)f_0(\underline{\theta})$$
The constant of proportional is determined by the requirement that f_1 is a probability density function (i.e. the integral is 1).

Words and Expressions

integration by substitution 换元积分法
Jacobian 雅可比行列式,函数行列式
integration by parts 分部积分法
Taylor series expansion 泰勒级数展开式
kth Taylor series expansion k 阶泰勒级数展开式
row $n.$ 行
column $n.$ 列
identity matrix 单位矩阵
inverse $n.$ 逆
transpose $n.$ 转置

positive definite matrix 正定矩阵
positive semidefinite matrix 半正定矩阵
negative definite matrix 负定矩阵
negative semidefinite matrix 半负定矩阵
Bayes' theorem 贝叶斯定理
partition $n.$ 分割
posterior distribution 后验分布
law (or theorem) of total probability 全概率定律
prior probability 先验概率
posterior probability 后验概率

Exercises

Part A: Translate the Following Material
1. What is Statistics?

(1) What is Statistics

Statistics is the study of the collection, organization, analysis, interpretation and presentation of data. It deals with all aspects of data including the planning of data collection in terms of the design of surveys and experiments. When analyzing data, it is possible to use one of two statistics methodologies: descriptive statistics or inferential statics. ——Wikipedia

"Statistics is a way to get information from data" (Fig. 2.6).

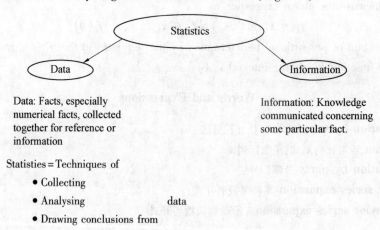

Fig. 2.6

(2) what is the difference between Probability and Statistics?

Probability is a measure of the likelihood of an event to occur. Since probability is a quantified measure, it has to be developed with the mathematical background. Specifically, this mathematical build of the probability is known as the probability theory.

Statistics is the discipline of collection, organization, analysis, interpretation, and presentation of data. Most statistical models are based on experiments and hypotheses, and probability is integrated into the theory, to explain the scenarios better.

· Probability and statistics can be considered two opposite processes, or rather two inverse processes.

· Using probability theory, the randomness or uncertainty of a system is measured by means of its random variables. As a result of the comprehensive model developed, the behaviour of the individual elements can be predicted.

But in statistics, a small number of observations is used to predict the behaviour of a larger set whereas, in probability, limited observations are selected at random from the population (the larger set).

· More clearly, it can be stated that using probability theory the general results can be used to interpret individual, events and the properties of the population are used to determine the properties of a smaller set. The probability model provides the data regarding the population.

· In statistics, the general model is based on specific events, and the sample properties are used to infer the characteristics of the population. Also, the statistical model is based on the observations/data. See the following Fig. 2.7.

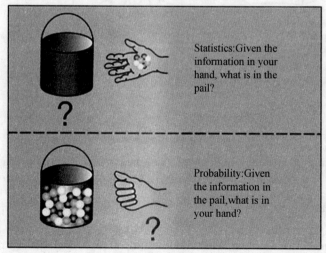

(a)

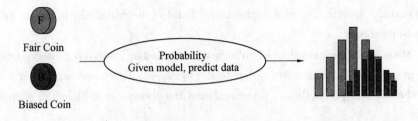
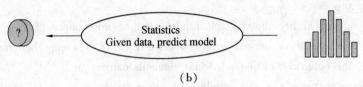

(b)

Fig. 2.7 Statistics vs Probability

(3) Statistics and Artificial Intelligence (Fig. 2.8)

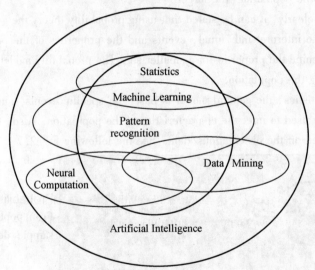

Fig. 2.8 Statistics and Artificial Intelligence

· Machine Learning: Creation of a model that uses training data or past experience

· Data Mining: application of learning methods to large datasets (ex. physics, astronomy, biology, etc.)

—Text mining = machine learning applied to unstructured textual data (ex. sentiment analysis, social media monitoring, etc. Text Mining, Wikipedia)

· Artificial intelligence: a model that can adapt to a changing environment.

· Statistics: Machine learning uses the theory of statistics in building mathematical models, because the core task is making inference from a sample.

Is there a Different Between Analytics and Analysis?

Even though the two terms analytics and analysis are often used interchangeably, they are not the same.

Basically, analysis refers to the process of separating a whole problem into its parts so that the parts can be critically examined at the granular level. It is often used when the investigation of a complete system is not feasible or practial, and the system needs to be simplified by being decomposed into more basic components. Once the improvements at the granular level are realized and the examination of the parts is complete, the whole system(either a conceptual or physical system) can then be put together using a process called synthesis.

Analytics, on the other hand, is a variety of methods, technologies, and associated tools for creating new knowledge/insight to solve complex problems and make better and faster decisions. In essence, analytics is a multifaceted and multidisciplinary approach to addressing complex situations. Analytics take advantage of data and mathematical models to make sense of the complicated world we are living in. Even though analytics includes the act of analysis at different stages of the discovery process, it is not just analysis but also includes synthesis and other complementing tasks and processes in. Even though analytics includes the act of analysis at differerent stages of the discovery process, it is not just analysis but also includes synthesis and other complementing tasks and processes.

2. Mathematical Theory of Statistics

The primary purpose of having a mathematical theory of statistics is to provide mathematical models for random experiments. Once a model for such an experiment has been provided and the theory worked out in detail, the statistician may, within this framework, make inferences (that is, draw conclusions) about the random experiment. The construction of such a model requires a theory of probability.

The subject of probability theory is the foundation upon which all of statistics is built, providing a means for modeling populations, experiments, or almost anything else that could be considered a random phenomenon. Through these models, statisticians are able to draw inferences about populations, inferences bases on examination of only a part of the whole.

3. Statistical Modeling Cultures

Statistics starts with data. Think of the data as being generated by a black box in which a vector of input variables x (independent variables) go in one side, and on the other side the response variables y come out. Inside the black box, nature functions to associate the predictor variables with the response variables, so the picture is like Fig. 2.9.

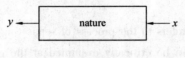

Fig. 2.9

There are two goals in analyzing the data:

Prediction: To be able to predict what the responses are going to be to future input variables;

Information: To extract some information about how nature is associating the response variables to the input variables.

There are two different approaches toward these goals:

(1) The Data Modeling Culture

The analysis in this culture starts with assuming a stochastic data model for the inside of the black box. For example, a common data model is that data are generated by independent draws from

response variables = f(predictor variables, random noise, parameters)

The values of the parameters are estimated from the data and the model then used for information and/or prediction. Thus the black box is filled in like Fig. 2.10.

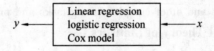

Fig. 2.10

Model validation: Yes-no using goodness-of-fit tests and residual examination.

Estimated culture population. 98% of all statisticians.

(2) The Algorithmic Modeling Culture

The analysis in this culture considers the inside of the box complex and unknown. Their approach is to find a function $f(x)$—an algorithm that operates on x to predict the responses y. Their black box looks Fig. 2.11.

Model validation. Measured by predictive accuracy.

Estimated culture population. 2% of statisticians.

4. Statistical Paradoxes

The world of statistics is full of paradoxes which have generated a lot of interest

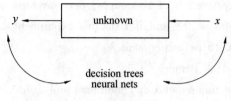

Fig. 2.11

and debate for many years. One of the main themes that these paradoxes take are related to the topic of probability and more specifically, conditional probability. These paradoxes demonstrate quirks which have significant implications on data analysis in research. The literature is full of examples were researchers fell foul of the pitfalls that these paradoxes illustrate.

(1) The two Envelopes Paradox

I have two identical envelopes containing cash. The amount of cash in one envelope is twice the amount in the second. I pick one envelope and I have a the chance to open it or swap for the second. I reason that if the amount in the envelope in my hand is X, the amount in the other envelope is either $2X$ or $X/2$, each having a probability of 1/2. The expected value of the amount in the second envelope is therefore

$$\frac{1}{2} \times 2X + \frac{1}{2} \times \frac{X}{2} = \frac{5}{2} \times X$$

which is higher than X. It is therefore in my advantage to sway. But then I apply the same reasoning to the second envelope and swap again, and go on swapping forever. Where did I go wrong? The problem is in my assumption that the amount in the envelope in my hand is X and making my calculations based on that assumption. However, X is a random value so $1.25X$ is also a random value.

Another way to look at it is that we were told that one envelope contains twice the amount of the second. We therefore defined the sample space at the start of the problem as $\{X, 2X\}$. Once we made a prior assumption about the first envelope (which we also called X just to be confusing), we based our assumption for the second envelope relative to the first and our sample space is now $\{X, 2X\}$. This sample space violates the condition of the original question as $2X$ is four times $X/2$ and not twice. The correct way to look at it is that each envelope has either X or $X/2$ with a probability of 1/2 so the expected value of each envelope is

$$\frac{1}{2} \times X + \frac{1}{2} \times 2X = \frac{3}{2} \times X$$

This is certainly true. If, for example, one envelope contains £ 10 and the other contains £ 20 ($X = 20$) and if I do this experiment 1,000 times, then on average I will gain £ 15 per experiment.

(2) The Monty Hall Paradox

This is an interesting paradox on conditional probability. Supposing you were in a game show and the host shows you three doors; 1, 2 and 3. Behind one of these doors is a car. You pick a door at random, say 1. Before the host opens door 1, he says 'let me open another door an show you that it does not contain the car', just to add suspense. He then opens door 3 and shows that it does not contain the car. He then gives you the option to stay with door 1 or swap to door 2. What should you do? The most logical answer is that the probability of the car being behind door 1 is equal to the probability of it being behind door 2, which is 1/2. Wrong! By swapping to door 2, you actually double your chances of winning.

Here is why. Each door has a probability of 1/3 of containing the car. Supposing that the car was indeed behind door 1. The host can open either door 2 or door 3, each with a probability of 1/2. The total probability of the car being behind door 1 and the host opening door 2 or door 3 is

$$1/3 \times 1/2 + 1/3 \times 1/2 = 1/3$$

In this case, if you swap you will lose. Now, if the car was behind door 2, the host can only open door 3 because if he opens door 2 he will reveal the car. The total probability of the car being behind door 2 and the host opening door 3 is therefore $1 \times 1/3$. In this case, if you swap you will win. The same argument holds if the car was behind door 3. There is therefore a 2/3 chance that you will win if you swap and a 1/3 chance that you will lose.

To put it mathematically, if the probability of the car being behind door 2 is $P(C=2)$, the probability of you selecting door 1 is $P(S=1)$, the probability of the host opening door 3 is $P(H=3)$, using Bayes theorem

$$P(C=2 \mid H=3, S=1) = \frac{P(H=3 \mid C=2, S=1) \times P(C=2 \mid S=1)}{\sum_{n=1}^{3} P(H=3 \mid c=n, S=1) \times P(C=n \mid S=1)} =$$

$$\frac{1 \times \frac{1}{3}}{\frac{1}{2} \times \frac{1}{3} + 1 \times \frac{1}{3} + 0 \times \frac{1}{3}} = \frac{2}{3}$$

Here again, the original sample space is $\{1/3, 2/3\}$, the probability of winning or losing. The host did not open a door at random. He opened a door knowing that it is not the one you picked and that it does not contain the prize, so the original sample space remains unchanged.

5. Relations of between Explanatory Variable and Response Variable.

Explanatory Variable	Response Variable		
	Continuous	Count	Proportion
Continuous	Regression	· square-root transform ation · GLM (Log-linear Regression)	· Arcsine transformation · GLM (Logistic regression)
Categorical	Student's; ANOVA	Contingency Table	· Arcsine transformation · GLM (Logistic analysis of deviance)
Continuous and Categorical	ANCOVA	· Square-root transformation · GLM (Poisson Errors)	· Arcsine transformation · GLM (Binomial Errors)
Time	Time Series Analysis		

6. Comparison of Statistical Tests.

	Parametric	Nonparametric	Frequency
Data type	Ratio Interval	Ordinal	Nominal
Single sample	z-test t-test	Sign test*, K-S test*	χ^2 Goodness-of-fit
Two independent samples	z-test t-test (2 types)	Wilcoxon Rank Sum (Mann-Whitney U)	
Two dependent samples	Paired t-test	Paired Sign, Wilcoxon Signed-rank	
More than two independent samples	One-way ANOVA	Kruskall-Wallis H	
Two factors	Two-way ANOVA		χ^2 Test of Independence
Correlation	Pearson r	Spearman p	Phi(ϕ)*

7. Flow Chart for Selecting Commonly Used Statistical Tests.

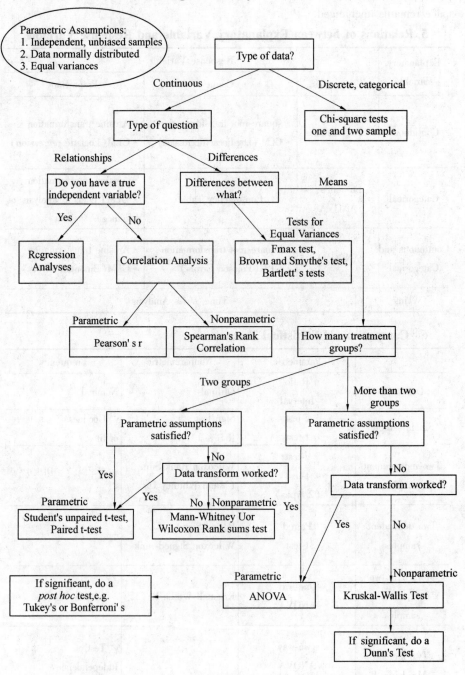

8. Data Science

Data science is the study of the generalizable extraction of knowledge from data yet the key word is science. ——Wikipedia

"Data scientists are inquisitive: exploring, asking questions, doing" what if analysis, questioning existing assumptions and processes. Armed with data and analytical results, a top-tier data scientist will then communicate informed conclusions and recommendations across an organization's leadership structure." (Fig. 2.12)

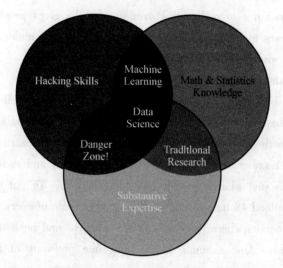

Fig. 2.12 Data Science. Source: Drew Conway

• Math & Statistics Knowledge: Once you have acquired and cleaned the data, the next step is to actually extract insight from it. You need to apply appropriate math and statistics methods, which requires at least a baseline familiarity with these tools.

• Hacking Skills: Data is a commodity traded electronically, therefore, in order to be in this market you need to speak hacker. Far from 'black hat' activities, data hackers must be able to manipulate text files at the command-line, thinking algorithmically, and be interested in learning new tools.

• Substantive Expertise: Science is about discovery and building knowledge, which requires some motivating questions about the world and hypotheses that can be brought to data and tested with statistical methods. Questions first, then data.

Machine Learning: Data plus math is machine learning, which is fantastic if that is what you if that is what you are interested in, but not if you are doing data science.

· Traditional Research: Substantive expertise plus math and statistics knowledge is where most traditional researcher falls. Doctoral level researchers spend most of their time acquiring expertise in these earas, but very little time learning about technology.

· Danger Zone!: This is where I place people who, 'know enough to be dangerous,' and is the most problematic area of the diagram. It is from this part of the diagram that the phrase 'lies, damned lies, and statistics' emanates, because either through ignorance or malice this overlap of skills gives people the ability to create what appears to be a legitimate analysis without any understanding of how they got there or what they have created.

9. What exactly is Big Data?

Simply put, big data is data that's too large or complex to be effectively handled by standard database technologies currently found in most organisations.

According to the conventional definition, for data to be regarded as "big", it should possess a number of key attributes-volume, velocity and variety:

· Volume is just what it sounds like: lots of data. To put this in context, YouTube users upload 48 hours of new video every minute of every day.

· Velocity occurs where the data is time-sensitive and needs to be processed and stored quickly. One example is the real-time probiling of internet display adverts that are customised according to your usage pattern.

· Variety covers the various forms that data can take, from neatly-structured tabular data, to unstructured data containing items such as images, emails, spreadsheets, social media conversations and streaming media. Currently, there is no universally accepted "one-size-fits-all" approach to handling this data variety.

What about the other Vs?

Given the prerequisite Vs of Volume, Velocity and Variety, that brings us to some of the other, lesser considered but probably more important Vs that can be associated with Big Data, these being Validity, Veracity, Value and Visibility. If the result of your Big Data processes is critical to you in your business, you may want to ensure these additional 4 Vs are rigorously assessed throughout your Big Data processes:

· Validity-the interpreted data having a sound basis in logic or fact-is a result of the logical inferences from matching data. One of the most common errors being the confusion between correlation and causation.

Volume−Validity=Worthlesness?

· Veracity−conformity to facts; accuracy−Do we need a spell checker to get data consistency?

Big Data−Veracity=Incorrect inferences being drawn?

· Value-the importance, worth, or usefulness of the data to those consuming it is probably the most relevant to organisations. Data in and of itself has no value.

Big Data=Data+Value?

· Visibility−the state of being able to see or be seen−is implied. Data from disparate sources need to be stitched together where they are visible to the technology stack making up Big Data. Critical data that is otherwise available, but not visible to the processes of Big Data may be one of the Achilles Heels of the Big Data paradigm. Conversely, unauthorised visibility is a risk.

Big Data−visibility=Black Hole?

In summary, Big Data, just like Cloud and other business technology ecosystems has it's place, and can be a game changer and deliver real value. Trick is to ensure your Big Data delivers what's expected and is not only a Black Hole for cost and effort, but most importantly, also does not elevate your risk profile resulting from incorrect decisions making because some of the key Vs were not clearly understood.

Part B: Multile-Choice Questions

1. In the scatterplot of y versus x shown in Fig. 2.13, the least squares regression line is superimposed on the plot, Which of the following points has the largest residual?

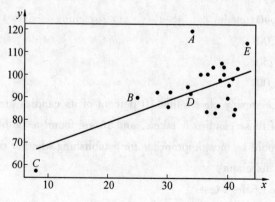

Fig. 2.13

(A) A
(B) B
(C) C
(D) D
(E) E

2. Under which of the following conditions is it preferable to use stratified random sampling rather that simple random sampling?

(A) The population can be divided into a large number of strata so that each stratum contains only a few individuals.

(B) The population can be divided into a small number of strata so that each stratum contains a large number of individuals.

(C) The population can be divided into strata so that the individuals in each stratum are as much alike as possible.

(D) The population can be divided into strata so that the individuals in each stratum are as different as possible.

(E) The population can be divided into strata of equal sizes so that each individual in the population still has the same chance of being selected.

3. All bags entering a research facility are screened. Ninety-seven percent of the bags that contain forbidden material trigger an alarm. Fifteen percent of the bags that do not contain forbidden material also trigger the alarm. If 1 out of every 1,000 bags entering the building contains forbidden material, what is the probability that a bag that triggers the alarm will actually contain forbidden material?

(A) 0.000,97
(B) 0.006,40
(C) 0.030,00
(D) 0.145,50
(E) 0.970,00

4. A candy company claims that 10 percent of its candies are blue. A random sample of 200 of these candies is taken, and 16 are found to be blue. Which of the following tests would be most appropriate for establishing whether the candy company needs to change its claim?

(A) Matched pairs t-test
(B) One-sample proportion z-test
(C) Two-sample t- test
(D) Two-sample proportion z-test

(E) Chi-square test of association

5. In a test of $H_0: \mu = 8$ versus $H_a: \mu \neq 8$, a sample of size 220 leads to a p-value of 0.034. Which of the following must be true?

(A) A 95% confidence interval for μ calculated from these data will not include $\mu = 8$.

(B) At the 5% level if H_0 is rejected, the probability of a Type II error is 0.034.

(C) The 95% confidence interval for μ calculated from these data will be centered at $\mu = 8$.

(D) The null hypothesis should not be rejected at the 5% level.

(E) The sample size is insufficient to draw a conclusion with 95% confidence.

6. A summer resort rents rowboats to customers but does not allow more than four people to a boat. Each boat is designed to hold no more than 800 pounds. Suppose the distribution of adult males who rent boats, including their clothes and gear, is normal with a mean of 190 pounds and standard deviation of 10 pounds. If the weights of individual passengers are independent, what is the probability that a group of four adult male passengers will exceed the acceptable weight limit of 800 pounds?

(A) 0.023
(B) 0.046
(C) 0.159
(D) 0.317
(E) 0.977

7. Consider a data set of positive values, at least two of which are not equal. Which of the following sample statistics will be changed when each value in this data set is multiplied by a constant whose absolute value is greater than 1?

I. The mean
II. The median
III. The standard deviation

(A) I only
(B) II only
(C) III only
(D) I and II only
(E) I, II and III

8. Each person in a simple random sample of 2,000 received a survery, and

317 people returned their survey. How could nonresponse cause the results of the survey to be biased?

(A) Those who did not respond reduced the sample size, and small samples have more bias than large samples.

(B) Those who did not respond caused a violation of the assumption of independence.

(C) Those who did not respond were indistinguishable from those who did not receive the survey.

(D) Those who did not respond represent a stratum, changing the simple random sample into a stratified random sample.

(E) Those who did respond may differ in some important way from those who did not respond.

9. In a certain game, a fair die is rolled and a player gains 20 points if the die shows a "6." If the die does not show a "6," the player loses 3 points. If the die were to be rolled 100 times, what would be the expected total gain or loss for the player?

(A) A gain of about 1,700 points

(B) A gain of about 583 points

(C) A gain of about 83 points

(D) A gain of about 250 points

(E) A gain of about 300 points

10. The Attila Barbell Company makes bars for weight lifting. The weights of the bars are independent and are normally distributed with a mean of 720 ounces (45 pounds) and a standard deviation of 4 ounces. The bars are shipped 10 in a box to the retailers. The weights of the empty boxes are normally distributed with a mean of 320 ounces and a standard deviation of 8 ounces. The weights of the boxes filled with 10 bars are expected to be normally distributed with a mean of 7,520 ounces and a standard deviation of

(A) $\sqrt{12}$ ounces

(B) $\sqrt{80}$ ounces

(C) $\sqrt{224}$ ounces

(D) 48 ounces

(E) $\sqrt{1,664}$ ounces

11. Exercise physiologists are investigating the relationship between lean body

mass (in kilograms) and the resting metabolic rate (in calories per day) in sedentary males.

Based on the computer output Table 2.4, which of the following is the best interpretation of the value of the slope of the regression line?

Table 2.4

Predictor	Coef	StDev	T	P
Constant	264.0	276.9	0.95	0.363
Mass	22.563	6.360	3.55	0.005

$S = 144.9 \quad R^2 = 55.7\% \quad R^2(\text{adj}) = 51.3\%$

(A) For each additional kilogram of lean body mass, the resting metabolic rate increases on average by 22.563 calories per day.

(B) For each additional kilogram of lean body mass, the resting metabolic rate increases on average by 264.0 calories per day.

(C) For each additional kilogram of lean body mass, the resting metabolic rate increases on average by 144.9 calories per day.

(D) For each additional calorie per day for the resting metabolic rate, the lean body mass increases on average by 22.563 kilograms.

(E) For each additional calorie per day for the resting metabolic rate, the lean body mass increases on average by 264.0 kilograms.

12. An investigator was studying a territorial species of Central American termites, *Nasutitermes corniger*. Forty-nine termite pairs were randomly selected; both members of each of these pairs were from the same colony. Fifty-five additional termite pairs were randomly selected; the two members in each of these pairs were from different colonies. The pairs were placed in petri dishes and observed to see whether they exhibited aggressive behavior. The results are shown in Table 2.5.

Table 2.5

	Aggressive	Nonaggressive	Total
Same colony	40(33.5)	9(15.5)	49
Different colonies	31(37.5)	24(17.5)	55
Total	71	33	104

A Chi-square test for homogeneity was conducted, resulting in $\chi^2 = 7.638$. The expected counts are shown in parentheses in the table. Which of the following sets of statements follows from these results?

(A) χ^2 is not significant at the 0.05 level.

(B) χ^2 is significant, $0.01 < p < 0.05$; the counts in the table suggest that termite pairs from the same colony are less likely to be aggressive than termite pairs from different colonies.

(C) χ^2 is significant, $0.01 < p < 0.05$; the counts in the table suggest that termite pairs from different colonies are less likely to be aggressive than termite pairs from the same colony.

(D) χ^2 is significant, $p < 0.01$; the counts in the table suggest that termite pairs from the same colony are less likely to be aggressive than termite pairs from different colonies.

(E) χ^2 is significant, $p < 0.01$; the counts in the table suggest that termite pairs from different colonies are less likely to be aggressive than termite pairs from the same colony.

13. Consider n pairs of numbers $(x_1, y_1), (x_2, y_2), \cdots,$ and (x_n, y_n). The mean and standard deviation of the x-values are $\bar{x} = 5$ and $s_x = 4$, respectively. The mean and standard deviation of the y-values are $\bar{y} = 10$ and $s_y = 10$, respectively. Of the following, which could be the least squares regression line?

(A) $\hat{y} = -5.0 + 3.0 x$

(B) $\hat{y} = 3.0x$

(C) $\hat{y} = 5.0 + 2.5x$

(D) $\hat{y} = 8.5 + 0.3x$

(E) $\hat{y} = 10.0 + 0.4x$

14. The mayor of a large city will run for governor if he believes that more than 30 percent of the voters in the state already support him. He will have a survey firm ask a random sample of n voters whether or not they support him. He will use a large sample test for proportions to test the null hypothesis that the proportion of all voters who support him is 30 percent or less against the alternative that the percentage is higher than 30 percent. Suppose that 35 percent of all voters in the state sactually support him. In which of the following situations would the power for this test be highest?

(A) The mayor uses a significance level of 0.01 and $n = 250$ voters.

(B) The mayor uses a significance level of 0.01 and $n = 500$ voters.

(C) The mayor uses a significance level of 0.01 and $n = 1,000$ voters.

(D) The mayor uses a significance level of 0.05 and $n = 500$ voters.

(E) The mayor uses a significance level of 0.05 and $n = 1,000$ voters.

15. George and Michelle each claimed to have the better recipe for chocolate chip cookies. They decided to conduct a study to determine whose cookies were

really better. They each baked a batch of cookies using their own recipe. George asked a random sample of his friends to taste his cookies and to complete a questionnaire on their quality. Michelle asked a random sample of her friends to complete the same questionnaire for her cookies. They then compared the results. Which of the following statements about this study is false?

(A) Because George and Michelle have a different population of friends, their sampling procedure makes it difficult to compare the recipes.

(B) Because George and Michelle each used only their own respective recipes, their cooking ability is confounded with the recipe quality.

(C) Because George and Michelle each used only the ovens in their houses, the recipe quality is confounded with the characteristics of the oven.

(D) Because George and Michelle used the same questionnaire, their results will generalize to the combined population of their friends.

(E) Because George and Michelle each baked one batch, there is no replication of the cookie recipes.

16. A large company is considering opening a franchise in St. Louis and wants to estimate the mean household income for the area using a simple random sample of households. Based on information from a pilot study, the company assumes that the standard deviation of household incomes is $\sigma = \$7,200$. Of the following, which is the least number of households that should be surveyed to obtain an estimate that is within $200 of the true mean household income with 95 percent confidence?

(A) 75
(B) 1,300
(C) 5,200
(D) 5,500
(E) 7,700

17. Courtney has constructed a cricket out of paper and rubber bands. According to the instructions for making the cricket, when it jumps it will land on its feet half of the time and on its back the other half of the time. In the first 50 jumps, Courtney's cricket landed on its feet 35 times. In the next 10 jumps, it landed on is feet only twice. Based on this experience, Courtney can conclude that

(A) the cricket was due to land on its feet less than half the time during the final 10 jumps, since it had landed too often on its feet during the first 50 jumps

(B) a confidence interval for estimating the cricket's true probability of landing on its feet is wider after the final 10 jumps than it was before the final 10 jumps

(C) a confidence interval for estimating the cricket's true probability of landing on its feet after the final 10 jumps is exactly the same as it was before the final 10 jumps

(D) a confidence interval for estimating the cricket's true probability of landing on its feet is more narrow after the final 10 jumps than it was before the final 10 jumps

(E) a confidence interval for estimating the cricket's true probability of landing on its feet based on the initial 50 jumps does not include 0.2, so there must be a defect in the cricket's construction to account for the poor showing in the final 10 jumps

18. A researcher has a theory that the average age of managers in a particular industry is over 35-years-old, and he wishes to prove this. The null hypothesis to conduct a statistical test on this theory would be _____.

(A) the population mean is $\leqslant 35$
(B) the population mean is $\geqslant 35$
(C) the population mean is $=35$
(D) the population mean is >35

19. A company produces an item that is supposed to have a six inch hole punched in the center. A quality control inspector is concerned that the machine which punches the hole is "out-of-control" (hole is too large or too small). In an effort to test this, the inspector is going to gather a sample punched by the machine and measure the diameter of the hole. The alternative hypothesis used to statistical test to determine if the machine is out-of-control is

(A) the mean diameter is >6 inches
(B) the mean diameter is <6 inches
(C) the mean diameter is $=6$ inches
(D) the mean diameter is not equal to 6 inches

20. A company believes that it controls more than 30% of the total market share for one of its products. To prove this belief, a random sample of 144 purchases, of this product are contacted. It is found that 50 of the 144 purchased this company's brand of the product. If a researcher wants to conduct a statistical test for this problem, the alternative hypothesis would be _____.

(A) the population proportion is less than 0.30
(B) the population proportion is greater than 0.30
(C) the population proportion is not equal to 0.30

(D) the population mean is less than 40

21. In a two-tailed hypothesis about a population mean with a sample size of 100 and $\alpha=0.05$, the rejection region would be _____.

(A) $z>1.64$

(B) $z>1.96$

(C) $z<-1.96$ and $z>1.96$

(D) $z<-1.64$ and $z>1.64$

22. A researcher is testing a hypothesis of a single mean. The critical z value for $\alpha=0.5$ and a two-tailed test is $+1.96$. The observed test statistic value from sample data is -1.85. The decision made by the researcher based on this information is to _____ the null hypothesis

(A) reject

(B) do not reject

(C) redefine

(D) change the alternate hypothesis

23. A Type II error is committed when

(A) we reject a null hypothesis that is true.

(B) we don't reject a null hypothesis that is true.

(C) we reject a null hypothesis that is false.

(D) we don't reject a null hypothesis that is false.

24. A Type I error is committed when

(A) we reject a null hypothesis that is true.

(B) we don't reject a null hypothesis that is false.

(C) we reject a null hypothesis that is false.

(D) we don't reject a null hypothesis that is false.

25. If a test of hypothesis has a Type I error probability (α) of 0.01, we mean

(A) if the null hypothesis is true, we don't reject it 1% of the time.

(B) if the null hypothesis is true, we reject it 1% of the time.

(C) if the null hypothesis is false, we don't reject it 1% of the time.

(D) if the null hypothesis is false, we reject it 1% of the time.

26. How many Kleenex should the Kimberly Clark Corporation package of tissues contain? Researchers determined that 60 tissues is the average number of tissues used during a cold. Suppose a random sample of 100 Kleenex users yielded the following data on the number of tissues used during a cold: mean = 52, $s=22$.

Using the sample information provided, calculate the value of the test statistic.

(A) $t = (52-60)/22$
(B) $t = (52-60)/(22/100)$
(C) $t = (52-60)/(22/100^2)$
(D) $t = (52-60)/(22/10)$

27. A pharmaceutical company claims that its weight loss drug allows women to lose 8.5 lb after one month of treatment. If we want to conduct an experiment to determine if the patients are losing less weight than advertised, which of the following hypotheses should be used?

(A) $H_0: \mu = 8.5; H_a: \mu > 8.5$
(B) $H_0: \mu = 8.5; H_a: \mu = 8.5$
(C) $H_0: \mu = 8.5; H_a: \mu < 8.5$
(D) $H_0: \mu \neq 8.5; H_a: \mu > 8.5$
(E) $H_0: \mu \neq 8.5; H_a: \mu < 8.5$

28. It is possible to directly compare the results of a confidence interval estimate to the results obtained by testing a null hypothesis if:

(A) a two-tailed test is used.
(B) a one-tailed test is used.
(C) both of the previous statements are true.
(D) none of the previous statements is true.

29. Suppose a 95% confidence interval for the proportion of Americans who exercise regularly is 0.29 to 0.37. Which one of the following statements is FALSE?

(A) It is reasonable to say that more than 25% of Americans exercise regularly.

(B) It is reasonable to say that more than 40% of Americans exercise regularly.

(C) The hypothesis that 33% of Americans exercise regularly cannot be rejected.

(D) It is reasonabe to say that fewer than 40% of Americans exercise regularly.

30. A hypothesis test is done in which the alternative hypothesis is that more than 10% of a population is left-handed. The p-value for the test is calculated to be 0.25. Which statement is correct?

(A) We can conclude that more than 10% of the population is left-handed.

(B) We can conclude that more than 25% of the population is left-handed.

(C) We can conclude that exactly 25% of the population is left-handed.

(D) We cannot conclude that more than 10% of the population is left-handed.

31. What is the value for the test statistic for the following hypothesis test? $Ho: p = 0.09$; $Ha: p < 0.09$; $n = 60$; the sample proportion is 0.085 and $\alpha = 0.05$.

(A) −0.130,9

(B) −0.132,6

(C) −0.135,3

(D) −0.137,7

32. A statistics professor used X = "number of class days attended" (out of 30) as an independent variable to predict Y = "score received on final exam" for a class of his students. The resulting regression equation was $Y = 39.4 + 1.4 \times X$.

Which of the following statements is true?

(A) If attendance increases by 1.4 days, the expected exam score will increase by 1 point

(B) If attendance increases by 1 days, the expected exam score will increase by 39.4 point

(C) If attendance increases by 1 days, the expected exam score will increase by 1.4 point

(D) If the student does not attend at all, the expected exam score is 1.4.

33. In a multiple regression analysis involving 40 observations and 5 independent variables, SST = 350 and SSE = 30. The coefficient of determination (R^2) is:

(A) 0.940,8

(B) 0.857,1

(C) 0.914,3

(D) 0.852,9

34. Given the regression equation $\hat{Y} = -4.3 + 5.9X$, which of the following statements is incorrect?

(A) The R^2 value could be less than 0.

(B) The correlation between x and y is positive.

(C) The slope of the line is 5.9.

(D) Given an X value of 2, the predicted value of Y is 7.5.

(E) The intercept value is less than 0.

35. In simple linear regression, what is the difference between b_1 and β_1?

(A) b_1 stands for the slope of the regression line for the sample, while β_1 stands for the slope of the regression line for the population.

(B) b_1 stands for the slope of the regression line for the population, while β_1 stands for the slope of the regression line for the sample.

(C) b_1 and β_1 are just two different ways of referring to the slope of the regression line for the sample.

(D) b_1 stands for the residual variance, β_1 stands for the residual standard deviation.

36. Sixteen student volunteers at Ohio State University drank a randomly assigned number of cans of beer. Thirty minutes later, their blood alcohol content (BAC) was measured by a police officer. The fitted regression line is

$$\hat{y} = -0.012,3 + 0.018,0(x)$$

where y is BAC and x is the number of cans of beer.

Which of the following is FALSE:

(A) As the number of cans of beer increases, so does BAC.

(B) The predicted BAC after 5 beers is about 0.08.

(C) The predicted BAC for someone who has had no beer is $-0.012,3$

(D) The predicted BAC after 1 beer is about 0.006

(E) For every can of beer consumed, BAC is expected to go up by 0.012,3.

Part C: Calculate

1. Let X be a random variable with range space $\{1;2;3\}$ with $P(X = 1) = P(X = 2) = 0.4$.

   (A) What is $P(X = 3)$?

   (B) Find the mean of X, $E(X)$.

   (C) Find the variance of X.

2. Let Y be a random variable with probability density function (p.d.f.) $f(y)$ given by

$$f(y) = \begin{cases} y/2, & 0 \leqslant y < 2 \\ 0, & \text{otherwise} \end{cases}$$

   (A) Find the probability that Y is between $1/2$ and 1.

   (B) Find the distribution function of Y, $F(y)$.

   (C) Find the mean and variance of Y.

3. A standard fair dice is rolled 8 times. Let X be the number of sixes rolled.

   (A) Which standard distribution (and which parameters) would you expect X to have?

(B) Under your assumption, what is $P(X=2)$?

4. Let $f(\theta) = e^{-\theta^2+4\theta}$. Calculate the first and second derivatives of $f(\theta)$ with respect to θ, and hence find the value of θ which maximises $f(\theta)$.

5. Let $f(x;y) = e^{-(x+y)}$. Find

(A) $\int_{x=0}^{1} \int_{y=0}^{1} f(x,y) \, dy dx$;

(B) $\int_{x=0}^{\infty} f(x;y) \, dx$.

6. Let

$$A = \begin{pmatrix} 1 & -1 \\ 2 & 1 \end{pmatrix} \text{ and } \Sigma = \begin{pmatrix} 4 & -1 \\ -1 & 9 \end{pmatrix}$$

Find $A\Sigma A^T$.

7. X_1 and X_2 are independent random variables with $N(\mu;1)$ and $N(\mu;4)$ distributions respectively, where μ is an unknown parameter. Let T_1, T_2 and T_3 be defined by

$$T_1 = \frac{X_1+X_2}{2}$$

$$T_2 = 2X_1 - X_2$$

$$T_3 = \frac{4X_1+X_2}{5}$$

Find the mean and variance of T_1, T_2 and T_3. Which would you prefer to use as an estimator of μ, and why?

Univariate distribution theory

8. The discrete random variable X has the probability function

$$p(x) = \begin{cases} \frac{1}{x(x+1)}, & \text{for } x = 1, 2, 3, \cdots \\ 0, & \text{otherwise} \end{cases}$$

(A) Find, using partial fractions, the distribution function F of X, and sketch its graph.

(B) Evaluate $P(10 \leq X \leq 20)$.

(C) Find the smallest x such that $P(X \geq x) \leq 0.01$.

(D) What happens if you attempt to calculate $E(X)$?

9. Let

$$F(x) = \frac{e^x}{1+e^x}, \quad \text{for all real } x$$

(A) Show that F satisfies properties (A) and (B) of a distribution function.

(As it is continuous, it also satisfies (C).)

(B) Show that the corresponding probability density function f is symmetrical about zero, in the sense that $f(-x)=f(x)$ for all x.

(C) If X is a random variable with this distribution, evaluate $P(|X|>2)$.

10. Sketch graphs of each of the following two functions, and explain why each of them is not a distribution function.

(A) $F(x) = \begin{cases} 0, & \text{for } x \leq 0 \\ x, & \text{for } x > 0 \end{cases}$

(B) $F(x) = \begin{cases} 0, & \text{for } x < 0 \\ x + \dfrac{1}{4}\sin 2\pi x, & \text{for } 0 \leq x < 1 \\ 1, & \text{for } x \geq 1 \end{cases}$

11. The probability density function $f(x)$ is given by

$$f(x) = \begin{cases} 1+x, & \text{for } -1 \leq x < 0 \\ 1-x, & \text{for } 0 \leq x < 1 \\ 0, & \text{otherwise} \end{cases}$$

Find the corresponding distribution function $F(x)$ for all real x.

12. Find the coefficients of skewness for the random variables X and Y described in questions 1 and 2.

13. X is a random variable with hypergeometric distribution, parameters $N=10; N^*=7; n=5$. What are the values that X can take? Find the probabilities that X takes each of these values. Find the mean and variance of X.

14. Let F be the d. f. of a life length and suppose it possesses a p. d. f. f. The hazard function at age t is defined as

$$h(t) = \frac{f(t)}{1-F(t)}, \quad \text{for } t \geq 0$$

[This may be interpreted as an instantaneous failure rate at age t.]

(A) Given that the exponential distribution has p. d. f. $f(x) = \lambda e^{-\lambda x}$, for $x \geq 0$ and parameter $\lambda > 0$, show that the exponential distribution has constant hazard function.

(B) Show that the distribution given by

$$F(t) = \frac{t}{1+t}, \quad \text{for } t \geq 0$$

has hazard function which decreases with age.

(C) Show that the distribution given by

$$F(t) = 1 - e^{-t^2}, \quad \text{for } t \geq 0$$

has hazard function which increases with age.

15. If X is a random variable with $Ga(\alpha;\beta)$ distribution, and k is a positive integer, show that
$$E(X^k) = \frac{\alpha(\alpha+1)\cdots(\alpha+k-1)}{\beta^k}$$
Hence confirm that the mean and variance of $Ga(\alpha;\beta)$ and find the coefficient of skewness.

16. Let X be a random variable following the beta distribution $Be(\alpha;\beta)$.

(A) For any $c>0$ find the p.d.f. of the random variable $Y=c/X$.

(B) Calculate the mean of Y, stating any restrictions on the parameter space of α or β.

17. Use R to investigate how the shape of the p.d.f. of a Gamma distribution varies with the difierent parameter values. In particular, fix a value of β, see how the shape changes as you vary α, and see how this relates to the value for the coeficient of skewness that you found in question 15. Note that in R you can obtain a plot of, for example, the p.d.f. of a $Ga(3;2)$ random variable between 0 and 10 with curve(dgamma(x, shape=3, scale=2), from=0, to=10).

18. Let X be a random variable with the p.d.f. $f(x)$ defined in question 11. Find the p.d.f.s of

(A) $Y=5X+3$.

(B) $Z=|X|$ (hint: first find $F_Z(z) = P(Z \leqslant z)$).

19. Let X have a $Be(\alpha;1)$ distribution, and let $Y = \sqrt[r]{X}$ for some positive integer r. Show that Y also has a Beta distribution, and find the parameters.

20. Let Θ be an angle chosen according to a uniform distribution on $(-\frac{\pi}{2}; \frac{\pi}{2})$, and let $X = \tan\Theta$. Use the theory on transformations of random variables to show that X has the Cauchy distribution.

21. Let S be the square $\{(u;v): 0 \leqslant u \leqslant 1; 0 \leqslant v \leqslant 1\}$, and let U and V have joint probability density function
$$f_{U;V}(u;v) = \begin{cases} \frac{4u+2v}{3}, & (u;v) \in S \\ 0, & \text{otherwise} \end{cases}$$

(A) Find $P(U+V \leqslant 1)$.

(B) Find the marginal p.d.f. of U.

(C) Find the marginal p.d.f. of V.

In each case check that your answer really is a p. d. f.

22. Let $(X;Y)$ be a random vector with joint probability density function
$$f_{X;Y}(x;y) = \begin{cases} ke^{-(x+y)}, & x>y>0 \\ 0, & \text{otherwise} \end{cases}$$

(A) Find the value of k.

(B) Find the marginal p. d. f. of Y, and hence describe the distribution of Y as a standard distribution.

23. For the random variables U and V in Exercise 21:

(A) Find the conditional p. d. f. of U given $V=v$.

(B) If the conditional expectation $E(U|V)$ is written in the form $g(V)$, find the function g.

24. Let $(X;Y)$ be a random vector with joint probability density function
$$f_{X;Y}(x;y) = \begin{cases} \dfrac{x+y}{2}, & 0 \leqslant x \leqslant 1, 0 \leqslant y \leqslant 1 \\ \dfrac{y-x}{2}, & -1 \leqslant x \leqslant 0, 0 \leqslant y \leqslant 1 \\ 0, & \text{otherwise} \end{cases}$$

Show that X and Y are not independent but that they have correlation coefficient zero.

25. In a particular location the amount of sunshine S (in hours) in the growing season is distributed as $S \sim Ga(\alpha, \beta)$ and, conditional on S, the change in weight, C of a certain plant during the growing season is distributed as $C \sim N(kS, \sigma^2)$ (for some constant k). Find the mean and variance of C (in terms of α, β, σ^2 and k).

26. The random variables X and Y have joint p. d. f. given by
$$f_{XY}(x;y) = \begin{cases} \dfrac{1}{2}(x+y)e^{(-x+y)}, & \text{for } x, y \geqslant \\ 0, & \text{elsewhere} \end{cases}$$

Find, using a suitable bivariate transformation, the p. d. f. of the random variable $U = X+Y$. Hence evaluate $E[(X+Y)^5]$.

27. Let (X, Y) be a random vector with joint p. d. f. $f(x,y)$ as in question 22.

(A) If $U = X-Y$ and $V = Y/2$, find the joint p. d. f. of (U, V).

(B) Are U and V independent?

(C) Describe the distributions of U and V as standard distributions.

28. Let X and Y be independent random variables with distributions $Ga(\alpha_1, \beta)$

and $Ga(\alpha_2,\beta)$ respectively. Show that the random variables $U=\dfrac{X}{X+Y}$ and $V=X+Y$ are independent with distributions $Be(\alpha_1,\alpha_2)$ and $Ga(\alpha_1+\alpha_2,\beta)$ respectively.

29. Question 28 showed that if X and Y are independent random variables with $X \sim Ga(\alpha_1,\beta)$ and $Y \sim Ga(\alpha_2,\beta)$, then $X+Y \sim Ga(\alpha_1+\alpha_2,\beta)$.

(A) Use induction to show that for $n \geqslant 2$, if $X_1, X_2, \cdots, X_n$ are independent random variables with $X_i \sim Ga(\alpha_i,\beta)$ then
$$\sum_{i=1}^{n} X_i \sim Ga(\sum_{i=1}^{n} \alpha_i, \beta)$$

(B) Hence show that for $n \geqslant 1$, if $Z_1, Z_2, \cdots, Z_n$ are independard standaral normal random variables then
$$\sum_{i=1}^{n} Z_i^2 \sim \chi_n^2$$

(Hint that this was true in the case $n = 1$, and recall that the χ^2 distribution is a special case of the Gamma.)

30. Random variables X, Y and Z have means 3, -4 and 6 respectively and variances 1, 1 and 25 respectively. X and Y are uncorrelated; the correlation coefficient between X and Z is $\dfrac{1}{5}$ and that between Y and Z is $-\dfrac{1}{5}$. Let $U=X+Y-Z$ and $W=2X+Z-4$.

(A) Write down the mean vector and covariance matrix of $(X,Y,Z)^T$.
(B) Find the mean vector and covariance matrix of $(U,W)^T$.
(C) Evaluate $E(2X+Z-6)^2$.

31. Let X and Y be independent standard normal random variables.

(A) Write down the covariance matrix of the random vector $\boldsymbol{X}=\begin{pmatrix}X\\Y\end{pmatrix}$.

(B) Let $\boldsymbol{R}$ be the rotation matrix
$$\begin{pmatrix}\cos\theta & -\sin\theta\\ \sin\theta & \cos\theta\end{pmatrix}$$
and show that $\boldsymbol{RX}$ has the same covariance matrix as $\boldsymbol{X}$.

32. Suppose that the random vector $\boldsymbol{X}=\begin{pmatrix}X_1\\X_2\end{pmatrix}$ follows the bivariate normal distribution with $\mu_1=\mu_2=0$, $\sigma_1^2=1$, $\sigma_{12}=2$ and $\sigma_2^2=5$.

(A) Calculate the correlation coefficient of X_1 and X_2. Are X_1 and X_2 independent?

(B) Find the mean and the covariance matrices of

and
$$Y = (1 \ 2)X$$
$$Z = \begin{pmatrix} 1 & 2 \\ 3 & 4 \end{pmatrix} X$$

What are the distributions of Y and Z?

33. Let X_1 and X_2 be bivariate normally distributed random variables each with mean 0 and variance 1, and with correlation coeffcient ρ.

(A) By integrating out the variable x_2 in the joint p. d. f., verify that the marginal distribution of X_1 is indeed that of a standard univariate normal random variable.

(B) Show by direct derivation of the conditional p. d. f. that the conditional distribution of X_2 given $X_1 = x_1$ is $N(\rho x_1, 1-\rho^2)$.

34. Let $X = (X_1, X_2)^T$ have a $N_2(\mu, \Sigma)$ distribution with $\mu = (\mu_1, \mu_2)^T$ and
$$\Sigma = \begin{pmatrix} \sigma_1^2 & \sigma_{12} \\ \sigma_{12} & \sigma_2^2 \end{pmatrix}$$

Let
$$A = \begin{pmatrix} 1 & \dfrac{\sigma_1}{\sigma_2} \\ \dfrac{\sigma_2}{\sigma_1} & 1 \end{pmatrix}$$

Find the distribution of $Y = AX$, and deduce that any bivariate normal random vector can be transformed by a linear transformation into a vector of independent normal random variables.

35. An observation from a $Bi(n, \theta)$ distribution gives the value 4.

(A) Assuming that n is known to be 9 and that θ is unknown, write down the likelihood function of θ (for $0 \leq \theta \leq 1$) and plot a graph of it. (You may use R or Maple to do the plot.)

(B) Assuming that θ is known to be $\dfrac{3}{4}$ and that n is unknown, write down a formula for the likelihood function of n (for integers $n \geq 4$) and calculate its values for $n = 4, 5, 6$ and 7.

36. Given the random sample $x = (x_1, x_2, \cdots, x_n)^T$, for some $n > 0$, write down the likelihood function $L(\theta, x)$, in each of the following cases. In each case you should give both the function and the parameter set Θ.

(A) The data are a random sample from the exponential distribution $Exp(\lambda)$

with $\lambda = 1/\theta$.

(B) The data are a random sample from the binomial $Bi(m,\theta)$ distribution, where m is known.

(C) The data are a random sample from the normal $N(\mu,\theta)$, where μ is known.

37. Repeat question 36 for the following: (A) The data are a random sample from the gamma distribution $Ga(\theta,4)$.

(B) The data are a random sample from the inverted gamma distribution $IGa(1,\theta)$. [The $IGa(\alpha,\beta)$ distribution is the distribution of $1 = U$ if $U \sim Ga(\alpha,\beta)$.]

(C) The data are a random sample from the beta distribution $Be(\theta,\theta)$.

38. For each of the cases of question 36, find the log likelihood, and simplify it as much as you can.

39. A random sample $(x_1, x_2, x_3)^T$ of three observations from a Poisson distribution with parameter λ, where λ is known to be in $\Lambda = \{1,2,3\}$, gives the values $x_1 = 4, x_2 = 0, x_3 = 3$. Find the likelihood of each of the possible values of λ, and hence find the maximum likelihood estimate.

40. As in question 35, an observation from a $Bi(n,\theta)$ distribution gives the value 4.

(A) Assuming that n is known to be 9 and that θ is unknown, find the maximum likelihood estimate of θ.

(B) Assuming that θ is known to be $\frac{3}{4}$ and that n is unknown (but is known to be an integer satisfying $n \geq 4$), find the maximum likelihood estimate of n.

41. Find the maximum likelihood estimate of θ when the data $x = (x_1, x_2, \cdots, x_n)^T$ are a random sample from the binomial $Bi(m,\theta)$ distribution, where m is known, as in question 36(b).

42. Find the maximum likelihood estimate of θ when the data $x = (x_1, x_2, \cdots, x_n)^T$ are a random sample from the normal $N(\mu,\theta)$, where μ is known, as in question 36(C). Show that this estimator is unbiased.

43. Find the maximum likelihood estimate when the data $x = (x_1, x_2, \cdots, x_n)^T$ are a random sample from the gamma distribution $Ga(3,\theta)$. If $\bar{x} = 3$, calculate the maximum likelihood estimate $\hat{\theta}$ and show that it does not depend on the sample size n.

44. A random sample $x = (x_1, x_2, \cdots, x_n)^T$ is taken from a population with a Pareto distribution with parameters α and β so that

$$f(x_i|\theta) = \frac{\alpha\beta^\alpha}{x_i^{\alpha+1}}, \quad x_i \geq \beta > 0, \alpha > 0$$

where $\theta = (\alpha, \beta)^T$.

Find the maximum likelihood estimate of θ based on the above sample.

45. A random sample $x = (x_1, x_2, \cdots, x_n)^T$ is taken from a population with a logarithmic distribution with parameters α and β so that

$$f(x_i|\theta) = \frac{\log x_i}{\beta(\log \beta - 1) - \alpha(\log \alpha - 1)}, \quad 1 \leq \alpha \leq x_i \leq \beta$$

where $\theta = (\alpha, \beta)^T$.

Find the maximum likelihood estimate of θ based on the above sample.

46. A random sample $x = (x_1, x_2, \cdots, x_n)^T$ is taken from a population with a geometric distribution with parameter θ, so that the probability function of X_i is

$$p(x_i) = P(X_i = x_i) = (1-\theta)^{x_i}\theta, \quad x_i = 0, 1, 2, \cdots, 0 < \theta < 1$$

Find the maximum likelihood estimate of θ based on the above sample.

47. A random sample $x = (x_1, x_2, \cdots, x_n)^T$ is taken from a population with an inverse Gaussian distribution (known also as the Wald distribution), with p. d. f.

$$f(x_i) = \sqrt{\frac{\theta}{2\pi x_i^3}} \exp\left(-\frac{\theta(x_i - \mu)^2}{2\mu^2 x_i}\right), \quad x_i > 0, \mu, \theta > 0$$

(A) Assuming that μ is known, find the maximum likelihood estimate of θ based on the above sample.

(B) If both μ and θ are unknown, find the maximum likelihood estimate of (μ, θ) based on the above sample.

48. (A) As in question 35(A) an observation from a $Bi(n, \theta)$ distribution with $n = 9$ gives the value $x = 4$.

i. Find the approximate range of values for which the log likelihood is within 2 of its maximum value. [You may do this either by inspection of a plot, or by using a computer package to solve the inequality numerically.]

ii. A traditional approximate 95% confidence interval here would be of the form $\hat{\theta} \pm 1.96\sqrt{\frac{\hat{\theta}(1-\hat{\theta})}{n}}$, where $\hat{\theta} = x/n$. Compare your answer to (A) to what this would give.

(B) Repeat (A) for $n = 90$ and $x = 40$.

49. Suppose that two random variables X and Y are linked through a third random variable Z by the relationship $Y = 2X + Z$, where X is independent of Z and $Z \sim N(0; 1)$. Assuming that $E(X) = 1$ and $\text{Var } X = 2$, verify the relationships

$$E\{E(Y|X)\} = E(Y)$$
$$E\{\mathrm{Var}(Y|X)\} + \mathrm{Var}\{E(Y|X)\} = \mathrm{Var}\, Y$$

Explain how you have used the fact that X and Z are independent.

50. Suppose that the random sample $x = (x_1, \cdots, x_n)^\mathrm{T}$ is taken from the negative binomial distribution, so that each X_i has probability function

$$p(x_i) = P(X_i = x_i) = \binom{x_i + r - 1}{r - 1} \theta^r (1-\theta)^{x_i}$$

for some "success" probability θ satisfying $0 \leq \theta \leq 1$; where $x_i = 0, 1, 2, \cdots$ and r is the total number of "successes". If r is known, find the maximum likelihood estimate of θ.

> Statistics are like a bikini. What they reveal is suggestive, but what they conceal is vital.
> ——Professor in Baruch College, Aaron Levenstein

Unit Three Index Numbers

3.1 Introduction

Index numbers are the most commonly-used instruments to measure changes in levels of various economic variables. Index numbers relating to various economic phenomena are regularly compiled and published. The consumer price index (CPI), which measures the changes in prices of a range of consumer goods and services, is the most widely-used economic indicator. Other important index numbers include the price deflators for national income aggregates; indices of import and export prices; financial indices such as the All Ordinaries Index (Australia) and the Dow Jones Index (U.S.A.).

The principal aim of this chapter is to provide a simple exposition to various index numbers that are relevant in the context of measuring productivity changes over time and space. It is evident that measuring productivity changes necessarily involves measuring changes in the levels of output and the associated changes in the input usage. Such changes are easy to measure in the case of a single input and a single output, but are more difficult when multi-input and multi-output cases are considered.

We see three principal areas in productivity measurement where index numbers play a major role. The first and foremost is the use of index numbers in the measurement of changes in total factor productivity (TFP) leading to the popular TFP index numbers. TFP index numbers in turn require separate input and output quantity index numbers.

The second use of index numbers in productivity measurement is an indirect role. It concerns the use of index numbers in generating the required data that required data that can be used in the application of data envelopment analysis (DEA) or in the estimation of the stochastic frontiers. Application of these techniques using very detailed data on inputs and outputs may pose estimation problems from the loss of degrees of freedom due to inclusion of a large number of input and output categories. In most practical applications of these techniques, it is necessary to "aggregate" data into a smaller number of input and output variables. For example, different types of labour inputs are usually aggregated into one single labour input. Outputs of commodities that belong to a particular group are usually aggregated into a single output aggregate for the group. For example, in agriculture, items such as wheat, rice, etc., are grouped to form the output of "cereals". This type of aggregation, which is essentially an intermediate step in the process of assessing efficiency and productivity change, requires the use of index numbers. Usually, such aggregates take the form of "*value aggregates at constant prices*" or just "*constant price series*".

The third area concerns the type of index numbers that are required in handling panel data sets, with price and quantity data over time and space. Comparison of spatial observations usually requires some basic consistency requirements such as "transitivity" and "base invariance". These requirements, in turn, stipulate that the formulae used for the purpose of generating index numbers, of the type discussed in the preceding two paragraphs, need to satisfy some additional requirements.

Words and Expressions

index numbers 指数
consumer price index (CPI) 消费价格指数
national income aggregates 国民总收入
price deflator 价格紧缩指数,价格平减指数
Dow Jones Index (U.S.A.) 道琼斯指数
total factor productivity (TFP) 全要素生产率
productivity measurement 生产率测量;生产率测算
value aggregates at constant prices 不变价格下的总价值
constant price series 不变价格序列
transitivity *n.* 传递性
base invanance 基不变性
generating index numbers 生成指数

stochastic frontiers 随机前沿
degrees of freedom 自由度
data envelopment analysis（DEA） 数据包络分析（数学规划的一个分支领域）
panel data 面板数据,平行数据
consistency n. 一致性

3.2 Conception and Notation

An index number is defined as a real number that measures changes in a set of related variables. Conceptually, index numbers may be used for comparisons over time or space or both. Index numbers are used to measure price and quantity changes over time, as well as to measure differences in the levels across firms, industries, regions of countries. Price index numbers may refer to consumer prices, input and output prices, export and import prices, etc., whereas quantity index numbers may be measuring changes in quantities of outputs produced or inputs used by a firm or industry over time or across firms.

Index numbers have a long and distinguished history in economics, with some of the most important contributions due to Laspeyres and Paasche, dating back to the late nineteenth century. The Laspeyres and Paasche formula are still commonly used by national statistical offices around the world. But it is the work of Irving Fisher and his book, *the Making of Index Numbers*, published in 1922, that recognised the possibility of using many statistical formula to derive appropriate index numbers. The Törnquist (1936) index is a formula that plays a major role in productivity measurement. Chapter 2 of Diewert and Nakamura (1993) provides an excellent exposition of the historical background to index number construction.

Notation

We use the following notation throughout this chapter. Let p_{mj} and q_{mj} represent the price and quantity, respectively, of the m-th commodity in the M commodities being considered ($m = 1, 2, \ldots, M$) in the j-th period ($j = s, t$). Without loss of generality, s and t may refer to two firms instead of time periods, and quantities may refer to either input or output quantities.

Conceptually, all index numbers measure changes in the levels of a set of variables from a reference period. The reference period is denoted at the "base period". The period for which the index is calculated is referred to as the "current period". Let I_{st} represent a general index number for current period, t, with s as the base period. Similarly, let V_{st}, P_{st} and Q_{st} represent value, price and quantity index numbers, respectively.

The General Index Number Problem

The value change from period s to t is the ratio of the value of commodities in periods s and t, valued at respective prices. Thus

$$V_{st} = \frac{\sum_{i=1}^{N} p_{it} q_{it}}{\sum_{i=1}^{N} p_{is} q_{is}} \tag{3.1}$$

the index, V_{st}, measures the change in the value of the basket of quantities of M commodities from period s to period t. Obviously, V_{st} is the result of changes in the two components, prices and quantities. While V_{st} is easy to measure, it is more difficult to disentangle the effects of price and quantity changes. We may want to disentangle these effects so that, for example, the quantity component can be used in measuring the quantity change.

If we are operating in a single-commodity world, then such a decomposition is very simple to achieve. We have

$$V_{st} = \frac{p_t q_t}{p_s q_s} = \frac{p_t}{p_s} \times \frac{q_t}{q_s}$$

Here the ratios p_t/p_s and q_t/q_s measure the relative price and quantity changes and there is no index number problem.

In generally, when we have $M \geq 2$ commodities, we have a problem of aggregation. The price relative, p_{mt}/p_{ms}, measures the change in the price level of the m-th commodity, and the quantity relative, q_{mt}/q_{ms}, measures the change in the quantity level of m-th commodity ($m=1,2,\ldots,M$).

Now the problem is one of combining the M different measures of price (quantity) changes, into a single real number, called a *price (quantity) index*. This problem is somewhat similar to the problem of selecting a suitable measure of central tendency. In the next two sections, we briefly examine some of the more commonly-used formula for measuring price and quantity index changes.

Words and Expressions

generating index numbers 生成指数
reference period 参考时期
base period 基期
current period 现期,计算期,报告期

disentangle *v.* 解脱,解开;解决(纠纷等);清理(破产公司等)
refer to 参照,涉及,提及
decomposition *n.* 分解
central tendency 中心趋势,集中趋势
be similar to 类似于……,相似于……
generating index numbers 综合指数
price index 价格指数
quantity index 数量指数

3.3 Formula for Price Index Numbers

We first focus on the price index numbers and then illustrate how these formula can also be used in the construction of quantity index numbers.

Laspeyres and Paasche Index Numbers

These index numbers represent the most widely used indices in practice. The Laspeyres price index uses the base-period quantities as weights, whereas, the Paasche index uses the current-period weights to define the index.

$$\text{Laspeyres index} = P_{st}^L = \frac{\sum_{m=1}^{M} p_{mt} q_{ms}}{\sum_{m=1}^{M} p_{ms} q_{ms}} = \sum_{m=1}^{M} \frac{p_{mt}}{p_{ms}} \times \omega_{ms} \qquad (3.2)$$

where $\omega_{ms} = p_{ms} q_{ms} / \sum_{m=1}^{M} p_{ms} q_{ms}$ is the value share of m-th commodity in the base period.

Equation (3.2) suggests two alternative interpretations. First, the Laspeyres index is the ratio of two value aggregates resulting from the valuation of the base-period quantities at current- and base-period prices. The second interpretation is that the index is a value-share weighted average of the M price relatives. The value shares reflect the relative importance of each commodity in the set involved. The value shares used here refer to the base period.

A natural alternative to the use of base-period quantities, in the definition of the Laspeyres index, is to the use current-period quantities. The Paasche index number, which makes use of the current-period quantities, is given by

$$\text{Paasche index} = P_{st}^P = \frac{\sum_{m=1}^{M} p_{mt} q_{mt}}{\sum_{m=1}^{M} p_{ms} q_{mt}} = \frac{1}{\sum_{m=1}^{M} \frac{p_{ms}}{p_{mt}} \times \omega_{mt}} \qquad (3.3)$$

The first part of equation (3.3) shows that the Paasche index is the ratio of the two value aggregate resulting from the valuation of current period-t quantities at the prices prevailing in periods t and s. Alternatively, the last part of the equation suggests that the Paasche index is a weighted harmonic mean of price relatives, with current-period value shares as weights.

From equations (3.2) and (3.3), it can be seen that the Laspeyres and Paasche formula, in a sense, represent two extremes, one formula placing emphasis on base-period quantities and the other on current-period quantities. These two indices coincide if the price relatives do not exhibit any variation, that is, if $p_{mt}/p_{ms}=c$, then the Laspeyres and Paasche indices are both equal to the constant c. These indices tend to diverge when price relatives exhibit a large variation. The extent of divergence also depends on quantity relatives and the statistical correlation between price and quantity relatives. Bortkiewicz (1924) provides a decomposition of the Laspeyres-Paasche gap.

The Laspeyres and Paasche indices are quite popular since they are easy to compute and they provide "bounds" for the *true index* that is defined using economic theory. Most national statistical agencies use there formula or some minor variations in computing various indices, such as the CPI. In particular, use of the Laspeyres index is more prevalent. We note that if published price indices are being used for purposes of deflating a given value series, then the resulting deflated series will exhibit definite characteristics depending on which formula is used in constructing the price index numbers. This issue is further elaborated in Section 3.4, where the indirect measurement of quantity changes are discussed.

The Fisher Index

The gap between the Laspeyres and Paasche indices led Fisher (1922) to define a geometric mean of the two indices as possible index number formula

$$\text{Fisher index} = P_{st}^F = \sqrt{P_{st}^L \times P_{st}^P} \tag{3.4}$$

Though the Fisher index is an artificial construct, which has value between the two extremes, it possesses a number of desirable statistical and economic theoretic properties. Diewert (1992) demonstrates the versatility of the Fisher index. In view of the many favourable properties it has, the Fisher index is also known as the *Fisher ideal index*.

The Törnqvist index

The Törnqvist index has been used in many total factor productivity studies that have been conducted in the last decade. In this section, we define the Törnqvist price index, while we define the Törnqvist quantity index in the next section. The Törnqvist price index is a weighted geometric average of the price relatives, with weights given by the simple average of the value shares in periods s and t

$$P_{st}^T = \prod_{m=1}^{M} \left[\frac{p_{mt}}{p_{ms}} \right]^{\frac{\omega_{ms}+\omega_{mt}}{2}} \quad (3.5)$$

The Törnqvist index is usually presented and applied in its log-change form

$$\ln P_{st}^T = \sum_{m=1}^{M} \left(\frac{\omega_{ms} + \omega_{mt}}{2} \right) [\ln p_{mt} - \ln p_{ms}] \quad (3.6)$$

The log-change form offers a convenient computational form. In log-change form, the Törnqvist index is a weighted average of logarithmic price changes. Furthermore, the log-change in the price of the m-th commodity, given by

$$\ln p_{mt} - \ln p_{ms} = \ln \frac{p_{mt}}{p_{ms}} \approx \left(\frac{p_{mt}}{p_{ms}} - 1 \right)$$

represents the percentage change in the price of the m-th commodity. Hence, the Törnqvist price index, in its log-change form, provides an indication of the overall growth rate in prices (inflation rate).

There are many more formula in index number literature but we restrict our attention to these four formula as they represent the most commonly-used formula. We return to discuss some of the properties of these index numbers in Section 3.5, after a brief description of quantity index numbers.

Words and Expressions

makes use of 利用,使用
prevailing *adj.* 主要的,流行的
weighted harmonic mean 加权调和平均(值)
resulting *adj.* 所得到的,作为结果的
variation *n.* 变异,变化,变更
deflated series 紧缩序列,平减序列
ideal index 理想指数
versatility *n.* 多功能性;多面性;多才多艺;易变性
weighted geometric average 加权几何平均(值)

logarithmic *adj.* 对数的
log-change form 对数变化形式
percentage *n.* 百分数,百分率,百分比
growth rate 增长率
inflation rate 通货膨胀率
indication *n.* 指示,指出,迹象,指标
restrict...to 限制,约束

3.4 Quantity Index Numbers

Two approaches can be used in measuring quantity changes. The first approach is a direct approach, where we derive a formula that measures overall quantity changes from individual commodity-specific quantity changes, measured by q_{mt}/q_{ms}. The Laspeyres, Paasche, Fisher and Törnqvist indices can be applied directly to quantity relatives. The second approach is an indirect approach, which uses the basic idea that price and quantity changes are two components that make up the value change over the periods s and t. So, if price changes are measured directly using the formula in the previous section, then quantity changes can be indirectly obtained after deflating the value change for the price change. This approach is discussed below in Section 3.4.2.

3.4.1 The Direct Approach

Various quantity index formula may be defined using price index numbers, by simply interchanging prices and quantities. The formula described above yield

$$Q_{st}^L = \frac{\sum_{m=1}^{M} p_{ms} q_{mt}}{\sum_{m=1}^{M} p_{ms} q_{ms}}, Q_{st}^P = \frac{\sum_{m=1}^{M} p_{mt} q_{mt}}{\sum_{m=1}^{M} p_{mt} q_{ms}}$$

and

$$Q_{st}^F = \sqrt{Q_{st}^L \times Q_{st}^P} \tag{3.7}$$

The Törnqvist quantity index, in its multiplicative and additive (log-change) forms, is given below

$$Q_{st}^T = \prod_{m=1}^{M} \left[\frac{q_{mt}}{q_{ms}}\right]^{\frac{\omega_{ms}+\omega_{mt}}{2}} \tag{3.8}$$

$$\ln Q_{st}^T = \sum_{m=1}^{M} \left(\frac{\omega_{ms}+\omega_{mt}}{2}\right) [\ln q_{mt} - \ln q_{ms}] \tag{3.9}$$

The Törnqvist index in equation (3.8) is the most popular index number used in measuring changes in output quantities produced and input quantities used in production over two time periods s and t. The log-change form of the Törnqvist index in equation (3.9) is the formula generally used for computational purposes. Preference for the use of the Törnqvist index formula is due to the many important economic-theoretic properties attributed to the index by Diewert (1976, 1981) and Caves, Chirstensen and Diewert (1982).

3.4.2 The Indirect Approach

The indirect approach is commonly used for purposes of quantity comparisons over time. This approach uses the basic premise that the measurement of the price and quantity changes must account for value changes

$$\text{Value change} = \text{Price change} \times \text{Quantity change}$$

$$V_{st} = P_{st} \times Q_{st} \tag{3.10}$$

Since V_{st} is defined from data directly as the ratio of values in periods t and s, Q_{st} can be obtained as a function of P_{st}, as shown below in equation (3.11)

$$Q_{st} = \frac{V_{st}}{P_{st}} = \frac{\sum_{m=1}^{M} P_{mt} q_{mt}}{\sum_{m=1}^{M} P_{ms} q_{ms}} \Bigg/ P_{st} = \frac{\sum_{m=1}^{M} P_{mt} q_{mt}/P_{st}}{\sum_{m=1}^{M} P_{ms} q_{ms}} =$$

$$\frac{\text{value in period } t, \text{ adjusted for price change}}{\text{value in period } s} \tag{3.11}$$

so $$Q_{st} = \frac{\text{value in period } t \text{ (at constant prices in period } s)}{\text{value in period } s \text{ (at price in period } s)}$$

The numerator in this expression corresponds to the constant price series that are commonly used in many statistical publications. Basically, this approach states that quantity indices can be obtained from ratios of values, aggregated after removing the effect of price movements over the period under consideration.

A few important features and applications of indirect quantity comparisons are discussed below.

Constant Price Aggregates and Quantity Comparison

A direct implication of equation (3.11) and the indirect approach is that value aggregates, adjusted for price changes over time, can be considered as aggregate quantities or quantities of a composite commodity. Such price deflated series are abundant in the publications of statistical agencies. Examples of such aggregates are: gross domestic product (GDP); output of sectors, such as agriculture and manufacturing; investment series; and exports and imports of good and services.

Time series and cross-section data on such aggregates are often used as data series for use in the estimation of least-squares econometric production models, stochastic frontiers, and also in DEA calculations, where it is necessary to reduce the dimensions of the output and input vectors. This means that, even if index number methodology is not used in measuring productivity changes directly, it is regularly used in creating intermediate data series.

"Self-Duality" of Formula for Direct and Indirect Quantity Comparisons

We examine the implications of the choice of formula for price comparisons on indirect quantity comparisons. Suppose, we construct our price index numbers using the Laspeyres formula. Then, the indirect quantity index, defined in equation (3.11), can be algebraically shown to be the Paasche quantity index, defined in equation (3.7). This means that the Laspeyres price index and the Paasche quantity index form a pair that together exactly decompose the value change. In that sense, the Paasche quantity index can be considered as the dual of the Laspeyres price index.

It is also easy to show that the Paasche price index and the Laspeyres price quantity index together decompose the value index, and, therefore, are dual to each other. An important question that arises is: "are there self-dual index number formulae such that the same formula for price and quantity index numbers decomposes the value index exactly?" The answer to this is in the affirmative. The Fisher index for prices and the Fisher index for quantities form a dual pair. This implies that the direct quantity index obtained using the Fisher formula is identical to the indirect quantity index derived by deflating the value change by the Fisher price index. This property is sometimes referred to as the *factor reversal test*. We consider this property in the next section.

The Törnqvist index, due to the geometric nature of its formula, does not have the property of self-duality. This means that if we use the Törnqvist price index, then the indirect quantity index that is derived would be different from the quantity index derived using the Törnqvist index in equation (3.8) directly.

If the direct and indirect approaches lead to different answers, or different numerical measures of quantity changes, a problem of choice often arises as to which approach should be used in a given practical application. This problem is discussed below.

Direct versus Indirect Quantity Comparisons

Some of the analytical issues involved in a choice between direct and indirect quantity comparisons are discussed in Allen and Diewert (1981). From a practical point of view, such a choice depends on the type of data available, the variability in the price and quantity relatives, as well as the theoretical framework used in the quantity comparisons.

From a practical point of view, a research rarely has the luxury of choosing between direct and indirect comparisons. If the problem involves the use of aggregative data, then quantity data are usually only available in the form of constant price series. In such cases, data unavailability solves the problem.

The second point concerns the reliability of the underlying index. Since an index number is a scalar-valued representation of changes that are observed for different commodities, the reliability of such a representation depends upon the variabilities that are observed in the price and quantity changes for the different commodities. If price changes tend to be uniform over different commodities, then the price index provides a reliable measure of the price changes. A similar conclusion can be drawn for quantity index numbers. The relative variability in the price and quantity ratios, p_{mt}/p_{ms} and q_{mt}/q_{ms} ($m = 1, 2, \ldots, M$) provides a useful clue as to which index is more reliable. If the price ratios exhibit less variability (relative to the quantity ratios), then a indirect quantity index is advocated, and if quantity relatives show less variability, then a direct quantity index is preferred. Variability in these ratios can be measured using standard variance measures.

Following on from this important consideration, it is worth noting that price changes over time tend to be more uniform across commodities than commodity changes. Price changes for different commodities are usually deviations from an underlying rate of overall price change. In contrast, quantity ratios tend to exhibit considerable variation across different commodities, even in the case of changes over time.

Another point of significance is that if price (quantity) ratios exhibit little variability then most index number formula lead to very similar measures of price (quantity) change. There is more concurrence of results arising out of different formula, and, therefore, the choice of a formula has less impact on the measure of price (quantity) change derived.

Finally, in the context of output and productivity comparisons, direct quantity comparisons may offer theoretically more meaningful indices as they utilise the constraints underlying the production technologies. Diewert (1976, 1983) and Caves, Christensen and Diewert (1982) suggest that direct input and output quantity indices, based on the Törnqvist index formula, are theoretically superior under certain conditions. Diewert (1992) shows that the Fisher index performs very well with respect to both theoretical and test properties. An additional point in favour of the Fisher index is that it is self-dual, in that it satisfies the factor-reversal test. In addition, the Fisher index is defined using the Lasperyres and Paasche indices. Therefore, the index is easier to understand and it is also capable of handing zero quantities in the data set.

Balk (1998) suggests that under the assumption of behaviour under revenue constraints, productivity indices are best computed using indirect quantity measures. Given these results, from a theoretical point of view, the choice between direct and indirect quantity (input or output) comparisons should be based on the assumptions on the behaviour of the firm or decision making unit.

All the evidence and discussion on this issue of choice between direct and indirect quantity comparisons suggests that a decision needs to be made on pragmatic considerations as well as on pure analytical grounds.

Words and Expressions

direct approach 直接方法
indirect approach 间接方法
multiplicative *adj.* 乘法的,增加的
additive *adj.* 加法的,可加的
gross domestic product（GDP）国内生产总值
time series 时间序列
cross-section 横截面,截面
least-squares 最小二乘法
econometric production models 经济计量生产模型
factor reversal test 要素逆检验
self-duality 自对偶性
scalar-valued 数量值,纯量值
revenue constraints 收入约束

pragmatic *adj.* 实际的,注重实效的
analytical grounds 解析基础,分析基础

3.5 Properties of Index Numbers: The Test Approach

In view of the existence of numerous index number formula, Fisher (1922) proposed a number of intuitively meaningful criteria, called *tests*, to be satisfied by the formula. These tests are used in the process of choosing a formula for purposes of constructing price and quantity index numbers. An alternative (yet closely related) framework is to state a number of properties, in the form of axioms, and then to find an index number that satisfies a given set of axioms. This approach is known as the *axiomatic approach* to index numbers. Eichorn and Voeller (1976) and Balk (1995) provide summaries of the axiomatic approach, the latter giving emphasis to price index number theory. Diewert (1992) provides a range of axioms for consideration in productivity measurement and recommends the use of the Fisher index. It is not within the scope of this book to provide details of the axiomatic approach or to delve deeply into various tests originally proposed by Fisher. The main purpose of this brief section is to provide an intuitive and non-rigorous treatment of some of the tests and state two results of some importance to productivity measurement.

Let P_{st} and Q_{st} represent price and quantity index numbers, which are both real-valued functions of the prices and quantities (M commodities) observed in periods s and t, denoted M-dimensional column vectors, $\boldsymbol{p}_s, \boldsymbol{p}_t, \boldsymbol{q}_s, \boldsymbol{q}_t$. Some of the basic and commonly-used axioms are listed below.

Positivity: The index (price or quantity) should be everywhere positive.

Continuity: The index is a continuous function of the prices and quantities.

Proportionality: If all prices (quantities) increase by the same proportion then $P_{st}(Q_{st})$ should increase by this proportion.

Commensurability or Dimensional Invariance: The price (quantity) index must be independent of the units of measurement of quantities (prices).

Time-reversal Test: For two periods s and t: $P_{st} = 1/P_{ts}$.

Mean-value Test: The price (or quantity) index must lie between the respective minimum and maximum changes at the commodity level.

Factor-reversal Test: A formula is said to satisfy this test if the same formula is used for direct price and quantity indices and the product of the resulting indices is equal to the value ratio.

Circularity Test (Transitivity): For any three periods, s, t and r, this test requires that: $P_{st} = P_{sr} \times P_{rt}$. That is, a direct comparison though period s and t yields the same index as an indirect comparison through period r.

The following two results describe the properties of the Fisher and Törnqvist indices, and thus offer justification for the common use of these indices in the context of productivity measurement.

Result 4.1

The Fisher index satisfies all the properties listed above, with the exception of the circularity test (transitivity).

In fact, Diewert (1992) shows that the Fisher index satisfies many more properties. The Fisher index satisfies the factor-reversal test which guarantees a proper decomposition of value change into price and quantity changes. This justifies the label of "ideal index" attached to the Fisher formula. The factor-reversal property shows that the direct Fisher quantity index is the same as the indirect quantity index derived by deflating the value index by the Fisher price index. The Fisher index exhibits the "self-dual" property. Diewert (1976, 1981) shows that the Fisher index is *exact* and *superlative*.

Result 4.2

The Törnqvist index satisfies all the tests listed above with the exception of the factor-reversal and circularity tests.

This result and other results are proved in Eichorn and Voeller (1983). Proofs of these statements are highly mathematical but the final results are quite useful. Theil (1973, 1974) shows that the Törnqvist index fails the factor-reversal test by only a small order of approximation. Failure to satisfy the factor-reversal test is not considered to be very serious as there is no necessity for the price and quantity index numbers to be *self-dual*, and no real analytical justification for the use of the same type of formula for price as well as quantity comparisons.

Fixed Base versus Chain Base Comparisons

We now briefly touch upon the issue of comparing prices, quantities and productivity over time. In the case of temporal comparisons, in particular, within the context of productivity measurement, we are usually interested in comparing each year with the previous year, and then combining annual changes in productivity to measure changes over a given period. The index constructed using this procedure is known as a *chain index*. To facilitate a formal definition, let $I(t, t+1)$ define an index of interest for period $t+1$ with t as the base period. The index can be applied to a time series with $t = 0, 1, 2, \cdots, T$. Then, a comparison between period t and a fixed base period, 0, can be made using the following chained index of comparisons for consecutive periods

$$I(0,t) = I(0,1) \times I(1,2) \times \cdots \times (t-1,t)$$

As an alternative to the chain-base index, it is possible to compare period 0 with period t using any one of the formula described earlier. The resulting index is known as the *fixed-base index*.

Most national statistical offices make use of a fixed-base Laspeyres index mainly because the weights remain the same for all the fixed-base index computations. Usually, the base periods are shifted on a regular basis.

There is a considerable index number literature focusing on the relative merits of fixed-and chain-base indices. A good survey of the various issues can be found in Forsyth (1978), Forsyth and Fowler (1981) and Szulc (1983). From a practical angle, especially with respect to productivity measurement, a chain index is more suitable than a fixed-base index. Since the chain index involves only comparisons with consecutive periods, the index is measuring smaller changes. Therefore, some of the approximations involved in the derivation of theoretically meaningful indices are more likely to hold. Another advantage is that comparisons over consecutive periods mean that the Laspeyres-Paasche spread is likely to be small indicating that most index number formula result in indices which are very similar in magnitude. The only drawback associated with the chain index is that the weights used in the indices need to be revised every year.

The use of a chained index does not result in transitive index numbers. Even though transitivity is not considered essential for temporal comparisons, it is necessary in the context of multilateral comparisons.

Which Formula to Choose

The foregoing discussion indicates that the choice of formula is essentially between the Fisher and Törnqvist indices. Both of these indices possess important properties and satisfy a number of axioms. If published aggregated data are used then it is necessary to check what formula was used in creating the series. It is very likely that Laspeyres or Paasche indices are used in such data series. If the indices are being computed for periods which are not far apart then differences in the numerical values of the Fisher and the Törnqvist indices are likely to be quite minimal. Further, both of these indices also have important theoretical properties. While, in practice, the Törnqvist index seems to be preferred, use of the Fisher index is recommended due to its additional self-dual property and its ability to accommodate zeros in the data.

Words and Expressions

axiomatic approach 公理化方法，公理方法
real-valued function 实值函数
positivity n. 正值性；确实；确信；积极性
continuity n. 连续性；继续；联结，连合
proportionality n. 比例(性)；均衡(性)；相称
commensurability n. 可公度性，可通约性，有公度性
dimensional invariance 维数不变性；维度不变性
mean-value test 均值检验
circularity n. 环比性；圆状，环状
superlative adj. 最优的，最高的
deflating n. 收缩，紧缩(通货)
chain index 环比指数，链指数
fixed-base index 固定基指数
be likely to (do) that 可能，大概
temporal adj. 时间的，暂时的
foregoing adj. 前述的，在前的
multilateral adj. 多边的，多国的
accommodate v. 供应，供给；使适应，调节

Genius is one per cent inspiration and ninety nine per cent perspiration.
—— T. A. Edison

4

Unit Four Missing Data and Imputation

4.1 Introduction

The problem of **missing data** in survey data is one of long standing, arising from nonresponse or partial response to survey questions. Reasons for nonresponse include unwillingness to provide the information asked for, difficulty of recall of events that occurred in the past, and not knowing the correct response. **Imputation** is the process of estimating or predicting the missing observations.

In this chapter we deal with the regression setup with data vector (y_i, x_i), $i = 1, \ldots, N$. For some of the observations some elements of x_i or of both (y_i, x_i) are missing. A number of questions are considered. When can we proceed with an analysis of only the complete observations, and when should we attempt to fill the gaps left by the missing observations? What methods of imputation are available? When imputed values for missing observations are obtained, how should estimation and inference then proceed?

If a data set has missing observations, and if these gaps can be filled by a statistically sound procedure, then benefit comes from a larger and possibly more representative sample and, under ideal circumstances, more precise inference. The cost of estimating missing data comes from having to make (possibly wrong) assumptions to support a procedure for generating proxies for the missing observations, and from the approximation error inherent in any such procedure. Further, statistical inference that follows data augmentation after imputed values replace missing data is more complicated because such inference must take into account the approximation errors introduced by imputation.

Gaps in data as the result of survey nonresponse and attrition from panels occur frequently. Imputation of missing values may be done by agencies for creating and maintaining the public-use survey databases or by those who use the data for modeling. In the former case the agency may have more extensive information, including confidential information, that can be harnessed in the imputation process. In the latter case the modeler may have a specific modeling framework that can be exploited in the imputation process. In both cases model-based imputation procedures are feasible.

An interesting example of missing data arises in the context of the Survey of Consumer Finances (Kennickell, 1998). Because of the sensitivity of the issue of consumer finances the survey exhibits many gaps in information on income and wealth. Analysts at the U. S. Federal Reserve have developed and implemented complex imputation algorithms for continuous and discrete variables using both publicly available survey information on income and wealth as well as confidential information from census data.

Fig. 4.1 shows some potential patterns of missing data on the regressors. The data set has a scalar dependent variable y and three regressors: x_1, x_2, and x_3 for each observation, then stacked as (y, x_1, x_2, x_3). In panel A, there are complete data on (y, x_2, x_3) but a block of observations on x_1 are missing. In panel B there are complete data on (y, x_3) but there are missing blocks of data on (x_1, x_2) such that x_1 and x_2 are never simultaneously observed. In panel C there is a general pattern of missing observations with missing observations on all three regressors, but there is no particular pattern of missingness.

The simplest way of handling missing data is to delete them and analyze only the reduced sample of "complete" observations. For example, in the case of panel A, the complete sample would be the subset of (y, x_1, x_2, x_3) formed by all available data on x_1 and the corresponding observations on (y, x_2, x_3). In the case of panel B, however, following this approach one would leave no usable observations, unless one excluded (x_1, x_2) from the analysis. In panel C the complete data set is formed after deleting any observation that contains a missing data point on any of the three regressors.

The procedure just described is called **listwise deletion**. It is widely followed and is often a default option in statistical software. It is not necessarily innocuous; the consequences depend on the missing data mechanism, and the conclusions

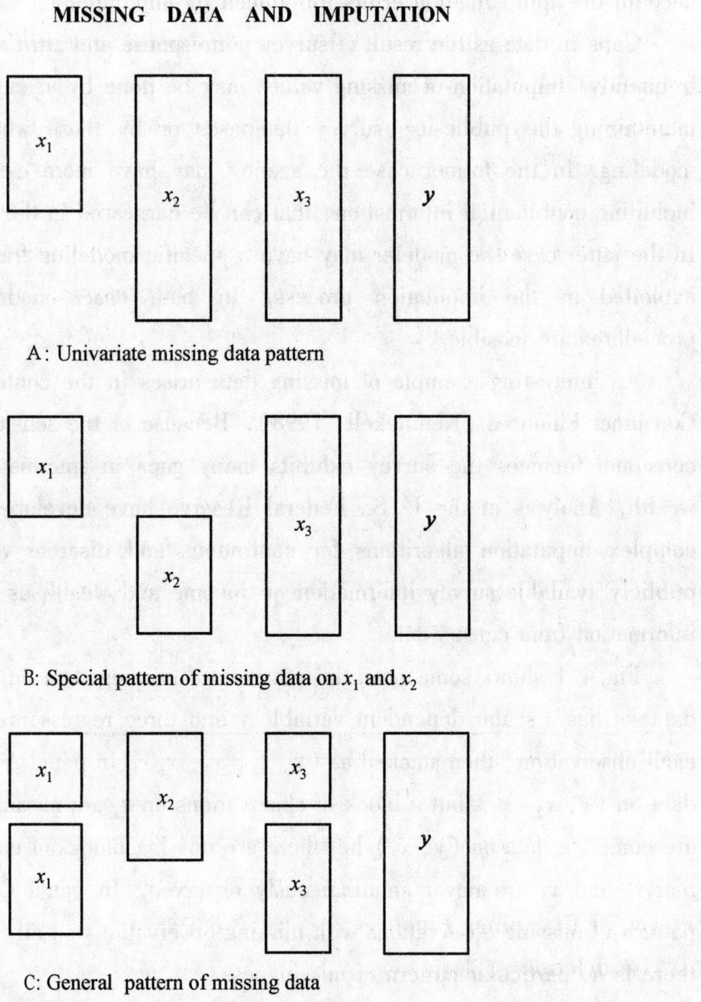

MISSING DATA AND IMPUTATION

A: Univariate missing data pattern

B: Special pattern of missing data on x_1 and x_2

C: General pattern of missing data

Fig. 4.1 Missing data: examples of missing regressors

drawn from such studies might be seriously flawed. Of course, in general throwing away data means throwing away information, and that reduces efficiency in estimation. Hence, provided the gaps attributed to missing data can be filled without creating distortion, listwise deletion seems worth trying. This chapter with study alternative approaches and their limitations.

Broadly, there are two approaches to imputation, one that is **model-based** and one that is not. The modern approach prefers model-based approaches. These use a model to impute the missing observations and then use the subsequent full data set to obtain better estimates of the model parameters. The process is iterative. Single and multiple imputation are feasible. A key feature of the modern approach is to regard missing data as random variables and then to replace them with multiple draws from the assumed underlying distribution; the process is called **multiple imputation**. Simulation methods may be used to approximate such a distribution.

This topic warrants a separate short introductory chapter as imputation is an important aspect of microeconometric work. Survey data inevitably include missing data, and the common practice of listwise deletion is an imputation method. Better imputation methods are available. An important caveat, however, is that all imputation methods are based on assumptions that in some applications may be too strong.

Most of the chapter deals with model-based approaches. Section 4.2 provides an introduction to the terminology and assumptions that are firmly entrenched in the imputation literature. Section 4.3 gives a brief treatment of missing data methods that do not use models. Section 4.4 begins with the first of the model-based methods, maximum likelihood. Section 4.5 considers the regression framework and EM-type methods of imputation.

Words and Expressions

missing adj. 缺掉的;失踪的;找不到的;不在的,缺席的
imputation n. 归罪;负责;非难;污名;[统] 估算,派算,补算
agency n. 代办处,经销处,代理机构;专业行政机构,局,署,处,社
harness v. 给……上挽具;套(马)[(+to)];治理,利用
Survey of Consumer Finances 消费者财务状况调查
listwise deletion 成列删除
model-based 基于模型方法
multiple imputation 多重估算,多重设算

4.2 Missing Data Assumptions

Some of the basic terminology and formal definitions widely used in the imputation literature are due to Rubin(1976), who introduced two key missing data mechanisms, missing at random and missing completely at random, that serve as useful benchmarks.

Rubin's setup involves Y, and $N \times p$ matrix consisting of a complete data set, which may not be fully observed. Denote by Y_{obs} the observed part and by Y_{mis} the nonobserved (missing) part. In the context of a regression model Y refers to both the regressors and the response (dependent) variables. Therefore, the analysis covers the general case of missing data. Let R denote an $N \times p$ matrix of indicator variables whose elements are zero or one depending on whether corresponding values in the Y matrix are missing or observed.

For regression with single dependent variable, Y contains data on the response variable y and the $(p-1)$ regressors X. The probability that x_{ki}, the ith observation on variable x_k, is missing may be (i) independent of its realized value, (ii) dependent on its realized value, (iii) dependent on x_{kj}, $j \neq i$, or (iv) dependent on x_{lj}, $j \neq i$, $l \neq k$.

Assumptions about the structure of missingness follow.

4.2.1 Missing at Random

Suppose $x_i (i=1, \ldots, N)$ is an observation on a variable in the data set under study. The **missing at random (MAR) assumption** is that the "missingness" in x_i does not depend on its value but may depend on the values of $x_j (j \neq i)$. Formally

$$x_i \text{ is MAR} \Rightarrow \Pr[x_i \text{ is missing } | x_i, x_j \forall j \neq i] =$$
$$\Pr[x_i \text{ is missing } | x_j \forall j \neq i] \qquad (4.1)$$

After controlling for other observations on x, the probability of missingness of x_i is unrelated to the value of x_i.

Rubin's (1976) even more formal definition states the following: The MAR assumption implies that the probability model for the indicator variable R does not depend on Y_{mis}, that is

$$\Pr[R | Y_{obs}, Y_{mis}, \psi] = \Pr[R | Y_{obs}, \psi]$$

where ψ is the underlying (vector) parameter of the missingness mechanism.

Under MAR no nonresponse bias is induced in a likelihood-based inference that ignores the missing data mechanism, although the resulting estimates may be inefficient. If the MAR assumption fails, however, the probability of missingness depends on the unobserved missing values. The MAR restriction is not testable because the values of the missing data are unknown. Because MAR is a strong assumption, sensitivity analyses based on different assumptions about missingness are desirable.

A separate issue is whether the pattern of missing data is purely random. In practice, we might expect that observations missing inside clusters of data, in the sense of Chapter 24, may be correlated. However, this issue is not related to that of nonresponse bias resulting from the missingness being connected to data values.

4.2.2 Missing Completely at Random

Missing completely at random (MCAR) is a special case of MAR. It means that Y_{obs} is a simple random sample of all potentially observable data values (Schafter, 1997).

Again suppose x_i is an observation on a variable in the data set under study. Then the data on x_i is said to be MCAR if the probability of missing data on x_i depends neither on its own values nor on the values of other variables in the data set. Formally

$$x_i \text{ is MCAR} \Rightarrow Pr[x_i \text{ is missing} \mid x_i, x_j \, \forall j \neq i]$$
$$= Pr[x_i \text{ is missing}] \quad (4.2)$$

For example, MCAR is violated if (a) those who do not report income are younger, on average, than those who do or if (b) typically small (large) values are missing.

For cases (i) ~ (iv) mentioned at the outset in this section, case (i) satisfies both MCAR and MAR, cases (iii) and (iv) satisfy MAR, and (ii) does not satisfy MAR.

MCAR implies that the observed data are a random subsample of the potential full sample. If the assumptions were valid no biases would result from ignoring incomplete observations, that is, observations with missing values.

The corollary is that the failure of MCAR implies a sample selection type of bias. MAR is a weaker assumption that still aids imputation as it assumes that the missing data mechanism depends only on observed quantities.

4.2.3 Ignorable and Nonignorable Missingness

A missing data mechanism is said to be **ignorable** if (a) the data set is MAR and (b) the parameters for the missing data-generating process, ψ, are unrelated to the parameters θ that we want to estimate.

This condition, which is similar to that of **weak exogeneity**, implies that the parameters θ of the model are distinct from parameters ψ of the missingness mechanism. Thus, if the missing data are ignorable, then there is no need to model the dgp for missing data as an essential part of the modeling exercise. MAR and "ignorability" are often treated as equivalent under the assumption that condition (b) for ignorability is almost always satisfied (Allison, 2002).

A **nonignorable** missing data mechanism arises if the MAR assumption is violated for (y, x), but it would not be violated if MAR is violated only for x. In that case the dgp for missing data must be modeled along with be overall model to obtain consistent estimates of the parameters θ. To avoid the possibility of selection bias, estimators such as Heckman's two-stage procedure must be used.

The imputation literature focues on ignorable missingness. If additionally the data set is MCAR then missing data cause no problem, aside from efficiency loss that might be reduced by imputation. If instead the data set is only MAR then imputation methods may be needed to ensure consistency, as well as to increase efficiency.

Words and Expressions

missing at random (MAR) assumption 随机缺失假设
missing completely at random 完全随机缺失
ignorable adj. 可忽略的
nonignorable adj. 不可忽略的
be distinct from 和……不同,与……有别
aside from 除……以外(尚有);除……之外;此外,除……还有

4.3 Handling Missing Data without Models

If no models are to be used, then one can simply analyze the available data or one can analyze data after non-model-based imputation.

4.3.1 Using Available Data Only

Listwise deletion or complete case analysis means the deletion of the observations(cases) that have missing values on one or more of the variables in the data set. Under the MCAR assumption, the remaining sample after listwise deletion remains a random sample from the original population; therefore the estimates based on it are consistent. However, the standard errors will be inflated because less information is used. If the number of regressors is large, then the total effect of listwise deletion can lead to very substantial reduction in the total number of observations. This might encourage one to leave out of the analysis variables with a high proportion of missing observations, but the results generated by such practice are potentially misleading.

If MCAR is not satisfied and the missing data are only MAR, then the estimates will be biased. Thus listwise deletion is not robust to the violations of MCAR. However, listwise deletion is robust to the violations of MAR among the independent variables (regressors) in regression analysis, that is, when the probability of missing data on any regressor does not depend on the values of the dependent variable. Briefly, listwise deletion is acceptable if incomplete cases attributable to missing data comprise a small percentage, say 5% or less, of the number of total cases (Schafter, 1996). It is important that the sample after listwise deletion is representative of the population under study.

Pairwise deletion or available-case analysis is often considered a better method than listwise deletion. The idea here is to use all possible pairs of observations (x_{1i}, x_{2i}) in estimating joint sample moments of (x_1, x_2) and to use all observations on an individual variable in estimating marginal moments. Thus, in a linear regression, under pairwise deletion we would estimate ($X'X$) and ($X'y$) using all possible pairs of regressors, whereas under listwise deletion we would estimate the same after deleting all cases with *any* missing observations. It is clear that we lose less information under pairwise deletion. The proposal here is to use maximum information to estimate individual summary statistics such as means and covariances and then to use these summary statistics to compute the regression estimates.

There are two important limitations of pairwise deletion: (1) Conventionally estimated standard errors and test statistics are biased and (2) the resulting regressor covariance matrix ($X'X$) may not be positive definite.

4.3.2 Imputation without Models

There are a number of ad hoc or weakly justified procedures often implemented in statistical software.

Mean imputation or **mean substitution** involves replacing missing observations by the average of the available values. It is mean-preserving but will have impact on the marginal distribution of the data. It is obvious that the probability mass in the center of the marginal distribution will increase. It will also affect the covariances and correlations with other variables.

Simple hot deck imputation involves replacement of the missing value by a randomly drawn value from the available observed values of that variable, somewhat like a bootstrap procedure. It preserves the marginal distribution of the variable, but it distorts the covariances and correlations between variables.

In a regression setting neither of these two well-known approaches are attractive despite their simplicity.

Words and Expressions

pairwise deletion 成对删除

available-case analysis 也叫 observed case analysis，就是根据观察到的数据进行分析，这里翻译成可用案例分析。此外，还有一种称为 **complete case analysis**，则是指把那些有缺失值的受试者全部排除，只分析有完整数据的受试者。这其实是处理缺失值最简单也是最粗糙的方法。

mean-preserving 均值不变的，均值保持不变的

simple hot deck 简单替补，热平台法

4.4 Observed-Data Likelihood

The modern approach to missing data is to impute values for missing observations by making single or multiple draws from the estimated distribution based on the postulated observed data model and the model for the missing data mechanism. The Bayesian variants of this procedure make the draws from the posterior distribution, which uses both the likelihood and the prior distribution of the parameters.

The first important issue involves the role played by the missing data mechanism in the imputation procedure and especially whether the missing data mechanism is ignorable.

Let θ denote the parameters of the dgp for $Y = (Y_{obs}, Y_{mis})$ and let ψ denote the parameters of the missing data mechanism. For convenience of notation it is assumed that (Y_{obs}, Y_{mis}) are continuous variables. Then the joint distribution of (R, Y_{obs}) is given by

$$\Pr[R, Y_{obs} | \theta, \psi] = \int \Pr[R, Y_{obs}, Y_{mis} | \theta, \psi] dY_{mis} =$$

$$\int \Pr[R | Y_{obs}, Y_{mis}, \psi] \Pr[Y_{obs}, Y_{mis} | \theta] dY_{mis} =$$

$$\Pr[R | Y_{obs}, \psi] \int \Pr[Y_{obs}, Y_{mis} | \theta] dY_{mis} =$$

$$\Pr[R | Y_{obs}, \psi] \Pr[Y_{obs} | \theta] \qquad (4.3)$$

The first equality derives the joint probability of (R, Y_{obs}) by integrating out (or averaging over) Y_{mis} from the joint probability of all data and R. The second line factors the joint probability into conditional and marginal components, the conditioning being with respect to Y_{obs} and Y_{mis}. The third line separates the missing data mechanism from the observed data mechanism; this step is justified by the

MAR assumption. The last line means that θ and ψ are distinct parameters and hence inference about θ can ignore the missing data mechanism and depends on Y_{obs} alone.

The **observed-data likelihood** is proportional to the last factor in the fourth line

$$\text{L}[\theta | Y_{\text{obs}}] \propto \Pr[Y_{\text{obs}} | \theta] \tag{4.4}$$

It involves only the observed data Y_{obs} even though the parameters θ appear in the dgp for all observations (observed and missing). The constant of proportionality does not appear in (4.4).

Under the MAR assumption the **joint posterior probability** of (θ, ψ) is written as the product of $\Pr[R, Y_{\text{obs}} | \theta, \psi]$ and the joint prior distribution $\pi(\theta, \psi)$ as follows

$$\begin{aligned}\Pr[\theta, \psi | Y_{\text{obs}}, R] &= k\Pr[R, Y_{\text{obs}} | \theta, \psi] \pi(\theta, \psi) \\ &\propto \Pr[R | Y_{\text{obs}}, \psi] \Pr[Y_{\text{obs}} | \theta] \pi(\theta, \psi) \\ &\propto \Pr[R | Y_{\text{obs}}, \psi] \Pr[Y_{\text{obs}} | \theta] \pi_\theta(\theta, \psi) \pi_\psi(\psi)\end{aligned} \tag{4.5}$$

where k in the first line is a constant of proportionality free of (θ, ψ). The second line uses the factorization given in (4.3), and the third line uses the asumption of independent priors for θ and ψ.

As our main interest is in θ, we derive the marginal posterior for θ by integrating out ψ from the joint posterior. This yields the **observed-data** posterior

$$\begin{aligned}\Pr[\theta | Y_{\text{obs}}, R] &= \int \Pr[\theta, \psi | Y_{\text{obs}}, R] d\psi \\ &\propto \Pr[Y_{\text{obs}} | \theta] \pi_\theta(\theta) \int \Pr[R | Y_{\text{obs}}, \psi] \pi_\psi(\psi) d\psi \\ &\propto \text{L}[\theta | Y_{\text{obs}}] \pi_\theta(\theta)\end{aligned} \tag{4.6}$$

where the second line separates θ and ψ, and the last line absorbs the integral expression into the constant of proportionality. Therefore, the last line does not involve ψ and is independent of the missing data mechanism R.

Words and Expressions

observed-data posterior 后验观测数据

4.5 Regression-Based Imputation

In this section we consider a least-squares based imputation. The key component is use of the EM algorithm.

The EM algorithm consists of the expectation step and the maximization step.

The structure of the EM algorithm is closely related to Bayesian MCMC and data augmentation methods. Therefore, rather than providing a fully operational method for handling missing data, we will introduce an example that brings out the motivation behind modern multiple imputation techniques and suggests the major features of such an approach.

4.5.1 Linear Regression Example with Missing Data on a Dependent Variable

In practice one can have missing observations on dependent (endogenous) variables and/or explanatory variables. We consider a regression example that has missing data on the dependent variable, with

$$\begin{bmatrix} y_1 \\ y_{\mathrm{mis}} \end{bmatrix} = \begin{bmatrix} X_1 \\ X_2 \end{bmatrix} \beta + \begin{bmatrix} u_1 \\ u_2 \end{bmatrix} \tag{4.7}$$

where $E[u \mid X] = 0$ and $E[uu' \mid X] = \sigma^2 I_N$. The complication is that a block of observations on the dependent variable y, denoted y_{mis}, is missing. We assume that the available complete observations are a random sample from the population, so that the missing data are asumed to be MAR though not MCAR.

Given the MAR assumption and $N_1 > K$, the first block of N_1 observations can be used to consistently estimate the K-dimensional parameter β and σ^2. The maximum likelihood estimates of (β, σ^2) under Gaussian errors and $\hat{\beta} = [X'_1 X_1]^{-1} X'_1 y_1$ and $s^2 = (y_1 - X_1 \hat{\beta})'(y_1 - X_1 \hat{\beta})/N_1$. By standard theory, and under the normality assumption, $\beta \mid \mathrm{data} \sim N[\beta, \sigma^2 [X'_1 X_1]^{-1}]$ and $s^2/\sigma^2 \mid \hat{\beta} \sim (N_1 - K) \cdot \chi^2_{N_1 - K}$.

First, consider a naive single-imputation procedure for generating the missing observations. Conditional on X_2, the predicted values of y_{miss}, denoted $\hat{y}_{\mathrm{mis}}$, are given by $X_1 \hat{\beta}$, where $\hat{\beta}$ is the preceding estimate obtained using only the first N_1 observations. Then

$$\hat{E}[y_{\mathrm{mis}} \mid X_2] = \hat{y}_{\mathrm{mis}} = X_2 \hat{\beta}$$
$$\hat{V}[\hat{y}_{\mathrm{mis}}] \equiv \hat{V}[\hat{y} \mid X_2] = s^2 (I_{N_2} + X_2 [X'_1 X_1]^{-1} X'_2) \tag{4.8}$$

where $s^2 I_{N_2}$ is an estimate of $V_{[u_2]}$.

In the naive method one would generate the N_2 predicted values of y_{mis}, and then apply standard regression methods to the full sample of $N = N_1 + N_2$ observations.

The two steps in the naive method correspond to the two steps of the **EM algorithm**. The prediction step is the **E-step**, and the second-step application of least squares to the augmented sample is the **M-step**.

However, this solution has flaws. First, consider the data augmentation step.

Because the generated values $\hat{y}_{mis}$ lie *exactly* on the least-squares fitted plane, the addition of $(\hat{y}_{mis}, X_2)$ to the sample to produce a new estimate, $\hat{\beta}_A$, does not change the previous estimate $\hat{\beta}$

$$\hat{\beta}_A = [X'_1 X_1 + X'_2 X_2]^{-1} [X'_1 y_1 + X'_2 \hat{y}_{mis}] =$$
$$[X'_1 X_1 + X'_2 X_2]^{-1} [X'_1 X_1 \hat{\beta} + X'_2 X_2 \hat{\beta}_{mis}] = \hat{\beta}$$

Second, the estimate of σ^2 obtained by the standard formula to the residuals from the augmented sample yields an estimate that is too small because the additional N_2 residuals are zero by construction

$$s_A^2 = (y - X\hat{\beta}_A)'(y - X\hat{\beta}_A)/N =$$
$$(y_1 - X_1 \hat{\beta})'(y_1 - X_1 \hat{\beta})/N < s^2 \tag{4.9}$$

where s^2 correctly divides by N_1 rather than N.

Finally, as can be seen from the expression for the sampling variance of $\hat{y}_{mis}$, the generated predictions are heteroskedastic, unlike the y_1, and hence the variance of $\hat{\beta}_A$ cannot be estimated using the least-squares formula in the usual way. The observations $\hat{y}_{mis}$ are draws from a distribution with a different variance. The naive method does not make allowance for the uncertainty attached to the estimates of $\hat{y}_{mis}$.

To fix these problems modifications are needed. First, the estimation of $\hat{y}_{mis}$ should take account of uncertainty regarding $\hat{\beta}$. This may be done by adjusting $\hat{y}_{mis}$ and adding some "noise" to the generated predictions such that the estimates of missing data more closely mimic a draw from the (estimated or conditional) distribution of y_1. A standardization step can use the fact that an estimate of $V[\hat{y}_{mis}], \hat{V}$, is available from (4.8). Hence the components of the transformed variable $\hat{V}^{-1/2} \hat{y}_{mis}$ have unit variance. To mimic the distribution of y_1, we can make a Monte Carlo draw from $N[0, s^2]$ distribution and multiply it by $\hat{V}^{-1/2} \hat{y}_{mis}$.

The revised algorithm is as follows.

1. Estimate $\hat{\beta}$ using the N_1 complete observations as before.
2. Generate $\hat{y}_{mis} = X_2 \hat{\beta}$.
3. Generate adjusted values of $\hat{y}_{mis}^a = (\hat{V}^{-1/2} \hat{y}_{mis}) \odot u_m$ of $\hat{y}_{mis}$, where u_m is a Monte Carlo draw from the $N[0, s^2]$ distribution and $\odot$ denotes element-by-element multiplication.
4. Using the augmented sample obtain a revised estimate of $\hat{\beta}$.
5. Repeat step 1~4 where in step 1 the revised estimate of $\hat{\beta}$ is used.

The revised algorithm, also an EM-type algorithm, continues until it converges in the sense that the changes in the coefficients or the changes in regression residual sum of squares become arbitrarily small.

Words and Expressions

data augmentation(method) 增广数据法。这是一个比较新的统计学术语,最早由 Dempster, Laird 和 Rubin 于 1997 年在一篇关于 **EM algorithm for maximizing a likelihood function** 论文中引入的。(**The term data augmentation refers to methods for constructing iterative optimization or sampling algorithms via the introduction of unobserved data or latent variables.**)

mimic v. (通过学样)戏弄;模仿,学……子;照样子画;与……极相似

To understand God's thoughts we must study statistics, for these are the measure of His purpose.
—— Florence Nightingale

Unit Five Advanced Topics

In the unit we present some basic notations, notions and definitions that a reader must absolutely know in order to further study advanced topics in mathematical statistics and its application.

5.1 Measures and Measure Spaces

We start with the definition of a σ-algebra.

Definition 5.1

A collection F of subsets of a set Ω is a σ-algebra, if

(1) When $A \in F$, then $A^c = (\Omega - A) \in F$;

(2) Given a finite or infinite sequence $\{A_k\}$ of subsets of $\Omega, A_k \in F$, then the union $\cup_k A_k \in F, k = 1, 2, \ldots$

(3) $\Omega \in F$.

From this definition it follows immediately, by properties (1) and (3), that the empty set $\varnothing$ belongs to F, since $\varnothing = \Omega^c$. Further, given a sequence $\{A_k\}$, $A_k \in F$, then the intersection $\cap_k A_k \in F$. To see this, note that

$$\cap_k A_k = \Omega - \cup_k (\Omega - A_k)$$

and then apply properties (1) and (2). Finally, the difference $A - B$ of two sets A and B that belong to F also belongs to F because

$$A - B = A \cap (\Omega - B)$$

Definition 5.2

A real-valued function μ defined on a σ-algebra is a measure, if

(1) $\mu(\varnothing) = 0$;

(2) $\mu(A) \geq 0$ for all $A \in F$, and

(3) $\mu(\cup_k A_k) = \sum_k \mu(A_k)$ if $\{A_k\}$ is finite or infinite sequence of pairwise disjoint sets from F, that is, $A_i \cap A_j = \emptyset$ for $i \neq j$.

We do not exclude the possibility that $\mu(A) = \infty$ for some $A \in F$.

Remark 5.1

This definition of a measure and the properties of σ-algebra F as detailed in definition 5.1 ensure that ① if we know the measure of a set Ω and a subset A of Ω we can determine the measure of $\Omega - A$; and ② if we know the measure of each disjoint subset A_k of F we can calculate the measure of their union.

Definition 5.3

If F is a σ-algebra of subsets of Ω and if μ is a measure on F, then the triple (Ω, F, μ) is called a *measure space*. The sets belonging to F are called *measurable sets* because, for them, the measure is defined.

Remark 5.2

A simple example of a measure space is the finite set $\Omega = \{x_1, \ldots, x_N\}$, in which the σ-algebra is all possible subsets of Ω and the measure is defined by ascribing to each element $x_i \in \Omega$ a nonnegative number, say p_i. From this it follows that the measure of a subset $\{x_{\alpha_1}, \ldots, x_{\alpha_k}\}$ of Ω is just $p_{\alpha_1} + \ldots + p_{\alpha_k}$. If $p_i = 1$, then the measure is called a *counting measure* because it counts the number of elements in the set.

Remark 5.3

If $\Omega = [0, 1]$ or R, the real line, then the most natural σ-algebra is the σ-algebra B of Borel sets (the *Borel σ-algebra*), which, by definition, is the smallest σ-algebra containing intervals. (The word smallest means that any other σ-algebra that contains intervals also contains any set contained in B) It can be proved that on the Borel σ-algebra there exists a unique measure, called the Borel measure, such that $([a, b]) = b - a$. Whenever considering spaces $\Omega = R$ or $\Omega = R^d$ or subsets of these (intervals, squares, etc.) we always assume the Borel measure and will not repeat this assumption again.

As presented, definition 5.3 is extremely general. In almost all applications a more specific measure space is adequate, as follow.

Definition 5.4

A measure space (Ω, F, μ) is called σ-*finite* if there is a sequence $\{A_k\}$, $A_k \in F$, satisfying

$$\Omega = \bigcup_{k=1}^{\infty} A_k \text{ and } \mu(A_k) < \infty \text{ for all } k$$

Remark 5.4

If $\Omega = R$, the real line, and μ is the Borel measure, then the A_k may be chosen as intervals of the form $[-k, k]$. In the d-dimensional space R^d, the A_k may be chosen as balls of radius k.

Definition 5.5

A measure space (Ω, F, μ) is called *finite* if $\mu(\Omega) < \infty$. In particular, if $\mu(\Omega) = 1$, then the measure space is said to be *normalized* or *probabilistic*.

Remark 5.5

We have defined a hierarchy of measure spaces from the most general (Definition 5.3) down to the most specific (Definition 5.5).

Words and Expressions

σ-algebra σ 代数
union *n*. 并集
intersection *n*. 交集
pairwise disjoint sets 两两不相交的集
disjoint subset 不相交子集
triple *n*. 三元组
measure space 测度空间
measurable set 可测集
counting measure 可数测度
Borel sets 波莱尔集
Borel σ-algebra 波莱尔 σ 代数
σ-finite σ 有限的
real line 实线
radius *n*. 半径;半径范围
normalized *n*. 正规化
hierarchy *n*. 层次
down to 直到,降到

5.2 Random Variables and Distributions

Let (Ω, F, P) be a probability space, where $\Omega = \{\omega\}$ is a set of elementary events, F is a σ-algebra of events, and P is a probability measure defined on (Ω, F). Further, let B denote an element of the Borel σ-algebra of subsets of the real line R.

Definition 5.6

A finite single-value function $X = X(\omega)$ which maps Ω into R is called a *random variable* if for and Borel set B in R, the inverse image of B, i.e.
$$X^{-1}(B) = \{\omega : X(\omega) \in B\}$$
belongs to the σ-algebra F.

It means that all Borel sets, one can define probabilities
$$P\{X \in B\} = P\{X^{-1}(B)\}$$
In particular, if for any $x(-\infty < x < \infty)$ we take $B = (-\infty, x]$, then the function
$$F(x) = P\{X \leqslant x\} \tag{5.1}$$
is defined for the random variable X.

Definition 5.7

The function $F(x)$ is called the *distribution function* or *cumulative distribution function* (c.d.f.) of the random variable X.

Remark 5.6

Quite often, the cumulative distribution function of a random variable X is defined as
$$G(x) = P\{X < x\}$$
Most of the properties of both these versions of c.d.f. (i.e., F and G) coincide. Only one important difference exists between functions $F(x)$ and $G(x)$: F is right continuous, while G is left continuous. In our treatment we use the c.d.f. as given in definition 5.7.

There are three types of distributions: absolutely continuous, discrete and singular, and any c.d.f. $F(x)$ can be represented as a mixture
$$F(x) = p_1 F_1(x) + p_2 F_2(x) + p_3 F_3(x) \tag{5.2}$$
of absolutely continuous F_1 discrete F_2 and singular F_3 c.d.f.'s, with nonnegative weights p_1, p_2, and p_3 such that $p_1 + p_2 + p_3 = 1$. In this chapter we restrict ourselves to distributions which are either purely absolutely continuous or purely discrete.

Definition 5.8

A random variable X is called to have *discrete distribution* if there exists a countable set $B = (x_1, x_2, \ldots)$ such that
$$P\{X \in B\} = 1$$

Remark 5.7

To determine a random variable having a discrete distribution, one must fix two sequences: a sequence of values $x_1, x_2, \ldots$ and a sequence of probabilities $p_k = P$

$\{X = x_k\}$, $k = 1, 2, \ldots$, such that
$$\sum_k p_k = 1$$

In this case, the c.d.f. of X is given by
$$F(x) = P\{X \leqslant x\} = \sum_{k \in \{k \mid x_k \leqslant x\}} p_k \tag{5.3}$$

Definition 5.9

A random variable X with a c.d.f. F is said to have *absolutely continuous distribution* if there exists a nonnegative function $p(x)$ such that
$$F(x) = \int_{-\infty}^{x} p(t)\,\mathrm{d}t \tag{5.4}$$
for any real x.

Remark 5.8

The function $p(x)$ then satisfies the condition
$$\int_{-\infty}^{+\infty} p(t)\,\mathrm{d}t = 1 \tag{5.5}$$
and it is called the *probability density function* (p.d.f.) of X. Note that any nonnegative function $p(x)$ satisfying (5.5) can be the p.d.f. of some random variable X.

Remark 5.9

If a random variable X has an absolutely continuous distribution, then its c.d.f. $F(x)$ is continuous.

Definition 5.10

We say that random variable X and Y have same distribution and write
$$X^d = Y \tag{5.6}$$
if the c.d.f.'s of X and Y (i.e., F_X and F_Y) coincide; that is
$$F_X(x) = P(X \leqslant x) = P(Y \leqslant x) = F_Y(x), \forall x$$

The *quantile function* of a random variables X with c.d.f. $F(x)$ is defined by
$$Q(u) = \inf\{x \mid F(x) \geqslant u\}, 0 < u < 1$$
In the case when X has an absolutely continuous distribution, then the quantile function $Q(u)$ may simply be written as
$$Q(u) = F^{-1}(u), 0 < u < 1$$
The corresponding *quantile density function* is given by
$$q(u) = \frac{\mathrm{d}Q(u)}{\mathrm{d}u} = \frac{1}{p(Q(u))}, 0 < \mu < 1$$
where $p(x)$ is the p.d.f. corresponding to the c.d.f. $F(x)$.

It should be noted that just as forms of $F(x)$ may be used to propose families of distributions, general forms of the quantile function $Q(u)$ may also be used to propose families of statistical distributions. Interested readers may refer to the recent by Gilchrist (2000) for a detailed discussion on statistical modeling with quantile functions.

Words and Expressions

coincide *v.* 一致,符合
singular *adj.* 单一的,非凡的,异常的
singular distribution 奇异积分
countable set 可数集
fix *v.* 固定,注视,决定,选定,确定
absolutely continuous distribution 绝对连续分布
nonnegative function 非负函数
quantile function 分位数函数
quantile density function 分位数密度函数

5.3 Type of Distribution

Definition 5.11

Random variable X and Y are said to belong to the same type of distribution if there exist constants a and $h>0$ such that
$$Y^d = a + hX \tag{5.7}$$
Note then that the c. d. f. 's F_X and F_Y of the random variables X and Y satisfy the relation
$$F_Y = F_X\left(\frac{x-a}{h}\right), \forall x \tag{5.8}$$
One can, therefore, choose a certain c. d. f. F as the standard distribution function of a certain distribution family. Then this family would consist of all c. d. f. 's of the form
$$F(x, a, h) = F\left(\frac{x-a}{h}\right), -\infty < x < +\infty, h>0 \tag{5.9}$$
and $$F(x) = F(x, 0, 1)$$
Thus, we have a two-parameter family of c. d. f. 's $F(x, a, h)$, where a is called the *location parameter* and h is the *scale parameter*.

For absolutely continuous distribution, one can introduce the correspond two-parameter families of probability density functions
$$p(x, a, h) = \frac{1}{h} p\left(\frac{x-a}{h}\right) \tag{5.10}$$

where $p(x) = p(x, 0, 1)$ corresponds to the random variable X with c. d. f. F, and $p(x, a, h)$ corresponds to the random variable $Y = a + hX$ with c. d. f. $F(x, a, h)$.

Words and Expressions

location parameter 位置参数
scale parameter 尺度参数,标度参数

5.4 Moment Characteristics

There are some classical numerical characteristics of random variables and their distributions. The most popular ones are expected values and variables. More general characteristics are the moments. Among them, we emphasize moments about zero (about origin) and central moments.

Definition 5.12

For a discrete random variable X taking on values $x_1, x_2, \ldots$ with probabilities
$$p_k = P\{X = x_k\}, k = 1, 2, \ldots$$
we define the mth moment of X about zero as
$$\alpha_n = EX^n = \sum_k x_k^n p_k \tag{5.11}$$
We say that α_n, exists if
$$\sum_k |x_k|^n p_k < \infty$$
Note that the expected value EX is nothing but α_1. EX is also called the mean of X or the *mathematical expectation* of X.

Definition 5.13

The nth *central moment* of X is defined as
$$\beta_n = E(X - EX)^n = \sum_k (x_k - EX)^n p_k \tag{5.12}$$
given that
$$\sum_k |x_k - EX|^n p_k < \infty$$

If a random variable X has an absolutely continuous distribution with a p. d. f. $p(x)$, then the moments about zero and the central moments have the following expressions
$$\alpha_n = EX^n = \int_{-\infty}^{+\infty} x^n p(x) \, dx \tag{5.13}$$
and
$$\beta_n = E(X - EX)^n = \int_{-\infty}^{+\infty} (x - EX)^n p(x) \, dx \tag{5.14}$$

We say that moments (5.13) exists if
$$\int_{-\infty}^{+\infty} |x|^n p(x)\,dx < \infty \tag{5.15}$$

The variance of X is simply the second central moment
$$\text{Var } X = \beta_2 = E(X - EX)^2 \tag{5.16}$$

Central moments are easily expressed in terms of moments about zero as follows
$$\beta_n = E(X - EX)^n = \sum_{k=0}^{n} (-1)^n \binom{n}{k} (EX)^k EX^{n-k} =$$
$$\sum_{k=0}^{n} (-1)^n \binom{n}{k} \alpha_1^k \alpha_{n-k} \tag{5.17}$$

In particular, we have
$$\text{Var } X = \beta_2 = \alpha_2 - \alpha_1^2 \tag{5.18}$$
and
$$\beta_3 = \alpha_3 - 3\alpha_1\alpha_2 + 2\alpha_1^3 \text{ and } \beta_4 = \alpha_4 - 4\alpha_1\alpha_3 + 6\alpha_1^2\alpha_2 - 3\alpha_1^4 \tag{5.19}$$

Note that the first central moment $\beta_1 = 0$.

The inverse problem cannot be soled, however, because all ventral moments save no information about; hence, the expected value cannot be expressed in terms of $\beta_n (n = 1, 2, \ldots)$. Nevertheless, the relation
$$\alpha_n = EX^n = E[(X - EX) + EX]^n =$$
$$\sum_{k=0}^{n} \binom{n}{k} (EX)^k E(X - EX)^{n-k} =$$
$$\sum_{k=0}^{n} \binom{n}{k} \alpha_1^k \beta_{n-k} \tag{5.20}$$

will enable us to express $\alpha_n (n = 2, 3, \ldots)$ in terms of $\alpha_1 = EX$ and central moments $\beta_2, \ldots, \beta_n$. In particular, we have
$$\alpha_2 = \beta_2 + \alpha_1^2 \tag{5.21}$$
$$\alpha_3 = \beta_3 + 3\beta_2\alpha_1 - \alpha_1^3 \text{ and } \alpha_4 = \beta_4 + 4\beta_3\alpha_1 + 6\beta_2\alpha_1^2 + \alpha_1^4 \tag{5.22}$$

Let X and Y belong to the same type of distribution (see equation (5.7)), meaning that
$$Y^d = a + hX$$
for some constants a and $h > 0$. Then, the following equalities allow us to express moments of Y in terms of the corresponding moments of X
$$EY^n = E(a + hX)^n = \sum_{k=0}^{n} \binom{n}{k} a^k h^{n-k} EX^{n-k} \tag{5.23}$$
and

$$E(Y-EY)^n = E[h(X-EX)^n] = h^n E(X-EX)^n \qquad (5.24)$$

Note that the central moments of Y do not depend on the location parameter a. As particular cases of (5.23) and (5.24), we have

$$EY = a + hEX \qquad (5.25)$$
$$EY^2 = a^2 + 2ahEX + h^2 EX^2, \text{ Var } Y = h^2 \text{ Var } X \qquad (5.26)$$
$$EY^3 = a^3 + 3a^2 hEX + 3ah^2 EX^2 + h^2 EX^3 \qquad (5.27)$$
$$EY^4 = a^4 + 4a^3 hEX + 6a^2 h^2 EX^2 + 4ah^3 EX^3 + h^4 EX^4 \qquad (5.28)$$

Definition 5.14

For random variable taking on values $0, 1, 2, \ldots$, the *factorial moments of positive order* are defined as

$$\mu_r = EX(X-1)\ldots(X-r+1), \, r=1,2,\ldots \qquad (5.29)$$

while the *factorial moments of negative order* are defined as

$$\mu_{-r} = E\left[\frac{1}{(X+1)(X+2)\ldots(X+r)}\right], \, r=1,2,\ldots \qquad (5.30)$$

While dealing with discrete distributions, it is quite often convenient to work with these factorial moments rather than regular moments. For this reason, it is useful to note the following relationships between the factorial moments and moments

$$\mu_1 = \alpha_1 \qquad (5.31)$$
$$\mu_2 = \alpha_2 - \alpha_1 \qquad (5.32)$$
$$\mu_3 = \alpha_3 - 3\alpha_2 + 2\alpha_1 \qquad (5.33)$$
$$\mu_4 = \alpha_4 - 6\alpha_3 + 11\alpha_2 - 6\alpha_1 \qquad (5.34)$$
$$\alpha_2 = \mu_2 + \mu_1 \qquad (5.35)$$
$$\alpha_3 = \mu_3 + 3\mu_2 + \mu_1 \qquad (5.36)$$
$$\alpha_4 = \mu_4 + 6\mu_3 + 7\mu_2 + \mu_1 \qquad (5.37)$$

Words and Expressions

moments about zero (about origin) 原点矩
central moments 中心矩
second central moments 二阶中心矩
first central moments 一阶中心矩
factorial moments of positive order 正的阶乘矩
factorial moments of negative order 负的阶乘矩
factorial moments 阶乘矩

5.5 Shape Characteristics

For any distribution, we are often interested in some characteristics that are associated with the shape of distribution. For example, we may be interested in finding out whether it is unimodal, skewed, and so on. Two important measures in this respect are Pearson's measures of skewness and kurtosis.

Definition 5.15

Pearson's measures of skewness and kurtosis are given by

$$\gamma_1 = \frac{\beta_3}{\beta_2^{3/2}}$$

and

$$\gamma_2 = \frac{\beta_4}{\beta_2^2}$$

Since these measures are functions of ventral moments, it is clear that they are free of the location. Similarly, due to the fractional form of the measures, it can readily be verified that they are free of scale as well. It can also be seen that the measure of skewness γ_1 may take on positive or negative values depending on whether β_3 is positive or negative, respectively. Obviously, when the distribution is symmetric about its mean, we may note that β_3 is 0, in which case the measure of skewness is also 0. Hence, distributions with $\gamma_1 > 0$ are said to be *positively skewed distributions*, while those with $\gamma_2 < 0$ are said to be *negatively skewed distributions*.

Now, without loss of generality, let us consider an arbitrary distribution with mean 0 and variance 1. Then, by writing

$$\left[\int x^3 p(x) \, dx \right]^2 = \left[\int \{ x \sqrt{p(x)} \} \{ (x^2 - 1) \sqrt{p(x)} \} \, dx \right]$$

and applying the Cauchy-Schwarz inequality, we readily obtain the inequality

$$\gamma_2 = \gamma_1^2 + 1$$

Later, we will observe the coefficient of kurtosis of a normal distribution to be 3. Based on this value, distribution with $\gamma_3 > 3$ are called *leptokurtic distributions*, while those with $\gamma_3 < 3$ are called *platykurtic distributions*. Incidentally, distributions for which $\gamma_3 = 3$ (which clearly includes the normal) are called *mesokuritic distributions*.

Remark 5.10

Karl Pearson (1895) designed a system of continuous distributions wherein the p.d.f. of every member satisfies a differential equation. By studying their moment properties and, in particular, their coefficients of skewness and kurtosis, he proposed seven families of distributions which all occupied different regions of the (γ_1, γ_2)-plane. Several prominent distributions (such as beta, gamma, normal and t distributions) belong to those families. This development was the first and historic attempt to propose a unified mechanism for developing different families of statistical distributions.

Words and Expressions

unimodal *adj.* 单峰的
skewness *n.* 偏度,偏斜度
kurtosis *n.* 峰度
positively skewed distributions 正的斜分布
negatively skewed distributions 负的斜分布
leptokurtic distributions 尖峰态分布
platykurtic distributions 低峰态分布
mesokuritic distributions 常峰态分布
wherein *adv.* 在何处,在其中
plane *n.* 平面

5.6 Entropy

One more useful characteristic of distributions (called *entropy*) was introduced by Shannon.

Definition 5.16

For a discrete random variable X taking on values $x_1, x_2, \ldots$, with probabilities $p_1, p_2, \ldots$, the entropy $H(X)$ is defined as

$$H(X) = -\sum p_n \log p_n \tag{5.38}$$

If X has an absolutely continuous distribution with p.d.f. $p(x)$, then the entropy is defined as

$$H(X) = -\int_D p(x) \log p(x) \, dx \tag{5.39}$$

where

$$D = \{x \mid p(x) > 0\}$$

In the case of discrete distributions, the transformation

$$Y = a + hX, \quad -\infty < x < +\infty, h > 0$$

does not change the probabilities p_n and consequently, we have

$$H(Y) = H(X)$$

On the other hand, if X has a p.d.f. $p(x)$, then $Y = a + hX$ has the p.d.f.

$$g(x) = \frac{1}{h} p\left(\frac{x-a}{h}\right)$$

and

$$H(Y) = -\int_{D_1} g(x)\log g(x)\,dx$$

where

$$D_1 = \{x \mid g(x) > 0\} = \left\{x \mid p\left(\frac{x-a}{h}\right) > 0\right\} = \left\{x \mid \frac{x-a}{h} \in D\right\}$$

It is then easy to verify that

$$H(X) = -\int_{D_1} \frac{1}{h} p\left(\frac{x-a}{h}\right) \log\left\{\frac{1}{h} p\left(\frac{x-a}{h}\right)\right\} dx =$$

$$-\int_D p(x)\log\left\{\frac{1}{h}p(x)\right\} dx =$$

$$\log h \int_D p(x)\,dx - \int_D p(x)\log p(x)\,dx =$$

$$\log h + H(X) \tag{5.40}$$

Words and Expressions

entropy *n.* 熵

verify *v.* 核实,检验,校验,查证

5.7 Generating Function and Characteristic Function

In this section we present some functions that are useful in generating the probabilities or the moments of the distribution in a simple and unified manner. In addition, they may also help in identifying the distribution of an underlying random variable of interest.

Definition 5.17

Let X taking on values $0, 1, 2, \ldots$ with probabilities $p_n = P\{X = n\}$, $n = 0, 1, \ldots$ All the information about this distribution is contained in the *generating function*, which is defied as

$$P(s) = Es^X = \sum_{n=0}^{\infty} p_n s^n \tag{5.41}$$

with the right-hand side (RHS) of (5.41) converging at least for $|s| \leq 1$.

Some important properties of generating function are as following

(1) $P(1) = 1$;

(2) for $|s| < 1$, there exist derivatives of $P(s)$ of any order;

(3) for $0 \leq s < 1$, and all its derivatives $P^{(k)}(s)$, $k = 1, 2, \ldots$, are nonnegative increasing convex functions;

(4) the generating function $P(s)$ uniquely determines probabilities p_n, $n = 1$,

$2, \ldots$ and the following relations are valid
$$p_0 = P(0)$$
$$p_n = \frac{P^{(n)}(0)}{n!}, \quad n = 1, 2, \ldots$$

(5) if random variables $X_1, \ldots, X_n$ are independent and have generating functions
$$P_k(s) = Es^{X_k}, \quad k = 1, \ldots, n$$
then the generating function of the sum $Y = X_1 + \ldots + X_n$ satisfies the relation
$$P_Y(s) = \prod_{k=1}^{n} P_k(s) \tag{5.42}$$

(6) the factorial moments can be determined from the generating function as
$$\mu_k = EX(X-1)\ldots(X-k+1) = P^{(k)}(1) \tag{5.43}$$
where
$$P^{(k)}(1) = \lim_{s \to 1} P^{(k)}(s)$$

Definition 5.18

The *characteristic function* $f(t)$ of a random variables X is defied as
$$f(t) = E \exp\{itX\} = E\cos tX + E\sin tX \tag{5.44}$$
If X takes on values $x_k (k = 1, 2, \ldots)$ with probabilities $p_k = P\{X = x_k\}$, then
$$f(t) = \sum_k \exp(itx_k) p_k = \sum_k \cos(itx_k) p_k + i \sum_k \sin(itx_k) p_k \tag{5.45}$$
For a random variable having a p.d.f. $p(x)$, the characteristic function takes on an analogous form
$$f(t) = \int_{-\infty}^{+\infty} e^{itx} p(x) \, dx$$
$$f(t) = \int_{-\infty}^{+\infty} \cos(tx) p(x) \, dx + i \int_{-\infty}^{+\infty} \sin(tx) p(x) \, dx \tag{5.46}$$

For random variables taking on $0, 1, 2, \ldots$, there exists the following relation between the characteristic function and the generating function
$$f(t) = P(e^{it}) \tag{5.47}$$

Some of useful properties of characteristic function are as following

(1) $f(0) = 1$;

(2) $|f(t)| \leq 1$;

(3) $f(t)$ is uniformly continuous;

(4) $f(t)$ uniquely determines the distribution of the corresponding random variables X;

(5) if X has the characteristic function f, then $Y = a + hX$ has the characteristic function

$$g(t) = e^{iat} f(ht)$$

(6) if random variables $X_1, \ldots, X_n$ are independent and their characteristic function are $f_1(t), \ldots, f_n(t)$, respectively, then characteristic function of sum $Y = X_1 + \ldots + X_n$ is given by

$$f_Y(t) = \prod_{k=1}^{n} f_k(t) \tag{5.48}$$

(7) if the nth moment EX^n of the random variable X exists, then the characteristic function $f(t)$ of X has the first n derivatives, and

$$\alpha_k = EX^k = \frac{f^{(k)}(0)}{i^k}, k = 1, 2, \ldots, n \tag{5.49}$$

Moreover, in the situation, the following expansion is valid for the characteristic function

$$f(t) = 1 + \sum_{k=1}^{n} f^{(k)}(0) t^k + r_n(t) =$$

$$1 + \sum_{k=1}^{n} \alpha_k (it)^k + r_n(t) \tag{5.50}$$

where
$$r_n(t) = o(t^n)$$
as $t \to 0$;

(8) let random variables $X, X_1, X_2, \ldots$, have c. d. f.'s $F, F_1, F_2, \ldots$ and characteristic functions $f, f_1, f_2, \ldots$, respectively. If for any fixed t, as $n \to \infty$

$$f_n(t) \to f(t) \tag{5.51}$$

then
$$F_n(t) \to F(t) \tag{5.52}$$

for any x, where the limiting c. d. f. is continuous. Note that (5.52) also implies (5.51).

There exist inversion formulas for characteristic functions which will enable us to determine the distribution that corresponds to a certain characteristic function. For example, if

$$\int_{-\infty}^{+\infty} |f(t)| \, dt < \infty$$

where $f(t)$ is the characteristic function of a random variable X, then X has the p. d. f. $p(x)$ given by

$$p(x) = \frac{1}{2\pi} \int_{-\infty}^{+\infty} e^{-itx} f(t) \, dt \tag{5.53}$$

Remark 5.11

Instead of working with characteristic functions, one could define the moment generating function of a random variable X as $E \exp\{tX\}$ (a real function this time, see Section 2.5) and work with it. However, there are instances where this moment generating function may not exist, while the characteristic function always exists. Nonetheless, when the moment generating function does exist, it uniquely determines the distribution just as the characteristic function does.

Words and Expressions

derivative *n.* 导数,微商
generating function 生成函数,母函数
converging *adj.* 收敛的;趋同的
convex functions 凸函数
characteristic function 特征函数
uniformly continuous 一致连续
limiting c. d. f. 极限 c. d. f.
instead of 而不,代替
just as 正像,正当……的时候
nonetheless = never the less *adv.* 仍然;虽然如此;不过;依然

5.8 Decomposition of Distributions

Definition 5.19

We say that a random variable X is *decomposable* if there are two independent nondegenerate random variables Y and Z such that $X \stackrel{d}{=} Y+Z$.

Remark 5.12

An equivalent definition can be given in terms of characteristic function as follows. A characteristic function f is decomposable if there are two nondegenerate characteristic functions f_1 and f_2 such that

$$f(t) = f_1(t) f_2(t) \tag{5.54}$$

Note that degenerate characteristic functions have the e^{ict}, which corresponds to the degenerate random variable taking on the value c with probability 1.

Definition 5.20

If for any $n = 1, 2, \ldots$, a characteristic function f satisfies the relation

$$f(t) = \{f_n(t)\}^n \tag{5.55}$$

where $f_n(t)$ are characteristic function for any $n = 1, 2, \ldots$, then we say that f is an *infinitely divisible characteristic function*. A random variable is said to have an *infinitely divisible distribution* if its characteristic function $f(t)$ is infinitely divisible.

Remark 5.13

Note that if a random variable has a bounded support, it cannot be infinitely divisible. It should also be noted that an infinitely divisible characteristic function cannot zero values.

5.9 Stable Distributions

Definition 5.21

We say that characteristic function f is *stable* if, for any positive a_1 and a_2, there exist $a>0$ and b such that

$$f(a_1 t)f(a_2 t) = e^{ibt}f(at) \qquad (5.56)$$

A random variable is said to have a stable distribution if its characteristic function is stable.

Remark 5.14

It is of interest to note any stable distribution is absolutely continuous, and is also infinitely divisible.

Words and Expressions

decomposable *adj.* 可分解的
nondegenerate *adj.* 非退化的
degenerate *adj.* 退化的
infinitely divisible characteristic function 无限可分的特征函数
infinitely divisible distribution 无限可分的分布
stable distribution 稳定分布
absolutely continuous 绝对连续的
infinitely divisible 无限可分的

5.10 Random Vectors and Multivariate Distributions

Let (Ω, F, P) be a probability space, where $\Omega = \{\omega\}$ is a set of elementary events, F is a σ-algebra of events, and P is a probability measure defined on (Ω, F). Further, let B denote an element of the Bored σ-algebra of subsets of the n-dimensional Euclidean space R^n.

Definition 5.22

An n-dimensional vector $X = X(\omega) = (X_1(\omega), \ldots, X_n(\omega))$ which maps Ω into R^n is called a *random vector* (or an n-dimensional random variable) if, for any Bored set B in R^n, the inverse image of B given by

$$X^{-1}(B) = \{\omega \mid X(\omega) \in B\} = \{\omega \mid X_1(\omega), \ldots, X_n(\omega) \in B\}$$
belongs to the σ-algebra F.

This means that for any Borel set B, we can define probability as
$$P\{X \in B\} = P\{X^{-1}(B)\}$$
in particular, for any $x = (x_1, \ldots, x_n)$, the function
$$F(x) = F(x_1, \ldots, x_n) = P\{X_1 \leq x_1, \ldots, X_n \leq x_n\}$$
$$-\infty < x_1, \ldots, x_n < +\infty \tag{5.57}$$
is defined for the random vector $X = (X_1, \ldots, X_n)$.

Definition 5.23

The function $F(x) = F(x_1, \ldots, x_n)$ is called the *distribution function* of the random vector X.

Remark 5.15

The elements $X_1, \ldots, X_n$ of the random vector X can be considered as n univariate random variables having distribution functions
$$F_1(x) = F(x, \infty, \ldots, \infty) = P\{X_1 \leq x_1\}$$
$$F_2(x) = F(\infty, x, \ldots, \infty) = P\{X_2 \leq x_2\}$$
$$\vdots$$
$$F_n(x) = F(\infty, \ldots, \infty, x) = P\{X_n \leq x_n\}$$
respectively. Moreover, and set of n random variables $X_1, \ldots, X_n$ forms a random vector $X = (X_1, \ldots, X_n)$. Hence
$$F(x) = F(x_1, \ldots, x_n) = P\{X_1 \leq x_1, \ldots, X_n \leq x_n\}$$
is often called the joint distribution function of the variables $X_1, \ldots, X_n$.

If $F(x_1, \ldots, x_n)$ is the joint distribution function of the random variables $X_1, \ldots, X_n$, we can obtain from it the joint distribution function of any subset $X_{\alpha(1)}, \ldots, X_{\alpha(m)}$ rather easily. For example, we have
$$P\{X_1 \leq x_1, \ldots, X_m \leq x_m\} = F(x_1, \ldots, x_n, \infty, \ldots, \infty) \tag{5.58}$$
as the joint distribution function of $(X_1, \ldots, X_n)$.

Definition 5.24

The random variables $X_1, \ldots, X_n$ are said to be *independent random variables* if
$$P\{X_1 \leq x_1, \ldots, X_n \leq x_n\} = P\{X_k \leq x_k\} \tag{5.59}$$
For any $-\infty < x_k < +\infty$ ($k = 1, \ldots, n$).

Definition 5.25

The vector $X_1 = (X_1, \ldots, X_n)$ and $X_2 = (X_{n+1}, \ldots, X_{n+m})$ are said to be *independent* if
$$P\{X_1 \leq x_1, \ldots, X_{n+m} \leq x_{n+m}\} =$$

$$P\{X_1 \leqslant x_1, \ldots, X_n \leqslant x_n\} P\{X_{n+1} \leqslant x_{n+1}, \ldots, X_{n+m} \leqslant x_{n+m}\} \qquad (5.60)$$

For any $-\infty < x_k < +\infty$ ($k=1, \ldots, n+m$).

In the following discussion we restrict ourselves to the two-dimensional case. Let (X, Y) be a two-dimensional random vector and let $F(x, y) = P(X \leqslant x, Y \leqslant y)$ be the joint distribution function of (X, Y). Then, $F_X(x) = F(x, \infty)$ and $F_Y(x) = F(\infty, y)$ are the marginal distribution function. Now, as we did earlier in the univariate case, we shall discuss discrete and absolutely continuous cases separately.

Definition 5.26

A two-dimensional random vector (X, Y) is said to have a *discrete bivariate distribution* if there exists a countable set $B = \{(x_1, y_1), (x_2, y_2), \ldots\}$ such that $P\{(X, Y) \in B\} = 1$.

Remark 5.16

In order to two-dimensional random vector (X, Y) having a bivariate discrete distribution, we need to fix two sequences: a sequence of two-dimensional points $\{(x_1, y_1), (x_2, y_2), \ldots\}$ and a sequence of probabilities $p_k = P\{X \leqslant x_k, \ldots, Y \leqslant y_k\}$, $k = 1, 2, \ldots$, such that $\sum_k p_k = 1$. In this case, the joint distribution function $F(x, y)$ of (X, Y) is given by

$$F(x, y) = \sum_{k \in \{k \mid x_k \leqslant x, y_k \leqslant y\}} p_k \qquad (5.61)$$

also, the components of the vector (X, Y) are independent if

$$P\{X = x_k\} = P\{X = x_k\} P\{Y = y_k\} \text{ for any } k \qquad (5.62)$$

Definition 5.27

A two-dimensional random vector (X, Y) with a joint distribution function $F(x, y)$ is said to have an *absolutely continuous bivariate distribution* if there exists a nongenative function $p(u, v)$ such that

$$F(x, y) = \int_{-\infty}^{y} \int_{-\infty}^{x} p(u, v) \, du \, dv \qquad (5.63)$$

for any real x and y.

Remark 5.17

The function $p(u, v)$ satisfies the condition

$$\int_{-\infty}^{+\infty} \int_{-\infty}^{+\infty} p(u, v) \, du \, dv = 1$$

and it is called the *probability density function* (p.d.f.) of the bivariate random vector (X, Y) or the *joint probability density function* of the random variables X and Y. If $p(u, v)$ is the p.d.f. of the bivariate vector (X, Y), then the components X

and Y have one-dimensional (marginal) densities
$$p_X(u) = \int_{-\infty}^{+\infty} p(u,v) \, dv \tag{5.65}$$
and
$$p_Y(v) = \int_{-\infty}^{+\infty} p(u,v) \, du \tag{5.66}$$
respectively.

Also, the components of the absolutely continuous bivariate vector (X, Y) are independent if
$$p(u,v) = p_X(u) p_Y(v) \tag{5.67}$$
where $p_X(u)$ and $p_Y(v)$ are marginal densities as given in (5.65) and (5.66). Moreover, if the joint p.d.f. $p(u,v)$ of (X,Y) admits a factorization of the form
$$p(u, v) = q_1(u) q_2(v) \tag{5.68}$$
Then the components X and Y are independent, and there exists a nonzero constant c such that
$$p_X(u) = c q_1(u) \quad \text{and} \quad p_Y(v) = \frac{1}{c} q_2(v)$$

Words and Expressions

n-dimensional *adj.* n 维的
Euclidean space 欧几里得空间
inverse image 逆象
factorization *n.* 把……化为因子,因式分解法
nonzero *adj.* 非零的

5.11 Conditional Distributions

Let (X, Y) be a random vector having a discrete bivariate distribution concentrated on some points (x_i, y_j), and let
$$p_{ij} = P\{X = x_i, Y = y_j\}, \quad q_i = P\{X = x_i\} > 0, \text{ and } r_j = P\{Y = y_j\} > 0$$
for $i, j = 1, 2, \ldots$. Then, for any $y_j (j = 1, 2, \ldots)$, the *conditional distribution* of X, given $Y = y_j$, is defined as
$$P\{X = x_i \mid Y = y_j\} = \frac{P\{X = x_i, Y = y_j\}}{P\{Y = y_j\}} = \frac{p_{ij}}{r_j} \tag{5.69}$$
Similarly, for any $x_i (i = 1, 2, \ldots)$, the conditional distribution of Y, given $X = x_i$, is defined as
$$P\{Y = y_j \mid X = x_i\} = \frac{P\{X = x_i, Y = y_j\}}{P\{X = x_i\}} = \frac{p_{ij}}{q_i} \tag{5.70}$$

Next, let (X, Y) be an absolutely continuous bivariate random vector with a joint p. d. f. $p(x,y)$ and marginal p. d. f. 's $p_X(x)$ and $p_Y(y)$. In the case, for any value y at which $p_Y(y)$ is continuous and positive, the conditional p. d. f. of X, given $Y=y$, is defined as

$$p_{X|Y}(x|y) = \frac{p(x,y)}{p_Y(y)} \qquad (5.71)$$

Similarly, for any value x at which $p_X(x)$ is continuous and positive, the conditional p. d. f. of Y, given $X=x$, is defined as

$$p_{Y|X}(x|y) = \frac{p(x,y)}{p_X(x)} \qquad (5.72)$$

Remark 5.18

Though the derivation of conditional distributions from a specified bivariate distribution is rather straightforward, the reverse is not so, however. The construction of a bivariate distribution with specified conditional distribution requires solutions of functional equations; for a detailed discussed, one may refer to the book by Arnold, Castillo, and Sarabia (1999).

In an analogous manner, we can also define conditional distributions for the general case of n-dimensional random vectors $(X_1, \ldots, X_n)$ with p. d. f. $p_X(x_1, \ldots, x_n)$. For example, let us consider the case when the n-dimensional random vector $X = (X_1, \ldots, X_n)$ has an absolutely continuous distribution. Let $U = (X_1, \ldots, X_m)$ and $V = (X_{m+1}, \ldots, X_n)$ ($m<n$) be the random vectors corresponding to the first m and the last $n-m$ components of the random vector X. we can define the p. d. f. 's $p_U(x_1, \ldots, x_m)$ and $p_V(x_{m+1}, \ldots, x_n)$ in this case in Eqs. (5.58) and (5.63). Then, the conditional p. d. f. of the random vector V, given $U=(x_1, \ldots, x_m)$, is defined as

$$p_{V|U}(x_{m+1}, \ldots, x_n \mid x_1, \ldots, x_m) = \frac{p_X(x_1, \ldots, x_n)}{p_U(x_1, \ldots, x_m)} \qquad (5.73)$$

for any $(x_1, \ldots, x_m)$ at which $p_U(x_1, \ldots, x_m) > 0$.

Words and Expressions

concentrate $v.$ 集中在;专心于(on)

5.12 Moment Characteristics of Random Vectors

Let (X, Y) be a bivariate discrete random vector concentrating on points (x_i, y_j) with probabilities $p_{ij} = P\{X = x_i, Y = y_j\}$ for $i,j = 1, 2. \ldots$ For any measurable function $g(x,y)$, we can find the expected value of $Z = g(X,Y)$ as

$$EZ = Eg(X,Y) = \sum_i \sum_j g(x_i, y_j) p_{ij} \qquad (5.74)$$

Similarly, if (X, Y) has an absolutely continuous bivariate distribution with the density function $p(x, y)$, then we have the expected value of $Z = g(X, Y)$ as

$$EZ = Eg(X,Y) = \int_{-\infty}^{+\infty} \int_{-\infty}^{+\infty} g(x,y) p(x,y) \mathrm{d}x \mathrm{d}y \qquad (5.75)$$

Of course, as in the univarite case, we say that $EZ = Eg(X, Y)$ defined in Eqs. (5.74) and (5.75) exist if

$$\sum_i \sum_j g(x_i, y_j) p_{ij} < \infty \quad \text{and} \quad \int_{-\infty}^{+\infty} \int_{-\infty}^{+\infty} g(x,y) p(x,y) \mathrm{d}x \mathrm{d}y$$

respectively. In particular, if $g(x,y) = x^k y^l$, we obtain $EZ = Eg(X, Y) = EX^k Y^l$, which is said to be the product moment of order (k, l). Similarly, the moment $E(X-EX)^k (Y-EY)^l$ is said to be the central product moment of order (k, l), and the special case of $E(X-EX)(Y-EY)$ is called the covariance between X and Y and is denoted by Cov (X, Y). Based on the covarivance, we can define another measure of association which invariant with respect to both location and scale of variables X and Y (measuring that it is not affected if the means and variances of the variables are changed). Such a measure is the correlation coefficient between X and Y and is defined as

$$\rho = \rho(X,Y) = \frac{\mathrm{Cov}(X,Y)}{\sqrt{\mathrm{Var}(X)\mathrm{Var}(Y)}}$$

It can easily be shown that $|\rho| \leq 1$.

If we are dealing with a general n-dimensional random vector $\boldsymbol{X} = (X_1, \ldots, X_n)$, then the following moment characteristics of $\boldsymbol{X}$ will be of interest to us: the mean vector $\boldsymbol{m} = (m_1, \ldots, m_n)$, where $m_i = EX_i (i=1, \ldots, n)$, the covariance matrix $\sum = ((\sigma_{ij}))_{i,j=1}^n$, where $\sigma_{ij} = \sigma_{ji} = \mathrm{Cov}(X_i, X_j)$ (for $i \neq j$) and $\sigma_{ii} = \mathrm{Var}(X_i)$, and the correlation matrix $\rho = ((\rho_{ij}))_{i,j=1}^n$, where $\rho_{ij} = \sigma_{ij}/\sqrt{\sigma_{ii}\sigma_{jj}}$. Note that the diagonal elements of the correlation matrix are all 1.

Words and Expressions

product moment of order (k, l) (k, l)阶的积矩
central product moment of order (k, l) (k, l)阶的中心积矩
invariant adj. 不变的
diagonal adj. 对角的
diagonal element 对角元素

5.13 Conditional Expectations

In section 5.10 we introduced conditional expectations in the case of discrete as well as absolutely continuous multivariate distributions. Based on those conditional expectations, we describe in this section *conditional expectations*.

For this purpose, let us first consider the case when (X, Y) has a discrete bivariate distribution concentrating on points (x_i, y_j) (for $i,j = 1, 2, \ldots$), and as before, let $p_{ij} = P\{X = x_i, Y = y_j\}$ and $r_j = P\{Y = y_j\} > 0$. Suppose also that EX exists. Then, based on the definition of conditional expectation of X, given $Y = y_j$, presented in Eq. (5.69), we readily have the conditional mean of X, given $Y = y_j$, as

$$E(X \mid Y = y_j) = \sum_i x_i P\{X = x_i, Y = y_j\} = \sum_i x_i \frac{p_{ij}}{r_j} \qquad (5.76)$$

More generally, for and measurable function $h(\cdot)$ for which $Eh(X)$ exists, we have the conditional expectation of $h(X)$, given $Y = y_j$, as

$$E\{h(X) \mid Y = y_j\} = \sum_i h(x_i) P\{X = x_i, Y = y_j\} = \sum_i h(x_i) \frac{p_{ij}}{r_j} \qquad (5.77)$$

Based on (5.76), we can introduce the conditional expectation of X, given Y, denoted by $E(X|Y)$, as a new random variable which takes on the value $E(X|Y = y_j)$ when Y takes on the value y_j (for $j = 1, 2, \ldots$). Hence, the conditional expectation of X, given Y, as a random variable takes on the values

$$E(X \mid Y = y_j) = \sum_i x_i \frac{p_{ij}}{r_j}$$

with probabilities $r_j (j = 1, 2, \ldots)$. Consequently, we readily observe that

$$E\{E(X \mid Y)\} = \sum_j E(X \mid Y = y_j) r_j = \sum_j r_j \sum_i x_i \frac{p_{ij}}{r_j} =$$

$$\sum_i x_i \sum_j p_{ij} = \sum_i x_i P\{X = x_i\} = EX$$

Similarly, if the conditional expectation $E\{h(X) \mid Y\}$ is a random variable which takes on values $E\{h(X) \mid Y = y_j\}$ when Y takes on the values y_j (for $j = 1, 2, \ldots$) with probabilities r_j, we can show that

$$E\{E[h(X) \mid Y]\} = E\{h(X)\}$$

Next, let us consider the case when ten random vector (X, Y) has an absolutely continuous bivariate distribution with p.d.f. $p(x, y)$, and let $p_Y(y)$ be the marginal density function of Y. Then, from Eq. (5.71), we have the conditional mean of X, given $Y = y$, as

$$E(X \mid Y = y) = \int_{-\infty}^{+\infty} x p_{X\mid Y}(x \mid y) \, dx = \int_{-\infty}^{+\infty} x \frac{p(x,y)}{p_Y(y)} dx \quad (5.78)$$

provided that EX exists. Similarly, if $h(\cdot)$ is a measurable function for which $Eh(X)$ exists, we have the conditional expectation of $h(X)$, given $Y=y$, as

$$E(h(X) \mid Y = y) = \int_{-\infty}^{+\infty} h(x) p_{X\mid Y}(x \mid y) \, dx =$$

$$\int_{-\infty}^{+\infty} h(x) \frac{p(x,y)}{p_Y(y)} dx \quad (5.79)$$

As in the discrete case, we can regard $E(X\mid Y)$ and $E\{h(X)\mid Y\}$ as random variables which takes on the values

$$E(X \mid Y = y) = \int_{-\infty}^{+\infty} x \frac{p(x,y)}{p_Y(y)} dx, \quad E(h(X) \mid Y = y) =$$

$$\int_{-\infty}^{+\infty} h(x) \frac{p(x,y)}{p_Y(y)} dx$$

when the random variable Y takes on the value y. In the case, too, it can be shown that

$$E\{E(X\mid Y)\} = EX \text{ and } E\{E[h(X)\mid Y]\} = E\{h(X)\}$$

5.14 Regressions

In Eqs. (5.76) and (5.78) we defined the conditional expectation $E(X\mid Y=y)$ provided that EX exists. From this conditional expectation, we may consider the function

$$a(y) = E(X\mid Y=y) \quad (5.80)$$

which is called the *regression function of X on Y*. Similarly, when EY exists, the function

$$b(x) = E(Y\mid X=x) \quad (5.81)$$

is called the *regression function of Y on X*.

Note that when the random variables X and Y are independent, then

$$a(y) = E(X\mid Y=y) = EX \text{ and } b(x) = E(Y\mid X=x) = EY$$

are simply the unconditional means of X and Y, and do not depend on y and x, respectively.

5.15 Generating Function of Random Vectors

Let $X = (X_1, \ldots, X_n)$ be a random vector, elements of which takes on values $0, 1, 2, \ldots$. In this case, the generating function $P(s_1, \ldots, s_n)$ is defined as

$$P(s_1, \ldots, s_n) = E s_1^{X_1} \ldots s_n^{X_n} =$$

$$\sum_{j_1=0}^{\infty}\cdots\sum_{j_n=0}^{\infty}P\{X_1=j_1,\ldots,X_n=j_n\}s_1^{j_1}\ldots s_n^{j_n} \tag{5.82}$$

Although the following properties can be presented for this general case, we present them for notational simplicity only for the bivariate case ($n=2$).

Let $P_{X,Y}(s,t)$, $P_X(s)$, and $P_Y(t)$ be the generating function of the bivariate random vector (X, Y), the marginal generating function of X, and the marginal generating function of Y, defined by

$$P_{X,Y}(s,t) = Es^X t^Y = \sum_{j=0}^{\infty}\sum_{k=0}^{\infty}P\{X=j, Y=k\}s^j t^k \tag{5.83}$$

$$P_X(s) = Es^X = \sum_{j=0}^{\infty}P\{X=j\}s^j \tag{5.84}$$

$$P_Y(t) = Et^Y = \sum_{k=0}^{\infty}P\{Y=k\}t^k \tag{5.85}$$

respectively. Then, the following properties of $P_{X,Y}(s,t)$ can be established easily

(1) $P_{X,Y}(1,1) = 1$;

(2) $P_{X,Y}(s,1) = P_X(s)$ and $P_{X,Y}(1,t) = P_Y(t)$;

(3) $P_{X,Y}(s,s) = P_{X+Y}(s)$, where $P_{X+Y}(s) = Es^{X+Y}$ is the generating function of the variable $X+Y$;

(4) $P_{X,Y}(s,t) = P_X(s)P_Y(t)$ if and only if X are Y independent;

(5) $\dfrac{\partial^{k+l}P_{X,Y}(s,t)}{\partial s^k \partial t^l}\bigg|_{s=t=1} = E\{X\ldots(X-k+1)Y\ldots(Y-l+1)\}$ and, in particular, we have

$$\frac{\partial^2 P_{X,Y}(s,t)}{\partial s \partial t}\bigg|_{s=t=1} = E\{XY\}$$

Next, for the random vector $X = (X_1,\ldots,X_n)$, we define the characteristic function $f(t_1,\ldots,t_n)$ as

$$f(t_1,\ldots,t_n) = Ee^{i(t_1 X_1+\ldots+t_n X_n)} =$$

$$\sum_{j_1=0}^{\infty}\sum_{j_n=0}^{\infty}P\{X_1=j_1,\ldots,X_n=j_n\}e^{i(t_1 j_1+\ldots+t_n j_n)} \tag{5.86}$$

Similarly, in the case when the random vector $X = (X_1,\ldots,X_n)$ has an absolutely continuous distribution with density function $p(x_1,\ldots,x_n)$, then its characteristic function $f(t_1,\ldots,t_n)$ is defined as

$$f(t_1,\ldots,t_n) = Ee^{i(t_1 X_1+\ldots+t_n X_n)} =$$

$$\int_{-\infty}^{+\infty}\cdots\int_{-\infty}^{+\infty}e^{i(t_1 x_1+\ldots+t_n x_n)}p(x_1,\ldots,x_n)dx_1\ldots dx_n \tag{5.87}$$

Once again, although the following properties can be presented for this general

n-dimensional case, we present them for notational simplicity only for the bivariate case ($n=2$).

Let $f_{X,Y}(s,t)$, $f_X(s)$, and $f_Y(t)$ be the characteristic function of the bivariate random vector (X,Y), the marginal characteristic function of X, and the marginal characteristic function of Y, defined by

$$f_{X,Y}(s,t) = \int_{-\infty}^{+\infty}\int_{-\infty}^{+\infty} e^{i(sx+ty)} p_{X,Y}(x,y) \mathrm{d}x\mathrm{d}y \tag{5.88}$$

$$f_X(s) = \int_{-\infty}^{+\infty} e^{i(sx)} p_X(x) \mathrm{d}x \tag{5.89}$$

$$f_Y(t) = \int_{-\infty}^{+\infty} e^{i(ty)} p_Y(y) \mathrm{d}y \tag{5.90}$$

respectively. Then, the following properties of $f_{X,Y}(s,t)$ can be established easily

(1) $f_{X,Y}(0,0) = 1$;

(2) $f_{X,Y}(s,0) = f_X(s)$ and $f_{X,Y}(0,t) = f_Y(t)$;

(3) $f_{X,Y}(s,s) = f_{X+Y}(s)$, where $f_{X+Y}(s) = E\, e^{is(X+Y)}$ is the characteristic function of the variable $X+Y$;

(4) $f_{X,Y}(s,t) = f_X(s)f_Y(t)$ if and only if X are Y independent;

(5) $\left.\dfrac{\partial^{k+l} f_{X,Y}(s,t)}{\partial s^k \partial t^l}\right|_{s=t=0} = i^{k+l} = E(X^k Y^l)$ and, in particular, we have

$$\left.\dfrac{\partial^2 f_{X,Y}(s,t)}{\partial s \partial t}\right|_{s=t=0} = -E\{XY\}$$

Words and Expressions

marginal characteristic function 边际特征函数

if and only if 当且仅当

Appendix 5A Properties of Conditional Expectations

Property CE 1 Let $a_1(x), \ldots, a_G(x)$ and $b(x)$ be scalar functions of x, and let $y_1, \ldots, y_G$ be random scalars. Then

$$E\Big(\sum_{j=1}^{G} a_j(x) y_j + b(x) \,\big|\, x\Big) = \sum_{j=1}^{G} a_j(x) E(y_j \,|\, x) + b(x)$$

provided that, $E(|y_j|) < \infty$, $E(|a_j(x) y_j|) < \infty$, and $E(|b(x)|) < \infty$. This is the sense in which the expectation is a linear operator.

Property CE 2 $E(y) = E[E(y|x)] \equiv E[\mu(x)]$.

Property CE 2 is the simplest version of the law of iterated expectations. As an illustration, suppose that x is a discrete random vector taking on values with p_1, $p_2, \ldots, p_M$ probabilities $c_1, c_2, \ldots, c_M$. Then the LIE says

$$E(y) = p_1 E(y \mid x_1 = c_1) + p_2 E(y \mid x_2 = c_2) + \ldots + p_M E(y \mid x_M = c_M)$$

In the other, $E(y)$ is simply a weighted average of the $E(y \mid x = c_j)$, where the weight p_j is the probability that x takes on the value c_j.

Property CE 3 (1) $E(y \mid x) = E[E(y \mid w) \mid x]$, where x and w are vectors with $x = f(w)$ for some nonstochastic function $f(\cdot)$. (This is the general version of the law of iterated expectations)

(2) As a special case of part 1, $E(y \mid x) = E[E(y \mid x, z) \mid x]$ for vectors x and z.

Property CE 4 If $f(x) \in R^J$ is a function of x such that for some scalar function $g(\cdot)$, then $E[y \mid f(x)] = E(y \mid x)$.

Property CE 5 If the vector (u, v) is independent of the vector x, then $E(u \mid x, v) = E(u \mid v)$.

Property CE 6 If $u \equiv y - E(y \mid x)$, then for any function $g(x)$, *provided that* $E(|g_j(x) u|) < \infty$, $j = 1, \ldots, K$ and $E(|u|) < \infty$. In particular, $E(u) = 0$ and $\text{Cov}(xj, u) = 0$, $j = 1, \ldots, K$.

Proof First, note that
$$E(u \mid x) = E[(y - E(y \mid x)) \mid x] = E[(y - \mu(x)) \mid x] =$$
$$E(y \mid x) - \mu(x) = 0$$

Next, by property CE 2, $E(g(x) u) = E(E(g(x) u \mid x)) = E(g(x) E(u \mid x))$
(by property CE 1) $= 0$ because $E(u \mid x) = 0$.

Property CE 7 (*Conditional Jensen's inequality*) If $c: R \to R$ is a convex function defined on R and $E[|y|] < \infty$, then
$$c[E(y \mid x)] \leq E[c(y) \mid x]$$

Technically, we should add the statement "almost surely-Px", which means that the inequality holds for all x in a set that a in a set that has probability equal to one. As a special case, $[E(y)]^2 \leq E(y^2)$. Also, if $y > 0$, then $-\log[E(y)] \leq E[-\log(y)]$, or $E[\log(y)] \leq \log[E(y)]$.

Property CE 8 If $E(y^2) < \infty$ and $\mu(x) \equiv E(y \mid x)$, then μ is a solution to
$$\min_{m \in M} E[(y - m(x))^2]$$
where M is the set of functions $m: R^K \to R$, such that $[m(x)^2] < \infty$. In other words, μ is the best mean square predictor of y based on information contained in x.

Proof By the conditional Jensen's inequality, if follows that $E(y^2) < \infty$ implies $E[(\mu - m(x))^2] < \infty$, so that $\mu \in M$. Next, for any $m \in M$, write
$$E[(y - m(x))^2] = \{E[(y - \mu(x)) + (\mu(x) - m(x))^2]\} =$$
$$E[(y - \mu(x))^2] + E[(\mu(x) - m(x))^2] +$$

$$2E[\mu(x)]$$
where $u \equiv y-\mu(x)$, Thus, by CE 6,
$$E[(y-m(x))^2] = E(u^2) + E[(\mu(x)-m(x))^2]$$
The right-hand side is clearly minimized at $m \equiv \mu$.

Appendix 5B Properties of Conditional Variances

The conditional variance of y given x is defined as
$$\text{Var}(y \mid x) \equiv \sigma^2(x) \equiv E\{[y-E(y \mid x)]^2 \mid x\} = E(y^2 \mid x) - [E(y \mid x)]^2$$
The last representation is often useful for computing $\text{Var}(y \mid x)$. As with the conditional expectation, $\sigma^2(x)$ is a random variable when x is viewed as a random vector.

Property CV 1 $\text{Var}[a(x)y+b(x) \mid x] = [a(x)]^2 \text{Var}(y \mid x)$.

Property CV 2 $\text{Var}(y) = E[\text{Var}(y \mid x)] + \text{Var}[E(y \mid x)] = E[\sigma^2(x)] + \text{Var}[\mu(x)]$.

Proof $\text{Var}(y) \equiv E[(y-E(y))^2] = E[(y-E(y \mid x) + E(y \mid x) - E(y))^2] =$
$$E[(y-E(y \mid x))^2] + E[(E(y \mid x) - E(y))^2] + 2E[(y-E(y \mid x))(E(y \mid x) - E(y))]$$
By CE 6, $E[(y-E(y \mid x))(E(y \mid x) - E(y))] = 0$; so
$$\text{Var}(y) = E[(y-E(y))^2] + E[(E(y \mid x) - E(y))^2] = E\{E[(y-E(y))^2 \mid x]\} + E[(E(y \mid x) - E[E(y \mid x)])^2]$$
by the law of iterated expectations
$$\text{Var}(y) \equiv E[\text{Var}(y \mid x)] + \text{Var}[E(y \mid x)]$$
An extension of Property CV 2 is often useful, and its proof is similar.

Property CV 3 $\text{Var}(y \mid x) = E[\text{Var}(y \mid x,z) \mid x] + \text{Var}[E(y \mid x,z) \mid x]$.

Consequently, by the law of iterated expectations CE 2,

Property CV 4 $E[\text{Var}(y \mid x)] \geqslant E[\text{Var}(y \mid x,z)]$.

For any function $m(\cdot)$, define the mean squared error as $\text{MSE}(y; m) \equiv E[(y-m(x))^2]$. Then CV 4 can be loosely stated as $\text{MSE}[y; E(y \mid x)] \geqslant \text{MSE}[y; E(y \mid x,z)]$. In other words, in the population one never does worse for predicting y when additional variables are conditioned on. In particular, if $\text{Var}(y \mid x)$ and $\text{Var}(y \mid x, z)$ are both constant, then $\text{Var}(y \mid x) \geqslant \text{Var}(y \mid x, z)$.

How about "Statistician"?

A statistician is someone who works with theoretical or applied statistics.

The profession exists in both the private and public sectors. It is common to combine statistical knowledge with expertise in other subjects. ——Wikipedia

Unit Six Data Science and Big data

6.1 From Data to Wisdom

We know that information is extracted from data, knowledge is extracted from information etc.. Do you know what means "DUKW"? Data Information Knowledge and Wisdom can be abbreviated as DIKW. In other words, DUKW stands for data, information, knowledge, and wisdom. There is a four layer hierarchy from data to wisdom, where each layer adds certain attributed over and above the previous one (see Fig. 6.1).

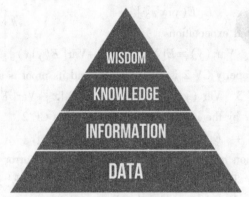

Fig. 6.1 DIKW Pyramid

Data is the most basic level; Information adds context; Knowledge adds how to use it; Wisdom adds when and why to use it. A further elaboration of Ackoff's definitions follows: Data is raw. It can exist in any form, usable or not. It does not have meaning of itself.

Information is data that has been given meaning by way of relational connection. This "Meaning" can be useful, but does not have to be. Knowledge is the appropriate collection of information, such that its intent is to be useful. Knowledge is a deterministic process. This knowledge has useful meaning to them, but it does not provide for, in and of itself, integration such as would infer further knowledge. Understanding is an interpolative and probabilistic process. It is cognitive and analytical. It is the process by which people can take knowledge and synthesize new knowledge from the previously held knowledge.

Wisdom is an extrapolatiove and non-deterministic, non-probabilistic process, look at Fig. 6.2. It calls upon all the previous levels of consciousness, and specifically upon special types of human programming (moral, ethical codes, etc.).

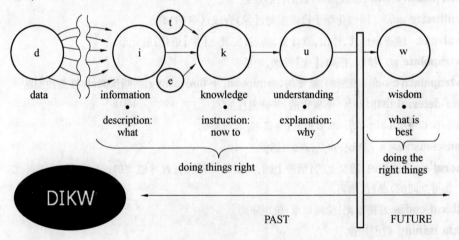

Fig. 6.2 from data to Wisdom

In the meaning of hierarchy of DIKW the data just a basic fact and raw that will be useful only let them evolve to the information, knowledge and wisdom. In the previous two levels of data and information we may use a lot of methods such as data mining, text mining, web mining and tools such as data base, data warehouse and management information system to let them to be useful. In order to move forward to the third level of knowledge we should use KDD, knowledge engineering and management, intelligent knowledge. Given large-scale databases, intelligent knowledge management enables to generate "special" knowledge, called intelligent knowledge base on the hidden patterns created by data mining.

The process of intelligent knowledge mangagemen—a new proposition from original data, rough knowledge, intelligent knowledge, and actionable knowledge is proposed. Especially in considering the expert experiences to let the knowledge extracted by some methods like data mining to be more useful, we use so-called domain driven data mining. For the sake of fully utilize the expert experience we propose expert mining, by which people may use properly the data, information and knowledge.

Words and Expressions

abbreviate *vt.* 缩写;缩短;缩写为;简称
wisdom *n.* 智慧;明智;才智;学问
elaboration *n.* 认真做;推敲;精巧;细致的工作[作品]
pyramid *n.* 锥体;(古埃及)金字塔;棱锥体;金字塔形的物体
interpolative *adj.* 篡改的,内插的,插入的
synthesize *adj.* (通过化学手段或生物过程)合成;(音响)合成
evolve *vt.* 使逐步形式,作出,设计出,制定;发展。【生】进化;进化形成
extrapolate *vt.* 推断,推知;【统】外推,外插
extrapolative *adj.* 推断的,推知的;extrapolative-forecasting 推断预测;外推测预测法
non-deterministic *adj.* 不确定的,非确定性的
non-probabilistic *adj.* 非概率的;非概率,非机率的
consciousness *n.* 意识;知觉;观念;感觉
moral *adj.* 道德的,道义上的;精神上的;无疑的,当然的;教导道德的;*n.* 寓意,教训;(尤指男女间的)品行;格言
ethical codes 道德准则;伦理规章;伦理守则
data mining 数据挖掘
text mining 文本挖掘;文本数据挖掘
web mining 网络挖掘;网络信息挖掘;网路探勘
management information system 管理信息系统
data base 数据库
data warehouse 数据仓库,可简写为 DW 或 DWH。(数据仓库是为企业所有级别的决策制定过程提供支持的所有类型数据的战略集合)
hidden pattern 隐藏模式;隐含模式;隐性模式
KDD(Knowledge Discovery and Data Mining) 知识发现和数据挖掘
KDD(Knowledge Discovery from Databases) 知识发现;数据库知识发现
large-scale databases 大规模数据库,大规模资料库

intelligent knowledge 智能知识
intelligent knowledge-based system 【计】知识智能系统
actionable knowledge 可行动知识,操作型知识
expert experience 专家经验
domain driven data mining 领域挖掘;领域驱动数据挖掘
expert mining 数据挖掘专家

6.2　Data Science

Data Science is a composite of a number of pre-existing disciplines. It is a young profession and academic discipline. The term was first coined in 1998. C. E. Jeff Wu first introduced the term "data science" in 1998 as a discipline that encompasses statistical analysis, science, and advanced computing.

Its popularity has exploded since 2010, pushed by the need for teams of people to analyze the big data that corporations and governments are collecting. The Google search engine is a classic example of the power of data science.

The term "Data Science was coined at the beginning of the 21st Century. It is attributed to William S. Cleveland who, in 2001, wrote "Data Science: An Action Plan for Expanding the Technical Areas of the Field of Statistics." About a year later, the International Council for Science: Committee on Data for Science and Technology started publishing the *CODATA Data Science Journal* beginning April 2002. Shortly thereafter, in January of 2003, Columbia Unviersity began publishing *The Journal of Data Science*.

The following timeline traces the evolution of the term "Data Science" and its use, attempts to define it, and related terms. (Fig. 6.3)

Words and Expressions

generalizable *adj.* 概括性;可概括的;可概括性
C. F. Jeff Wu 吴建民,(Coca-Cola Chair in Engineering Statistics and Professor) 教授,统计家,1949 年 1 月 15 日,1971 年毕业于台湾大学数学系,1976 年在美国伯克利(Berkeley)加州大学获得统计学博士。2004 年作为第一位统计学者当选美国国家工程院院士,也是第一位华人统计学者获此殊荣。吴教授在世界一流期刊上发表学术论文超过一百篇,其研究成果被很多专业期刊杂志广泛引用。著作包括,与 M. Hamada 合著 *Experiments: Planning, Analysis, and Parameter Design Optimization*, 2nd (Wiley, 2009) 以及 R. Mukerjee 合著 *A Modern Theory of Factorial Designs* (Springer,2006) 等。
pre-existing *adj.* *pre-existent* 的变体,先前存在的,已有的
Coin *vt.* 创造;提出;铸造(货币);制造;*n.* 硬币;铸币;[俚语]金钱;现金

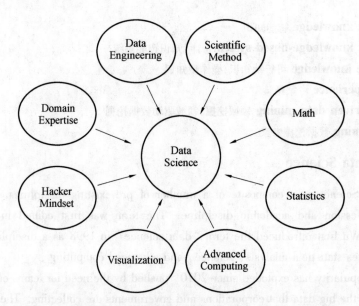

Fig. 6.3 The Disciplines of Data Science, Source: Calvin Andrus

CODATA 国际科技数据委员会；国际科学技术数据委员会；国际科学数据委员会。(The Committee on Data for Science and Technology (CODATA) was established in 1966 as an interdisciplinary committee of the International Council for Science. It seeks to improve the compilation, critical evaluation, storage, and retrieval of data of importance to science and technology.) 中国全国委员会的网址：www.codata.cn

CODATA Data Science Journal *CODATA* 官方电子期刊《数据科学期刊》

6.2.1 A Short History of Data Science

The story of how data scientists became sexy is mostly the story of the coupling of the mature discipline of statistics with a very young one-computer science. The term "Data Science" has emerged only recently to specifically designate a new profession that is expected to make sense of the vast stores of big data. But making sense of data has a long history and has been discussed by scientists, statisticians, librarians, computer scientists and others for years. The following timeline traces the evolution of the term "Data Science" and its use, attempts to define it, and related terms.

Data Science in 1962

1962 John W. Tukey writes in "The Future of Data Analysis": "For a long time I thought I was a statistician, interested in inferences from the particular to the general. But as I have watched mathematical statistics evolve, I have had cause to wonder and doubt... I have come to feel that my central interest is in data analysis... Data analysis, and the parts of statistics which adhere to it, must... take on the characteristics of science rather than those of mathematics... data analysis is intrinsically an empirical science... How vital and how important... is the rise of the stored-program electronic computer? In many instances the answer may surprise many by being 'important but not vital,' although in others there is no doubt but what the computer has been 'vital. '"

In 1947, Tukey onined the term "bit" which Claude Shannon used in his 1948 paper "*A Mathematical Theory of Communications.*" In 1977, Tukey published *Exploratory Data Analysis*, arguing that more emphasis needed to be placed on using data to suggest hypothese to test and that *Exploratory Data Analysis* and *Confirmatory Data Aanalysis* "can-and should-proceed side by side." (Fig. 6.4)

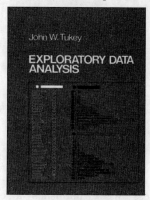

Fig. 6.4

Data Science in 1974

1974 Peter Naur (2005 Turing award winner) publishes *Concise Survey of Computer Methods* in Sweden and the United States. The book is a survey of contemporary data processing methods that are used in a wide range of applications. It is organized around the concept of data as defined in the IFIP Guide to Concepts and Terms in Data Processing: "[Data is] a representation of facts or ideas in a formalized manner capable of being communicated or manipulated by some process. "The Preface to the book tells the reader that a course plan was presented at the IFIP Congress in 1968, titled "Datalogy, the science of data and of data processes and its place in education, "and that in the text of the book," the term 'data science' has been used freely." Naur offers the following definition of data science: "The science of dealing with data, once they have been established, while the relation of the data to what they represent is delegated to other fields and sciences."

1977 The International Association for Statistical Computing (IASC) is established as a Section of the ISI. "It is the mission of the IASC to link traditional statistical methodology, modern computer technology, and the knowledge of domain experts in order to donvert data into information and knowledge."

Data Science in 1989

1989 Gregory Piatetsky-Shapiro organizes and chairs the first Knowledge Discovery in Databases (KDD) workshop. In 1995, it became the annual ACM SIGKDD Conference on Knowledge Discovery and Data Mining (KDD). (Fig. 6.5)

Fig. 6.5

September 1994 Business Week publishes a cover story on "*Database Marketing*": "*Companies are collecting mountains of information about you, crunching it to predict how likely you are to buy a product, and using that knowledge to craft a marketing message precisely calibrated to get you to do so... An earlier flush of enthusiasm prompted by the spread of checkout scanners in the 1980s ended in widespread disappointment: Many companies were too overwhelmed by the sheer quantity of data to do anything useful with the information... Still, many companies believe they have no choice but to brave the database-marketing frontier.*"

1996 Members of the International Federation of Classification Societies (IFCS) meet in Kobe, Japan, for their biennial conference. For the first time, the term "data science" is included in the title of the conference ("*Data Science, Classification, and Related Methods*"). The IFCS was founded in 1985 by six country-and language-specific classification societies, one of which, The Classfication Society, was founded in 1964. The classification societies have variously used the terms data analysis, data mining, and data science in their publications. (Fig. 6.6)

Fig. 6.6

1996 Usama Fayyad, Gregory Piatetsky-Shapiro, and Padhraic Smyth publish "*From Data Mining to Knowledge Discovery in Databases.*" They write: "Historically, the notion of finding useful patterns in data has been given a variety of names, including data mining, knowledge extraction, information discovery, information harvesting, data archeology, and data pattern processing... In our view, KDD [Knowledge Discovery in Databass] refers to the overall process of discovering useful knowledge from data, and data mining refers to a particular step in this process. Data mining is the application of specific algorithms for extracting patterns from data... the additional steps in the KDD process, such as data preparation, data selection, data cleaning, incorporation of appropriate prior knowledge, and proper interpretation of the results of mining, are essential to ensure that useful knowledge is derived from the data. Blind application of data-mining methods(rightly criticized as data dredging in the statistical literature) can be a dangerous activity, easily leading to the discovery of meaningless and invalid patterns."

Data Science in 1997

1997 In his inaugural lecture for the H. C. Carver Chair in Statistics at the University of Michigan, Professor C. F. Jeff Wu(currently at the Georgia Institute of Technology), calls for statistics to be renamed data science and statisticians to be renamed data scientistis.

1997 The journal *Data Mining and Knowledge Discovery* is launched; the reversal of the order of the two terms in its title reflecting the ascendance of "data mining" as the more popular way to designate "extracting information from large databases."

December 1999 Jacob Zahavi is quoted in "*Mining Data for Nuggets of Knowledge*" in Knowledge@Wharton: "Conventional statistical methods work well with small data sets. Today's databases, however, can involve millions of rows and scores of data... Scalability is a huge issue in data mining. Another technical challenge is edeveloping models that can do a better job analyzing data, detecting non-linear relationships and interaction between element... Special data mining tools may have to be developed to address web-site decisions."

Words and Expressions

designate *vt.* 指明,指出;指派;表明,意味着;把……定名为。*adj.* 指定而尚未上任的;选出而尚未上任的

timeline *n.* 时间轴,时间表

John W. Tukey 约翰·图基(1915—2000)统计学家,他对统计学的做出了巨大的贡献,在时间序列、稳健性、方差分析、实验设计和多重比较方面开展了基础性的工作。他发明了探索性数据分析(exploratory data analysis)。

Confirmatory Data Analysis 验证数据分析

datalogy *n.* 数据科学

intrinsically *adv.* 真正;从本质上来说;内在的;固有的

stored-program 存储程序

stored-program electronic computer 储程式电子计算机

Claude Shannon 克劳德·香农(1916年4月30日—2001年2月26日),美国数学家、信息论的创始人,他的《通讯的数学原理》*A Mathematical Theory of Communications* 于1948年发表,奠定了现代通信理论的基础,这是一部20世纪最重大的贡献之一。香农有两大贡献:一是信息理论、信息熵的概念;另一是符号逻辑和开关理论。

Peter Naur 彼得·诺尔(1928年10月25日—),计算机领域的专家,获得2005年图灵奖,以表彰其,对Algol 60编程语言的设计与定义,对编译器设计和计算机编程领域的理论与实践的基础性贡献。

programming language 编程语言

IFIP(**International Federation for Information Pocessing**,缩写 **IFIP**)国际信息处理联合会是一个从事于信息处理的非政府的,非营利的国际组织。

IASC, **The International Association for Statistical Computing** 国际统计计算协会

ISI, **International Statistical Institure** 国际统计研究所

Usama Fayyad 尤萨马·菲亚德

Gregory Piatetsky-Shapiro 美国数据挖掘技术开拓者,数据挖掘领域的著名专家。

ACM(Association for Computing Machinery 美国计算机协会是世界性的计算机专业组织,创立于 1947 年,是世界上影响力最强的科学性及教育性计算机组织。ACM 每年都出版大量计算机科学的高水平专门期刊,并在各项计算机专业领域都有分会,称为 SIG(Special Interest Group),他曾任前主席(2005~2008)SIG KDD 是国际数据挖掘界最著名的组织,其中 KDD(Knowledge Discovery and Data Mining,知识发现与数据挖掘)一词首次出现在 1989 年 8 月举行的第 11 届国际联合人工智能学术会议(IJCAI)上,由 Piatetsky Sharpiro 正式提出)。

Padhraic Smyth 加州大学欧文分校计算机科学系教授
International Federation of Classification Societies(IFCS) 国际分类学会联合会
craft *vt.* 工艺;船;手艺;飞行器;*vt.* 手工制作;精巧地制作
data archeology 数据考古
information harvesting 信息收获
chairs *vt.* 使入座;使就认要职;担任(会议、委员会)主席
checkout scanners 条码扫描器
disappointment *n.* 失望;挫折;伤心;令人失望的事
overwhelm *vt.* 征服,压倒;压服;推翻;淹没
Knowledge Discovery in Databases 数据库知识发现
brave *adj.* 勇敢的,无畏的;炫耀的;壮观的,极好的;*vt.* 勇敢地面对
Kobe *n.* 神户(日本的城市)
knowledge extraction 知识提取,知识抽取
data dredging 数据疏浚,有时候指的是数据捕鱼(*data fishing*),它是一种数据挖掘实践,分析其中大批量的数据来寻找数据间可能的关系。相反的,传统科学方法以假设开始,紧接着测试数据。
inaugural *adj.* 就职的,就任的,首次的
ascendance *n.* 优势,支配(地位)
scalability 可量测性
web-site 万维网站点
Jacob Zahavi 雅克布·扎哈维,沃顿商学院客座教授
Knowledge@ Wharton 沃顿知识在线

Data Science in 2001

2001 William S. Cleveland publishes *Data Science: An Action Plan for Expanding the Technical Areas of the Field of Statistics*. It is a plan "to enlarge the major areas of technical work of the field of statistics. Because the plan is ambitious and implies substantial change, the altered field will be called 'data science.'" Cleveland puts the proposed new discipline in the context of computer science and the contemporary work in data mining: "... the benefit to the data analyst has been limited, because the knowledge among computer scientists about how to think of and approach the analysis of data is limited, just as the knowledge of computing environments by statisticians is limited. A merger of knowledge bases would produce a powerful force for innovation. This suggests that statisticians should look to computing for knowledge today just as data science looked to mathematics in the past... departments of data science should contain faculty members who devote their careers to advances in computing with data and who form partnership with computer scientists. "

2001 Leo Breiman publishes *Statistical Modeling: The Two Cultures*: "There are two cultures in the use of statistical modeling to reach conclusions from data. One assumes that the data are generated by a given stochastic data model. The other uses algorithmic models and treats the data mechanism as unknown. The statistical community has been committed to the almost exclusive use of data models. This commitment has led to irrelevant theory, questionable conclusions, and has kept statisticians from working on a large range of interesting current problems. Algorithmic modeling, both in theory and practice, has developed rapidly in fields outside statistics. It can be used both on large complex data sets and as a more accurate and informative alternative to data modeling on smaller data sets. If our goal as a field is to use data to solve problems, then we need to move away from exclusive dependence on data models and adopt a more diverse set of tools. "

Data Science in 2002

April 2002 *Launch of Data Science* Journal, publishing papers on " the management of data and databases in Science and Technology. The scope of the Journal includes descriptions of data systems, their publication on the internet, applications and legal issues. " The journal is published by the Committee on Data for Science and Technology (CODATA) of the International Council for Science (ICSU).

January 2003 Launch of Journal of *Data Science*: " By *Data Science* we mean almost everything that has something to do with data: Collecting, analyzing, modeling... yet the most important part is its applications—all sorts of applications. This journal is devoted to applications of statistical methods at large... The Journal of *Data Science* will provide a platform for all data workers to present their views and exchange ideas. ' "

Data Science in 2005

May 2005 Thomas H. Davenport, Don Cohen, and Al Jacobson publish *Competing on Analytics*, a Babson College Working Knowledge Research Center report, describing "the emergence of a new form of competition based on the extensive use of analytics, data, and fact-based decision making... Instead of competing on traditional factors, companies are beginning to employ statistical and quantitative analysis and predictive modeling as primary elements of competition." The research is later published by Davenport in the Harvard Business Review (January 2006) and is expanded (with Jeanne G. Harris) into the book Competing on *Analytics The New Science of Winning* (March 2007).

September 2005 The National Science Board publishes *Long-lived Digital Data Collections: Enabling Research and Education in the 21st Century*. One of the recommendations of the report reads: "The NSF, working in partnership with collection managers and the community at large, should act to develop and mature the career path for data scientists and to ensure that the research enterprise includes a sufficient number of high-quality data scientists." The report defines data scientists as "the information and computer scientists, database and software engineers and programmers, disciplinary experts, curators and expert annotators, librarians, archivists, and others, who are crucial to the successful management of a digital data collection."

Data Science in 2007

2007 The Research Center for Dataology and Data Science is established at Fudan University, Shanghai, China. In 2009, two of the center's researchers, YangyongZhu and Yun Xiong, publish *Introduction to Dataology and Data Science*, in which they state "Different from natural science and social science, Dataology and Data Science takes data in cyberspace as its research object. It is a new science." The center holds annual symposiums on Dataology and Data Science (2013 第四届数据科学国际研讨会)。

July 2008 The JISC publishes the final report of a study it commissioned to "examine and make recommendations on the role and career development of data scientists and the associated supply of specialist data curation skills to the research community." The study's final report, *The Skills, Role & Career Structure of Data Scientists & Curators: Assessment of Current Practice & Future Needs*, defines data scientists as "people who work where the research is carried out or, in the case of data centre personnel, in close collaboration with the creators of the data and may be involved in creative enquiry and analysis, enabling others to work with digital data, and developments in data base technology."

Words and Expressions

William S. Cleveland 威廉·克利夫兰,在贝尔实验室中研究统计
Leo Breiman 利奥·布莱曼(1928年1月27日—2005年7月5日)统计学家
the International Council for Science(ICSU) 国际科学理事会
Thomas H. Davenport 托马斯·达文波特
Don Cohen 唐·科恩
Al Jacobson 阿尔·雅各布森
annotator n. 注解者,注释者
archivist n. 档案保管员
curator n. （博物馆、图书馆）馆长,主任
analytics 分析学
Babson College Working Knowledge Research Center 巴布森商学院知识管理研究中心
The National Science Board, NSF 国家科学委员会,美国国家科学局
The NSF 美国国家科学基金会
ZhuYangyong 朱扬勇,复旦大学数据科学研究中心研究员
XiongYun 熊赟,复旦大学数据科学研究中心研究员
cyberspace n. 计算机空间,网络语言
cybers- 前缀表示计算机的;网络的。如 cybershop vi. 网络购物;
cyberspeak n. 网络用语,网络语言
curation n. 治疗,治疗。【IT】(对数字信息的)综合处理,指对数字信息的选择,保存,管理等一系列处理行为,其目的是建立完善的查询机制和提供可靠的参考数据
data curation 这是一个专业术语【计】,国内翻译成:数据管理;数据监管;数据监护;数据存管等。国内学者及研究机构对 data curation 定义的研究主要可归纳为两点:一方面指对科学数据的选择、注释、组织和存储;另一方面具有产生附加价值和知识的功能。
enable vt. 使能够,使可行,为……提供条件(机会、手段)

Data Science in 2009

January 2009 Harnessing the Power of Digital Data for Science and Society is published. This report of the Interagency Working Group on Digital Data to the Committee on Science of the National Science and Technology Council states that

"The nation needs to identify and promote the emergence of new disciplines and specialists expert in addressing the complex and dynamic challenges of digital preservation, sustained access, reuse and repurposing of data. Many disciplines are seeing the emergence of a new type of data science and management expert, accomplished in the computer, information, and data sciences arenas and in another domain science. These individuals are key to the current and future success of the scientific enterprise. However, these individuals often receive little recognition for their contributions and have limited career paths."

January 2009 Hal Varian, Google's Chief Economist, tells the McKinsey Quarterly: "I keep saying the sexy job in the next ten years will be statisticians. People think I'm joking, but who would've guessed that computer engineers would've been the sexy job of the 1990s? The ability to take data to be able to understand it, to process it, to extract value from it, to visualize it, to communicate it—that's going to be a hugely important skill in the next decades... Becase now we really do have essentially free and ubiquitous data. So the complimentary scarce factor is the ability to understand that data and extract value from it... I do think those skills—of being able to access, understand, and communicate the insights you get from data analysis—are going to be extremely important. Managers need to be able to access and understand the data themselves."

March 2009 Kirk D. Borne and other astrophysicists submit to the Astro 2010 Decadal Survey a paper titled *The Revolution in Astronomy Eduction: Data Science for the Masses* "Training the next generation in the fine art of derving intelligent understanding from data is needed for the success of sciences, communities, projects, agences, businesses, and economies. This is true for both specialists (scientists) and non-specialists(everyone else: the public, educators and students, workforce). Specialists must learn and apply new data science research techniques in order to advance our understanding of the Universe. Non-specialists require information literacy skills as productive members of the 21st century workforce, integrating foundational skills for lifelong learning in a world increasingly dominated by data."

May 2009 Mike Driscoll writes in *The Three Sexy Skills of Data Geeks*: "... with the Age of Data upon us, those who can model, munge, and visually communicate data-call us statisticians or data geeks-are a hot commodity."

June 2009 Nathan Yau writes in *Rise of the Data Scientist*: "As we've all read by now, Google's chief economist Hal Varian commented in January that the next sexy job in the next sexy job in the next 10 years would be statisticians. Obviously, I whole-heartedly agree. Heck, I'd go a step further and say they're sexy now—mentally and physically. However, if you went on to read the rest of Varian's interview, you'd know that by statisticians, he actually meant it as a general title for someone sho is able to extract information from large datasets and then present something of use to non-data experts... [Ben] Fry... argues for an entirely new field that combines the skills and talents from often disjoint areas of expertise... [computer science; mathematics, statistics, and data mining; graphic design; infovis and human-computer interaction]. And after two years of highlighting visualization on Flowing Data, it seems collaborations between the fields are growing more common, but more importantly, computational information design edges closer to reality. We're seeing data scientists—people who can do it all—emerge from the rest of the pack."

June 2009 Troy Sadkowsky creates the data scientists group on LinkedIn as a companion to his website, datasceintists. com (which later became datascientists. net).

Data Science in 2010

February 2010 Kenneth Cukier writes in The Economist Special Report *Data, Data Everywhere*: "... a new kind of professional has emerged, the data scientist, who combines the skills of software programmer, statistician and storyteller/artist to extract the nuggets of gold hidden under mountains of data."

June 2010 Mike Loukides writes in *What is Data Science?*: "Data scientists combine entrepreneurship with patience, the willingness to build data probucts incrementally, the ability to explore, and the ability to iterate over a solution. They are inherently interdisciplinary. They can tackle all aspects of a problem, from initial data collection and data conditioning to drawing conclusions. They can think outside the box to come up with new ways to view the problem, or to work with very broadly defined problems: 'here's a lot of data, what can you make from it?'"

September 2010 Hilary Mason and Chirs Wiggins write in *A Taonomy of Data Science*: "... we thought it would be useful to propose one possible taxonomy... of what a data scientist does, in roughly chronological order: Obtain, Scrub, Explore, Model, and iNterpret... Data science is clearly a blend of the hackers' arts... statistics and machine learning... and the expertise in mathematics and the domain of the data for the analysis to be interpretable... It requires creative decisions and open-mindedness in a scientific context."(Fig. 6.7)

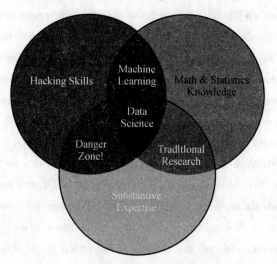

Fig. 6.7 Data Science, Source: Drew Conway

September 2010 Drew Conway writes in *The Data Science Venn Diagram*: "... one needs to learn a lot as they aspire to become a fully competent data scientist. Unfortunately, simply enumerating texts and tutorials does not untangle the knots. Therefore, in an effort to simplify the discussion, and add my own thoughts to what is already a crowded market of ideas, I present the Data Science Venn Diagram... Hacking skills, math and stats knowledge, and substantive expertise."

Data Science in 2011

May 2011 Pete Warden writes in *Why the term 'data science' is flawed but useful*: "There is no widely accepted boundary for what's inside and outside of data science's scope. Is it just a faddish rebranding of statistics? I don't think so, but I also don't have a full definition. I believe that the recent abundance of data has sparked something new in the world, and when I look around I see people with shared characteristics who don't fit into traditional categories. These people tend to work beyond the narrow specialties that dominate the corporate and instiutional world, handling everything from finding the data, processing it at scale, visualizing it and writing it up as a story. They also seem to start by looking at what the data can tell them, and then picking interesting threads to follow, rather than the traditional scientist's approach of choosing the problem first and then finding data to shed light on it."

May 2011 David Smith writes in 'Data Science': What's in a name?: "The terms Data Science and Data Scientist have only been in common usage for a little over a year, but they've really taken off since then: many companies are now hiring for Data Scientists, and entire conferences are run under the name of 'data science'. But despite the widespread adoption, some have resisted the change from the more traditional terms like 'statistician' or 'quant' or 'data analyst'... I think Data Science better describes what we actually do: a combination of computer hacking, data analysis, and problem solving.'"

June 2011 Matthew J. Graham talks at the Astrostatistics and Data Mining in Large Astronomical Databases workshop about The Art of Data Science. He says: "To flourish in the new data-intensive environment of 21st century science, we need to evolve new skills... We need to understand what rules [data] obeys, hot it is symbolized and communicated and what its relationship to physical space and time is."

September 2011 Harlan Harris writes in Data Science, Moore's Law, and Moneyball: "Data Science is defined as what Data Scientists do. What Data Scientists do has been very well covered, and it runs the gamut from data collection and munging, through application of statistics and machine learning and related techniques, to interpretation, communication, and visualization of the results. Who Data Scientists are may be the more fundamental question... I tend to like the idea that Data Science is defined by its practitioners, that it's a career path rather than a category of activities. In my conversations with people, it seems that people who consider themselves Data Scientists typically have eclectic career paths, that might in some ways seem not to make much sense.'"

September 2011 D. J. Patil writes in Building Data Science Teams: "Starting in 2008, Jeff Hammerbacher(@hackingdata) and I sat down to share our experiences building the data and analytics groups at Facebook and LinkedIn. In many was, that meeting was the start of data science as a distinct professional specialization... we realized that as our organizations grew, we both had to figure out what to call the people on our teams. 'Business analyst' seemed too limiting. 'Data analyst' was a contender, but we felt that title might limit what people could do. After all, many of the people on our teams had deep engineering expertise. 'Research scientist' was a reasonable job title used by companies like Sun, HP, Xerox, Yahoo, and IBM. However, we felt that most research scientists worked on projects that were futuristic and abstract, and the work was done in labs that were isolated from the product development teams. It might take years for lab research to affect key products, if it ever did. Instead, the focus of our teams was to work on data applications that would have an immediate and massive impact on the business. The term that seemed to fit best was data scientist: those who use both data and science to create something new."

September 2012 Tom Davenport and D. J. Patil publish *Data Scientist*: *The Sexiest Job of the 21st Century* in the Haravard Business Review.

Words and Expressions

the Committee on Science of the National Science and Technology Council 美国众议院科学委员会的国家科学技术委员会

Hal Varian 谷歌的首席经济学家

the McKinsey Quarterly 麦肯锡季刊

Kirk D. Borne 柯克·博恩

astronomy 天文学

Universe *n.* 宇宙,天地(这里第一个字母大写,意指特定术语)【数】全域。【统】总体,母体

Mike Driscoll 迈克·德里斯科尔

Nathan Yau 邱南森,目前加州大学洛杉矶分校统计学专业在读博士、超级数据迷,专注于数据可视化与个人数据收集。(N. Yau. Seeing Your Life in Data, Beautiful Data O'Reilly [J]. Media, Inc., July 2009)

Troy Sadkowsky 特洛伊·萨德科夫斯基,数据科学家,网站 *www.datascientists.net* 的创建者

Kenneth Cukier 肯尼斯·库克耶,《经济学人》*The Economist* 数据编辑,是一位著名大数据发展评论员

tackle *vt.* 处理;阻截;与某人交涉;向某人提起(问题或困难情况)

Mike Loukides 迈克·劳克德斯,奥莱利出版社副总裁

Hilary Mason 希拉里·梅森

blend *n.* 混合,混杂;混合物。*vt.* 使混合在一起,使混合,使交融

open-minded *adj.* 虚心的;思想开朗的;无先入之见的;无偏见的

open-mindness *n.* 思想开阔,无偏见;开明

scrub *vt. & vi.* 用力擦洗,刷洗;取消(原有安排)

Chris Wiggins 克里斯·威金斯

taxonomy *n.* 分类学;分类法;分类系统

chronological order 按日期顺序排列;编排顺序;按年月的次序;年月日次序

Drew Conway 德鲁·康维

aspire *vi.* 渴望;追求;有志于(*for*,*to*,*after*)

untangle *vt.* 解开;事理;理清

crowded *adj.* 人(太)多的;拥挤的;充满的;充满的。"*crowd*"的过去分词和过去式
Pete Warden 皮特·沃登
faddish *adj.* 流行一时的;喜爱时尚的
rebranding 品牌重塑;品牌再造;重塑品牌
shed light on 为……提供线索;对……透露情况;使……清楚地显出;阐明
David Smith 戴维·史密斯
take off 启程,离去;取消;减去;移送;致死
Matthew J. Graham 马修·格雷厄姆
Astrostatistics 天文统计学
Large Astronomical Databases 大型天文数据库
data-intensive 数据密集型
Harlan Harris 哈伦·哈里斯
obey *vt.* 服从,顺从;遵从,执行(命令)
gamut *n.* 全部;整个范围。【音乐】全音阶;长音阶
munging *n.* 作不合需要的修改
Jeff Hammerbacher 杰夫·哈默巴切
thread *n.* 线,细丝;思路,思绪;【复】各组成部分
figure out 算出,理解,解决
eclectic *adj.* 折中的;不拘一格的;(从不同学科,方法中)兼收并蓄的
futuristic *adj.* 未来主义的,超前先进的,未来派的
contender *n.* 竞争者,争夺者
Harvard Business Review 哈佛商业评论

6.2.2 Data Science

Data science is, in general terms, the extraction of knowledge from data. The key word in this job title is "science," with the main goals being to extract meaning from data and to produce data products. It employs techniques and theories drawn from many fields within the broad areas of mathematics, statistics, and information technology, including signal processing, pobability models, machine learning, statistical learning, computer programming, data engineering, pattern recognition, visualization, uncertainty modeling, data warehousing, and high performance computing.

The discipline is not restricted only to so-called big data, although an important aspect of data science is its ability to easily cope with large amounts of data. The developent of machine learning, a branch of artificial intelligence used to uncover patterns in data from which practical and usable predictive models can be developed, has enhanced the growth and importance of data science. (Fig. 6.8)

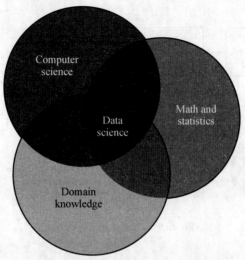

Fig. 6.8 Data science is all the rage

http://www.ibm.com/developerworks/jp/opensource/library/os-datascience/figure1.png

A practitioner of data science is known as a data scientist. Data scientists investigate complex problems through expertise in disciplines within the fields of mathematics, statistics, and computer science. These areas represent great breadth and diversity of knowledge, and a data scientist will most likely be expert in only one or at most two of these areas and merely proficient in the other(s). Therefore a data scientist typically works as part of a team whose other members have knowledge and skills which complement his or hers.

Data scientists use the ability to find and interpret rich data sources, manage large amounts of data despite hardware, software, and bandwidth constraints, merge data sources, ensure consistency of datasets create visualizations to aid in understanding data, build mathematical models using the data, present and communicate the data insights/findings to specialists and scientists in their team and if required to a non-expert audience.

Data science techniques affect research in many domains, including the biological sciences, medical informatics, health care, social sciences and the humanities. It heavily influences economics, business and finance. From the business perspective, data science is an integral part of competitive intelligence, a newly emerging field that encompasses a number of activities, such as data mining and data analysis. (Fig. 6.9)

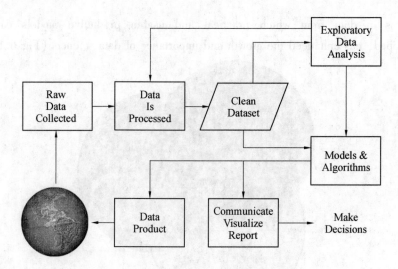

Fig. 6. 9 Data science process

6.3 Big Data

We are in a flood of data today. Statistics show that daily, we create around 2.5 Exabyte's of data that is 90% of the total world's data has been created in the last two years, and it is growing exponentially. Just to have an idea of the amount of data being generated, one Exabyte's (EB) equals 10^{18} bytes, meaning 10^9 GB.

6.3.1 What is Big Data?

The term "Big Data" was first introduced to the computing world by Roger Magoulas from O'Reilly media in 2005 in order to define a great amount of data that traditional data management techniques cannot manage and process due to the complexity and size of this data.

Big Data is the large amounts of data that is collected with time and is difficult to analyze using the traditional database system tools. This data comes from everywhere: posts from social media sites, digital videos and pictures, sensors used to gather climate information, cell phone GPS signals, and online purchase transaction records, to name a few.

Big Data is defined by its size, comprising a large, complex and independent collection of data sets, each with the potential to interact. In addition, an important aspect of Big Data is the fact that it cannot be handled with standard data management techniques due to the inconsistency and unpredictability of the possible combinations. (Table 6. 1)

Table 6.1 Big Data and Small Data

Category	Big Data	Small Data
Data Sources	Data generated outside the enterprise from nontraditional data sources. Include: · Social media · Sensor data · Log data · Device data · Video, Images, etc.	Traditional enterprise data. Include: · Enterprise Resource Planning transactions data · Customer Relationship Management (CRM) systems · Web transactions · Financial data e. g. general ledger data
Volume	· Terabytes(10^{12}) · Petabytes(10^{15}) · Exabytes(10^{18}) · Zettabytes(10^{21})	· Gigabytes(10^{9}) · Terabytes(10^{12})
Velocity	· Often real-time · Requires immediate response	· Batch or near real-time · Does not always require immediate response
Variety	· Structured · Unstructured · Multi-structured	· Structured · Unstructured

6.3.2 A Short History of Big Data

The story of how data became big starts many years before the current tide around big data. Already seventy years ago we encounter the first attempts to quantify the growth rate in the volume of data or what has popularly been known as the "information explosion". The following are the several phases in the history of sizing data volumes plus other "firsts" in the evolution of the idea of "big data"; we adopt most information from G. Press with minor modifications.

· 1944 Fremont Rider, Wesleyan University Librarian, publishes *The Scholar and the Future of the Research Library*. He estimates that American university libraries were doubling in size every sixteen years. Given this growth rate, Rider speculates that the Yale Library in 2040 will have "approximately 200,000,000 volumes, which will occupy over 6,000 miles of shelves... [requiring] a cataloging staff of over six thousand persons."

· 1949 Claude Shannon, known as the "Father of Information", carried out research on big storage capacity on items such as punch cards and photographic data. One of the largest items on Shannon's list was the Library of Congress, measuring over 100 trillion bits of data.

· 1961 Derek Price publishes *Science Since Bbylon*, in which he charts the growth of scientific knowledge by looking at the growth in the number of scientific journals and papers. He concludes that the number of new journals has grown exponentially rather than linearly, doubling every fifteen years and increasing by a factor of ten during every half-century. Price calls this the "law of exponential increase," explaining that "each [scientific] advance generates a new series of advances at a reasonably constant birth rate, so that the number of births is strictly proportional to the size of the population of discoveries at any given time."

· 1967 November 1967 B. A. Marron and P. A. D. de Maine publish "*Automatic Data compression*" in the Communications of the ACM, stating that "The 'information explosion' noted in recent years makes it essential that storage requirements for all information be kept to a minimum." The paper describes "a fully automatic and rapid three-part compressor which can be used with 'any' body of information to greatly reduce slow external storage requirements and to increase the rate of information transmission through a computer."

· 1971 Arthur R. Miller, author of the book "*The Assault on Privacy*", identified that "Too many information handlers seem to measure a man by the number of bits of storage capacity his dossier will occupy."

· 1975 The Ministry of Posts and Telecommunications in Japan began conducting the Information Flow Census, tracking the volume of information circulating in Japan (the idea was first suggested in a 1969 paper). The census introduces "amount of words" as the unifying unit of measurement across all media.

· 1981 The Hungarian Central Statistics Office carried out a research project that is still on-going today. This involved accounting for the country's information for industries via measuring data volume in bits.

· 1983 August 1983 Ithiel de Sola Pool publishes *Tracking the Flow of Information* in *Science*. Looking at growth trends in 17 major communications media from 1960 to 1977, and concluded that the flow of information had exponentially grown by 2.9% throughout that period due to broadcasting and media.

· 1996 Digital storage becomes more cost-effective for storing data than paper according to R. J. T. Morris and B. J. Truskowski, in *The Evolution of Storage Systems*, IBM Systems Journal, *July* 1, 2003.

· 1997 M. Cox and D. Ellsworth in their article mentions that "data sets are generally quite large, taxing the capacities of main memory, local disk, and even remote disk. We call this the problem of big data. When data sets do not fit in main memory(in core), or when they do not fit even on local disk, the most common solution is to acquire more resources." It is the first article to use the term "big data."

• 1997 M. Lesk publishes "How much information is there in the world?" he concludes that "There may be a few thousand petabytes(PB) of information."

• 2000 P. Lyman and H. R. Varian publish "*How Much Information?*" It is the first comprehensive study to quantify, in computer storage terms, the total amount of new and original information(not counting copies) created in the world annually and stored in four physical media: paper, film, optical (CDs and DVDs), and magnetic. The study finds that in 1999, the world produced about 1.5 exabytes (equal=1,500PB) of unique information, A similar study conduceted in 2003 by the same researchers found that the world produced about 5 exabytes of new information in 2002.

• 2001 D. Laney, publishes a research note titled *3D Data Management: Controlling Data Volume, Velocity, and Variety*. A decade later, the "3Vs" have become the generally-accepted three defining dimensions of big data, although the term itself does not appear in Laney's note.

• 2007 J. F. Gantz, D. Reinsel and other researchers make estimation and forecast the amount of digital data in 2006, the world created 161 exabytes of data and forecasts that between 2006 and 2010, the information added annually to the digital universe will increase more than six fold to 988 exabytes, or doubling every 18 months. According to the 2010 and 2012 releases of the same study, the amount of digital data created annually surpassed this forcast, reaching 1,227 exabytes in 2010, and growing to 2,837 exabytes in 2012.

• 2008 Bret Swanson and George Gilder estimates that U. S. IP traffic could reach one zettabyte by 2015 and that the U. S. internet of 2015 will be at least 50 times larger than it was in 2006.

2008 Cisco predicted that "IP traffic will nearly double every two years through 2012" and that it will reach half a zettabyte in 2012. The forecast held well, as Cisco's latest report (May 30,2012) estimates IP traffic in 2012 at just over half a zettabyte."

• 2009 R. E. Bohn and J. E. Short publish *How Much Information? 2009 Report on American Consumers*. The study finds that in 2008, "Americans consumed information for about 1.3 trillion hours, an average of almost 12 hours per day. Consumption totaled 3.6 Zettabytes and 10,845 trillion words, corresponding to 100,500 words and 34 gigabytes for an average person on an average day." (Fig. 6.10)

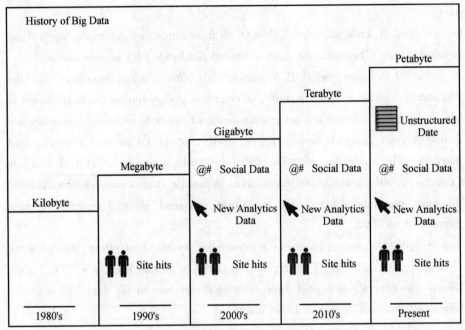

Fig. 6.10　Data science process

· After 2010

2011 Martin Hilbert and Priscilla Lopez, estimated that the world's information storage capacity grew at a compound annual growth rate of 25% per year between 1986 and 2007. They also estimated that in 1986, 99.2% of all storage capacity was analog, but by 2007, 94% of all storage capacity was digital.

2012 D. Boyd and K. Crawford publish *Critical Questions for Big Data*. They define big data as "a cultural, technological, and scholarly phenomenon that rests on the interplay of: (1) Technology: maximizing computation power and algorithmic accuracy to gather, analyze, link, and compare large data sets. (2) Analysis: drawing on large data sets to identify patterns in order to make economic, social, technical, and legal claims. (3) Mythology: the widespread belief that large data sets offer a higher form of intelligence and knowledge that can generate insights that were previously impossible, with the aura of truth, objectivity, and accuracy."

2013 Businesses are beginning to implement new in-memory technoloty such as

SAP HANA to analyze and optimize mass quantities of data. Companies are becoming ever more reliant on utilizing data as a business asset to gain competitive advantage, with big data leading the charge as arguably and make use of in order to remain relevant in today's rapidly changing market.

We find that for the volume of big data, its magnitude are PB, EB, even ZB, and for the specific features now in big data there appeared 4Vs, the first three Volume, Velocity, and Variety are the same in 2001, but the last V some says it is Veracity, most mentions Value, probably they will add some more features, see following paragraph.

For order of magnitude of data, there is in Table 6.2 listing the abbreviations of magnitude of data.

Table 6.2 Order of magnitude of data

Value	Abbreviation	Metric
$1,000$	KB	kilobytes
$1,000^2$	MB	megabyte
$1,000^3$	GB	gigabyte
$1,000^4$	TB	terabyte
$1,000^5$	PB	petabyte
$1,000^6$	EB	exabyte
$1,000^7$	ZB	zettabyte
$1,000^8$	YB	yottabyte

Words and Expressions

exabyte = 1,024**PB**, 5*EB* 相当于至今全世界人类所讲过的话语
sensor *n*. 传感器,灵敏元件
to name a few 举几个来说
storage capacity 存储容量;存储能力;储存溶量
Fremont Rider 弗里蒙特·赖特
Derek Price 德里克·普里奇
B. A. Marron 马伦
P. A. D. de Maine
R. Miller 米勒
The Ministry of Posts and Telecommunications in Japan 日本政府邮电省

The Hungarian Central Statistics Office 匈牙利中央统计局
Ithiel de Sola Pool 伊锡尔·德·索拉·普尔
R. J. T. Morris 莫里斯
B. J. Truskowski 特鲁斯科维奇
M. Cox 考克斯
D. Ellsworth 埃尔斯沃斯
M. Lesk 莱斯克
P. Lyman 莱曼
H. R. Varian 瓦里安
D. Laney 兰尼
J. F. Gantz 甘茨
D. Reinsel 莱茵泽尔
Bret Swanson 布雷特·斯旺森
George Gilder 乔治·吉尔德
Cisco 西斯科
R. E. Bohn 波恩
J. E. Short 肖特
Martin Hibert 马丁·希尔波特
Priscilla Lopez 普丽西拉·洛佩斯
D. Boyd 博伊德
K. Crawford 克劳福德
mythology *n.* （统称）神话；某文化（或社会等）的神话；虚幻的想法
aura *n.* 氛围；气氛；气质

6.3.3 Characteristics of Big Data

In general, there are three characteristics of Big Data: Volume, Velocity, and Variety. Now, someone gives other Veracity, Variability, and Value.

· **Volume**: Volume is the first and most notorious feature. In the year 2000, 800,000 petabytes of data were stored in the world. This number is expected to reach 35 zeta bytes by 2020. Twitter and Face book generate around 7 TB and 10 TB of data every day respectively. Some organizations generate data in terms of terabytes per hour. As implied by the term "Big Data", organizations are facing large volumes of data. Organizations which do not know how to mange this large data are facing a big problem. But organizations can ue analytical tools to analyze the data and make best use of it for the organization's growth.

· **Variety**: Variety refers to different types of data. With the increased use of smart devices, sensors, as well as social collaboration technologies, data has become large and complex, because it includes not only traditional relational data, but also semi-structured, and unstructured data from different sources such as web pages, search indexes, e-mail, documents, sensor data, social media forums, web log files(including click-stream data) etc. Organizations should choose an analytical tool consisting of both traditional and nontraditional methods of data analysis as traditional analytical tools are limited to structured data analysis. The organization's success is dependent on its ability to analyze both relational and non-relational data.

· **Velocity**: It refers to how quickly the data is generated and stored, and its associated rates of processing and retrieval. Now a days, organizations are dealing with data sizes in terms of hundreds of terabytes, petabytes, Exabyte's etc. and this data is getting generated at an ever-increaing rate; it has become impossible for traditional systems to handle it. So organizations must be able to analyze this large and varied data in real-time or near real time to find insights in this data. So organizations must choose better analytical tool to deal effectively with Big Data. (Fig. 6.11)

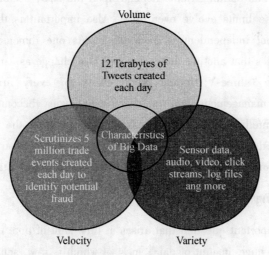

Fig. 6.11 Characteristics of Big Data

In addition to the three Vs, other dimensions of big data have also been mentioned. These include:

· **Veracity**: Refers to the degree in which a leader trusts the used information in order to take decision. So getting the right correlations in Big Data is very important for the business future.

In addition, in Gartner's IT Glossary Big Data is defined as high volume, velocity and variety information assets that demand cost-effective, innovative forms of information processing for enhanced insight and decision making.

· **Variability**(and complexity). SAS introduced Variability and Complexity as two additional dimensions of big data. Variability refers to the variation in the data flow rates. Often, big data velocity is not consistent and has periodic peaks and troughs. Complexity refers to the fact that big data are generated through a myriad of sources. This imposes a critical challenge: the need to connect, match, cleanse and transform data received from different sources.

· **Value**. Oracle introduced Value as a defining attribute of big data. Based on Oracle's definition, big data are often characterized by relatively "low value density". That is, the data received in the original form usually has a low value relative to its volume. However, a high value can be obtained by analyzing large volumes of such data.

The relativity of big data volumes discussed earlier applies to all dimensions. Thus, universal benchmarks do not exist for volume, variety, and velocity that define big data. The defining limits depend upon the size, sector, and location of the firm and these limits evolve over time. Also important is the fact that these dimensions are not independent of each other. As one dimension changes, the likelihood increases that another dimension will also change as a result.

However, a "three-V tipping point' exists for every firm beyond which traditional data management and analysis technologies become inadequate for deriving timely intelligence. The Three-V tipping point is the threshold beyond which firms start dealing with big data. The firms should then trade-off the future value expected from big data technologies against their implementation costs. "

6.3.4 Managing Big Data

The most important question that arises at this point of time is how do we store and process such huge amount of data; most of which is raw, semi structured, and may be unstructured. Big data platforms are categorized depending on how to store and process them in a scalable fault tolerant and efficient manner. Two important information management styles for handling big data are relational DBMS products enhanced for systematic workloads(often known as analytic RDBMSs, or ADBMSs) and non-relational techniques(sometimes known as NOSQL systems) for handling raw, semi structured and unstructured data. Non-relational techniques can be used to produce statistics from big data, or to preprocess big information before it is combined into a data warehouse. (Fig. 6.12)

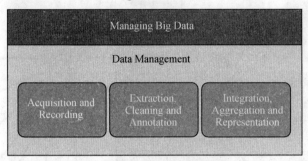

Fig. 6.12 Big Data Management

Words and Expressions

Database Management System 缩写为 DBMS,数据库管理系统,是一种操纵和管理数据库的大型软件

RDBMS 关系数据库管理系统

ADBMS 主动数据库管理系统

NOSQL 有时也称作 Not Only SQL 的缩写,是对不同于传统的关联式数据库的数据库管理系统统称

click-stream data 点击流数据

6.4 Analytics

6.4.1 Business Intelligence (BI)

Business intelligence (or BI for short) is the set of techniques and tools for the transformation of raw data into meaningful and useful information for business analysis purposes. BI technologies are capable of handling large amounts of unstructured data to help identify, develop and otherwise create new strategic business opportunities. The goal of BI is to allow for the easy interpretation of these large volumes of data. Identifying new opportunities and implementing an effective strategy based on insights can provide businesses with a competitive market advantage and long-term stability. See Fig. 6.13.

BI technologies provide historical, current and predictive views of business operations. Common functions of business intelligence technologies are reporting, online analytical processing, analytics, data mining, process mining, complex event processing, business performance management, benchmarking, text mining,

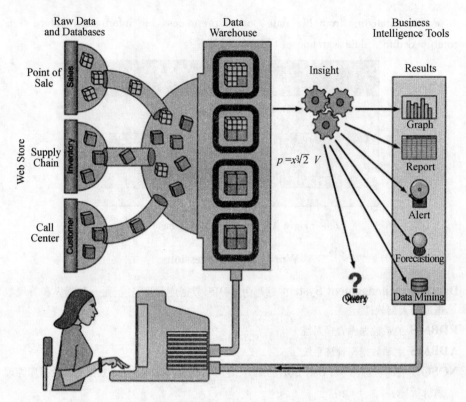

Fig. 6.13 A Basic Understanding of BI (Source: Jayanthi Ranjan)

predictive analytics and prescriptive analytics.

BI can be used to support a wide range of business decisions ranging from operational to strategic. Basic operating decisions include product positioning or pricing. Strategic business decisions include priorities, goals and directions at the broadest level. In all cases, BI is most effective when it combines data derived from the market in which a company operates (external data) with data from company sources internal to the business such as financial and operations data (internal data). When combined, external and internal data can provide a more complete picture which, in effect, creates an "intelligence" that cannot be derived by any singular set of data.

In the widest sense it can be defined as a collection of approaches for gathering, storing, analyzing and providing access to data that helps users to gain insights and make better fact-based business decisions. See Fig. 6.14.

Organizations use Business intelligence to gain data-driven insights on anything related to business performance. It is used to understand and improve performance and to cut costs and identify new business opportunities, this can include, among

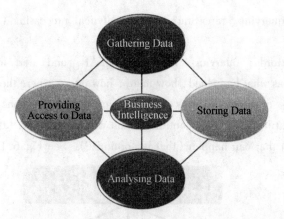

Fig. 6.14　Overview of Business Analytics

many other things:
- Analysing customer behaviours, buying patterns and sales trends.
- Measuring, tracking and predicting sales and financial performance
- Budgeting and financial planning and forecasting
- Tracking the performance of marketing campaigns
- Optimising processes and operational performance
- Improving delivery and supply chain effectiveness
- Web and e-commerce analytics
- Customer relationship management
- Risk analysis
- Strategic value driver analysis

6.4.2　Business Analytics (BA)

Business analytics (BA) refers to the skills, technologies, practices for continuous iterative exploration and investigation of past business performance to gain insight and drive business planning. Business analytics focuses on developing new insights and understanding of business performance based on data and statistical methods. In contrast, business intelligence traditionally focuses on using a consistent set of metrics to both measure past performance and guide business planning, which is also based on data and statistical methods.

Business analytics makes extensive use of statistical analysis, including explanatory and predictive modeling, and fact-based management to drive decision making. It is therefore closely related to management science. Analytics may be used as input for human decisions or may drive fully automated decisions. Business intelligence is querying, reporting, online analytical processing (OLAP), and " alerts. "

In other words, querying, reporting, OLAP, and alert tools can answer questions such as what happened, how many, how often, where the problem is, and what actions are needed. Business analytics can answer questions like why is this happening, what if these trends continue, what will happen next (that is, predict), what is the best that can happen (that is, optimize). See Fig. 6. 15.

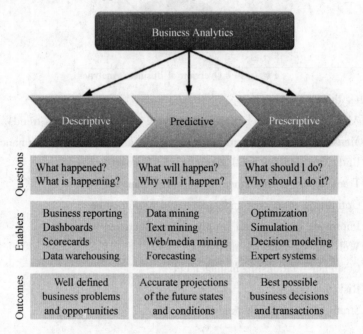

Fig. 6. 15　Three Types of Business Analytics

Business analytics is used by companies committed to data-driven decision making. BA is used to gain insights that inform business decisions and can be used to automate and optimize business processes. Data-driven companies treat their data as a corporate asset and leverage it for competitive advantage. Successful business analytics depends on data quality, skilled analysts who understand the technologies and the business and an organizational commitment to data-driven decision making.

Examples of BA uses include:

● Exploring data to find new patterns and relationships (data mining)

● Explaining why a certain result occurred (statistical analysis, quantitative analysis)

● Experimenting to test previous decisions (A/B testing, multivariate testing)

● Forecasting future results (predictive modeling, predictive analytics)

Once the business goal of the analysis is determined, an analysis methodology is selected and data is acquired to support the analysis. Data acquisition often involves extraction from one or more business systems, cleansing, and integration into a single repository such as a data warehouse or data mart.

The analysis is typically performed against a smaller sample set of data. Analytic tools range from spreadsheets with statistical functions to complex data mining and predictive modeling applications. As patterns and relationships in the data are uncovered, new questions are asked and the analytic process iterates until the business goal is met. Deployment of predictive models involves scoring data records (typically in a database) and using the scores to optimize real-time decisions within applications and business processes. BA also supports tactical decision making in response to unforeseen events, and in many cases the decision making is automated to support real-time responses.

Prescriptive analytics incorporates both structured and unstructured data, and uses a combination of advanced analytic techniques and disciplines to predict, prescribe, and adapt. Prescriptive analytics automatically synthesizes big data, multiple disciplines of mathematical sciences and computational sciences, and business rules, to make predictions and then suggests decision options to take advantage of the predictions, see Fig. 6.16.

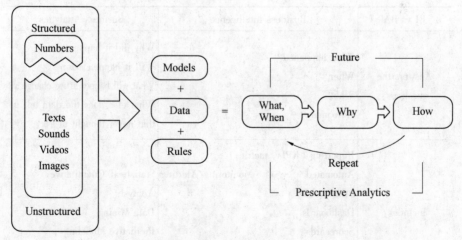

Fig. 6.16　Prescriptive Analytics

Business analytics involves tools as simple as reports and graphs, as well as some that are as sophisticated as optimization, data mining, and simulation. In practice, companies that apply analytics often follow a trajectory similar to that shown in Fig. 6.17. Organizations start with basic analytics in the lower left. As they realize the advantages of these analytic techniques, they often process to more sophisticated techniques in an effort to reap the derived competitive advantages. Predictive and prescriptive analytics are sometimes therefore referred to as advanced analytics. Not all companies reach that level of usage, but those that embrace analytics as a competitive strategy often do. See Fig. 6.17.

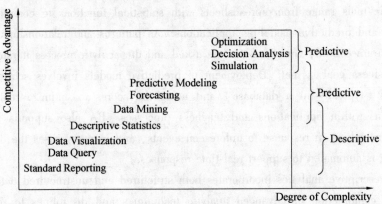

Fig. 6.17 the spectrum of business analytics

● While the terms business intelligence and business analytics are often used interchangeably, there are some key differences: see Table 6.3.

Table 6.3 Business Intelligence and Business Analytics

BI vs BA	Business Intelligence	Business Analytics
Answers the questions:	What happened? When? Who? How many?	Why did it happen? Will it happen again? What will happen if we change x? What else does the data tell us that never thought to ask?
Includes:	Reporting (KPIs, metrics) Automated Monitoring/Alerting (thresholds) Dashboards Scorecards OLAP (Cubes, Slice & Dice, Drilling) Ad hoc query	Statistical/Quantitative Analysis Data Mining Predictive Modeling Multivariate Testing

6.4.3 Analytics

According to the Merriam-Webster dictionary, analytics is "the method of logical analytics." This is a very broad definition of analytics, without an explicitly stated end-goal. A view of analytics within the business community is that analytics describes a process (a method or a analysis) that transforms (hopefully, logically) raw data into actionable knowledge in order to guide strategic decision-making. Along this line, technology research guru Gartner defines analytics as methods that "leverage data in a particular functional process (or application) to enable context-specific insight that is actionable." See Fig. 6.18.

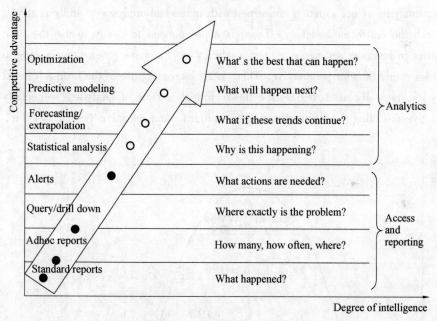

Fig. 6.18 Business intelligence and analytics

Analytics is the discovery and communication of meaningful patterns in data. Especially valuable in areas rich with recorded information, analytics relies on the simultaneous application of statistics, computer programming and operations research to quantify performance. Analytics often favors data visualization to communicate insight. Therefore, analytics is guide decision making by discovering patterns in data using statistics, programming, and operations research.

Firms may commonly apply analytics to business data, to describe, predict, and improve business performance. Specifically, arenas within analytics include predictive analytics, enterprise decision management, retail analytics, store assortment and stock-keeping unit optimization, marketing optimization and marketing mix modeling, web analytics, sales force sizing and optimization, price and promotion modeling, predictive science, credit risk analysis, and fraud analytics. Since analytics can require extensive computation, the algorithms and software used for analytics harness the most current methods in computer science, statistics, and mathematics.

Analytics is amulti-dimensional discipline. There is extensive use of mathematics and statistics, the use of descriptive techniques and predictive models to gain valuable knowledge from data—data analysis. The insights from data are used to recommend action or to guide decision making rooted in business context. Thus, analytics is not so much concerned with individual analyses or analysis steps, but with the entire methodology. There is a pronounced tendency to use the term analytics in business settings e. g. text analytics vs. the more generic text mining to emphasize this broader perspective. There is an increasing use of the term advanced analytics, typically used to describe the technical aspects of analytics, especially predictive modeling, machine learning techniques, and neural networks. See Fig. 6.19.

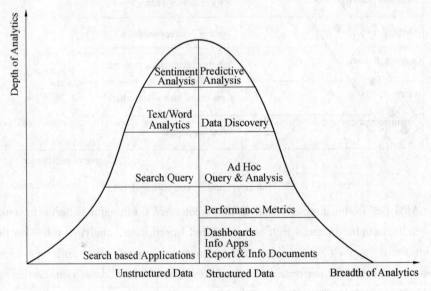

Fig. 6.19 Depth of Analytics and Breadth of Analytics

6.4.4 Analytics Process Model

The following Fig. 6.20 gives a high-level overview of the analytics process model. As a first step, a thorough definition of the business problem to be solved with analytics is needed. Next, all source data need to be identified that could be of potential interest. This is a very important step, as data is the key ingredient to any analytical exercise and selection of data will have a deterministic impact on the analytical models that will be built in a subsequent step. All data will then be gathered in a staging area, which could be, for example, a data mart or data warehouse.

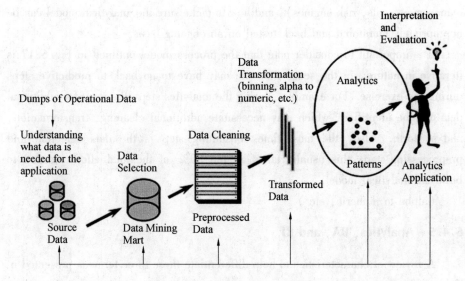

Fig. 6.20 Analytics process model

Some basic exploratory analysis can be considered here using, for example, online analytical process (OLAP) facilities for multidimensional data analysis (e.g., roll-up, drill down, slicing and dicing). This will be followed by a data cleaning step to get rid of all inconsistencies, such as missing value, outliers, and duplicate data. Additional transformations may also be considered, such as binning, alphanumeric to numeric coding, geographical aggregation, and so forth. In the analytics step, an analytical model will be estimated on the preprocesses and transformed data. Differential types of analytics can be considered here (e.g., to do churn prediction, fraud detection, customer segmentation, market basket analytics).

Finally, once the model has been built, it will be interpreted and evaluated by the business experts. Usually, many trivial patterns will be detected by the model. For example, in a market basket analysis setting, one many find that spaghetti and spaghetti sauce are often purchased together. These patterns are interesting because they provide some validation of model. But of course, the key issue here is to find the unexpected yet interesting and actionable patterns (sometimes also referred to as knowledge diamonds) that can provide added value in the business setting. Once the analytical model has been appropriately validated and approved, it can be put into production as an analytics application (e. g., decision support system, scoring engine). It is important to consider here how to represent the model output in a user-friendly way, how to integrate it with other applications (e. g. campaign management tools, risk engines), and how to make sure the analytical model can be appropriately monitored and back tested on an ongoing basis.

It is important to consider note that the process model outlined in Fig. 6. 17 is iterative in nature, in the sense that one may have to go back to predictive steps during the exercise. For example, during the analytics step, the need for additional data may be identified, which may necessitate additional cleaning, transformation, and so forth. Also, the most time consuming step is the data selection and preprocessing step; this usually takes around 80% of the total efforts needed to build an analytical model.

(alpha to numeric, etc)

6.4.5 Analytics, BA, and BI

A review of characteristics to help differentiate these three terms is presented in Table 6.4.

Table 6.4 Characteristics of analytics, business analytics, and business inelligence

Characteristics	Analytics	Business Analytics	Business Intelligence
Business performance planning role	What is happening, and what will be happening?	What is happening now, what will be happening, and what is the best strategy to deal with it?	What is happening now, and what have we done in the past to deal with it?
Use of descriptive analytics as a major component of analysis	Yes	Yes	Yes

Table 6.4 (Continued)

Characteristics	Analytics	Business Analytics	Business Intelligence
Use of predictive analytics as a major component of analysis	Yes	Yes	No (only historically)
Use of prescriptive analytics as a major component of analysis	Yes	Yes	No (only historically)
Use of all three in combination	No	Yes	No
Business focus	Maybe	Yes	Yes
Focus of storing and maintaining data	No	No	Yes
Required focus of improving business value and performance	No	Yes	Yes

6.4.6 Analytics Applications

To summarize, the relevance, importance, and impact of analytics are now bigger than ever before and, given that more and more data are being collected and that there is strategic value in know what is hidden in data, analytics will continue to grow. Without claiming to be exhaustive, table 6.5 presents some examples of how analytics is applied in various settings

Table 6.5 Example analytics applications

Marketing	Risk Management	Government	Web	Logistics	other
Response modeling	Credit modeling	Tax avoidance	Web analytics	Demand forecasting	Text analytics
Net lift modeling	Market risk modeling	Social security fraud	Social media analytics	Supply chain analytics	Business Process analytics
Retention modeling	Operational Risk modeling	Money laundering	Multivariate testing		
Market basket analytics	Fraud detection	Terrorism detection			

Table 6.5 (Continued)

Marketing	Risk Management	Government	Web	Logistics	other
Recommender systems					
Customer segmentation					

Words and Expressions

data warehousing 数据仓库；数据仓库系统
database 数据库
and otherwise 等等，及其他
query *vt.* 问，询问；怀疑；表示疑虑
  n. 问题；疑问；询问；质问。*query language*【计】查询语言。*Ad hoc query*【计】即席查询，数据库应用最普遍的一种查询，利用数据仓库技术，让用户随时可以面对数据库，获取所希望的数据。
alert *vt.* 向……报警；使警觉；使警惕；使戒备 *n.* 警报；警惕；警戒；戒备；预警
priority *n.* 优先；重点；优先权；优先事项
online analytical process（OLAP） 在线分析处理；联机分析处理；联机分析处理系统，意指由数据库所联结出来的在线分析处理程序。OLAP 概念最早是由关系数据库之父 E. F. Codd 于 1993 年提出的，他同时提出了关于 OLAP 的 12 条准则。OLAP 与数据挖掘（Data Mining）两者是截然不同的，其差异在于数据挖掘用在产生假设，OLAP 则用于查证假设。简单来说，OLAP 是由使用者所主导，使用者先有一些假设，然后利用 OLAP 来查证假设是否成立；而数据挖掘则是用来帮助使用者产生假设。所以，在使用 OLAP 或其他 Query 的工具时，使用者是自己在做探索（exploration），但数据挖掘是用工具在帮助做探索。OLAP 的基本多维分析操作有钻取（roll up 与 drill down）、切片（slice）与切块（dice）、以及旋转（pivot，drill across，drill through）等。钻取是改变维的层次，变换分析的粒度。数据立方体（Data Cube），是数据立方体只是多维模型的一种形象说法。

当今，数据处理大致可分成两大类：联机事务处理（或称为在线事务处理、联机事务处理系统）OLTP（online transaction processing）和联机分析处理 OLAP（online analytical processing）。这两者的差异如下表：

OLAP 与 OLTP 的差异比较

数据处理类型	OLTP	OLAP
面向对象	业务开发人员	分析决策人员
功能实现	日常事物处理	面向分析决策
数据模型	关系模型	多维模型
数据量	几条或几十条记录	成百上千记录
操作类型	查询、插入、更新、删除	查询为主

data-driven 数据驱动的

cut *vt.* 切;割;剪切,减少,消减。cut cost 减少成本

track *n.* 足迹;踪迹;跟踪。【铁】轨道,线路。【体】跑道
  vt. 跟踪;追踪;追随(潮流、趋势)

among many other things 除了别的以外,其中(包括)

marketing campaigns 推销运动;市场推广活动;营销活动

strategic cost driver analysis 战略成本动因分析

iterative *adj.* 重复的,反反复复的。【数】迭代(的),逐次迭代的

commit *vt.* 犯罪;忠于;承诺

inform *vt.* 通知;告知;报告;使了解,使熟悉 (*of*)

corporate asset 公司资产

leverage *n.* 杠杆,杠杆作用,影响力,杠杆比率
  vt. 使举债经营;为 融资;充分利用

cleansing *n.* 清洗;清洁;净化;(家禽等的)胎衣

data mart 数据集市;资料超市

meet *vt.* 满足;迎接;遇见;相遇,*n.* 运动会;体育比赛;猎狐运动

repository *n.* 仓库;存放处;贮藏室

tactical *adj.* 战术(性)的;有策略的,手段高明的;方式方法上的

tactical decision making 战术决策

prescribe *vt.* 规定;指定,*vi.* 适合;改造

take advantage of 占便宜;利用;欺骗

business intelligence(**BI**) 商务智能(或商业智能)意指用来帮助企业更好地利用数据提高决策质量的技术集合,是从大量的数据中抽取信息与知识的过程。商业智能概念于 1996 年最早由加特纳集团(Gartner Group)提出,加特纳集团将商业智能定义为:商业智能描述了一系列的概念和方法,通过应用基于事实的支持系统来辅助商业决策的制定。商业智能技术提供使企业迅速分析数据的技术和方法,包括收集、管理和分析数据,将这些数据转化为有用的信息,然后分发到企业各处。

business analytics (BA) 直译是商业分析学(或商业分析方法)。BI 和 BA 两者都是方法,概括地讲,针对的目标是企业决策支持方面,二者都与数据有关,不同之处在于二者的分析视角、切入点以及着重点不一样。具体说来,可把"商业智能"理解为将数据转化为知识的分析工具,而把"商业分析学"理解为基于知识的决策方法。
在实际应用中,二者的范围是交叠和关联的。"商业智能"是从技术层面入手的数据分析方法,是对企业数据进行整理、分析和展示,以帮助企业做出智能化决策的一整套方法和工具。"商业分析"则是从企业的业务决策层面入手的信息应用方法,包括对企业业务进行分析、建模、模拟计算和预测。BI 重在数据分析,BA 重在信息应用;BI 着重于从数据中发现已经发生了什么,从而提醒决策者采取行动,BA 着重于从信息中洞察为什么发生并预测将来的趋势,从而计划下一步的行动。可以看出,BI 和 BA 本质的区别在于对业务领

域的关注和支持程度不同,BA 是建立在 BI 基础之上的高端分析拓展,而且更侧重与业务领域的应用。

reap *vt.* 获得,取得

embrace *vt.* 接受,采纳

KPIs 关键绩效指标;关键性能指标;关键业绩指标

analytics 数据分析学(或分析学)是利用数学、运筹学、统计学及计算机技术来探寻数据之间的关系,提取洞察力来提高商业价值,改进决策制定和理解社会关系的一种方法。

descriptive analysis 描述性分析,将信息的主要特征总结出来

predictive analytics 预测性分析,利用建模,机器学习,数据挖掘等技术,通过分析历史数据对未来或特定假设进行预测

prescriptive analytics 指导性分析,通过模拟和最优化(**optimazion**)找到最理想决策

prescriptive *adj.* 指定的;规定的;规范的;约定俗成的

spectrum *n.* 谱;光谱;频谱;波谱

cube *n.* 立方体;立方形;立方形的东西(尤指食物);三次幂
  vt. 使成立方体;将切成小方块;求……的立方

roll-up 向上钻取,是在某一维上将低层次的细节数据概括到高层次的汇总数据,或者减少维数。

drill down 向下钻取,与 **roll-up** 相反,它从汇总数据深入到细节数据进行观察或增加新维。

slicing 数据切片

dicing 数据切块

assortment *n.* 分类;各种各样

harness *n.* 马具;挽具;保护带,*vt.* 利用(或控制) 以产生动力,利用;<喻>驾驭,抑制

ingredient *n.* 成分;要素;组成部分;成分

get rid of 除去;除掉;扔掉;摆脱

duplicate data 复制数据;数据复制;将原始数据列复制

churn prediction 客户流失预测

fraud detection 欺诈甄别;发现欺诈;侦测诈欺行为;检测欺诈

customer segmentation 顾客细分;客户细分;客户区分;客户群体划分

market basket analytics 市场购物篮分析,是指通过这些购物篮子(购物篮意指超级市场内供顾客购物时使用的装商品篮子,当顾客付款时这些购物篮内的商品被营业人员通过收款机——登记结算并记录)所显示的信息来研究顾客的购买行为。其主要的目的在于找出什么样的东西应该放在一起。借由顾客的购买行为来了解是什么样的顾客以及这些顾客为什么买这些产品,找出相关的联想(association)规则,企业借由这些规则的挖掘获得利益与建立竞争优势。

stock-keeping unit 最小存货单位,或库存量单位。在连锁零售门店中,有时称单品为一个 SKU(简称 SKU),即保存库存控制的最小可用单位。例如,纺织品中 SKU 通常表示规

格、颜色、款式。

retention *n.* 保留；记忆力，保持力；滞留，扣留

machine learning 机器学习，是一门多领域交叉学科，涉及概率论、统计学、逼近论、凸分析、算法复杂度理论等多门学科，它是人工智能的核心，是使计算机具有智能的根本途径，其应用遍及人工智能的各个领域，主要使用归纳、综合而不是演绎。

neural network 神经网络

response modeling 响应建模

net lift modeling 净提升建模。这是 SAS 编程中经常用到一种方法。

terrorism detection 检测恐怖主义

money laundering 洗钱；洗黑钱；洗黑钱活动

tax avoidance 合法避税；逃税；避税行为

logistics *n.* 后勤学；现代物流；物流学；物流

heap *n.* 大量；(凌乱的)一堆，许多；破旧汽车

untapped *adj.* 未利用的；未开发的；蕴藏的

initiative *adj.* 创始的，*n.* 倡议；主动性；积极性；主动权

web server log 【计】网站伺服器的纪录档，web 服务器日志

unstructured data 非结构化数据

structured data 结构化数据

massively parallel 【计】大规模并行的，巨量并行的

massively parallel processing 【计】大规模并行处理。是多个处理器处理同一程序的不同部分时该程序的协调过程，工作的各处理器运用自身的操作系统和内存。

SQL (Structured Query Language) 【计】结构化查询语言，是一种特殊目的的编程语言，是一种数据库查询和程序设计语言，用于存取数据以及查询、更新和管理关系数据库系统。

NoSQL database 【计】泛指非关系型的数据库，NoSQL = Not Only SQL，意思是不仅仅是 SQL。NoSQL 并没有一个明确的范围和定义。

Hadoop 【计】是一个分布式系统基础架构，由 Apache 基金会开发，Hadoop 是一种能对大量数据进行分布式处理的软件框架。

MapReduce 【计】分布式计算系统；并行编程技术；分布式编程环境

streaming *n.* 流出，流动

vacuum *n.* 真空；空白；空虚。*in a vacuum* 在封闭状态中，与外界隔绝。

diverse *adj.* 各种各样的，形形色色的

vendor *n.* 供应商；小贩

6.5 Big Data Analytics

Analytics is, and always has been, about discovering insights that lead to better business decisions. The range of technologies and use cases that inhabit this area is wide: statistical analysis, data and process mining, predictive analytics and modeling, and complex event processing.

What is now referred to as big data has pushed analytics beyond the capabilities of traditional solution. "Big analytics" has organizations diving into large heaps of data that previously was not available or usable.

The primary goal of big data analytics is help companies make better business decisions by enabling data scientist and other users to analyze huge volumes of transaction data as well as other data sources that may be left untapped by conventional business intelligence (BI) programs. These other data sources may include Web server logs and Internet clickstream data, social media activity reports, mobile-phone call detail records and information captured by sensors. Some people exclusively associate big data and big data analytics with unstructured data of that sort, but consulting firms like Gartner Inc. and Forrester Research Inc. also consider transactions and other structured data to be valid forms of big data. See Fig. 6.21.

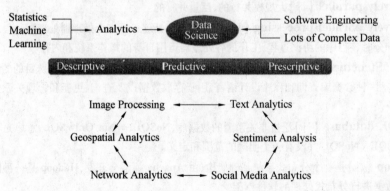

Fig. 6.21 Overview of big data analytics

Big data analytics can be done with the software tolls commonly used as part of advanced analytics disciplines such as predictive analytics and data mining. But the unstructured data sources used for big data analytics may not fit in traditional data warehouse. Furthermore, traditional data warehouse may not be able to handle the processing demands posed by big data. As a result, a new class of big data technology has emerged and is being used in many big data analytics environments. The technologies associated with big data analytics include NoSQL database,

Hadoop and MapReduce. These technologies form the core of an open source software framework that supports the processing of large data sets across clustered systems. See Fig. 6.22.

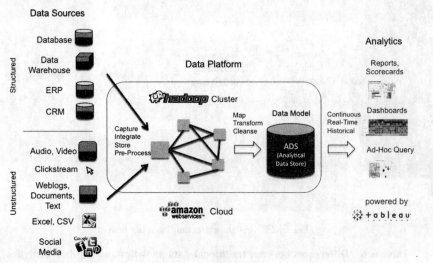

Fig. 6.22 Big data analytics

Potential pitfalls that can trip up organizations on big data initiatives include a lack of internal analytics skills and the high cost of hiring experienced analytics professional, plus challenges in integrating Hadoop systems and data warehouses, although vendors are starting to offer software connectors between those technologies. See Fig. 6.23.

Given the characteristics of big data's datasets, the methods used to analyze these datasets are different from traditional methods. One prominent difference is data structure. While traditional structured data is always used after it has been collected and organized neatly, big data takes any form of data structure and it can be at rest or in motion. Another big difference is the analysis sample.

In traditional data analysis, research question(s) are posed before analysis, and then data is collected to seek answers for those pre-designed questions. A sample is taken from a known population to conduct the analysis in a relational database environment. Big data analytics, however, works with a framework such as Hadoop that performs data analysis of entire known or unknown populations. Further, big data analytics handle data that is streaming and non-stop, offering opportunities to seek answers for questions either already posed or newly raised during the process-questions we may otherwise not be able to ask. Table 6.6 below summarizes the major differences between the two.

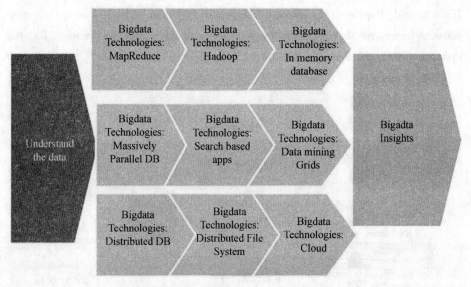

Fig. 6.23 Insight extraction from big data

Table 6.6 Differences between traditional data analytics and big data analytics

	Traditional Data Analytics	Big Data Analytics
Data features	· Environment suitable for structured data only · Usual unit of volume is megabyte/gigabyte	· Environment suitable for any data structured, semi −/multi −/unstructured data from multiple sources · Usual unit of volume is terabyte or petabyte
Population of analysis and questions to ask	· Sample data analysis of known populations · Answering questions we know that we don't know	· Non−sample data analysis of unknown populations · Answering questions we don't know we don't know
Technologies	· SQL approach to data · Relational database (data to function model) · No open source · Batch processing (offline) of "historical," static data	· Massively parallel processing and NoSQL approach to data, but almost SQL compliant · Hadoop framework (function to data model) · Open source · Stream processing (online) of (near) real time, live data
Research & Development	· Individual manufacturer/developer can work independently	· Nobody works alone; all related parties must work together

(Source: from Jean Yan, 2013)

Big data are worthless in a vacuum. Its potential value is unlocked only when leveraged to drive decision making. To enable such evidence-based decision making, organizations need efficient processes to turn high volumes of fast-moving and diverse data into meaningful insights. The overall process of extracting insights from big data can be broken down into five stages, shown in Fig. 6.24. These five stages form the two main sub-processes: data management and analytics. Data management involves processes and supporting technologies to acquire and store data and to prepare and retrieve it for analysis. Analytics, on the other hand, refers to techniques used to analyze and acquire intelligence from big data. Thus, big data analytics can be viewed as a sub-process in the overall process of 'insight extraction' from big data.

In the following sections, we briefly review big data analytical techniques for structured and unstructured data. Given the breadth of the techniques, an exhaustive list of techniques is beyond the scope of a single paper. Thus, the following techniques represent a relevant subset of the tools available for big data analytics.

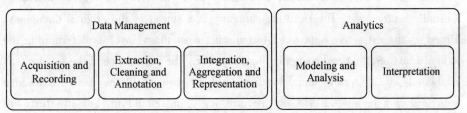

Fig. 6.24 Processes for extracting insights from big data

6.5.1 Text Analytics

Text analytics (text mining) refers to techniques that extract information from textual data. Socail network feeds, emails, blogs, online forums, survey responses, corporate documents, news, and call center logs are examples of textual data held by organizations.

Text analytics involve statistical analysis, computational linguistics, and machine learning. Text analytics enable businesses to convert large volums of human generated text into meaningful summaries, which support evidence-based decision-making. For instance, text analytics can be used to predict stock market based on information extracted from financial news. We present a brief review of text analytics methods below.

Information extraction(IE) techniques extract structured data from unstructured text. For example, IE algorithms can extract structured information such as drug name, dosage, and frequency from medical prescriptions. Two sub-tasks in IE are Entity Recognition(ER) and Relation Extraction(RE). ER finds names in text and classifies them into predefined categories such as person, data, location, and organization. RE finds and extracts semantic relationships between entities (e. g. persons, organizations, drugs, genes, etc.) in the text. For example, given the sentence "Steve Jobs co-founded Apple Inc. in 1976", an RE system can extract relations such as Founder Of[Steve Jobs, Apple Inc.] or FoundedIn[Apple Inc., 1976].

Text summarization techniques automatically produce a succinct summary of a single or multiple documents. The resulting summary conveys the key information in the original text (s). Applications include scientific and news articles, advertisements, emails, and blogs. Broadly speaking, summarization follows two approaches: the extractive approach and the abstractive approach.

In extractive summarization, a summary is created from the original text units (usually sentences). The resulting summary is a subset of the original document. Based on the extractive approach, formulating a summary involves determining the salient units of a text and stringing them together. The importance of the text units is evaluated by analyzing their location and frequency in the text. Extractive summarization techniques do not require an 'understanding' of the text. In contrast, abstractive summarization techniques involve extracting semantic information from the text. The summaries contain text units that are not necessarily present in the original text. In order to parse the original text and generate the summary, abstractive summarization incorporates advanced Natural Language Processing(NLP) techniques. As a result, abstractive systems tend to generate more coherent summaries than the extractive systems do. However, extractive systems are easier to adopt, especially for big data.

Question answering(QA) techniques provide answers to questions posed in natural language. Apple's Siri and IBM's Watson are examples of commercial QA systems. These systems have been implemented in healthcare, finance, marketing, and education.

Similar to abstractive summarization, QA systems rely on complex NLP techniques. QA techniques are further classified into three categories: the information retrieval(IR)-based approach, the knowledge-based approach, and the hybrid approach. IR-based QA systems often have three sub-components. First is the question processing, used to determine details, such as the question type, question focus, and the answer type, which are used to create a query. Second is document processing which is used to retrieve relevant pre-written passages from a set of existing documents using the query formulated in question processing. Third is answer processing, used to extract candidate answers from the output of the previous component, rank them, and return the highest-ranked candidate as the output of the QA system. Knowledge-based QA systems generate a semantic description of the question, which is then used to query structured resources. The Knowledge-based QA systems are particularly useful for restricted domains, such as tourism, medicine, and transportation, where large volumes of pre-written documents do not exist. Such domains lack data redundancy, which is required for IR-based QA systems. Apple's Siri is an example of a QA system that exploits the knowledge-based approach. In hybrid QA systems, like IBM's Watson, while the question is semantically analyzed, candidate answers are generated using the IR methods.

Sentiment analysis (opinion mining) techniques analyze opinionated text, which contains people's opinions toward entities such as products, organizations, individuals, and events. Businesses are increasingly capturing more data about their customers' sentiments that has led to the proliferation of sentiment analysis. Marketing, finance, and the political and social sciences are the major application areas of sentiment analysis.

Sentiment analysis techniques are further divided into three subgroups, namely document-level, sentence-level, and aspect-based. Document-level techniques determine whether the whole document expresses a negative or a positive sentiment. The assumption is that the document contains sentiments about a single entity. While certain techniques categorize a document into two classes negative and positive, others incorporate more sentiment classes (like the Amazon's five-star system). Sentence-level techniques attempt to determine the polarity of a single sentiment about a known entity expressed in a single sentence.

Sentence-level techniques must first distinguish subjective sentences from objective ones. Hence, sentence-level techniques tend to be more complex compared to document-level techniques. (Fig. 6.25)

Aspect-based techniques recognize all sentiments within a document and identify the aspects of the entity to which each sentiment refers. For instance, customer product reviews usually contain opinions about different aspects (or

374 English in Statistics

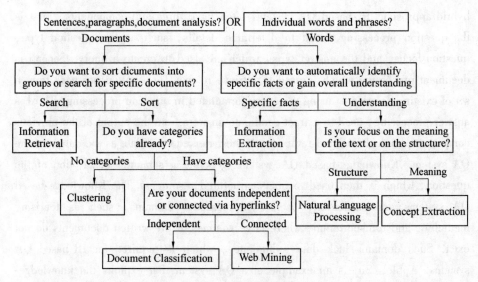

Fig. 6.25 Text Aanalytics Application

features) of a product. Using aspect-based techniques, the vendor can obtain valuable information about different features of the product that would be missed if the sentiment is only classified in terms of polarity.

6.5.2 Audio Analytics

Audio analytics analyze and extract information from unstructured audio data. When applied to human spoken language, audio analytics is also referred to as speech analytics. Since these techniques have mostly been applied to spoken audio, the terms audio analytics and speech analytics are often used interchangeably.

Currently, customer call centers and healthcare are the primary application areas of auio analytics. Call centers use audio analytics for efficient analysis of thousands or even millions of hours of recorded calls. These techniques help improve customer experience, evaluate agent performance, enhance sales turnover rates, monitor compliance with different policies (e. g. , privacy and security policies), gain insight into customer behavior, and identify product or service issues, among many other tasks. Audio analytics systems can be designed to analyze a live call, formulate cross/up-selling recommendations based on the customer's past and present interactions, and provide feedback to agents in real time. In addition, automated call centers use the Interactive Voice Response (IVR) platforms to identify and handle frustrated callers.

In healthcare, audio analytics support diagnosis and treatment of certain medical conditions that affect the patient's communication patterns (e. g., depression, schizophrenia, and cancer). Also, audio analytics can help analyze an infant's cries, which contain information about the infant's health and emotional status. The vast amount of data recorded through speech-driven clinical documentation systems is another driver for the adoption of audio analytics in healthcare.

Speech analytics follows two common technological approaches: the transcript-based approach (widely known as large-vocabulary continuous speech recognition, LVCSN) and the phonetic-based approach. These are explained below.

· LVCSR systems follow a two-phase process: indexing and searching. In the first phase, they attempt to transcribe the speech content of the audio. This is performed using automatic speech recognition (ASR) algorithms that match sounds to words. The words are identified based on a predefined dictionary. If the system fails to find the exact word in the dictionary, it returns the most similar one. The output of the system is a searchable index file that contains information about the sequence of the words spoken in the speech. In the second phase, standard text-based methods are used to find the search term in the index file.

· Phonetic-based systems work with sounds or phonemes. Phonemes are the perceptually distinct units of sound in a specified language that distinguish one word from another (e. g., the phonemes/k/and/b/differentiate the meanings of "cat" and "bat"). Phonetic-based systems also consist of two phases: phonetic indexing and searching. In the first phase, the system translates the input speech into a sequence of phonemes. This is in contrast to LVCSR systems where the speech is converted into a sequence of words. In the second phase, the system searches the output of the first phase for the phonetic representation of the search terms.

Words and Expressions

document processing 文件处理；文书处理；文献自动处理

retrieve vt. 重新得到；领会；【计算机】检索

sentiment analysis 情感分析；情绪分析；感情分析

polarity n. 【物】(分)极性，磁性引力；(光的)偏极；极体；【数】配极(变换)；【生】(茎与根的)反向性，极性。(性格的)正反对。

Natural Language Processing(NLP) 自然语言处理，是人工智能和语言学领域的分支学科。在这些领域中，探讨如何处理及运用自然语言；自然语言认知则是指让电脑"懂"人类的语言。

Information Extraction(IE) 信息抽取
Entity Recognition(ER) 实体识别
Relation Extraction(RE) 关系抽取
audio analytics 音频分析
speech analytics 语音分析
Interactive Voice Response(IVR) 交互式语音应答;交谈式语音回复系统;自动语音应答产品
transcript-based approach 基于记录的方法
large-vocabulary continuous speech recognition,**LVCSR** 大词汇量连续语音识别系统;大词汇量连续语音的识别;大词汇量连续语音识别
automatic speech recognition(ASR) 自动语音识别服务;自动声音识别;语音辨识服务
phonetic *adj.* 语音的,语言学的;*n.* [语]音位,语音
phonetic-based systems 基于语音的系统
video content analysis(VCA) 视频内容分析
closed-circuit television(CCTV) 闭路电视
surveillance *n.* 监督;监控;监测
feed *vt.* 喂养,维持,增长,满足。*n.* 喂养,饲养;饲料;[口语]饭食,吃饭;传送,送料,加水
salient *adj.* 显著的,突出的;*n.* 凸角,突出部分
parse *vt.* 从语法上分析(句子)。【计】对进行语法分析。*n.*【计】语法分析

6.5.3 Video Analytics

Video analytics, also known as video content analysis (VCA), involves a variety of techniques to monitor, analyze, and extract meaningful information from video streams. Although video analytics is still in its infancy compared to other types of data mining, various techniques have already been developed for processing real-time as well as pre-recorded videos.

The increasing prevalence of closed-circuit television (CCTV) cameras and the booming popularity of video-sharing websites are the two leading contributors to the growth of computerized video analysis. A key challenge, however, is the sheer size of video data. To put this into perspective, one second of a high-definition video, in terms of size, is equivalent to over 2,000 pages of text.

Now consider that 100 hours of video are uploaded to YouTube every minute (YouTube Statistics, n. d.). Big data technologies turn this challenge into opportunity. Obviating the need for cost-intensive and risk-prone manual processing, big data technologies can be leveraged to automatically sift through and draw intelligence from thousands of hours of video. As a result, the big data technology is the third factor that has contributed to the development of video analytics. The primary application of video analytics in recent years has been in automated security and surveillance systems. In addition to their high cost, labor-based surveillance systems tend to be less effective than automatic systems (e. g. Hakeem et al., 2012 report that security personnel cannot remain focused on surveillance tasks for more than 20 minutes). Video analytics can efficiently and effectively perform surveillance functions such as detecting breaches of restricted zones, identifying objects removed or left unattended, detecting loitering in a specific area, recognizing suspicious activities, and detecting camera tampering, to name a few. Upon detection of a threat, the surveillance system may notify security personnel in real time or trigger an automatic action (e. g. sound alarm, lock doors, or turn on lights).

The data generated by CCTV cameras in retail outlets can be extracted for business intelligence. Marketing and operations management are the primary application areas. For instance, smart algorithms can collect demographic information about customers, such as age, gender, and ethnicity. Similarly, retailers can count the number of customers, measure the time they stay in the store, detect their movement patterns, measure their dwell time in different areas, and monitor queues in real time. Valuable insights can be obtained by correlating this information with customer demographics to drive decisions for product placement, price, assortment optimization, promotion design, cross-selling, layout optimization, and staffing.

Another potential application of video analytics in retail lies in the study of buying behavior of groups. Among family members who shop together, only one interacts with the store at the cash register, causing the traditional systems to miss data on buying patterns of other members. Video analytics can help retailers address this missed opportunity by providing information about the size of the group, the group's demographics, and the individual members' buying behavior.

Automatic video indexing and retrieval constitutes another domain of video analytics applications. The widespread emergence of online and offline videos has highlighted the need to index multimedia content for easy search and retrieval. The indexing of a video can be performed based on different levels of information available in a video including the metadata, the soundtrack, the transcripts, and the visual content of the video. In the metadata-based approach, relational database management systems (RDBMS) are used for video search and retrieval. Audio analytics and text analytics techniques can be applied to index a video based on the associated soundtracks and transcripts, respectively.

In terms of the system architecture, there exist two approaches to video analytics, namely server-based and edge-based:

· Server-based architecture. In this configuration, the video captured through each camera is routed back to a centralized and dedicated server that performs the video analytics. Due to bandwidth limits, the video generated by the source is usually compressed by reducing the frame rates and/or the image resolution. The resulting loss of information can affect the accuracy of the analysis. However, the server-based approach provides econmies of scale and facilitates easier maintenance.

· Edge-based architecture. In this approach, analytics are applied at the 'edge' of the system. That is, the video analytics is performed locally and on the raw data captured by the camera. As a result, the entire content of the video stream is available for the analysis, enabling a more effective content analysis. Edge-based systems, however, are more costly to maintain and have a lower processing power compared to the server-based systems.

Words and Expressions

infancy n. 婴儿期；初期；幼稚阶段
unattended adj. 没有出席的,无人陪伴的
loiter vi. 闲逛,游荡；徘徊
to name a few 举几个例子,仅举数例
metadata n. 【计】元数据(描述数据的数据,主要是描述数据属性的信息,用来支持如指示存储位置、历史数据、资源查找、文件记录等功能)
soundtrack n. 电影配乐；电影原声带
promotion design 推广宣传设计
layout optimization 布局优化；优化布局；布置优化
relational database management systems(RDBMS) 关系数据库管理系统
server-based 基于服务器；基于服务器网络；基于服务器的网络
edge-based 以边缘为基础；边缘基础

6.5.4 Social Media Analytics

Social media analytics refer to the analysis of structured and unstructured data from social media channels. Social media is a broad term encompassing a variety of online platforms that allow users to create and exchange content. Social media can be categorized into the following types: Social networks (e.g. Facebook and LinkedIn), blogs (e.g., Blogger and WordPress), microblogs (e.g., Twitter and Tumblr), social news (e.g., Digg and Reddit), social bookmarking (e.g., Delicious and StumbleUpon), media sharing (e.g. Instagram and You Tube), wikis (e.g., Wikipedia and Wikihow), question-and-answer sites (e.g., Yahoo! Answers and Ask.com) and review sites (e.g., Yelp, TripAdvisor). Also, many mobile apps, such as Find My Friend, provide a platform for social interactions and, hence, serve as social media channels.

Although the research on social networks dates back to early 1920s, nevertheless, social media analytics is a nascent field that has emerged after the advent of Web 2.0 in the early 2000s. The key characteristic of the modern social media analytics is its data-centric nature. The research on social media analytics spans across several disciplines, including psychology, sociology, anthropology, computer science, mathematics, physics, and economics. Marketing has been the primary application of social media analytics in recent years. This can be attributed to the widespread and growing adoption of social media by consumers worldwide, to the extent that Forrester Research, Inc., projects social media to be the second-fastest growing marketing channel in the US between 2011 and 2016.

User-generated content (e.g., sentiments, images, videos, and bookmarks) and the relationships and interactions between the network entities (e.g., people, organizations, and products) are the two sources of information in social media. Based on this categorization, the social media analytics can be classified into two groups:

· **Content-based analytics.** Content-based analytics focuses on the data posted by users on social media platforms, such as customer feedback, product reviews, images, and videos. Such content on social media is often voluminous, unstructured, noisy, and dynamic. Text, audio, and video analytics, as discussed earlier, can be applied to derive insight from such data. Also, big data technologies can be adopted to address the data processing challenges.

· **Structure-based analytics.** Also referred to as social network analytics, this type of analytics are concerned with synthesizing the structural attributes of a social network and extracting intelligence from the relationships among the participating entities. The structure of a social network is modeled through a set of nodes and edges, representing participants and relationships, respectively. The model can be visualized as a graph composed of the nodes and the edges. We review two types of network graphs, namely social graphs and activity graphs.

In social graphs, an edge between a pair of nodes only signifies the existence of a link(e.g., friendship) between the corresponding entities. Such graphs can be mined to identify communities or determine hubs(i.e., the users with a relatively large number of direct and indirect social links). In activity networks, however, the edges represent actual interactions between any pair of nodes. The interactions involve exchanges of information (e.g., likes and comments). Activity graphs are preferable to social graphs, because an active relationship is more relevant to analysis than a mere connection.

Various techniques have recently emerged to extract information from the structure of social networks. We briefly discuss these below.

· **Community detection**, also referred to as community discovery, extracts implicit communities within a network. For online social networks, a community refers to a sub-network of users who interact more extensively with each other than with the rest of the network. Often containing millions of nodes and edges, online social networks tend to be colossal in size. Community detection helps to summarize huge networks, which then facilitates uncovering existing behavioral patterns and predicting emergent properties of the network. In this regard, community detection is similar to clustering, a data mining technique used to partition a data set into disjoint subsets based on the similarity of data points. Community detection has found several application areas, including marketing and the World Wide Web. For example, community detection enables firms to develop more effective product recommendation systems.

Social influence analysis refers to techniques that are concerned with modeling and evaluating the influence of actors and connections in a social network. Naturally, the behavior of an actor in a social network is affected by others. Thus, it is desirable to evaluate the participants' influence, quantify the strength of connections, and uncover the patterns of influence diffusion in a network. Social influence analysis techniques can be leveraged in viral marketing to efficiently enhance brand awareness and adoption.

A salient aspect of social influence analysis is to quantify the importance of the network nodes. Various measures have been developed for this purpose, including degree centrality, betweenness centrality, closeness centrality, and eigenvector centrality. Other measures evaluate the strength of connections represented by edges or model the spread of influence in social networks. The Linear Threshold Model (LTM) and Independent Cascade Model (ICM) are two well-known examples of such frameworks.

Link prediction specifically addresses the problem of predicting future linkages between the existing nodes in the underlying network. Typically, the structure of social networks is not static and continuously grows through the creation of new nodes and edges. Therefore, a natural goal is to understand and predict the dynamics of the network. Link prediction techniques predict the occurrence of interaction, collaboration, or influence among entities of a network in a specific time interval. Link prediction techniques outperform pure chance by factors of 40 ~ 50, suggesting that the current structure of the network surely contains latent information about future links.

In biology, link prediction techniques are used to discover links or associations in biological networks (e.g., protein-protein interaction networks), eliminating the need for expensive experiments. In security, link prediction helps to uncover potential collaborations in terrorist or criminal networks. In the context of online social media, the primary application of link prediction is in the development of recommendation systems, such as Facebook's People you May Kow", YouTube's "Recommended for You", and Netflix's and Amazon's recommender engines.

Words and Expressions

social networks 社会网络
anthropology n. 人类学
Forrester Research, Inc 福瑞斯特研究公司
content-based analytics 基于内容的分析；内涵式分析
structure-based analytics 基于结构的分析
node n. 结点，节点
network graphs 网络图
hub n. 中心，轮轴；焦点
community detection 社团发现算法；社团挖掘；团体发现
colossal adj. 巨大的；庞大的

Social influence analysis 社会影响分析
actor *n.* 行动者
Linear Threshold Model(LTM) 线性门限模型
Independent Cascade Model(ICM) 独立级联模型
degree centrality 度中心性
betweenness centrality 阶数中心性
closeness centrality 接近中心性;亲近中心性;紧密中心性
eigenvector centrality 特征微量中心性
protein *n.* 蛋白质
voluminous *adj.* 浩繁的,构成多卷的;长篇的
signify *vt.* 表示……的意思;有……的意思;表示;表明
hub *n.* 中心,轮轴;焦点
terrorist *n.* 恐怖(主义)分子;威胁者

6.5.5 Predictive Analytics

Predictive analytics comprise a variety of techniques that predict future outcomes based on historical and current data. In practice, predictive analytics can be applied to almost all disciplines-from predicting the failure of jet engines based on the stream of data from several thousand sensors, to predicting customers' next moves based on what they buy, when they buy, and even what they say on social media.

At its core, predictive analytics seek to uncover patterns and capture relationships in data. Predictive analytics techniques are subdivided into two groups. Some techniques, such as moving averages, attempt to discover the historical patterns in the outcome variable(s) and extrapolate them to the future. Others, such as linear regression, aim to capture the interdependencies between outcome variable(s) and explanatory variables, and exploit them to make predictions.

Based on the underlying methodology, techniques can also be categorized into two groups: regression techniques (e.g., multinomial logit models) and machine learning techniques (e.g., neural networks). Another classification is based on the type of outcome variables: techniques such as linear regression address continuous outcome variables (e.g., sale price of houses), while others such as Random Forests are applied to discrete outcome variables (e.g., credit status).

Predictive analytics techniques are primarily based on statistical methods.

Several factors call for developing new statistical methods for big data. First, conventional statistical methods are rooted in statistical significance: a small sample is obtained from the population and the result is compared with chance to examine the significance of a particular relationship. The conclusion is then generalized to the entire population. In contrast, big data samples are massive and represent the majority of, if not the entire, population. As a result, the notion of statistical significance is not that relevant to big data. Secondly, in terms of computational efficiency, many conventional methods for small samples do not scale up to big data. The third factor corresponds to the distinctive features inherent in big data: heterogeneity, noise accumulation, spurious correlations, and incidental endogeneity.

We describe these below:

· **Heterogeneity.** Big data are often obtained from different sources and represent information from different sub-populations. As a result, big data are highly heterogeneous. The sub-population data in small samples are deemed outliers because of their insufficient frequency. However, the sheer size of big data sets creates the unique opportunity to model the heterogeneity arising from sub-population data, which would require sophisticated statistical techniques.

· **Noise accumulation.** Estimating predictive models for big data often involve the simultaneous estimation of several parameters. The accumulated estimation error (or noise) for different parameters could dominate the magnitudes of variables that have true effects within the model. In other words, some variables with significant explanatory power might be overlooked as a result of noise accumulation.

· **Spurious correlation.** For big data, spurious correlation refers to uncorrelated variables being falsely found to be correlated due to the massive size of the dataset. Fan and Lv (2008) show this phenomenon through a simulation example, where the correlation coefficient between independent random variables is shown to increase with the size of the dataset. As a result, some variables that are scientifically unrelated (due to their independence) are erroneously proven to be correlated as a result of high dimensionality.

· **Incidental endogeneity.** A common assumption in regression analysis is the exogeneity assumption: the explanatory variables, or predictors, are independent of the residual term. The validity of most statistical methods used in regression analysis depends on this assumption. In other words, the existence of incidental endogeneity (i.e., the dependence of the residual term on some of the predictors) undermines the validity of the statistical methods used for regression analysis. Although the exogeneity assumption is usually met in small samples, incidental endogeneity is commonly present in big data. It is worthwhile to mention that, in contrast to spurious correlation, incidental endogeneity refers to a genuine relationship between variables and the error term.

The irrelevance of statistical significance, the challenges of computational efficiency, and the unique characteristics of big data discussed above highlight the need to develop new statistical techniques to gain insights from predictive models.

Technological advances in storage and computations have enabled cost-effective capture of the informational value of big data in a timely manner. Consequently, one observes a proliferation in real-world adoption of analytics that were not economically feasible for large-scale applications prior to the big data era. For example, sentiment analysis(opinion mining) have been known since the early 2000s.

However, big data technologies enabled businesses to adopt sentiment analysis to glean useful insights from millions of opinions shared on social media. The processing of unstructured text fueled by the massive influx of social media data is generating business value by adopting conventional(pre-big data) sentiment analysis techniques, which may not be ideally suited to leverage big data.

Although major innovations in analytical techniques for big data have not yet taken place, one anticipates the emergence of such novel analytics in the near future. For instance, real-time ananlytics will likely become a prolific field of research because of the growth in location-aware social media and mobile apps. Since big data are noisy, highly interrelated, and unreliable, it will likely lead to the development of statistical techniques more readily apt for mining big data while remaining sensitive to the unique characteristics. Going beyond samples, additional valuable insights could be obtained from the massive volumes of less 'trustworthy' data.

Words and Expressions

multinomial logit models 多项式 *logit* 模型
heterogeneity *n.* 异质性,不均匀性,不纯一性
spurious correlation 伪相关
exogeneity *n.* 外生性
pre-big data 前大数据
mobile apps 移动应用;移动应用程序

trustworthy *adj.* 可靠的；值得信任的
overlook *vi.* 瞭望；监督；忽视
undermine *vt.* 在……下面掘地道，暗掘；冲蚀；削弱……的基础；暗中破坏
genuine *adj.* 真的；非人造的；名副其实的
glean *vt.* 慢慢地收集；耐心地搜集；查明，弄清

第Ⅲ部分 参考译文

第3单元 指数译文

3.1 引 言

指数是指用于测算各种经济变量变化的最常用的工具。与各种经济现象相联系的指数会定期被编辑与出版。消费物价指数(consumer price index, CPI)测算了一系列消费品与服务的价格变化,它是应用最广泛的一种经济指数。其他重要的指数,还包括国民总收入(national income aggregates)的价格紧缩指数(price deflator);进出口价格指数;金融指数,诸如所有普通指数(澳大利亚)以及道琼斯指数(美国)。

本章主要目的是对测算随时间与空间变化的生产率相关的各种各样指数提供一种简单解释。显然,测算生产率的变化必然包含测算产出水平的变化以及与此相关的投入变化。在单投入、单产出情况下,这些变化很容易测算,但是在涉及到多投入与多产出时就更为困难。

我们看到,指数在生产率测量领域中起着三个方面的重要作用。第一个也是最重要的一个,是指数用于对全要素生产率(total factor productivity, TFP)变化的测量,这就产生了广为流行的 TFP 指数。反过来,TFP 指数要求分离投入与产出的数量指数。

指数在生产率测量中的第二个作用是一种间接作用。它关系到指数用于数据包络分析(Data Envelopment Analysis, DEA)或估计随机前沿(Stochastic Frontiers)之中生成所需要的数据方面。利用非常详细的投入与产出数据的这些技术,提出了起因于包括大量的投入与产出种类而自由度损失的估计问题。在这些技术的大多数实际应用中,将数据"综合"成投入与产出变量更小的集合显得很有必要。例如,不同类型的劳动投入通常被综合成一种单一劳动投入。属于一个特定分组的商品产出通常被综合成这个分组的一个单一集合产出。例如,在农业中,诸如小麦、稻米等的这类商品就被综合成谷类产出。这种类型的综合实质上是评价效率与生产率变化过程的一个中间步骤,它需要使用指数。通常,这种综合采用的形式是"不变价格下的总价值"(value aggregates at constant prices)或者就是"不变价格序列"(constant price series)。

第三个问题所涉及需要处理平行数据集合的指数类型,即价格与数量的数据随时间以及空间不同而变化的情况。对空间观测值的比较经常要提出一些基本的一致性要求,诸如"传递性"与"基不变性"。反过来,这些要求规定了对于生成指数来说所用到的前两段曾讨论的公式需要满足的一些附加要求。

3.2 概念与符号

把指数(index number)定义成是对一组相关变量之中变化进行测算的一个实数。从概念上讲,指数可以用来比较随时间或者空间或随两者同时变化的量。指数用来测算随时间变化的价格与数量,也可以用来衡量不同厂商、行业、地区或国家的水平差异。价格指数可以指消费者物价、投入与产出价格、进出口价格等等,而数量指数可以测算一个厂商或行业随时间变化或者不同厂商在产出商品以及所用投入上的数量变化。

指数在经济学上有着悠久的且与众不同的历史,一些最重要的贡献归功于早在19世纪晚期的Laspeyres与Paasche的研究。Laspeyres公式与Paasche公式仍旧被全世界一些国家统计局所广泛应用。但是,正是欧文·费希尔(Irving Fisher)的工作以及他的著作——在1922年出版的《编制指数》——认识到使用许多统计公式生成适当的指数的可能性。Törnqvist指数(1936)在生产率测量中起到重要作用。Diewert和Nakamura(1993)书中的第2章提供了极好的阐明指数构建的历史背景。

符号

在这一章中,我们自始至终地使用下述符号。设 p_{mj} 与 q_{mj} 分别表示第 m 种($m = 1, 2, \cdots, M$)商品在第 j 个($j=s,t$)时期中的价格与数量。为了不失一般性,s 与 t 除了可以表示时期之外,还可以指两家厂商,而数量可以是投入量,也可以是产出量。

从概念上讲,所有指数测算了来自于一个参考时期的一组变量水平的变化。参考时期由"基期"(base period)表示。用于计算指数的时期称为"现期"(current period,又称计算期、报告期,译者注)。设 I_{st} 表示以 s 为基期的现期 t 的综合指数。类似地,设 V_{st}、P_{st} 以及 Q_{st} 分别表示价值指数、价格指数以及数量指数。

综合指数问题

从时期 s 到时期 t 的价值变化是在时期 s 与 t 的商品价值之比值,价值由各自的价格衡量。因而

$$V_{st} = \frac{\sum_{i=1}^{N} p_{it} q_{it}}{\sum_{i=1}^{N} p_{is} q_{is}} \tag{3.1}$$

指数 V_{st} 测算了从时期 s 到 t 的 M 种商品集合数量价值的变化。显然,V_{st} 是两种成分即价格变化与数量变化的结果。尽管 V_{st} 容易测算时,但是要剔除价格变化与数量变化的影响就非常难。我们想要剔除这种影响,因此,比如说,使数量成分可以用于测算数量的变化。

如果我们在单一商品的世界里处理问题,那么这种分解就很容易做到。我们有

$$V_{st} = \frac{p_t q_t}{p_s q_s} = \frac{p_t}{p_s} \times \frac{q_t}{q_s}$$

其中比值 p_t/p_s 与 q_t/q_s 测算了相关的价格变化与数量变化,从而不存在指数问题。

通常,当商品数 $M \geq 2$ 时,我们就有了综合问题。相对价格 p_{mt}/p_{ms} 测算了第 m 种商品价格水平的变化,而相对数量 p_{mt}/p_{ms} 测算了第 m 种商品数量水平的变化 ($m = 1, 2, \cdots, M$)。

现在的问题是,如何将这 M 种不同的价格(数量)变化的测量合成一个简单实数,称之为价格(数量)指数(price (quantity) index)。这个问题有点类似于选择一种合适的中心趋势来测量。在下面两节中,我们简要地阐明测算价格指数与数量指数变化的一些最常用的公式。

3.3 价格指数公式

首先,我们关注价格指数的构建,然后阐明这些公式是如何用于构建数量指数的。

Laspeyres 指数与 Paasche 指数

这两个公式在实践中是应用最为广泛的公式。Laspeyres 价格指数使用基期的数量作为权数,而 Paasche 指数使用现期的数量作为权数来定义指数。

$$\text{Laspeyres 指数} = P_{st}^L = \frac{\sum_{m=1}^{M} p_{mt} q_{ms}}{\sum_{m=1}^{M} p_{ms} q_{ms}} = \sum_{m=1}^{M} \frac{p_{mt}}{p_{ms}} \times \omega_{ms} \quad (3.2)$$

其中 $\omega_{ms} = p_{ms} q_{ms} / \sum_{m=1}^{M} p_{ms} q_{ms}$ 表示基期第 m 种商品的价值份额。

式(3.2) 给出了两种可供选择的解释。第一种解释是，Laspeyres 指数是两个取基期的数量、现期与基期的价格之价值的综合值的比值。第二种解释是，N 种相关价格的价值份额权数的平均值。价值份额反映了每一种商品在集合中的相对重要性。这里所用的价值份额是参照基期而计算的。

在定义 Laspeyres 指数中所使用了基期数量，一个自然的可供选择就是使用现期数量的指数公式。利用现期数量的 Paasche 指数是由公式

$$\text{Paasche 指数} = P_{st}^P = \frac{\sum_{m=1}^{M} p_{mt} q_{mt}}{\sum_{m=1}^{M} p_{ms} q_{mt}} = \frac{1}{\sum_{m=1}^{M} \frac{p_{ms}}{p_{mt}} \times \omega_{mt}} \quad (3.3)$$

给出的。

式(3.3) 的第一部分表明，Paasche 指数是两个取现期 t 的数量、现期与基期的价格之价值的综合值的比值。另一方面，等式的后一部分表明，Paasche 指数是一些以现期价值份额作为权数的相关价格的加权调和平均值。

由式(3.2) 与 (3.3) 可以看出，在某种意义上说，Laspeyres 公式与 Paasche 公式代表了两个极端，一个公式将重点放在基期的数量上，而另一个的重点则在现期的数量上。如果相关价格不发生任何变化，那么这两个指数相一致，也就是说，如果 $p_{it}/p_{is} = c$，那么 Laspeyres 指数与 Paasche 指数相一致，均为常数 c。当相关价格变动较大时，这两种指数也会有较大差别。差别的程度同样依赖于相应数量以及相应价格与数量的统计相关性。Bortkiewicz(1924) 提供了对 Laspeyres-Paasche 差异的一种分解。

Laspeyres 指数与 Paasche 指数应用广泛，主要是因为它们计算简单，并且它们给出了利用经济原理所定义的真实指数(true index) 的"范围"(bounds)。相当多数的国家统计机构都使用这两个公式或者用这两种指数稍微变化之后的形式来计算各种各样的指数，比如 CPI。特别是，Laspeyres 指数应用更加广泛。我们注意到，如果已公布的价格指数被用作对给定价值序列的紧缩目的，那么得到的紧缩序列将表现出有限的特性，这些特性依赖于在构建价格指数中所使用的那个公式。这个问题将会在 3.4 节中进一步阐述，其中讨论了数量变化的间接测量。

Fisher 指数

Laspeyres 指数与 Paasche 指数之间的差异引发了费希尔(1922)将这两种指数的几何平均值作为一个可能的指数公式

$$\text{Fisher 指数} = P_{st}^F = \sqrt{P_{st}^L \times P_{st}^P} \tag{3.4}$$

虽然 Fisher 指数是人为构建的,它介于两个极端之间,它拥有许多理想的统计性质与经济理论性质。Diewert(1992)曾阐明 Fisher 指数的多功能性。考虑到 Fisher 指数具有如此之多的令人满意的特点,所以 Fisher 指数以 Fisher 理想指数而著称。

Törnqvist 指数

在过去十年多里,Törnqvist 指数应用于全要素生产率的研究之中。这一节中,我们定义 Törnqvist 价格指数,而在下一节定义 Törnqvist 数量指数。Törnqvist 价格指数是一些相关价格的加权几何平均值,时期 s 与时期 t 中的价值份额的简单平均值作为权系数

$$P_{st}^T = \prod_{m=1}^{M} \left[\frac{p_{mt}}{p_{ms}}\right]^{\frac{\omega_{ms}+\omega_{mt}}{2}} \tag{3.5}$$

Törnqvist 指数经常以它的对数变化形式出现,并得以应用

$$\ln P_{st}^T = \sum_{m=1}^{M} \left(\frac{\omega_{ms}+\omega_{mt}}{2}\right)(\ln p_{mt} - \ln p_{ms}) \tag{3.6}$$

对数变化形式提供了一种方便的计算式。在对数变化形式中,Törnqvist 指数是价格变化对数的加权平均值。此外,第 m 种商品价格的对数变化量

$$\ln p_{mt} - \ln p_{ms} = \ln \frac{p_{mt}}{p_{ms}} \approx \left(\frac{p_{mt}}{p_{ms}} - 1\right)$$

表示第 m 种商品价格的变化率。因此,用对数变化形式表示的 Törnqvist 价格指数提供了一种价格方面整体增长率的指标(通货膨胀率)。

在指数文献中存在许多公式,我们把讨论范围限定在这四种公式上,因为它们代表着应用最广泛的公式。在简要描述数量指数之后,在 3.5 节中我们回过头来讨论一下这些指数的性质。

3.4 数量指数

存在两种方法用于测算数量变化。第一种方法是直接方法,我们通过用 q_{mt}/q_{ms} 测算单个商品特定数量变化的方法来推导出测算全部数量变化的一个公式。Laspeyres 公式、Paasche 公式、Fisher 公式以及 Törnqvist 公式可以直接应

用于相关的数量指数上。第二种方法是间接法,基本思想是价格变化与数量变化是导致价值在时期 s 与 t 上生成变化的两个原因。因此,如果价格变化可以通过前面所讨论的公式得到测量,那么将价格变化所引起的价值变化排除掉就可以间接地获得数量变化。这种方法将在下面的 3.4.2 中讨论。

3.4.1 直接方法

通过简单变换价格与数量的位置,就可以利用价格指数定义各种各样的数量指数。由上面描述的公式可得到

$$Q_{st}^L = \frac{\sum_{m=1}^{M} p_{ms} q_{mt}}{\sum_{m=1}^{M} p_{ms} q_{ms}}, \quad Q_{st}^P = \frac{\sum_{m=1}^{M} p_{mt} q_{mt}}{\sum_{m=1}^{M} p_{mt} q_{ms}}, \quad \text{以及} \quad Q_{st}^F = \sqrt{Q_{st}^L \times Q_{st}^P} \quad (3.7)$$

Törnqvist 数量指数的乘法形式以及加法(对数变化形式)形式由下面

$$Q_{st}^T = \prod_{m=1}^{M} \left(\frac{q_{mt}}{q_{ms}}\right)^{\frac{\omega_{ms}+\omega_{mt}}{2}} \quad (3.8)$$

$$\ln Q_{st}^T = \sum_{m=1}^{M} \left(\frac{\omega_{ms}+\omega_{mt}}{2}\right)(\ln q_{mt} - \ln q_{ms}) \quad (3.9)$$

给出。在对两个时期 s 与 t 的生产过程测算生产的产出量与用于生产的投入数量时,等式(3.8)Törnqvist 数量指数是应用最为广泛的指数。等式(3.9)所给出的 Törnqvist 数量指数的对数变化形式主要用于计算目的。优先选择 Törnqvist 数量指数的原因是,许多重要的归属于 Diewert(1976,1981),Caves,Christensen 和 Diewert(1982)所发现的指数经济理论的性质。

3.4.2 间接方法

间接方法通常用来比较不同时间的数量变化情况。这种方法的一个基本前提是,所测量到的价格变化与数量变化一定会引起价值的变化。

$$\text{价值变化} = \text{价格变化} \times \text{数量变化}$$

$$V_{st} = P_{st} \times Q_{st} \quad (3.10)$$

由于 V_{st} 可以由数据直接定义为时期 t 与 s 价值的比值,Q_{st} 可以通过作为 P_{st} 的函数而得到,如下面式(3.11)所示

$$Q_{st} = \frac{V_{st}}{P_{st}} = \frac{\sum_{m=1}^{M} p_{mt} q_{mt}}{\sum_{m=1}^{M} p_{ms} q_{ms}} \bigg/ P_{st} = \frac{\sum_{m=1}^{M} p_{mt} q_{mt}/P_{st}}{\sum_{m=1}^{M} p_{ms} q_{ms}} =$$

$$\frac{\text{经过价格变化调整后的时期 } t \text{ 的价值}}{\text{时期 } s \text{ 的价值}} \quad (3.11)$$

所以
$$Q_{st} = \frac{\text{时期 } t \text{ 的价值（以时期 } s \text{ 的不变价格计算）}}{\text{时期 } s \text{ 的价值（以时期 } s \text{ 的价格计算）}}$$

这个表达式中的分子对应于不变价格序列，这种不变价格序列经常在许多统计出版物中得到应用。基本上，这种方法认为数量指数可以通过价值比值获得，这里的价值已经排除掉了所考虑时期的价格变化所带来的影响。

下面讨论间接数量比较的一些重要的特征与应用。

不变价格综合与数量比较

式(3.11)与间接方法的直接含义，就是由随时间变化的价格调整的价值综合可以被看成综合数量或者是合成商品的数量。这种价格通货紧缩序列在统计机构发行物中经常出现。这种综合的例子有：国内生产总值(GDP)；部门产出，诸如农业、制造业；投资序列以及进出口货物或服务。

这种时间序列与横截面数据的综合经常被当作数据序列，用于估计最小二乘法计量经济生产模型、随机前沿，也应用于 DEA 的计算，在 DEA 的计算中必须降低投入向量与产出向量的维数。这意味着，即使指数方法不能直接用于测算生产率的变化，但是它总是用于生成中间的数据序列。

直接数量与间接数量比较的公式"自对偶性"

我们审视一下在间接数量比较中选择价格公式时所涉及的一些问题。假定我们使用 Laspeyres 公式构建价格指数。于是，经过代数计算，可以证明，式(3.11)所定义的间接数量指数就是式(3.7)中所定义的 Paasche 数量指数。这意味着，Laspeyres 价值指数与 Paasche 数量指数可以组成一个指数对，此指数对一起精确地分解了价值变化。从这个意义上说，Laspeyres 价值指数与 Paasche 数量指数可以看成是对偶的。

容易证明，Laspeyres 价值指数与 Paasche 数量指数一起分解了价值指数，因此，它们互为对偶。一个很重要的问题就出现了："是否存在自对偶指数公式，使得由同一个公式生成的价格指数与数量指数可以精确分解价值指数呢？"答案是肯定的。由 Fisher 公式生成的价格指数与数量指数组成一个对偶对。这蕴含着由 Fisher 公式直接生成的数量指数与利用 Fisher 价格指数紧缩通货价值变化所间接推导出的数量指数是相同的。此特征有时称为"要素逆检验"(factor reversal test)。在下一节中我们会讨论这一特征。

Törnqvist 指数因其自身的几何特性而并不具有自对偶性的性质。这意味着，如果我们使用 Törnqvist 价格指数，那么间接数量指数不同于直接利用等式(3.8)中的 Törnqvist 指数所推导出的数量指数。

如果直接方法与间接方法导致了不同的答案，或者不同的数量变化的数值测量，那么就会引发关于哪一种方法应该用于给定的实际应用选择问题。这个问题下面讨论。

直接数量与间接数量的比较

Allen 和 Diewert(1981)讨论了,在直接数量方法或间接数量方法之间选择时所涉及的一些解析性问题。从实用角度讲,这种选择依赖于可用数据的类型,相关价格与数量的可用性以及用于数量比较中的理论框架上。

从实践角度讲,研究者很少奢侈到可以在直接方法与间接方法中进行选择。如果问题涉及综合数据的应用,那么数量数据通常仅在不变价格序列下是可利用的。在这种情况下,数据的不可获得性解决了选择的问题。

关注的第二点是,这种基本指数的可靠性。因为指数代表了所观测的不同商品变化的数量值,这种代表的可靠性取决于在不同商品的价格与数量变化中所观测到的可变性。如果不同商品的价格变化趋于一致,那么价格指数就可以提供价格变化的有效测量。对于数量指数而言,可以得到同样的结论。价格与数量比值 p_{mt}/p_{ms} 及 q_{mt}/q_{ms}($m=1,2,\cdots,M$)的相关可变性为哪一种指数的成为更可靠的提供了一条有用的线索。如果价格比值表现出(相对于数量指数而言)较小的可变性,那么提倡使用间接数量指数,如果相应的数量比值可变性较小,那么使用直接数量指数更合适。这些比值的可变性可用标准方差测量法进行测算。

鉴于这个重要的考虑,值得关注的是随不同商品的价格变化比起商品的变化更加趋向于一致。不同商品的价格变化通常会背离全部价格的基本变化率。与之相比,即使是在随不同时间而变化的情形中,不同商品的数量比值趋向于反映出很大的可变性。

还有一点很重要,如果价格(数量)比值表现出很小的可变性,那么大部分的指数公式都会给出很相近的价格(数量)变化的测量。不同的公式会生成更多的一致性结果,因此,公式的选择对测量价格(数量)变化就不会生成太大的影响。

最后,在产出与生产率的比较背景下,直接数量的比较在理论上会提供更有意义的指数,因为它们利用了支撑生产技术基础的一些约束。Diewert (1976,1983),Caves 以及 Christensen 和 Diewert(1982)提出,在某种条件下,基于 Törnqvist 指数公式所得到的直接投入与产出数量指数从理论上讲是最优的(superior)。Diewert(1992)证明,Fisher 指数在理论与检验性质上的效果都很好。偏爱 Fisher 指数的另一个原因是它是自对偶的,因为它满足要素逆检验。此外,Fisher 指数是利用 Laspeyres 指数与 Paasche 指数定义的。因此,理解这种指数就更容易,并且它也能处理数据集合中的零数量。

Balk(1998)建议,在收入约束行为假设下,生产率指数可以通过利用直接数量测量而得到最好的测算。有了这些结果,从理论角度讲,直接数量与间接数量(投入或产出)的选择应建立在关于厂商或决策单元行为假设的基础之上。

对直接数量与间接数量之间选择比较问题的所有根据及讨论都表明,一个决策制定需要建立在实用考虑与纯分析基础之上。

3.5 指数性质:检验方法

考虑到存在大量的指数公式,Fisher(1922)提出了许多公式要求在直观意义上满足的一些准则,称之为检验(tests)。这些检验标准用在选择公式构建价格指数与数量指数的过程中。另一种(相关性较强的)框架是以公理形式提出一些性质,然后找到满足这些公理的指数。这种方法称为指数构建的公理化方法(axiomatic approach)。Eichorn 和 Voeller(1976)以及 Balk(1995)给出一个公理方法的概述,后者突出强调价格指数理论。Diewert(1992)为生产率测量中所要考虑的问题给出了一系列公理,并且建议使用 Fisher 指数。本小节的主要目的是,简要向读者提供一种直观的而不严谨的一些检验方法,并且提出对生产率测量有意义重大的两个结论。

设 P_{st} 与 Q_{st} 分别表示价格指数与数量指数,它们都是在时期 s 与时期 t 中观测到的价格与数量(M 种商品)的实数函数,由 M 维列向量 p_s, p_t, q_s, q_t 表示。下面列出一些基本又常用的公理。

正值性(Positivity):指数(价格或数量)总为正的。

连续性(Continuity):指数是价格与数量的连续函数。

比例性(Proportionality):如果所有的价格(数量)以相同的比例增长,那么 $P_{st}(Q_{st})$ 也应以这个比例增长。

可公度性或维数不变性(Commensurability or Dimensional Invariance):价格(数量)指数必须不依赖于数量(价格)的度量单位。

逆时检验(Time-reversal Test):对于两个时期 s 与时期 t:$P_{st}=1/P_{ts}$。

价值均值检验(Mean-value Test):价格(或数量)指数必须介于商品变化的最大值与最小值之间。

要素逆检验(Factor-reversal Test):如果直接构建价格值数与数量指数用的是同一个公式,并且指数比值相同,那么这个公式就满足这个检验。

环比性检验(传递性)(Circularity Test(Transitivity)):对于任意三个时期 s, t 以及 r,这个检验需要:$P_{st}=P_{sr}\times P_{rt}$。也就是说,时期 s 与时期 t 之间直接的比较与通过时期 r 进行间接比较所得到的结果是一样的。

接下来的两个结论描述 Fisher 指数与 Törnqvist 指数的性质,并指出在生产率测量中使用这两种指数的理由。

结论 4.1 除了环比检验(传递性)之外,Fisher 指数具有上述性质。

事实上，Diewert(1992)指出，Fisher 指数具有更多性质。Fisher 指数满足要素逆检验保证了可以将价值变化适当分解成价格变化与数量变化。这就证明，将"理想指数"的称号赋予 Fisher 指数是合适的。要素逆性质使得直接计算的 Fisher 数量指数与通过 Fisher 价格指数紧缩价值指数得到的间接 Fisher 数量指数是相同的。Fisher 指数表现出自对偶性。Diewert(1976,1981)指出，Fisher 指数是精确的(exact)、最佳的(superlative)。

结论 4.2 除了要素逆检验与环比检验之外，Törnqvist 指数满足上述所有检验。

Eichorn 和 Voeller(1983)证明本结论与其他结论。这些命题的证明具有非常强的数学性，但是最终结果却十分有用。Theil(1973, 1974)指出，Törnqvist 指数不满足要素逆检验仅仅是因为不满足一个近似要求。通常人们认为，不满足要素逆检验并不是非常严重的，因为没有必要要求价格指数与数量指数具有自对偶性质(self-dual)，而且没有分析表明，使用相同类型的公式进行价格与数量比较是合理的。

固定基与链基的比较

现在，我们简要了解一下比较不同时间的价格、数量以及生产率。在不同时间的比较中，尤其是要进行生产率测量时，我们经常感兴趣于将每年的情况与其前一年情况的比较，然后将每一年的生产率变化结合起来用以测算一段给定的时期内生产率的变化。以这种过程构建的指数称为环比指数(chain index，又称为链指数，译者注)。为给出一个正式的定义，设 $I(t, t+1)$ 表示一个以 t 为基期的所关注的 $t+1$ 时期指数。这个指数可以应用于一个时间序列 $t = 0,1,2,\cdots,T$。这样时期 t 与固定基期 0 的比较可以由下面的连续时期的环比指数比较得到

$$I(0,t) = I(0,1) \times I(1,2) \times \cdots \times I(t-1,t)$$

除使用链基准指数，应用前面所提到的任何一种公式来比较时期 0 与时期 t 都是可能的。作为结果的指数称为固定基指数(fixed-base index)。

大多数的国家统计局都使用固定基 Laspeyres 指数，主要是因为对于所有的固定基指数的计算权系数保持一致。通常基期在固定基础上变动。

指数文献存在相当多的集中讨论固定基与链基指数的相关优点。关于各种各样问题的优秀调查研究可以参看 Forsyth(1978)，Forsyth 和 Fowler(1981)以及 Szulc(1983)。从实用角度上讲，尤其是涉及生产率测量时，环比指数比固定基指数更合适。因为环比指数仅包括连续时期的比较，所以这种指数测算了更小的变化。因此，在生成具有理论意义指数的过程中所包含的一些近似就更可能被控制。另一个优点是，在连续时期上的比较意味着 Laspeyres 指数与 Paasche 指数之间的差别较小，潜在的、大部分的指数公式所生成的指数在数量

上是十分相近的。环比指数的唯一缺陷是指数中的权数每年都需要加以修正。

利用环比指数并不能生成传递指数。即使传递性在时间比较中并不被认为是必需的,但是在进行多边比较时仍是必要的。

选择哪一个公式

前面的讨论表明,公式的选择本质上是在 Fisher 指数与 Törnqvist 指数之间进行的。这两个公式都具有一些重要的性质并且都满足许多公理。如果使用公布的已经综合数据,那么就需要检验生成这组序列使用的是什么公式。这样的数据序列很可能使用的是 Laspeyres 指数或 Paasche 指数。如果在距离不是很远的时期上计算这些指数,那么 Fisher 指数与 Törnqvist 指数之间的数值差别可能是相当小的。此外,这两种指数还都具有一些重要的理论性质。实践中好像更偏爱 Törnqvist 指数,但是提倡使用 Fisher 指数,因为它还具有自对偶性,并且它能处理数据中包含零数值的问题。

第 4 单元 缺失数据与估算

4.1 引言

调查数据出现缺失现象问题是一个因调查问题无回答或部分回答而引起的一个古老问题。无回答的理由包括：不愿意提供所问信息、很难回忆起过去发生的事件、不知道正确的回答。估算(imputation，又称借补、设算，译者注)是一种估计或预测缺失观测值的过程。

在这一章，我们研究含有数据向量的回归背景，这里的数据向量为 $(y_i, x_i), i = 1, \cdots, N$。对于某些观测值来说，$x_i$ 的某些元素或 (y_i, x_i) 两个元素之中的某些元素出现缺失。因而，需要考虑一系列问题。什么时候我们应着手分析仅有完整观测值，又什么时候应试图填上由缺失观测值而引起的缺口呢? 什么样的估算方法可以利用呢? 一旦获得缺失观测值的估算，又怎样进行估计与推断呢?

假如数据集出现缺失观测值，而且这些缺口能利用统计上合理的方法加以填补，则这样做的益处源于拥有更大的且可能更有代表性的样本，并在理想环境下可实施更准确推断。估计缺失数据的成本来自做出支撑生成缺失观测值代表性方法的(可能错误)假设，还有来自任何这种方法所固有的近似误差。另外，在用估算值代替缺失数据之后，由数据扩充而引发的统计推断会更加复杂，因为此类推断必须考虑到因估算而引入的近似误差。

作为调查无回答与因(对一组有代表性进行的调查)一组调查对象损耗而出现数据缺口的情况经常发生。对缺失值估算可能由官方机构来完成，以此生成与维护公用调查数据库，或者由那些使用数据建模者完成。在前者情况下，官方机构可以拥有更广泛的信息，包括机密信息／秘密信息，这些信息能在估算过程中得到了利用。在后者情况下，建模者具有特定的建模框架，在估算过程时，则要利用此种建模框架。

一个有趣的缺失数据例子是，在消费者财务状况调查下(Survey of Consumer Finances)[肯尼克尔(Kennickell, 1998)]出现的问题。因为消费者财务问题极为敏感，所以调查表出现收入与财富信息的大量缺口，美国联邦储备的分析人员针对连续变量与离散变量，发展并实施一些复杂估算算法，既利用公开可用的收入与财富的调查信息，又有来自人口普查数据的保密信息。

图 4.1 给出回归元出现缺失数据的某些潜在模式。某一个数据集具有一个纯量因变量 y、三个回归元：x_1、x_2、x_3，它们中每一个都有观测值，那么将它们叠放成 (y, x_1, x_2, x_3)。在 A 组调查对象中，观测值都是完整数据，但 x_1 有一些缺失，B 组调查 (y, x_3) 是完整数据，数据 (x_1, x_2) 出现缺失值，使得 x_1 与 x_2 永远不会同时被观测到。C 组调查是全部三个回归元都出现缺失观测值时的一般缺失观测值模式，但却不存在特定的缺失模式。

处理缺失数据的一种最简单方法是删除缺失数据，然后仅仅分析简化的"完整"观测值样本。例如，在 A 组调查对象中，完整样本是由 x_1 的所有可利用数据所构成的 (y, x_1, x_2, x_3) 的子集。不过，在 B 组调查对象中，当沿用该种方法时，人们舍弃无用的观测值，除非人们从分析中去掉 (x_1, x_2)。在 C 组调查对象中，完整数据集是通过删除任何包括三个回归元当中任一个出现缺失数据的观测值之后而形成的。

上面所述方法被称为成列删除(listwise deletion)。该方法已被广泛采用，并且经常是统计软件的默认选项。此方法不一定没有什么害处；其结果依赖于缺失数据机制，而且从这种研究所得出的结论可能出现严重缺陷。当然，一般地讲，丢掉数据意味着丢掉信息，同时将降低估计效率。因此，倘若归因于缺失数据的缺口以能不产生曲解的方式得以填补，则成列删除看起来似乎值得尝试，本章将研究其他的一些可供选择方法及其局限性。

广义地讲，估算存在两种方法，一种是基于模型方法(model-based)，另一种则不是基于模型方法。第一种方法运用模型对缺失观测值加以设定，然后使用得到的完整数据集去获得模型参数的更好估计。该过程是一种反反复复的。单个估算与多重估算都是可行的。现代方法的一个重要特征是，将缺失数据处理成随机变量，然后用从所假定的基本分布中抽取的多重值代替，这种过程被称为多重估算(multiple imputation)。利用模拟方法可逼近这类分布。

由于估算是微观经济计量研究中的一个重要方面，所以有必要将此专题作为一个独立又简短的介绍章节。调查数据不可避免地包含缺失数据，一种普遍作法即成列删除就是一个估算方法。而且，还可利用更好的估算方法。不过，我们应该注意到：所有估算方法均建立在假设基础上，而在某些应用中，有些估算假设是根本站不住脚的。

本章大部分内容研究基于模型方法。4.2 节介绍估算文献里占据主导地位的术语与假设的。4.3 节给出不使用模型来处理缺失数据方法的一个简述。4.4 节首先以基于模型的方法开始，然后讨论极大似然法。4.5 节考察估算的回归框架及 EM 形式方法。

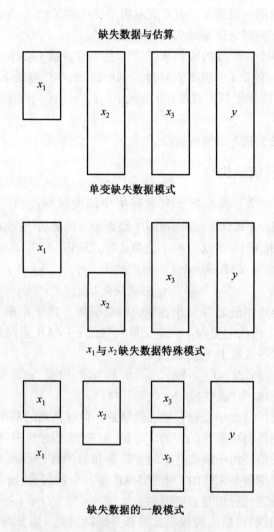

图4.1 缺失数据:缺失回归元的例子

4.2 缺失数据假设

估算文献广泛使用的某些基本术语与正式定义都要归功于鲁宾(Rubin, 1976)的研究工作,他曾引入两种重要的缺失数据机制,一种是随机缺失,另一种是完全随机缺失,这两种机制成为有用的基准。

鲁宾的设置背景包括 Y,Y 是由完整数据集所构成的 $N \times p$ 矩阵,它可能不是全部被观测到的。用 Y_{obs} 表示观测部分,Y_{mis} 表示非观测到(缺失)部分。在回归模型背景下,Y 既可以指回归元,又可以指响应(因)变量。因此,该分析涵盖了缺失数据的一般情况。设 R 表示指示变量的 $N \times p$ 矩阵，R 的元素是0或1，这要依据 Y 中的对应值是缺失的还是观测的。

对于含有单个因变量的回归来说，Y 包括响应变量 y 与 $(p-1)$ 个回归元 X 的数据。变量 x_k 的第 i 个观测值记为 x_{ki}，缺失的概率可能是下述情形：① 与其实观值独立；② 依赖于其实观值；③ 依赖于 $x_{kj}, j \neq i$；④ 依赖于 $x_{lj}, j \neq i, l \neq k$。

下面给出关于缺失结构的假设。

4.2.1 随机缺失

设 $x_i (i = 1 \ldots N)$ 表示所研究数据集中的变量观测值。随机缺失假设（missing at random(MAR) assumption）是指如下的缺失情况，x_i 缺失并不依赖于 x_i 之值，但可能依赖于 $x_j (j \neq i)$ 之值。正式地讲，

$$x_i \text{ 是 MAR 的} \Rightarrow \Pr[x_i \text{ 出现缺失} \mid x_i, x_j, \forall j \neq i] \quad (4.1)$$
$$\Rightarrow \Pr[x_i \text{ 出现缺失} \mid x_j, \forall j \neq i]$$

在控制 x 的其他观测值之后，x_i 出现缺失的概率与 x_i 之值不相关。

鲁宾(1976)给出的更为正式定义可表叙如下：MAR 假设蕴含着指示变量 R 的概率模型并不依赖于 Y_{mis}，也就是

$$\Pr[R \mid Y_{\text{obs}}, Y_{\text{mis}}, \psi] = \Pr[R \mid YY_{\text{obs}}, \psi]$$

其中 ψ 表示缺失机制的基本(向量)参数。

在 MAR 条件下，无响应被包括在忽略缺失信息机制的基于似然推断之中，尽管所得到的估计值可能是无效的。可是，若 MAR 假设失效，则缺失概率依赖于非观测的缺失值。由于缺失数据的值是未知的，所以 MAR 约束不是可检验的。因为缺失数据值是未知的。由于 MAR 是一个强假设，所以基于缺失性各种不同假设的敏感性分析是值得做的。

一个单独问题是，缺失数据模式是否是纯随机的。在实际应用时，我们希望观测值缺失处于数据聚集内部，在第24章意义下，观测值可能是相关的。可是，该问题并不与因缺失性及数据值有联系而产生的无响应偏倚。

4.2.2 完全随机缺失

完全随机缺失(Missing completely at random，记为 MCAR)是 MAR 的一种特殊情况。它意味着，Y_{obs} 是所有潜在可观测数据值的一个简单随机样本(谢弗(Schafer)，1997)。

再次假定 x_i 是正在研究数据集中变量的一个观测值。于是，x_i 的数据被称为 MCAR，如果 x_i 缺失数据的概率既不依赖于 x_i 之值，也不依赖于数据中其他变量的值。正式地讲

$$x_i \text{ 是 MCAR 的} \Rightarrow \Pr[\,x_i \text{ 出现缺失} \mid x_i,\ x_j,\ \forall j \neq i\,] \quad (4.2)$$
$$\Rightarrow \Pr[\,x_i \text{ 出现缺失}\,]$$

例如,如果(a) 没有报告收入的那些人,平均地讲,比报告收入的人要年轻;(b) 典型小的(大的)值出现缺失,那么就违背了 MCAR。

对于本小节前面所提及的情况(i) 至(v),情况(i) 既满足 MCAR 又满足 MAR,情况(iii) 与(iv) 均满足 MAR,而情况(ii) 则不满足 MAR。

MCAR 蕴含,观测数据是所有样本的一个随机子样本。当假设有效,因忽略不完整观测值,也就是观测值含有缺失值时,就不会产生偏倚。

一个推论是,MCAR 失效蕴含样本有选择偏倚形式。MAR 虽是一个较弱假设,但仍有助于估算,这是因为它假定缺失数据机制仅依赖于观测量。

4.2.3 可忽略缺失与不可忽略缺失

缺失数据机制被称为可忽略的(ignorable),如果 (a) 数据集是 MAR 的;(b) 缺失数据生成过程的参数 ψ 与我们要估计的参数不相关。

这个条件类似于弱外生性条件,意味着模型参数 θ 与缺失机制参数 ψ 截然不同。因而,如果缺失数据是可忽略的,那么就不需要所将缺失数据的缺口建模成建立模型演算的一个基础性部分。在可忽略缺失条件 (b) 几乎总是得到满足的假设下,MAR 与"可忽略性"经常被处理成等价的(阿利森(Allison),2002)。

如果对于(y, x)来说,MAR 假设被违背了,那么就产生非可忽略的缺失数据机制,但是若仅对 x 来说被违背时,则没有违背非可忽略的缺失数据机制。在那种情况下,为了获得参数 θ 的一致估计,必须对缺失数据生成过程以及整个模型加以建模。为了避免选择偏倚的可能性,必须使用诸如赫克曼两阶段方法的估计量。

估算文献关注可忽略缺失性。若数据集是 MCAR,则撇开可通过估算减少的效率损失不谈,缺失数据并不会引起什么问题。相反,如果数据集仅仅是 MAR,那么为确保一致性与提高效率或许必用估算方法。

4.3 非模型处理缺失数据

倘若没有模型可以利用,则人们直接分析可用数据,或者分析经过基于非模型估算之后的数据。

4.3.1 只利用可用数据

成列删除或完整个案分析意指,删除数据中有缺失值的一个或多个变量的那种观测值(个案)。在 MCAR 假设下,经过成列删除之后,所保留的样本仍是源自最初总体的一个随机样本;因此,基于该样本的估计是一致的。不过,其标准误差将会扩大,因为所用信息甚少。若回归元个数很多,则成列删除的总效果导致总观测值会剧烈减少。这激发人们脱离那种对拥有高比例缺失观测值的变量进行分析,可是,由该种方法所产生的结果却潜在的使人误导。

如果 MCAR 得不到满足且缺失数据仅仅是 MAR,那么估计将是有偏的。因而,成列删除对违背 MCAR 而言不是稳健的。不过,成列删除对回归分析中各个自变量(回归元)违背 MAR 而言是稳健的,也就是,当任何回归元出现缺失数据的概率并不依赖于因变量之值。简略地讲,成列删除是可接受的,如果归因于缺失数据的不完全情况构成了各种各样总情况的比例很小,比如说5%或更少(谢弗,1996)。重要的是,成列删除之后的样本是所研究总体的代表。

成对删除(pairwise deletion)或可用案例分析,时常被认为是比成列删除更好的一种方法。其思想是估计(x_1, x_2)的联合样本矩时,运用观测值(x_{1i}, x_{2i})的全部可能对,并且估计边缘矩时运用个体变量的全部观测值。因而,在线性回归中,在成对删除下我们运用回归元的所可能对估计$(X'X)$与$(X'y)$,而在成列删除下,要在删除任何拥有缺失观测值的全部情况后才能估计$(X'X)$与$(X'y)$。很明显,在成对删除下,我们损失较少信息。这里建议要运用最大信息量去估计个体概括统计量,诸如均值与协方差,然后使用这些概括统计量去计算回归估计。

成对删除有两个重要局限性:(1) 一般地讲,估计标准误差与检验统计量都是有偏的;(2) 所得到的回归元协方差矩阵 $(X'X)$ 可能不是正定的。

4.3.2 不用模型的估算

统计软件经常执行一系列专门或勉强证明合理的方法。

均值估算(mean imputation)或均值替补(mean substitution)意指,运用可利用值的平均值代替缺失观测值。该方法是均值保持不变的,但将对数据的边缘分布产生影响。很明显,边缘分布中心概率质量表现出增大。该方法也影响到协方差以及与其他变量的相关性。

简单替补(simple hot deck,或称热平台法,译者注)估算意指,用来自从那种有观测值的变量中随机抽取到的值代替缺失值,有点像自助法。该方法维持了那个变量的边缘分布,但却扭曲了变量之间的协方差与相关性。

在回归背景下,这两个著名方法虽然具有简单性,但却没有一个引人注目。

4.4 观测数据似然函数

缺失数据的现代方法是,通过从基于假定观测数据模型或缺失数据机制中抽取的单个或多重值来估算缺失观测值。该种方法的贝叶斯变形是从后验分布中采样,既使用似然函数又使用参数的先验分布。

第一个重要问题涉及估算方法中缺失数据机制所起的作用,特别是,缺失数据机制是否是可忽略的。

设 θ 表示 $Y = (Y_{obs}, Y_{mis})$ 数据生成过程的参数,并设 ψ 表示缺失数据机制的参数。为于符号简单起见,假定 (Y_{obs}, Y_{mis}) 均是连续变量。于是, (R, Y_{obs}) 的联合分布由

$$\Pr[R, Y_{obs} | \theta, \psi] = \int \Pr[R, Y_{obs}, Y_{mis} | \theta, \psi] d Y_{mis} \qquad (4.3)$$

$$= \int \Pr[R | Y_{obs}, Y_{mis}, \psi] \Pr[Y_{obs}, Y_{mis} | \theta] d Y_{mis}$$

$$= \Pr[R | Y_{obs}, \psi] \int \Pr[Y_{obs}, Y_{mis} | \theta] d Y_{mis}$$

$$= \Pr[R | Y_{obs}, \psi] \Pr[Y_{obs} | \theta]$$

第一个等式是从所有数据与 R 的联合概率中通过对 Y_{mis} 进行积分(或者平均),进而推导出 (R, Y_{obs}) 的联合概率。第二行将联合概率因式分解以 Y_{obs} 与 Y_{mis} 为条件的、条件成分及边缘成分。第三行从观测数据机制中分离出缺失数据机制;该步由 MAR 假设得出。最后一行意味着, θ 与 ψ 是截然不同的参数,从而对 θ 进行推断能忽略缺失数据机制,而仅仅依赖于 Y_{obs}。

观测数据似然是与第四行的最后因子成比例

$$L[\theta | Y_{obs}] \propto \Pr[Y_{obs} | \theta] \qquad (4.4)$$

该观测数据似然只涉及观测数据 Y_{obs},尽管参数 θ 出现在全部观测值(观测到数据与缺失数据)的数据生成过程中。比例常值没有出现在(4.4)之中。

在 MAR 假设下, (θ, ψ) 的联合后验概率可被写成 $\Pr[R, Y_{obs} | \theta, \psi]$ 与先验联合分布 $\pi(\theta, \psi)$ 的如下乘积形式:

$$\Pr[\theta, \psi | Y_{obs}, R] = k \Pr[R, Y_{obs} | \theta, \psi] \pi(\theta, \psi) \qquad (4.5)$$

$$\propto \Pr[R | Y_{obs}, \psi] \Pr[Y_{obs} | \theta] \pi(\theta, \psi)$$

$$\propto \Pr[R | Y_{obs}, \psi] \Pr[Y_{obs} | \theta] \pi\theta(\theta) \pi\psi(\psi)$$

其中第一行中的 k 表示与 (θ, ψ) 无关的一个比例性常值。第二行用到了(4.3)给出的因式分解,而第三行则使用了 θ 与 ψ 是独立先验的假设。

因为主要关注内容在于 θ,所以从联合后验中通过对 ψ 进行积分推导 θ 的边缘后验。从而,得出后验观测数据(observed-data posterior)

$$\Pr[\boldsymbol{\theta} \mid \boldsymbol{Y}_{\text{obs}}, \boldsymbol{R}] = k \Pr[\boldsymbol{\theta}, \boldsymbol{\psi} \mid \boldsymbol{Y}_{\text{obs}}, \boldsymbol{R}] \mathrm{d}\boldsymbol{\psi} \quad (4.6)$$
$$\propto \Pr[\boldsymbol{Y}_{\text{obs}} \mid \boldsymbol{\psi}] \boldsymbol{\pi}_\theta(\boldsymbol{\theta}) \int \Pr[\boldsymbol{R} \mid \boldsymbol{Y}_{\text{obs}}, \boldsymbol{\psi}) \boldsymbol{\pi}_\psi(\boldsymbol{\psi}) \mathrm{d}\boldsymbol{\psi}$$
$$\propto L[\boldsymbol{\theta} \mid \boldsymbol{Y}_{\text{obs}}] \boldsymbol{\pi}_\theta(\boldsymbol{\theta})$$

其中第二行将 $\boldsymbol{\theta}$ 与 $\boldsymbol{\psi}$ 分离开,而最后一行将积分表达式合并到比例性常值之中。因此,最后一行没有包含 $\boldsymbol{\psi}$,从而与缺失数据机制 $\boldsymbol{R}$ 独立。

4.5 基于回归的估算

在本节,我们考察基于最小二乘法的估算。其重要组成部分是运用 EM 算法。

EM 算法由期望步骤与求极大值步骤组成。EM 算法的结构与贝叶斯 MCMC 及增广数据方法紧密地联系。因此,将引入一个例子,阐述支撑现代多重估算方法的动因,并给出这类方法的重要特性,而不是提供处理缺失数据的完整操作方法。

4.5.1 因变量出现缺失数据的线性回归例子

在实际应用中,因变量(内生变量)与/或者解释变量可能出现缺失观测值。我们考察一个回归例子,其中因变量有缺失观测值,即

$$\begin{bmatrix} y_1 \\ y_{\text{mis}} \end{bmatrix} = \begin{bmatrix} X_1 \\ X_2 \end{bmatrix} \beta + \begin{bmatrix} u_1 \\ u_2 \end{bmatrix} \quad (4.7)$$

其中 $E[\boldsymbol{u} \mid \boldsymbol{X}] = 0, E[\boldsymbol{u}\boldsymbol{u}' \mid \boldsymbol{X}] = \sigma^2 I_N$。新出现的困难是,因变量 y 观测值的一部分出现缺失,将此缺失部分记为 $\boldsymbol{Y}_{\text{mis}}$。我们假定,可利用的完全观测值是来自总体的一个随机样本,因而假定缺失数据虽不是 MCAR 的,但却是 MAR 的。

已知 MAR 假设,且 $N_1 > K$,N_1 的第一分块能用于一致地估计出 K 维参数。在高斯误差条件下,(β, σ^2) 的极大似然估计是 $\hat{\beta} = [X_1'X_1]^{-1}X_1'y_1$。借助于标准理论知识,并在正态性假设下,得到 $\hat{\beta} \mid$ 数据 $\sim \mathcal{N}[\beta, \sigma^2 [X_1'X_1]^{-1}]$ 与 $s^2/\sigma^2 \mid \hat{\beta} \sim (N_1 - K)\chi^2_{N_1-K}$。

首先,考察生成缺失观测值的一种朴素单一估算方法。以 X_2 为条件,Y_{mis} 的预测值记为 $\hat{y}_{\text{mis}}$,$\hat{y}_{\text{mis}}$ 由 $X_2\hat{\beta}$ 给出,其中 $\hat{\beta}$ 表示仅利用前面 N_1 个观测所获得的先前估计值。于是

$$\hat{E}[\boldsymbol{y}_{\text{mis}} \mid \boldsymbol{X}_2] = \hat{y}_{\text{mis}} = X_2\hat{\beta} \quad (4.8)$$
$$\hat{V}[\boldsymbol{Y}_{\text{mis}} \mid \boldsymbol{X}_2] \equiv \hat{V}[\hat{y} \mid \boldsymbol{X}_2] = s^2(I_{N_2} + X_2[X_1'X_1]X_2')$$

其中 $s^2 I_{N_2}$ 表示 $V_{[u_2]}$ 的估计值。

就上面朴素方法而言,可生成 N_2 个 y_{mis} 的预测值,然后将标准回归方法应用到 $N = N_1 + N_2$ 观测值的全部样本上。

朴素方法的两个步骤对应于 EM 算法的两个步骤。预测步是 E 步骤,而将最小二乘应用于扩大样本的第二步则是 M 步骤。

不过,这种解显得不精细。第一,考虑数据扩大步骤。由于生成值 $\hat{y}_{\text{mis}}$ 准确地位于最小二乘拟合平面上,为了得到一个新的估计值 $\hat{\beta}_A$ 将 $(\hat{y}_{\text{mis}}, X_2)$ 加入样本之中并不会改变先前估计值 $\hat{\beta}$

$$\hat{\beta}_A = [X'_1X_1 + X'_2X_2]^{-1}[X'_1y_1 + X'_2\hat{y}_{\text{mis}}] =$$
$$[X'_1X_1 + X'_2X_2]^{-1}[X'_1X_1\hat{\beta} + X'_2X_2\hat{\beta}] = \hat{\beta}$$

第二,因为由构造知,添加的 N_2 个残差均为 0,通过标准公式所获得的来自扩大样本的 σ^2 估计值,该估计值显得太小,即

$$s_A^2 = (y - X\hat{\beta}_A)'(y - X\hat{\beta}_A)/N =$$
$$(y - X\hat{\beta}_A)'(y - X\hat{\beta}_A)/N < s^2 \qquad (4.9)$$

正确地讲,其中 s^2 应被 N_1 而不是 N 除。

最后,正如从 $\hat{y}_{\text{mis}}$ 的抽样方差中所看到的,与 y_1 不同,生成预测都是异方差的,从而 $\hat{\beta}_A$ 的方差不能利用通常最小二乘公式加以估计。观测值 $\hat{y}_{\text{mis}}$ 是从具有不同方差的分布中抽取的。这种朴素方法没有考虑到依附于 $\hat{y}_{\text{mis}}$ 估计的不确定性。

为了确定这些问题,就需要校正。首先,$\hat{y}_{\text{mis}}$ 的估计应考虑到 $\hat{\beta}$ 的不确定性。通过调整 $\hat{y}_{\text{mis}}$ 可达到此目的,并将某些"噪声"加入到生成预测之中,使得缺失数据估计值更紧密地酷似从 y_1 的(估计或条件)分布所抽取的值。标准化步骤用到了下面事实: $V[\hat{y}_{\text{mis}}]$ 的估计值 $\hat{V}$ 可从 (4.8) 式得出。因此,变换变量 $\hat{V}^{-1/2}\hat{y}_{\text{mis}}$ 的成分拥有单位方差。为了类似 y_1 的分布,我们能运用从 $\mathcal{N}[0, s^2]$ 分布实施蒙特卡罗抽样,并用 $\hat{V}^{-1/2}\hat{y}_{\text{mis}}$ 乘以它。

修正算法如下:

1. 利用前面 N_1 个完整观测值估计值 $\hat{\beta}$。
2. 生成 $\hat{y}_{\text{mis}} = X_2\hat{\beta}$。
3. 生成 $\hat{y}_{\text{mis}}^a = (\hat{V}^{-1/2}\hat{y}_{\text{mis}}) \odot u_m$ 的调整值,其中 u_m 表示由 $N[0, s^2]$ 分布得出的蒙特卡罗抽样值,而 $\odot$ 表示元素对元素逐一乘法。
4. 运用扩大样本得到 $\hat{\beta}$ 的修正估计值。
5. 重复第 1 步至第 4 步,第一步将用到 $\hat{\beta}$ 的修正估计。

修正算法也称为 EM 类型算法,该方法不断实施,一直到它在下述意义下收敛为止:系数变化或回归残差平方和变化可变得任何小。

附 录

附录 I 常用数学运算和统计学常用的符号及读法

表 1 常用数学运算和关系符号

符号	读法	含义
+	plus, add	加法, addition; 和, sum
-	minus, subtract	减法, subtraction; 差, difference
×·	times, multiply	乘法, multiplication; 积, product
÷ /	divided by	除法, division; 商, quotient
=	equals	$1+2=3$, one plus two equals three
≠	not equal to	$1 \neq 2$, one is not equal to two
≈	almost equal to	约等于, $e \approx 2.71828$
≡	identical to	恒等于, 同余于
<	less than	$1<2$, one is less than two
≪	much less than	远小于
>	greater than	$1+1>1$, one plus one is greater than one
≫	much greater than	远大于
(	left parenthesis	左小括号
)	right parenthesis	右小括号
[	left bracket	左中括号
]	right bracket	右中括号
{	left brace	左大括号
}	right brace	右大括号
.	period	句号
,	comma	逗号
:	colon	冒号
;	semicolon	分号
…	dot dot dot	省略号, 数学上只用三个点就好

表2　常用统计计算符号

符号	读法	含义
$\bar{x}$	x bar	x 的平均值（传说中的"x 拨"）
$\tilde{x}$	x tilde	x 的中位数
$\hat{x}$	x hat	x 的估计值
x_i	x sub i	第 i 个 x
$\sum$	sigma	求和符号，大写的 σ
$\sum_{i=1}^{n} x_i$	summation from x sub 1 to x sub n	从 x_1 一直加到 x_n
$\prod$	pi	求积符号，大写的 π
$\prod_{i=1}^{n} x_i$	product from x sub 1 to x sub n	从 x_1 一直乘到 x_n

表3　常用集合逻辑关系符号

符号	读法	含义
$\cup$	union	并集，取两个集合的所有元素
$\cap$	intersection	交集，取两个集合共有的元素
$\subset$	contained in or subset of	包含于，$A \subset B$，A 包含于 B
$\supset$	contains or superset of	包含，$A \supset B$，A 包含 B
$\rightarrow$	arrow	箭头
$\Rightarrow$	implies	意味着，推导出
$\Leftrightarrow$	equivalent	等价于
$\propto$	proportional to	正比于
∞	infinity	无限
Δ	delta	判别式
$\forall$	for all	对于任意
$\exists$	there exists	存在

表4 常用运算关系和微积分计算符号

符号	读法	含义
$\|a\|$	absolute volve of a	a 的绝对值
a^*	a star	also as a asterisk
$\dfrac{a}{b}$	a over b	分子, numerator; 分母, denominator
a^2	a square	a 的平方
a^3	a cube	a 的立方
a^n	a to the nth power	a 的 n 次方
$\sqrt{a}$	square root of a	(二次)根号 a
$\sqrt[3]{a}$	cubic root of a	三次根号 a
$\sqrt[n]{a}$	nth root of a	n 次根号 a
$\log_b a$	logarithm base b of a	以 b 为底 a 的对数
$\lg x$	logarithm base 10 of x or lg of x	x 的常用对数, common logarithm(德国和俄罗斯的传统)
$\ln x$	logarithm base e of x or ln of x	x 的自然对数, natural logarithm(e, 欧拉数, Euler's number)
$\lim\limits_{x \to a} f(x) = b$	limit as x approaches a of $f(x)$ equals b	当 $x \to a$ 时, $f(x)$ 的极限是 b
$\dfrac{dy}{dx}$	dy by dx	x 的微分, 莱布尼兹的记号(the derivative of y with respect of x, Leibniz's notation)
y'	y prime	y 的导数, 拉格朗日的记号(Lagrange's notation)
$\dot{y}$	y dot	y 的导数, 牛顿的记号(Newton's notation)
$\int f(x) dx$	integral of $f(x)$	$f(x)$ 的不定积分(indefinite integral)
$\int_a^b f(x) dx$	from a to b	$f(x)$ 的定积分(definite integral)

表5 常用三角函数符号

符号	读法	含义
sin	sine	正弦, 对边与斜边的比值
cos	cosine	余弦, 邻边与斜边的比值
tan	tangent	正切, 对边与邻边的比值(切线)
cot	cotangent	余切, 邻边与对边的比值
sec	secant	正割, 斜边与邻边的比值(割线)
csc	cosecant	余割, 斜边与对边的比值
arcsin	arcus sine	反正弦, 正弦函数的反函数
f^{-1}	inverse function of f	f 的反函数

附录 II 概率论数理统计惯用符号及其含义

X, Y random variables　　随机变量

$P(X\leqslant 2)$, $Pr(X\leqslant 2)$ probability that $X\leqslant 2$　　$X\leqslant 2$ 的概率

$P(X\leqslant 2|Y\geqslant 1)$, conditional probability　　条件概率

$E(X\leqslant 2)$, $E(X)$ expectation of X　　X 的期望值

$E(X|Y\geqslant 1)$ conditional expectation　　条件期望值

c. d. f. /cdf cumulative distribution function　　累计分布函数

p. d. f. /pdf probability density function　　概率密度函数

p. g. f. /pgf probability generating functions　　概率生成函数

c. f. /cf characteristic function　　特征函数

m. g. f. /mgf moment generating function　　矩生成函数(矩母函数)

$\bar{x}$ mean (especially, sample mean)　　平均值(特别是样本平均值)

σ/s. d. standard deviation　　标准偏差

σ^2, Var, var, variance　　方差

μ_1, μ_2, μ_3, μ_i, μ_{ij} moments of a distribution　　分布矩

ρ coefficient of correlation　　相关系数

$\rho_{12,34}$ partial correlation coefficient　　偏相关系数

附录Ⅲ 统计学常用英文词汇汉译表

A

abnormal distribution 非正态分布
abnormal observation 反常观测值
absence of correlation 无相关,没有相关
absence of multicollinearity 无多重共线性
abscissa 横坐标
abscissa axis 横轴
absence rate 缺勤率
absolute accuracy 绝对精度
absolute deviation 绝对离差
absolute frequency 绝对频数
absolute number 绝对数
absolute value 绝对值
absolute residuals 绝对残差
absolutely continuous distribution 绝对连续分布
acceleration life testing 加速寿命试验
acceptable region 接受域
acceptable hypothesis 可接受假设
accident error 偶然误差
accumulated frequency 累积频数,累计频率
accumulation 积累,累积,累计
accuracy 准确度,准确性
actual figures 实际数字
adaptive estimator 自适应估计量
addition 增加,加法
addition theorem 加法定理
additivity 可加性
additivity of probability 概率的可加性
adjusted index 校正指数,调整指数
adjusted mean 校正平均数,调整平均数
adjusted R^2 调整的 R^2

adjusted rate 调整率
adjusted value 校正值
admissibility 容许性
admissibility of minimax rules 极小极大法则的容许性
admissible error 容许误差
aggregate 合计,总计,集合体,合计的,集合的
aggregate data 总量数据,综合资料
aggregation 综合,汇总,聚合
aggregation bias 归并偏倚,归并偏误
allowance error 容许误差
almost everywhere 几乎处处
almost surely 几乎必然
alternative hypothesis 对立假设,备择假设
among class variation 组间变异
amounts 合计,总数,数量
analysis of correlation 相关分析
analysis of covariance 协方差分析
analysis of data 分析数据
analysis of regression 回归分析
analysis of time series 时间序列分析
analysis of variance (ANOVA) 方差分析
angular transformation 角变换
ANOVA(analysis of variance) 方差分析
ANOVA Models 方差分析模型
applied statistics 应用统计学
approximate distribution 近似分布
approximate error 近似误差
approximation 近似,逼近,近似值,逼近值
area under the curve 曲线下的面积
arithmetic expression 算术表达式
arithmetic mean 算术平均数,算术均值
artificial data 虚构数据
ascending sort 升序排列,升序排序
aspect ratio 长宽比,纵横比
association analysis 关联性分析

associative law 结合律
asymmetrical distribution 非对称分布
asymmetry 非对称性
asymptote (asymptotic line) 渐近线
asymptotic analysis 渐近分析
asymptotic bias 渐近偏倚
asymptotic efficiency 渐近效率
asymptotic variance 渐近方差
asymptotic theory 渐近理论
asymptotical variance 渐近正态性
asymptotically 渐近地
asymptotically unbiased estimator 渐近无偏估计量
asymptotics 渐近性
attribute data 属性数据,属性资料
attribute inspection 属性检验
auto correlation function 自相关函数
auto covariance 自协方差函数
auto regression process 自回归过程
automatic data processing (ADP) 自动化数据处理
auxiliary regression 辅助回归
auxiliary variable 辅助变量
average 平均,平均数
average confidence interval length 平均置信区间长度
average deviation (AD) 平均离差
average growth rate 平均增长率
average sample size (ASS) 平均样本量,平均样本大小
axiomatic approach 公理化方法,公理方法
axiom 公理,公设
axiom of complete induction 完全归纳法公理,数学归纳法公理
axis of abscissas 横坐标轴
axis of ordinates 纵坐标轴

B

bar chart 条形图,条线图
bar graph 条形图,条线图

base period 基期,基本周期
basevector 基向量
base-period value 基期值
basic data 原始数据,基本数据
basic econometric technique 基本经济计量方法
basic hypothesis 基本假设
Bayes analysis 贝叶斯分析
Bayes theorem 贝叶斯定理
bell-shaped curve 钟形曲线
benchmark 基准,水平基点
Bernoulli distribution 伯努利分布
Bernoulli experiment 伯努利试验
Bernoulli theorem 伯努利定理
best estimate 最佳估计,最佳估计值
best linear unbiased estimator (BLUE) 最佳线性无偏估计量
beta coefficient β 系数
beta distribution β 分布
between variation 组间变差
bias 偏性,偏倚,偏差
biased downward 向下偏倚
biased error 偏倚误差,有偏误差
biased estimator 有偏估计量
biased statistic 有偏统计量,偏倚统计量
biased upward 向上偏倚,上偏
biaxial coordinates 双轴坐标
bilinear form 双线性型
bilinear function 双线性函数
bimodal curve 双峰曲线
binary bit 二进位
binary logistic regression 二元逻辑斯蒂回归
binary random variable 二元随机变量
binomial coefficient 二项式系数
binomial distribution 二项分布
binomial theorem 二项式定理
biometrics 生物测量学,生物统计学

bivariate 双变量的,二元的,二维的
bivariate correlate 二变量相关
bivariate data 二元数据
bivariate normal distribution 二元变量正态分布
bivariate normal population 二元变量正态总体
block 区组,区,块,分组,分块
bootstrap 自助法,自举法
Borel set 波莱尔集
box plots 盒须图,箱线图
breakdown bound 崩溃点
broken line 折线,虚线
broken line graph 折线图,虚线图
Brownian motion 布朗运动
business efficiency 经营效率
business index 商业指数
business statistics 工商业统计
buying power index 购买力指数

C

calculation 计算,演算
calculator 计算器,计算员
calculus 微积分,微积分学,演算
canonical correlation 典型相关
canonical mean 典型均值
cap "冒"符号,"交"运算符(∩)
caption 标题,说明,加上标题
cartogram 比较统计地图,统计图
case study 案例研究,个案研究
case-control study 个案控制研究
case mortality rate 致命率
case method 个案法,案例法,举例法
case study 个案研究,案例研究
casting 投掷
categorical variable 分类变量
catenary 悬链线

Cauchy distribution 柯西分布
cause-and-effect relationship 因果关系
cell 单元，网格
censored data 删失数据
censored distribution 删失分布
censored regression 删失回归
censoring 删失
censoring time 删失时间
census 普查，全面调查
census family 普查家庭
census of agriculture 农业普查
center of location 定位，中心原点
center of symmetry 对称中心
centering 集中，中心化
centering the data 集中数据，数据中心化
centile 百分位数
central feature 主要特征
central limit theorem 中心极限定理
central moment 中心矩
central tendency 集中趋势
central value 中心值
chain 环，链，连锁
chain base 环比基期
chain base index 环比指数，环基指数
chance 机会，机遇
chance error 随机误差
chance variable 随机变量
characteristic equation 特征方程
characteristic function 特征函数
characteristic root 特征根
characteristic vector 特征向量
Chebyshev criterion of fit 拟合的切比雪夫准则
Chebyshev's inequality 切比雪夫不等式
Chernoff faces 切尔诺夫脸谱图
chi-square test 卡方检验

Choleskey decomposition 乔洛斯基分解
circle chart 圆图
class boundaries 组界
class limits 组限
class interval 组区间,组距
class mid-value 组中值
class upper limit 组上限
class width 组距
classification 分组,分类
classified variable 分类变量
cluster analysis 聚类分析
cluster sampling 整群抽样
code 代码,编码
coded data 编码数据
coding 编码
coefficient 系数
coefficient matrix 系数矩阵
coefficient of auto-correlation 自相关系数
coefficient of contingency 列联系数
coefficient of determination 决定系数
coefficient of multiple correlation 多重相关系数
coefficient of partial correlation 偏相关系数
coefficient of production-moment correlation 积差相关系数
coefficient of rank correlation 等级相关系数
coefficient of regression 回归系数
coefficient of skewness 偏度系数
coefficient of variation 变异系数
cohort study 队列研究
collection of data 收集数据,数据收集
column 列(栏)
column effect 列效应
column factor 列因素
combination pool 合并
combinative table 组合表
common factor 公因子,公共因子

common regression coefficient 公共回归系数
common ratio 公比
common value 共同值
common variance 共同方差
communality variance 公因子方差
comparability 可比性
comparison method 比较法
comparison principle 比较原理
comparison value 比较值
complement of set 余集
complement of an event 事件的补，补事件
complete additivity 完全可加性
complete data 完备数据
complete independence 完全独立
complete statistics 完备统计量
completely randomized design（CRD）完全随机化设计
composite alternative hypothesis 复合备择假设
composite error 综合误差，总和误差
composite event 联合事件，复合事件
composite hypothesis 复合假设
concave function 凹函数
concavity 凹性
condition variance 条件方差
conditional density 条件密度
conditional distribution 条件分布
conditional equation 条件方程式
conditional expectation 条件期望
conditional expected value 条件期望值
conditional independence 条件独立性
conditional likelihood 条件似然
conditional probability 条件概率
conditional probability function 条件概率函数
conditional test 条件检验
confidence interval 置信区间
confidence level 置信水平

confidence limit 置信限
confidence lower limit 置信下限
confidence upper limit 置信上限
confidentiality 保密性
confirmatory 稳定
confirmatory data analysis 证实性数据分析
confirmatory research 证实性研究
confounding 混杂
confounding factor 混杂因素
conjoint sets 相交集
consistency 一致性，相合性，相容性
consistency check 一致性核查
consistent asymptotically normal estimate 一致渐近正态估计(值)，相合渐近正态估计(值)
consistent estimate 一致估计(值)，相合估计(值)
constrained nonlinear regression 受约束非线性回归
constraint 约束
consumer price index (CPI) 消费价格指数
contaminated distribution 污染分布
contaminated Gaussian distribution 污染高斯分布
contaminated normal distribution 污染正态分布
contamination 污染
contamination model 污染模型
contingency table 列联表
continuity 连续性
contour 轮廓，周线，等高线
contour line 等值线
contribution rate 贡献率
control 控制
control chart 控制图
control parameter 控制参数
controlled experiments 受控实验
conventional data 常规数据，常规资料
conventional depth 常规深度
converge 收敛

converge weakly 弱收敛
convergence 收敛，收敛性
convergence in distribution 依分布收敛
convergence in probability 依概率收敛
convolution 卷积
corrected factor 校正因子
corrected mean 校正均值
correction coefficient 校正系数
correctness 正确性
correlation coefficient 相关系数
correlation index 相关指数
correspondence 对应
counting 计数
covariance 协方差
covariant 协变量
Cox Regression Cox 回归
Cramer-Rao inequality Cramer-Rao 不等式
criteria for fitting 拟合准则
criteria of least squares 最小二乘准则
critical ratio 临界比
critical region 拒绝域
critical value 临界值
cross-over design 交叉设计
cross-section 横截面，截面
cross-section analysis 横截面分析，截面分析
cross-section survey 横截面调查
cross tabs 交叉表
cross-tabulation table 横列表，交叉分组表
cube root 立方根
cumulative distribution function 累计分布函数
cumulative frequency 累积频率
cumulative frequency polygon 累加次数多边形图
cumulative probability 累计概率
curvature 曲率，弯曲
curve fit 曲线拟和

curve fitting 曲线拟合
curvilinear regression 曲线回归
curvilinear relation 曲线关系
cut-and-try method 尝试法
cutoff point 截止点，截尾点
cycle 周期，循环，一段时间
cycle period 周转期
cyclical test 循环检验

D

D test　D 检验
data 数据，资料
data acquisition 数据收集，资料收集
data bank 数据库
data capacity 数据容量
data deficiencies 数据缺乏
data envelopment analysis（DEA）数据包络分析
data handling 数据处理
data manipulation 数据处理
data processing 数据处理
data reduction 数据缩减
data set 数据集
data sources 数据来源
data transformation 数据变换
data validity 数据有效性
data-in 数据输入
data-out 数据输出
dead time 停滞期
decile 十分位数，十分位值
degree of freedom 自由度
degree of precision 精确度
degree of reliability 可靠性程度
degression 递减，减速，下降
density function 密度函数
density of data points 数据点的密度

dependent variable 应变量，因变量
depth 深度
derivative matrix 导数矩阵
derivative-free methods 无导数方法
design 设计
determinacy 确定性
determinacy principle 确定性原理
determinant 行列式
determinant identity 行列式恒等式
determinant rank 行列式秩
deviation 偏差，变差，离差
deviation from average 平均离差，平均偏差
deviation from an estimate 估计偏差
deviation from regression 回归偏差
deviation point 偏差点
diagnostic plot 诊断图
diagonal block 对角块
diagonal block matrix 对角分块矩阵
diagonal sum 对角和
dichotomous classification 二元分类，二项分类
dichotomous population 二元总体，两分总体
difference 差异，差别，差分，微分的，
difference between two means 两个均值之差
difference with significance 差别显著
differential equation 微分方程
dimensional invariance 维数不变性，维度不变性
direct standardization 直接标准化法
discrete variable 离散型变量
discriminant 判断式，判别的
discriminant analysis 判别分析
discriminant coefficient 判别系数
discriminant function 判别函数
discriminant of quadratic form 二次型的判别式
discriminantor 判别子，判别式函数
dispersion 离散，离散度，离中趋势，离差

dispersion index 离散指数
disposable income (DI) 可支配收入
disproportion 不成比例，不均衡
disproportionate sampling 非比例抽样，不按比例抽样
disproportionate sub-class numbers 不成比例的小组含量
distance 距离
distance between samples 样本间距离
distance function 距离函数
distributed 分布的
distributed parameter 分布参数
distribution 分布，分配
distribution-free method 非参数方法，无分布方法
distribution-free test 非参数检验，无分布检验
distribution law 分布律
distributive law 分配律
distribution shape 分布形状
disturbance term 扰动，扰动项
disturbed 扰动，干扰，受扰动的
domain 域，范围，定义域，领域
dose response method 剂量效果反应法
dose response curve 剂量反应曲线
dot 点
dot diagram 点图
double blind method 双盲法
double blind trial 双盲试验
double difference 二重差分
double limit 二重极限
double logarithmic 双对数的
double sampling plan 二次抽样方案
double sum 二重和
Dow Jones index 道琼斯指数
downward bais 向下偏倚，向下偏误，下偏
downward cumulation 向下累加
downward rank 降秩
downward trend 向下趋势

drift 漂移，变化，偏移
dual-space plot 对偶空间图
duration model 持续期限模型
dynamic data 动态数据
dynamic indicator 动态指标
dynamics 动态学，动力学

E

econometrics 经济计量学，计量经济学
econometric analysis 经济计量分析
econometric jargon 经济计量学术语
econometric model 经济计量模型
economic growth 经济增长
economic model 经济模型
economic parameter 经济参数
economic reasoning 经济推理
economic series 经济序列
effect 效应，作用，效果，影响
effect of interaction 交互作用的效应，交叉作用的影响
effective data 有效数据
effective period 有效期
effectiveness 效力，有效性，效果
effectiveness of investment 投资效益
efficiency 有效性，效益，效率
efficiency estimation 效率估计
efficiency index 效率指数
efficiency of estimator 估计量的有效性
eigen vector (EV) 特征向量
eigenelement 特征元素
eigenvalue 特征值
elasticity 弹性
ellipse 椭圆
empirical assumption 经验假设
empirical distribution 经验分布
empirical probability 经验概率

enumeration data 计数资料
equal sun-class number 相等次级组含量
equally likely 等可能
equal variance 同变性
error 误差,错误
error of estimate 估计误差
error type I 第一类错误
error type II 第二类错误
estimate 估计,估计值
estimated error mean squares 估计误差均方
estimated error sum of squares 估计误差平方和
estimator of location 位置估计量
estimator of scale 尺度估计量
Euclidean distance 欧几里得距离
event 事件
event space 事件空间
Eviews (Econometric Views)   Eviews 软件
ex ante forecasting 事前预测
examination of residual 残差检查,剩余检查
exceptional point 例外点
exceptional sample 例外样本
exclusive events 互斥事件
exogeneity 外生性
exogenous 外生的,外部的,局部的
exogenous lagged variable 外生滞后变量
expectation 期望,预期
expectation function 期望函数
expectation of life 平均寿命
expectation operator 期望算子
expected deviation 期望离差,期望偏差
expected loss 期望损失
expected utility 期望效用
expected value 期望值
expected value of sample 样本期望值
experiment 实验,试验

experiment design 实验设计,试验设计
experiment error 实验误差,试验误差
experimental group 实验组
experimental sampling 实验抽样
experimental unit 实验单位
explained deviation 可解释变异,可解释离差
explained variable 被解释变量
explanatory variable 说明变量,解释变量
exploratory data analysis 探索性数据分析
exponential curve 指数曲线
exponential distribution 指数分布
exponential growth 指数式增长
extended model 扩展模型
extra parameter 附加参数
extrapolation 外推法
extreme observation 极端观测值
extreme 尽头的,极端的,极度的
extreme value 极端值, 极值

F

F distribution F 分布
F test F 检验
factor 因素,要素,因子
factor analysis 因子分析,因素分析
factor level 因子水平,因子水准
factor score 因子得分
factorial 阶乘;阶乘的
factorial design 析因设计,因子设计
false data 虚假数据
false negative 假阴性
false negative error 假阴性错误
family of distributions 分布族
family of estimators 估计量族
fanning 扇面
fatality rate 病死率

field investigation 现场调查
field survey 现场调查
finite population 有限总体
finite sample 有限样本
first derivative 一阶导数,一阶微商
first order condition 一阶条件
first order equation 一阶方程
first principal component,第一主成分
first quadrant 第一象限
first quartile 第一四分位数
Fisher information 费雪信息(量)
fitted value 拟合值
fitting a curve 曲线拟合
fixed base 定基
fluctuation 随机起伏
forecast 预测
fourfold table 四重表
fourth 第四
fractile 分位数,分位点
fractile graphical analysis 分位数图形分析
fraction defective 次品率
fractional error 部分误差,相对误差
frequency 频率
frequency distribution 频数分布
frequency polygon 频数多边图
frontier point 前沿点,界限点
function relationship 函数关系
future value 未来值

G

Gamma distribution 伽玛分布
Gaussian curve 高斯曲线
Gauss increment 高斯增量
Gaussian distribution 高斯分布,正态分布
Gauss-Newton increment 高斯-牛顿增量

general census 全面普查
generalized liner models 广义线性模型
geometric distribution 几何分布
geometric mean 几何平均数
Gini's mean difference 基尼均差
general liner models 一般线性模型
general price index 总物价水平
general solution 通解
generalized 广义的,一般的
generalized inverse matrix 广义逆矩阵
generalized least squares (GLS) 广义最小二乘法
generalized liner models 广义线性模型
geometrical mean 几何平均数
geometry 几何学
given 给定的,已知的,特定的,
given value 给定值,已知值
global maximum 全局极大值
global minimum 全局极小值
goodness of fit 拟合优度,拟合度
goodness of fit test 拟合优度检验
gradient 梯度,斜度
gradient of determinant 行列式的梯度
graph 图形,图示,图解
graphic chart 图,图表,图解
grand mean 总均值,总平均数
gross amount 总量,总额
gross book value 账面价值总额
gross error ratio 总误差比
gross domestic product (GDP) 国内生产总值
gross national product (GNP) 国民生产总值
gross national product per capita 人均国民生产总值
group 组,类,群
group averages 分组平均数
group index 分组指数,类指数
group mean 组平均值

grouped data 分组数据,分组资料
grouped frequency 群频率,分组频率
growth curve 增长曲线
growth rate 增长率
guess value 估价,估值,估算
guessed 猜想的,假定的
guessed mean 假定平均数

H

half-normal distribution 半正态分布
half-period 半周期
half-range 半极差,半距
half line 半(直)线,射线
harmonic average 调和平均数
harmonic average index number 调和平均指数
harmonic index 调和指数
harmonic mean 调和平均,调和中项
hazard function 风险函数,危险函数
hazard rate 风险率,危险率
heading 标题,项目
health statistics 卫生统计学,健康统计学
heavy-tail 重尾,厚尾
heavy-tailed distribution 重尾分布,厚尾分布
Hessian matrix 海塞矩阵
heterogeneity 异质性,非均匀性,非齐次性
heterogeneity of variance 方差异质性,方差非齐次性
heterogeneity test 异质性检验,非均匀性检验
heteroscedasticity 异方差性
heteroscedastic model 异方差模型
hierarchical classification 层次分类
hierarchical clustering method 层次聚类法
hierarchy 层,层系,层次,谱系
high-leverage point 高杠杆率点
high order approximation 高阶近似
histogram 直方图

historical data 历史数据
homogeneity 同质性，齐性，齐次性
homogeneity of variance 方差同质性，方差齐性
homogeneity test 同质性检验，齐性检验
homogeneous 齐次的，同质的，均匀的
homogeneous equation system 齐次方程组
homogeneous polynomial 齐次多项式
homogeneous transition probability 齐次转移概率
Huber M-estimators Huber M 估计量
hyper 超
hyperbola 双曲线
hypergeometric distribution 超几何分布
hypernormal 超正态
hypernormality 超正态性
hyperplane 超平面
hypothesis testing 假设检验
hypothetical universe 假设总体，全域
hypothetical value 假设值

I

ideal index formula 理想指数公式
idempotent matrix 幂等矩阵
identical distribution 同分布
identical equal 恒等，全等
identical relation 恒等式，恒等关系
identification 识别，判定
identification condition 识别条件
identity 恒等，恒等式
identity law 同一律
identity equation 恒等式
identity matrix 单位矩阵
if and only if 当且仅当
iff (if and only if) 当且仅当
iid (IID) 独立同分布
impossible event 不可能事件

IMS (Institute of Mathematical Statistics) 数理统计学会
incidence correspondence 关联,对应
incidence matrix 关联矩阵
incidence rate 发病率
incomplete data 不完全数据
incomplete statistics 不完全统计,不完全统计资料
incompleteness 不完全性
inconsistency 不相容性
increasing function 递增函数
indefinite form 不定型
indefinite integral 不定积分
independence 独立,独立性
independence assumption 独立性假设
independence of random variable 随机变量的独立性
independent 独立的,无关的
independent event 独立事件
independent experiment 独立实验
independent random variable 独立随机变量
independent and identical distribution (iid, IID) 独立同分布
independently identically distribution sample 独立同分布样本
independent variable 自变量
index 指数,指标
index number 指数
index(number) of price 物价指数
index(number) of wholesale price 批发价格指数
indirect estimate 间接估计,间接估计值,间接推算
indirect sampling 间接抽样
indirect standardization 间接标准化法
individual 个体,个别
individual income 个体所得
individual measurement 个别测量值
induced 诱导的,导出的
induced measure 诱导测度
inductive approach 归纳法
inductive statistics 归纳统计学

infection rate 感染率
inferential statistics 推断统计学
inference band 推断带
infinite population 无限总体
infinite sample 无穷样本
infinite set 无穷集
infinitely great 无穷大,无限大
infinitely small 无穷小,无限小
infinity 无穷,无穷大
influence curve 影响曲线
influence function 影响函数
information capacity 信息容量
initial condition 初始条件
initial data 原始数据
initial estimate 初始估计值
initial level 最初水平
interaction 交互作用
interaction terms 交互作用项
intercept 截距
interpolation 内插法
interquartile range (IQR) 四分位数间距,四分位距
interval estimation 区间估计
intervals of equal probability 等概率区间
interval scale 区间尺度,区间标度
intraclass 组内,群内
intraclass correlation 组内相关,群内相关
intrinsic curvature 固有曲率
invariance 不变性
inverse correlation 逆相关
inverse distribution 逆分布
inverse function 反函数
inverse matrix 逆矩阵
inverse operation 逆运算
inverse probability 逆概率
inverse ratio 反比

inverse transformation 逆变换
isoquant 等量
isoquant curve 等量曲线
iteration 迭代
iteration method 迭代法
instrumental variables method 工具变量法

J

Jacobian determinant 雅可比行列式
joint density 联合密度
joint distribution function 联合分布函数
joint dependence 联合相依
joint hypothesis 联合假设
joint of events 事件并, 事件和
joint probability 联合概率
joint probability distribution 联合概率分布
just-identified equation 恰好识别方程
just-identified model 恰好识别模型

K

Kalman filter 卡尔曼滤子, 卡尔曼滤波器
Kaplan-Meier estimator Kaplan-Meier 估计量
Kaplan-Merier chart Kaplan-Merier 图
Kendall's coefficient Kendall 系数
Kendall's rank correlation Kendall 等级相关
kernel 核
kernel estimation 核估计
kernel function 核函数
kinetic 运动的, 动力学的
known quantity 已知量
known variance 已知方差
Kolmogorov theorem 柯尔莫哥洛夫定理
Kolmogorov-Smirnove test 柯尔莫哥洛夫—斯米尔诺夫检验
Kruskal and Wallis test Kruskal 与 Wallis 检验
kurtosis 峰度

kurtosis coefficient 峰度系数

L

lack of fit 拟合不佳
lack of sample 样本不足
ladder index 阶梯指数
lag 滞后
lag correlation 滞后相关
lag covariance 滞后协方差
lagged value 滞后值
Lagrange multiplier 拉格朗日乘子
large sample 大样本
large sample test 大样本检验
Latin square 拉丁方
Latin square design 拉丁方设计
law of large numbers theorem 大数定律
leading diagonal 主对角线
leakage 泄漏,漏损
least favorable configuration 最不利构形
least favorable distribution 最不利分布
least significant difference 最小显著差数
least square method 最小二乘法
least-absolute-residuals estimates 最小绝对残差估计
least-absolute-residuals fit 最小绝对残差拟合
least-absolute-residuals line 最小绝对残差线
legend 图例,表列,符号表
L-estimator L 估计量
L-estimator of location 位置 L 估计量
level 水平,水准
level line 水平线
level of confidence 置信水平
life expectance 预期寿命
life table 寿命表
life table method 生命表法
light-tailed distribution 轻尾分布,窄尾分布

likelihood function 似然函数
likelihood ratio 似然比
likelihood ratio test 似然比检验
line graph 线图
linear correlation 直线相关
linear equation 线性方程
linear programming 线性规划
linear regression 直线回归，线性回归
linear regression equation 直线回归方程
linear trend 线性趋势
link index (number) 环比指数
link relative ratio 环比
list of charts 统计图
location parameter 位置参数
location-scale parameter 位置尺度参数
location invariance 位置不变性
log likelihood 对数似然
log-rank test 对数秩检验
logarithmic curve 对数曲线
logarithmic normal distribution 对数正态分布
logarithmic scale 对数尺度，对数标度
logarithmic transformation 对数变换
logic check 逻辑检查
logistic distribution 逻辑斯蒂分布
Logit transformation   Logit 变换
lognormal distribution 对数正态分布
loss function 损失函数
low correlation 低度相关
lower bound 下界
lower confidence limit 下置信限，置信下限
lower control limit (LCL)   控制下限，下控制线
lower limit 下极限，下限
lowest-attained variance 最小可达方差
lurking variable 潜在变量

M

magnitude of variation 变异的大小，变异量
main effect 主效应，主作用
major heading 主标目，大标题
marginal density function 边缘密度函数
marginal probability 边缘概率
marginal probability distribution 边缘概率分布
matched data 配对资料
matched distribution 匹配分布
matched pair design 配对设计
matching of distribution 分布的匹配
matching of transformation 变换的匹配
mathematical expectation 数学期望
mathematical model 数学模型
mathematical statistics 数理统计学，数理统计
maximum L-estimator 极大 L 估计量
maximum likelihood method 最大似然法，极大似然法
mean 平均数，均数，均值，平均值
mean deviation（MD）平均绝对差，平均离差
mean square between groups 组间均方
mean square error（MSE）均方误差
mean square within group 组内均方
measure space 测度空间
measure of dependence 相依测度
measure of dispersion 离差测度
measure of central tendency 集中趋势测度
measure of goodness of fit 拟合优度度量
measurable 可测的
measurable function 可测函数
measurable space 可测空间
measurement data 计量数据
measurement value 测定值
measurement variable 测定变量
median 中位数

median polish 中位数平滑

median test 中位数检验

microdata 微观数据

mid-point 中点

mid-point of cell 组中值

mid-value 中间值

mid-value of class 组中值

minimal ancillary statistic 最小辅助统计量

minimal sufficient statistic 最小充分统计量

minimum distance estimation 最小距离估计

minimum effective dose 最小有效量,最小有效剂量

minimum variance bound (MVB)最小方差限

minimum variance estimator 最小方差估计量

MINITAB 统计软件包

minor heading 小标目,次标题

missing data 缺失数据,遗漏资料

mode 众数

model specification 模型设定

models for outliers 异常值模型,离群值模型

modified log odds 修正对数优比

modified mean 修正平均数

modulus of continuity 连续性模

moment 矩,动差

moment about the mean 中心矩

moment about the origin 原点矩

moment distribution 矩分布

morbidity 患病率,发病率

mortality 死亡率,死亡人数

most favorable configuration 最有利构形

multidimensional Scaling (ASCAL) 多维尺度,多维标度

multinomial Logistic Regression 多项逻辑斯蒂回归

multiple comparison 多重比较

multiple correlation 复相关

multiple covariance 多元协方差

multiple linear regression 多元线性回归

multiple response 多重选项
multiple sampling 多重抽样，多次抽样
multiple solutions 多解，多重解
multiple statistical analysis 多元统计分析
multiplication theorem 乘法定理
multi response 多元响应
multi-stage sampling 多阶段抽样
multivariate 多变量的，多元的
multivariate multinomial distribution 多元多项分布
mutual exclusive 互不相容
mutual independence 互相独立

N

natality 出生率
national income aggregates 国民总收入
natural boundary 自然边界
natural dead 自然死亡
natural logarithm 自然对数
natural zero 自然零
negative correlation 负相关
negative linear correlation 负线性相关
negatively skewed 负偏的
Newman-Keuls method Newman-Keuls 方法
NK method NK 方法
no statistical significance 无统计意义
nominal variable 名义变量
nonlinear regression 非线性相关
nonparametric statistics 非参数统计
nonparametric test 非参数检验
normal deviate 正态离差
normal distribution 正态分布
normal equation 正规方程组
normal ranges 正常范围
normal value 正常值
normalization 正规化

normal curve 正态曲线
normal deviate 正态离差
normal distribution 正态分布
normal kurtosis 正态峰
normal population 正态总体
normal probability curve 正态概率曲线
normal range 正常范围
normal value 正常值
normality test 正态性检验
nuisance parameter 多余参数，讨厌参数
null hypothesis 零假设，原假设
numerical variable 数值变量

O

objective function 目标函数
observation unit 观察单位，观测单位
observed value 观察值，观测值
one sided test 单侧检验
one-way analysis of variance 单因素方差分析
one way ANOVA 单因素方差分析
open sequential trial 开放型序贯设计
order statistics 顺序统计量
ordered categories 有序分类
ordinal 序数，序数的
ordinal function 序数函数
ordinal logistic regression 序数逻辑斯蒂回归
ordinal number 序数
ordinal variable 有序变量
orthogonal basis 正交基
orthogonal design 正交试验设计
orthogonal matrix 正交矩阵
orthogonal projection 正交投影
orthogonality 正交性
orthogonality conditions 正交条件，正交性条件
orthogonalization 正交化

outlier 离群值，异常值
outlier test 离群值检验
over identification 过度识别
over identified parameter 过度识别参数
output data 输出数据
output variable 输出变量

P

p value p 值
pair 配对,对偶,双
pair test 成对检验
paired design 配对设计
paired sample 成对样本,配对样本
pairwise 两两,成对,配对
pairwise comparison 成对比较,两两对比
pairwise independent 两两独立的
panel data 面板数据,平行数据
parabola 抛物线
parallel test 平行检验,替换检验
parameter 参数
parameter equation 参数方差
parameter space 参数空间
parameter test 参数检验
parameter of distribution 分布参数
parameter of regularity 正则参数,正则性参数
partial correlation 偏相关
partial derivation 求偏导数
partial derivative 偏导数,偏微商
partial regression 偏回归
partial replacement 部分放回(抽样)
partial replication 部分重复
partial sum 部分和
partials variance 偏方差
pattern 模式
pattern classification 模式分类

pattern recognition 模式识别
Pearson curves 皮尔逊曲线
percent (= per cent) 百分率,百分比,百分数
percent defective 不合格品百分率
percentage 百分法,百分比,百分数,百分数
percentage diagram 百分数图
percentage point 百分点
percentile 百分位数
percentile curves 百分位数曲线
percentile measure 百分位数度量
periodicity 周期性
permutation 排列
pie graph 圆形图,饼分图
Pitman estimator 皮特曼估计量
pivot 主元,枢轴量
planar (可)平面的
planar set 平面集
point density 点密度
point elasticity 点弹性
point estimation 点估计
point of discontinuity 不连续点
Poisson distribution 泊松分布
Poisson parameter 泊松参数
polled standard deviation 合并标准差
polled variance 综合方差,合并方差
poller 民意测验
polygon 多边图
polynomial 多项式
polynomial curve 多项式曲线
population 总体
positive correlation 正相关
positive definite 正定的,正的
positive skewness 正偏态,正偏斜度
positively skewed 正偏态,正偏斜
possible outcome 可能结果

post testing 事后试验,事后检验
posterior distribution 后验分布
power of a test 检验的功效,检验力
power series 幂级数
pre-sample value 预置样本值
precision 精密度,精度
predicted value 预测值,推测值
prediction 预测,推测
predictor 预测式,预估量,预报因子
preliminary analysis 初步分析
preliminary data 初步数据,初步资料
premultiply 自左乘
price deflator 价格紧缩指数
price level 物价水平,物价水准
pricing by quality 按质论价
primary data 原始数据,原始资料
primary index 原始指数,初级指数,未调整指数
primary sample 初级样本,原始样本
primary sampling units (PSUs) 初级抽样单位
principal axis 主轴
principal component analysis 主成分分析
principal indicators 主要指标
prior 先验的,居先的
prior distribution 先验分布
prior density 先验密度
prior hypothesis 先验假设
prior probability 先验概率
probabilistic model 概率模型
probability 概率,几率,或然率,可能性
probability a posterior 后验概率
probability a prior 先验概率
probability density 概率密度
probability density function (PDF) 概率密度函数
probability limits (Plim) 概率极限
probability plot 概率图

probability space 概率空间
probability weight 概率权数
probit 概率单位
probit regression 概率单位回归
product cost 产品成本
product line 生产线
product matrix 积矩阵
product moment correlation 乘积矩相关
productivity measurement 生产率测量；生产率测算
profile curve 纵断面曲线,轮廓曲线
proportion 比,比例,比率,部分,平衡
proportion by inverse 反比
proportion of failure 失败比例
proportion of success 成功比例
proportional 成比例的,比例的,平衡的,比例项
proportional mean 比例中项
proportional sampling 按比例抽样
prospective study 前瞻性调查
proximity 近似性,邻近,接近
pseudo 假的,伪的,拟的
pseudo correlation 伪相关
pseudo random number 伪随机数
pure error 纯误差
purposive sampling 有目的抽样,有意抽样

Q

quadrant 象限,四分之一圆
quadratic 二次的,
quadratic approximation 二次近似
quadratic differential 二次微分
qualitative 定性的,质量的
qualitative characteristics 品质特征
qualitative classification 定性分类,属性分类
qualitative index 质量指数
qualitative method 定性方法

quality control (QC) 质量控制,质量管理,品质控制
quantile 分位数,分位点
quantile-quantile plot 分位数-分位数图,Q-Q 图
quantity index 数量指数
quantitative analysis 定量分析,数量分析
quartile 四分位数,四分位点
quartile coefficient 四分位系数
quasi 准,拟,半
quasi-auto correlation 拟自相关
quasi-linear equation 准线性方程
questionnaire 问卷,调查表,征询意见表

R

radial 径向的
radial curve 径向曲线
radian 弧度
radical sign 根号
radius 半径
radix 底,根,基数
radix point 小数点
random allocation 随机配置,随机分配
random dependent variable 随机因变量
random effect 随机效应,随机效果
random event 随机事件
random number 随机数,随机号码
random process 随机过程
random residual 随机残差
random sampling 随机抽样
random variable 随机变量
randomization 随机化
randomization blocks 随机化区组,随机化区集
randomness test 随机性检验
range 极差,全距,范围
rank correlation 秩相关,等级相关
rank sum test 秩和检验

ranked 分等的,分级的
ranked data 分级数据,分级资料
rate 比率
rate of discount 贴现率,折扣率
rate of increment 增长率
rate of unemployment 失业率
ratio 比率,比例,比值
ratio scale 比例尺度
ratio test 比率检验
raw data 原始数据,原始资料
real root 实根
real wage index 实际工资指数
real-time data processing 实时数据处理
real-value function 实值函数
reciprocal 倒数,相反的,相互的,互逆的
reciprocal transformation 倒数变换
rectangle 矩形,长方形
reduced form 简化形式
reduced form equation 简化形式方程
reference 参考,比较,基准
reference data 参考数据
reference set 参考集
reference value 参考值
region of acceptance 接受域
regression coefficient 回归系数
regression function 回归函数
regression parameter 回归参数
regression slope 回归斜率
regression sum of square 回归平方和
regressor 回归量,回归元
regressand 回归子(应变量)
regret 损耗
regularity 正则性,规则性,定期性
regularity conditions 正则性条件
reject limit 拒绝限

rejection error 拒绝误差
rejection region 拒绝域
related chart 相关图
relatedness 关联性
relative dispersion 相对离势,相对离散度
relative index 相对相关指数
reliability 可靠性,可靠度
reliability theory 可靠性理论
repeatability 重复性
replication 完全重复,重复次数,再抽样
report period 报告期
reported data 报告数据
residual sum of square 剩余平方和
resistance 耐抗性
resistant line 耐抗线
resistant technique 耐抗技术
retrospective study 回顾性调查
ridge estimate,岭估计
root square (sqrt) 平方根
root mean square 均方根
root mean square error 均方根误差
rotation 轮换,轮流,循环
rotation sample 轮换样本
rounding 舍入,四舍五入,取整
row 行,排,横行
row and column constraints 行和列的约束
row effect 行效应
row vector 行向量
rule of thumb method 经验法则

S

sample 样本,样品
sample average 样本平均数
sample bias 样本偏误
sample central moment 样本中心矩

sample covariance 样本协方差
sample data 样本数据
sample error 样本误差
sample estimate 样本估计值
sample frame 样本框,样本结构
sample mode 样本众数
sample regression coefficient 样本回归系数
sample regression function 样本回归函数
sample size 样本量
sample space 样本空间
sample standard deviation 样本标准差
sample statistic 样本统计量
sampling error 抽样误差
sampling rate 抽样率
sampling statistic 抽样统计量
sampling table 抽样表
SAS (Statistical analysis system) SAS 统计软件包
scalar-valued 数量值,纯量值
scale 尺度,标度,比率,比例
scatter diagram 散点图
schematic model 图解模型
score test 得分检验
screening 筛选,分开
screening inspection 筛选检验,筛选检查
seasonal adjustment series 季节调整序列
second derivative 二阶导数
second principal component 第二主成分
SEM (structural equation modeling) 结构方程模型
semi-logarithmic graph 半对数图
semi-logarithmic paper 半对数格纸
sensitivity curve 敏感度曲线
sequential analysis 贯序分析
sequential design 贯序设计
sequential sample 贯序样本
sequential sampling method 贯序抽样法,逐次抽样法

sequential test 贯序检验,逐次检验
serial correlation test 序列相关检验
serial test 序列检验
short-cut method 简捷法
short-cut run 短期
Sigmoid curve S形曲线
sign function 符号函数
sign test 符号检验
signed rank 符号秩
significance test 显著性检验
significant figure 有效数字
significant level 显著性水平
simple cluster sampling 简单整群抽样
simple correlation 单相关
simple random sampling 简单随机抽样,纯随机抽样
simple regression 简单回归
simple table 简单表,单项表
single-tailed test 单尾检验
size of sample 样本量,样本容量,样本大小
skew 偏斜,偏
skewness 偏度,偏斜度,偏态
slope 斜率,斜度
slope coefficient 斜率系数
small sample estimation 小样本估计
smallest sample value 最小样本值
solution 解,解法
solution set 解集
sources of variation 变异来源
standard deviation(SD) 标准差
standard error (SE)标准误
standard error of estimate 标准估计误差
standard error of the mean 平均数的标准误
standardization 标准化
standardized rate 标化率
standardized normal distribution 标准正态分布

stata 一种统计软件包
statistic 统计量
statistics 统计学
statistical induction 统计归纳
statistical inference 统计推断
statistical map 统计图，统计地图
statistical method 统计方法
statistical survey 统计调查
statistical table 统计表
statistical test 统计检验
statistical treatment 统计处理
stratified sampling 分层抽样
stochastic frontiers 随机前沿
stochastic variable 随机变量
sum of distribution 分布和
sum of mean squares 均方和
sum of ranks 秩和
sum of residuals 残差和
sum of squared residuals (SSR) 残差平方和
sum of the deviation 离差和
superior limit 上限
survival rate 生存率
symmetry 对称，对称性
system correction 系统校正
system of equations 方程组
system of indices 指标体系
systematic error 系统误差
systematic estimation 系统估计
systematic risk 系统风险
systematic sampling 系统抽样，机械抽样
systematic variation 系统变差，系统变异

T

t distribution t 分布
t test t 检验

tabulation system 表列制度
tabulation value 表值
technical equation 技术方程
test statistics 检验统计量
test of goodness of fit 拟合优度检验
test of homogeneity 齐次性检验
test of independence 独立性检验
test of normality 正态性检验
test of randomness 随机性检验
test of one-sided 单侧检验
test of one-tailed 单尾检验
test of significance 显著性检验
test of two-sided 双侧检验
test of two-tailed 双尾检验
testing procedures 检验方法，检验程序
theoretical frequency 理论频数
theoretical number 理论数
total factor productivity（TFP）全要素生产率
transitivity 传递性
treatment 处理
treatment effect 处理效果
treatment effect linear model 处理效果线性模型
treatment of data 数据处理
trend 趋势，倾向，动向
trend adjusted indexes 趋势调整指数
trend correction method 趋势修正法
trend model 趋势模型
trimmed mean 调整平均，修削平均
truncated data 截尾数据
truncated distribution 截尾分布
truncated regression 截尾回归
truncated sample 截尾样本
two-dimensional 二维的
two-dimensional space 二维空间
two-factor analysis of variance 双因素方差分析

two-sample test 二样本检验
two-sided test 双侧检验
two-stage method 两步法
two-stage sampling 二次抽样
two-tailed test 双尾检验
type I error 第一类误差
type II error 第二类误差
typical sampling 典型抽样

U

U-shaped curve U形曲线
U test U 检验
unbiased error 无偏误差
unbiased estimate 无偏估计值
unbiased estimator 无偏估计量
unbiased statistic 无偏统计量
unbiasedness 无偏性
unbiasedness in estimation 估计的无偏性
unbounded 无界的 不受限制的
unclassified data 未分组数据
unconditional expectation 无条件期望
uniform distribution 均匀分布，一致分布
uniformly best distance power (UBDP) 一致最佳距离功效
uniformly most powerful (UMP) 一致最大功效
uniformly most powerful test 一致最大功效检验
unimodal 单峰，单峰的
unimodal distribution 单峰分布
union of events 事件并集
union set 并集
unique solution 唯一解
unit matrix 单位阵
unit variance 单位方差
univariate 单变量，单变量的，一元的，
univariate distribution 一元分布，单变量分布
univariate linear regression 一元线性回归

univariate normal distribution 一元正态分布
universe 总体，全域
ungrouped data 未分组资料
unknown parameter 未知参数
unknown quantity 未知量
unobservable random disturbance 不可观测的随机扰动
unobservable random variable 不可观测的随机变量
unobservable value 不可观测的值
unrestricted model 无约束模型
unrestricted variable 无约束变量
unstable distribution 不稳定分布
unstable solution 不稳定解
unweighted index number 未加权指数
upper bound 上限，上界
upper limit 上限
upper value 上值
upward bias 向上偏倚，上偏误，偏高
upward cumulation 向上累计

V

vacancy 空闲,空额,空位
vacancy rate 空闲率
valid figure 有效数字
validity 有效性
validity of the normal approximation 正态近似的有效性
value added 增加值,增加价值
value aggregates at constant prices 不变价格下的总价值
value at current price 按现价计算
value of output 产值
VAR(vector autoregressive) model 向量自回归(VAR)模型
variability 变异性
variable 变量,变数,可变的,变量的
variable error 变量误差
variable selection 变量选择
variance 方差，变差，差异，变异

variance analysis 方差分析
variance between classes 组间方差
variance between clusters 群间方差
variance component 方差分量
variance matrix 方差矩阵
variance-covariance matrix 方差协方差矩阵
variance of a random variable 随机变量的方差
variance of estimated variance 估计方法的方差
variance of estimator 估计量的方差
variance of ratio 比率的方差
variance ratio 方差比
variance test 方差检验
variance within classes 组内方差
variance within clusters 群内方差
variate 变量,随机变量
variate transformation 变量变换
variation 变异,变差,差异,变动
variation between clusters 群间变异
variation within clusters 群内变异
variation within samples 样本内变异
variational calculus 变分学,变分法
vector 向量, 矢量
vector components 向量分量
vector correlation 向量相关
velocity 速率, 速度, 周转率
velocity of development 发展速度
velocity of increase 增长速度
volume 体积,容积,数额,量
volume chart 体积图
volume index 物量指数, 数量指数

W

wage rate 工资率
wage per day 日工资
wage per year 年工资

Wald test 沃尔德检验
Weibull distribution 威布尔分布
Weibull model 威布尔模型
weight 权，权数
weighted arithmetic mean 加权算术平均数
weighted average 加权平均，加权平均数
weighted geometric average 加权几何平均数
weighted least squares (WLS) 加权最小二乘法
weighted mean 加权平均数，加权均数
white noise 白噪声
White test 怀特检验
Wiener process 维纳过程
wild observation 野值
within-class variation 组内变差
within-cluster regression 组内回归
without bias 无偏误，无偏倚
WLS (weighted least squares) 加权最小二乘法
Wold's decomposition 沃尔德分解
WPI (wholesale price index) 批发物价指数

Z

zero 零，零点，零元
zero correlation 零相关
zero correlation criterion 零相关准则
zero element 零元，零元素
zero-mean random variable 零均值随机变量
zero of a function 函数的零点
zero-one distribution 零一分布

附录Ⅳ 网上概率和统计学期刊

Probability and Statistics Journals on the Web

Here * indicates browsable table of contents, ** indicates browsable abstacts, *** indicates downloadable papers.

Some publishers require registration to browse abstracts. Others require a current subscription to the journal by you or your institution. Most browsable titles, abstracts and papers are only for the past year or so.

For abstracts, one may also try the Web of Science citation databases of the Institute for Scientific Information. One might also try Zentralblatt Math Database.

Probability Journals

- Advances in Applied Probability, Applied Probability Trust *
- Annales de l'Institut Henri Poincaré, Gauthier-Villars ***
- Annals of Applied Probability, Institute of Mathematical Statistics ***
- Annals of Probability, Institute of Mathematical Statistics ***
- Applied Stochastic Models in Business and Industry, Wiley ***
- Electronic Journal of Probability and Electronic Communications in Probability, IMS ***
- Journal of Applied Probability, Applied Probability Trust *
- Journal of Theoretical Probability, Springer ***
- Markov Processes and Related Fields, Odysseus **
- Methodology and Computing in Applied Probability, Springer **
- Probability in the Engineering and Informational Sciences, Cambridge University Press *
- Probability Surveys, Electronic Journal, IMS and Bernouli Society ***
- Probability Theory and Related Fields, Springer ***
- Random Operators and Stochastic Equations, de Gruyter *
- Stochastic Analysis and Applications, Taylor and Francis **
- Stochastic Models, Taylor and Francis **
- Stochastic Processes and their Applications, Elsevier ***
- Stochastics: An International Journal of Probability and Stochastic Processes, Taylor and Francis **
- Theory of Probability and its Applications, SIAM ***

Statistics Journals

- Advances and Applications in Statistics, Pushpa Publishing House**
- Advances in Statistical Analysis, Springer
- American Statistician, American Statistical Association **
- Annals of Applied Statistics, Institute of Mathematical Statistics *
- Annals of the Institute of Statistical Mathematics, Springer **
- Annals of Statistics, Institute of Mathematical Statistics
- Australian and New Zealand Journal of Statistics, Statistical Society of Australia **
- Bayesian Analysis, International Society of Bayesian Analysis ***
- Bernoulli, Bernoulli Society *
- Biometrics, International Biometric Society *
- Biometrika, Imperial College, ***
- Brazilian Journal of Probability and Statistics Brazilian Statistical Society *
- Canadian Journal of Statistics, Statistical Society of Canada, **
- Chance, Springer *
- Communications in Statistics-Simulation and Computation, Taylor and Francis **
- Communications in Statistics-Theory and Methods, Taylor and Francis **
- Computational Statistics, Springer **
- Computational Statistics and Data Analysis, Elsevier*
- Current Index to Statistics, IMS, ASA.
- Econometrica, Econometric Society* (经济计量学家)
- Electronic Journal of Statistics, Institute of Mathematical Statistics***
- ESAIM: Probability and Statistics, SMAI *
- Far East Journal of Theoretical Statistics, Pushpa Publishing House**
- IMS Bulletin. IMS
- International Statistical Review, International Statistical Institute
- InterStat, Statistics on the Internet ***
- Journal of Applied Statistics, Taylor and Francis **
- Journal of Computational and Graphical Statistics, IMS, ASA, Interface ** Abstracts and Data Sets
- Journal of Data Science, Beijing, New York and Taipei ***
- Journal of Multivariate Analysis, Science Direct *** (多元统计分析期刊)
- Journal of Nonparametric Statistics, Taylor and Francis ** (非参数统计学期

刊)
- Journal of Probability and Statistical Science, Susan River's Cultural Institute **
- Journal of Statistical Computation and Simulation, * (统计计算与模拟期刊)
- Journal of Statistical Planning and Inference, Elsevier **
- Journal of Statistical Software, UCLA *** (统计软件期刊)
- Journal of Statistics Education, ASA *** (统计教育期刊)
- Journal of the American Statistical Association, ASA ** (Data Archive)
- Journal of the Japan Statistical Society, Scipress ***
- Journal of the Korean Statistical Society, Korean Statistical Society *
- Journal of the Royal Statistical Society, Series A, General, Royal Statistical Society **
- Journal of the Royal Statistical Society, Series B, Methodology, Royal Statistical Society **
- Journal of the Royal Statistical Society, Series C, Applied Statistics, Royal Statistical Society **
- Journal of the Royal Statistical Society, Series D, The Statistician, Royal Statistical Society **
- Journal of Time Series Analysis, Blackwell **
- JP Journal of Biostatistics, Pushpa Publishing House **
- Latin American Journal of Probability and Mathematical Statistics, IMPA and IMS ***
- Metrika, Springer ***
- Metron, Università deli Studi di Roma "La Sapienza" *
- Probability and Mathematical Statistics, Wroclaw University ***
- Psychometrika, College of William and Mary, Williamsburg **
- Rivista Statistica, Università di Bologna, **
- Sankhya, Indian Statistical Institute *
- Scandinavian Journal of Statistics, Blackwell **
- Sequential Analysis, Taylor and Francis **
- Significance, Wiley-Blackwell Publishing ***
- Statistica Neerlandica, Vereniging voor Statistiek **
- Statistica Sinica, Institute of Statistical Science Academia Sinica **
- Statistical Inference for Stochastic Processes, Springer **

- Statistical Papers, Springer
- Statistical Science, Institute of Mathematical Statistics
- Statistics: A Journal of Theoretical and Applied Statistics, Taylor and Francis **
- Statistics and Computing, Springer ***
- Statistics and Decisions, Oldenbourg Verlag*
- Statistics and Probability Letters, Elsevier **
- Statistics Surveys, Electronic Journal, IMS and Bernoulli Society ***
- StatLib - Applied Statistics Algorithms, Statistics, CMU ***
- Stats, The Magazine for Students of Statistics, ASA **
- Survey Methodology, Statistics Canada
- Technometrics, ASA **
- Test, Spanish Statistical and Operations Research Society ***
- Theory of Probability and Mathematical Statistics, AMS Translations

Related Journals

- American Mathematical Monthly, Mathematical Association of America **
- American Journal of Epidemiology, Society for Epidemiologic Research **
- Annals of Operations Research, Springer ***
- Applied Mathematics and Optimization, Springer ***
- Applied Mathematics and Computation, Elsevier ***
- Artificial Intelligence, Elsevier ***
- Astin Bulletin, Peeters ***
- Biometrical Journal, Wiley-VCH ***
- British Journal of Mathematical and Statistical Psychology, British Pyschological Society ***
- Chemometrics and Intelligent Laboratory Systems, Elsevier ***
- Combinatorics, Probability and Computing, Cambridge University Press ***
- Computational Optimization and Applications, Springer ***
- Computer Methods and Programs in Biomedicine, Elsevier ***
- Computers and Operations Research, Elsevier **
- Contemporary Clinical Trials, Elsevier **
- Econometric Reviews, Taylor and Francis **
- Econometric Theory, Cambridge University Press ***
- Econometrics Journal, Royal Econometrics Society *
- Electronic Journal of Combinatorics, WWW ***

- Environmental and Ecological Statistics, Springer ***
- Environmetrics, Wiley ***
- European Journal of Operations Research, Elsevier *
- Extremes, Springer ***
- Finance and Stochastics, Springer **
- Games and Economic Behavior, Elsevier ***
- IEEE Transactions on Automatic Control, IEEE *
- IEEE Transactions on Pattern Analysis and Machine Intelligence, IEEE **
- IEEE Transactions on Reliability, IEEE
- IEEE Transactions on Signal Processing, IEEE *
- Insurance Mathematics and Economics, Elsevier **
- Interfaces, INFORMS ***
- International Game Theory Review, World Scientific **
- International Journal of Biostatistics, Bepress ***
- International Journal of Epidemiology, Oxford University Press **
- International Journal of Forecasting, Elsevier **
- International Journal of Game Theory, Springer ***
- International Journal of Statistics and Management Science, Serial Publications
- Journal of Agricultural, Biological, and Environmental Statistics, ASA **
- Journal of Applied Econometrics, Wiley, Interscience ***
- Journal of Biopharmaceutical Statistics, Taylor and Francis **
- Journal of Business and Economic Statistics, ASA **
- Journal of Chemometrics, Wiley ***
- Journal of Classification, Springer **
- Journal of Combinatorial Designs, Wiley ***
- Journal of Combinatorial Optimization, Springer **
- Journal of Combinatorial Theory-Series A, Elsevier ***
- Journal of Combinatorial Theory-Series B, Elsevier ***
- Journal of Consulting and Clinical Psychology, American Psychological Association *
- Journal of Econometrics, Elsevier **
- Journal of Economic Theory, Elsevier. ***
- Journal of Educational and Behavioral Statistics, American Educational Research Association *

- Journal of Forecasting, Wiley ***
- Journal of Interdisciplinary Mathematics, TARU Publications *
- Journal of Machine Learning, MIT Press ***
- Journal of the Operational Research Society, Palmgrave **
- Journal of Optimization Theory and Applications, Springer ***
- Journal of Quantitative Analysis in Sports, Bepress ***
- Journal of Risk and Uncertainty, Kluwer ***
- Journal of Statistics and Management Systems, TARU Publications *
- Journal of the Association for Computing Machinery, ACM **
- Machine Learning, Springer ***
- Management Science, INFORMS ***
- Mathematical Biosciences, Elsevier ***
- Mathematical Geology, Springer ***
- Mathematical Methods of Operations Research, Springer ***
- Mathematical Scientist, Applied Probability Trust **
- Mathematical Spectrum, Applied Probability Trust **
- Mathematics of Operations Research, INFORMS ***
- Naval Research Logistics, Wiley ***
- Operations Research, INFORMS ***
- Operations Research Letters, Elsevier *
- Optimization, Taylor and Francis **
- Optimization Methods and Software, Taylor and Francis **
- OR-Spektrum, Springer ***
- Pattern Recognition, Elsevier ***
- Pattern Recognition Letters, Elsevier ***
- Probabilistic Engineering Mechanics, Elsevier *
- Psychological Bulletin, American Psychological Association **
- Quality Progress, American Society for Quality Control *
- Queueing Systems, Baltzer *
- Random Structures and Algorithms, Wiley ***
- Reliability Engineering and System Safety, Elsevier *
- Review of Economics and Statistics, MIT Press **
- Risk Analysis, Society for Risk Analysis ***
- SIAM Journal on Scientific Computing, SIAM ***

- SIAM Journal on Control and Optimization, SIAM ***
- SIAM Journal on Matrix Analysis and Applications, SIAM ***
- SIAM Journal on Optimization, SIAM ***
- SIAM Review, SIAM ***
- Statistical Applications in Genetics and Molecular Biology, Bepress ***
- Statistical Communications in Infectious Diseases, Bepress ***
- Statistical Methods and Applications, Springer
- Statistical Methods in Medical Research, Sage ***
- Statistical Modelling, Sage ***
- Statistics Education Research Journal, IASE ***
- Statistics in Medicine, Wiley ***
- Stochastic Environmental Research and Risk Assessment, Springer ***
- Theoretical Computer Science, Elsevier ***
- Theoretical Population Biology, Elsevier ***
- Transactions on Modeling and Computer Simulation, ACM ***

附录V 统计学专业软件

Statistical software（统计学专业软件）

Below are links to statistical software providers. If your interest is in subroutines for use in SAS, SPSS, STATA, etc. see statistical subroutines providers in SAS, SPSS, STATA, etc..

AM Statistical Software

AM is a statistical software package for analyzing data from complex samples, especially largescale assessments such as the National Assessment of Educational Progress (NAEP) and the Third International Mathematics and Science Studies (TIMSS).

AM offers sophisticated statistics with an easy-to-use drag and drop interface, and an integrated help system that explains the statistics as well as how to use the system.

AM offers sophisticated statistics with an easy-to-use drag and drop interface, and an integrated help system that explains the statistics as well as how to use the system.

AM includes statistical procedures for analyzing assessment and survey data, including models estimated via marginal maximum likelihood (MML). MML procedures recognize that tests can't pinpoint proficiency, but instead define a probability distribution over the proficiency scale. AM will also analyze the "plausible values" used in programs like NAEP.

AM includes procedures for analyzing non-assessment survey data as well.

All of AM's procedures automatically provides appropriate standard errors for complex samples. All procedures are available with a Taylor-series approximation for the standard errors, and a few offer an option to use a jackknife or other replication technique.

AM is completely free and may be shared and copied. It was developed, in part, with funding from the National Center for Education Statistics.

(American Institutes for Research) http://am.air.org

Blossom Statistical Software

Blossom is an interactive program for making statistical comparisons with distance-function based permutation tests developed by P. W. Mielke, Jr. and colleagues at Colorado State University (Mielke and Berry 2001) and for testing parameters estimated in linear models with permutation procedures developed by B. S. Cade and colleagues at the Fort Collins Science Center, U. S. Geological Survey (known as the Midcontinent Ecological Science Center prior to 2002).

http://www.fort.usgs.gov/products/software/Blossom

Epi Info

Physicians, nurses, epidemiologists, and other public health workers lacking a background in information technology often have a need for simple tools that allow the rapid creation of data collection instruments and data analysis, visualization, and reporting using epidemiologic methods. Epi Info™, a suite of lightweight software tools, delivers core ad-hoc epidemiologic functionality without the complexity or expense of large, enterprise applications.

Epi Info™ is easily used in places with limited network connectivity or limited resources for commercial software and professional IT support. Epi Info™ is flexible, scalable, and free while enabling data collection, advanced statistical analyses, and geographic information system (GIS) mapping capability.

Since its initial release, Epi Info™ users have self-registered in over 181 countries covering all continents including Antarctica. Epi Info™ has been translated in more than 13 languages.

（Epi Info 是由美国疾病控制与预防中心（Centers for Disease Control and Prevention,（CDCUS)所研制的统计软件,是最常用的公共卫生领域的相关研究。）

http://www.cdc.gov/epiinfo/

EQS

Developed by one of the world's leading authorities on the subject, Dr. Peter M. Bentler, EQS provides researchers and statisticians with a simple method for conducting the full range of structural equations models including multiple regression, multivariate regression, confirmatory factor analysis, structured means analysis, path analysis, and multiple population comparisons. Users agree that EQS is more complete and much easier to use than other products such as LISREL. With EQS, no knowledge of matrix algebra is required!

EQS provides the most accurate known statistics for analysis on data that may not be multivariate normally distributed (real data are typically non-normal!) with the Satorra-Bentler scaled chi-square, robust standard errors, and the Yuan-Bentler distribution-free statistics. These features are not available in other modeling programs.

EQS now includes polyserial and polychoric correlations for treating categorical data, additional exploration functions, enhancements to the RETEST and WTEST options, and the ability to import weight matrices.

(EQS V 6.1 是由该领域在国际间享负盛名的 Peter M. Bentler 教授，EQS 提供研究人员与统计学家简单建构结构方程模型的最佳工具，包含复回归分析、多变量回归、验证性因素分析、结构分析路径分析以及多重母体比较。使用过的 EQS 的学者一致认同本软件的提供完整且简单操作接口。使用 EQS，人们可以不用具备任何矩阵代数的知识，就能轻易操作这个软件。)

(Multivariate Software, Inc.) http://www.mvsoft.com

Eviews

A combination of power and ease-of-use make EViews 7 the ideal package for anyone working with time series, cross-section, or longitudinal data. With EViews, you can quickly and efficiently manage your data, perform econometric and statistical analysis, generate forecasts or model simulations, and produce high quality graphs and tables for publication or inclusion in other applications.

Featuring an innovative graphical object-oriented user-interface and a sophisticated analysis engine, EViews blends the best of modern software technology with the features you've always wanted. The result is a state-of-the art program that offers unprecedented power within a flexible, easy-to-use interface.

Find out for yourself why EViews is the worldwide leader in Windows-based econometric software and the choice of those who demand the very best.

- An Intuitive, Easy-to-Use Interface
- Powerful Analytic Tools
- Sophisticated Data Management
- Presentation Quality Output
- Traditional Command Line and Programming Interface

(Eviews 是美国 QMS 公司研制的在 Windows 下专门从事数据分析、回归分析和预测的工具。使用 Eviews 可以迅速地从数据中寻找出统计关系，并用得到的关系去预测数据的未来值。Eviews 的应用范围包括：科学实验数据分析与评估、金融分析、宏观经济预测、仿真、销售预测和成本分析等。

(Quantitative Micro Software) http://www.eviews.com

GAUSS

The GAUSS Mathematical and Statistical System is a fast matrix programming language widely used by scientists, engineers, statisticians, biometricians, econometricians, and financial analysts.

Designed for computationally intensive tasks, the GAUSS system is ideally suited for the researcher who does not have the time required to develop programs in C or FORTRAN but finds that most statistical or mathematical "packages" are not flexible or powerful enough to perform complicated analysis or to work on large problems.

As a complete programming language, the GAUSS system is both flexible and powerful. Immediately available to the GAUSS user is a wide variety of statistical, mathematical and matrix handling routines. GAUSS can be used either interactively for short one-off commands or by creating large programs consisting of several files and libraries of functions, or anything in between.

(Aptech Systems) http://www.aptech.com

Latent GOLD, GOLDMineR, SI-CHAID

Statistical Innovations Inc. (SI) is a Boston-based consulting and software development company specializing in innovative applications of **statistical modeling**. Beginning in 1981 with the development of the highly popular SPSS CHAID tree-based segmentation program, SI offers statistical software packages that truly represent the state-of-the-art in statistical modeling.

Latent GOLD 4.5 is a powerful latent class and finite mixture program. Latent GOLD contains separate modules for estimating three different model structures—LC Cluster models, D Factor models, and LC Regression models. Which are useful in somewhat different application areas? Latent GOLD 4.5 comes in either a Basic or Advanced version.

(Statistical Inovations, Inc.) http://www.statisticalinnovations.com

LIMDEP, NLOGIT

LIMDEP and NLOGIT are at the forefront of econometrics and offer statistical tools not found in other programs.

NLOGIT Version 4.0 is an extension of LIMDEP that provides programs for estimation, model simulation and analysis of multinomial choice data, such as brand choice, transportation mode, and all manner of survey and market data in which consumers choose among a set of competing alternatives. NLOGIT has become the premier package for estimation and simulation of multinomial discrete choice models.

NLOGIT 4.0 is a full information maximum likelihood estimator for, among other models, up to four level nested logit models. Many other formulations are included in NLOGIT, including random parameters (mixed logit), latent class, multinomial probit, many forms of the nested logit model, and several new formulations for panel data.

NLOGIT offers a complete set of tools for econometric analysis. In addition to the estimation programs, NLOGIT provides:

• Data management, including input from all standard sources (such as Excel), all manner of transformations and sample controls

• Built-in estimation programs plus a programming language, matrix algebra package and scientific calculator that allow you to write your own estimators, test statistics and simulation and analysis programs

• Random number, vector and matrix capabilities for bootstrapping, Gibbs sampling and Monte Carlo simulation

• A wide range of graphical and numeric descriptive statistics capabilities

• Optimization tools that allow you to construct your own likelihood, GMM, or maximum simulated likelihood estimators

• Analysis tools including graphics, numerical analysis and post estimation tools for specification and hypothesis testing

• An extensive hard copy documentation set, with over 3,000 pages, containing full reference guides for the programs, background econometrics, and sample applications

(Econometric Software, Inc.) http://www.limdep.com

Maple

Maple™ is the essential technical computing software for today's engineers, mathematicians, and scientists. Whether you need to do quick calculations, develop design sheets, teach fundamental concepts, or produce sophisticated high-fidelity simulation models, Maple's world-leading computation engine offers the breadth, depth, and performance to handle every type of mathematics.

The result of over 25 years of cutting-edge research and development, Maple combines the world's most powerful mathematical computation engine with an intuitive, "clickable" user interface. Its smart document environment automatically captures all of your technical knowledge in an electronic form that seamlessly integrates calculations, explanatory text and math, graphics, images, sound, and diagrams. (Maple 14, up to 2010)

International Sales and Support in China.
Cybernet Systems China, Room 908, No. 777 Zhao Jia Bang Road, Shanghai
Tel: +86 21 6471 6031, Fax: +86 21 6471 6050. http://www.cca-es.com
(Waterloo Maple, Inc.) http://www.maplesoft.com

Mathematica

Mathematica is a computational software program used in scientific, engineering, and mathematical fields and other areas of technical computing. It was conceived by Stephen Wolfram and is developed by Wolfram Research of Champaign, Illinois.

Mathematica is split into two parts, the "kernel" and the front end. The kernel interprets expressions (Mathematica code) and returns result expressions.

The front end, designed by Theodore Gray, provides a GUI, which allows the creation and editing of Notebook documents containing program code with pretty printing, formatted text together with results including typeset mathematics, graphics, GUI components, tables, and sounds. All contents and formatting can be generated algorithmically or interactively edited. Most standard word processing capabilities are supported, but there is only one level of "undo".

Almost any workflow involves computing results, and that's what Mathematica does—from building a hedge fund trading website or publishing interactive engineering textbooks to developing embedded image recognition algorithms or teaching calculus.

Mathematica is renowned as the world's ultimate application for computations. But it's much more—it's the only development platform fully integrating computation into complete workflows, moving you seamlessly from initial ideas all the way to deployed individual or enterprise solutions. Mathematica 8.0 (November 15, 2010)

(Wolfram Research, Inc.) http://www.wri.com

mathStatica

mathStatica was designed to solve the algebraic/symbolic problems that are of primary interest in mathematical statistics. It does so by building upon the incredible symbolic computational power of *Mathematica* to create a sophisticated toolset specially designed for doing mathematical statistics.

By contrast, packages like SPSS, Systat, SAS, Gauss, JMP, R and S-Plus provide a numerical/graphical toolset. They can illustrate, they can simulate, and they can find approximate numerical solutions to numerical problems, but they generally cannot find exact symbolic solutions to statistical problems.

Features include: a complete suite for manipulating arbitrary pdf's
- univariate and multivariate
- automated expectations, probability, plotting
- automated transformations (functions of random variables)
- products of random variables
- Maximum / Minimum of random variables
- generating functions
- inversion theorems
- symbolic maximum likelihood estimation
- numerical maximum likelihood estimation
- automated Pearson curve fitting
- Johnson curve fitting
- Gram-Charlier expansions
- non-parametric kernel density estimation
- moment conversion formulae
- component-mix and parameter-mix distributions
- stable distributions
- copulae
- random number generation
- asymptotics
- decision theory
- order statistics
- order statistics for non-identical distributions
- Fisher Information
- h-statistics, k-statistics, polykays
- checking and correction of textbook formulae

(Mathstatica Pty Ltd.) http://www.mathstatica.com

MATLAB

MATLAB (matrix laboratory) is a numerical computing environment and fourth-generation programming language. Developed by Math Works, MATLAB allows matrix manipulations, plotting of functions and data, implementation of algorithms, creation of user interfaces, and interfacing with programs written in other languages, including C, C++, and Fortran.

Although MATLAB is intended primarily for numerical computing, an optional toolbox uses the MuPAD symbolic engine, allowing access to symbolic computing capabilities. An additional package, Simulink, adds graphical multi-domain simulation and Model-Based Design for dynamic and embedded systems.

(MATLAB 和 Mathematica、Maple 并称为三大数学软件。它在数学类科技应用软件中在数值计算方面首屈一指。MATLAB 可以进行矩阵运算、绘制函数和数据、实现算法、创建用户界面、连接其他编程语言的程序等,主要应用于工程计算、控制设计、信号处理与通讯、图像处理、信号检测、金融建模设计与分析等领域。)

中国公司网址 http://www.mathworks.cn/

(The MathWorks, Inc.) http://www.mathworks.com

Meta Analysis

Meta-analysis is the statistical procedure for combining data from multiple studies. When the treatment effect (or effect size) is consistent from one study to the next, meta-analysis can be used to identify this common effect. When the effect varies from one study to the next, meta-analysis may be used to identify the reason for the variation.

Decisions about the utility of an intervention or the validity of a hypothesis cannot be based on the results of a single study, because results typically vary from one study to the next. Rather, a mechanism is needed to synthesize data across studies. Narrative reviews had been used for this purpose, but the narrative review is largely subjective (different experts can come to different conclusions) and becomes impossibly difficult when there are more than a few studies involved. Meta-analysis, by contrast, applies objective formulas (much as one would apply statistics to data within a single study), and can be used with any number of studies.

Meta-Analysis in applied and basic research

Pharmaceutical companies use meta-analysis to gain approval for new drugs, with regulatory agencies sometimes requiring a meta-analysis as part of the approval process. Clinicians and applied researchers in medicine, education, psychology, criminal justice, and a host of other fields use meta-analysis to determine which interventions work, and which ones work best. Meta analysis is also widely used in basic research to evaluate the evidence in areas as diverse as sociology, social psychology, sex differences, finance and economics, political science, marketing, ecology and genetics, among others.

(Biostat) http://www.Meta-Analysis.com

Microfit

Microfit 5.0 is an interactive, menu-driven program with a host of facilities for estimating, hypothesis testing, forecasting, data processing, file management, and graphic display. These features make Microfit 5.0 one of the most powerful menu-driven time-series econometric packages currently available. It is a major advance over Microfit 4.0 and offers a unique built-in interactive, searchable econometric text. It provides users with technical, functional and tutorial help throughout the package, and can be used at different levels of technical sophistication.

Microfit 5.0 is suitable for classroom teaching of undergraduate and postgraduate courses in applied econometrics. For experienced users of econometric programs, it offers a variety of univariate methods, multivariate techniques for cointegration, principal components, canonical correlations and multivariate volatility modelling, and provides a large number of diagnostic and non-nested tests not readily available on other packages. The interaction of excellent graphics and estimation capabilities in Microfit 5.0 allows important econometric research to be carried out in a matter of days rather than weeks.

(Microfit 是用于计量经济模型建立的软件。程序是由剑桥大学的经济学者 Dr. Hashem Pesaran 和 Dr. Bahram Pesaran 所设计,新增的数据分析功能,可以预估设计高等的单变量(Univariate)及多变量(multivariate)时间序列的模型。Microfit 的使用手册包含了 76 个教学范例,使用 25 种不同的财务及经济数据。Microfit 是交谈式,选单驱动的评估预测软件。非常适合企业、银行、教学及研究使用。)

Bahram Pesaran, Time Series Econometrics using Microfit 5,
Oxford University Press, October 2009. Book and Software.

ISBN13: 9780199581511,
ISBN10: 0199581517,
ISBN13: 9780199563531;
ISBN10: 0199563535 (single, multiple, and network use)
http://www.oup.co.uk/microfit/

Minitab

Minitab is the leading provider of software for statistics education and Lean, Six Sigma, and quality improvement projects. For nearly 40 years we have been helping world-class organizations analyze problems, transform their business, and train their students.

(Minitab Inc.) http://www.minitab.com

Ox, PcGive, OxMetrics

OxMetrics™ is a family of of software packages providing an integrated solution for the econometric analysis of time series, forecasting, financial econometric modelling, or statistical analysis of cross-section and panel data. OxMetrics consists of a front-end program called OxMetrics, and individual application modules such as PcGive, STAMP, etc.

OxMetrics™ is the "desktop" for the OxMetrics modules. OxMetrics displays reports and graphics, which can be manipulated on screen, offers a calculator and algebraic language for transforming data, and enables the user to open multiple databases. A batch language allows for the automation of many of these tasks.

(Jurgen A. Doornik, Nuffield College) http://www.doornik.com

PASW Statistics (formerly SPSS)

SPSS (originally, Statistical Package for the Social Sciences) was released in its first version in 1968 after being developed by Norman H. Nie and C. Hadlai Hull. Norman Nie was then a political science postgraduate at Stanford University, and now Research Professor in the Department of Political Science at Stanford and Professor Emeritus of Political Science at the University of Chicago. SPSS is among the most widely used programs for statistical analysis in social science. It is used by market researchers, health researchers, survey companies, government, education researchers, marketing organizations and others.

The original SPSS manual (Nie, Bent & Hull, 1970) has been described as one of "sociology's most influential books". In addition to statistical analysis, data management (case selection, file reshaping, creating derived data) and data documentation (a metadata dictionary is stored in the datafile) are features of the base software.

SPSS is acomputer program used for statistical analysis. Between 2009 and 2010 the premier vendor for SPSS was called PASW (Predictive Analytics SoftWare) Statistics, while copyright issues for the name were settled. The company announced July 28, 2009 that it was being acquired by IBM for US＄1.2 billion. As of January 2010, it became "SPSS: An IBM Company".

（SPSS 是统计产品与服务解决方案（Statistical Product and Service Solutions)的简称,SPSS 公司推出的一系列用于统计学分析运算、数据挖掘、预测分析和决策支持任务的软件产品及相关服务的总称。中国公司网址:http://www.spss.com.cn/index.aspx)

http://www.spss.com/

R

R is a language and environment for statistical computing and graphics. It is a GNU project which is similar to the S language and environment which was developed at Bell Laboratories (formerly AT&T, now Lucent Technologies) by John Chambers and colleagues. R can be considered as a different implementation of S. There are some important differences, but much code written for S runs unaltered under R.

R provides a wide variety of statistical (linear and nonlinear modelling, classical statistical tests, time-series analysis, classification, clustering...) and graphical techniques, and is highly extensible. The S language is often the vehicle of choice for research in statistical methodology, and R provides an Open Source route to participation in that activity.

One of R's strengths is the ease with which well-designed publication-quality plots can be produced, including mathematical symbols and formulae where needed. Great care has been taken over the defaults for the minor design choices in graphics, but the user retains full control.

R is available as Free Software under the terms of the Free Software Foundation's GNU General Public License in source code form. It compiles and runs on a wide variety of UNIX platforms and similar systems (including FreeBSD and Linux), Windows and MacOS.

(Robert Gentleman, Ross Ihaka, et al.) University of Auckland
http://www.r-project.org

SAS, JMP

SAS has helped organizations across all industries realize the full potential of their greatest asset: data. Simply put, SAS allows you to transform data about customers, performance, financials and more into information and predictive insight that lays the groundwork for solid and coherent decisions. That's why SAS is used at more than 50,000 sites in over 100 countries, including 93 of the top 100 companies on the 2010 FORTUNE Global 500® list.

You can with SAS® business analytics software and services. SAS has delivered proven solutions that drive innovation and improve performance since 1976. With consistent revenue growth and an unwavering dedication to helping customers make better, fact-based decisions, privately held SAS continues to provide organizations with THE POWER TO KNOW®.

中国公司网址 http://www.sas.com/offices/asiapacific/china/index.html
(SAS Institute Inc.) http://www.sas.com

Stat/Transfer

Stat/Transfer knows about statistical data—it handles missing data, value and variable labels and all of the other details that are necessary to move as much information as is possible from one file format to another.

Stat/Transfer allows you to select output variables and control their storage types, allows case selection and random sampling, and provides a variety of options to let you tailor Stat/Transfer to match your needs and the nature of your data. The Stat/Transfer user interface lets you do routine transfers with just a few clicks.

Stat/Transfer provides both an easy-to-use menu interface and a powerful batch facility. Whether you are moving a simple table from Excel to SAS or moving megabytes of survey data between statistical packages, Stat/Transfer will save you time and money.

(Circle Systems Inc.) http://www.stattransfer.com

Stata

Stata is a complete, integrated statistical package that provides everything you need for data analysis, data management, and graphics. Stata is not sold in pieces, which means you get everything you need in one package without annual license fees.

With apoint-and-click interface, an intuitive command syntax, and online help, Stata is easy to use, fast, and accurate (see certification results and FDA document compliance for details). All analyses can be reproduced and documented for publication and review.

Broad suite of statistical capabilities

Stata puts hundreds of statistical tools at your fingertips, from advanced techniques, such as survival models with frailty, dynamic panel data (DPD) regressions, generalized estimating equations (GEE), multilevel mixed models, models with sample selection, multiple imputation, ARCH, and estimation with complex survey samples; to standard methods, such as linear and generalized linear models (GLM), regressions with count or binary outcomes, ANOVA/MANOVA, ARIMA, cluster analysis, standardization of rates, case-control analysis, and basic tabulations and summary statistics.

Stata is distributed in more than 150 countries and is used by professionals in manyfields of research. See what research professionals say about Stata. Our certified distributors offer services such as basic technical support and training.

(StataCorp LP) http://www.stata.com

Statistica

The STATISTICA line of software provides a comprehensive and integrated set of tools and solutions for:

- Data analysis and reporting, data mining and predictive modeling, business intelligence, simple and multivariate QC, process monitoring, analytic optimization, simulation, and for applying a large number of statistical and other analytic techniques to address routine and advanced data analysis needs
- Data visualization, graphical data analysis, visual data mining, visual querying, and simple and advanced scientific and business graphing; in fact, STATISTICA has been acknowledged as the "king of data visualization software" (by the editors of "PC Graphics & Video")
- Simple and advanced desktop analyses and computing for business, engineering, research institutions, universities, laboratories, and for applications

ranging from CRM and predictive modeling to the application of multivariate model-based quality control

• Role-based and guided enterprise-wide analytic computing and reporting, using Web-enabled server-based computations managed by a mature, robust, scalable, and open-architected server platform that can take advantage of the most powerful hardware, multi-core servers, and server farms, to perform mission critical analytic tasks (in validated manufacturing environments) that in many cases cannot be accomplished by any other analytic solution platform

• Quickly deploying enterprise data analysis or predictive modeling solutions, credit scoring solutions, multivariate SPC and advanced process monitoring solution on 32-bit or 64-bit platforms, in various languages, and supported by local offices and training centers world-wide (StatSoft, Inc.)

http://www.statsoft.com

Statistix

Statistix is a powerful statistical analysis program you can use to quickly analyze your data. This incredibly easy-to-use program offers the basic and advanced statistics you want—plus powerful data manipulation tools—at one affordable price.

Statistix **FEATURES**:

• **Easy to Learn and Use**

Completely menu-driven, procedures are specified using concise Windows-style dialog boxes.

"Statistix is very easy... an inexpensive no-nonsense package that delivers."

—PC Magazine Editor's Choice award

• **Reliable**

Developed in 1985, Statistix has more than 30,000 users. It's an accurate, proven program with favorable press reviews.

"Statistix is computationally robust. I'm happy to recommend this package."

—The Professional Statistician

• **Comprehensive**

Statistix performs all the basic and advanced statistics needed by most users.

"Statistix gives the user easy access to all the common tools of data analysis as well as many less common ones."

—Chance Magazine

- **Fast**

Computes lightening fast. No time consuming disk access needed. Data are memory resident.

"Statistix is fast, very fast."

—The American Statistician

(Analytical software)

http://www.statistix.com

TSP

TSP™ is a complete language for the estimation and simulation of econometric models. It is a world-wide standard for econometric estimation, with over 2,000 installations. What follows is a general overview; detailed lists of features and commands can be found elsewhere. TSP stands for "Time Series Processor", although the program is also frequently used for cross section and panel data. TSP happens to be a common acronym with alternative definitions.

TSP FEATURES:

- Easy-to-use free format command and data input
- All the standard econometric estimation methods, such as OLS, instrumental variables, LIML, nonlinear systems estimation, generalized methods of moments, FIML, maximum likelihood for qualitative dependent variable models, ARIMA, Kalman filter, ARCH, VAR, and other time series techniques (complete feature list).
- Extensive diagnostics and testing facilities.
- Flexible data transformation with many built-in functions and matrix algebra.
- Offers a choice between interactive use or full programming language for econometric methods development.

COMMON APPLICATIONS OF TSP

- Applied econometrics
- Macroeconomic research and forecasting
- Sales forecasting
- Financial analysis
- Cost analysis and forecasting
- Monte Carlo simulation
- Estimation and simulation of economic models

Although TSP was originally and continues to be developed primarily by economists, there is nothing in its design limiting it to economic times series. Any data consisting of repeated observations of the same variable for different units may be analyzed with TSP.

(TSP International) http://www.tspintl.com/

附录Ⅵ 希腊字母读音表

序号	大写	小写	英文注音	国际音标注音	中文注音
1	A	α	alpha	aːlf	阿尔法
2	B	β	beta	bet	贝塔
3	Γ	γ	gamma	gaːm	伽马
4	Δ	δ	delta	delt	德尔塔
5	E	ε	epsilon	ep'silon	伊普西龙
6	Z	ζ	zeta	zat	截塔
7	H	η	eta	eit	艾塔
8	Θ	θ	thet	θit	西塔
9	I	ι	iot	aiot	约塔
10	K	κ	kappa	kap	卡帕
11	Λ	λ	lambda	lambd	兰布达
12	M	μ	mu	mju	缪
13	N	ν	nu	nju	纽
14	Ξ	ξ	xi	ksi	克西
15	O	o	omicron	omik'ron	奥密克戎
16	Π	π	pi	pai	派
17	P	ρ	rho	rou	肉
18	Σ	σ	sigma	'sigma	西格马
19	T	τ	tau	tau	套
20	Y	υ	upsilon	jup'silon	宇普西龙
21	Φ	φ	phi	fai	佛爱
22	X	χ	chi	phai	西
23	Ψ	ψ	psi	psai	普西
24	Ω	ω	omega	o'miga	欧米伽

附录VII 基数与序数的英文表示汇总表

Cardinal number(基数)			Ordinal number(序数)	
zero	0			
one	1	I	first	1st
two	2	II	second	2nd
three	3	III	third	3rd
four	4	IV	fourth	4th
five	5	V	fifth	5th
six	6	VI	sixth	6th
seven	7	VII	seventh	7th
eight	8	VIII	eighth	8th
nine	9	IX	ninth	9th
ten	10	X	tenth	10th
eleven	11	XI	eleventh	11th
twelve	12	XII	twelfth	12th
thirteen	13	XIII	thirteenth	13th
fourteen	14	XIV	fourteenth	14th
fifteen	15	XV	fifteenth	15th
sixteen	16	XVI	sixteenth	16th
seventeen	17	XVII	seventeenth	17th
eighteen	18	XVIII	eighteenth	18th
nineteen	19	XIX	nineteenth	19th
twenty	20	XX	twentieth	20th
twenty-one	21	XXI	twenty-first	21st
thirty	30	XXX	thirtieth	30th
forty	40	XL	fortieth	40th
fifty	50	L	fiftieth	50th
sixty	60	LX	sixtieth	60th
seventy	70	LXX	seventieth	70th
eighty	80	LXXX	eightieth	80th
ninety	90	XC	ninetieth	90th
one hundred	100	C	one hundredth	100th
one thousand	1,000	M	one, thousandth	1,000th
ten thousand	10,000	$\overline{X}$	ten thousandth	10,000th
one hundred thousand	100,000	$\overline{C}$	one hundred thousandth	100,000th
one million	1,000,000	$\overline{M}$	one millionth	1,000,000th

附录Ⅷ 概率论及统计学历史大事

- 1545年,意大利数学家(Girolamo Cardano)出版《大术》,标志近代数学的开端,后来出版的《游戏机遇的学说》是第一本概率书。
- 1654年,法国数学家帕斯卡(Blaise Pascal)为概率论奠定了基础。
- 1657年,荷兰数学家惠更斯(Christian Huygens)出版《论赌博中的计算》,这是第一部十分有影响的、关于概率的论著。
- 1693年,英国数学家哈雷(Edmund Hallet)对德国布雷斯劳的死亡率进行了统计研究。
- 1718年,法国数学家隶莫弗(Abraham de Moivre)发表《机会论》(The Doctrine of Chance)。后来,在1738年和1756年又发表2个扩展版本。
- 1733年,隶莫弗发表一部著作,表明正态曲线是二项分布的近似。
- 1763年,英国数学家贝叶斯(Thomas Bayes)发表关于概率的文章。
- 1785年,法国数学家孔多塞(Condocet)将概率论用于分析陪审团评判和选举系统。
- 1806年,法国数学家勒让德(Adrien-Marie Legendre)使用最小二乘法拟合数据。
- 1809年,德国数学家高斯(C. F. Gauss)在研究天文学问题中使用最小二乘法。
- 1812年,法国数学家拉普拉斯(Pierre-Simon Laplace)发表2卷《概率的解析理论》(Analytical Theory of Probabilities)这是19世纪最有影响的概率论著作。
- 1820年,高斯在天文学中使用正态分布作为误差法则。
- 1835年,比利时数学家、统计学家凯特莱(Adolphe Quetelet)在他的社会学著作中使用正态曲线衡量和'平均人'之间的偏差。
- 1837年,法国数学家、物理学家泊松(Simeon-Denis Poisson)描述了以他名字命名的泊松分布。
- 1885年,国际统计学会(The International Statistical Institute)成立。
- 1885年~1887年,英国数学家高尔顿(Francis Galton)提出回归和相关。
- 1887年,国际统计学会在罗马举行第1届国际统计学大会。
- 1896年,英国数学家皮尔逊(Karl Pearson)发表关于回归和相关的文献,他推广高尔顿的相关结论和方法。
- 1904年,英国统计学家斯皮尔曼(C. E. Spearman)在心理学研究中使用秩相关工具。

- 1912 年,凯恩斯发表《关于概率的论文》(Treatise on Probabilities),该书对他后来在经济学和统计学方面的理论产生重要影响。
- 1933 年,柯尔莫哥洛夫(A. N. Kolmogorov)发表《一般测度论和概率论》,第一次将概率论建立在稳固的公理基础上。
- 1937 年,意大利统计学家德·费奈蒂(Bruno de Finetti)提倡将主观概率作为频率学说的另一选择。
- 1950 年,美国数学家吉姆·萨维奇(Jimmy Savage)和丹尼斯·林力(Dennis Lindley)带头发起现代贝叶斯运动。
- 20 世纪 50 年代,"贝叶斯学派"一词第一次出现。
- 1975 年,贝叶斯协会(Bernoulli Society)成立,是国际统计学会的一个分支学会。

附录Ⅸ 数据阶常用英文表示法
Order of magnitude of data

In words	Value	Power of ten	Order of magnitude	Prefix	Metric	Abbreviation	中文
one	1	10^0	0	—	—	—	—
ten	10	10^1	1	deca-	—	—	—
hundred	100	10^2	2	hector-	—	—	—
thousand	1,000	10^3	3	kilo-	kilobytes	KB	千字节
million	$1,000^2$	10^6	6	mega-	megabyte	MB	兆字节
billion	$1,000^3$	10^9	9	giga-	gigabyte	GB	吉字节
trillion	$1,000^4$	10^{12}	12	tera-	terabyte	TB	太字节
quadrillion	$1,000^5$	10^{15}	15	peta-	petabyte	PB	拍字节
quintillion	$1,000^6$	10^{18}	18	exa-	exabyte	EB	艾字节
sextillion	$1,000^7$	10^{21}	21	zetta-	zettabyte	ZB	择字节
septillion	$1,000^8$	10^{24}	24	yotta-	yottabyte	YB	尧字节

注释:(1)bit:比特,二进制的位,存放一位二进制数,即 0 或 1。(2)byte:字节,字组,作为一个单位来操作(运算)的二进制字符串,通常 8 bits 组成一个字节,也就是 1 byte=8 bits,byte 简写为 B。

附录 X 计算机系统存储单位数据表示
Data representation in computer systems storage unit

单位名称	换算等式	形象注释
Bit（位）	存放一位二进制数，即 0 或 1	最小的存储单位
Byte（字节）记为 B	8 个二进制为一个字节（B）	常用的单位，一个汉字占 2 个字节
KB（千字字）	1KB = 1,024 B	1 千个字节约等于 512 个汉字的存储
MB（兆字节）	1MB = 1,024 KB	1 兆字节约等于存储 52 万多个汉字，相当于存储一本 50 多万字的书
GB（吉字节）	1GB = 1,024 MB	1GB 相当于存储 1 千多本 50 多万字的书
TB（太字节）	1TB = 1,024 GB	1TB 相当于存储 100 万本 50 多万字的书
PB（拍字节）	1PB = 1,024 TB	1PB 相当于存储 10 亿多本 50 多万字的书
EB（艾字节）	1EB = 1,024 PB	1EB 相当于存储全球所有图书
ZB（泽字节）	1ZB = 1,024 EB	1ZB 相当于存储全球目前所有互联网数据信息
YB（尧字节）	1YB = 1,024 ZB	1YB 相当于存储全球人类所有数据信息。人类目前的所有互联网数据、移动数据、书籍数据加起来都不够 1YB 的存储容量

附录XI 大数据常用术语(含定义)表
Big data glossary

术 语	定 义
算法(Algorithm)	应用数据分析数据。通常而言,算法一般是计算的步骤集合,也是可以一个用于计算某个函数的指令列表
分析法(Analytics)	应用数学从数据中提取内在价值
分析学平台(Analytics)	拥有强大的计算能力,并依托一系列分析工具进行各类数据的查询和处理
设备(Appliance)	用于从事某些特定活动的优化后的软件和硬件
序列化系统(Avro)	数据序列化系统(Apache Avro)是一个数据序列化系统,它允许对 Hadoop 文件模式进行编码。它擅长分析数据,是 Apache Hadoop 的组成部分
批处理(Batch)	无需人工干预、在后台运行的工作或处理过程
大数据(Big Data)	大数据事实上的标准定义是指超越了传统数据3个维度(数量、种类、速率)限制的数据,这3个维度结合起来使得数据更难吸收、处理和可视化
大数据洞察力(Big Insights)	带有企业级增值组件的 IBM Hadoop 商业分布
非关系数据库(Cassandra)	由 Apache 软件管理的开源阵列数据库
Clojure	发音为"closure",是一种基于 LISP 的动态编程语言
云(Cloud)	用于泛指任何计算资源——软件、硬件、服务——这些都是作为网络服务被交付的
Cloudera	第一家 Hadoop 商业提供商。Cloudera 在交付 Hadoop 时提供企业级增值组件
陈列数据库(Columnar database)	通过阵列存储、优化数据。对于基于列存储的数据分析处理特别有用
复杂事件处理(Complex Event Processing, CEP)	当事件发生时对事件进行分析和处理的进程
数据挖掘(Data Mining)	使用机器学习从数据中发现结构、趋势、关系的进程
分布式处理(Distributed Processing)	在多台 CPU 上完成一个项目的处理方式

续表 1

术　语	定　义
Dremel	Dremel 是一个可伸缩的、交互式点对点问答系统，它能以每秒运转上兆行的速度进行聚合查询
Flume	Flume 是一个从 Web 服务器、应用服务器和移动设备上聚集 Hadoop 数据的框架
Grid	联合在一起，可以并行计算的松散耦合服务器
Hadapt	为 Hadoop 提供相关附加物的商业提供商，而 Hadoop 上的数据通过一个高速载体在 HDFS 和关系型数据库之间移动
Hadoop	一个可以在集群（Grid）上存储大量非结构性数据（HDFS）、处理非结构性数据（MapReduce）的开源项目
HANA	来源于 SAP（用于大量交易和实时分析）的内存处理计算平台
Hbase	一个分布式、阵列型非关系型（NoSQL）数据库
HDFS	Hadoop 的文件系统，即 Hadoop 的存储机制
Hive	Hadoop 上类似于 SQL 的查询语言
Horton Works	带有用企业级附加价值的 Hadoop 商业交付组件
HPC	即高性能计算（High-Performance Computing），通俗讲是指设计用于高速浮点处理、多硬盘并行存储的设备
Hstreaming	Hadoop 上提供实时 CEP 处理的商业附加物
机器学习（Machine Learning）	即这样一种算法技术：学习经验数据，然后使用经验数据的规律来预测新数据的分析结果
Mahout	一个为 Hadoop 的 MapReduce 创建可伸缩的、机器学习算法库的 Apache 项目
MapR	一个带有企业级附加价值的 Hadoop 商业交付组件
MapReduce	Hadoop 的并行计算批处理框架，一般使用 Java 编程。大型问题被分解为若干小型片段，并沿服务器群进行负荷分布，以便可以同时进行分析工作（这就是 mapper 完成的工作）。管理单元（Reducer）收集所有中期处理结果并综合为最终结果
大规模并行处理（Massively Paraller Processing，MPP）	协调同步程序执行的系统（操作系统、处理器、存储器）
MPP Appliance	用于处理并行计算的，带有处理器、内存、硬盘和软件的融合平台
MPP Database	用于优化 MPP 环境的数据库
MongoDB	用 C++ 编写的可伸缩的、高性能的、开源的开关系数据库（NoSQL）

续表 2

术 语	定 义
NoSQL 数据库 (NoSQL Database)	指任何一种不使用 SQL 进行数据查询的数据库。非关系数据库限制了传统功能,用于设计可伸缩的、高性能的查询和数据扩展。典型地,NoSQL 数据库采用 key-value 的模式存储数据,这对于非结构化的数据是很有效的
Oozie	Oozie 是允许用户自定义一系列用 Mapreduce、Pig、Hive 等编程语言编写的工作单元的工作流处理系统
Pig	使用查询语言(Pig Latin)来实施数据转换的分布式处理框架。目前为了在 Hadoop 上执行,Pig Latin 被翻译为 Mapreduce 处理单元
R	R 是一种统计计算与制图的开源语言和环境
实时 (Real-Time)	现在口语中的 Real-Time 被定义为"实时处理"。实时处理起源于 20 世纪 50 年代,当时多任务机器提供了打断当前任务、执行高优先级任务的能力。这些机器占据了太空项目、军事应用和许多商业系统
关系数据库 (Relational Darabase)	通过行、列来存储和优化数据
评分(Scoring)	通过预测模型来预测新数据的分析结果
半结构化数据 (Semistructured Data)	通过可用的格式化描述可以用于某种结构的非结构化数据
Spark	用于内存分析计算处理(经常用于实时查询)的高性能处理框架
SQL(structured Query Language)	在关系数据库之间存储、获取、处理数据的语言
Sqoop	SQL-to-Hadoop 是向 Hadoop 文件中导入单个表格或整个表格的命令行工具
Storm	用于分布式、容错、实时分析处理的开源框架
结构化数据 (Structured Data)	具有预设格式的数据
非结构化数据 (Unstructured Data)	没有预设格式的数据
Whirr	Apache Whirr 是运行云服务的数据库
YARN	YARN 是 Apache Hadoop 的下一代计算框架,它除了支持 Mapreduce 外还支持其他编程范式

附录XII 数据科学与统计学的比较
Data Science vs Statistics Comparison Table

The differences between data science vs statistics are explained in the points presented below

Basis for Comparison	Data Science	Statistics
Meaning	● An interdisciplinary area of scientific techniques ● Similar to data mining uses processes, algorithms, and systems ● Extract insight information from data (structured or unstructured)	● Provides a collection of methods in representing data ● A branch in mathematics ● Provide methods for designing experiments ● Plans data collection, analysis and representation for further evaluations
Concept	● Based on scientific computing techniques ● Encompasses machine learning, other analytics processes, business models ● Uses advanced mathematics and statistics to derive new information from big data ● A wide discipline which involves programming, understanding of business models, trends, and so on	● Statistics is the science of data ● It is used to measure or estimate an attribute ● Applies statistical functions or algorithms on sets of data to determine values as appropriate for the problem being studied
Basis of formation	● To solve data related problems ● Model big data for analysis towards understanding trends, patterns behaviors and business performance ● Supports in decision making	● To design and formulate real world questions based on data ● Represent data in the form of tables, charts, graphs ● Understand techniques in data analysis ● Support for decision making

续表

Basis for Comparison	Data Science	Statistics
Application areas	● Healthcare systems ● Finance ● Fraud and intrusion detection ● Manufacturing, engineering ● Market analysis, etc.	● Commerce and trade ● Industry ● Population studies, economics ● Psychology ● Biology and physical sciences ● Astronomy, etc.
Approach	● Apply scientific methods in problem solving using random data ● Identifies data requirements for a given problem. ● Identify techniques to obtain desired results ● Provide value to organizations using data	● Use of mathematical formulas models and concepts ● Analysis of random data ● Estimate values for different data attributes ● To determine behaviors based on data

Conclusion–Data science vs statistics

In summary, it may be noted that Data science and statistics are indistinguishable and are closely linked. It is clear that statistics is a tool or method fordata science, while data science is a wide domain where a statistical method is an essential component. Data science and statistics will continue to exist and there is a big overlap between these two disciplines. Also to note, all statisticians cannot become data scientists and vice-versa. Data science has developed recently with big data and will continue to grow in the coming years as data growth seems to be never-ending.

附录XIII 数据科学各构成部分关系框架
(The Data Science competence groups interrelations)

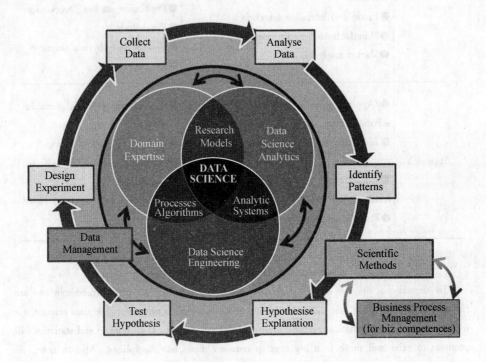

附录 XIV 哈佛大学统计系本科生及研究生课程纵览
Harvard Undergraduate Statistics Courses Family Tree

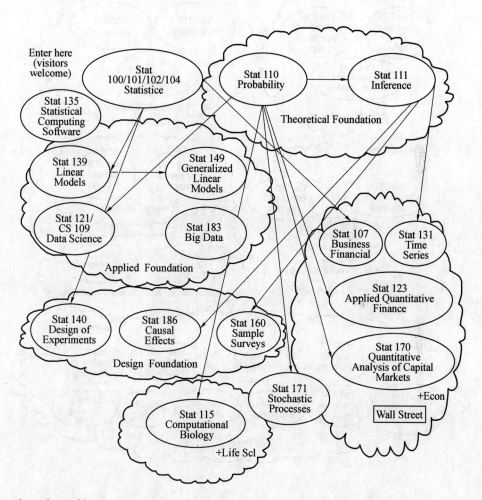

Seconday Field: Stat 110 and 111, two more Stat Courses abore 111 C_{107} also counts.

Concentration: Sta 110 and 111, five more Stat courses, five related courses.

Honors-eligible: Concentration requirements thesis, and two more related courses

Harvard Graduate Statistics Courses Family Tree

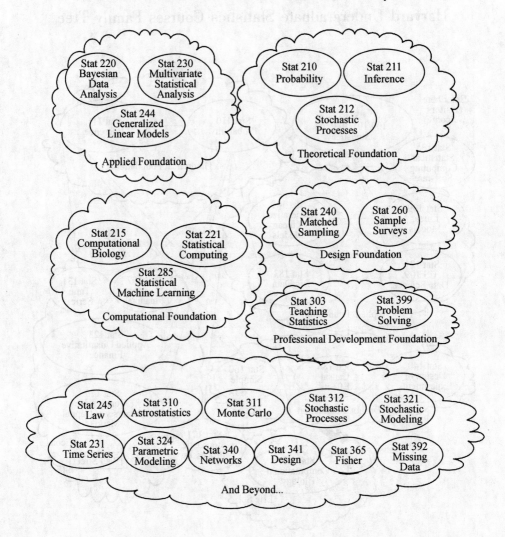

附录XV 生日与星座
Birthdays and the Signs of the Zodiac

Birthdays	The Signs of the Zodiac	
Jan. 20 ~ Feb. 18	Aquarius	宝瓶座/水瓶座
Feb. 19 ~ Mar. 20	Pisces	双鱼座
Mar. 20 ~ Apr. 19	Aries	白羊座/牡羊座
Apr. 20 ~ May. 20	Taurus	金牛座
May 21 ~ June 21	Gemini	双子座
June 22 ~ July 22	Cancer	巨蟹座
July. 23 ~ Aug. 22	Leo	狮子座
Aug. 23 ~ Sept. 22	Virgo	处女座
Sept. 23 ~ Oct. 22	Libra	天秤座
Oct. 23 ~ Nov. 21	Scorpio	天蝎座
Nov. 22 ~ Dec. 21	Sagittarius	射手座/人马座
Dec. 22 ~ Jan. 19	Capricorn	摩羯座/山羊座

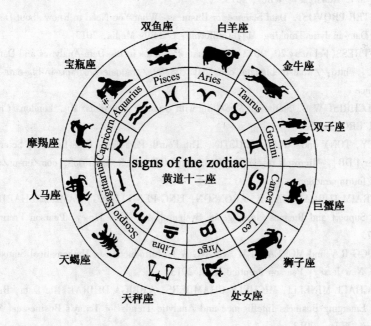

参考文献

[1] BREIMAN, LOE. Statistical Modeling: The Two Cultures[J]. Statistical Science, 2001, Vol. 16, No. 3, 199-231.

[2] CAMERON, COLIN A and PRAVIN K TRIVEDI. Microeconometrics: Methods and Applications[M]. Cambridge: Cambridge University Press, 2005.

[3] CASELLA, GEORGE and BERGER, ROGER L. Statistical Inference[M]. 2nd. Melbourne: Cengage Learning, 2001.

[4] COELLI T J. An Introduction to Efficiency and Productivity Analysis[M]. 2nd. NewYork: Springer, 2005.

[5] DAVENPORT, THOMAS H and HARRIS, JEANNE G. Competing on Analytics: The New Science of Winning[M]. Bosten: Harvard Business Review Press, 2007.

[6] DAVENPORT, THOMAS H and PATIL D J. Data Scientist: The Sexiest Job of the 21st Century[M]. Besten: Harvard Business Review Pree, 2012.

[7] ERIC SIEGEL. Predictive Analytics: The Power to Predict Who Will Click, Buy, Lie, or Die[M]. NewJersey: Wiley, 2013.

[8] FOSTER PROVOST. Data Science for Business: What You Need to Know about Data Mining and Data-analytic Thinking[M]. California: O'Reilly Media, 2013.

[9] GIL PRESS(February 20, 2013). Graduate Programs in Big Data Analytics and Data Science [OL]. http://whatsthebigdata.com/2012/08/09/graduate-programs-in-big-data-and-data-science.

[10] GILCHRIST W G. Statistical Modelling with Quantile Functions[M]. London: Chapman & Hall/CRC, 2000.

[11] HEY, TONY and TOLLE, KRISTIN. The Fourth Paradigm: Data-Intensive Scientific Discovery[DB]. Microsoft research, 2010. http://hesearch.microsoft.com/en-us/collaboration/fourthparadigm.

[12] EFRAIM TURBAN, JAY E, ARONSON, TING-PENG LIANG, RAMESH SHARDA. Decision Support and Business Intelligence Systems[M]. New Jersey: Pearson Pretince Hall, 2007.

[13] HOGG R V and MCKEAN J W, CRAIG A T. Introduction to Mathematical Statistics[M]. 7th. New Jersey: Pearson Prentice Hall, 2013.

[14] MICHAEL MINELLI, MICHELE CHAMBERS, AMBIGA DHIRAJ. Big Data, Big Analytics: Emerging Business Intelligence and Analytic Trends for Today's Businesses[M]. New Jersey: Wiley, 2013.

[15] TABAK, JOHN. Probability and Statistics: The Science of Uncertainty[M]. New York:

Checkmark Books,2005.
[16] THOMAS H, DAVENPORT and JEANNE G, HARRIS. Competing on Analytics: The New Science of Winning[M]. Bosten: Harvard Business Review Press, 2007.
[17] WOOLDRIDGE J M. Econometric Analysis of Cross Section and Panel Data[M]. Cambridge: MIT Press, 2002.
[18] 李文文,陈雅,国内外 Data Curation 研究综述[J].《情报资料工作》,2013(5):35-38.
[19] 田文杰.科技英语教程[M].西安:西安交通工业出版社,2008.
[20] 张鸿林,葛显良.英汉数学词汇[M].2版.北京:清华大学出版社,2010.
[21] 张晓峒.英汉数量经济学词汇[M].北京:机械工业出版社,2006.
[22] 吴艳.实用电脑英汉词典[M].北京:人民邮电出版社,2008.

刘培杰数学工作室
已出版(即将出版)图书目录——初等数学

书　　名	出版时间	定　价	编号
新编中学数学解题方法全书(高中版)上卷(第2版)	2018—08	58.00	951
新编中学数学解题方法全书(高中版)中卷(第2版)	2018—08	68.00	952
新编中学数学解题方法全书(高中版)下卷(一)(第2版)	2018—08	58.00	953
新编中学数学解题方法全书(高中版)下卷(二)(第2版)	2018—08	58.00	954
新编中学数学解题方法全书(高中版)下卷(三)(第2版)	2018—08	68.00	955
新编中学数学解题方法全书(初中版)上卷	2008—01	28.00	29
新编中学数学解题方法全书(初中版)中卷	2010—07	38.00	75
新编中学数学解题方法全书(高考复习卷)	2010—01	48.00	67
新编中学数学解题方法全书(高考真题卷)	2010—01	38.00	62
新编中学数学解题方法全书(高考精华卷)	2011—03	68.00	118
新编平面解析几何解题方法全书(专题讲座卷)	2010—01	18.00	61
新编中学数学解题方法全书(自主招生卷)	2013—08	88.00	261
数学奥林匹克与数学文化(第一辑)	2006—05	48.00	4
数学奥林匹克与数学文化(第二辑)(竞赛卷)	2008—01	48.00	19
数学奥林匹克与数学文化(第二辑)(文化卷)	2008—07	58.00	36'
数学奥林匹克与数学文化(第三辑)(竞赛卷)	2010—01	48.00	59
数学奥林匹克与数学文化(第四辑)(竞赛卷)	2011—08	58.00	87
数学奥林匹克与数学文化(第五辑)	2015—06	98.00	370
世界著名平面几何经典著作钩沉——几何作图专题卷(上)	2009—06	48.00	49
世界著名平面几何经典著作钩沉——几何作图专题卷(下)	2011—01	88.00	80
世界著名平面几何经典著作钩沉(民国平面几何老课本)	2011—03	38.00	113
世界著名平面几何经典著作钩沉(建国初期平面三角老课本)	2015—08	38.00	507
世界著名解析几何经典著作钩沉——平面解析几何卷	2014—01	38.00	264
世界著名数论经典著作钩沉(算术卷)	2012—01	28.00	125
世界著名数学经典著作钩沉——立体几何卷	2011—02	28.00	88
世界著名三角学经典著作钩沉(平面三角卷Ⅰ)	2010—06	28.00	69
世界著名三角学经典著作钩沉(平面三角卷Ⅱ)	2011—01	38.00	78
世界著名初等数论经典著作钩沉(理论和实用算术卷)	2011—07	38.00	126
发展你的空间想象力(第2版)	2019—11	68.00	1117
空间想象力进阶	2019—05	68.00	1062
走向国际数学奥林匹克的平面几何试题诠释.第1卷	2019—07	88.00	1043
走向国际数学奥林匹克的平面几何试题诠释.第2卷	2019—09	78.00	1044
走向国际数学奥林匹克的平面几何试题诠释.第3卷	2019—03	78.00	1045
走向国际数学奥林匹克的平面几何试题诠释.第4卷	2019—09	98.00	1046
平面几何证明方法全书	2007—08	35.00	1
平面几何证明方法全书习题解答(第2版)	2006—12	18.00	10
平面几何天天练上卷·基础篇(直线型)	2013—01	58.00	208
平面几何天天练中卷·基础篇(涉及圆)	2013—01	28.00	234
平面几何天天练下卷·提高篇	2013—01	58.00	237
平面几何专题研究	2013—07	98.00	258

刘培杰数学工作室
已出版(即将出版)图书目录——初等数学

书　名	出版时间	定　价	编号
最新世界各国数学奥林匹克中的平面几何试题	2007—09	38.00	14
数学竞赛平面几何典型题及新颖解	2010—07	48.00	74
初等数学复习及研究(平面几何)	2008—09	58.00	38
初等数学复习及研究(立体几何)	2010—06	38.00	71
初等数学复习及研究(平面几何)习题解答	2009—01	48.00	42
几何学教程(平面几何卷)	2011—03	68.00	90
几何学教程(立体几何卷)	2011—07	68.00	130
几何变换与几何证题	2010—06	88.00	70
计算方法与几何证题	2011—06	28.00	129
立体几何技巧与方法	2014—04	88.00	293
几何瑰宝——平面几何 500 名题暨 1000 条定理(上、下)	2010—07	138.00	76,77
三角形的解法与应用	2012—07	18.00	183
近代的三角形几何学	2012—07	48.00	184
一般折线几何学	2015—08	48.00	503
三角形的五心	2009—06	28.00	51
三角形的六心及其应用	2015—10	68.00	542
三角形趣谈	2012—08	28.00	212
解三角形	2014—01	28.00	265
三角学专门教程	2014—09	28.00	387
图天下几何新题试卷.初中(第 2 版)	2017—11	58.00	855
圆锥曲线习题集(上册)	2013—06	68.00	255
圆锥曲线习题集(中册)	2015—01	78.00	434
圆锥曲线习题集(下册·第 1 卷)	2016—10	78.00	683
圆锥曲线习题集(下册·第 2 卷)	2018—01	98.00	853
圆锥曲线习题集(下册·第 3 卷)	2019—10	128.00	1113
论九点圆	2015—05	88.00	645
近代欧氏几何学	2012—03	48.00	162
罗巴切夫斯基几何学及几何基础概要	2012—07	28.00	188
罗巴切夫斯基几何学初步	2015—06	28.00	474
用三角、解析几何、复数、向量计算解数学竞赛几何题	2015—03	48.00	455
美国中学几何教程	2015—04	88.00	458
三线坐标与三角形特征点	2015—04	98.00	460
平面解析几何方法与研究(第 1 卷)	2015—05	18.00	471
平面解析几何方法与研究(第 2 卷)	2015—06	18.00	472
平面解析几何方法与研究(第 3 卷)	2015—07	18.00	473
解析几何研究	2015—01	38.00	425
解析几何学教程.上	2016—01	38.00	574
解析几何学教程.下	2016—01	38.00	575
几何学基础	2016—01	58.00	581
初等几何研究	2015—02	58.00	444
十九和二十世纪欧氏几何学中的片段	2017—01	58.00	696
平面几何中考.高考.奥数一本通	2017—07	28.00	820
几何学简史	2017—08	28.00	833
四面体	2018—01	48.00	880
平面几何证明方法思路	2018—12	68.00	913
平面几何图形特性新析.上篇	2019—01	68.00	911
平面几何图形特性新析.下篇	2018—06	88.00	912
平面几何范例多解探究.上篇	2018—04	48.00	910
平面几何范例多解探究.下篇	2018—12	68.00	914
从分析解题过程学解题:竞赛中的几何问题研究	2018—07	68.00	946
从分析解题过程学解题:竞赛中的向量几何与不等式研究(全 2 册)	2019—06	138.00	1090
二维、三维欧氏几何的对偶原理	2018—12	38.00	990
星形大观及闭折线论	2019—03	68.00	1020
圆锥曲线之设点与设线	2019—05	60.00	1063
立体几何的问题和方法	2019—11	58.00	1127

刘培杰数学工作室
已出版(即将出版)图书目录——初等数学

书　名	出版时间	定　价	编号
俄罗斯平面几何问题集	2009-08	88.00	55
俄罗斯立体几何问题集	2014-03	58.00	283
俄罗斯几何大师——沙雷金论数学及其他	2014-01	48.00	271
来自俄罗斯的5000道几何习题及解答	2011-03	58.00	89
俄罗斯初等数学问题集	2012-05	38.00	177
俄罗斯函数问题集	2011-03	38.00	103
俄罗斯组合分析问题集	2011-01	48.00	79
俄罗斯初等数学万题选——三角卷	2012-11	38.00	222
俄罗斯初等数学万题选——代数卷	2013-08	68.00	225
俄罗斯初等数学万题选——几何卷	2014-01	68.00	226
俄罗斯《量子》杂志数学征解问题100题选	2018-08	48.00	969
俄罗斯《量子》杂志数学征解问题又100题选	2018-08	48.00	970
俄罗斯《量子》杂志数学征解问题	2020-05	48.00	1138
463个俄罗斯几何老问题	2012-01	28.00	152
《量子》数学短文精粹	2018-09	38.00	972
用三角、解析几何等计算解来自俄罗斯的几何题	2019-11	88.00	1119
谈谈素数	2011-03	18.00	91
平方和	2011-03	18.00	92
整数论	2011-05	38.00	120
从整数谈起	2015-10	28.00	538
数与多项式	2016-01	38.00	558
谈谈不定方程	2011-05	28.00	119
解析不等式新论	2009-06	68.00	48
建立不等式的方法	2011-03	98.00	104
数学奥林匹克不等式研究(第2版)	2020-07	68.00	1181
不等式研究(第二辑)	2012-02	68.00	153
不等式的秘密(第一卷)(第2版)	2014-02	38.00	286
不等式的秘密(第二卷)	2014-01	38.00	268
初等不等式的证明方法	2010-06	38.00	123
初等不等式的证明方法(第二版)	2014-11	38.00	407
不等式·理论·方法(基础卷)	2015-07	38.00	496
不等式·理论·方法(经典不等式卷)	2015-07	38.00	497
不等式·理论·方法(特殊类型不等式卷)	2015-07	48.00	498
不等式探究	2016-03	38.00	582
不等式探秘	2017-01	88.00	689
四面体不等式	2017-01	68.00	715
数学奥林匹克中常见重要不等式	2017-09	38.00	845
三正弦不等式	2018-09	98.00	974
函数方程与不等式:解法与稳定性结果	2019-04	68.00	1058
同余理论	2012-05	38.00	163
[x]与{x}	2015-04	48.00	476
极值与最值.上卷	2015-06	28.00	486
极值与最值.中卷	2015-06	38.00	487
极值与最值.下卷	2015-06	28.00	488
整数的性质	2012-11	38.00	192
完全平方数及其应用	2015-08	78.00	506
多项式理论	2015-10	88.00	541
奇数、偶数、奇偶分析法	2018-01	98.00	876
不定方程及其应用.上	2018-12	58.00	992
不定方程及其应用.中	2019-01	78.00	993
不定方程及其应用.下	2019-02	98.00	994

刘培杰数学工作室
已出版(即将出版)图书目录——初等数学

书　名	出版时间	定价	编号
历届美国中学生数学竞赛试题及解答(第一卷)1950—1954	2014—07	18.00	277
历届美国中学生数学竞赛试题及解答(第二卷)1955—1959	2014—04	18.00	278
历届美国中学生数学竞赛试题及解答(第三卷)1960—1964	2014—06	18.00	279
历届美国中学生数学竞赛试题及解答(第四卷)1965—1969	2014—04	28.00	280
历届美国中学生数学竞赛试题及解答(第五卷)1970—1972	2014—06	18.00	281
历届美国中学生数学竞赛试题及解答(第六卷)1973—1980	2017—07	18.00	768
历届美国中学生数学竞赛试题及解答(第七卷)1981—1986	2015—01	18.00	424
历届美国中学生数学竞赛试题及解答(第八卷)1987—1990	2017—05	18.00	769
历届中国数学奥林匹克试题集(第2版)	2017—03	38.00	757
历届加拿大数学奥林匹克试题集	2012—08	38.00	215
历届美国数学奥林匹克试题集：1972～2019	2020—04	88.00	1135
历届波兰数学竞赛试题集.第1卷,1949～1963	2015—03	18.00	453
历届波兰数学竞赛试题集.第2卷,1964～1976	2015—03	18.00	454
历届巴尔干数学奥林匹克试题集	2015—05	38.00	466
保加利亚数学奥林匹克	2014—10	38.00	393
圣彼得堡数学奥林匹克试题集	2015—01	38.00	429
匈牙利奥林匹克数学竞赛题解.第1卷	2016—05	28.00	593
匈牙利奥林匹克数学竞赛题解.第2卷	2016—05	28.00	594
历届美国数学邀请赛试题集(第2版)	2017—10	78.00	851
全国高中数学竞赛试题及解答.第1卷	2014—07	38.00	331
普林斯顿大学数学竞赛	2016—06	38.00	669
亚太地区数学奥林匹克竞赛题	2015—07	18.00	492
日本历届(初级)广中杯数学竞赛试题及解答.第1卷(2000～2007)	2016—05	28.00	641
日本历届(初级)广中杯数学竞赛试题及解答.第2卷(2008～2015)	2016—05	38.00	642
360个数学竞赛问题	2016—08	58.00	677
奥数最佳实战题.上卷	2017—06	38.00	760
奥数最佳实战题.下卷	2017—05	58.00	761
哈尔滨市早期中学数学竞赛试题汇编	2016—07	28.00	672
全国高中数学联赛试题及解答:1981—2019(第4版)	2020—07	138.00	1176
20世纪50年代全国部分城市数学竞赛试题汇编	2017—07	28.00	797
国内外数学竞赛题及精解:2017～2018	2019—06	45.00	1092
许康华竞赛优学精选集.第一辑	2018—08	68.00	949
天问叶班数学问题征解100题.Ⅰ,2016—2018	2019—05	88.00	1075
天问叶班数学问题征解100题.Ⅱ,2017—2019	2020—07	98.00	1177
美国初中数学竞赛：AMC8准备(共6卷)	2019—07	138.00	1089
美国高中数学竞赛：AMC10准备(共6卷)	2019—08	158.00	1105
高考数学临门一脚(含密押三套卷)(理科版)	2017—01	45.00	743
高考数学临门一脚(含密押三套卷)(文科版)	2017—01	45.00	744
高考数学题型全归纳:文科版.上	2016—05	53.00	663
高考数学题型全归纳:文科版.下	2016—05	53.00	664
高考数学题型全归纳:理科版.上	2016—05	58.00	665
高考数学题型全归纳:理科版.下	2016—05	58.00	666

刘培杰数学工作室
已出版(即将出版)图书目录——初等数学

书　名	出版时间	定价	编号
王连笑教你怎样学数学:高考选择题解题策略与客观题实用训练	2014—01	48.00	262
王连笑教你怎样学数学:高考数学高层次讲座	2015—02	48.00	432
高考数学的理论与实践	2009—08	38.00	53
高考数学核心题型解题方法与技巧	2010—01	28.00	86
高考思维新平台	2014—03	38.00	259
30分钟拿下高考数学选择题、填空题(理科版)	2016—10	39.80	720
30分钟拿下高考数学选择题、填空题(文科版)	2016—10	39.80	721
高考数学压轴题解题诀窍(上)(第2版)	2018—01	58.00	874
高考数学压轴题解题诀窍(下)(第2版)	2018—01	48.00	875
北京市五区文科数学三年高考模拟题详解:2013～2015	2015—08	48.00	500
北京市五区理科数学三年高考模拟题详解:2013～2015	2015—09	68.00	505
向量法巧解数学高考题	2009—08	28.00	54
高考数学解题金典(第2版)	2017—01	78.00	716
高考物理解题金典(第2版)	2019—05	68.00	717
高考化学解题金典(第2版)	2019—05	58.00	718
我一定要赚分:高中物理	2016—01	38.00	580
数学高考参考	2016—01	78.00	589
2011～2015年全国及各省市高考数学文科精品试题审题要津与解法研究	2015—10	68.00	539
2011～2015年全国及各省市高考数学理科精品试题审题要津与解法研究	2015—10	88.00	540
最新全国及各省市高考数学试卷解法研究及点拨评析	2009—02	38.00	41
2011年全国及各省市高考数学试题审题要津与解法研究	2011—10	48.00	139
2013年全国及各省市高考数学试题解析与点评	2014—01	48.00	282
全国及各省市高考数学试题审题要津与解法研究	2015—02	48.00	450
高中数学章节起始课的教学研究与案例设计	2019—05	28.00	1064
新课标高考数学——五年试题分章详解(2007～2011)(上、下)	2011—10	78.00	140,141
全国中考数学压轴题审题要津与解法研究	2013—04	78.00	248
新编全国及各省市中考数学压轴题审题要津与解法研究	2014—05	58.00	342
全国及各省市5年中考数学压轴题审题要津与解法研究(2015版)	2015—04	58.00	462
中考数学专题总复习	2007—04	28.00	6
中考数学较难题常考题型解题方法与技巧	2016—09	48.00	681
中考数学难题常考题型解题方法与技巧	2016—09	48.00	682
中考数学中档题常考题型解题方法与技巧	2017—08	68.00	835
中考数学选择填空压轴好题妙解365	2017—05	38.00	759
中考数学:三类重点考题的解法例析与习题	2020—04	48.00	1140
中小学数学的历史文化	2019—11	48.00	1124
初中平面几何百题多思创新解	2020—01	58.00	1125
初中数学中考备考	2020—01	58.00	1126
高考数学之九章演义	2019—08	68.00	1044
化学可以这样学:高中化学知识方法智慧感悟疑难辨析	2019—07	58.00	1103
如何成为学习高手	2019—09	58.00	1107
高考数学:经典真题分类解析	2020—04	78.00	1134
从分析解题过程学解题:高考压轴题与竞赛题之关系探究	2020—08	88.00	1179

刘培杰数学工作室
已出版(即将出版)图书目录——初等数学

书 名	出版时间	定 价	编号
中考数学小压轴汇编初讲	2017—07	48.00	788
中考数学大压轴专题微言	2017—09	48.00	846
怎么解中考平面几何探索题	2019—06	48.00	1093
北京中考数学压轴题解题方法突破(第5版)	2020—01	58.00	1120
助你高考成功的数学解题智慧:知识是智慧的基础	2016—01	58.00	596
助你高考成功的数学解题智慧:错误是智慧的试金石	2016—04	58.00	643
助你高考成功的数学解题智慧:方法是智慧的推手	2016—04	68.00	657
高考数学奇思妙解	2016—04	38.00	610
高考数学解题策略	2016—05	48.00	670
数学解题泄天机(第2版)	2017—10	48.00	850
高考物理压轴题全解	2017—04	48.00	746
高中物理经典问题25讲	2017—05	28.00	764
高中物理教学讲义	2018—01	48.00	871
2016年高考文科数学真题研究	2017—04	58.00	754
2016年高考理科数学真题研究	2017—04	78.00	755
2017年高考理科数学真题研究	2018—01	58.00	867
2017年高考文科数学真题研究	2018—01	48.00	868
初中数学、高中数学脱节知识补缺教材	2017—06	48.00	766
高考数学小题抢分必练	2017—10	48.00	834
高考数学核心素养解读	2017—09	38.00	839
高考数学客观题解题方法和技巧	2017—10	38.00	847
十年高考数学精品试题审题要津与解法研究.上卷	2018—01	68.00	872
十年高考数学精品试题审题要津与解法研究.下卷	2018—01	58.00	873
中国历届高考数学试题及解答.1949—1979	2018—01	38.00	877
历届中国高考数学试题及解答.第二卷,1980—1989	2018—10	28.00	975
历届中国高考数学试题及解答.第三卷,1990—1999	2018—10	48.00	976
数学文化与高考研究	2018—03	48.00	882
跟我学解高中数学题	2018—07	58.00	926
中学数学研究的方法及案例	2018—05	58.00	869
高考数学抢分技能	2018—07	68.00	934
高一新生常用数学方法和重要数学思想提升教材	2018—06	38.00	921
2018年高考数学真题研究	2019—01	68.00	1000
2019年高考数学真题研究	2020—05	88.00	1137
高考数学全国卷16道选择、填空题常考题型解题诀窍.理科	2018—09	88.00	971
高考数学全国卷16道选择、填空题常考题型解题诀窍.文科	2020—01	88.00	1123
高中数学一题多解	2019—06	58.00	1087

新编640个世界著名数学智力趣题	2014—01	88.00	242
500个最新世界著名数学智力趣题	2008—06	48.00	3
400个最新世界著名数学最值问题	2008—09	48.00	36
500个世界著名数学征解问题	2009—06	48.00	52
400个中国最佳初等数学征解老问题	2010—01	48.00	60
500个俄罗斯数学经典老题	2011—01	28.00	81
1000个国外中学物理好题	2012—04	48.00	174
300个日本高考数学题	2012—05	38.00	142
700个早期日本高考数学试题	2017—02	88.00	752
500个前苏联早期高考数学试题及解答	2012—05	28.00	185
546个早期俄罗斯大学生数学竞赛题	2014—03	38.00	285
548个来自美苏的数学好问题	2014—11	28.00	396
20所苏联著名大学早期入学试题	2015—02	18.00	452
161道德国工科大学生必做的微分方程习题	2015—05	28.00	469
500个德国工科大学生必做的高数习题	2015—05	28.00	478
360个数学竞赛问题	2016—08	58.00	677
200个趣味数学故事	2018—02	48.00	857
470个数学奥林匹克中的最值问题	2018—10	88.00	985
德国讲义日本考题.微积分卷	2015—04	48.00	456
德国讲义日本考题.微分方程卷	2015—04	38.00	457
二十世纪中叶中、英、美、日、法、俄高考数学试题精选	2017—06	38.00	783

刘培杰数学工作室
已出版(即将出版)图书目录——初等数学

书 名	出版时间	定 价	编号
中国初等数学研究 2009卷(第1辑)	2009—05	20.00	45
中国初等数学研究 2010卷(第2辑)	2010—05	30.00	68
中国初等数学研究 2011卷(第3辑)	2011—07	60.00	127
中国初等数学研究 2012卷(第4辑)	2012—07	48.00	190
中国初等数学研究 2014卷(第5辑)	2014—02	48.00	288
中国初等数学研究 2015卷(第6辑)	2015—06	68.00	493
中国初等数学研究 2016卷(第7辑)	2016—04	68.00	609
中国初等数学研究 2017卷(第8辑)	2017—01	98.00	712
初等数学研究在中国.第1辑	2019—03	158.00	1024
初等数学研究在中国.第2辑	2019—10	158.00	1116
几何变换(Ⅰ)	2014—07	28.00	353
几何变换(Ⅱ)	2015—06	28.00	354
几何变换(Ⅲ)	2015—01	38.00	355
几何变换(Ⅳ)	2015—12	38.00	356
初等数论难题集(第一卷)	2009—05	68.00	44
初等数论难题集(第二卷)(上、下)	2011—02	128.00	82,83
数论概貌	2011—03	18.00	93
代数数论(第二版)	2013—08	58.00	94
代数多项式	2014—06	38.00	289
初等数论的知识与问题	2011—02	28.00	95
超越数论基础	2011—03	28.00	96
数论初等教程	2011—03	28.00	97
数论基础	2011—03	18.00	98
数论基础与维诺格拉多夫	2014—03	18.00	292
解析数论基础	2012—08	28.00	216
解析数论基础(第二版)	2014—01	48.00	287
解析数论问题集(第二版)(原版引进)	2014—05	88.00	343
解析数论问题集(第二版)(中译本)	2016—04	88.00	607
解析数论基础(潘承洞,潘承彪著)	2016—07	98.00	673
解析数论导引	2016—07	58.00	674
数论入门	2011—03	38.00	99
代数数论入门	2015—03	38.00	448
数论开篇	2012—07	28.00	194
解析数论引论	2011—03	48.00	100
Barban Davenport Halberstam 均值和	2009—01	40.00	33
基础数论	2011—03	28.00	101
初等数论100例	2011—05	18.00	122
初等数论经典例题	2012—07	18.00	204
最新世界各国数学奥林匹克中的初等数论试题(上、下)	2012—01	138.00	144,145
初等数论(Ⅰ)	2012—01	18.00	156
初等数论(Ⅱ)	2012—01	18.00	157
初等数论(Ⅲ)	2012—01	28.00	158

刘培杰数学工作室
已出版(即将出版)图书目录——初等数学

书　名	出版时间	定　价	编号
平面几何与数论中未解决的新老问题	2013—01	68.00	229
代数数论简史	2014—11	28.00	408
代数数论	2015—09	88.00	532
代数、数论及分析习题集	2016—11	98.00	695
数论导引提要及习题解答	2016—01	48.00	559
素数定理的初等证明.第2版	2016—09	48.00	686
数论中的模函数与狄利克雷级数(第二版)	2017—11	78.00	837
数论:数学导引	2018—01	68.00	849
范氏大代数	2019—02	98.00	1016
解析数学讲义.第一卷,导来式及微分、积分、级数	2019—04	88.00	1021
解析数学讲义.第二卷,关于几何的应用	2019—04	68.00	1022
解析数学讲义.第三卷,解析函数论	2019—04	78.00	1023
分析・组合・数论纵横谈	2019—04	58.00	1039
Hall 代数:民国时期的中学数学课本:英文	2019—08	88.00	1106
数学精神巡礼	2019—01	58.00	731
数学眼光透视(第2版)	2017—06	78.00	732
数学思想领悟(第2版)	2018—01	68.00	733
数学方法溯源(第2版)	2018—08	68.00	734
数学解题引论	2017—05	58.00	735
数学史话览胜(第2版)	2017—01	48.00	736
数学应用展观(第2版)	2017—08	68.00	737
数学建模尝试	2018—04	48.00	738
数学竞赛采风	2018—01	68.00	739
数学测评探营	2019—05	58.00	740
数学技能操握	2018—03	48.00	741
数学欣赏拾趣	2018—02	48.00	742
从毕达哥拉斯到怀尔斯	2007—10	48.00	9
从迪利克雷到维斯卡尔迪	2008—01	48.00	21
从哥德巴赫到陈景润	2008—05	98.00	35
从庞加莱到佩雷尔曼	2011—08	138.00	136
博弈论精粹	2008—03	58.00	30
博弈论精粹.第二版(精装)	2015—01	88.00	461
数学 我爱你	2008—01	28.00	20
精神的圣徒 别样的人生——60位中国数学家成长的历程	2008—09	48.00	39
数学史概论	2009—06	78.00	50
数学史概论(精装)	2013—03	158.00	272
数学史选讲	2016—01	48.00	544
斐波那契数列	2010—02	28.00	65
数学拼盘和斐波那契魔方	2010—07	38.00	72
斐波那契数列欣赏(第2版)	2018—08	58.00	948
Fibonacci 数列中的明珠	2018—06	58.00	928
数学的创造	2011—02	48.00	85
数学美与创造力	2016—06	48.00	595
数海拾贝	2016—01	48.00	590
数学中的美(第2版)	2019—04	68.00	1057
数论中的美学	2014—12	38.00	351

— 8 —

刘培杰数学工作室
已出版(即将出版)图书目录——初等数学

书　　名	出版时间	定　价	编号
数学王者　科学巨人——高斯	2015—01	28.00	428
振兴祖国数学的圆梦之旅:中国初等数学研究史话	2015—06	98.00	490
二十世纪中国数学史料研究	2015—10	48.00	536
数字谜、数阵图与棋盘覆盖	2016—01	58.00	298
时间的形状	2016—01	38.00	556
数学发现的艺术:数学探索中的合情推理	2016—07	58.00	671
活跃在数学中的参数	2016—07	48.00	675
数学解题——靠数学思想给力(上)	2011—07	38.00	131
数学解题——靠数学思想给力(中)	2011—07	48.00	132
数学解题——靠数学思想给力(下)	2011—07	38.00	133
我怎样解题	2013—01	48.00	227
数学解题中的物理方法	2011—06	28.00	114
数学解题的特殊方法	2011—06	48.00	115
中学数学计算技巧	2012—01	48.00	116
中学数学证明方法	2012—01	58.00	117
数学趣题巧解	2012—03	28.00	128
高中数学教学通鉴	2015—05	58.00	479
和高中生漫谈:数学与哲学的故事	2014—08	28.00	369
算术问题集	2017—03	38.00	789
张教授讲数学	2018—07	38.00	933
陈永明实话实说数学教学	2020—04	68.00	1132
中学数学学科知识与教学能力	2020—06	58.00	1155
自主招生考试中的参数方程问题	2015—01	28.00	435
自主招生考试中的极坐标问题	2015—04	28.00	463
近年全国重点大学自主招生数学试题全解及研究.华约卷	2015—02	38.00	441
近年全国重点大学自主招生数学试题全解及研究.北约卷	2016—05	38.00	619
自主招生数学解证宝典	2015—09	48.00	535
格点和面积	2012—07	18.00	191
射影几何趣谈	2012—04	28.00	175
斯潘纳尔引理——从一道加拿大数学奥林匹克试题谈起	2014—01	28.00	228
李普希兹条件——从几道近年高考数学试题谈起	2012—10	18.00	221
拉格朗日中值定理——从一道北京高考试题的解法谈起	2015—10	18.00	197
闵科夫斯基定理——从一道清华大学自主招生试题谈起	2014—01	28.00	198
哈尔测度——从一道冬令营试题的背景谈起	2012—08	28.00	202
切比雪夫逼近问题——从一道中国台北数学奥林匹克试题谈起	2013—04	38.00	238
伯恩斯坦多项式与贝齐尔曲面——从一道全国高中数学联赛试题谈起	2013—03	38.00	236
卡塔兰猜想——从一道普特南竞赛试题谈起	2013—06	18.00	256
麦卡锡函数和阿克曼函数——从一道前南斯拉夫数学奥林匹克试题谈起	2012—08	18.00	201
贝蒂定理与拉姆贝克莫斯尔定理——从一个拣石子游戏谈起	2012—08	18.00	217
皮亚诺曲线和豪斯道夫分球定理——从无限集谈起	2012—08	18.00	211
平面凸图形与凸多面体	2012—10	28.00	218
斯坦因豪斯问题——从一道二十五省市自治区中学数学竞赛试题谈起	2012—07	18.00	196

刘培杰数学工作室
已出版(即将出版)图书目录——初等数学

书　名	出版时间	定　价	编号
纽结理论中的亚历山大多项式与琼斯多项式——从一道北京市高一数学竞赛试题谈起	2012—07	28.00	195
原则与策略——从波利亚"解题表"谈起	2013—04	38.00	244
转化与化归——从三大尺规作图不能问题谈起	2012—08	28.00	214
代数几何中的贝祖定理(第一版)——从一道 IMO 试题的解法谈起	2013—08	18.00	193
成功连贯理论与约当块理论——从一道比利时数学竞赛试题谈起	2012—04	18.00	180
素数判定与大数分解	2014—08	18.00	199
置换多项式及其应用	2012—10	18.00	220
椭圆函数与模函数——从一道美国加州大学洛杉矶分校(UCLA)博士资格考题谈起	2012—10	28.00	219
差分方程的拉格朗日方法——从一道 2011 年全国高考理科试题的解法谈起	2012—08	28.00	200
力学在几何中的一些应用	2013—01	38.00	240
从根式解到伽罗华理论	2020—01	48.00	1121
康托洛维奇不等式——从一道全国高中联赛试题谈起	2013—03	28.00	337
西格尔引理——从一道第 18 届 IMO 试题的解法谈起	即将出版		
罗斯定理——从一道前苏联数学竞赛试题谈起	即将出版		
拉克斯定理和阿廷定理——从一道 IMO 试题的解法谈起	2014—01	58.00	246
毕卡大定理——从一道美国大学数学竞赛试题谈起	2014—07	18.00	350
贝齐尔曲线——从一道全国高中联赛试题谈起	即将出版		
拉格朗日乘子定理——从一道 2005 年全国高中联赛试题的高等数学解法谈起	2015—05	28.00	480
雅可比定理——从一道日本数学奥林匹克试题谈起	2013—04	48.00	249
李天岩-约克定理——从一道波兰数学竞赛试题谈起	2014—06	28.00	349
整系数多项式因式分解的一般方法——从克朗耐克算法谈起	即将出版		
布劳维不动点定理——从一道前苏联数学奥林匹克试题谈起	2014—01	38.00	273
伯恩赛德定理——从一道英国数学奥林匹克试题谈起	即将出版		
布查特—莫斯特定理——从一道上海市初中竞赛试题谈起	即将出版		
数论中的同余数问题——从一道普特南竞赛试题谈起	即将出版		
范•德蒙行列式——从一道美国数学奥林匹克试题谈起	即将出版		
中国剩余定理:总数法构建中国历史年表	2015—01	28.00	430
牛顿程序与方程求根——从一道全国高考试题解法谈起	即将出版		
库默尔定理——从一道 IMO 预选试题谈起	即将出版		
卢丁定理——从一道冬令营试题的解法谈起	即将出版		
沃斯滕霍姆定理——从一道 IMO 预选试题谈起	即将出版		
卡尔松不等式——从一道莫斯科数学奥林匹克试题谈起	即将出版		
信息论中的香农熵——从一道近年高考压轴题谈起	即将出版		
约当不等式——从一道希望杯竞赛试题谈起	即将出版		
拉比诺维奇定理	即将出版		
刘维尔定理——从一道《美国数学月刊》征解问题的解法谈起	即将出版		
卡塔兰恒等式与级数求和——从一道 IMO 试题的解法谈起	即将出版		
勒让德猜想与素数分布——从一道爱尔兰竞赛试题谈起	即将出版		
天平称重与信息论——从一道基辅市数学奥林匹克试题谈起	即将出版		
哈密尔顿—凯莱定理:从一道高中数学联赛试题的解法谈起	2014—09	18.00	376
艾思特曼定理——从一道 CMO 试题的解法谈起	即将出版		

刘培杰数学工作室
已出版(即将出版)图书目录——初等数学

书 名	出版时间	定 价	编号
阿贝尔恒等式与经典不等式及应用	2018—06	98.00	923
迪利克雷除数问题	2018—07	48.00	930
幻方、幻立方与拉丁方	2019—08	48.00	1092
帕斯卡三角形	2014—03	18.00	294
蒲丰投针问题——从2009年清华大学的一道自主招生试题谈起	2014—01	38.00	295
斯图姆定理——从一道"华约"自主招生试题的解法谈起	2014—01	18.00	296
许瓦兹引理——从一道加利福尼亚大学伯克利分校数学系博士生试题谈起	2014—08	18.00	297
拉姆塞定理——从王诗宬院士的一个问题谈起	2016—04	48.00	299
坐标法	2013—12	28.00	332
数论三角形	2014—04	38.00	341
毕克定理	2014—07	18.00	352
数林掠影	2014—09	48.00	389
我们周围的概率	2014—10	38.00	390
凸函数最值定理:从一道华约自主招生题的解法谈起	2014—10	28.00	391
易学与数学奥林匹克	2014—10	38.00	392
生物数学趣谈	2015—01	18.00	409
反演	2015—01	28.00	420
因式分解与圆锥曲线	2015—01	18.00	426
轨迹	2015—01	28.00	427
面积原理:从常庚哲命的一道CMO试题的积分解法谈起	2015—01	48.00	431
形形色色的不动点定理:从一道28届IMO试题谈起	2015—01	38.00	439
柯西函数方程:从一道上海交大自主招生的试题谈起	2015—02	28.00	440
三角恒等式	2015—02	28.00	442
无理性判定:从一道2014年"北约"自主招生试题谈起	2015—01	38.00	443
数学归纳法	2015—03	18.00	451
极端原理与解题	2015—04	28.00	464
法雷级数	2014—08	18.00	367
摆线族	2015—01	38.00	438
函数方程及其解法	2015—05	38.00	470
含参数的方程和不等式	2012—09	28.00	213
希尔伯特第十问题	2016—01	38.00	543
无穷小量的求和	2016—01	28.00	545
切比雪夫多项式:从一道清华大学金秋营试题谈起	2016—01	38.00	583
泽肯多夫定理	2016—03	38.00	599
代数等式证题法	2016—01	28.00	600
三角等式证题法	2016—01	28.00	601
吴大任教授藏书中的一个因式分解公式:从一道美国数学邀请赛试题的解法谈起	2016—06	28.00	656
易卦——类万物的数学模型	2017—08	68.00	838
"不可思议"的数与数系可持续发展	2018—01	38.00	878
最短线	2018—01	38.00	879
幻方和魔方(第一卷)	2012—05	68.00	173
尘封的经典——初等数学经典文献选读(第一卷)	2012—07	48.00	205
尘封的经典——初等数学经典文献选读(第二卷)	2012—07	38.00	206
初级方程式论	2011—03	28.00	106
初等数学研究(Ⅰ)	2008—09	68.00	37
初等数学研究(Ⅱ)(上、下)	2009—05	118.00	46,47

刘培杰数学工作室
已出版（即将出版）图书目录——初等数学

书　　名	出版时间	定价	编号
趣味初等方程妙题集锦	2014—09	48.00	388
趣味初等数论选美与欣赏	2015—02	48.00	445
耕读笔记(上卷)：一位农民数学爱好者的初数探索	2015—04	28.00	459
耕读笔记(中卷)：一位农民数学爱好者的初数探索	2015—05	28.00	483
耕读笔记(下卷)：一位农民数学爱好者的初数探索	2015—05	28.00	484
几何不等式研究与欣赏.上卷	2016—01	88.00	547
几何不等式研究与欣赏.下卷	2016—01	48.00	552
初等数列研究与欣赏·上	2016—01	48.00	570
初等数列研究与欣赏·下	2016—01	48.00	571
趣味初等函数研究与欣赏.上	2016—09	48.00	684
趣味初等函数研究与欣赏.下	2018—09	48.00	685
火柴游戏	2016—05	38.00	612
智力解谜.第 1 卷	2017—07	38.00	613
智力解谜.第 2 卷	2017—07	38.00	614
故事智力	2016—07	48.00	615
名人们喜欢的智力问题	2020—01	48.00	616
数学大师的发现、创造与失误	2018—01	48.00	617
异曲同工	2018—09	48.00	618
数学的味道	2018—01	58.00	798
数学千字文	2018—10	68.00	977
数贝偶拾——高考数学题研究	2014—04	28.00	274
数贝偶拾——初等数学研究	2014—04	38.00	275
数贝偶拾——奥数题研究	2014—04	48.00	276
钱昌本教你快乐学数学(上)	2011—12	48.00	155
钱昌本教你快乐学数学(下)	2012—03	58.00	171
集合、函数与方程	2014—01	28.00	300
数列与不等式	2014—01	38.00	301
三角与平面向量	2014—01	28.00	302
平面解析几何	2014—01	38.00	303
立体几何与组合	2014—01	28.00	304
极限与导数、数学归纳法	2014—01	38.00	305
趣味数学	2014—03	28.00	306
教材教法	2014—04	68.00	307
自主招生	2014—05	58.00	308
高考压轴题(上)	2015—01	48.00	309
高考压轴题(下)	2014—10	68.00	310
从费马到怀尔斯——费马大定理的历史	2013—10	198.00	I
从庞加莱到佩雷尔曼——庞加莱猜想的历史	2013—10	298.00	II
从切比雪夫到爱尔特希(上)——素数定理的初等证明	2013—07	48.00	III
从切比雪夫到爱尔特希(下)——素数定理 100 年	2012—12	98.00	III
从高斯到盖尔方特——二次域的高斯猜想	2013—10	198.00	IV
从库默尔到朗兰兹——朗兰兹猜想的历史	2014—01	98.00	V
从比勃巴赫到德布朗斯——比勃巴赫猜想的历史	2014—02	298.00	VI
从麦比乌斯到陈省身——麦比乌斯变换与麦比乌斯带	2014—02	298.00	VII
从布尔到豪斯道夫——布尔方程与格论漫谈	2013—10	198.00	VIII
从开普勒到阿诺德——三体问题的历史	2014—05	298.00	IX
从华林到华罗庚——华林问题的历史	2013—10	298.00	X

— 12 —

刘培杰数学工作室
已出版(即将出版)图书目录——初等数学

书　名	出版时间	定　价	编号
美国高中数学竞赛五十讲.第1卷(英文)	2014—08	28.00	357
美国高中数学竞赛五十讲.第2卷(英文)	2014—08	28.00	358
美国高中数学竞赛五十讲.第3卷(英文)	2014—09	28.00	359
美国高中数学竞赛五十讲.第4卷(英文)	2014—09	28.00	360
美国高中数学竞赛五十讲.第5卷(英文)	2014—10	28.00	361
美国高中数学竞赛五十讲.第6卷(英文)	2014—11	28.00	362
美国高中数学竞赛五十讲.第7卷(英文)	2014—12	28.00	363
美国高中数学竞赛五十讲.第8卷(英文)	2015—01	28.00	364
美国高中数学竞赛五十讲.第9卷(英文)	2015—01	28.00	365
美国高中数学竞赛五十讲.第10卷(英文)	2015—02	38.00	366
三角函数(第2版)	2017—04	38.00	626
不等式	2014—01	38.00	312
数列	2014—01	38.00	313
方程(第2版)	2017—04	38.00	624
排列和组合	2014—01	28.00	315
极限与导数(第2版)	2016—04	38.00	635
向量(第2版)	2018—08	58.00	627
复数及其应用	2014—08	28.00	318
函数	2014—01	38.00	319
集合	2020—01	48.00	320
直线与平面	2014—01	28.00	321
立体几何(第2版)	2016—04	38.00	629
解三角形	即将出版		323
直线与圆(第2版)	2016—11	38.00	631
圆锥曲线(第2版)	2016—09	48.00	632
解题通法(一)	2014—07	38.00	326
解题通法(二)	2014—07	38.00	327
解题通法(三)	2014—05	38.00	328
概率与统计	2014—01	28.00	329
信息迁移与算法	即将出版		330
IMO 50年.第1卷(1959—1963)	2014—11	28.00	377
IMO 50年.第2卷(1964—1968)	2014—11	28.00	378
IMO 50年.第3卷(1969—1973)	2014—09	28.00	379
IMO 50年.第4卷(1974—1978)	2016—04	38.00	380
IMO 50年.第5卷(1979—1984)	2015—04	38.00	381
IMO 50年.第6卷(1985—1989)	2015—04	58.00	382
IMO 50年.第7卷(1990—1994)	2016—01	48.00	383
IMO 50年.第8卷(1995—1999)	2016—06	38.00	384
IMO 50年.第9卷(2000—2004)	2015—04	58.00	385
IMO 50年.第10卷(2005—2009)	2016—01	48.00	386
IMO 50年.第11卷(2010—2015)	2017—03	48.00	646

刘培杰数学工作室
已出版(即将出版)图书目录——初等数学

书名	出版时间	定价	编号
数学反思(2006—2007)	即将出版		915
数学反思(2008—2009)	2019-01	68.00	917
数学反思(2010—2011)	2018-05	58.00	916
数学反思(2012—2013)	2019-01	58.00	918
数学反思(2014—2015)	2019-03	78.00	919
历届美国大学生数学竞赛试题集.第一卷(1938—1949)	2015-01	28.00	397
历届美国大学生数学竞赛试题集.第二卷(1950—1959)	2015-01	28.00	398
历届美国大学生数学竞赛试题集.第三卷(1960—1969)	2015-01	28.00	399
历届美国大学生数学竞赛试题集.第四卷(1970—1979)	2015-01	18.00	400
历届美国大学生数学竞赛试题集.第五卷(1980—1989)	2015-01	28.00	401
历届美国大学生数学竞赛试题集.第六卷(1990—1999)	2015-01	28.00	402
历届美国大学生数学竞赛试题集.第七卷(2000—2009)	2015-08	18.00	403
历届美国大学生数学竞赛试题集.第八卷(2010—2012)	2015-01	18.00	404
新课标高考数学创新题解题诀窍:总论	2014-09	28.00	372
新课标高考数学创新题解题诀窍:必修1~5分册	2014-08	38.00	373
新课标高考数学创新题解题诀窍:选修2-1,2-2,1-1,1-2分册	2014-09	38.00	374
新课标高考数学创新题解题诀窍:选修2-3,4-4,4-5分册	2014-09	18.00	375
全国重点大学自主招生英文数学试题全攻略:词汇卷	2015-07	48.00	410
全国重点大学自主招生英文数学试题全攻略:概念卷	2015-01	28.00	411
全国重点大学自主招生英文数学试题全攻略:文章选读卷(上)	2016-09	38.00	412
全国重点大学自主招生英文数学试题全攻略:文章选读卷(下)	2017-01	58.00	413
全国重点大学自主招生英文数学试题全攻略:试题卷	2015-07	38.00	414
全国重点大学自主招生英文数学试题全攻略:名著欣赏卷	2017-03	48.00	415
劳埃德数学趣题大全.题目卷.1:英文	2016-01	18.00	516
劳埃德数学趣题大全.题目卷.2:英文	2016-01	18.00	517
劳埃德数学趣题大全.题目卷.3:英文	2016-01	18.00	518
劳埃德数学趣题大全.题目卷.4:英文	2016-01	18.00	519
劳埃德数学趣题大全.题目卷.5:英文	2016-01	18.00	520
劳埃德数学趣题大全.答案卷:英文	2016-01	18.00	521
李成章教练奥数笔记.第1卷	2016-01	48.00	522
李成章教练奥数笔记.第2卷	2016-01	48.00	523
李成章教练奥数笔记.第3卷	2016-01	38.00	524
李成章教练奥数笔记.第4卷	2016-01	38.00	525
李成章教练奥数笔记.第5卷	2016-01	38.00	526
李成章教练奥数笔记.第6卷	2016-01	38.00	527
李成章教练奥数笔记.第7卷	2016-01	38.00	528
李成章教练奥数笔记.第8卷	2016-01	48.00	529
李成章教练奥数笔记.第9卷	2016-01	28.00	530

刘培杰数学工作室
已出版(即将出版)图书目录——初等数学

书　名	出版时间	定　价	编号
第19～23届"希望杯"全国数学邀请赛试题审题要津详细评注(初一版)	2014—03	28.00	333
第19～23届"希望杯"全国数学邀请赛试题审题要津详细评注(初二、初三版)	2014—03	38.00	334
第19～23届"希望杯"全国数学邀请赛试题审题要津详细评注(高一版)	2014—03	28.00	335
第19～23届"希望杯"全国数学邀请赛试题审题要津详细评注(高二版)	2014—03	38.00	336
第19～25届"希望杯"全国数学邀请赛试题审题要津详细评注(初一版)	2015—01	38.00	416
第19～25届"希望杯"全国数学邀请赛试题审题要津详细评注(初二、初三版)	2015—01	58.00	417
第19～25届"希望杯"全国数学邀请赛试题审题要津详细评注(高一版)	2015—01	48.00	418
第19～25届"希望杯"全国数学邀请赛试题审题要津详细评注(高二版)	2015—01	48.00	419
物理奥林匹克竞赛大题典——力学卷	2014—11	48.00	405
物理奥林匹克竞赛大题典——热学卷	2014—04	28.00	339
物理奥林匹克竞赛大题典——电磁学卷	2015—07	48.00	406
物理奥林匹克竞赛大题典——光学与近代物理卷	2014—06	28.00	345
历届中国东南地区数学奥林匹克试题集(2004～2012)	2014—06	18.00	346
历届中国西部地区数学奥林匹克试题集(2001～2012)	2014—07	18.00	347
历届中国女子数学奥林匹克试题集(2002～2012)	2014—08	18.00	348
数学奥林匹克在中国	2014—06	98.00	344
数学奥林匹克问题集	2014—01	38.00	267
数学奥林匹克不等式散论	2010—06	38.00	124
数学奥林匹克不等式欣赏	2011—09	38.00	138
数学奥林匹克超级题库(初中卷上)	2010—01	58.00	66
数学奥林匹克不等式证明方法和技巧(上、下)	2011—08	158.00	134,135
他们学什么:原民主德国中学数学课本	2016—09	38.00	658
他们学什么:英国中学数学课本	2016—09	38.00	659
他们学什么:法国中学数学课本.1	2016—09	38.00	660
他们学什么:法国中学数学课本.2	2016—09	28.00	661
他们学什么:法国中学数学课本.3	2016—09	38.00	662
他们学什么:苏联中学数学课本	2016—09	28.00	679
高中数学题典——集合与简易逻辑·函数	2016—07	48.00	647
高中数学题典——导数	2016—07	48.00	648
高中数学题典——三角函数·平面向量	2016—07	48.00	649
高中数学题典——数列	2016—07	58.00	650
高中数学题典——不等式·推理与证明	2016—07	38.00	651
高中数学题典——立体几何	2016—07	48.00	652
高中数学题典——平面解析几何	2016—07	78.00	653
高中数学题典——计数原理·统计·概率·复数	2016—07	48.00	654
高中数学题典——算法·平面几何·初等数论·组合数学·其他	2016—07	68.00	655

刘培杰数学工作室
已出版(即将出版)图书目录——初等数学

书　名	出版时间	定　价	编号
台湾地区奥林匹克数学竞赛试题.小学一年级	2017—03	38.00	722
台湾地区奥林匹克数学竞赛试题.小学二年级	2017—03	38.00	723
台湾地区奥林匹克数学竞赛试题.小学三年级	2017—03	38.00	724
台湾地区奥林匹克数学竞赛试题.小学四年级	2017—03	38.00	725
台湾地区奥林匹克数学竞赛试题.小学五年级	2017—03	38.00	726
台湾地区奥林匹克数学竞赛试题.小学六年级	2017—03	38.00	727
台湾地区奥林匹克数学竞赛试题.初中一年级	2017—03	38.00	728
台湾地区奥林匹克数学竞赛试题.初中二年级	2017—03	38.00	729
台湾地区奥林匹克数学竞赛试题.初中三年级	2017—03	28.00	730
不等式证题法	2017—04	28.00	747
平面几何培优教程	2019—08	88.00	748
奥数鼎级培优教程.高一分册	2018—09	88.00	749
奥数鼎级培优教程.高二分册.上	2018—04	68.00	750
奥数鼎级培优教程.高二分册.下	2018—04	68.00	751
高中数学竞赛冲刺宝典	2019—04	68.00	883
初中尖子生数学超级题典.实数	2017—07	58.00	792
初中尖子生数学超级题典.式、方程与不等式	2017—08	58.00	793
初中尖子生数学超级题典.圆、面积	2017—08	38.00	794
初中尖子生数学超级题典.函数、逻辑推理	2017—08	48.00	795
初中尖子生数学超级题典.角、线段、三角形与多边形	2017—07	58.00	796
数学王子——高斯	2018—01	48.00	858
坎坷奇星——阿贝尔	2018—01	48.00	859
闪烁奇星——伽罗瓦	2018—01	58.00	860
无穷统帅——康托尔	2018—01	48.00	861
科学公主——柯瓦列夫斯卡娅	2018—01	48.00	862
抽象代数之母——埃米·诺特	2018—01	48.00	863
电脑先驱——图灵	2018—01	58.00	864
昔日神童——维纳	2018—01	48.00	865
数坛怪侠——爱尔特希	2018—01	68.00	866
传奇数学家徐利治	2019—09	88.00	1110
当代世界中的数学.数学思想与数学基础	2019—01	38.00	892
当代世界中的数学.数学问题	2019—01	38.00	893
当代世界中的数学.应用数学与数学应用	2019—01	38.00	894
当代世界中的数学.数学王国的新疆域(一)	2019—01	38.00	895
当代世界中的数学.数学王国的新疆域(二)	2019—01	38.00	896
当代世界中的数学.数林撷英(一)	2019—01	38.00	897
当代世界中的数学.数林撷英(二)	2019—01	48.00	898
当代世界中的数学.数学之路	2019—01	38.00	899

刘培杰数学工作室
已出版(即将出版)图书目录——初等数学

书　名	出版时间	定　价	编号
105 个代数问题:来自 AwesomeMath 夏季课程	2019—02	58.00	956
106 个几何问题:来自 AwesomeMath 夏季课程	即将出版		957
107 个几何问题:来自 AwesomeMath 全年课程	2020—07	58.00	958
108 个代数问题:来自 AwesomeMath 全年课程	2019—01	68.00	959
109 个不等式:来自 AwesomeMath 夏季课程	2019—04	58.00	960
国际数学奥林匹克中的 110 个几何问题	即将出版		961
111 个代数和数论问题	2019—05	58.00	962
112 个组合问题:来自 AwesomeMath 夏季课程	2019—05	58.00	963
113 个几何不等式:来自 AwesomeMath 夏季课程	即将出版		964
114 个指数和对数问题:来自 AwesomeMath 夏季课程	2019—09	48.00	965
115 个三角问题:来自 AwesomeMath 夏季课程	2019—09	58.00	966
116 个代数不等式:来自 AwesomeMath 全年课程	2019—04	58.00	967
紫色彗星国际数学竞赛试题	2019—02	58.00	999
数学竞赛中的数学:为数学爱好者、父母、教师和教练准备的丰富资源.第一部	2020—04	58.00	1141
数学竞赛中的数学:为数学爱好者、父母、教师和教练准备的丰富资源.第二部	2020—07	48.00	1142
澳大利亚中学数学竞赛试题及解答(初级卷)1978~1984	2019—02	28.00	1002
澳大利亚中学数学竞赛试题及解答(初级卷)1985~1991	2019—02	28.00	1003
澳大利亚中学数学竞赛试题及解答(初级卷)1992~1998	2019—02	28.00	1004
澳大利亚中学数学竞赛试题及解答(初级卷)1999~2005	2019—02	28.00	1005
澳大利亚中学数学竞赛试题及解答(中级卷)1978~1984	2019—03	28.00	1006
澳大利亚中学数学竞赛试题及解答(中级卷)1985~1991	2019—03	28.00	1007
澳大利亚中学数学竞赛试题及解答(中级卷)1992~1998	2019—03	28.00	1008
澳大利亚中学数学竞赛试题及解答(中级卷)1999~2005	2019—03	28.00	1009
澳大利亚中学数学竞赛试题及解答(高级卷)1978~1984	2019—05	28.00	1010
澳大利亚中学数学竞赛试题及解答(高级卷)1985~1991	2019—05	28.00	1011
澳大利亚中学数学竞赛试题及解答(高级卷)1992~1998	2019—05	28.00	1012
澳大利亚中学数学竞赛试题及解答(高级卷)1999~2005	2019—05	28.00	1013
天才中小学生智力测验题.第一卷	2019—03	38.00	1026
天才中小学生智力测验题.第二卷	2019—03	38.00	1027
天才中小学生智力测验题.第三卷	2019—03	38.00	1028
天才中小学生智力测验题.第四卷	2019—03	38.00	1029
天才中小学生智力测验题.第五卷	2019—03	38.00	1030
天才中小学生智力测验题.第六卷	2019—03	38.00	1031
天才中小学生智力测验题.第七卷	2019—03	38.00	1032
天才中小学生智力测验题.第八卷	2019—03	38.00	1033
天才中小学生智力测验题.第九卷	2019—03	38.00	1034
天才中小学生智力测验题.第十卷	2019—03	38.00	1035
天才中小学生智力测验题.第十一卷	2019—03	38.00	1036
天才中小学生智力测验题.第十二卷	2019—03	38.00	1037
天才中小学生智力测验题.第十三卷	2019—03	38.00	1038

刘培杰数学工作室
已出版(即将出版)图书目录——初等数学

书　名	出版时间	定　价	编号
重点大学自主招生数学备考全书:函数	2020—05	48.00	1047
重点大学自主招生数学备考全书:导数	2020—08	48.00	1048
重点大学自主招生数学备考全书:数列与不等式	2019—10	78.00	1049
重点大学自主招生数学备考全书:三角函数与平面向量	即将出版		1050
重点大学自主招生数学备考全书:平面解析几何	2020—07	58.00	1051
重点大学自主招生数学备考全书:立体几何与平面几何	2019—08	48.00	1052
重点大学自主招生数学备考全书:排列组合·概率统计·复数	2019—09	48.00	1053
重点大学自主招生数学备考全书:初等数论与组合数学	2019—08	48.00	1054
重点大学自主招生数学备考全书:重点大学自主招生真题.上	2019—04	68.00	1055
重点大学自主招生数学备考全书:重点大学自主招生真题.下	2019—04	58.00	1056
高中数学竞赛培训教程:平面几何问题的求解方法与策略.上	2018—05	68.00	906
高中数学竞赛培训教程:平面几何问题的求解方法与策略.下	2018—06	78.00	907
高中数学竞赛培训教程:整除与同余以及不定方程	2018—01	88.00	908
高中数学竞赛培训教程:组合计数与组合极值	2018—04	48.00	909
高中数学竞赛培训教程:初等代数	2019—04	78.00	1042
高中数学讲座:数学竞赛基础教程(第一册)	2019—06	48.00	1094
高中数学讲座:数学竞赛基础教程(第二册)	即将出版		1095
高中数学讲座:数学竞赛基础教程(第三册)	即将出版		1096
高中数学讲座:数学竞赛基础教程(第四册)	即将出版		1097

联系地址:哈尔滨市南岗区复华四道街 10 号　哈尔滨工业大学出版社刘培杰数学工作室
网　　址:http://lpj.hit.edu.cn/
邮　　编:150006
联系电话:0451—86281378　　　13904613167
E-mail:lpj1378@163.com